THEORY OF FINITE AUTOMATA

with an INTRODUCTION to FORMAL LANGUAGES

JOHN CARROLL

San Diego State University

DARRELL LONG

University of California, Santa Cruz

PRENTICE HALL, Englewood Cliffs, New Jersey 07632

Library of Congress Cataloging-in-Publication Data

CARROLL, JOHN
Theory of finite automata.

Bibliography: p.
Includes index.
1. Sequential machine theory. 2. Formal languages. I. Long, Darrell II. Title.
QA267.5.S4C35 1989 511 88-22416
ISBN 0-13-913708-4

for Bonnie
for Mary

Editorial/production supervision: Kathleen Schiaparelli and Joan McCulley
Manufacturing buyer: Mary Noonan

Printed in the United States of America

10 9 8 7 6 5 4 3 2 1

ISBN 0-13-913708-4

PRENTICE-HALL INTERNATIONAL (UK) LIMITED, *London*
PRENTICE-HALL OF AUSTRALIA PTY. LIMITED, *Sydney*
PRENTICE-HALL CANADA INC., *Toronto*
PRENTICE-HALL HISPANOAMERICANA, S.A., *Mexico*
PRENTICE-HALL OF INDIA PRIVATE LIMITED, *New Delhi*
PRENTICE-HALL OF JAPAN, INC., *Tokyo*
SIMON & SCHUSTER ASIA PTE. LTD., *Singapore*
EDITORA PRENTICE-HALL DO BRASIL, LTDA, *Rio de Janeiro*

CONTENTS

PREFACE

It often seems that mathematicians regularly provide answers well before the rest of the world finds reasons to ask the questions. The operation of the networks of relays used in the first computers is exactly described by Boolean functions. George Boole thereby made his contribution to computer science in the mid-1800s, and Boolean algebra is used today to represent modern TTL (transistor–transistor logic) circuits. In the 1930s, Alan Turing formalized the concept of an algorithm with his presentation of an abstract computing device and characterized the limitations of such machines. In the 1950s, the abstraction of the concepts behind natural language grammars provided the theoretical basis for computer languages that today guides the design of compilers.

These three major foundations of computer science, the mathematical description of computational networks, the limitations of mechanical computation, and the formal specification of languages are highly interrelated disciplines, and all require a great deal of mathematical maturity to appreciate. A computer science undergraduate is often expected to deal with all these concepts, typically armed only with a course in discrete mathematics.

This presentation attempts to make it possible for the average student to acquire more than just the facts about the subject. It is aimed at providing a reasonable level of understanding about the methods of proof and the attendant thought processes, without burdening the instructor with the formidable task of simplifying the material. The majority of the proofs are written with a level of detail that should leave no doubt about how to proceed from one step to the next. These same proofs thereby provide a template for the exercises and serve as examples of how to produce formal proofs in the mathematical areas of computer science. It is not unreasonable to expect to read and understand the material presented here in a nonclassroom setting. The text is therefore a useful supplement to those approaching a course in computation or formal languages with some trepidation.

This text develops the standard mathematical models of computational devices, and investigates the cognitive and generative capabilities of such machines. The engineering viewpoint is addressed, both in relation to the construction of such devices and in the applications of the theory to real-world machines such as traffic controllers and vending machines. The software viewpoint is also considered, providing insight into the underpinnings of computer languages. Examples and applications relating to compiler construction abound.

This material can be tailored to several types of courses. A course in formal languages that stressed the development of mathematical skills could easily span two semesters. At the other extreme, a course designed as a prerequisite for a formal languages sequence might cover Chapters 1 through 7 and parts of Chapters 8 and 12. In particular, Chapter 8 is written so that the discussion of the more robust grammars (Section 8.1) can be entirely omitted. Section 12.1 is exclusively devoted to results pertaining to the constructs described in the earlier chapters, and Section 12.3 provides a natural introduction to the theory of computability by developing the halting problem without relying on Turing machine concepts.

Several people played significant roles in shaping this text. The book grew out of a set of lecture notes taken by Jack Porter, a student in a one-semester course on finite automata taught by Sara Baase at San Diego State in the 1970s. Baase's course was based on five weeks of lectures by Richard M. Karp at the University of California, Berkeley. The lecture notes were revised by William Root during the semesters he taught the course at San Diego State. The authors are also indebted to the many students who helped refine the presentation by suggesting clarifications and identifying typos, inaccuracies, and sundry other sins. Special thanks to Jon Barwise and John Etchemendy at Stanford University for their permission to incorporate examples from their Turing's World Macintosh software package, available from Kinko's Academic Courseware Exchange, 255 West Stanley Ave., Ventura, CA 93001. Robin Fishbaugh was instrumental in shepherding the class notes through their various electronic forms; her numerous contributions are greatfully acknowledged.

Courtesy of Alexis A. Gilliland

CHAPTER

0

PRELIMINARIES

This chapter reviews some of the basic concepts used in this text. Many can be found in standard texts on discrete mathematics. Much of the notation employed in later chapters is also presented here.

0.1 LOGIC AND SET THEORY

A basic familiarity with the nature of formal proofs is assumed; most proofs given in this text are complete and rigorous, and the reader is encouraged to work the exercises in similar detail. A knowledge of logic circuits would be necessary to construct the machines discussed in this text. Important terminology and techniques are reviewed here.

Unambiguous *statements* that can take on the values **True** or **False** (denoted by **1** and **0**, respectively) can be combined with *connectives* such as *and* ($\wedge$), *or* ($\vee$), and *not* ($\neg$) to form more complex statements. The truth tables for several useful connectives are given in Figure 0.1, along with the symbols representing the physical devices that implement these connectives.

As an example of a complex statement, consider the assertion that two statements p and q take on the same value. This can be rephrased as:

Either (p is true and q is true) or (p is false and q is false).

As the truth table for *not* shows, a statement r is false exactly when $\neg$r is true; the above assertion could be further refined to:

Either (p is true and q is true) or ($\neg$p is true and $\neg$q is true).

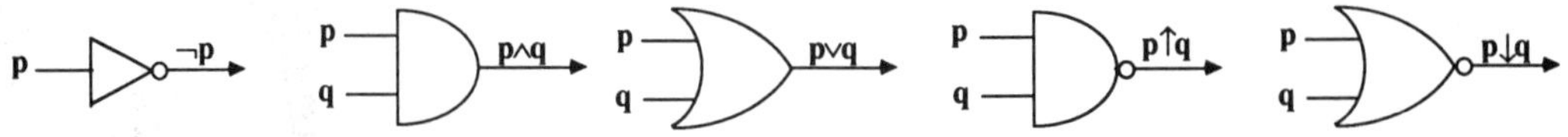

NOT gate

p	¬p
1	**0**
0	**1**

AND gate

p	q	p∧q
1	**1**	**1**
1	**0**	**0**
0	**1**	**0**
0	**0**	**0**

OR gate

p	q	p∨q
1	**1**	**1**
1	**0**	**1**
0	**1**	**1**
0	**0**	**0**

NAND gate

p	q	p ↑ q
1	**1**	**0**
1	**0**	**1**
0	**1**	**1**
0	**0**	**1**

NOR gate

p	q	p ↓ q
1	**1**	**0**
1	**0**	**0**
0	**1**	**0**
0	**0**	**1**

Figure 0.1 Common logic gates and their truth tables

In symbols, this can be abbreviated as:

$$(p\wedge q)\vee(\neg p\wedge\neg q)$$

The truth table covering the four combinations of truth values of p and q can be built from the truth tables defining $\wedge$, $\vee$, and $\neg$, as shown in Figure 0.2. The truth table shows that the assertion is indeed true in the two cases where p and q reflect the same values, and false in the two cases where the values assigned to p and q differ. When the statement that r and s always take on the same value is indeed true, we often write r *iff* s (r if and only if s). It can also be denoted by $r\Leftrightarrow s$ (r is *equivalent* to s).

p	q	¬p	¬q	¬p∧¬q	p∧q	(p∧q)∨(¬p∧¬q)
1	**1**	**0**	**0**	**0**	**1**	**1**
1	**0**	**0**	**1**	**0**	**0**	**0**
0	**1**	**1**	**0**	**0**	**0**	**0**
0	**0**	**1**	**1**	**1**	**0**	**1**

Figure 0.2 Truth tables for various compound expressions

Consider the statement $(p\wedge q)\vee(p\downarrow q)$. Truth tables can be constructed to verify that $(p\wedge q)\vee(\neg p\wedge\neg q)$ and $(p\wedge q)\vee(p\downarrow q)$ have identical truth tables, and thus $(p\wedge q)\vee(\neg p\wedge\neg q)\Leftrightarrow(p\wedge q)\vee(p\downarrow q)$.

EXAMPLE 0.1

Circuitry for realizing each of the above statements is displayed in Figure 0.3. Since the two statements were equivalent, the circuits will exhibit the same behavior for all combinations of input signals p and q. The second circuit would be less costly to build since it contains fewer components, and tangible benefits therefore arise when equivalent but less cumbersome statements can be derived. Techniques for *minimizing* such circuitry are presented in most discrete mathematics texts.

Example 0.1 shows that it is straightforward to implement statement formulas by circuitry. Recall that the location of the **1** values in the truth table can be used to find the corresponding *principal disjunctive normal form* (PDNF) for the expression

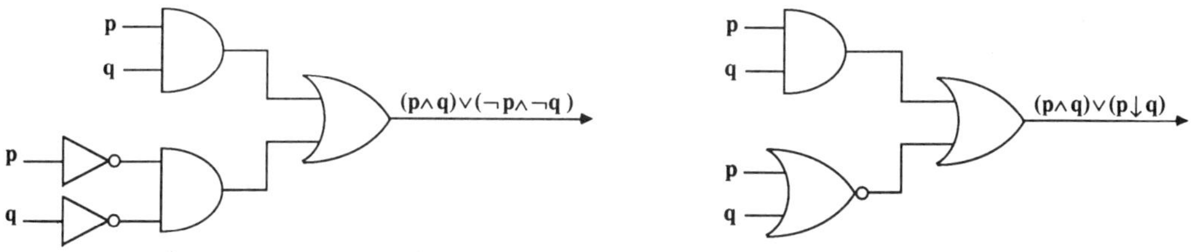

Figure 0.3 Functionally equivalent circuits

represented by the truth table. For example, the truth table corresponding to NAND has 3 rows with **1** values ($p = \mathbf{1}$, $q = \mathbf{0}$; $p = \mathbf{0}$, $q = \mathbf{1}$; $p = \mathbf{0}$, $q = \mathbf{0}$), leading to three *terms* in the PDNF expression: $(p \wedge \neg q) \vee (\neg p \wedge q) \vee (\neg p \wedge \neg q)$. This formula can be implemented as the circuit illustrated in Figure 0.4, and thus a NAND gate can be replaced by this combination of three ANDs and one OR gate. This circuit relies on the assurance that a quantity of interest (such as p) will generally be available in both its negated and unnegated forms. Hence we can count on access to an input line representing $\neg p$ (rather than feeding the input for p into a NOT gate).

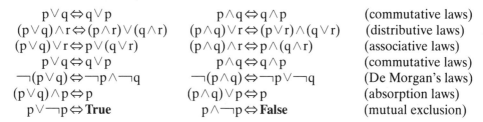

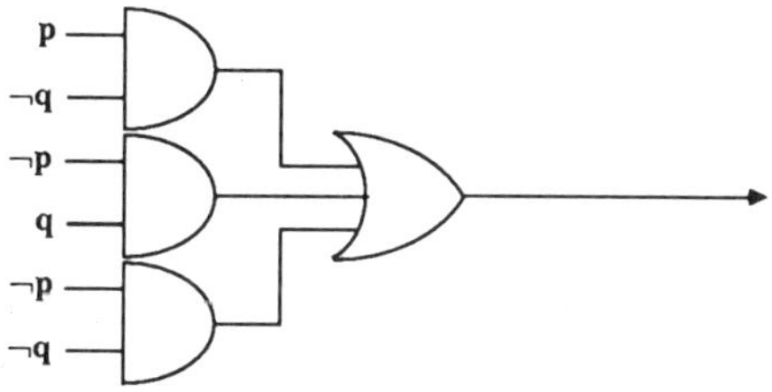

Figure 0.4 A circuit equivalent to a single NAND gate

In a similar fashion, *any* statement formula can be represented as a group of AND gates feeding a single OR gate. In larger truth tables, there may be many more **1** values, and hence more complex statements may need many AND gates. Regardless of the statement complexity, however, circuits based on the PDNF of an expression will allow for a fast response to changing input signals, since no signal must propagate through more than two gates.

Other useful equivalences are given in Figure 0.5. Each rule has a *dual*, written on the same line.

$p \vee q \Leftrightarrow q \vee p$	$p \wedge q \Leftrightarrow q \wedge p$	(commutative laws)
$(p \vee q) \wedge r \Leftrightarrow (p \wedge r) \vee (q \wedge r)$	$(p \wedge q) \vee r \Leftrightarrow (p \vee r) \wedge (q \vee r)$	(distributive laws)
$(p \vee q) \vee r \Leftrightarrow p \vee (q \vee r)$	$(p \wedge q) \wedge r \Leftrightarrow p \wedge (q \wedge r)$	(associative laws)
$p \vee q \Leftrightarrow q \vee p$	$p \wedge q \Leftrightarrow q \wedge p$	(commutative laws)
$\neg(p \vee q) \Leftrightarrow \neg p \wedge \neg q$	$\neg(p \wedge q) \Leftrightarrow \neg p \vee \neg q$	(De Morgan's laws)
$(p \vee q) \wedge p \Leftrightarrow p$	$(p \wedge q) \vee p \Leftrightarrow p$	(absorption laws)
$p \vee \neg p \Leftrightarrow$ **True**	$p \wedge \neg p \Leftrightarrow$ **False**	(mutual exclusion)

Figure 0.5 Some useful equivalences and their duals

Predicates are often used to make statements about certain *objects*, such as the numbers in the set $\mathbb{I}$ of integers. For example, Q might represent the property of being less than 5, in which case Q(x) will represent the statement "x is less than 5." Thus, Q(3) is true, while Q(7) is false. It is often necessary to make global statements such as: *All* integers have the property P, which can be denoted by $(\forall x \in \mathbb{I})\mathrm{P}(x)$. Note that the *dummy* variable x was used to state the concept in a convenient form; x is not meant to represent a particular object, and the statement could be equivalently phrased as $(\forall i \in \mathbb{I})\mathrm{P}(i)$. For the predicate Q defined above, the statement $(\forall x \in \mathbb{I})\mathrm{Q}(x)$ is false, while when applied to more restricted domains, $(\forall x \in \{1,2,3\})\mathrm{Q}(x)$ is true, since it is in this case equivalent to $\mathrm{Q}(1)\wedge\mathrm{Q}(2)\wedge\mathrm{Q}(3)$, or $(1<5)\wedge(2<5)\wedge(3<5)$.

In a similar fashion, the statement that *some* integers have the property P will be denoted by $(\exists i \in \mathbb{I})\mathrm{P}(i)$. For the predicate Q defined above, $(\exists i \in \{4,5,6\})\mathrm{Q}(i)$ is true, since it is equivalent to $\mathrm{Q}(3)\vee\mathrm{Q}(5)\vee\mathrm{Q}(6)$, or $(4<5)\vee(5<5)\vee(6<5)$. The statement $(\exists y \in \{7,8,9\})\mathrm{Q}(y)$ is false.

Note that asserting that it is not the case that all objects have the property P is equivalent to saying that there is at least one object that does not have the property P. In symbols, we have

$$\neg(\forall x \in \mathbb{I})\mathrm{P}(x) \Leftrightarrow (\exists x \in \mathbb{I})(\neg\mathrm{P}(x))$$

Similarly,

$$\neg(\exists x \in \mathbb{I})\mathrm{P}(x) \Leftrightarrow (\forall x \in \mathbb{I})(\neg\mathrm{P}(x))$$

Given two statements A and B, if B is true whenever A is true, we will say that A *implies* B, and write $\mathrm{A}\Rightarrow\mathrm{B}$. For example, the truth tables show that $\mathrm{p}\wedge\mathrm{q}\Rightarrow\mathrm{p}\vee\mathrm{q}$, since for the case where $\mathrm{p}\wedge\mathrm{q}$ is true ($\mathrm{p}=\mathbf{1}$, $\mathrm{q}=\mathbf{1}$), $\mathrm{p}\vee\mathrm{q}$ is true, also. In the cases where $\mathrm{p}\wedge\mathrm{q}$ is false, the value of $\mathrm{p}\vee\mathrm{q}$ is immaterial.

A basic knowledge of set theory is assumed. Some standard special symbols will be repeatedly used to designate common sets.

∇ **Definition 0.1**

The set of *natural numbers* is given by $\mathbb{N} = \{0,1,2,3,4,\ldots\}$.

The set of *integers* is given by $\mathbb{I} = \{\ldots -2,-1,0,1,2,\ldots\}$.

The set of *rational numbers* is given by $\mathbb{Q} = \{a/b \mid a \in \mathbb{I}, b \in \mathbb{I}, b \neq 0\}$.

The set of *real numbers* (points on the number line) will be denoted by $\mathbb{R}$.

Δ

The following concepts and notation will be used frequently throughout the text.

∇ **Definition 0.2.** Let A and B be sets. A is a *subset* of B if every element of A also belongs to B; that is, $A \subseteq B$ ***iff*** $(\forall x)(x \in A \Rightarrow x \in B)$.

Δ

∇ **Definition 0.3.** Two sets A and B are said to be *equal* if they contain exactly the same elements; that is, $A = B$ ***iff*** $(\forall x)(x \in A \Leftrightarrow x \in B)$.

Δ

Thus, two sets A and B are equal *iff* $A \subseteq B$ and $B \subseteq A$. The symbol $\subset$ will be used to denote a *proper* subset: $A \subset B$ *iff* $A \subseteq B$ and $A \neq B$.

∇ **Definition 0.4.** For sets A and B, the *cross product* of A with B, is the set of all ordered pairs from A and B; that is, $A \times B = \{\langle a, b\rangle \mid a \in A \wedge b \in B\}$.
Δ

0.2 RELATIONS

Relations are used to describe relationships between members of sets of objects. Formally, a relation is just a subset of a cross product of two sets.

∇ **Definition 0.5.** Let X and Y be sets. A relation R from X to Y is simply a subset of $X \times Y$. If $\langle a, b\rangle \in \mathrm{R}$, we write $a\mathrm{R}b$. If $\langle a, b\rangle \notin \mathrm{R}$, we write $a\not\mathrm{R}b$. If $X = Y$, we say R is a relation *in* X.
Δ

EXAMPLE 0.2

Let $X = \{1, 2, 3\}$. The familiar relation $<$ (less than) would then consist of the following ordered pairs: $<$: $\{\langle 1, 2\rangle, \langle 1, 3\rangle, \langle 2, 3\rangle\}$, by which we mean to indicate that $1 < 2$, $1 < 3$, and $2 < 3$. $\langle 3, 3\rangle \notin <$ since $3 \not< 3$.

Some relations have special properties. For example, the relation "less than" is *transitive*, by which we mean that for any numbers x, y, and z, if $x < y$ and $y < z$, then $x < z$. Definition 0.6 describes an important class of relations that have some familiar properties.

∇ **Definition 0.6**

A relation is *reflexive* ***iff*** $(\forall x)(x\mathrm{R}x)$.

A relation is *symmetric* ***iff*** $(\forall x)(\forall y)(x\mathrm{R}y \Rightarrow y\mathrm{R}x)$.

A relation is *transitive* ***iff*** $(\forall x)(\forall y)(\forall z)((x\mathrm{R}y \wedge y\mathrm{R}z) \Rightarrow x\mathrm{R}z)$.

An *equivalence relation* is a relation that is reflexive, symmetric, and transitive.

Δ

EXAMPLE 0.3

$<$ is not an equivalence relation; while it is transitive, it is not reflexive since $3 \not< 3$. (It is also not symmetric, since $2 < 3$, but $3 \not< 2$.)

EXAMPLE 0.4

Let $X = \mathbb{N}$. The familiar relation $=$ (equality) *is* an equivalence relation.

$$=:\{\langle 0, 0\rangle, \langle 1, 1\rangle, \langle 2, 2\rangle, \langle 3, 3\rangle, \langle 4, 4\rangle, \ldots\},$$

and it is clear that $(\forall x)(\forall y)(x = y \Rightarrow y = x)$. The equality relation is therefore symmetric, and it is likewise obvious that = is also reflexive and transitive.

∇ **Definition 0.7.** Let R be an equivalence relation in X, and let $h \in X$. Then $[h]_R$ refers to the *equivalence class* consisting of all entities that are related to h by the equivalence relation R; that is, $[h]_R = \{y \mid y \, R \, h\}$.
Δ

EXAMPLE 0.5

The equivalence classes for = are singleton sets: $[1]_= = \{1\}$, $[5]_= = \{5\}$, and so on.

EXAMPLE 0.6

Let $X = \mathbb{I}$, and define the relation R in $\mathbb{I}$ by

$$\langle u, v\rangle \, R \, \langle w, x\rangle \textit{ iff } ux = vw$$

If $\langle x, y\rangle$ is viewed as the fraction x/y, then R is the relation that identifies equivalent fractions: 2/3 R 14/21, since $2\cdot 21 = 3\cdot 14$. In this sense, R can be viewed as the *equality* operator on the set of rational numbers $\mathbb{Q}$.

Note that in this context the equivalence class $[2/8]_R$ represents the set of all "names" for the point one-fourth of the way between 0 and 1; that is,

$$[2/8]_R = \{\ldots, -3/-12, -2/-8, -1/-4, 1/4, 2/8, 3/12, 4/16, 5/20, \ldots\}$$

There are therefore many other ways of designating this same set; for example,

$$[1/4]_R = \{\ldots, -3/-12, -2/-8, -1/-4, 1/4, 2/8, 3/12, 4/16, 5/20, \ldots\}$$

EXAMPLE 0.7

Let $X = \mathbb{N}$ and choose an $n \in \mathbb{N}$. Define R_n by

$$x \, R_n \, y \textit{ iff } (\exists i \in \mathbb{I})(x - y = i\cdot n)$$

That is, two numbers are related if their difference is a multiple of n. Equivalently, x and y must have the same remainder upon dividing each of them by n if we are to have $x \, R_n \, y$.

R_n can be shown to be an equivalence relation for each natural number n. The equivalence classes of R_2, for example, are the two familiar sets, the even numbers and the odd numbers. The equivalence classes for R_3 are

$$[0]_{R_3} = \{0, 3, 6, 9, 12, 15, \ldots\}$$

$$[1]_{R_3} = \{1, 4, 7, 10, 13, \ldots\}$$

$$[2]_{R_3} = \{2, 5, 8, 11, 14, \ldots\}$$

R_n is often called *congruence modulo n*, and $x \, R_n \, y$ is commonly denoted by $x \equiv y \pmod{n}$ or $x \equiv_n y$.

If R is an equivalence relation in X, then every element of X belongs to exactly one equivalence class of R. X is therefore comprised of the union of the equivalence classes of R, and in this sense R *partitions* the set X into disjoint subsets. Conversely, a partition of X defines an equivalence relation in X; the sets of the partition can be thought of as the equivalence classes of the resulting relation.

∇ **Definition 0.8.** Given a set X and sets $A_1, A_2, \ldots, A_n$, $P = \{A_1, A_2, \ldots, A_n\}$ is a *partition* of X if the sets in P are all *subsets* of X, they *cover* X, and are *pairwise disjoint*. That is, the following three conditions are satisfied:

$$(\forall i \in \{1, 2, \ldots, n\})(A_i \subseteq X)$$

$$(\forall x \in X)(\exists i \in \{1, 2, \ldots, n\} \ni x \in A_i)$$

$$(\forall i, j \in \{1, 2, \ldots, n\})(i \neq j \Rightarrow A_i \cap A_j = \emptyset)$$

Δ

∇ **Definition 0.9.** Given a set X and a partition $P = \{A_1, A_2, \ldots, A_n\}$ of X, the relation $\mathrm{R}(P)$ in X induced by P is given by

$$(\forall x \in X)(\forall y \in X)(x\ \mathrm{R}(P)\ y \Leftrightarrow (\exists i \in \{1, 2, \ldots, n\} \ni x \in A_i \wedge y \in A_i))$$

Δ

$\mathrm{R}(P)$ thus relates elements that belong to the same subset of P.

EXAMPLE 0.8

Let $X = \{1, 2, 3, 4, 5\}$ and consider the relation $\mathrm{Q} = \mathrm{R}(S)$ induced by the partition $S = \{\{1, 2\}, \{3, 5\}, \{4\}\}$. Since 1 and 2 are in the same set, they should be related by Q, while $1 \not{\mathrm{Q}} 4$ because 1 and 4 belong to different sets of the partition. Q can be described by

$$\mathrm{Q} = \{\langle 1, 1\rangle, \langle 1, 2\rangle, \langle 2, 1\rangle, \langle 2, 2\rangle, \langle 3, 3\rangle, \langle 3, 5\rangle, \langle 4, 4\rangle, \langle 5, 3\rangle, \langle 5, 5\rangle\}$$

It is straightforward to check that Q satisfies the three properties needed to qualify as an equivalence relation, and the equivalence classes of Q are

$$[1]_{\mathrm{Q}} = \{1, 2\}$$

$$[2]_{\mathrm{Q}} = \{1, 2\}$$

$$[3]_{\mathrm{Q}} = \{3, 5\}$$

$$[4]_{\mathrm{Q}} = \{4\}$$

$$[5]_{\mathrm{Q}} = \{3, 5\}$$

The set of *distinct* equivalence classes of Q can be used to partition X; note that these three classes comprise P. In a similar manner, the three distinct equivalence classes of R_3 in Example 0.7 form a partition of $\mathbb{N}$.

A "finer" partition of X can be obtained by breaking up the equivalence classes of Q into smaller (and hence more numerous) sets. The resulting relation is called a *refinement* of Q.

∇ **Definition 0.10.** Given two equivalence relations R and Q in a set X, R is a *refinement* of Q ***iff*** $\mathrm{R} \subseteq \mathrm{Q}$; that is, $(\forall x \in X)(\forall y \in X)(\langle x, y\rangle \in \mathrm{R} \Rightarrow \langle x, y\rangle \in \mathrm{Q})$.
Δ

EXAMPLE 0.9

Consider $\mathrm{Q} = \{\langle 1,1\rangle, \langle 1,2\rangle, \langle 2,1\rangle, \langle 2,2\rangle, \langle 3,3\rangle, \langle 3,5\rangle, \langle 4,4\rangle, \langle 5,3\rangle, \langle 5,5\rangle\}$ and $\mathrm{S} = \{\langle 1,1\rangle, \langle 2,2\rangle, \langle 3,3\rangle, \langle 3,5\rangle, \langle 4,4\rangle, \langle 5,3\rangle, \langle 5,5\rangle\}$. S is clearly a subset of Q, and hence S refines Q. Note that the partition induced by S, $\{\{1\}, \{2\}, \{3,5\}, \{4\}\}$, indeed splits up the partition induced by Q, which was $\{\{1,2\}, \{3,5\}, \{4\}\}$. While it may at first seem strange, the fact that S contained *fewer* ordered pairs than Q guarantees that S will yield *more* equivalence classes than Q.

0.3 FUNCTIONS

A *function* f is a special type of relation in which each first coordinate is associated with one and only one second coordinate, in which case we can use functional notation $f(x)$ to indicate the unique element f associates with a given first coordinate x. In the previous section we concentrated on relations *in* X, that is, subsets of $X \times X$. The set of first coordinates of a function f (the *domain* X) is often different from the set of possible second coordinates (the *codomain* Y), and hence f will be a subset of $X \times Y$.

∇ **Definition 0.11.** A *function* f: $X \to Y$ is a subset of $X \times Y$ for which

1. $(\forall x \in X)(\exists y \in Y \ni x f y)$.
2. $(\forall x \in X)((x f y_1 \wedge x f y_2) \Rightarrow y_1 = y_2)$.

Δ

When a pair of elements are related by a function, we will write $f(a) = b$ instead of $a f b$ or $\langle a, b\rangle \in f$. The criteria for being a function could then be rephrased as $(\forall x \in X)(\exists y \in Y \ni f(x) = y)$, and $(\forall x_1 \in X)(\forall x_2 \in X)(x_1 = x_2 \Rightarrow f(x_1) = f(x_2))$.

EXAMPLE 0.10

Let n be a positive integer. Define $f_n : \mathbb{N} \to \mathbb{N}$ by $f_n(j)$ = the smallest natural number i for which $j \equiv i \bmod n$. $f_3(j)$, for example, is a function and is represented by the ordered pairs f_3: $\{\langle 0,0\rangle, \langle 1,1\rangle, \langle 2,2\rangle, \langle 3,0\rangle, \langle 4,1\rangle, \ldots\}$. This implies that $f_3(0) = 0$, $f_3(1) = 1$, $f_3(2) = 2$, $f_3(3) = 0$, and so on.

Note that f_3 is a subset of the relation R_3 given in Example 0.7. If R_3 were presented as a function, it would not be *well defined*; that is, R_3 does not satisfy Definition 0.11. For example, $2\,\mathrm{R}_3\,5$ and $2\,\mathrm{R}_3\,8$, but $5 \neq 8$, and so $\mathrm{R}_3(2)$ is not a meaningful expression, since there is no unique object that R_3 associates with 2. In this case, R_3 violated Definition 0.11 by associating *more* than one object with a given first coordinate; in general, a proposed relation may also fail to be well defined by associating *no* objects with a potential first coordinate.

EXAMPLE 0.11

Consider the "function" $g: \mathbb{Q} \to \mathbb{N}$ defined by $g(m/n) = m$. This apparently straightforward definition is fundamentally flawed. According to the formula, $g(2/8) = 2$, $g(7/9) = 7$, $g(5/10) = 5$, and so forth. However, $2/8 = 5/20$, but $g(2/8) = 2 \neq 5 = g(5/20)$, and Definition 0.11 is again violated; $g(0.25)$ is not a well defined quantity, and thus the "function" g is not well defined. Had g truly been a function, it would have passed the test: if $x = y$, then $g(x) = g(y)$.

The problem with this seemingly innocent definition is that 0.25 is actually an *equivalence class* of fractions (recall Example 0.6), and the definition of g was based on just one *representative* of that class. We observed that two representatives (2/8 and 5/20) of the *same* class gave conflicting answers (2 and 5) for the value that g associated with their class (0.25). While it is possible to define functions on a set of equivalence classes in a consistent manner, it will always be important to verify that such functions are *single valued*.

Selection criteria, which determine whether a candidate does or does not belong to a given set, are special types of functions.

∇ **Definition 0.12.** Given a set A, the *characteristic function* χ_A associated with A is defined by

$$\chi_A(x) = 1 \text{ if } x \in A \quad \text{and} \quad \chi_A(x) = 0 \text{ if } x \notin A$$

Δ

EXAMPLE 0.12

The characteristic function for the set of odd numbers is the function f_2 given in Example 0.10.

To say that a *set* is well defined essentially means that the characteristic function associated with that set is a well-defined function. A set of equivalence classes can be ill defined if the definition is based on the representatives of those equivalence classes.

EXAMPLE 0.13

Consider the "set" of fractions that have odd numerators, whose characteristic "function" is defined by:

$$\chi_B(m/n) = 1 \text{ if } m \text{ is odd}$$

and

$$\chi_B(m/n) = 0 \text{ if } m \text{ is even}$$

This characteristic function suffers from flaws similar to those found in the function g in Example 0.11. 1/4 = 2/8 and yet $\chi_B(1/4) = 1$ while $\chi_B(2/8) = 0$, which implies that the fraction 1/4 belongs to B, while 2/8 is not an element of B. Due to this ambiguous definition of set membership, B is not a well-defined set. B failed to pass the test: if $x = y$, then ($x \in B$ *iff* $y \in B$).

The definition of a relation requires the specification of the domain, codomain, and the ordered pairs comprising the relation. For relations that are functions, every domain element must occur as a first coordinate. However, the set of elements that occurs as second coordinates need not include all the codomain (as was the case in the function f_n in Example 0.10).

∇ **Definition 0.13.** The *range* of a function $f\colon X \to Y$ is given by

$$\{y \in Y \mid \exists x \in X \ni f(x) = y\}.$$

Δ

Conditions similar to those imposed on the behavior of first coordinates of a function may also be placed on second coordinates, yielding specialized types of functions. Functions for which the range encompasses all the codomain, for example, are called *surjective*.

∇ **Definition 0.14.** A function $f\colon X \to Y$ is *onto* or *surjective iff*

$$(\forall y \in Y)(\exists x \in X \ni f(x) = y);\text{ that is,}$$

a set of ordered pairs representing an *onto* function must have at least one first coordinate associated with any given second coordinate.

Δ

EXAMPLE 0.14

The function $g\colon \{1,2,3\} \to \{a,b\}$ defined by $g(1) = a$, $g(2) = b$, and $g(3) = a$ is onto since both codomain elements are part of the range of g. However, the function $h\colon \{1,2,3\} \to \{a,b,c\}$ defined by $h(1) = a$, $h(2) = b$, and $h(3) = a$ is *not* onto since no domain element maps to c.

The function $f\colon \mathbb{N} \to \mathbb{N}$ defined by $f(i) = i + 1$ $(\forall i = 0, 1, 2, \ldots)$ is not onto since there is no element x for which $f(x) = 0$.

∇ **Definition 0.15.** A function $f\colon X \to Y$ is *one to one* or *injective iff*

$$(\forall x_1 \in X)(\forall x_2 \in X)(f(x_1) = f(x_2) \Rightarrow x_1 = x_2);\text{ that is,}$$

an *injective* function must not have more than one first coordinate associated with any given second coordinate.

Δ

EXAMPLE 0.15

The function f: $\mathbb{N} \to \mathbb{N}$ defined by $f(i) = i + 1$ ($\forall i = 0, 1, 2, \ldots$) is clearly injective since if $f(i) = f(j)$ then $i + 1 = j + 1$, and so i must equal j.

The function g: $\{1, 2, 3\} \times \{a, b\}$ defined by $g(1) = a$, $g(2) = b$, and $g(3) = a$ is not one to one since $g(1) = g(3)$, but $1 \neq 3$.

∇ **Definition 0.16.** A function is a *bijection* ***iff*** it is one to one and onto (injective and surjective); that is, it must satisfy

1. $(\forall x_1 \in X)(\forall x_2 \in X)(f(x_1) = f(x_2) \Rightarrow x_1 = x_2)$.
2. $(\forall y \in Y)(\exists x \in X \ni f(x) = y)$.

Δ

A *bijective* function must therefore have *exactly* one first coordinate associated with any given second coordinate.

EXAMPLE 0.16

The function f: $\mathbb{N} \to \mathbb{N}$ defined by $f(i) = i + 1$ ($\forall i = 0, 1, 2, \ldots$) is injective but not surjective, so it is not a bijection. However, the function b: $\mathbb{I} \to \mathbb{I}$ defined by $b(i) = i + 1$ ($\forall i = \ldots, -2, -1, 0, 1, 2, \ldots$) is a bijection. Note that while the rule for b remains the same as for f, both the domain and range have been expanded, and many more ordered pairs have been added to form b.

It is often appropriate to take the results produced by one function and apply the rule specified by a second function. For example, we may have a list associating students with their height in inches (that is, we have a function relating names with numbers). The conversion rule for changing inches into centimeters is also a function (associating any given number of inches with the corresponding length in centimeters), which can be applied to the heights given in the student list to produce a new list matching student names with their height in centimeters. This new list is referred to as the *composition* of the original two functions.

∇ **Definition 0.17.** The *composition* of two functions f: $X \to Y$ and g: $Y \to Z$ is given by

$$g \circ f = \{\langle x, z\rangle \mid \exists y \in Y \ni \langle x, y\rangle \in f \text{ and } \langle y, z\rangle \in g\}$$

Δ

Note that the composition is not defined unless the codomain of the first function matches the domain of the second function. In functional notation, $g \circ f = \{\langle x, z\rangle \mid \exists y \in Y \ni f(x) = y \text{ and } g(y) = z\}$, and therefore when $g \circ f$ is defined, it can be described by the rule $g \circ f(x) = g(f(x))$.

EXAMPLE 0.17

Consider the functions f_3 from Example 0.10 and f from Example 0.14, where $f_3 : \mathbb{N} \to \mathbb{N}$ was defined by $f_3(j)$ = the smallest natural number i for which $j \equiv i \bmod 3$, and the function f: $\mathbb{N} \to \mathbb{N}$ is defined by $f(i) = i + 1$. $f_3 \circ f$ consists of the ordered pairs $\{\langle 0,1\rangle, \langle 1,2\rangle, \langle 2,3\rangle, \langle 3,1\rangle, \langle 4,2\rangle, \langle 5,3\rangle, \ldots\}$ and is represented by the rule $f \circ f_3(j) = f_3(j) + 1$, which happens to be the smallest *positive* number that is congruent to $j + 1 \bmod 3$. Note that $f_3 \circ f(j) = f_3(j + 1)$, which happens to be the smallest *natural* number that is congruent to $j + 1 \bmod 3$. This represents the different set of ordered pairs $\{\langle 0,1\rangle, \langle 1,2\rangle, \langle 2,0\rangle, \langle 3,1\rangle, \langle 4,2\rangle, \langle 5,0\rangle, \ldots\}$. In most cases, $f \circ g \neq g \circ f$.

∇ **Theorem 0.1.** Let the functions f: $X \to Y$ and g: $Y \to Z$ be onto. Then $g \circ f$ is onto.

Proof. See the exercises.

Δ

∇ **Theorem 0.2** Let the functions f: $X \to Y$ and g: $Y \to Z$ be one to one. Then $g \circ f$ is one to one.

Proof. See the exercises.

Δ

∇ **Definition 0.18.** The *converse* of a relation R, written ~R, is defined by

$$\sim R = \{\langle y,x\rangle \mid \langle x,y\rangle \in R\}$$

The converse of a function f is likewise

$$\sim f = \{\langle y,x\rangle \mid \langle x,y\rangle \in f\}$$

If $\sim f$ happens to be a function, it is called the *inverse* of f and is denoted by f^{-1}.

Δ

When the inverse exists, it is appropriate to use functional notation for f^{-1} also, and we therefore have, for any elements a and b, $f^{-1}(b) = a$ *iff* $f(a) = b$. Note that if f: $X \to Y$ then f^{-1}: $Y \to X$.

EXAMPLE 0.18

Consider the ordered pairs for the relation $<$: $\{\langle 1,2\rangle, \langle 1,3\rangle, \langle 2,3\rangle\}$. The converse is then $\sim<$: $\{\langle 1,2\rangle, \langle 1,3\rangle, \langle 2,3\rangle\}$. Thus, the converse of "less than" is the relation "greater than."

The function b: $\mathbb{I} \to \mathbb{I}$ defined by $b(i) = i + 1$ ($\forall i = \ldots, -2, -1, 0, 1, 2, \ldots$) has the inverse b^{-1}: $\mathbb{I} \to \mathbb{I}$ defined by $b^{-1}(i) = i - 1$ ($\forall i = \ldots, -2, -1, 0, 1, 2, \ldots$). The inverse of the function that increments integers by 1 is the function that decrements integers by the same amount.

The function f: □ → □ defined by $f(i) = i^2$ ($\forall i = \ldots, -2, -1, 0, 1, 2, \ldots$) has a converse that is not a function over the given domain and codomain; the inverse notation is inappropriate, since $f^{-1}(3)$ is not defined, nor is $f^{-1}(-4)$,

Not surprisingly, if the converse of f is to be a function, the codomain of f (which will be the new domain of f^{-1}) must satisfy conditions similar to those imposed on the domain of f. In particular:

∇ **Theorem 0.3.** Let f: $X \rightarrow Y$ be a function. The converse of f is a function *iff* f is a bijection.

Proof. See the exercises.

Δ

If f is a bijection, f^{-1} must exist and will also be a bijection. In fact, the compositions $f \circ f^{-1}$ and $f^{-1} \circ f$ are the *identity* functions on the domain and codomain, respectively (see the exercises).

0.4 CARDINALITY AND INDUCTION

The *size* of various sets will frequently be of interest in the topics covered in this text, and it will occasionally be necessary to consider the set of all subsets of a given set.

∇ **Definition 0.19.** Given a set A, the *power set* of A, denoted by $\rho(A)$ or 2^A, is

$$\rho(A) = \{X \mid X \subseteq A\}$$

Δ

EXAMPLE 0.19

$$\rho(\{a, b, c\}) = \{\emptyset, \{a\}, \{b\}, \{c\}, \{a, b\}, \{a, c\}, \{b, c\}, \{a, b, c\}\}$$

and

$$\rho(\{\ \}) = \{\emptyset\}.$$

Note that $\{\emptyset\} \neq \emptyset$.

∇ **Definition 0.20.** Two sets X and Y are *equipotent* if there exists a bijection f: $X \rightarrow Y$, and we will write $\|X\| = \|Y\|$. $\|X\|$ denotes the *cardinality* of X, that is, the number of elements in X.

Δ

That is, sets with the same cardinality or "size" are equipotent. The equipotent relation is reflexive, symmetric, and transitive and is therefore an equivalence relation.

EXAMPLE 0.20

The function g: $\{a, b, c\} \rightarrow \{x, y, z\}$ defined by $g(a) = z$, $g(b) = y$, and $g(c) = x$ is a bijection, and thus $\|\{a, b, c\}\| = \|\{x, y, z\}\|$. The equivalence class consisting of all sets that are equipotent to $\{a, b, c\}$ is generally associated with the *cardinal number* 3. Thus, $\|\{a, b, c\}\| = 3$; $\|\{\ \}\| = 0$. $\{a, b, c\}$ is not equipotent to $\{\ \}$, and hence $3 \neq 0$.

The subset relation allows the sizes of sets to be *ordered*: $\|A\| \leq \|B\|$ ***iff*** $(\exists C)(C \subseteq B \wedge \|A\| = \|C\|)$. We will write $\|A\| < \|B\|$ ***iff*** $(\|A\| \leq \|B\|$ and $\|A\| \neq \|B\|)$. The observations about $\{a, b, c\}$ and $\{\ \}$ imply that $0 < 3$.

For $\mathbb{N} = \{0, 1, 2, 3, 4, 5, 6, \ldots\}$ and $\mathbb{E} = \{0, 2, 4, 6, \ldots\}$, the function f: $\mathbb{N} \rightarrow \mathbb{E}$, defined by $f(x) = 2x$, is a bijection. The set of natural numbers $\mathbb{N}$ is *countably infinite*, and its size is often denoted by $\aleph_0 = \|\mathbb{N}\|$. The doubling function f shows that $\|\mathbb{N}\| = \|\mathbb{E}\|$. Similarly, it can be shown that $\mathbb{I}$ and $\mathbb{N} \times \mathbb{N}$ are also countably infinite (see the exercises). A set that is equipotent to one of its proper subsets is called an infinite set. Since $\|\mathbb{N}\| = \|\mathbb{E}\|$ and yet $\mathbb{N} \subset \mathbb{E}$, we know that $\mathbb{N}$ must be infinite. No such correspondence between $\{a, b, c\}$ and any of its proper subsets is possible, so $\{a, b, c\}$ is a finite set. 3 is therefore a finite cardinal number, while $\aleph_0$ represents an infinite cardinal number.

Theorem 0.4 compares the size of a set A with the number of subsets of A and shows that $\|A\| < \|\rho(A)\|$. For the sets in Example 0.19, we see that $3 < 8$ and $0 < 1$, which is not unexpected. It is perhaps surprising to find that the theorem will also apply to infinite sets, for example, $\|\mathbb{N}\| < \|\rho(\mathbb{N})\|$. This means that there are cardinal numbers larger than $\aleph_0$; there are infinite sets that are not countably infinite. Indeed, the next theorem implies that there is an unending progression of infinite cardinal numbers.

∇ **Theorem 0.4.** Let A be *any* set. Then $\|A\| < \|\rho(A)\|$.

Proof. There is a bijection between A and the set of all singleton subsets of A, as shown by the function s: $A \rightarrow \{\{x\} \mid x \in A\}$ defined by $s(z) = \{z\}$ for each $z \in A$. Since $\{\{x\} \mid x \in A\} \subseteq \rho(A)$, we have $\|A\| \leq \|\rho(A)\|$. It remains to show that $\|A\| \neq \|\rho(A)\|$. By definition of cardinality, we must show that there cannot exist a bijection between A and $\rho(A)$. The following proof by contradiction will show this.

Assume f: $A \rightarrow \rho(A)$ is a function; we will demonstrate that there must exist a set in $\rho(A)$ that is not in the range of f, and hence f cannot be onto. Consider an element z of A and the set $f(z)$ to which it maps. $f(z)$ is a subset of A, and hence z may or may not belong to $f(z)$. Define B to be the set $\{y \in A \mid y \notin f(y)\}$. B is then the set of all elements of A that do not appear in the set corresponding to their image under f. It is impossible for B to be in the range of f, for if it were then there would be an element of A that maps to this subset: assume $w \in A$ and $f(w) = B$. Since w is an element of A, it might belong to B, which is a subset of A. If $w \in B$, then $w \in f(w)$, since $f(w) = B$; but the elements for which $y \in f(y)$ were exactly the ones omitted from B, and thus we would have $w \notin B$, which is a contradiction. Our speculation that w might belong to B is therefore incorrect. The only other option is that w does not belong to B. But if $w \notin B = f(w)$, then w *is* one of the elements that

are supposed to be in B and we are again faced with the impossibility that $w \notin B$ and $w \in B$. In all cases, we reach a contradiction if we assume that there exists an element w for which $f(w) = B$. Thus, B was a member of the codomain that is not in the range of f, and f is therefore not a bijection.
Δ

Sets that are finite or are countably infinite are called *countable* or *denumerable* because their elements can be arranged one after the other (enumerated). We will often need to prove that a given statement is true in an infinite variety of cases that can be enumerated by the natural numbers $0, 1, 2, \ldots$. The assertion that the sum of the first n positive numbers can be predicted by multiplying n by the number one larger than n and dividing the result by 2 seems to be true for various test values of n:

$$1 + 2 + 3 = 3(3 = 1)/2$$

$$1 + 2 + 3 + 4 + 5 = 5(5 + 1)/2$$

and so on. We would like to show that the assertion is true for all values of $n = 1, 2, 3, \ldots$, but we clearly could never check the arithmetic individually for an infinite number of cases. The assertion, which varies according to the particular number n we choose, can be represented by the statement

$$\text{P}(n)\text{: } 1 + 2 + 3 + \cdots + (n - 2) + (n - 1) + n \text{ adds up to } (n + 1)n/2.$$

Note that $\text{P}(n)$ is *not* a number; it is the assertion that two numbers are the same and therefore will only take on the values **True** and **False**. We would like to show that $\text{P}(n)$ is true for each positive integer n; that is, $(\forall n)\text{P}(n)$. Notice that if you were to attempt to check out whether P(101) was true your work would be considerably simplified if you already knew how the first 100 numbers added up. If the first 100 summed to 5050, it is clear that $1 + 2 + \cdots + 99 + 100 + 101 = (1 + 2 + \cdots + 99 + 100) + 101 = 5050 + 101 = 5151$; the hard part of the calculation can be done *without* doing arithmetic with 101 separate numbers. Checking that $(101 + 1)101/2$ agrees with 5151 shows that P(101) is indeed true [that is, as long as we are sure that our calculations in verifying P(100) are correct]. Essentially, the same technique could have been used to show that P(6) followed from P(5). This trick of using the results of previous cases to help verify further cases is reflected in the principle of mathematical induction.

∇ **Theorem 0.5.** Let $\text{P}(n)$ be a statement for each natural number $n \in \mathbb{N}$. From the two hypotheses

i. P(0)
ii. $(\forall m \in \mathbb{N})(\text{P}(m) \Rightarrow \text{P}(m + 1))$

we can conclude $(\forall n \in \mathbb{N})\text{P}(n)$.
Δ

The fundamental soundness of the principle is obvious in light of the following analogy: Assume you can reach the basement of some building (hypothesis i). If you were assured that from *any* floor m you could reach the next higher floor (hypothesis ii), you would then be assured that you could reach any floor you wished $((\forall n \in \mathbb{N})\mathrm{P}(n))$.

Similar statements can be made from other starting points; for example, beginning with P(4) and $(\forall m > 4)(\mathrm{P}(m) \Rightarrow \mathrm{P}(m+1))$, we can derive the conclusion $(\forall m > 4)\mathrm{P}(n)$; had we started on the fourth floor of the building, we could reach *any* of the higher floors.

EXAMPLE 0.21

Consider the statement discussed above, where $\mathrm{P}(n)$ was the assertion that $1+2+3+\cdots+(n-2)+(n-1)+n$ adds up to $(n+1)n/2$. We will begin with P(1) (the *basis* step) and note that $1=(1+1)1/2$, so P(1) is indeed true. For the *inductive* step, let m be an arbitrary (but fixed) positive integer, and assume $\mathrm{P}((m+1)$ is true; that is, $1+2+3+\cdots+(m-2)+(m-1)+m$ adds up to $(m+1)m/2$. We need to show $\mathrm{P}(m+1)$: $1+2+3+\cdots+(m+1-2)+(m+1-1)+(m+1))$ adds up to $(m+1+1)(m+1)/2$. As in the case of proceeding from 100 to 101, we will use the fact that the first m integers add up correctly (the induction assumption) to see how the first $m+1$ integers add up. We have:

$$\begin{aligned}1+2+3+\cdots+(m+1-2)+(m+1-1)+(m+1)\\ &= (1+2+3+\cdots+(m+1-2)+(m+1-1))+(m+1)\\ &= (m+1)m/2+(m+1)\\ &= (m+1)m/2+(m+1)2/2\\ &= ((m+1)m+(m+1)2)/2\\ &= ((m+1)(m+2)/2\\ &= (m+1+1)(m+1)/2\end{aligned}$$

$\mathrm{P}(m+1)$ is therefore true, and $\mathrm{P}(m+1)$ indeed follows from $\mathrm{P}(m)$. Since m was arbitrary, $(\forall m)(\mathrm{P}(m) \Rightarrow \mathrm{P}(m+1))$ and, by induction, $(\forall n \geq 1)\mathrm{P}(n)$. The formula is therefore true for every positive integer n. It is interesting to note that, with the usual convention of defining the sum of *no* integers to be zero, the formula also holds for $n=0$, and P(0) could have been used as the basis step to prove $(\forall n \in \mathbb{N})\mathrm{P}(n)$.

EXAMPLE 0.22

Consider the statement

> Any statement formula using the n variables $p_1, p_2, \ldots, p_n$ has an equivalent expression that contains less than $n \cdot 2^n$ operators.

This can be proved by induction on the statement

P(n): Any statement formula using *n or fewer* variables has an equivalent expression that contains less than $n \cdot 2^n$ operators.

Basis step: A statement formula in one variable must be either be p, $\neg$p, **T**, or **F**, each of which requires at most one operator, and since $1 < 1 \cdot 2^1$, P(1) is true.

Inductive step: Assume P(m) is true; we need to prove that P(m + 1) is true, which is to say that we need to ensure that the statement holds not just for formulas with m or fewer variables, but also for formulas with m + 1 variables. Thus, choose an expression S containing the variables $p_1, p_2, \ldots, p_m, p_{m+1}$. Consider the principal disjunctive normal form (PDNF) of S. This expression is equivalent to S and has terms that can be separated into two categories: (1) those that contain the term p_{m+1}, and (2) those that contain the term $\neg p_{m+1}$. While the PDNF may very well contain more than the desired number of terms, the distributive law can be used to factor p_{m+1} out of all the terms in (1), leaving an expression of the form $C \wedge p_{m+1}$, where C is a formula containing only the terms $p_1, p_2, \ldots, p_m$. Similarly, $\neg p_{m+1}$ can be factored out of all the terms in (2), leaving an expression of the form $D \wedge \neg p_{m+1}$, where D is also a formula containing only the terms $p_1, p_2, \ldots, p_m$.

S can therefore be written as $(C \wedge p_{m+1}) \vee (D \wedge \neg p_{m+1})$, which contains the four operators $\wedge$, $\vee$, $\wedge$, and $\neg$ and the operators that comprise the formulas for C and D. However, since both C and D only contain the m variables $p_1, p_2, \ldots, p_m$, the induction assumption ensures that they each have equivalent representations using no more than $m \cdot 2^m$ operators. S can therefore be written in a form containing at most $4 + m \cdot 2^m + m \cdot 2^m$ operators, which can be shown to be less than $(m + 1) \cdot 2^{m+1}$ for all positive numbers m. Since S was an arbitrary expresson with $m + 1$ operators, we have shown that *any* statement formula using exactly m + 1 variables has an equivalent expression that contains no more than $(m + 1) \cdot 2^{m+1}$ operators.

Since P(m) was assumed true, we likewise know that any statement formula using m or fewer variables also has an equivalent expression that contains no more than $m \cdot 2^m$ operators. P(m + 1) is therefore true, and P(m + 1) indeed follows from P(m). Since m was an arbitrary positive integer, $(\forall m > 1)(P(m) \Rightarrow P(m + 1))$ and by induction $(\forall n > 1)P(n)$. The formula is therefore true for every natural number n.

0.5 RECURSION

Since this text will be dealing with devices that repeatedly perform certain operations, it is important to understand the recursive definition of functions and how to effectively investigate the properties of such functions. Recall that the factorial function ($f(n) = n!$) is defined to be the product of the first n integers. Thus,

$$f(1) = 1$$

$$f(2) = 1 \cdot 2 = 2$$

$$f(3) = 1 \cdot 2 \cdot 3 = 6$$

$$f(4) = 1 \cdot 2 \cdot 3 \cdot 4 = 24$$

and so on. Note that individual definitions get longer as n increases. If we adopt the convention that $f(0) = 1$, the factorial function can be *recursively* defined in terms of other values produced by the function.

∇ **Definition 0.21.** For $x \in \mathbb{N}$, define

$$f(x) = 1, \qquad \text{if } x = 0$$

$$f(x) = x \cdot f(x-1), \qquad \text{if } x > 0$$

Δ

This definition implies that $f(3) = 3 \cdot f(2) = 3 \cdot 2 \cdot f(1) = 3 \cdot 2 \cdot 1 \cdot f(0) = 3 \cdot 2 \cdot 1 \cdot 1 = 6$.

0.6 BACKUS–NAUR FORM

The syntax of programming languages is often illustrated with *syntax diagrams* or described in *Backus–Naur Form* (BNF) notation.

EXAMPLE 0.23

The constraints for integer constants, which may begin with a sign and must consist of one or more digits, are succinctly described by the following *productions* (replacement rules):

<sign> ::= **+** | **−**

<digit> ::= **0** | **1** | **2** | **3** | **4** | **5** | **6** | **7** | **8** | **9**

<natural> ::= <digit> | <digit><natural>

<integer> ::= <natural> | <sign><natural>

The symbol | represents "or," and the rule

<sign> ::= **+** | **−**

should be interpreted to mean that the token <sign> can be replaced by either the symbol **+** or the symbol **−**. A typical integer constant is therefore **+12**, since it can be derived by applying the above rules in the following fashion:

<real constant> → <integer>

<integer> → <sign><natural>

<sign><natural> → **+**<natural>

+<natural> → **+**<digit><natural>

+<digit><natural> → **+1**<natural>

+1<natural> → **+1**<digit>

+1<digit> → **+12**

Syntax diagrams for each of the four productions are shown in Figure 0.6. These can be combined to form a diagram that does not involve the intermediate tokens <sign>, <digit>, and <natural> (see Figure 0.7).

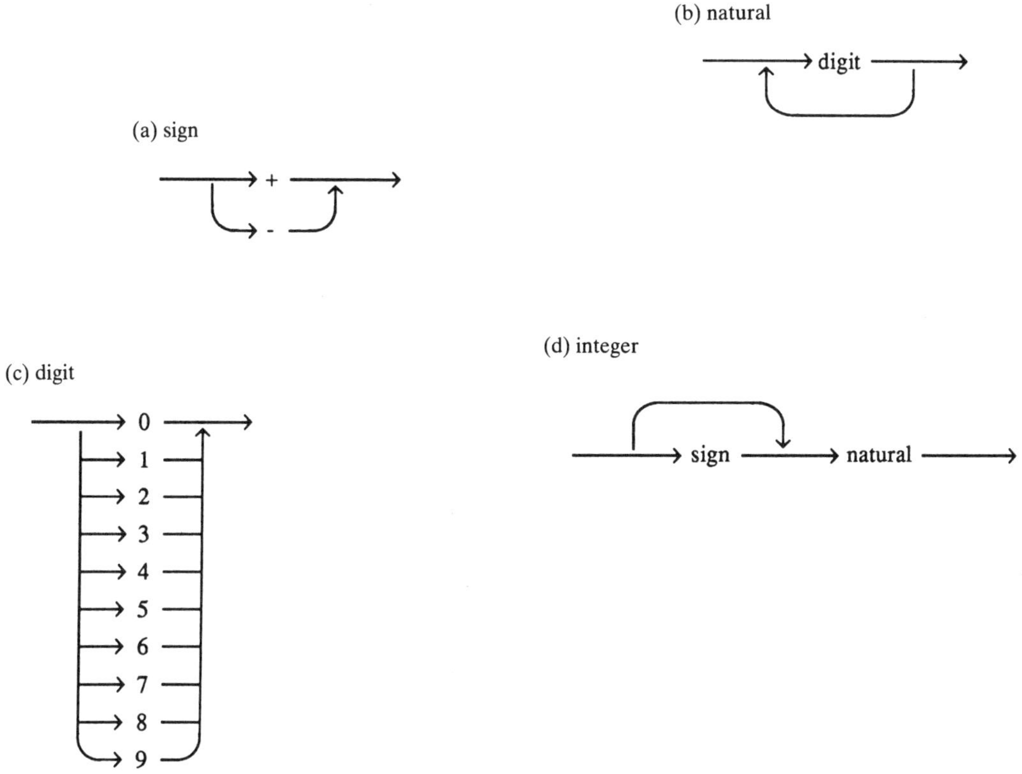

Figure 0.6 Syntax diagrams for the components of integer constants

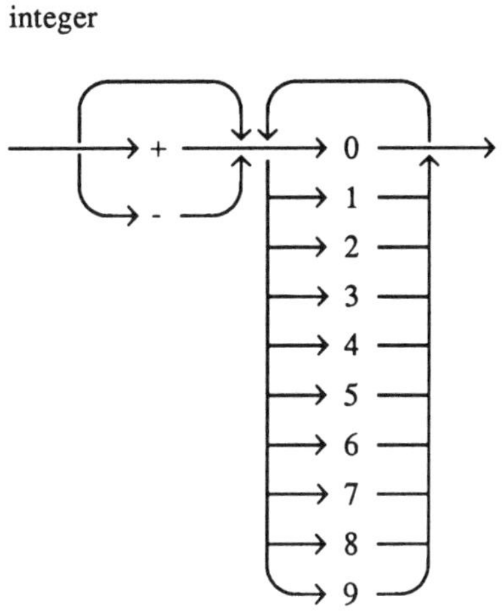

Figure 0.7 A syntax diagram for integer constants

EXERCISES

0.1. Construct truth tables for:
(a) $\neg r \vee (\neg p \downarrow \neg q)$
(b) $(p \wedge \neg q) \vee \neg(p \uparrow q)$

0.2. Draw circuit diagrams for:
(a) $\neg(r \vee (\neg p \downarrow \neg q)) \uparrow (s \wedge p)$
(b) $(p \wedge \neg q) \vee \neg(p \uparrow q)$

0.3. Show that the sets $\{1, 2\} \times \{a, b\}$ and $\{a, b\} \times \{1, 2\}$ are not equal.

0.4. Let $X = \{1, 2, 3, 4\}$.
(a) Determine the set of ordered pairs comprising the relation $<$.
(b) Determine the set of ordered pairs comprising the relation $=$.
(c) Since relations are sets of ordered pairs, it makes sense to union them together. Determine the set $= \cup <$.
(d) Determine the set of ordered pairs comprising the relation $\leq$.

0.5. Let n be a natural number. Show that congruence modulo n, $\equiv_n$, is an equivalence relation.

0.6. Let $X = \mathbb{N}$. Determine the equivalence classes for congruence modulo 0.

0.7. Let $X = \mathbb{N}$. Determine the equivalence classes for congruence modulo 1.

0.8. Let $X = \mathbb{R}$. Determine the equivalence classes for congruence modulo 1.

0.9. Let R be an arbitrary equivalence relation in X. Prove that the distinct equivalence classes of R form a partition of X.

0.10. Given a set X and a partition $P = \{A_1, A_2, \ldots, A_n\}$ of X, prove that X equals the union of the sets in P.

0.11. Given a set X and a partition $P = \{A_1, A_2, \ldots, A_n\}$ of X, prove that the relation $R(P)$ in X induced by P is an equivalence relation.

0.12. Let $X = \{1, 2, 3, 4\}$.
(a) Give an example of a partition P for which $R(P)$ is a function.
(b) Give an example of a partition P for which $R(P)$ is not a function.

0.13. The following "proof" seems to indicate that a relation that is symmetric and transitive must also be reflexive:

> By symmetry, $x\,R\,y \Rightarrow y\,R\,x$.
> Thus we have $(x\,R\,y \wedge y\,R\,x)$.
> By transitivity, $(x\,R\,y \wedge y\,R\,x) \Rightarrow x\,R\,x$.
> Hence $(\forall x)(x\,R\,x)$.

Find the flaw in this "proof" and give an example of a relation that is symmetric and transitive but not reflexive.

0.14. Let R be an arbitrary equivalence relation in X. Prove that the equality relation on X refines R.

0.15. Consider the "function" t: $\mathbb{R} \to \mathbb{R}$ defined by pairing x with the real number whose cosine is x.
(a) Show that t is not well defined.
(b) Adjust the domain and range of t to produce a valid function.

0.16. Consider the function s': $\mathbb{R} \to \mathbb{R}$ defined by $s'(x) = x^2$. Show that the converse of s' is not a function.

0.17. Let $\mathbb{P}$ be the set of nonnegative real numbers, and consider the function s: $\mathbb{P} \to \mathbb{P}$ defined by $s(x) = x^2$. Show that s^{-1} exists.

0.18. Let f: $X \times Y$ be an arbitrary function. Prove that the converse of f is a function ***iff*** f is a bijection.

0.19. **(a)** Let $\sim A$ denote the complement of a set A. Prove that $\sim(\sim A) = A$.
(b) Let $\sim$R denote the converse of a relation R. Prove that $\sim(\sim\mathrm{R}) = \mathrm{R}$.

0.20. Let the functions f: $X \to Y$ and g: $Y \to Z$ be one to one. Prove that $g \circ f$ is one to one.

0.21. Let the functions f: $X \to Y$ and g: $Y \to Z$ be onto. Prove that $g \circ f$ is onto.

0.22. Define two functions for which $f \circ g = g \circ f$.

0.23. Define, if possible, a bijection between:
(a) $\mathbb{N}$ and $\mathbb{I}$
(b) $\mathbb{N}$ and $\mathbb{N} \times \mathbb{N}$
(c) $\mathbb{N}$ and $\mathbb{Q}$
(d) $\mathbb{N}$ and $\{a, b, c\}$

0.24. Use induction to prove that the sum of the cubes of the first n positive integers adds up to $n^2(n+1)^2/4$.

0.25. Use induction to prove that the sum of the first n positive integers is less than n^2 (for $n > 1$).

0.26. Use induction to prove that, for $n > 3$, $n! > n^2$.

0.27. Use induction to prove that, for $n > 3$, $n! > 2^n$.

0.28. Use induction to prove that $1^2 + 2^2 + \cdots + n^2 = n(n+1)(2n+1)/6$.

0.29. Prove by induction that $X \cap (X_1 \cup X_2 \cup \cdots \cup X_n) = (X \cap X_1) \cup (X \cap X_2) \cup \cdots \cup (X \cap X_n)$.

0.30. Let $\sim A$ denote the complement of the set A. Prove $\sim(X_1 \cup X_2 \cup \cdots \cup X_n) = (\sim X_1) \cap (\sim X_2) \cap \cdots \cap (\sim X_n)$ by induction.

0.31. Use induction to prove that there are 2^n subsets of a set of size n; that is, for a finite set A, $\|\rho(A\| = 2^{\|A\|}$.

0.32. The principle of mathematical induction is often stated in the following form, which requires (apparently) stronger hypotheses to reach the desired conclusion: Let P(n) be a statement for each natural number $n \in \mathbb{N}$. From the two hypotheses
i. P(0)
ii. $(\forall m \in \mathbb{N})(((\forall i \le m)\mathrm{P}(i)) \Rightarrow \mathrm{P}(m+1))$
we can conclude $(\forall n \in \mathbb{N})\mathrm{P}(n)$. Prove that the strong form of induction is equivalent to the statement of induction given in the text. *Hint:* Consider the restatement of the hypothesis given in Example 0.22.

0.33. Determine what types of strings are defined by the following BNF:

<sign> ::= **+** | **−**
<digit> ::= **0** | **1** | **2** | **3** | **4** | **5** | **6** | **7** | **8** | **9**
<natural> ::= <digit> | <digit><natural>
<integer> ::= <natural> | <sign><natural>
<real constant> ::= <integer> |
<integer>**.** |
<integer>**.**<natural> |
<integer>**.**<natural>**E**<integer>

0.34. A set X is *cofinite* if the complement of X (with respect to some generally understood universal set) is finite. Let the universal set be $\mathbb{I}$. Give an example of

(a) A finite set
(b) A cofinite set
(c) A set that is neither finite nor cofinite

0.35. Consider the equipotent relation, which relates sets to other sets.
(a) Prove that this relation is reflexive.
(b) Prove that this relation is symmetric.
(c) Prove that this relation is transitive.

0.36. Define a function that will show that $\|\mathbb{N}\| = \|\mathbb{N} \times \mathbb{N}\|$.

0.37. Show that $\mathbb{N}$ is equipotent to $\mathbb{N}$.

0.38. Show that $\mathbb{N}$ is equipotent to $\mathbb{Q}$.

0.39. Show that $\rho(\mathbb{N})$ is equipotent to $\{f\colon \mathbb{N} \to \{\text{Yes}, \text{No}\} \mid f \text{ is a function}\}$.

0.40. Show that $\rho(\mathbb{N})$ is equipotent to $\mathbb{R}$.

0.41. Draw a circuit diagram that will implement the function q given by the truth table shown in Figure 0.8.

0.42. (a) Draw a circuit diagram that will implement the function q_1 given by the truth table shown in Figure 0.9.
(b) Draw a circuit diagram that will implement the function q_2 given by the truth table shown in Figure 0.9.
(c) Draw a circuit diagram that will implement the function q_3 given by the truth table shown in Figure 0.9.

p_1	p_2	p_3	q
0	0	0	0
0	0	1	0
0	1	0	1
0	1	1	0
1	0	0	1
1	0	1	0
1	1	0	0
1	1	1	1

Figure 0.8 The truth table for Exercise 0.41

p_1	p_2	p_3	p_4	q_1	q_2	q_3
0	0	0	0	1	1	1
0	0	0	1	0	1	0
0	0	1	0	1	0	0
0	0	1	1	1	1	0
0	1	0	0	0	1	1
0	1	0	1	1	0	0
0	1	1	0	1	1	0
0	1	1	1	0	0	0
1	0	0	0	1	0	1
1	0	0	1	1	0	0
1	0	1	0	0	1	0
1	0	1	1	0	0	0
1	1	0	0	1	1	1
1	1	0	1	0	1	0
1	1	1	0	0	1	1
1	1	1	1	0	0	0

Figure 0.9 The truth table for Exercise 0.42

CHAPTER

1

INTRODUCTION and BASIC DEFINITIONS

This chapter introduces the concept of a *finite automaton*, which is perhaps the simplest form of abstract computing device. Although finite automata theory is concerned with relatively simple machines, it is an important foundation of a large number of concrete and abstract applications. The finite-state control of a finite automaton is also at the heart of more complex computing devices such as *finite-state transducers* (Chapter 7), *pushdown automata* (Chapter 10), and *Turing machines* (Chapter 11).

Applications for finite automata can be found in the algorithms used for string matching in text editors and spelling checkers and in the lexical analyzers used by assemblers and compilers. In fact, the best known string matching algorithms are based on finite automata. Although finite automata are generally thought of as abstract computing devices, other noncomputer applications are possible. These applications include traffic signals and vending machines or any device in which there are a finite set of inputs and a finite set of things that must be "remembered" by the device.

Briefly, a *deterministic finite automaton*, also called a *recognizer* or *acceptor*, is a mathematical model of a finite-state computing device that recognizes a set of *words* over some alphabet; this set of words is called the *language* accepted by the automaton. For each word over the alphabet of the automaton, there is a unique path through the automaton; if the path ends in what is called a *final* or *accepting* state, then the word traversing this path is in the language *accepted* by the automaton.

Finite automata represent one attempt at employing a finite description to rigorously define a (possibly) infinite set of words (that is, a *language*). Given such a description, the criterion for membership in the language is straightforward and well-defined; there are simple algorithms for ascertaining whether a given word belongs to the set. In this respect, such devices model one of the behaviors we require of a compiler: recognizing syntactically correct programs. Actually, finite automata have inherent limitations that make them unsuitable for modeling the compilers of modern programming languages, but they serve as an instructive first approximation. Compilers must also be capable of producing object code from source code, and a model of a simple translation device is presented in Chapter 7 and enhanced in later chapters.

Logic circuitry can easily be devised to implement these automata in hardware. With appropriate data structures, these devices can likewise be modeled with software. An example is the highly interactive Turing's World, developed at Stanford University by Jon Barwise and John Etchemendy. This Apple® Macintosh graphics package and the accompanying tutorial are particularly useful in experimenting with many forms of automata. Both hardware and software approaches will be explored in this chapter. We begin our formal treatment with some fundamental definitions.

1.1 ALPHABETS AND WORDS

The devices we will consider are meant to react to and manipulate symbols. Different applications may employ different character sets, and we will therefore take care to explicitly mention the *alphabet* under consideration.

∇ **Definition 1.1.** Σ is an *alphabet* ***iff*** Σ is a finite nonempty set of symbols.
Δ

An element of an alphabet is often called a letter, although there is no reason to restrict symbols in an alphabet to consist solely of single characters. Some familiar examples of alphabets are the 26-letter English alphabet and the ASCII character set, which represents a standard set of computer codes. In this text we will usually make use of shorter, simpler alphabets, like those given in Example 1.1.

EXAMPLE 1.1

i. $\{\mathbf{0}, \mathbf{1}\}$
ii. $\{\mathbf{a}, \mathbf{b}, \mathbf{c}\}$
iii. $\{\langle \mathbf{0}, \mathbf{0}\rangle, \langle \mathbf{0}, \mathbf{1}\rangle, \langle \mathbf{1}, \mathbf{0}\rangle, \langle \mathbf{1}, \mathbf{1}\rangle\}$

It is important to emphasize that the elements (letters) of an alphabet are not restricted to single characters. In example (iii) above, the alphabet is composed of the ordered pairs in $\{\mathbf{0}, \mathbf{1}\} \times \{\mathbf{0}, \mathbf{1}\}$. Such an alphabet will be utilized in Chapter 7 when we use sequential machines to construct a simple binary adder.

Based on the definition of an alphabet, we can define composite entities called *words* or *strings*, which are finite sequences of symbols from the alphabet.

∇ **Definition 1.2.** For a given an alphabet Σ and a natural number n, a sequence of symbols $\mathbf{a}_1\mathbf{a}_2 \ldots \mathbf{a}_n$ is a *word* (or *string*) *over the alphabet* Σ *of length n* ***iff*** for each $i = 1, 2, \ldots, n$, $\mathbf{a}_i \in \Sigma$.
Δ

As formally specified in Definition 1.5, the order in which the symbols of the word occur will be deemed significant, and therefore a word of length 3 can be identified with an ordered triple belonging to $\Sigma \times \Sigma \times \Sigma$. Indeed, one may view the three-letter word **bca** as a convenient shorthand for the ordered triple $\langle \mathbf{b}, \mathbf{c}, \mathbf{a} \rangle$. A word over an alphabet is thus an ordered string of symbols, where each symbol in the string is an element of the given alphabet. An obvious example of words are what you are reading right now, which are words (or strings) over the standard English alphabet. In some contexts, these strings of symbols are occasionally called *sentences*.

EXAMPLE 1.2

Let $\Sigma = \{\mathbf{0}, \mathbf{1}, \mathbf{2}, \mathbf{3}, \mathbf{4}, \mathbf{5}, \mathbf{6}, \mathbf{7}, \mathbf{8}, \mathbf{9}\}$; some examples of words over this alphabet are

i. **42**
ii. **242342**

Even though only three different members of Σ occur in the second example, the length of **242342** is 6, as each symbol is counted each time it occurs. To easily and succinctly express these concepts, the absolute value notation will be employed to denote the length of a string. Thus, $|\mathbf{42}| = 2$, $|\mathbf{242342}| = 6$, and $|\mathbf{a}_1\mathbf{a}_2\mathbf{a}_3\mathbf{a}_4| = 4$.

∇ **Definition 1.3.** For a given alphabet Σ and a word $x = \mathbf{a}_1\mathbf{a}_2 \ldots \mathbf{a}_n$ over Σ, $|x|$ denotes the length of x. That is, $|\mathbf{a}_1\mathbf{a}_2 \ldots \mathbf{a}_n| = n$.
Δ

It is possible to join together two strings to form a composite word; this process is called *concatenation*. The concatenation of two strings of symbols produces one longer string of symbols, which is made up of the characters in the first string, followed immediately by the symbols of the second string.

∇ **Definition 1.4.** Given an alphabet Σ, let $x = \mathbf{a}_1 \ldots \mathbf{a}_n$ and $y = \mathbf{b}_1 \ldots \mathbf{b}_m$ be strings where each $\mathbf{a}_i \in \Sigma$ and each $\mathbf{b}_j \in \Sigma$. The *concatenation of the strings x and y*, denoted by $x \cdot y$, is the juxtaposition of x and y; that is, $x \cdot y = \mathbf{a}_1 \ldots \mathbf{a}_n\mathbf{b}_1 \ldots \mathbf{b}_m$.
Δ

Note in Definition 1.4 that $|x \cdot y| = n + m = |x| + |y|$. Some examples of string concatenation are

i. $\mathbf{aaa} \cdot \mathbf{bbb} = \mathbf{aaabbb}$
ii. $\mathbf{home} \cdot \mathbf{run} = \mathbf{homerun}$
iii. $\mathbf{a}^2 \cdot \mathbf{b}^3 = \mathbf{aabbb}$

Example (iii) illustrates a shorthand notation for denoting strings. Placing a superscript after a symbol means that this entity is a string made by concatenating it to itself the specified number of times. In a similar fashion, $(\mathbf{ac})^3$ is meant to express **acacac**. Note that an *equal* sign was used in the above examples. Formally, two strings are equal if they have the same number of symbols and these symbols match, character for character.

∇ **Definition 1.5.** Given an alphabet Σ, let $x = \mathbf{a}_1 \ldots \mathbf{a}_n$ and $y = \mathbf{b}_1 \ldots \mathbf{b}_m$ be strings over Σ. x and y are equal ***iff*** $n = m$ and for each $i = 1, 2, \ldots, n$, $\mathbf{a}_i = \mathbf{b}_i$.
Δ

The operation of concatenation has certain algebraic properties: it is associative, and it is not commutative. That is,

i. $(\forall x \in \Sigma^*)(\forall y \in \Sigma^*)(\forall z \in \Sigma^*)x \cdot (y \cdot z) = (x \cdot y) \cdot z$.
ii. For most strings x and y, $x \cdot y \neq y \cdot x$.

When the operation of concatenation is clear from the context, we will adopt the convention of omitting the symbol for the operator (as is done in arithmetic with the multiplication operator). Thus xyz refers to $x \cdot y \cdot z$. In fact, in Chapter 6 it will be seen that the operation of concatenation has many algebraic properties that are similar to those of arithmetic multiplication.

It is often necessary to count the number of occurrences of a given symbol within a word. The notation described in the next definition will be an especially useful shorthand in many contexts.

∇ **Definition 1.6.** Given an alphabet Σ, and some $\mathbf{b} \in \Sigma$, the *length of a word w with respect to $\mathbf{b}$*, denoted $|w|_{\mathbf{b}}$, is the number of occurrences of the letter **b** within that word.
Δ

EXAMPLE 1.3

i. $|\mathbf{abb}|_{\mathbf{b}} = 2$
ii. $|\mathbf{abb}|_{\mathbf{c}} = 0$
iii. $|\mathbf{1000000001118881888888}|_{\mathbf{1}} = 5$

∇ **Definition 1.7.** Given an alphabet Σ, the *empty word*, denoted by λ, is defined to be the (unique) word consisting of zero letters.
Δ

The empty word is often denoted by ϵ in other formal language texts. The empty string serves as the identity element for concatenation. That is, for all strings x,

$$x \cdot \lambda = \lambda \cdot x = x$$

Even though the empty word is represented by a single character, λ is a string but is *not* a member of any alphabet: $\lambda \notin \Sigma$.

A particular string x can be divided into *substrings* in several ways. If we choose to break x up into three substrings u, v, and w, there are many ways to accomplish this. For example, if $x = \mathbf{abccdbc}$, it could be written as $\mathbf{ab} \cdot \mathbf{ccd} \cdot \mathbf{bc}$; that is, $x = uvw$, where $u = \mathbf{ab}$, $v = \mathbf{ccd}$, and $w = \mathbf{bc}$. This x could also be written as $\mathbf{abc} \cdot \lambda \cdot \mathbf{cdbc}$, where $u = \mathbf{abc}$, $v = \lambda$, and $w = \mathbf{cdbc}$. In this second case, $|x| = 7 = 3 + 0 + 4 = |u| + |v| + |w|$.

A fundamental structure in formal languages involves sets of words. A simple example of such a set is Σ^k, the collection of all words of exactly length k (for some $k \in \mathbb{N}$) that can be constructed from the letters of Σ.

∇ **Definition 1.8.** Given an alphabet Σ and a nonnegative integer $k \in \mathbb{N}$, we define

$$\Sigma^k = \{x \mid x \text{ is a word over } \Sigma \text{ and } |x| = k\}$$

Δ

EXAMPLE 1.4

If

$$\Sigma = \{\mathbf{0}, \mathbf{1}\}$$

then

$$\Sigma^0 = \{\lambda\}$$
$$\Sigma^1 = \{\mathbf{0}, \mathbf{1}\}$$
$$\Sigma^2 = \{\mathbf{00}, \mathbf{01}, \mathbf{10}, \mathbf{11}\}$$
$$\Sigma^3 = \{\mathbf{000}, \mathbf{001}, \mathbf{010}, \mathbf{011}, \mathbf{100}, \mathbf{101}, \mathbf{110}, \mathbf{111}\}$$

λ is the only element of Σ^0, the set of all words containing zero letters from Σ. There is no difficulty in letting λ be an element (and the only element) of Σ^0, since each Σ^k is not necessarily an alphabet, but is instead a set of words; λ, according to the definition, is indeed a word consisting of zero letters.

∇ **Definition 1.9.** Given an alphabet Σ, define

$$\Sigma^* = \bigcup_{k=0}^{\infty} \Sigma^k = \Sigma^0 \cup \Sigma^1 \cup \Sigma^2 \cup \Sigma^3 \cup \dots$$

and

$$\Sigma^+ = \bigcup_{k=1}^{\infty} \Sigma^k = \Sigma^1 \cup \Sigma^2 \cup \Sigma^3 \cup \dots$$

Δ

Σ^* is the set of all words that may be constructed from the letters of an alphabet Σ. Σ^+ is the set of all *nonempty* words that may be constructed from Σ.

Σ^*, like the set of natural numbers, is an infinite set. Although Σ^* is infinite, each word in Σ^* is of finite length. This property follows from the definition of Σ^* and a property of natural numbers: any $k \in \mathbb{N}$ must by definition be a finite number. Σ^* is defined to be the union of all Σ^k, $k \in \mathbb{N}$. Since each such k is a finite number and every word in Σ^k is of length k, then every word in Σ^k must be of finite length. Furthermore, since Σ^* is the union of all such Σ^k, every word in Σ^* must also be of finite length. While Σ^* can contain arbitrarily long words, each of these words must be finite, just as every number in $\mathbb{N}$ is finite.

Since Σ^* is the union of all Σ^k for $k \in \mathbb{N}$, Σ^* must also contain Σ^0. In other words, besides containing all words that can be constructed from one or more letters of Σ, Σ^* also contains the empty word λ. While $\lambda \notin \Sigma$, $\lambda \in \Sigma^*$. λ represents a *string* and *not* a symbol, and thus the empty string cannot be in the alphabet Σ. However, λ is included in Σ^*, since Σ^* is not just an alphabet, but a collection of words over the alphabet Σ. Note, however, that Σ^+ is $\Sigma^* - \{\lambda\}$; Σ^+ specifically excludes λ.

1.2 DEFINITION OF A FINITE AUTOMATON

We now have the building blocks necessary to define deterministic finite automata. A *deterministic finite automaton* is a mathematical model of a machine that accepts a particular set of words over some alphabet Σ.

A useful visualization of this concept might be referred to as the *black box* model. This conceptualization is built around a black box that houses the *finite-state control*. This control reacts to the information provided by the *read head*, which extracts data from the *input tape*. The control also governs the operation of the output indicator, often depicted as an *acceptance light*, as shown in Figure 1.1.

There is no limit to the number of symbols that can be on the tape (although each individual word must be of finite length). As the input tape is read by the machine, *state transitions*, which alter the current *state* of the automaton, take place within the black box. Depending on the word contained on the input tape, the light bulb either lights or remains dark when the end of the input string is reached, indicating acceptance or rejection of the word, respectively. We assume that the input head can sense when it has passed the last symbol on the tape.

In some sense, a personal computer fits the finite-state control model; it reacts

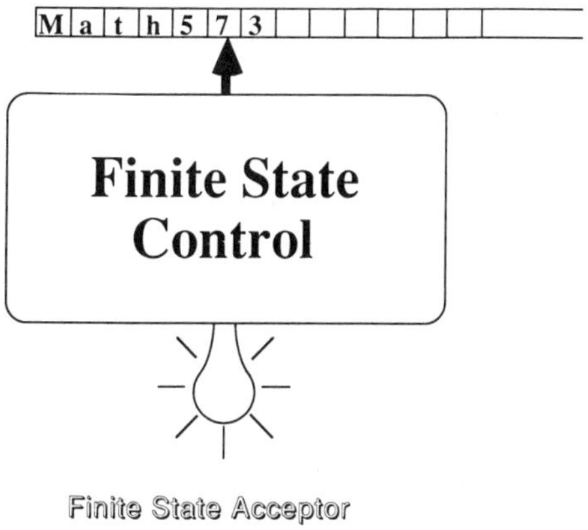

Figure 1.1 A model of a finite-state acceptor

to each keystroke entered from the keyboard according to the current state of the CPU and its own internal memory. However, the number of possible bit patterns that even a small computer can assume is so astronomically large that it is totally impractical to model a computer in this fashion. Finite-state machines can be profitably used to describe portions of a computer (such as parts of the arithmetic/logic unit, as discussed in Chapter 7, Example 7.15) and other devices that assume a reasonable number of states.

Although finite automata are usually thought of as processing strings of letters over some alphabet, the input can conceptually be elements from any finite set. A useful example is the "brain" of a vending machine, which, say, dispenses 30¢ candy bars.

EXAMPLE 1.5

The input to the vending machine is the set of coins {nickel, dime, quarter}, represented by **n**, **d**, and **q** in Figure 1.2. The machine may only "remember" a finite number of things; in this case, it will keep track of the amount of money that has been dropped into the machine. Thus, the machine may be in the "state" of remembering that no money has yet been deposited (denoted in this example by <0¢>), or that a single nickel has been inserted (the state labeled <5¢>), or that either a dime or two nickels have been deposited (<10¢>), and so on. Note that from state <0¢> there is an arrow labeled by the dime token **d** pointing to the state <10¢>, indicating that, at a time when the machine "believes" that no money has been deposited, the insertion of a dime causes the machine to transfer to the state that remembers that ten cents has been deposited. From the <0¢> state, the arrows in the diagram show that if two nickels (**n**) are input the machine moves through the <5¢> state and likewise ends in the state labeled <10¢>.

The vending machine thus counts the amount of change dropped into the machine (up to 50¢). The machine begins in the state labeled <0¢> and follows the arrows to higher-numbered states as coins are inserted. For example, depositing a nickel, a dime, and then a quarter would move the machine to the states <5¢>,

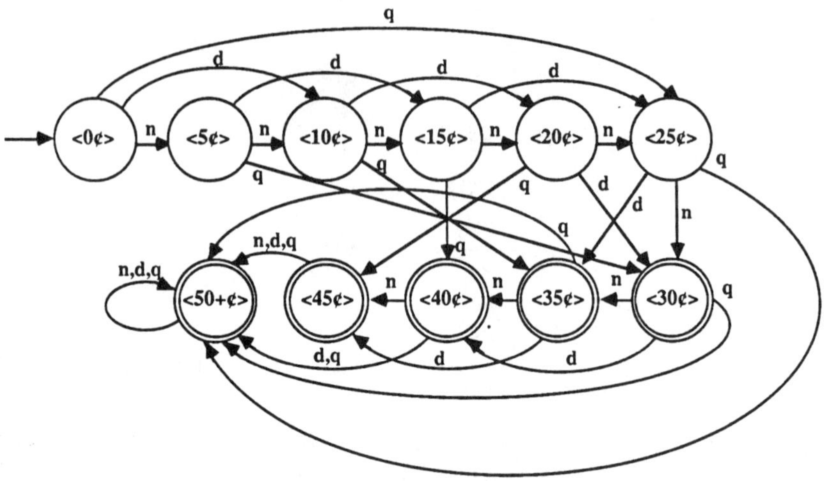

Figure 1.2 An implementation of a vending machine

<15¢>, and then <40¢>. The states labeled 30¢ and above are doubly encircled to indicate that enough money has been deposited; if 30¢ or more has been deposited, then the machine "accepts," indicating that a candy bar may be selected.

Finite automata are appropriate whenever there are a finite number of inputs and only a finite number of situations must be distinguished by the machine. Other applications include traffic signals and elevators (as discussed in Chapter 7). We now present a formal mathematical definition of a finite-state machine.

∇ **Definition 1.10.** A *deterministic finite automaton* or *deterministic finite acceptor* (DFA) is a quintuple $<\Sigma, S, s_0, \delta, F>$, where

- **i.** Σ is the *input alphabet* (a finite nonempty set of symbols).
- **ii.** S is a finite nonempty set of *states*.
- **iii.** s_0 is the *start* (or *initial*) state, an element of S.
- **iv.** δ is the *state transition function*; $\delta: S \times \Sigma \rightarrow S$.
- **v.** F is the set of *final* (or *accepting*) states, a (possibly empty) subset of S.

Δ

The input alphabet, Σ, for any deterministic finite automaton A, is the set of symbols that can appear on the input tape. Each successive symbol in a word will cause a transition from the present state to another state in the machine. As specified by the δ function, there is exactly one such state transition for each combination of a symbol $\mathbf{a} \in \Sigma$ and a state $s \in S$. This is the origin of the word "deterministic" in the phrase "deterministic finite automaton."

The various states represent the memory of the machine. Since the number of states in the machine is finite, the number of distinguishable situations that can be remembered by the machine is also finite. This limitation of the device's ability to store its past history is the origin of the word "finite" in the phrase "deterministic finite automaton." At any given time during processing, if the previous history of the machine is considered to be the reactions of the DFA to the letters that have already been read, then the current state represents all that is known about the history of the machine.

The start state of the machine is the state in which the machine always begins processing a string. From this state, successive input symbols from Σ are used by the δ function to arrive at successive states in the machine. Processing stops when the string of symbols is exhausted. The state in which the machine is left can either be a final state, in which case the word is *accepted*, or it can be any one of the other states of S, in which case the word is *rejected*.

To produce a formal description of the concepts defined above, it is necessary to enumerate each part of the quintuple that comprises the DFA. Σ, S, s_0, and F are easily enumerated, but the function δ can often be tedious to describe. One device used to display the mapping δ is the *state transition diagram*. Besides graphically displaying the transitions of the δ function, the state transition diagram for a deterministic finite automaton also illustrates the other four parts of the quintuple.

A finite automaton state transition diagram is a directed graph. The states of the machine represent the vertices of the graph, while the mapping of the δ function describes the edges. Final states are denoted by a doubly encircled state, and the start state is identified by a straight incoming arrow. Each domain element of the transition function corresponds to an edge in the directed graph. We formally define a finite automaton state transition diagram for $<\Sigma, S, s_0, \delta, F>$ as a directed graph $G = \langle V, E\rangle$, as follows:

i. $V = S$,

ii. $E = \{\langle s, t, \mathbf{a}\rangle \mid s, t \in S, \mathbf{a} \in \Sigma \wedge \delta(s, \mathbf{a}) = t\}$,

where V is the set of vertices of the graph, and E is the set of edges connecting these vertices. Each element of E is an ordered triple, $\langle s, t, \mathbf{a}\rangle$, such that s is the origin vertex, t is the terminus, and **a** is the letter from Σ labeling the edge. Thus, for any vertex there is exactly one edge leaving that vertex for each element of Σ.

EXAMPLE 1.6

In the DFA shown in Figure 1.3, the set of edges E of the graph G is given by $E = \{\langle s_0, s_1, \mathbf{a}\rangle, \langle s_0, s_2, \mathbf{b}\rangle, \langle s_1, s_1, \mathbf{a}\rangle, \langle s_1, s_2, \mathbf{b}\rangle, \langle s_2, s_1, \mathbf{a}\rangle, \langle s_2, s_0, \mathbf{b}\rangle\}$. The figure also shows that s_0 is the designated start state and that s_1 is the only final state. The state transition function for a finite automaton is often represented in the form of a *state transition table*. A state transition table is a matrix with the rows of the matrix labeled and indexed by the states of the machine, and the columns of the matrix labeled and indexed by the elements of the input alphabet; the entries in the table are the states to which the DFA will move. Formally, let T be a state transition table

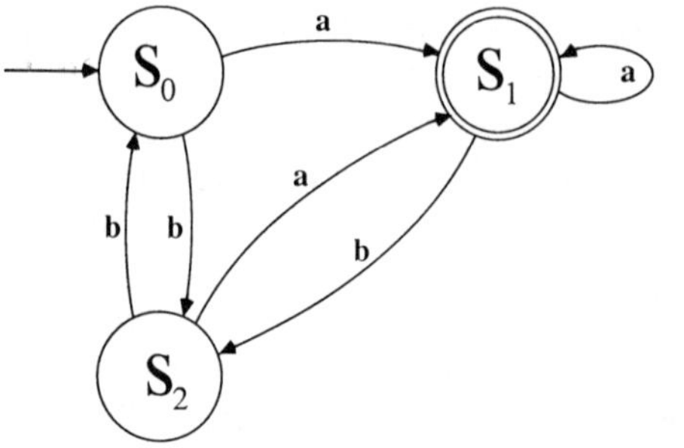

Figure 1.3 The DFA described in Example 1.6

for some deterministic finite automaton $A = <\Sigma, S, s_0, \delta, F>$, and let $s \in S$ and $\mathbf{a} \in \Sigma$. Then the value of each matrix entry is given by the equation

$$(\forall s \in S)(\forall \mathbf{a} \in \Sigma) T_{sa} = \delta(s, \mathbf{a})$$

For the automaton in Example 1.6, the state transition table is

δ	a	b
s_0	s_1	s_2
s_1	s_1	s_2
s_2	s_1	s_0

This table represents the following transitions:

$$\delta(s_0, \mathbf{a}) = s_1 \qquad \delta(s_0, \mathbf{b}) = s_2$$

$$\delta(s_1, \mathbf{a}) = s_1 \qquad \delta(s_1, \mathbf{b}) = s_2$$

$$\delta(s_2, \mathbf{a}) = s_1 \qquad \delta(s_2, \mathbf{b}) = s_0$$

State transition tables are the most common method of representing the basic structure of an automaton within a computer. When represented as an array in the memory of the computer, access is very fast and the structure lends itself easily to manipulation by the computer. Techniques such as depth-first search are easily and efficiently implemented when the state transition diagram is represented as a table. Figure 1.4 illustrates an implementation of the δ function via transition tables in Pascal.

```
type
   Sigma='a'..'c';
   State=(s0, s1, s2);
var
   TransitionTable=array [State, Sigma] of State;

function Delta(S:State; A:Sigma):State;
begin
   Delta:=TransitionTable [S, A]
end; {Delta}
```

Figure 1.4 A Pascal implementation of a state transition function

With δ, we can describe the state in which we will find ourselves after processing a single letter. We also want to be able to describe the state at which we will arrive after processing an entire string. We will extend the δ function to cover entire *strings* rather than just single *letters*; $\overline{\delta}(s, x)$ will be the state we wind up at when starting at s and processing, in order, all the letters of the string x. While this is a relatively easy concept to (vaguely) state in English, it is somewhat awkward to formally define. To facilitate formal proofs concerning DFAs, we use the following recursive definition.

∇ **Definition 1.11.** Given a DFA $A = <\Sigma, S, s_0, \delta, F>$, the *extended state transition function for* A, denoted $\overline{\delta}$, is a function $\overline{\delta}$: $S \times \Sigma^* \to S$ defined recursively as follows:

i. $(\forall s \in S)(\forall \mathbf{a} \in \Sigma) \qquad \overline{\delta}(s, \mathbf{a}) = \delta(s, \mathbf{a})$
ii. $(\forall s \in S) \qquad \overline{\delta}(s, \lambda) = s$
iii. $(\forall s \in S)(\forall x \in \Sigma^*)(\forall \mathbf{a} \in \Sigma) \qquad \overline{\delta}(s, \mathbf{a}x) = \overline{\delta}(\delta(s, \mathbf{a}), x)$

Δ

The $\overline{\delta}$ function extends the δ function from single letters to words. Whereas the δ function maps pairs of states and *letters* to other states, the $\overline{\delta}$ function maps pairs of states and *words* to other states. (i) is the observation that δ and $\overline{\delta}$ treat single letters the same; this fact is not really essential to the definition of $\overline{\delta}$, since it can be deduced from (ii) and (iii) (see the exercises).

The $\overline{\delta}$ function maps the current state s and the first letter $\mathbf{a}_1$ of a word $w = \mathbf{a}_1 \ldots \mathbf{a}_n$ via the δ function to some other state t. It is then recursively applied with the new state t and the remainder of the word, that is, with $\mathbf{a}_2 \ldots \mathbf{a}_n$. The recursion stops when the remainder of the word is the empty word λ. See Examples 1.7 and 1.11 for illustrations of computations using this recursive definition.

Since the recursion of the $\overline{\delta}$ function all takes place at the end of the string, $\overline{\delta}$ is called *tail recursive*. Tail recursion is easily transformed into iteration by applying the δ to successive letters of the input word and using the result of the previous application of $\overline{\delta}$ as an input to the current application.

Figure 1.5 gives an implementation of the $\overline{\delta}$ function in Pascal. Recursion has been replaced by iteration, and previous function results are saved in an auxiliary variable T. The function Delta, the input alphabet Sigma, and the state set State agree with the definitions given in Figure 1.4.

It stands to reason that if we start in state s and word y takes us to state r, and if we start in state r and word x takes us to state t, then the word yx should take us from state s all the way to t. That is, if $\overline{\delta}(s, y) = r$ and $\overline{\delta}(r, x) = t$, then $\overline{\delta}(s, yx)$ should equal t, also. We can indeed prove this, as shown with the following theorem.

∇ **Theorem 1.1.** Let $A = <\Sigma, S, s_0, \delta, F>$ be a DFA. Then

$$(\forall x \in \Sigma^*)(\forall y \in \Sigma^*)(\forall s \in S)(\overline{\delta}(s, yx) = \overline{\delta}(\overline{\delta}(s, y), x))$$

Proof. Define P(n) by

$$(\forall x \in \Sigma^*)(\forall y \in \Sigma^n)(\forall s \in S)(\overline{\delta}(s, yx) = \overline{\delta}(\overline{\delta}(s, y), x))$$

Basis step: P(0): Let $y \in \Sigma^0$ ($\Rightarrow y = \lambda$).

$$
\begin{aligned}
&= \overline{\delta}(\overline{\delta}(\mathrm{s}, y), x) && \text{(since } y = \lambda\text{)}\\
&= \overline{\delta}(\overline{\delta}(\mathrm{s}, \lambda), x) && \text{(by Definition 1.11ii)}\\
&= \overline{\delta}(\mathrm{s}, x) && \text{(since } x = \lambda \cdot x\text{)}\\
&= \overline{\delta}(\mathrm{s}, \lambda x) && \text{(since } y = \lambda\text{)}\\
&= \overline{\delta}(\mathrm{s}, yx)
\end{aligned}
$$

Inductive step: Assume P(m):

$$(\forall x \in \Sigma^*)(\forall y \in \Sigma^m)(\forall \mathrm{s} \in S)(\overline{\delta}(\mathrm{s}, yx) = \overline{\delta}(\overline{\delta}(\mathrm{s}, y), x)).$$

For any $z \in \Sigma^{m+1}$, $(\exists \mathbf{a} \in \Sigma^1)(\exists y \in \Sigma^m) \ni z = \mathbf{a}y$. Then

$$
\begin{aligned}
&\overline{\delta}(\mathrm{s}, zx) && \text{(by definition of } z\text{)}\\
&= \overline{\delta}(\mathrm{s}, \mathbf{a}yx) && \text{(by Definition 1.11iii)}\\
&= \overline{\delta}(\delta(\mathrm{s}, \mathbf{a}), yx) && \text{(since } (\exists \mathrm{t} \in S) \ni \delta(\mathrm{s}, \mathbf{a}) = \mathrm{t}\text{)}\\
&= \overline{\delta}(\mathrm{t}, yx) && \text{(by the induction assumption)}\\
&= \overline{\delta}(\overline{\delta}(\mathrm{t}, y), x) && \text{(by definition of t)}\\
&= \overline{\delta}(\overline{\delta}(\delta(\mathrm{s}, \mathbf{a}), y), x) && \text{(by Definition 1.11iii)}\\
&= \overline{\delta}(\overline{\delta}(\mathrm{s}, \mathbf{a}y), x) && \text{(by definition of } z\text{)}\\
&= \overline{\delta}(\overline{\delta}(\mathrm{s}, z), x)
\end{aligned}
$$

Therefore, P(m) $\Rightarrow$ P($m + 1$), and since this implication holds for any nonnegative integer m, by the principle of mathematical induction we can say that P(n) is true for all $n \in \mathbb{N}$. Since the statement therefore holds for any string y of any length, the assertion is indeed true for all y in Σ^*. This completes the proof of the theorem.
Δ

Note that the statement of Theorem 1.1 is very similar to the rule iii of the recursive definition of the extended state transition function (Definition 1.11) with the *string* y replacing the single *letter* **a**. We will see a remarkable number of situations like this, where a recursive rule defined for a single symbol extends in a natural manner to a similar rule for arbitrary strings.

As alluded to earlier, the state in which a string terminates is significant; in particular, it is important to determine whether the terminal state for a string happens to be one of the states that was designated to be a *final* state.

∇ **Definition 1.12.** Given a DFA A = $<\Sigma, S, \mathrm{s}_0, \delta, F>$, A *accepts* a word $w \in \Sigma^*$ *iff* $\overline{\delta}(\mathrm{s}_0, w) \in F$.
Δ

```
const
   MaxWordLength=255; {an arbitrary constraint}
type
   Word=record
      Length  :0..MaxWordLength;
      Letters:packed array [0..MaxWordLength] of Sigma
   end; {Word}

function DeltaBar(S:State; W:Word):State;
{uses the function Delta defined previously}
var
   T:State;
   I:0..MaxWordLength;
begin
   T:=S;
   if W.Length>0
      then
         for I:=1 to W.Length do
            T:=Delta(T,W.Letters[I]);
   DeltaBar:=T
end; {DeltaBar}
```

Figure 1.5 A Pascal implementation of the extended state transition function

We say a word w is accepted by a machine $A = <\Sigma, S, s_0, \delta, F>$ ***iff*** the extended state transition function $\overline{\delta}$ associated with A maps to a final state from s_0 when processing thc word w. This means that the path from the start state ultimately leads to a final state when the word w is presented to the machine. We will occasionally say that A *recognizes* w; a DFA is sometimes referred to as a *recognizer*.

∇ **Definition 1.13.** Given a DFA $A = <\Sigma, S, s_0, \delta, F>$, A *rejects* a word $w \in \Sigma^*$ ***iff*** $\overline{\delta}(s_0, w) \notin F$.
Δ

In other words, a word w is rejected by a machine $A = <\Sigma, S, s_0, \delta, F>$ ***iff*** the $\overline{\delta}$ function associated with A maps to a nonfinal state from s_0 when processing the word w.

EXAMPLE 1.7

Let

$$A = <\Sigma, S, s_0, \delta, F>$$

where

$$\Sigma = \{\mathbf{0}, \mathbf{1}\}$$

$$S = \{q_0, q_1\}$$

$$s_0 = q_0$$

$$F = \{q_1\}$$

and δ is given by the transition table

δ	**0**	**1**
q_0	q_0	q_1
q_1	q_1	q_0

The structure of this automaton is shown in Figure 1.6.

To see how some of the above definitions apply, let $x = \mathbf{0100}$:

$$\begin{aligned}
\bar{\delta}(q_0, x) &= \bar{\delta}(q_0, \mathbf{0100}) \\
&= \bar{\delta}(\delta(q_0, \mathbf{0}), \mathbf{100}) \\
&= \bar{\delta}(q_0, \mathbf{100}) \\
&= \bar{\delta}(\delta(q_0, \mathbf{1}), \mathbf{00}) \\
&= \bar{\delta}(q_1, \mathbf{00}) \\
&= \bar{\delta}(\delta(q_1, \mathbf{0}), \mathbf{0}) \\
&= \bar{\delta}(q_1, \mathbf{0}) \\
&= \delta(q_1, \mathbf{0}) \\
&= q_1
\end{aligned}$$

Thus, $\delta(q_0, x) = q_1 \in F$, which means that x is *accepted* by A; A *recognizes* x.

Now let $y = \mathbf{1100}$:

$$\begin{aligned}
\bar{\delta}(q_0, y) &= \bar{\delta}(q_0, \mathbf{1100}) \\
&= \bar{\delta}(\delta(q_0, \mathbf{1}), \mathbf{100}) \\
&= \bar{\delta}(q_1, \mathbf{100}) \\
&= \bar{\delta}(\delta(q_1, \mathbf{1}), \mathbf{00}) \\
&= \bar{\delta}(q_0, \mathbf{00}) \\
&= \bar{\delta}(\delta(q_0, \mathbf{0}), \mathbf{0}) \\
&= \bar{\delta}(q_0, \mathbf{0}) \\
&= \delta(q_0, \mathbf{0}) \\
&= q_0
\end{aligned}$$

Therefore, $\bar{\delta}(q_0, y) = q_0 \notin F$, which means that y is *not accepted* by A.

Following the Pascal conventions defined in the previous programming fragments, the function *Accept* defined in Figure 1.7 tests for acceptance of a string by consulting a FinalState set and using DeltaBar to refer to the TransitionTable.

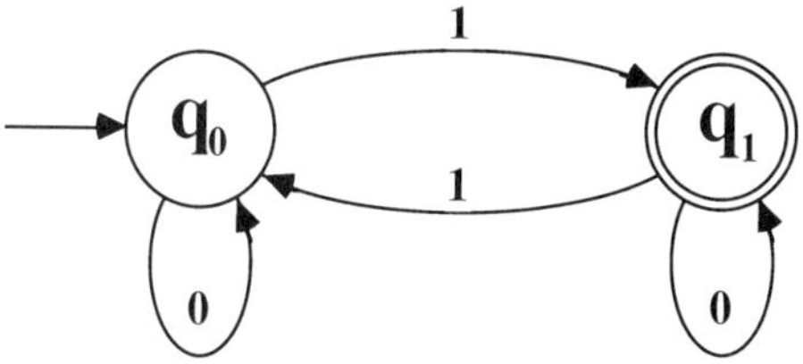

Figure 1.6 The DFA discussed in Example 1.7

The functions `Delta`, `DeltaBar`, and `Accept` can be combined to form a Pascal program that models a DFA. The sample fragments given in Figures 1.4, 1.5, and 1.7 rightly pass the candidate string as a parameter. A full program would be complicated by several constraints, including the awkward way in which strings must be handled in Pascal. To highlight the correspondence between the code modules and the automata definitions, the program given in Figure 1.8 handles input at the character level rather than at the word level. The definitions in the procedure `Initialize` reflect the structure of the DFA shown in Figure 1.9. Invoking this program will produce a response to a single input word. For example, a typical exchange would be

cba
Rejected

Running this program again might produce

cccc
Accepted

This behavior is essentially the same as that of the C program shown in Figure 1.10. The succinct coding clearly shows the relationship between the components of the quintuple for the DFA and the corresponding code.

∇ **Definition 1.14.** Given an alphabet Σ, L is a *language* over the alphabet Σ *iff* $L \subseteq \Sigma^*$.
Δ

A language is a collection of words over some alphabet. If the alphabet is denoted by Σ, then a language L over Σ is a subset of Σ^*. Since $L \subseteq \Sigma^*$, L may be finite or infinite. Clearly, the words used in the English language are a subset of

```
function Accept(W:Word):Boolean;
{returns TRUE iff W is accepted by the DFA}
begin
   Accept:=DeltaBar(s0,W) in FinalState
end; {Accept}
```

Figure 1.7 A Pascal implementation of a test for acceptance

```
program DFA(input, output);

{This program tests whether input strings are accepted by the }
{automaton displayed in Figure 1.9. The program expects input }
{from the keyboard, delimited by a carriage return. No error  }
{checking is done; letters outside ['a'..'c'] cause a range   }
{error.                                                        }

type
    Sigma='a'..'c';
    State=(s0, s1, s2);

var
    TransitionTable : array [State, Sigma] of State;
    FinalState      : set of State;

function Delta(s : State; c : Sigma) : State;
begin
    Delta :=TransitionTable[s,c]
end; { Delta }

function DeltaBar(s : State) : State;
var
    t : State;
begin

    t :=s;

    { Step through the keyboard input one letter at a time. }

    while not eoln(input) do
        begin
            t :=Delta(t, input^);
            get(input)
        end;
    DeltaBar :=t

end; { DeltaBar }

function Accept : boolean;

begin
    Accept :=DeltaBar(s0) in FinalState
end; { Accept }

procedure Initialize;
begin

    FinalState := [s2];

    { Set up the state transition table. }

    TransitionTable [s0,'a'] :=s1;
    TransitionTable [s0,'b'] :=s0;
```

```
    TransitionTable [s0,'c'] :=s2;
    TransitionTable [s1,'a'] :=s2;
    TransitionTable [s1,'b'] :=s0;
    TransitionTable [s1,'c'] :=s0;
    TransitionTable [s2,'a'] :=s0;
    TransitionTable [s2,'b'] :=s0;
    TransitionTable [s2,'c'] :=s1;

end; { Initialize }

begin { DFA }

    Initialize;
    if Accept then
        writeln(output, 'Accepted')
    else
        writeln(output, 'Rejected')

end. { DFA }
```

Figure 1.8 A Pascal program that emulates the DFA shown in Figure 1.9

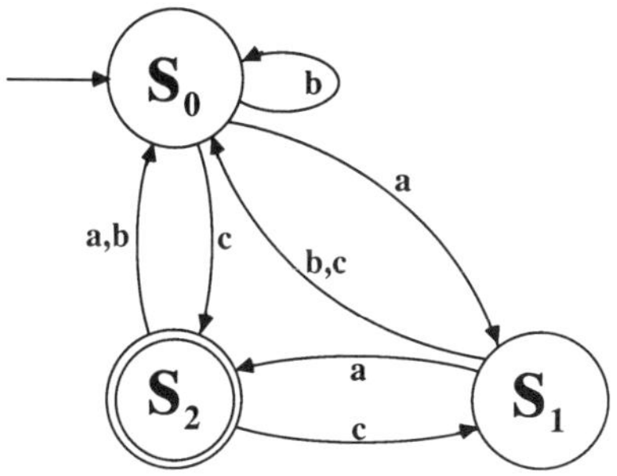

Figure 1.9 The DFA emulated by the programs in Figures 1.8 and 1.10

words over the Roman alphabet and this collection is therefore a language according to our definition. Note that a language L, in this context, is simply a list of words; neither syntax nor semantics are involved in the specification of L. Thus, a language as defined by Definition 1.14 has little of the structure or relationships one would normally expect of either a natural language (like English) or a programming language (like Pascal).

EXAMPLE 1.8

Some other examples of valid languages are

- **i.** $\emptyset$
- **ii.** $\{w \in \{\mathbf{0}, \mathbf{1}\}^* \mid |w| > 5\}$
- **iii.** $\{\lambda\}$
- **iv.** $\{\lambda, \mathbf{bilbo}, \mathbf{frodo}, \mathbf{samwise}\}$
- **v.** $\{x \in \{\mathbf{a}, \mathbf{b}\}^* \mid |x|_{\mathbf{a}} = |x|_{\mathbf{b}}\}$

```
# include     <stdio.h>

# define      to_int(c)        ((int) c-(int) 'a')

# define      FINAL_STATE    s_2

enum state { s_0, s_1, s_2 };
/*
** This table implements the state transition function and is indexed by
** the current state and the current input letter.
*/

enum state transition_table[3][3]={ { s_1, s_0, s_2 },
                                    { s_2, s_0, s_0 },
                                    { s_0, s_0, s_1 }

};

enum state delta(s, c)
enum state s;
char       c;
{
        return transition_table[ (int) s][ to_int(c)];
}

enum state delta_bar(s)
enum state s;
{
        enum state t;
        char       c;

        t=s;

/*
** Step through the input one letter at a time.
*/
        while ((char) (c = getchar()) != '\n')
              t=delta(t, c);
        return t;
}

main() {
        if (delta_bar(s_0) == FINAL_STATE)
              printf("Accepted\n");
        else
              printf("Rejected\n");
        exit(0);
}
```

Figure 1.10 A C program that emulates the DFA shown in Figure 1.9

The empty language, denoted by $\emptyset$ or { }, is different from {λ}, the language consisting of only the empty word λ. Whereas the empty language consists of zero words, the language consisting of λ contains one word (which contains zero letters). The distinction is analogous to an example involving sets of numbers: the set {0}, containing only the integer 0, is still a larger set than the empty set.

Every DFA differentiates between words that do not reach final states and words that do. In this sense, each automaton defines a language.

∇ **Definition 1.15.** Given a DFA $\mathsf{A} = <\Sigma, S, s_0, \delta, F>$, the *language accepted by* A, denoted $\boldsymbol{L}(\mathsf{A})$, is defined to be

$$\boldsymbol{L}(\mathsf{A}) = \{w \in \Sigma^* \mid \overline{\delta}(s_0, w) \in F\}$$

Δ

$\boldsymbol{L}(\mathsf{A})$, the language accepted by a finite automaton A, is the set of all words w from Σ^* for which $\overline{\delta}(s_0, w) \in F$. In order for a word w to be contained in $\boldsymbol{L}(\mathsf{B})$, the path through the finite automaton B, as determined by the letters in w, must lead from the start state to one of the final states.

For deterministic finite automata, the path for a given word w is unique: there is only one path since, at any given state in the automaton, there is exactly one transition for each $\mathbf{a} \in \Sigma$. This is not necessarily the case for another variety of finite automaton, the *nondeterministic* finite automaton, as will be seen in Chapter 4.

∇ **Definition 1.16.** Given an alphabet Σ, a language $\mathrm{L} \subseteq \Sigma^*$ is *finite automaton definable* (FAD) ***iff*** there exists some DFA $\mathsf{B} = <\Sigma, S, s_0, \delta, F>$, such that $\mathrm{L} = \boldsymbol{L}(\mathsf{B})$.
Δ

The set of all words over {**0**, **1**} that contain an odd number of **1**s is finite automaton definable, as evidenced by the automaton in Example 1.7, which accepts exactly this set of words.

1.3 EXAMPLES OF FINITE AUTOMATA

This section illustrates the definitions of the quintuples and the state transition diagrams for some nontrivial automata. The following example and Example 1.11 deal with the recognition of tokens, an important issue in the construction of compilers.

EXAMPLE 1.9

The set of FORTRAN identifiers is a finite automaton definable language. This statement can be proved by verifying that the following machine accepts the set of all valid FORTRAN 66 identifiers. These identifiers, which represent variable, subroutine, and array names, can contain from 1 to 6 (nonblank) characters, must begin with an alphabetic character, can be followed by up to 5 letters or digits, and may have embedded blanks. In this example, we have ignored the difference between capital and lowercase letters, and ◇ represents a blank.

$$\Sigma = \text{ASCII}$$

$$\Gamma = \text{ASCII} - \{\mathbf{a}, \mathbf{b}, \mathbf{c}, \ldots \mathbf{x}, \mathbf{y}, \mathbf{z}, \mathbf{0}, \mathbf{1}, \mathbf{2}, \mathbf{3}, \mathbf{4}, \mathbf{5}, \mathbf{6}, \mathbf{7}, \mathbf{8}, \mathbf{9}, \diamond\}$$

$$S = \{s_0, s_1, s_2, s_3, s_4, s_5, s_6, s_7\}$$

$$s_0 = s_0$$

δ	**a**	**b**	**c . . . y**	**z**	**0**	**1 . . . 8**	**9**	◇	**Γ**
s_0	s_1	s_1	s_1 . . . s_1	s_1	s_7	s_7 . . . s_7	s_7	s_0	s_7
s_1	s_2	s_2	s_2 . . . s_2	s_2	s_2	s_2 . . . s_2	s_2	s_1	s_7
s_2	s_3	s_3	s_3 . . . s_3	s_3	s_3	s_3 . . . s_3	s_3	s_2	s_7
s_3	s_4	s_4	s_4 . . . s_4	s_4	s_4	s_4 . . . s_4	s_4	s_3	s_7
s_4	s_5	s_5	s_5 . . . s_5	s_5	s_5	s_5 . . . s_5	s_5	s_4	s_7
s_5	s_6	s_6	s_6 . . . s_6	s_6	s_6	s_6 . . . s_6	s_6	s_5	s_7
s_6	s_7	s_7	s_7 . . . s_7	s_7	s_7	s_7 . . . s_7	s_7	s_6	s_7
s_7	s_7	s_7	s_7 . . . s_7	s_7	s_7	s_7 . . . s_7	s_7	s_7	s_7

$$F = \{s_1, s_2, s_3, s_4, s_5, s_6\}$$

The entries under the column labeled Γ show the transitions taken for each member of the set Γ. The state transition diagram of the machine corresponding to this quintuple is displayed in Figure 1.11. Note that, while each of the 26 letters transition from s_0 to s_1, a single arrow labeled **a-z** is sufficient to denote all these transitions. Similarly, the transition labeled Σ from s_7 indicates that every element of the alphabet follows the same path.

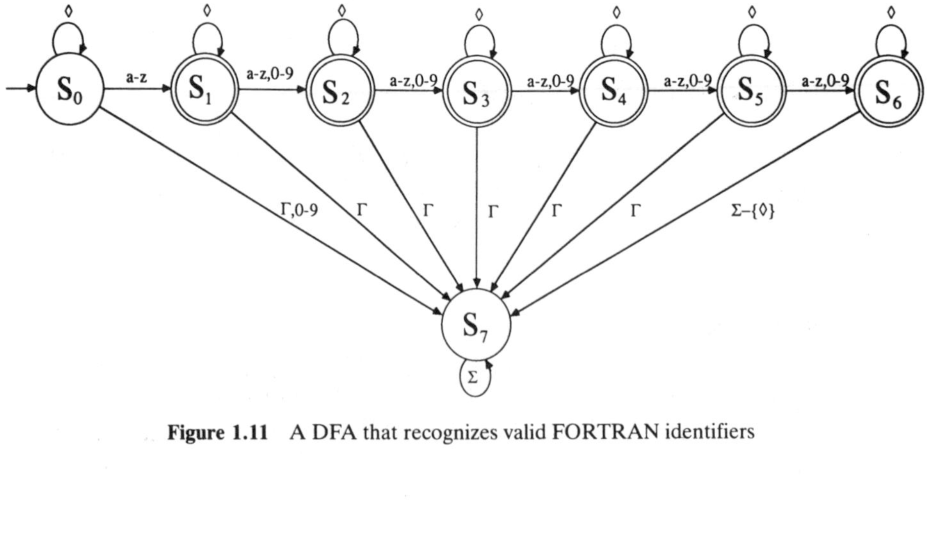

Figure 1.11 A DFA that recognizes valid FORTRAN identifiers

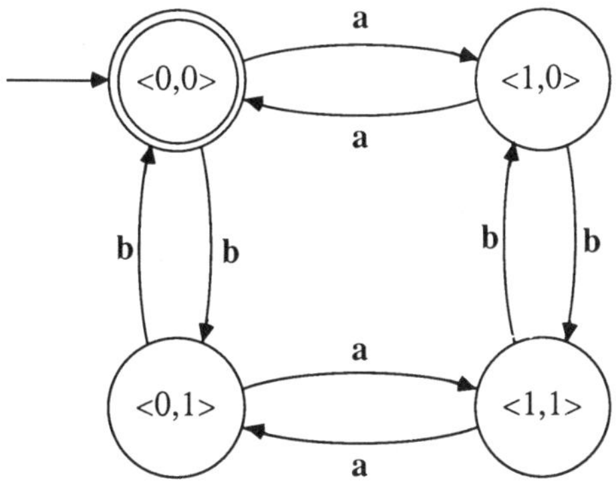

Figure 1.12 The DFA M discussed in Example 1.10

EXAMPLE 1.10

The DFA M shown in Figure 1.12 accepts only those strings that have an even number of **b**s and an even number of **a**s. Thus,

$$L(\mathsf{M}) = \{x \in \{\mathbf{a}, \mathbf{b}\}^* \mid |x|_{\mathbf{a}} \equiv 0 \bmod 2 \land |x|_{\mathbf{b}} \equiv 0 \bmod 2\}$$

The corresponding quintuple for $\mathsf{M} = <\Sigma, S, s_0, \delta, F>$ has the following components:

$$\Sigma = \{\mathbf{a}, \mathbf{b}\}$$

$$S = \{<0,0>, <0,1>, <1,0>, <1,1>\}$$

$$s_0 = <0,0>$$

δ	**a**	**b**
<0,0>	<1,0>	<0,1>
<0,1>	<1,1>	<0,0>
<1,0>	<0,0>	<1,1>
<1,1>	<0,1>	<1,0>

$$F = \{<0,0>\}$$

Note that the transition function can be succinctly specified by

$$\delta(<i,j>, \mathbf{a}) = <1-i, j> \text{ and } \delta(<i,j>, \mathbf{b}) = <i, 1-j> \text{ for all } i, j \in \{0,1\}$$

See the exercises for some other problems involving congruence modulo 2.

EXAMPLE 1.11

Consider a typical set of all real number constants in modified scientific notation format described by the BNF in Table 1.1.

TABLE 1.1

<sign> ::= **+** | **−**

<digit> ::= **0** | **1** | **2** | **3** | **4** | **5** | **6** | **7** | **8** | **9**

<natural> ::= <digit> | <digit><natural>

<integer> ::= <natural> | <sign><natural>

<real constant> ::= <integer> |
<integer>**.** |
<integer>**.**<natural> |
<integer>**.**<natural>**E**<integer>

This set of productions defines real number constants like **+192.**, since

<real constant> ⇒ <integer>**.**
<integer>**.** ⇒ <sign><natural>**.**
<sign><natural>**.** ⇒ **+**<natural>**.**
+<natural>**.** ⇒ **+**<digit><natural>**.**
+<digit><natural>**.** ⇒ **+1**<natural>**.**
+1<natural>**.** ⇒ **+1**<digit><natural>**.**
+1<digit><natural>**.** ⇒ **+1**<digit><digit>**.**
+1<digit><digit>**.** ⇒ **+1**<digit>**2.**
+1<digit>**2.** ⇒ **+192.**

Other possibilities are

1
3.1415
2.718281828
27.
42.42
1.0E-32

while the following strings do not qualify:

.01
1. + 1
8.E-10

The set of all real number constants that can be derived from the productions given in Table 1.1 is a FAD language. Let R be the deterministic finite automaton defined below. The corresponding state transition diagram is given in Figure 1.13.

$$\Sigma = \{\mathbf{0}, \mathbf{1}, \mathbf{2}, \mathbf{3}, \mathbf{4}, \mathbf{5}, \mathbf{6}, \mathbf{7}, \mathbf{8}, \mathbf{9}, \mathbf{+}, \mathbf{-}, \mathbf{E}, \mathbf{.}\}$$

$$S = \{s_0, s_1, s_2, s_3, s_4, s_5, s_6, s_7, s_8\}$$

$$s_0 = s_0$$

δ	**0**	**1**	**2**	**3**	**4**	**5**	**6**	**7**	**8**	**9**	**+**	**−**	**E**	**.**
s_0	s_2	s_2	s_2	s_2	s_2	s_2	s_2	s_2	s_2	s_2	s_1	s_1	s_7	s_7
s_1	s_2	s_2	s_2	s_2	s_2	s_2	s_2	s_2	s_2	s_2	s_7	s_7	s_7	s_7
s_2	s_2	s_2	s_2	s_2	s_2	s_2	s_2	s_2	s_2	s_2	s_7	s_7	s_7	s_3
s_3	s_8	s_8	s_8	s_8	s_8	s_8	s_8	s_8	s_8	s_8	s_7	s_7	s_7	s_7
s_4	s_5	s_5	s_5	s_5	s_5	s_5	s_5	s_5	s_5	s_5	s_6	s_6	s_7	s_7
s_5	s_5	s_5	s_5	s_5	s_5	s_5	s_5	s_5	s_5	s_5	s_7	s_7	s_7	s_7
s_6	s_5	s_5	s_5	s_5	s_5	s_5	s_5	s_5	s_5	s_5	s_7	s_7	s_7	s_7
s_7	s_7	s_7	s_7	s_7	s_7	s_7	s_7	s_7	s_7	s_7	s_7	s_7	s_7	s_7
s_8	s_8	s_8	s_8	s_8	s_8	s_8	s_8	s_8	s_8	s_8	s_7	s_7	s_4	s_7

$$F = \{s_2, s_3, s_5, s_8\}$$

The language accepted by R, that is $L(\mathsf{R})$, is exactly the set of all real number constants in modified scientific notation format described by the BNF in Table 1.1.

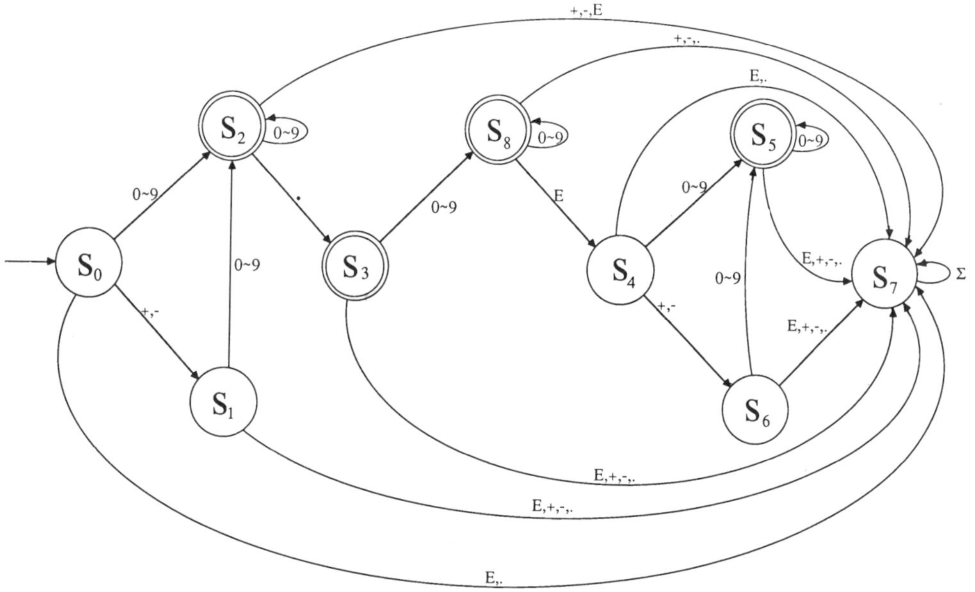

Figure 1.13 A DFA that recognizes real number constants

For example, let $x = \mathbf{3.1415}$:

$$\begin{aligned}
\overline{\delta}(s_0, x) &= \overline{\delta}(s_0, \mathbf{3.1415}) \\
&= \overline{\delta}(\delta(s_0, \mathbf{3}), \mathbf{.1415}) \\
&= \overline{\delta}(s_2, \mathbf{.1415}) \\
&= \overline{\delta}(\delta(s_2, \mathbf{.}), \mathbf{1415}) \\
&= \overline{\delta}(s_3, \mathbf{1415}) \\
&= \overline{\delta}(\delta(s_3, \mathbf{1}), \mathbf{415}) \\
&= \overline{\delta}(s_8, \mathbf{415}) \\
&= \overline{\delta}(\delta(s_8, \mathbf{4}), \mathbf{15}) \\
&= \overline{\delta}(s_8, \mathbf{15}) \\
&= \overline{\delta}(\delta(s_8, \mathbf{1}), \mathbf{5}) \\
&= \overline{\delta}(s_8, \mathbf{5}) \\
&= \delta(s_8, \mathbf{5}) \\
&= s_8
\end{aligned}$$

$s_8 \in F$, and therefore $\mathbf{3.1415} \in L(\mathsf{R})$.

While many important classes of strings such as numerical constants (Example 1.11) and identifiers (Example 1.9) are FAD, not all languages that can be described by BNF can be recognized by DFAs. These limitations will be investigated in Chapters 8 and 9, and a more capable type of automaton will be defined in Chapter 10.

1.4 CIRCUIT IMPLEMENTATION OF FINITE AUTOMATA

Now that we have described the mathematical nature of deterministic finite automata, let us turn to the physical implementation of such devices. We will investigate the sort of physical components that actually go into the "brain" of, say, a vending machine. Recall that the basic building blocks of digital logic circuits are *logic gates*; using **0** or **False** to represent a low voltage (ground) and **1** or **True** to represent a higher voltage (often +5 volts), the basic gates have the truth tables shown in Figure 1.14.

Since our DFA will examine one letter at a time, we will generally need some type of timing mechanism, which will be regulated by a *clock pulse*; we will read one letter per pulse and allow enough interim time for transient signals to propagate through our network as we change states and move to the next letter on the input tape. The clock pulse will alternate between high and low voltages, as shown in Figure 1.15. For applications such as vending machines, the periodic clock pulse

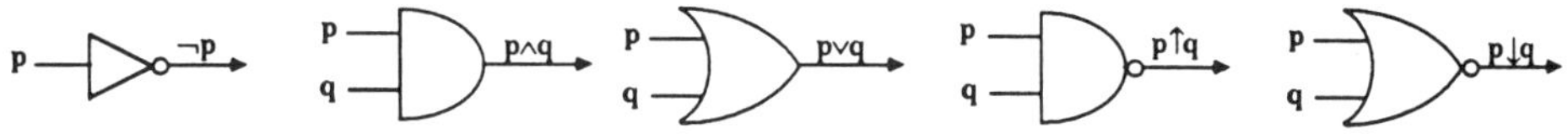

NOT gate

p	¬p
1	0
0	1

AND gate

p	q	p∧q
1	1	1
1	0	0
0	1	0
0	0	0

OR gate

p	q	p∨q
1	1	1
1	0	1
0	1	1
0	0	0

NAND gate

p	q	p ↑ q
1	1	0
1	0	1
0	1	1
0	0	1

NOR gate

p	q	p ↓ q
1	1	0
1	0	0
0	1	0
0	0	1

Figure 1.14 Common logic gates and their truth tables

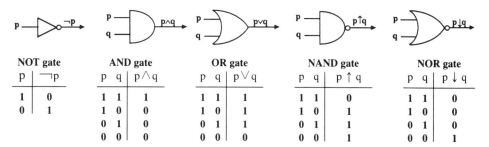

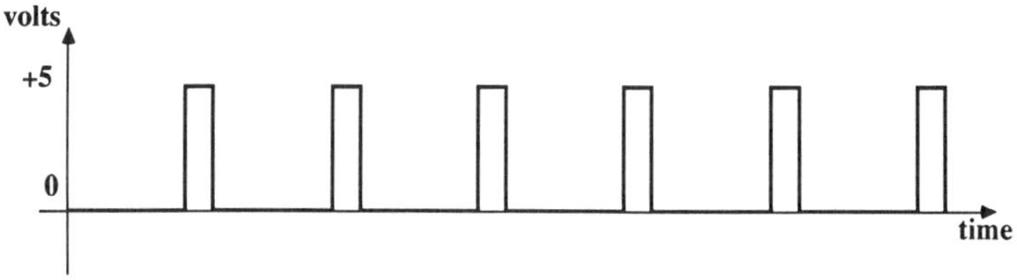

Figure 1.15 A typical clock pulse pattern for latched circuits

would be replaced by a device that pulsed whenever a new input (such as the insertion of a coin) was detected.

We need to retain the present status of the network (current state, letter, and so forth) as we move on to the next input symbol. This is achieved through the use of a *D flip-flop* (D stands for data or delay), which uses NAND gates and the clock signal to store the current value of, say, p', between clock pulses. The symbol for a D flip-flop (sometimes called a *latch*) is shown in Figure 1.16, along with the actual gates that comprise the circuit.

The output, p and $\neg p$, will reflect the value of the input signal p' *only* after the high clock pulse is received and will retain that value after the clock drops to low (even if p' subsequently changes) until the next clock pulse comes along, at which time the output will reflect the new current value of p'. This is best illustrated by referring to the NAND truth table and tracing the changes in the circuit. Begin with clock $= p = p' = \mathbf{0}$ and $\neg p = \mathbf{1}$, and verify that the circuit is stable. Now assume that p' changes to **1**, and note that, although some internal values may change, p and $\neg p$ remain at **0** and **1**, respectively; the old value of p' has been "remembered" by the D flip-flop. Contrast this with the behavior when we strobe the clock: assume that the clock now also changes to **1** so that we now have clock $= p' = \neg p = \mathbf{1}$, and $p = \mathbf{0}$. When the signal propagates through the network, we find that p and $\neg p$ have changed to reflect the new value of p'; clock $= p = p' = \mathbf{1}$, and $\neg p = \mathbf{0}$.

We will also have to represent the letters of our input alphabet by high and low voltages (that is, combinations of **0**s and **1**s). The ASCII alphabet, for example, is quite naturally represented by 8 bits, $\mathbf{a_1a_2a_3a_4a_5a_6a_7a_8}$, where **B**, for example, has the bit pattern **01000010** (binary 66). One of these bit patterns should be reserved for

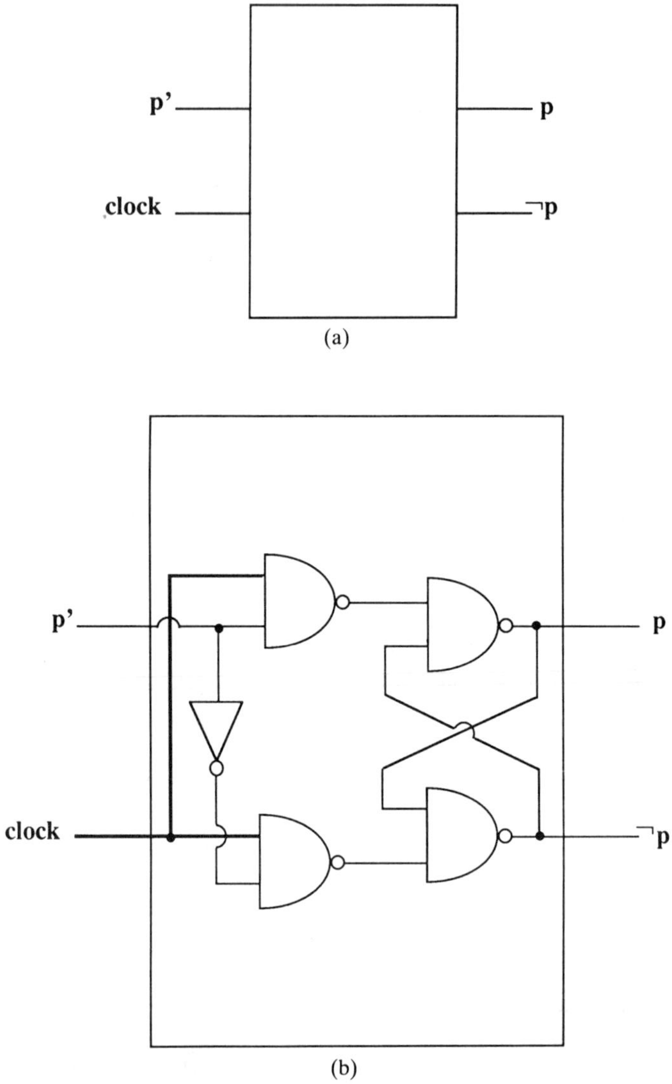

Figure 1.16 (a) A data flip-flop or latch (b) The circuitry for a D flip-flop

indicating the end of our input string <EOS>. Our convention will be to reserve binary zero for this role, which means our ASCII end of string symbol would be **00000000** (or NULL). In actual applications using the ASCII alphabet, however, a more appropriate choice for <EOS> might be **00001101** (a carriage return) or **00001001** (a line feed) or **00100000** (a space).

Our alphabets are likely to be far smaller than the ASCII character set, and we will hence need fewer than 8 bits of information to encode our letters. For example, if $\Sigma = \{\mathbf{b}, \mathbf{c}\}$, 2 bits, $\mathbf{a}_1$ and $\mathbf{a}_2$, will suffice. Our choice of encoding could be **00** = <EOS>, **01** = **b**, **10** = **c**, and **11** is unused.

In a similar fashion, we must encode state names. A machine with $S = \{r_0, r_1, r_2, r_3, r_4, r_5\}$ would need 3 bits (denoted by $\mathbf{t}_1$, $\mathbf{t}_2$, and $\mathbf{t}_3$) to represent the six states. The most natural encoding would be $r_0 = \mathbf{000}$, $r_1 = \mathbf{001}$, $r_2 = \mathbf{010}$, $r_3 = \mathbf{011}$, $r_4 = \mathbf{100}$, and $r_5 = \mathbf{101}$, with the combinations **110** and **111** left unused.

Finally, a mechanism for differentiating between final and nonfinal states must be implemented (although this need not be engaged until the <EOS> symbol is encountered). Recall that we must illuminate the "acceptance light" if the machine terminates in a final state and leave it unlit if the string on the input tape is instead rejected by the DFA. A second "rejection light" can be added to the physical model, and exactly one of the two will light when <EOS> is scanned by the input head.

EXAMPLE 1.12

When building a logical circuit from the definition of a DFA, we will find it convenient to treat <EOS> as an input symbol, and define the state transition function for it by $(\forall s \in S)(\delta(s, \text{<EOS>}) = s)$. Thus, the DFA in Figure 1.17a should be thought of as shown in Figure 1.17b. As we have only two states, a single state bit will suffice, representing s_0 by $\mathbf{t}_1 = \mathbf{0}$ and s_1 by $\mathbf{t}_1 = \mathbf{1}$. Since $\Sigma = \{\mathbf{b}, \mathbf{c}\}$, we will again use 2 bits, $\mathbf{a}_1$ and $\mathbf{a}_2$, to represent the input symbols. As before, $\mathbf{00}$ = <EOS>, $\mathbf{01} = \mathbf{b}$, $\mathbf{10} = \mathbf{c}$, and **11** is unused.

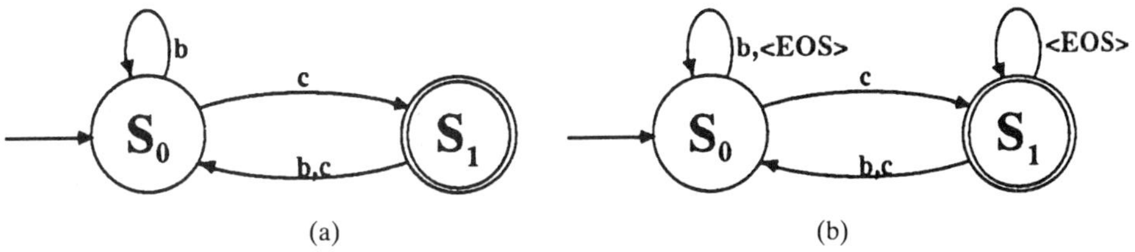

Figure 1.17 (a) The DFA discussed in Example 1.12 (b) The expanded state transition diagram for the DFA implemented in Figure 1.18

Determining the state transition function will require knowledge of the current state (represented by the status of $\mathbf{t}_1$) and the current input symbol (represented by the pair of bits $\mathbf{a}_1$ and $\mathbf{a}_2$. These three input values will allow the next state $\mathbf{t}_1'$ to be calculated. From the δ function, we know that

$$\delta(s_0, \mathbf{b}) = s_0$$

$$\delta(s_0, \mathbf{c}) = s_1$$

$$\delta(s_1, \mathbf{b}) = s_0$$

$$\delta(s_1, \mathbf{c}) = s_0$$

These specifications correspond to the following four rows of the truth table for $\mathbf{t}_1'$:

t_1	a_1	a_2	t_1'
0	0	1	0
0	1	0	1
1	0	1	0
1	1	0	0

which represents

t_1	a_1	a_2	t_1'
s_0	0	1 = b	s_0
s_0	1	0 = c	s_1
s_1	0	1 = b	s_0
s_1	1	0 = c	s_0

Adding the state transitions for <EOS> and using * to represent the outcome for the two rows corresponding to the unused combination $\mathbf{a}_1\mathbf{a}_2 = \mathbf{11}$ fills out the eight rows of the complete truth table, as shown in Table 1.2.

TABLE 1.2

t_1	a_1	a_1	t_1'
0	0	0	0
0	0	1	0
0	1	0	1
0	1	1	*
1	0	0	1
1	0	1	0
1	1	0	0
1	1	1	*

If we arbitrarily assume that the two don't-care combinations (*) are zero, the principle disjunctive normal form of $\mathbf{t}_1'$ contains just two terms: $(\neg\mathbf{t}_1\wedge\mathbf{a}_1\wedge\neg\mathbf{a}_2)\vee(\mathbf{t}_1\wedge\neg\mathbf{a}_1\wedge\neg\mathbf{a}_2)$. It is profitable to reassign the don't-care value in the fourth row to **1**, since the expression can then be shortened to $(\neg\mathbf{t}_1\wedge\mathbf{a}_1)\vee(\mathbf{t}_1\wedge\neg\mathbf{a}_1\wedge\neg\mathbf{a}_2)$ by applying standard techniques for minimizing Boolean functions. Incorporating this into a feedback loop with a D flip-flop provides the heart of the digital logic circuit representing the DFA, as shown in Figure 1.18.

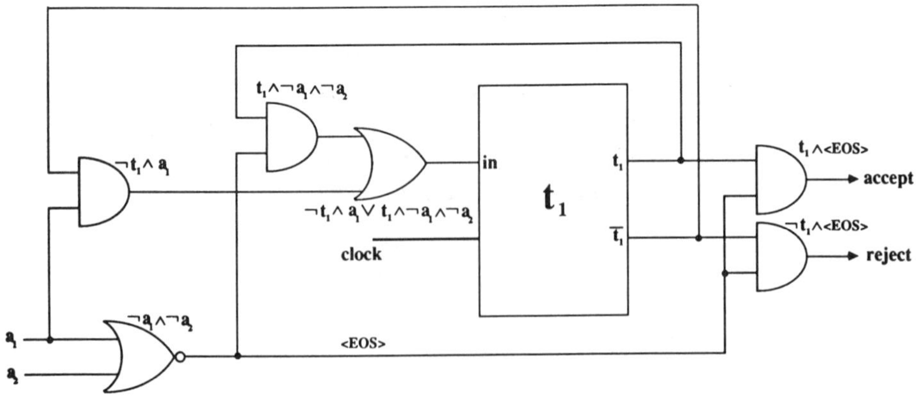

Figure 1.18 The circuitry implementing the DFA discussed in Example 1.12

The accept portion of the circuitry ensures that we do not indicate acceptance when passing through the final state; it is only activated when we are in a final state while scanning the <EOS> symbol. Similarly, the reject circuitry can only be activated when the <EOS> symbol is encountered. When there are several final states, this part of the circuitry becomes correspondingly more complex. It is instructive to follow the effect a string such as **bcc** has on the above circuit. Define $\mathbf{a}_i(j)$ as the jth value the bit $\mathbf{a}_i$ takes on as the string **bcc** is processed; that is, $\mathbf{a}_i(j)$ is the value of $\mathbf{a}_i$ during the jth clock pulse. We then have

$$\mathbf{a}_1(1) = \mathbf{0} \qquad \mathbf{a}_2(1) = 1 \qquad \Rightarrow \mathbf{b}$$
$$\mathbf{a}_1(2) = \mathbf{1} \qquad \mathbf{a}_2(2) = \mathbf{0} \qquad \Rightarrow \mathbf{c}$$
$$\mathbf{a}_1(3) = \mathbf{1} \qquad \mathbf{a}_2(3) = \mathbf{0} \qquad \Rightarrow \mathbf{c}$$
$$\mathbf{a}_1(4) = \mathbf{0} \qquad \mathbf{a}_2(4) = \mathbf{0} \qquad \Rightarrow \text{<EOS>}$$

Trace the circuit through four clock pulses (starting with $\mathbf{t}_1 = \mathbf{0}$), and observe the current values that $\mathbf{t}_1$ assumes, noting that it corresponds to the appropriate state of the machine as each input symbol is scanned.

Note that a six-state machine would require more and substantially larger truth tables. Since a state encoding would now need to specify $\mathbf{t}_1$, $\mathbf{t}_2$, and $\mathbf{t}_3$, three different truth tables (for $\mathbf{t}_1'$, $\mathbf{t}_2'$, and $\mathbf{t}_3'$) must be constructed to predict the next state transition. More significantly, the input variables would include $\mathbf{t}_1$, $\mathbf{t}_2$, $\mathbf{t}_3$, $\mathbf{a}_1$, and $\mathbf{a}_2$, making each table 32 rows long. Three D flip-flop feedback loops would be necessary to store the three values $\mathbf{t}_1$, $\mathbf{t}_2$, and $\mathbf{t}_3$.

Also, physical logic circuits of this type have the disconcerting habit of initializing to some random configuration the first time power is applied to the network. A true working model would thus need a *reset* circuit to initialize each $\mathbf{t}_i$ to **0** in order to ensure that the machine started in state s_0. Slightly more complex set–reset flip-flops can be used to provide a hardware solution to this problem. However, a simple algorithmic solution would require the input tape to have a *leading* start-of-string symbol <SOS>. The definition of the state transition function should be expanded so that scanning the <SOS> symbol from any state will automatically transfer control to s_0. We will adopt the convention that <SOS> will be represented by the highest binary code; in ASCII, for example, this would be **11111111**, while in the preceding example it would be **11**. To promote uniformity in the exercises, it is suggested that <SOS> should always be given the highest binary code and <EOS> be represented by binary zero; as in the examples given here, the symbols in Σ should be numbered sequentially according to their natural alphabetical order. In a similar fashion, numbered states should be given their corresponding binary codes. The reader should note, however, that other encodings might result in less complex circuitry.

EXAMPLE 1.13

As a more complex example of automaton circuitry, consider the DFA displayed in Figure 1.19. Two flip-flops $\mathbf{t}_1$ and $\mathbf{t}_2$ will be necessary to represent the three states,

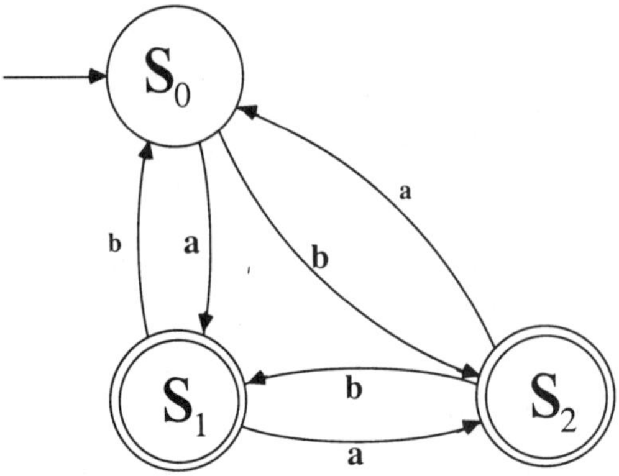

Figure 1.19 The DFA discussed in Example 1.13

most naturally encoded as $s_0 = \mathbf{00}$, $s_1 = \mathbf{01}$, $s_2 = \mathbf{10}$, **with** $s_3 = \mathbf{11}$ unused. Employing both <SOS> and <EOS> encodings yields the DFA in Figure 1.20.

Note that we must account for the possibility that the circuitry might be randomly initialized to $\mathbf{t_1} = \mathbf{1}$ and $\mathbf{t_2} = \mathbf{1}$; we must ensure that scanning the <SOS> symbol moves us back into the "real" part of the machine. Two bits of information ($\mathbf{a_1}$ and $\mathbf{a_2}$) are also needed to describe the input symbols. Following our conventions, we assign <EOS> = **00**, **a** = **01**, **b** = **10**, and <SOS> = **11**. The truth table for both the transition function and the conditions for acceptance is given in Table 1.3.

In the first row, $\mathbf{t_1} = \mathbf{0}$ and $\mathbf{t_2} = \mathbf{0}$ indicate state s_0, while $\mathbf{a_1} = \mathbf{0}$ and $\mathbf{a_2} = \mathbf{0}$ denote the <EOS> symbol. Since δ(s_0, <EOS>) = s_0, $\mathbf{t_1'} = \mathbf{0}$ and $\mathbf{t_2'} = \mathbf{0}$. We do not want to accept a string that ends in s_0, so **accept** = **0** also. The remaining rows are determined similarly. The (nonminimized) circuitry for this DFA is shown in Figure 1.21.

TABLE 1.3

t_1	t_2	a_1	a_2	t_1'	t_2'	accept
0	0	0	0	0	0	0
0	0	0	1	0	1	0
0	0	1	0	1	0	0
0	0	1	1	0	0	0
0	1	0	0	0	1	1
0	1	0	1	1	0	0
0	1	1	0	0	0	0
0	1	1	1	0	0	0
1	0	0	0	1	0	1
1	0	0	1	0	0	0
1	0	1	0	0	1	0
1	0	1	1	0	0	0
1	1	0	0	*	*	*
1	1	0	1	*	*	*
1	1	1	0	*	*	*
1	1	1	1	0	0	0

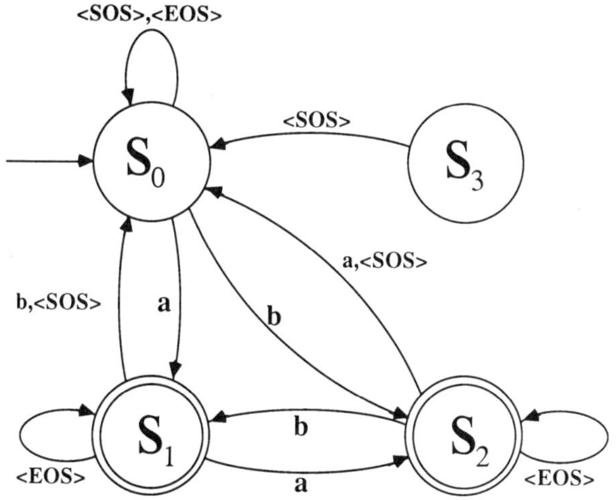

Figure 1.20 The expanded state transition diagram for the DFA implemented in Figure 1.21

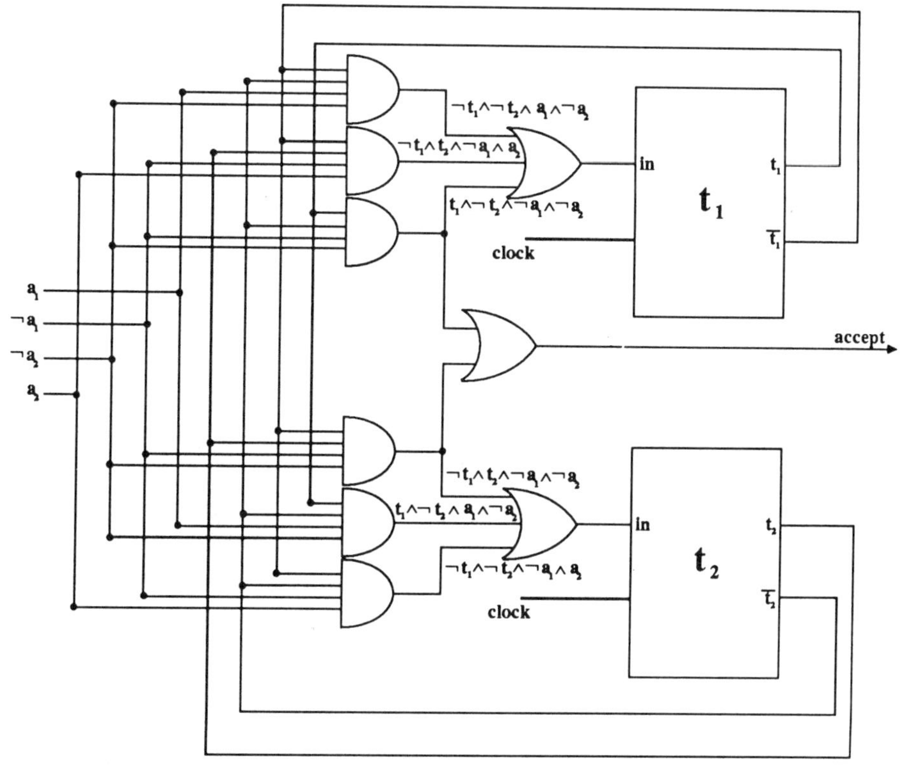

Figure 1.21 The circuitry implementing the DFA discussed in Example 1.13

1.5 APPLICATIONS OF FINITE AUTOMATA

In this chapter we have described the simplest form of finite automaton, the DFA. Other forms of automata, such as nondeterministic finite automata, pushdown automata, and Turing machines, are introduced later in the text. We close this chapter with three examples to motivate the material in the succeeding chapters.

When presenting automata in this chapter, we made no effort to construct the minimal machine. A *minimal* machine for a given language is one that has the least number of states required to accept that language.

EXAMPLE 1.14

In Example 1.5, the vending machine kept track of the amount of change that had been deposited up to 50¢. Since the candy bars cost only 30¢, there is no need to count up to 50¢. In this sense, the machine is not optimal, since a less complex machine can perform the same task, as shown in Figure 1.22. The corresponding quintuple is $<\{\mathbf{n}, \mathbf{d}, \mathbf{q}\}, \{s_0, s_5, s_{10}, s_{15}, s_{20}, s_{25}, s_{30}\}, s_0, \delta, \{s_{30}\}>$, where for each state s_i, δ is defined by

$$\delta(s_i, \mathbf{n}) = s_{\min\{30, i+5\}}$$

$$\delta(s_i, \mathbf{d}) = s_{\min\{30, i+10\}}$$

$$\delta(s_i, \mathbf{q}) = s_{\min\{30, i+25\}}$$

Note that the higher-numbered states in Example 1.6 were all effectively "remembering" the same thing, that enough coins had been deposited. These final states have been coalesced into a single final state to produce the more efficient machine in Figure 1.22. In the next two chapters, we develop the theoretical background and algorithms necessary to construct from an arbitrary DFA the minimal machine that accepts the same language.

As another illustration of the utility of concepts relating to finite-state machines, we will consider the formalism used by many text editors to search for a particular target string pattern in a text file. To find **ababb** in a file, for example, a

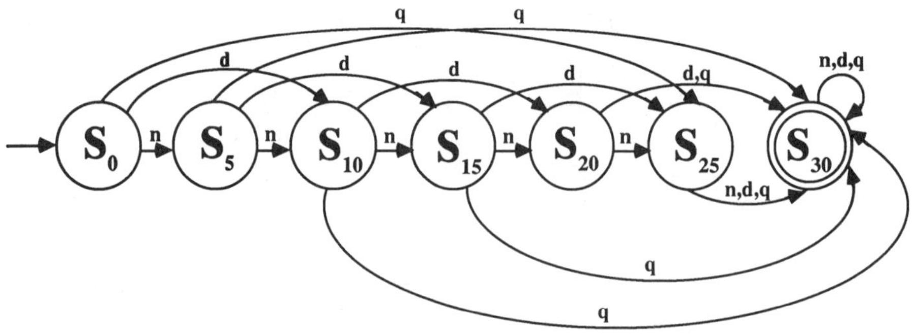

Figure 1.22 The automaton discussed in Example 1.14

naive approach might consist of checking whether the first five characters of the file fit this pattern, and next checking characters 2 through 6 to find a match, and so on. This results in examining file characters more than once; it ought to be possible to remember past values, and avoid such duplication. Consider the text string **aabababbb**. By the time the fifth character is scanned, we have matched the first four characters of **ababb**. Unfortunately, **a**, the sixth character of **aabababbb**, does not produce the final match; however, since characters 4, 5, and 6 (**aba**) now match the first three characters of the target string, it does allow for the possibility of characters 4 through 8 matching (as is indeed the case in this example). This leads to a general rule: If we have matched the first four letters of the target string, and the next character happens to be an **a** (rather that the desired **b**), we must remember that we have now matched the first three letters of the target string.

"Rules" such as these are actually the state transitions in the DFA given in the next example. State s_i represents having matched the first i characters of the target string, and the rule developed above is succinctly stated as $\delta(s_4, \mathbf{a}) = s_3$.

EXAMPLE 1.15

A DFA that accepts all strings that contain **ababb** as a substring is displayed in Figure 1.23. The corresponding quintuple is

$$<\{\mathbf{a}, \mathbf{b}\}, \{s_0, s_1, s_2, s_3, s_4, s_5\}, s_0, \delta, \{s_5\}>,$$

where δ is defined by

δ	a	b
s_0	s_1	s_0
s_1	s_1	s_2
s_2	s_3	s_0
s_3	s_1	s_4
s_4	s_3	s_5
s_5	s_5	s_5

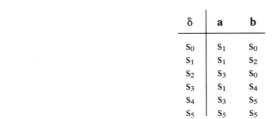

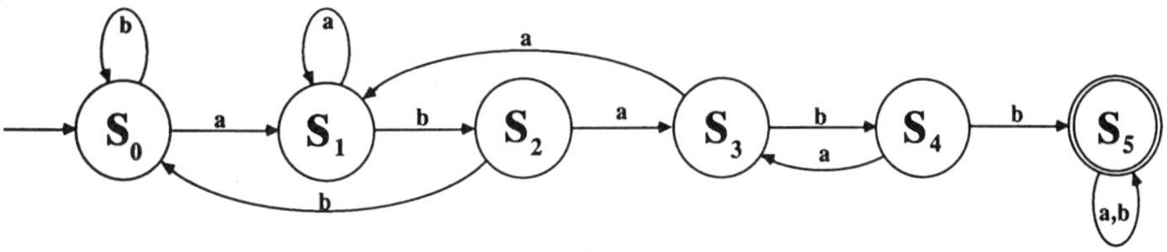

Figure 1.23 A DFA that accepts strings containing **ababb**

It is a worthwhile exercise to test the operation of this DFA on several text strings and verify that the automaton is indeed in state s_i exactly when it has matched the first i characters of the target string. Note that if we did not care what the third character of the substring was (that is, if we were searching for occurrences of **ababb** *or* **abbbb**), a trivial modification of the above machine would allow us to search for both substrings at once, as shown in Figure 1.24. The corresponding quintuple is $<\{\mathbf{a}, \mathbf{b}\}, \{s_0, s_1, s_2, s_3, s_4, s_5\}, s_0, \delta, \{s_5\}>$, where δ is defined by

δ	a	b
s_0	s_1	s_0
s_1	s_1	s_2
s_2	s_3	s_3
s_3	s_1	s_4
s_4	s_3	s_5
s_5	s_5	s_5

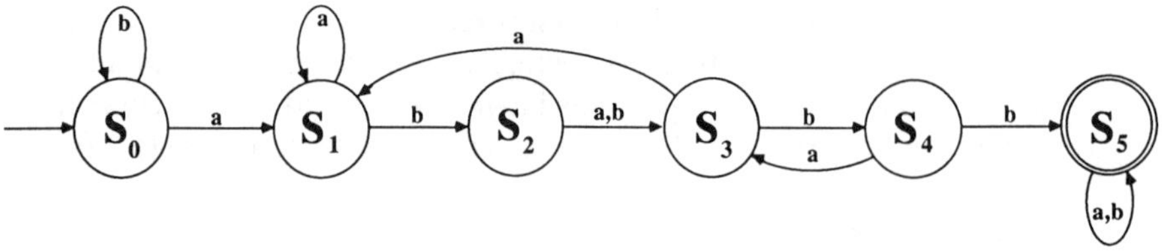

Figure 1.24 A DFA that accepts strings that contain either **ababb** or **abbbb**

In this case, we required one letter between the initial part of the search string (**ab**) and the terminal part (**bb**). It is possible to modify the machine to accept strings that contain **ab**, followed by any number of letters, followed by **bb**. This type of machine would be useful for identifying *comments* in many programming languages. For example, a Pascal comment is essentially of the form **(***, followed by most combinations of letters, followed by the first occurrence of ***)**.

It should be noted that the machine in Example 1.15 is highly specialized and tailored for the specific string **ababb**; other target strings would require completely different recognizers. While it appears to require much thought to generate the appropriate DFA for a given string, we will see how the tools presented in Chapter 4 can be used to automate the entire process.

Example 1.15 indicates how automata can be used to guide the construction of software for matching designated patterns. Finite-state machines are also useful in designing hardware that detects designated sequences. Example 4.7 will explore a communications application, and the following discussion illustrates how these concepts can be applied to help evaluate the performance of computers.

A computer program is essentially a linear list of machine instructions, stored in consecutive memory locations. Each memory location holds a sequence of bits that can be thought of as words comprised of **0**s and **1**s. Different types of instructions are represented by different patterns of bits. The CPU sequentially *fetches* these instructions and chooses its next action by examining the incoming bit pattern to determine the type of instruction that should be executed. The sequences of bits that encode the instruction type are called *opcodes*.

Various performance advantages can be attained when one part of the CPU *prefetches* the next instruction while another part executes the current instruction. However, computers must have the capability of altering the order in which instructions are executed; *branch* instructions allow the CPU to avoid the anticipated next instruction and instead begin executing the instructions stored in some other area of memory. When a branch occurs, the prefetched instruction will generally need to be replaced by the proper instruction from the new area of memory. The consequent delay can degrade the speed with which instructions are executed.

Irrespective of prefetching problems, it should be clear that a branch instruction followed immediately by another branch instruction is inefficient. If a CPU is found to be regularly executing two or more consecutive branch instructions, it may be worthwhile to consider replacing such series of branches with a single branch to the ultimate destination [FERR]. Such information would be determined by monitoring the instruction stream and searching for patterns that represented consecutive branch opcodes. This activity is essentially the pattern recognition problem discussed in Example 1.15.

It is unwise to try to collect the data representing the contents of the instruction stream on secondary storage so that it can be analyzed later. The volume of information and the speed with which it is generated preclude the collection of a sufficiently large set of data points. Instead, the preferred solution uses a specially tailored piece of hardware to monitor the contents of the CPU opcode register and increment a hardware counter each time the appropriate patterns are detected. The heart of this monitor can be built by transforming the appropriate automaton into the corresponding logic circuitry, as outlined in Section 1.4. Unlike the automaton in Example 1.15, the automaton model for this application would allow transitions out of the final state, so that it may continue to search for successive patterns. The resulting logic circuitry would accept as input the bit patterns currently present in the opcode register, and send a pulse to the counter mechanism each time the accept circuitry was energized.

Note that in this case we would not want to inhibit the accept circuitry by requiring an <EOS> symbol to be scanned. Indeed, we want the light on our conceptual black box to flicker as we process the data, since we are intent on counting the number of times it flickers during the course of our monitoring.

EXAMPLE 1.16

We close this chapter with an illustration of the manner in which computational algorithms can profitably use the automaton abstraction. Network communications between independent processors are governed by a *protocol* that implements a finite state control [TANE]. The *Kermit* protocol, developed at Columbia University, is widely employed to communicate between processors and is still most often used for its original purpose: to transfer files between micros and mainframes [DACR]. During a file transfer, the send portion of Kermit on the source host is responsible for delivering data to the receive portion of the Kermit process on the destination host. The receive portion of Kermit reacts to incoming data in much the same way as the machines presented in this chapter. The receive program *starts* in a state of waiting for a transfer request (in the form of an initialization packet) to signal the commencement of a file transfer (state R in Figure 1.25). When such a packet is received, Kermit *transitions* to the RF state, where it awaits a file-header

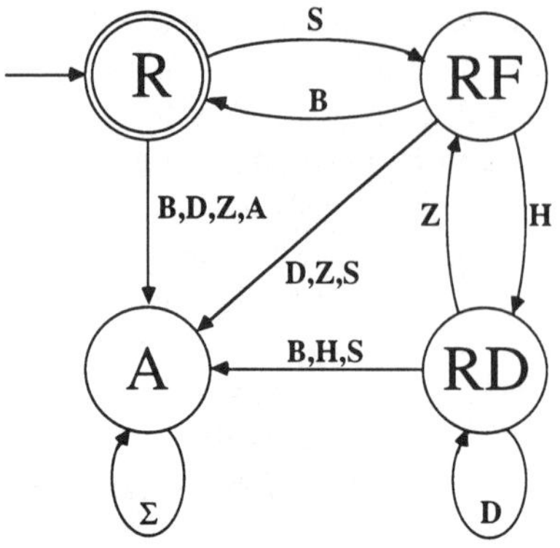

Figure 1.25 The state transition diagram for the receive portion of Kermit, as discussed in Example 1.16

packet (which specifies the name of the file about to be transferred). Upon receipt of the file-header packet, it enters the RD state, where it processes a succession of data packets (which comprise the body of the file being transferred). An EOF packet should arrive after all the data are sent, which can then be followed by another file-header packet (if there is a sequence of files to be transferred) or by a break packet (if the transfer is complete). In the latter case, Kermit reverts to the start state R and awaits the next transfer request. The send portion of the Kermit process on the source host follows the behavior of a slightly more complex automaton. The state transition diagram given in Figure 1.25 succinctly describes the logic of the receive portion of the Kermit protocol; for simplicity, timeouts and error conditions are not reflected in the diagram. The input alphabet is {B, D, Z, H, S}, where B represents a break, D is a data packet, Z is EOF, H is a file-header packet, and S is a send-intention packet. The state set is {A, R, RF, RD}, where A denotes the *a*bort state, R signifies *r*eceive, RF is *r*eceive *f*ileheader, and RD is *r*eceive *d*ata. Note that unexpected packets (such as a data packet received in the start state R or a break packet received when data packets are expected in state RD) cause a transition to the abort state A.

In actuality, the receive protocol does more than just observe the incoming packets; Kermit sends an acknowledgment (ACK or NAK) of each packet back to the source host. Receipt of the file header should also cause an appropriate file to be created and opened, and each succeeding data packet should be verified and its contents placed sequentially in the new file. A machine model that incorporates actions in response to input is the subject of Chapter 7, where automata with output are explored.

EXERCISES

1.1. Recall how we defined $\overline{\delta}$ in this chapter:

$$(\forall \mathrm{s} \in S)(\forall \mathbf{a} \in \Sigma) \qquad \overline{\delta}_t(\mathrm{s}, \mathbf{a}) = \delta(\mathrm{s}, \mathbf{a})$$
$$(\forall \mathrm{s} \in S) \qquad \overline{\delta}_t(\mathrm{s}, \lambda) = \mathrm{s}$$
$$(\forall \mathrm{s} \in S)(\forall x \in \Sigma^*)(\forall \mathbf{a} \in \Sigma) \qquad \overline{\delta}_t(\mathrm{s}, \mathbf{a}x) = \overline{\delta}_t(\delta(\mathrm{s}, \mathbf{a}), x)$$

$\overline{\delta}$, here denoted $\overline{\delta}_t$, was tail recursive. Tail recursion means that all recursion takes place at the end of the string. Let us now define an alternative extended transition function, $\overline{\delta}_h$, thusly:

$$(\forall s \in S)(\forall \mathbf{a} \in \Sigma) \qquad \overline{\delta}_h(s, \mathbf{a}) = \delta(s, \mathbf{a})$$
$$(\forall s \in S) \qquad \overline{\delta}_h(s, \lambda) = s$$
$$(\forall s \in S)(\forall \mathbf{a} \in \Sigma)(\forall x \in \Sigma^*) \qquad \overline{\delta}_h(s, x\mathbf{a}) = \delta(\overline{\delta}_h(s, x), \mathbf{a})$$

It is clear from the definition of $\overline{\delta}_h$ that all the recursion takes place at the head of the string. For this reason, $\overline{\delta}_h$ is called *head recursive*. Show that the two definitions result in the same extension of δ, that is, prove by mathematical induction that

$$(\forall s \in S)(\forall x \in \Sigma^*)(\overline{\delta}_t(s, x) = \overline{\delta}_h(s, x))$$

1.2. Consider Example 1.14. The vending machine accepts coins as input, but if you change your mind (or find you do not have enough change), it will not refund your money. Modify this example to have another input, <coin-return>, which is represented by **r** and which will conceptually return all your coins.

1.3. **(a)** Specify the quintuple corresponding to the DFA displayed in Figure 1.26.
(b) Describe the language defined by the DFA displayed in Figure 1.26.

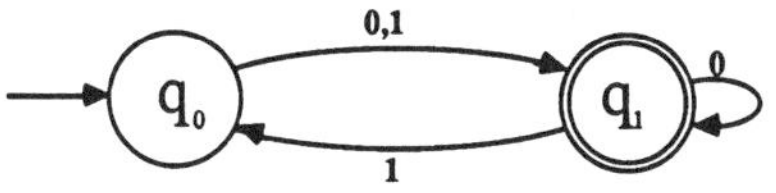

Figure 1.26 The automaton discussed in Exercise 1.3

1.4. Construct a state transition diagram and enumerate all five parts of a deterministic finite automaton $A = <\{\mathbf{a}, \mathbf{b}, \mathbf{c}\}, S, s_0, \delta, F>$ such that

$$L(A) = \{x \mid |x| \text{ is a multiple of 2 or 3}\}.$$

1.5. Let $\Sigma = \{\mathbf{0}, \mathbf{1}\}$. Construct deterministic finite automata that will accept each of the following languages, if possible.
(a) $L_1 = \{x \mid |x| \bmod 7 = 4\}$
(b) $L_2 = \Sigma^* - \{w \mid \exists n \geq 1 \ni w = a_1 \ldots a_n \wedge a_n = \mathbf{1}\}$
(c) $L_3 = \{y \mid |y|_0 = |y|_1\}$

1.6. Let $\Sigma = \{\mathbf{a}, \mathbf{b}\}$.
(a) Construct deterministic finite automata A_1, A_2, A_3, and A_4 such that:
i. $L(A_1) = \{x \mid (|x|_\mathbf{a} \text{ is odd}) \wedge (|x|_\mathbf{b} \text{ is even})\}$
ii. $L(A_2) = \{y \mid (|y|_\mathbf{a} \text{ is even}) \vee (|y|_\mathbf{b} \text{ is odd})\}$
iii. $L(A_3) = \{z \mid (|z|_\mathbf{a} \text{ is even}) \underline{\vee} (|z|_\mathbf{b} \text{ is even})\}$ ($\underline{\vee}$ represents exclusive-or)
iv. $L(A_4) = \{z \mid |z|_\mathbf{a} \text{ is even}\}$
(b) How does the structure of each of these machines relate to the one defined in Example 1.10?

1.7. Modify the machine M defined in Example 1.10 so that the language accepted by the machine consists of strings $x \in \{\mathbf{a}, \mathbf{b}\}^*$, where both $|x|_\mathbf{a}$ and $|x|_\mathbf{b}$ are even and $|x| > 0$, that is, the new machine should accept $L(M) - \{\lambda\}$.

1.8. Let $M = <\Sigma, S, s_0, \delta, F>$ be an (arbitrary) DFA that accepts the language $L(M)$. Write down a general procedure for modifying this machine so that it will accept $L(M) - \{\lambda\}$. (Specify the five parts of the new machine and justify your statements.) It may be helpful to do this for a specific machine (as in Exercise 1.7) before attempting the general case.

1.9. Let $M = <\Sigma, S, s_0, \delta, F>$ be an (arbitrary) DFA that accepts the language $L(M)$. Write down a general procedure for modifying this machine so that it will accept $L(\mathrm{M}) \cup \{\lambda\}$. (Specify the five parts of the new machine and justify your statements.)

1.10. Let $\Sigma = \{\mathbf{a}, \mathbf{b}, \mathbf{d}\}$ and $\Psi = \{x \in \Sigma^* \mid (x \text{ begins with } \mathbf{d}) \vee (x \text{ contains two consecutive } \mathbf{b}\text{s})\}$.
- **(a)** Draw a machine that will accept Ψ.
- **(b)** Formally specify the five parts of the DFA from part (a).

1.11. Let $\Sigma = \{\mathbf{a}, \mathbf{b}, \mathbf{c}\}$ and $\Phi = \{x \in \Sigma^* \mid \text{every } \mathbf{b} \text{ in } x \text{ is immediately followed by } \mathbf{c}\}$.
- **(a)** Draw a machine that will accept Φ.
- **(b)** Formally specify the five parts of the DFA from part (a).

1.12. Let $\Sigma = \{\mathbf{0}, \mathbf{1}, \mathbf{2}, \mathbf{3}, \mathbf{4}, \mathbf{5}, \mathbf{6}, \mathbf{7}, \mathbf{8}, \mathbf{9}\}$. Consider the base 10 numbers formed by strings from Σ^*: **14** represents fourteen, the three-digit string **205** represents two hundred and five, and so on. Let $\Omega = \{x \in \Sigma^* \mid \text{the number represented by } x \text{ is evenly divisible by } 7\} = \{\lambda, \mathbf{0}, \mathbf{00}, \mathbf{000}, \ldots, \mathbf{7}, \mathbf{07}, \mathbf{007}, \ldots, \mathbf{14}, \mathbf{21}, \mathbf{28}, \mathbf{35}, \ldots\}$.
- **(a)** Draw a machine that will accept Ω.
- **(b)** Formally specify the five parts of the DFA from part (a).

1.13. Let $\Sigma = \{\mathbf{0}, \mathbf{1}, \mathbf{2}, \mathbf{3}, \mathbf{4}, \mathbf{5}, \mathbf{6}, \mathbf{7}, \mathbf{8}, \mathbf{9}\}$. Let $\Gamma = \{x \in \Sigma^* \mid \text{the number represented by } x \text{ is evenly divisible by } 3\}$.
- **(a)** Draw a three-state machine that will accept Γ.
- **(b)** Formally specify the five parts of the DFA from part (a).

1.14. Let $\Sigma = \{\mathbf{0}, \mathbf{1}, \mathbf{2}, \mathbf{3}, \mathbf{4}, \mathbf{5}, \mathbf{6}, \mathbf{7}, \mathbf{8}, \mathbf{9}\}$. Let $\mathrm{K} = \{x \in \Sigma^* \mid \text{the number represented by } x \text{ is evenly divisible by } 5\}$.
- **(a)** Draw a five-state DFA that accepts K.
- **(b)** Formally specify the five parts of the DFA from part (a).
- **(c)** Draw a two-state DFA that accepts K.
- **(d)** Formally specify the five parts of the DFA from part (c).

1.15. Let $\Sigma = \{\mathbf{0}, \mathbf{1}, \mathbf{2}, \mathbf{3}, \mathbf{4}, \mathbf{5}, \mathbf{6}, \mathbf{7}, \mathbf{8}, \mathbf{9}\}$. Draw a DFA that accepts the first eight primes.

1.16.
- **(a)** Find all ten combinations of u, v, and w such that $uvw = \mathbf{cab}$ (one such combination is $u = \mathbf{c}$, $v = \lambda$, $w = \mathbf{ab}$).
- **(b)** In general, if x is of length n, and $uvw = x$, how many distinct combinations of u, v, and w will satisfy this constraint?

1.17. Let $\Sigma = \{\mathbf{a}, \mathbf{b}\}$ and $\Xi = \{x \in \Sigma^* \mid x \text{ contains (at least) two consecutive } \mathbf{b}\text{s} \wedge x \text{ does } \textit{not} \text{ contain two consecutive } \mathbf{a}\text{s}\}$. Draw a machine that will accept Ξ.

1.18. The FORTRAN identifier in Example 1.9 recognized *all* alphabetic words, including those like DO, DATA, END, and STOP, which have different uses in FORTRAN. Modify Figure 1.11 to produce a DFA that will also reject the words DO and DATA while still accepting all other valid FORTRAN identifiers.

1.19. Consider the machine defined in Example 1.11. This machine accepts most real-number constants in scientific notation. However, this machine does have some (possibly desirable) limitations. These limitations include requiring that a **0** precede the decimal point when specifying a number with a mantissa less than 1.
- **(a)** Modify Figure 1.13 so that it will accept the set of real-number constants described by the following BNF.

<sign> ::= **+** | **−**
<digit> ::= **0** | **1** | **2** | **3** | **4** | **5** | **6** | **7** | **8** | **9**
<natural> ::= <digit> | <digit><natural>
<integer> ::= <natural> | <sign><natural>
<real constant> ::= <integer> |

<integer>. |
.<natural> |
<sign>.<natural> |
.<natural>**E**<integer> |
<sign>.<natural>**E**<integer> |
<integer>.<natural> |
<integer>.<natural>**E**<integer>

(b) Write a program in your favorite programming language to implement the automaton derived in part (a). The program should read a line of text and state whether or not the word on that line was accepted.

1.20. Show that part (i) of Definition 1.11 is implied by parts (ii) and (iii) of that definition.

1.21. Develop a more succinct description of the transition function given in Example 1.9 (compare with the description in Example 1.10).

1.22. Let the universal set be {**a**, **b**}*. Give an example of
(a) A finite set.
(b) A cofinite set.
(c) A set that is neither finite nor cofinite.

1.23. Consider the DFA given in Figure 1.27.
(a) Specify the quintuple for this machine.
(b) Describe the language defined by this machine.

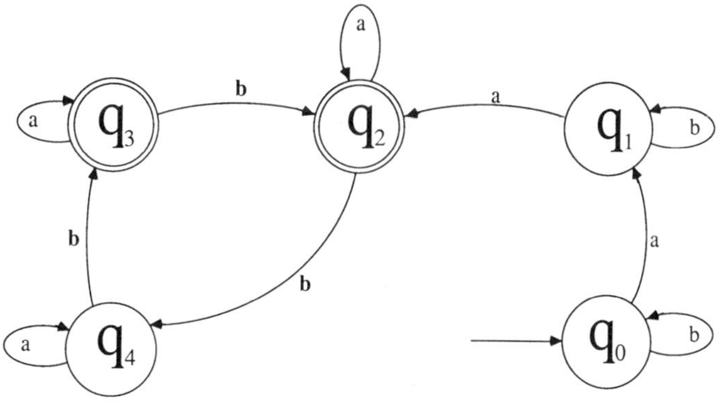

Figure 1.27 The DFA discussed in Exercise 1.23

1.24. Consider the set consisting of the names of everyone in China. Is this set a FAD language?

1.25. Consider the set of all legal infix arithmetic expressions over the alphabet {**A**, **B**, +, −, *, /} without parentheses (assume normal procedence rules apply). Is this set a FAD language? If so, draw the machine.

1.26. Consider an arbitrary deterministic finite automaton M.
(a) What aspect of the machine determines whether $\lambda \in L(\mathsf{M})$?
(b) Specify a condition that would guarantee that $L(\mathsf{M}) = \Sigma^*$.
(c) Specify a condition that would guarantee that $L(\mathsf{M}) = \emptyset$.

1.27. Construct deterministic finite automata to accept each of the following languages.

(a) $\{x \in \{\mathbf{a}, \mathbf{b}, \mathbf{c}\}^* \mid \mathbf{abc}$ is a substring of $x\}$

(b) $\{x \in \{\mathbf{a}, \mathbf{b}, \mathbf{c}\}^* \mid \mathbf{acaba}$ is a substring of $x\}$

1.28. Consider Example 1.14. The vending machine had as input nickels, dimes, and quarters. When 30¢ had been deposited, a candy bar could be selected. Modify this machine to also accept pennies, denoted by **p**, as an additional input. How does this affect the number of states in the machine?

1.29. **(a)** Describe the language defined by the following quintuple (compare with Figure 1.28).

$$\Sigma = \{\mathbf{a}, \mathbf{b}\} \qquad \delta(t_0, \mathbf{a}) = t_0$$
$$S = \{t_0, t_1\} \qquad \delta(t_0, \mathbf{b}) = t_1$$
$$s_0 = t_0 \qquad \delta(t_1, \mathbf{a}) = t_1$$
$$F = \{t_1\} \qquad \delta(t_1, \mathbf{b}) = t_0$$

(b) Rigorously *prove* the statement you made in part (a). *Hint:* First prove the inductive statement

$$P(n)\colon (\forall x \in \Sigma^n)((\bar{\delta}(t_0, x) = t_0 \Leftrightarrow |x|_{\mathbf{b}} \text{ is even}) \wedge (\bar{\delta}(t_0, x) = t_1 \Leftrightarrow |x|_{\mathbf{b}} \text{ is odd})).$$

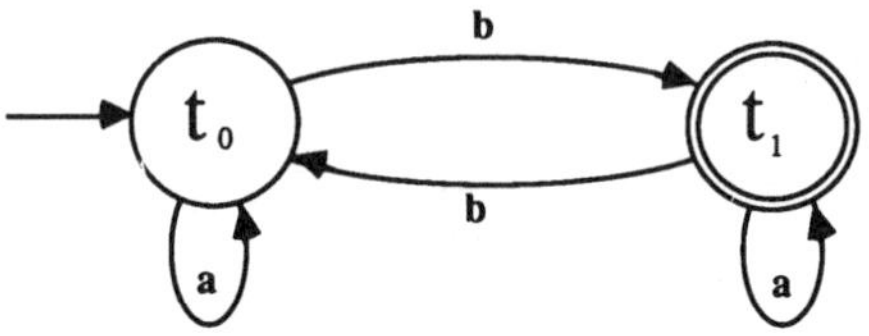

Figure 1.28 The DFA discussed in Exercise 1.29

1.30. Consider a vending machine that accepts as input pennies, nickels, dimes, and quarters and dispenses 10¢ candy bars.

(a) Draw a DFA that models this machine.

(b) Define the quintuple for this machine.

(c) How many states are absolutely necessary to build this machine?

1.31. Consider a vending machine that accepts as input nickels, dimes, and quarters and dispenses 10¢ candy bars.

(a) Draw a DFA that models this machine.

(b) How many states are absolutely necessary to build this machine?

(c) Using the standard encoding conventions, draw a circuit diagram for this machine (include <EOS> but not <SOS> in the input alphabet).

1.32. Using the standard encoding conventions, draw a circuit diagram that will implement the machine given in Exercise 1.29, as follows:

(a) Implements both <EOS> and <SOS>.

(b) Uses neither <EOS> nor <SOS>.

1.33. Using the standard encoding conventions, draw a circuit diagram that will implement the machine given in Exercise 1.7, as follows:

(a) Implements both <EOS> and <SOS>.

(b) Uses neither <EOS> nor <SOS>.

1.34. Modify Example 1.12 so that it correctly handles the <SOS> symbol; draw the new circuit diagram.

1.35. Using the standard encoding conventions, draw a circuit diagram that will implement the machine given in Example 1.6, as follows:

(a) Implements both <EOS> and <SOS>.
(b) Uses neither <EOS> nor <SOS>.

1.36. Using the standard encoding conventions, draw a circuit diagram that will implement the machine given in Example 1.10, as follows:
(a) Implements both <EOS> and <SOS>.
(b) Uses neither <EOS> nor <SOS>.

1.37. Using the standard encoding conventions, draw a circuit diagram that will implement the machine given in Example 1.14 (include <EOS> but not <SOS> in the input alphabet).

1.38. Using the standard encoding conventions, draw a circuit diagram that will implement the machine given in Example 1.16; include the <SOS> and <EOS> symbols.

1.39. Let $\Sigma = \{\mathbf{a}, \mathbf{b}, \mathbf{c}\}$. Let $L = \{x \in \{\mathbf{a}, \mathbf{b}, \mathbf{c}\}^* \mid |x|_{\mathbf{b}} = 2\}$.
(a) Draw a DFA that accepts L.
(b) Formally specify the five parts of a DFA that accepts L.

1.40. Draw a DFA accepting $\{x \in \{\mathbf{a}, \mathbf{b}, \mathbf{c}\}^* \mid$ every **b** in x is eventually followed by **c**$\}$; that is, x might look like **baabacaa**, or **bcacc**, and so on.

1.41. Let $\Sigma = \{\mathbf{a}, \mathbf{b}\}$. Consider the language consisting of all words that have neither consecutive **a**s nor consecutive **b**s.
(a) Draw a DFA that accepts this language.
(b) Formally specify the five parts of a DFA that accepts L.

1.42. Let $\Sigma = \{\mathbf{a}, \mathbf{b}, \mathbf{c}\}$. Let $L = \{x \in \{\mathbf{a}, \mathbf{b}, \mathbf{c}\}^* \mid |x|_{\mathbf{a}} \equiv 0 \bmod 3\}$.
(a) Draw a DFA that accepts L.
(b) Formally specify the five parts of a DFA that accepts L.

1.43. Let $\Sigma = \{\mathbf{a}, \mathbf{b}, (, *,)\}$. Recall that a Pascal comment is essentially of the form: **(*** followed by most combinations of letters followed by the first occurrence of ***)**. While the appropriate alphabet for Pascal is the ASCII character set, for simplicity we will let $\Sigma = \{\mathbf{a}, \mathbf{b}, (, *,)\}$. Note that **(*b(*b(a)b*)** is a single valid comment, since all characters prior to the first ***)** (including the second **(***) are considered part of the comment. Consequently, comments cannot be nested.
(a) Draw a DFA that recognizes all strings that contain exactly one valid Pascal comment (and no illegal portions of comments, as in **aa(*b*)b(*a**).
(b) Draw a DFA that recognizes all strings that contain zero or more valid (that is, unnested) Pascal comments. For example, **a(*b(*bb*)ba*)aa** and **a(*b** are not valid, while **a()a(**)b(*ab*)** is valid.

1.44. **(a)** Is the set of all postfix expressions over $\{\mathbf{A}, \mathbf{B}, +, -, *, /\}$ with two or fewer operators a FAD language? If it is, draw a machine.
(b) Is the set of all postfix expressions over $\{\mathbf{A}, \mathbf{B}, +, -, *, /\}$ with four or fewer operators a FAD language? If it is, draw a machine.
(c) Is the set of all postfix expressions over $\{\mathbf{A}, \mathbf{B}, +, -, *, /\}$ with eight or fewer operators a FAD language? If it is, draw a machine.
(d) Do you think the set of *all* postfix expressions over $\{\mathbf{A}, \mathbf{B}, +, -, *, /\}$ is a FAD language? Why or why not?

1.45. Let $\Sigma = \{\mathbf{a}, \mathbf{b}, \mathbf{c}\}$. Consider the language consisting of all words that begin and end with different letters.
(a) Draw a DFA that accepts this language.
(b) Formally specify the five parts of a DFA that accepts this language.

1.46. Let $\Sigma = \{\mathbf{a}, \mathbf{b}, \mathbf{c}\}$.

(a) Draw a DFA that rejects all words for which the last two letters match.

(b) Formally specify the five parts of the DFA.

1.47. Let $\Sigma = \{\mathbf{a}, \mathbf{b}, \mathbf{c}\}$.

(a) Draw a DFA that rejects all words for which the first two letters match.

(b) Formally specify the five parts of the DFA.

1.48. Prove that the empty word is unique; that is, using the definition of equality of strings, show that if x and y are empty words then $x = y$.

1.49. For any two strings x and y, show that $|xy| = |x| + |y|$.

1.50. **(a)** Draw the DFA corresponding to $\mathrm{C} = <\{\mathbf{a}, \mathbf{b}, \mathbf{c}\}, \{t_0, t_1\}, q_0, \delta, \{t_1\}>$, where

$$\begin{array}{ll} \delta(t_0, \mathbf{a}) = t_0 & \delta(t_1, \mathbf{a}) = t_0 \\ \delta(t_0, \mathbf{b}) = t_1 & \delta(t_1, \mathbf{b}) = t_1 \\ \delta(t_0, \mathbf{c}) = t_1 & \delta(t_1, \mathbf{c}) = t_0 \end{array}$$

(b) Describe $\boldsymbol{L}(\mathrm{C})$.

(c) Using the standard encoding conventions, draw a circuit diagram for this machine (include <EOS> but not <SOS> in the input alphabet).

1.51. Let $\Sigma = \{\mathbf{I}, \mathbf{V}, \mathbf{X}, \mathbf{L}, \mathbf{C}, \mathbf{M}\}$. Recall that **VVI** is not considered to be a Roman numeral.

(a) Draw a DFA that recognizes strict-order Roman numerals; that is, 9 must be represented by **VIIII** rather than **IX**, and so on.

(b) Draw a DFA that recognizes the set of all Roman numerals; that is, 9 can be represented by **IX**, 40 by **XL**, and so on.

(c) Write a Pascal program based on your answer to part (b) that recognizes the set of all Roman numerals.

1.52. Describe the set of words accepted by the DFA in Figure 1.9.

1.53. Let $\Sigma = \{\mathbf{0}, \mathbf{1}, \mathbf{2}, \mathbf{3}, \mathbf{4}, \mathbf{5}, \mathbf{6}, \mathbf{7}, \mathbf{8}, \mathbf{9}\}$. Let
$L_n = \{x \in \Sigma^* \mid \text{the sum of the digits of } x \text{ is evenly divisible by } n\}$. Thus,
$L_7 = \{\lambda, \mathbf{0}, \mathbf{7}, \mathbf{00}, \mathbf{07}, \mathbf{16}, \mathbf{25}, \mathbf{34}, \mathbf{43}, \mathbf{52}, \mathbf{59}, \mathbf{61}, \mathbf{68}, \mathbf{70}, \mathbf{77}, \mathbf{86}, \mathbf{95}, \mathbf{000}, \mathbf{007}, \ldots\}$.

(a) Draw a machine that will accept L_7.

(b) Formally specify the five parts of the DFA given in part (a).

(c) Draw a machine that will accept L_3.

(d) Formally specify the five parts of the DFA given in part (c).

(e) Formally specify the five parts of a DFA that will recognize L_n.

1.54. Consider the last row of Table 1.3. Unlike the preceding three rows, the outputs in this row are not marked with the don't-care symbol. Explain.

CHAPTER

2

CHARACTERIZATION of FAD LANGUAGES

Programming languages can be thought of, in a limited sense, as conforming to the definition of a language given in Chapter 1. We can consider a text file as being one long "word," that is, a string of characters (including spaces, carriage returns, and so on). In this sense, each Pascal program can be thought of as a single word over the ASCII alphabet. We might define the *language* Pascal as the *set* of all valid Pascal programs (that is, the valid "words" are those text files that would compile with no compiler errors). This and many other languages are too complicated to be represented by the machines described in Chapter 1. Indeed, even reliably matching an unlimited number of `begin` and `end` statements in a file is beyond the capabilities of a DFA.

The goals for this chapter are to develop some tools for identifying these non-FAD languages and to investigate the underlying structure of finite automaton definable languages. We begin with the exploration of the relations that describe that structure.

2.1 RIGHT CONGRUENCES

To characterize the structure of FAD languages, we will be dealing with relations over Σ^*, that is, we will relate strings to other strings. Recall that an *equivalence relation* must be *reflexive*, *symmetric*, and *transitive*. The *identity* relation over Σ^*, in which each string is related to itself but to no other string, is an example of an equivalence relation.

The main tool we will need to understand which kinds of languages can be represented by finite automata is the concept of a *right congruence*. If we allow the set of all strings that terminate in some given state to define an *equivalence class*, the states of a DFA naturally partition Σ^* into equivalence classes (as formally presented later in Definition 2.4). Due to the structure imposed on the machine, these classes have special relationships that are not found in ordinary equivalence relations. For example, if $\delta(\mathrm{s}, \mathbf{a}) = \mathrm{t}$, then, given *any* word x in the class corresponding to the state s, appending an **a** to this word to form $x\mathbf{a}$ is guaranteed to produce a word listed in the class corresponding to the state t. Right congruences, defined below, allow us to break up Σ^* in the same fashion that a DFA breaks up Σ^*.

∇ **Definition 2.1.** Given an alphabet Σ, a relation R between pairs of strings ($\mathrm{R} \subseteq \Sigma^* \times \Sigma^*$) is a *right congruence in* Σ^* ***iff*** the following four conditions hold:

$$(\forall x \in \Sigma^*) \qquad (x \mathrm{R} x) \qquad \text{(R)}$$

$$(\forall x, y \in \Sigma^*) \qquad (x \mathrm{R} y \Rightarrow y \mathrm{R} x) \qquad \text{(S)}$$

$$(\forall x, y, z \in \Sigma^*) \qquad (x \mathrm{R} y \wedge y \mathrm{R} z \Rightarrow x \mathrm{R} z) \qquad \text{(T)}$$

$$(\forall x, y \in \Sigma^*) \qquad (x \mathrm{R} y \Rightarrow (\forall u \in \Sigma^*)(xu \mathrm{R} yu)) \qquad \text{(RC)}$$

Δ

Note that if P is a right congruence then the first three conditions imply that P must be an equivalence relation; for example, if $\Sigma = \{\mathbf{a}, \mathbf{b}\}$, **aa** P **aa** by reflexivity, and if $\langle \mathbf{abb}, \mathbf{aba} \rangle \in \mathrm{P}$, then by symmetry $\langle \mathbf{aba}, \mathbf{abb} \rangle \in \mathrm{P}$, and so forth. Furthermore, if **abb** P **aba**, then the right congruence property guarantees that

abba P **abaa**	if $u = \mathbf{a}$
abbb P **abab**	if $u = \mathbf{b}$
abbaa P **abaaa**	if $u = \mathbf{aa}$
abbbbaabb P **ababbaabb**	if $u = \mathbf{bbaabb}$

and so on. Thus, the presence of just one ordered pair in P requires the existence of many, many more ordered pairs. This might seem to make right congruences rather rare objects; there are, however, an infinite number of them, many of them rather simple, as shown by the following examples.

EXAMPLE 2.1

Let $\Sigma = \{\mathbf{a}, \mathbf{b}\}$, and let R be defined by $x \mathrm{R} y \Leftrightarrow |x| - |y|$ is even. It is easy to show that this R is an equivalence relation (see the exercises) and partitions Σ^* into two equivalence classes: the even-length words and the odd-length words. Furthermore, R is a right congruence: for example, if $x = \mathbf{abb}$ and $y = \mathbf{baabb}$, then **abb** R **baabb**, since $|x| - |y| = 3 - 5 = -2$, which is even. Note that for *any* choice of u, **abb**u R **baabb**u, since $|xu| - |yu|$ will also be -2. Thus **abb**u R **baabb**u for every choice of u. The same is true for any other pair of words x and y that are related by R, and so R is indeed a right congruence.

EXAMPLE 2.2

Let $\Sigma = \{\mathbf{a}, \mathbf{b}, \mathbf{c}\}$, and let R_2 be defined by $x \; R_2 \, y \Leftrightarrow x$ and y end with the same letter. It is straightforward to show that R_2 is a right congruence (see the exercises) and partitions Σ^* into four equivalence classes: those words ending in **a**, those words ending in **b**, those words ending in **c**, and $\{\lambda\}$.

The relation R_2 was based on the placement of letters within words, while Example 2.1 was based solely on the length of the words. The following definition illustrates a way to produce a relation in Σ^* based on a given set of words L.

∇ **Definition 2.2.** Given an alphabet Σ and a language $L \subseteq \Sigma^*$, the *relation induced by L in* Σ^*, denoted by R_L, is defined by

$$(\forall x, y \in \Sigma^*)(x \, R_L \, y \Leftrightarrow (\forall u \in \Sigma^*)(xu \in L \Leftrightarrow yu \in L))$$

Δ

EXAMPLE 2.3

Let K be the set of all words over $\{\mathbf{a}, \mathbf{b}\}^*$ that are of odd length. Those strings that are in K are used to define exactly which pairs of strings are in R_K. For example, we can determine that **ab** R_K **bbaa**, since it is true that, for any $u \in \Sigma^*$, either $\mathbf{ab}u \notin K$ and $\mathbf{bbaa}u \notin K$ (when $|u|$ is even) or $\mathbf{ab}u \in K$ and $\mathbf{bbaa}u \in K$ (when $|u|$ is odd). Note that **ab** and **a** are not related by R_K, since there are choices for u that would violate the definition of R_K: $\mathbf{ab}\lambda \notin K$ and yet $\mathbf{a}\lambda \in K$. In this case, R_K turns out to be the same as the relation R defined in Example 2.1.

Recall that relations are sets of ordered pairs, and thus the claim that these two relations are equal means that they are equal as sets; an ordered pair belongs to R exactly when it belongs to R_K:

$$R = R_K \textit{ iff } (\forall x, y \in \Sigma^*)(x R y \Leftrightarrow x R_K y)$$

The strings **ab** and **bbaa** are related by R in Example 2.1, and they are likewise related by R_K. A similar statement is true for any other pair that was in the relation R; it will be in R_K, also. Additionally, it can be shown that elements that were not in R will not be in R_K either.

Notice that R_K relates more than just the words in K; neither **ab** nor **bbaa** belongs to K, and yet they were related to each other. This simple language K happens to partition Σ^* into two equivalence classes, corresponding to the language itself and its complement. Less trivial languages will often form many equivalence classes. The relation R_L defined by a language L has all the properties given in Definition 2.1.

∇ **Theorem 2.1.** Let Σ be an alphabet. If L is any language over Σ (that is, $L \subseteq \Sigma^*$), the relation R_L given in Definition 2.2 must be a right congruence.

Proof. See the exercises.

Δ

Note that the above theorem is very broad in scope: *any* language, no matter how complex, *always* induces a relation that satisfies all four properties of a right congruence. Thus, R_L always partitions Σ^* into equivalence classes. One useful measure of the complexity of a language L is the degree to which it fragments Σ^*, that is, the number of equivalence classes in R_L.

∇ **Definition 2.3.** Given an equivalence relation P, the *rank of P*, denoted *rk*(P), is defined to be the number of *distinct* (and nonempty) equivalence classes of P.
Δ

The ranks of the relation in Example 2.3 was 2, since there were two equivalence classes, the set of even-length words and the set of odd-length words. In Example 2.2, $rk(R_2) = 3$. The rank of R_L can be thought of as a measure of the complexity of the underlying language L. Thus, for K in Example 2.3, $rk(R_K) = 2$, and K might consequently be considered to be a relatively simple language. Some languages are too complex to be recognized by finite automata; this relationship will be explored in the subsequent sections.

While the way in which a language gives rise to a partition of Σ^* may seem mysterious and highly nonintuitive, a deterministic finite automaton naturally distributes the words of Σ^* into equivalence classes. The following definition describes the manner in which a DFA partitions Σ^*.

∇ **Definition 2.4.** Given a DFA $M = <\Sigma, S, s_0, \delta, F>$, define a relation R^M on Σ^* as follows:

$$(\forall x, y \in \Sigma^*)(x R^M y \Leftrightarrow \bar{\delta}(s_0, x) = \bar{\delta}(s_0, y))$$

Δ

R^M relates all strings that, when starting at s_0, wind up at the same state. It is easy to show that R^M will be an equivalence relation with (usually) one equivalence class for each state of M (remember that equivalence classes are by definition nonempty; what type of state might not have an equivalence class associated with it?). It is also straightforward to show that the properties of the state transition function guarantee that R^M is in fact a right congruence (see the exercises).

The equivalence classes of R^M are called *initial sets* and will be of further interest in later chapters. For a DFA $M = <\Sigma, S, s_0, \delta, F>$ and a given state t from M, $I(M, t) = \{x \mid \bar{\delta}(s_0, x) = t\}$. This initial set can be thought of as the language accepted by a machine similar to M, but which has t as its only final state. That is, if we define $M_t = <\Sigma, S, s_0, \delta, \{t\}>$, then $I(M, t) = L(M_t)$.

The notation presented here allows a concise method of denoting both relations defined by languages and relations defined by automata. It is helpful to observe that even in the absence of context, R_X indicates that a relation based on the *language* X is being described (since X occurs as a subscript), while the relation R^Y identifies Y as a *machine* (since Y occurs as a superscript).

Just as each DFA M gives rise to a right congruence R^M, many right congruences Q can be associated with a DFA, which will be called A_Q. It can be shown that, if some of the equivalence classes of Q are singled out to form a language L, A_Q will recognize L.

∇ **Definition 2.5.** Given a right congruence Q of finite rank and a language L that is the union of some of the equivalence classes of Q, A_Q is defined by

$$A_Q = <\Sigma, S_Q, s_{0_Q}, \delta_Q, F_Q>$$

where

$$S_Q = \{[x]_Q \mid x \in \Sigma^*\}$$

$$s_{0_Q} = [\lambda]_Q$$

$$F_Q = \{[x]_Q \mid x \in L\}$$

and δ_Q is defined by

$$(\forall x \in \Sigma^*)(\forall \mathbf{a} \in \Sigma)(\delta_Q([x]_Q, \mathbf{a}) = [x\mathbf{a}]_Q)$$

Δ

Note that this is a *finite*-state machine since $rk(Q) < \infty$, and that if L_1 were a different collection of equivalence classes of Q, A_Q would remain the same except for the placement of the final states. In other words, F_Q is the only aspect of this machine that depends on the language L (or L_1). As small as this change might be, it should be noted that A_Q is defined both by Q and the language L. It is left for the reader to show that A_Q is well-defined and that $L(A_Q) = L$ (see the exercises). The corresponding statements will be proved in detail in the next section for the important special case where $Q = R_L$.

EXAMPLE 2.4

Let $Q \subseteq \{\mathbf{a}\}^* \times \{\mathbf{a}\}^*$ be the equivalence relation with the following equivalence classes:

$$[\lambda]_Q = \{\lambda\} = \{\mathbf{a}\}^0$$

$$[\mathbf{a}]_Q = \{\mathbf{a}\} = \{\mathbf{a}\}^1$$

$$[\mathbf{aa}]_Q = \{\mathbf{a}\}^2 \cup \{\mathbf{a}\}^3 \cup \{\mathbf{a}\}^4 \cup \{\mathbf{a}\}^5 \cup \cdots$$

It is easy to show that Q is a right congruence (see the exercises). If L_1 were defined to be $[\lambda]_Q \cup [\mathbf{a}]_Q$, then A_Q would have the structure shown in Figure 2.1a. For the language defined by the different combination of equivalence classes given by $L_2 = [\lambda]_Q \cup [\mathbf{aa}]_Q$, A_Q would look like the DFA given in Figure 2.1b. This example illustrates that it is the right congruence Q that establishes the start state and the transitions, while the language L determines the final state set. It should also be clear why L must be a union of equivalence classes from Q. The figure shows that a machine with the structure imposed by Q cannot possibly both reject **aaa** and accept **aaaa**. Either the entire equivalence class for $[\mathbf{aa}]_Q$ must belong to L, or none of the strings from $[\mathbf{aa}]_Q$ can belong to L.

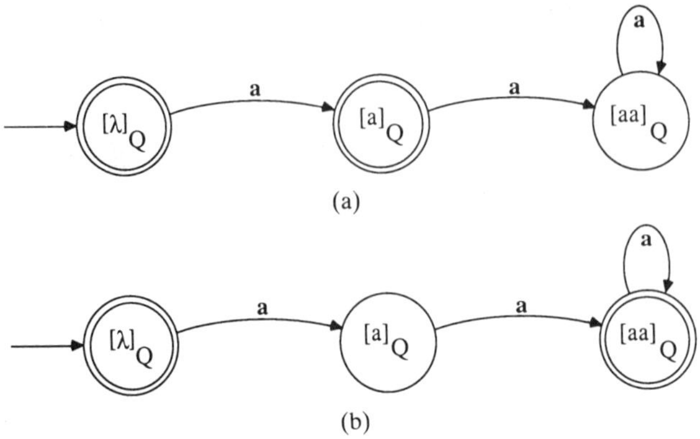

Figure 2.1 (a) The automaton for L_1 in Example 2.4 (b) The automaton for L_2 in Example 2.4

2.2 NERODE'S THEOREM

In this section, we will show that languages that partition Σ^* into a finite number of equivalence classes can be represented by finite automata, while those that yield an infinite number of classes would require a machine with an infinite number of states.

EXAMPLE 2.5

The language K given in Example 2.3 can be represented by a finite automaton with two states; all words that have an even number of letters eventually wind up at state s_0, while all the odd words are taken by $\overline{\delta}$ to s_1. This machine is shown in Figure 2.2.

It is no coincidence that these states split up the words of Σ^* into the same equivalence classes that R_K does. There is an intimate relationship between languages that can be represented by a machine with a finite number of states and languages that induce right congruences with a finite number of equivalence classes, as shown by the following theorem.

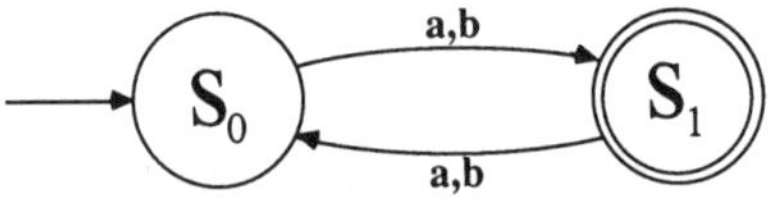

Figure 2.2 The DFA discussed in Example 2.5

∇ **Theorem 2.2: Nerode's Theorem.** Let L be a language over an alphabet Σ; the following statements are all equivalent:

1. L is FAD.
2. There exists a right congruence R on Σ^* for which L is the (possibly empty) union of some of the equivalence classes of R and $rk(R) < \infty$.
3. $rk(R_L) < \infty$.

Proof. Because of the transitivity of $\Rightarrow$, it will be sufficient to show only the three implications (1) $\Rightarrow$ (2), (2) $\Rightarrow$ (3), and (3) $\Rightarrow$ (1), rather than all six of them.

Proof of (1) $\Rightarrow$ (2): Assume (1); that is, let L be FAD. Then there is a machine that accepts L; that is, there exists a finite automaton $\mathsf{M} = \langle \Sigma, S, s_0, \delta, F \rangle$ such that $L(\mathsf{M}) = \mathrm{L}$. Consider the relation R^{M} on Σ^* based on this machine M as given in Definition 2.4: $(\forall x, y \in \Sigma^*)(x \mathrm{R}^{\mathsf{M}} y \Leftrightarrow \bar{\delta}(s_0, x) = \bar{\delta}(s_0, y))$.

This R^{M} will be the relation R we need to prove (2). For each $s \in S$, consider $I(\mathsf{M}, s) = \{x \in \Sigma^* \mid \bar{\delta}(s_0, x) = s\}$, which represents all strings that wind up at state s (from s_0). Note that it is easy to define automata for which it is impossible to reach certain states from the start state; for such states, $I(\mathsf{M}, s)$ would be empty. Then $\forall s \in S$, $I(\mathsf{M}, s)$ is either an equivalence class of R^{M} or $I(\mathsf{M}, s) = \emptyset$. Since there is at most one equivalence class per state, and there are a finite number of states, it follows that $rk(\mathrm{R}^{\mathsf{M}})$ is also finite: $rk(\mathrm{R}^{\mathsf{M}}) \le \|S\| < \infty$.

However, we have

$$\mathrm{L} = L(\mathsf{M}) = \{x \in \Sigma^* \mid \bar{\delta}(s_0, x) \in F\} = \bigcup_{f \in F} \{x \in \Sigma^* \mid \bar{\delta}(s_0, x) = f\} = \bigcup_{f \in F} I(\mathsf{M}, f)$$

That is, L is the union of some of the equivalence classes of the right congruence R^{M}, and R^{M} is indeed of finite rank, and hence (2) is satisfied. Thus (1) $\Rightarrow$ (2).

Proof of (2) $\Rightarrow$ (3): Assume that (2) holds; that is, there is a right congruence R for which L is the union of some of the equivalence classes of the right congruence R, and $rk(\mathrm{R}) < \infty$. Note that we no longer have (1) as an assumption; there is *no* machine (as yet) associated with L.

Case 1: It could be that L is the empty union; that is, that $\mathrm{L} = \emptyset$. In this case, it is easy to show that R_{L} has only one equivalence class (Σ^*), and thus $rk(\mathrm{R}_{\mathrm{L}}) = 1 < \infty$ and (3) will be satisfied.

Case 2: In the nontrivial case, L is the union of one or more of the equivalence classes of the given right congruence R, and it is possible to show that this R must then be closely related to the R_{L} induced by the original language L. In particular, for any strings x and y,

$$x \mathrm{R} y \Rightarrow \text{(since R is a right congruence)}$$
$$(\forall u \in \Sigma^*)(xu \,\mathrm{R}\, yu) \Leftrightarrow \text{(by definition of [ ])}$$
$$(\forall u \in \Sigma^*)([xu]_{\mathrm{R}} = [yu]_{\mathrm{R}}) \Rightarrow \text{(by definition of L as a union of [ ]'s)}$$
$$(\forall u \in \Sigma^*)(xu \in \mathrm{L} \Leftrightarrow yu \in \mathrm{L}) \Leftrightarrow \text{(by definition of } \mathrm{R}_{\mathrm{L}})$$
$$x \mathrm{R}_{\mathrm{L}} y$$

$(\forall x \in \Sigma^*)(\forall y \in \Sigma^*)(x \mathrm{R} y \Rightarrow x \mathrm{R}_{\mathrm{L}} y)$ means that R refines R_{L}, and thus each equivalence class of R is entirely contained in an equivalence class of R_{L}; that is, each equivalence class of R_{L} must be a union of one or more equivalence classes of R. Thus, there are more equivalence classes in R than in R_{L}, and so $rk(\mathrm{R}_{\mathrm{L}}) \le rk(\mathrm{R})$. But by hypothesis, $rk(\mathrm{R})$ is finite, and so R_{L} must be of finite rank also, and (3) is satisfied. Thus, in either case, (2) $\Rightarrow$ (3).

Proof of (3) $\Rightarrow$ (1): Assume now that condition (3) holds; that is, L is a language for which R_{L} is of finite rank. Once again, note that all we know is that R_{L} has a finite number of equivalence classes; we do not have either (1) or (2) as a hypothesis. Indeed, we wish to show (1) by proving that L is accepted by some finite automaton. We will base the structure of this automaton on the right congruence R_L, using Definition 2.5 with $Q = R_L$. A_{R_L} is then defined by

$$A_{R_L} = <\Sigma, S_{R_L}, s_{0_{R_L}}, \delta_{R_L}, F_{R_L}>$$

where

$$S_{R_L} = \{[x]_{R_L} \mid x \in \Sigma^*\}$$

$$s_{0_{R_L}} = [\lambda]_{R_L}$$

$$F_{R_L} = \{[x]_{R_L} \mid x \in L\}$$

and δ_{R_L} is defined by

$$(\forall x \in \Sigma^*)(\forall \mathbf{a} \in \Sigma)(\delta_{R_L}([x]_{R_L}, \mathbf{a}) = [x\mathbf{a}]_{R_L})$$

The basic idea in this construction is to define one state for each equivalence class in R_L, use the equivalence class containing λ as the start state, use those classes that were made up of words in L as final states, and define δ in a natural manner. We claim that this machine is really a well-defined finite automaton and that it does behave as we wish it to; that is, the language accepted by A_{R_L} really *is* L. In other words, $\boldsymbol{L}(A_{R_L}) = L$.

First, note that S_{R_L} is a finite set, since [by the only assumption we have in (3)] R_L consists of only a finite number of equivalence classes. It can be shown that F_{R_L} is well defined; if $[z]_{R_L} = [y]_{R_L}$, then either (both $z \in L$ and $y \in L$) or (neither z nor y belong to L) (why?). The reader should show that δ_{R_L} is similarly well defined; that is, if $[z]_{R_L} = [y]_{R_L}$, it follows that δ_{R_L} is forced to also take both transitions to the same state ($[z\mathbf{a}]_{R_L} = [y\mathbf{a}]_{R_L}$). Also, a straightforward induction on $|y|$ shows that the rule for δ_{R_L} extends to a similar rule for $\overline{\delta}_{R_L}$:

$$(\forall x \in \Sigma^*)(\forall y \in \Sigma^*)(\overline{\delta}_{R_L}([x]_{R_L}, y) = [xy]_{R_L})$$

With this preliminary work out of the way, it is possible to easily show that $\boldsymbol{L}(A_{R_L}) = L$. Let x be any element of Σ^*. Then

$$x \in \boldsymbol{L}(A_{R_L}) \Leftrightarrow \text{(by definition of L)}$$

$$\overline{\delta}_{R_L}(s_{0_{R_L}}, x) \in F_{R_L} \Leftrightarrow \text{(by definition of } s_{0_{R_L}})$$

$$\overline{\delta}_{R_L}([\lambda]_{R_L}, x) \in F_{R_L} \Leftrightarrow \text{(by definition of } \overline{\delta}_{R_L} \text{ and induction)}$$

$$[\lambda x]_{R_L} \in F_{R_L} \Leftrightarrow \text{(by definition of } \lambda)$$

$$[x]_{R_L} \in F_{R_L} \Leftrightarrow \text{(by definition of } F_{R_L})$$

$$x \in L$$

Consequently, L is exactly the language accepted by this finite automaton; so L must be FAD, and (1) is satisfied. Thus (3)$\Rightarrow$(1). We have therefore come full circle, and all three conditions are equivalent.

Δ

The correspondence described by Nerode's theorem can best be illustrated by an example.

EXAMPLE 2.6

Let L be the following FAD language: $L = \Sigma^* - \{\lambda\} = \Sigma^+$. There are many finite automata that accept L, one of which is the DFA given in Figure 2.3. This four-state machine gives rise to a four-equivalence class right congruence as described in $(1) \Rightarrow (2)$, where

$$[\lambda]_{R^N} = I(N, s_0) = \{\lambda\}, \text{ since } \lambda \text{ is the only string that ends up at } s_0$$

$$[\mathbf{1}]_{R^N} = I(N, s_1) = \{y \mid |y| \text{ is odd, and } y \text{ ends with a } \mathbf{1}\} = \{z \mid \bar{\delta}(s_0, z) = s_1\}$$

$$[\mathbf{11}]_{R^N} = I(N, s_2) = \{y \mid |y| \text{ is even}\} - \{\lambda\} = \{z \mid \bar{\delta}(s_0, z) = s_2\}$$

$$[\mathbf{000}]_{R^N} = I(N, s_3) = \{y \mid |y| \text{ is odd, and } y \text{ ends with a } \mathbf{0}\} = \{z \mid \bar{\delta}(s_0, z) = s_3\}$$

Note that L is indeed $I(N, s_1) \cup I(N, s_2) \cup I(N, s_3)$ which is the union of all the equivalence classes that correspond to final states in N, as required by (2). To illustrate $(2) \Rightarrow (3)$, let R be the equivalence relation R^N defined above, let L again be Σ^+, and note that (2) is satisfied: $L = [\mathbf{1}]_R \cup [\mathbf{11}]_R \cup [\mathbf{000}]_R$, the union of 3 of the equivalence class of a right congruence of rank 4 (which is finite).

As in the proof of $(2) \Rightarrow (3)$, R_L is refined by R, but in this case R and R_L are not equal. All the relations from R still hold, such as $\mathbf{11}\,R\,\mathbf{1111}$, so $\mathbf{11}\,R_L\,\mathbf{1111}$; $\mathbf{0}\,R\,\mathbf{000}$, and thus $\mathbf{0}\,R_L\,\mathbf{000}$, and so forth. It can also be shown that $\mathbf{11}\,R_L\,\mathbf{000}$, even though **11** and **000** were not related by R (apply the definition of R_L to convince yourself of this). Thus, everything in $[\mathbf{11}]_R$ is related *by* R_L to everything in $[\mathbf{000}]_R$; that is, all the strings belong to the same equivalence class *of* R_L, even though they formed separate equivalence classes *in R*. It may at first appear strange, but the fact that there are *more* relations in R_L means that there are *fewer* equivalence classes in R_L than in R. Indeed, R_L has only two equivalence classes, $\{\lambda\}$ and L. In this case, three equivalence classes of R collapse to form one large equivalence class of R_L. Thus $\{\lambda\} = [\lambda]_{R_L} = [\lambda]_R$ and $L = [\mathbf{11}]_{R_L} = [\mathbf{1}]_R \cup [\mathbf{11}]_R \cup [\mathbf{000}]_R$ and, as we were assured by $(2) \Rightarrow (3)$, R refines R_L.

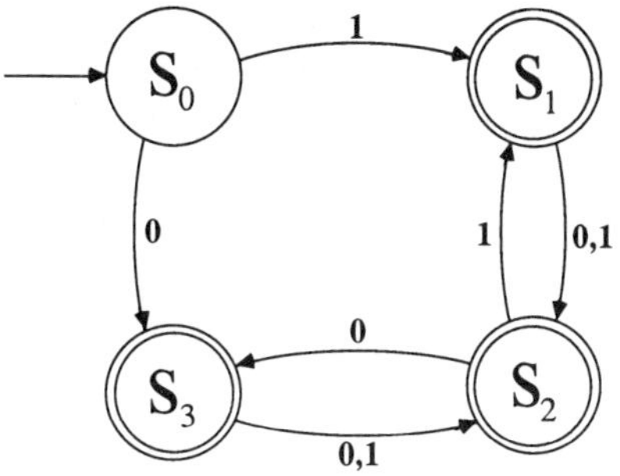

Figure 2.3 The DFA N discussed in Example 2.6

To illustrate $(3) \Rightarrow (1)$, let's continue to use the L and R_L given above. Since R_L is of rank 2, we are assured of finding a two-state machine that will accept L. A_{R_L} in this case would take the form of the automat P displayed in Figure 2.4. In this DFA, for example, $\delta([\mathbf{11}]_{R_L}, \mathbf{0}) = [\mathbf{110}]_{R_L} = [\mathbf{11}]_{R_L}$, and $[\lambda]_{R_L}$ is the start state. $[\mathbf{11}]_{R_L}$ is a final state since $\mathbf{11} \in L$. Verify that this machine accepts all words except λ; that is, $L(A_{R_L}) = L$.

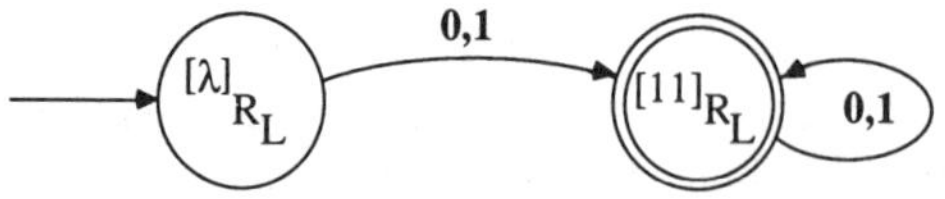

Figure 2.4 The DFA P discussed in Example 2.6

EXAMPLE 2.7

Assume Q is defined to be the right congruence R given in Example 2.4, and L is again Σ^+, which is the union of three of the equivalence classes of Q: $[\mathbf{1}]_Q$, $[\mathbf{11}]_Q$, and $[\mathbf{000}]_Q$. The automaton A_Q is given in Figure 2.5.

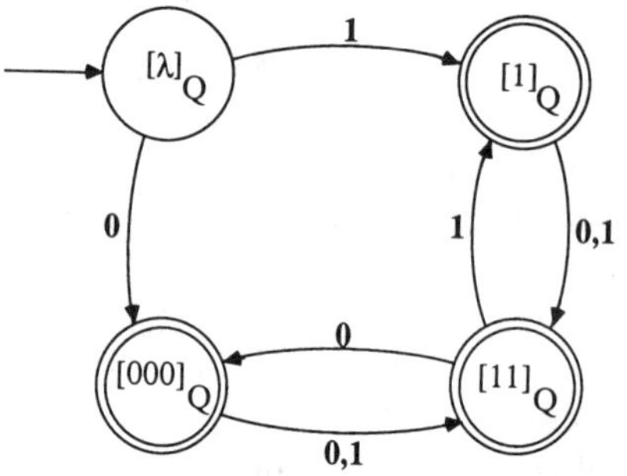

Figure 2.5 The automaton discussed in Example 2.7

If we were instead to begin with the same language L, but use the two-state machine P at the end of Example 2.6 to represent L, we would find that L would consist of only one equivalence class, R^P would have only two equivalence classes, and R^P would in this case be the same as R_L (see the exercises). R^P turns out to be as simple as R_L because the machine we started with was as "simple" as we could get and still represent L. In Chapter 3 we will characterize the idea of a machine being "as simple as possible," that is, *minimal*.

The two machines given in Example 2.6 accept the same language. It will be convenient to formalize this notion of distinct machines "performing the same task," and we therefore make the following definition.

∇ **Definition 2.6.** Two DFAs A and B are *equivalent iff* $L(A) = L(B)$.
Δ

EXAMPLE 2.8

The DFAs N from Example 2.6 and A_Q from Example 2.7 are equivalent since $L(N) = \Sigma^+ = L(A_Q)$.

∇ **Definition 2.7.** A DFA $A = <\Sigma, S_A, s_{0_A}, \delta_A, F_A>$ is *minimal iff* for every DFA $B = <\Sigma, S_B, s_{0_B}, \delta_B, F_B>$ for which $L(A) = L(B)$, $|S_A| \leq |S_B|$.
Δ

An automaton is therefore minimal if no equivalent machine has fewer states.

EXAMPLE 2.9

The DFA N from Example 2.6 is clearly not minimal since the automaton A_Q from Example 2.7 is equivalent and has fewer states than N. The techniques from Chapter 3 can be used to verify that the automaton A_Q from Example 2.7 is minimal. More importantly, minimization techniques will be explored in Chapter 3 that will allow an optimal machine (like this A_Q) to be produced from an inefficient automaton (like N).

2.3 PUMPING LEMMAS

As you have probably noticed by now, finding R_L and counting the equivalence classes is not a very practical way of verifying that a suspected language cannot be defined by a finite automaton. It would be nice to have a better way to determine if a given language is unwieldy. The *pumping lemma* will supply us with such a technique. It is based on the observation that if your automaton processes a "long enough" word it must eventually visit (at least) one state more than once.

Let $A = <\Sigma, S, s_0, \delta, F>$, and consider starting at some state s and processing a word x of length 5. We will pass through state s and perhaps five other states, although these states may not all be distinct if we visit some of them repeatedly while processing the five letters in x; thus the total will be six states (or less). Note that if A has 10 states ($\|S\| = 10$) and $|x| = 12$ we cannot go to 13 *different* states while processing x; (at least) one state must be visited more than once.

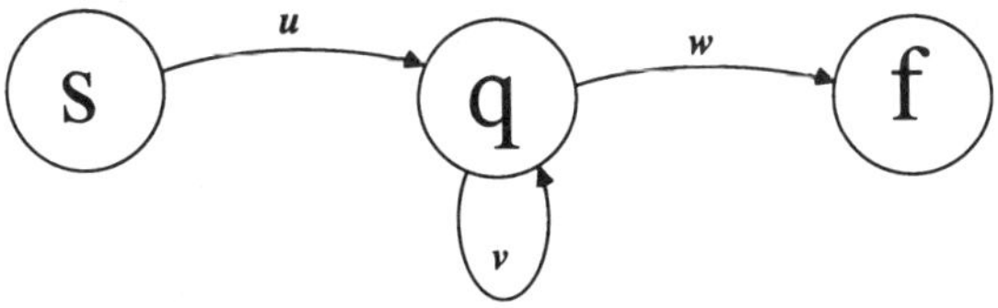

Figure 2.6 A path with a loop

In general, if $n = \|S\|$, then any string x whose length is equal to or greater than n must pass through some state q twice while being processed by A, as shown in Figure 2.6. Here the arrows are meant to represent the path taken while processing *several* letters, and the intermediate states are not shown. The strings u, v, and w are defined as

u = first few letters of x that take us to the state q

v = next few letters of x that will again take us back to q

w = rest of the string x

Then, with $x = uvw$, we have $\overline{\delta}(s, u) = q$, $\overline{\delta}(s, uv) = q$, and in fact $\overline{\delta}(q, v) = q$. Also, $\underline{\delta}(s, x) = \overline{\delta}(s, uvw) = f$ and $\overline{\delta}(q, w) = f$, as is clear from the diagram. Now consider the string uw, that is, the string x with the v part "removed":

$$\begin{aligned} \overline{\delta}(s, uw) &= \overline{\delta}(\overline{\delta}(s, u), w) \qquad \text{(why?)} \\ &= \overline{\delta}(q, w) \\ &= f \end{aligned}$$

That is, the string uw winds up in the same place uvw does; this is illustrated in Figure 2.7a. Note that a similar thing happens if uv^2w is processed:

$$\begin{aligned}\overline{\delta}(\mathrm{s}, uvvw) &= \overline{\delta}(\overline{\delta}(\mathrm{s}, u), vvw)\\ &= \overline{\delta}(\mathrm{q}, vvw)\\ &= \overline{\delta}(\overline{\delta}(\mathrm{q}, v), vw)\\ &= \overline{\delta}(\mathrm{q}, vw)\\ &= \overline{\delta}(\overline{\delta}(\mathrm{q}, v), w)\\ &= \overline{\delta}(\mathrm{q}, w)\\ &= \mathrm{f}\end{aligned}$$

This behavior is illustrated in Figure 2.7b.

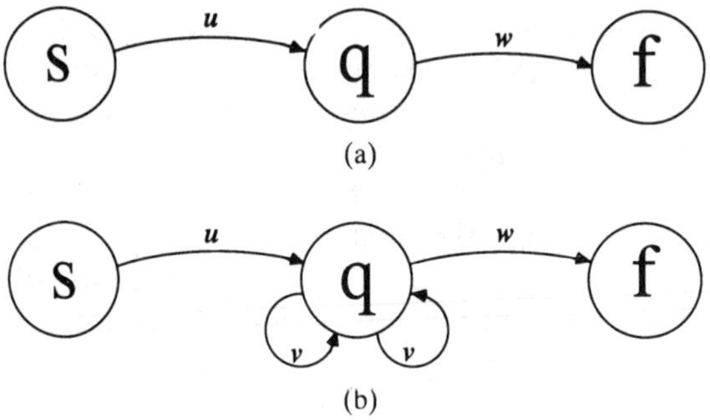

Figure 2.7 (a) The path that bypasses the loop (b) The path that traverses the loop twice

In general, it can be proved by induction that $(\forall i \in \mathbb{N})\{\overline{\delta}(\mathrm{s}, uv^iw) = \mathrm{f} = \overline{\delta}(\mathrm{s}, uvw)\}$. Notice that we do reach q two *distinct* times, which implies that the string v contains at least one letter; that is, $|v| \geq 1$. Also, after the first n letters of x, we must have already repeated a state, and thus some state q can be found such that $|uv| \leq n$. If s happens to be the start state s_0 and f is a final state, we have now shown that: If $\mathrm{A} = <\Sigma, S, \mathrm{s}_0, \delta, F>$, where $\|S\| = n$, then, given any string $x = \mathbf{a}_1\mathbf{a}_2\mathbf{a}_3 \ldots \mathbf{a}_m$, where $m \geq n$ and $\overline{\delta}(\mathrm{s}_0, x) = \mathrm{f} \in F$ [which implies $x \in L(\mathrm{A})$], the states $\overline{\delta}(\mathrm{s}_0, \lambda), \overline{\delta}(\mathrm{s}_0, \mathbf{a}_1), \overline{\delta}(\mathrm{s}_0, \mathbf{a}_1\mathbf{a}_2), \overline{\delta}(\mathrm{s}_0, \mathbf{a}_1\mathbf{a}_2\mathbf{a}_3), \ldots, \overline{\delta}(\mathrm{s}_0, \mathbf{a}_1\mathbf{a}_2 \ldots \mathbf{a}_n)$ cannot all be distinct, and so x can be broken up into strings u, v, and w such that

$$\begin{gathered}x = uvw\\ |uv| \leq n\\ |v| \geq 1\end{gathered}$$

and $(\forall i \in \mathbb{N})(\overline{\delta}(\mathrm{s}_0, uv^iw) = \mathrm{f})$, that is, $(\forall i \in \mathbb{N})(uv^iw \in L(\mathrm{A}))$. In other words, given any "long" string in $L(\mathrm{A})$, there is a part of the string that can be "pumped" to produce even longer strings in $L(\mathrm{A})$.

Thus, if L is FAD, there exists an automaton (with a finite number n of states), and thus for some $n \in \mathbb{N}$, the above statement should hold. We have just proved what is generally known as the *pumping lemma*, which we now state formally.

∇ **Theorem 2.3: The Pumping Lemma.** Let L be an FAD language over Σ^*. Then $(\exists n \in \mathbb{N})(\forall x \in L \ni |x| \geq n)(\exists u, v, w \in \Sigma^*) \ni$

$$x = uvw,$$

$$|uv| \leq n,$$

$$|v| \geq 1,$$

and

$$(\forall i \in \mathbb{N})(uv^i w \in L).$$

Proof. Given above.

Δ

EXAMPLE 2.10

Let E be the set of all even-length words over $\{\mathbf{a}, \mathbf{b}\}^*$. There is a two-state machine that accepts E, so E is FAD, and the pumping lemma applies if n is, say, 5. Then $\forall x \ni |x| > 5$, if $x = \mathbf{a}_1\mathbf{a}_2\mathbf{a}_3 \ldots \mathbf{a}_j \in E$ (that is, j is even), we can choose $u = \lambda$, $v = \mathbf{a}_1\mathbf{a}_2$, and $w = \mathbf{a}_3\mathbf{a}_4 \ldots \mathbf{a}_j$. Note that $|uv| = 2 \leq 5$, $|v| = 2 \geq 1$, and $|uv^i w| = j + 2(i-1)$, which is even, and so $(\forall i \in \mathbb{N})(uv^i w \in E)$.

If Example 2.10 does not appear truly exciting, there is good reason: The pumping lemma is generally not applied to FAD languages! (*Note:* We *will* see an application later.) The pumping lemma is often applied to show languages are *not* FAD (by proving that the language does not satisfy the pumping lemma). Note that the contrapositive of Theorem 2.3 is:

∇ **Theorem 2.4.** Let L be a language over Σ^*. **If** $(\forall n \in \mathbb{N})(\exists x \in L \ni |x| \geq n)(\forall u, v, w \in \Sigma^* \ni x = uvw, |uv| \leq n, |v| \geq 1)(\exists i \in \mathbb{N} \ni uv^i w \notin L)$, **then** L is *not FAD*.

Proof. See the exercises.

Δ

EXAMPLE 2.11

Consider $L_4 = \{y \in \{\mathbf{0}, \mathbf{1}\}^* \mid |y|_\mathbf{1} = |y|_\mathbf{0}\}$. We will use Theorem 2.4 to show L_4 is not FAD: Let n be given, and choose $x = \mathbf{0}^n \mathbf{1}^n$. Then $x \in L_4$, since $|x|_\mathbf{1} = n = |x|_\mathbf{0}$. It should be observed that x must be dependent on n, and we have *no* control over n (in particular, n cannot be replaced by some constant; similarly, while i may be chosen to be a fixed constant, a proof that covers all possible combinations of u, v, and w must be given).

Note that this choice of x is "long enough" in that $|x| = 2n \geq n$, as required by Theorem 2.4. For *any* combination of $u, v, w \in \Sigma^*$ such that $x = uvw$, $|uv| \leq n$, $|v| \geq 1$, we hope to find a value for i such that $uv^i w \notin L_4$. Since $|uv| \leq n$ and the first n letters of x are all zeros, this narrows down the choices for u, v, and w. They must be of the form $u = \mathbf{0}^j$ and $v = \mathbf{0}^k$ (since $|uv| \leq n$ and x starts with n zeros), and w must be the "rest of the string" and look something like $w = \mathbf{0}^m \mathbf{1}^n$. The constraints on u, v, and w imply that $j + k \leq n$, $k \geq 1$, and $j + k + m = n$. If $i = 2$, we have that

$uv^2w = \mathbf{0}^{n+k}\mathbf{1}^n \notin L_4$ (why?). Thus, by Theorem 2.4, L_4 is not FAD [or, alternately, because the conclusion of the pumping lemma (Theorem 2.3) does *not* hold, L_4 cannot be FAD].

It is instructive to attempt to build a DFA that attempts to recognize the language L_4. As you begin to see what such a machine must look like, it will become clear that no matter how many states you add (that is, no matter how large n becomes) there will always be some strings ("long" strings) that would require even more states. Your construction may also suggest what the equivalence classes of R_{L_4} must look like (see the exercises). How many equivalence classes are there? (You should be able to answer this last question without referring to any constructions.)

A similar argument can be made to show that no DFA can recognize the set of all fully parenthesized infix expressions (see the exercises). Matching parentheses, like matching **0**s and **1**s in the last example, requires unlimited storage. We have seen that DFAs are adequate vehicles for pattern matching and token identification, but a more complex model is clearly needed to implement functions like the parsing of arithmetic expressions. *Pushdown automata*, discussed in Chapter 10, augment the finite memory with an unbounded *stack*, allowing more complex languages to be recognized.

Intuitively, we would not expect *finite*-state machines to be able to differentiate between arbitrarily long integers. While *modular* arithmetic, which only differentiates between a finite number of remainders, should be representable by finite automata, unrestricted arithmetic is likely to be impossible. For example, $\{\mathbf{a}^i\mathbf{b}^j\mathbf{c}^k \mid i, j, k \in \mathbb{N} \text{ and } i + j = k\}$ cannot be recognized by any DFA, while the language $\{\mathbf{a}^i\mathbf{b}^j\mathbf{c}^k \mid i, j, k \in \mathbb{N} \text{ and } i + j \equiv k \bmod 3\}$ is FAD. Checking whether two numbers are relatively prime is likewise too difficult for a DFA, as shown by the proof in the following example.

EXAMPLE 2.12

Consider $L = \{\mathbf{a}^i\mathbf{b}^j \mid i, j \in \mathbb{N} \text{ and } i \text{ and } j \text{ are relatively prime}\}$. We will use Theorem 2.4 to show L is not FAD: Let n be given, and choose a prime p larger than $n + 1$ (we can be assured such a p exists since there are an infinite number of primes). Let $x = \mathbf{a}^p\mathbf{b}^{(p-1)!}$. Since p has no factors other than 1 and p, it has no nontrivial factor in common with $(p-1)\cdot(p-2)\cdot\ldots\cdot3\cdot2\cdot1$, and so p and $(p-1)!$ are relatively prime, which guarantees that $x \in L$. The length of x is clearly greater than n, so Theorem 2.3 should apply, which implies that there must exist a combination $u, v, w \in \Sigma^*$ such that $x = uvw$, $|uv| \leq n$, $|v| \geq 1$; we hope to find a value for i such that $uv^iw \in L$. Since $|uv| \leq n$ and the first n letters of x are all **a**s, there must exist integers j, k, and m for which $u = \mathbf{a}^j$ and $v = \mathbf{a}^k$, and w must be the "rest of the string"; that is, $w = \mathbf{a}^m\mathbf{b}^{(p-1)!}$. The constraints on u, v, and w imply that $j + k \leq n$, $k \geq 1$, and $j + k + m = p$. If $i = 0$, we have that $uv^0w = \mathbf{a}^{p-k}\mathbf{b}^{(p-1)!}$. But $p - k$ is a number between $p - 1$ and $p - n$ and hence must match one of the nontrivial factors in $(p-1)!$, which means that $uv^0w \notin L$ (why?). Therefore, Theorem 2.3 has been violated, so L could not have been FAD.

The details of the basic argument used to prove the pumping lemma can be varied to produce other theorems of a similar nature: for example, when processing x, there must be a state q′ repeated within the *last n* letters. This gives rise to the following variation of the pumping lemma.

∇ **Theorem 2.5.** Let L be a FAD language over Σ^*. Then

$$(\exists n \in \mathbb{N})(\forall x \in \mathrm{L} \ni |x| \geq n)(\exists u, v, w \in \Sigma^*) \ni$$

$$x = uvw$$

$$|vw| \leq n,$$

$$|v| \geq 1$$

and

$$(\forall i \in \mathbb{N})(uv^i w \in \mathrm{L})$$

Proof. See the exercises.

Δ

The new condition $|vw| \leq n$ reflects the constraint that some state must be repeated within the last n letters. The contrapositive of Theorem 2.5 can be useful in demonstrating that certain languages are not FAD. By repeating our original reasoning while assuming the string x takes us to a *non*final state, we obtain yet another variation.

∇ **Theorem 2.6.** Let L be a FAD language over Σ^*. Then

$$(\exists n \in \mathbb{N})(\forall x \notin \mathrm{L} \ni |x| \geq n)(\exists u, v, w \in \Sigma^*) \ni$$

$$x = uvw$$

$$|uv| \leq n$$

$$|v| \geq 1$$

and

$$(\forall i \in \mathbb{N})(uv^i w \notin \mathrm{L})$$

Proof. See the exercises.

Δ

Notice that Theorem 2.6 guarantees that if one "long" string is *not* in the language then there is an entire sequence of strings that cannot be in the language. There are some examples of languages in the exercises where Theorem 2.4 is hard to apply, but where Theorem 2.5 (or Theorem 2.6) is appropriate.

When $i = 0$, the pumping lemma states that given a "long" string (uvw) in L there is a shorter string (uw) that is also in L. If this new string is still of length greater than n, the pumping lemma can be reapplied to find a still shorter string, and so on. This technique is the basis for proving the following theorem.

∇ **Theorem 2.7.** Let M be an n-state DFA accepting L. Then

$$(\forall x \in \mathrm{L} \ni x = \mathbf{a}_1\mathbf{a}_2 \ldots \mathbf{a}_m \text{ and } m \geq n)(\exists \text{ an increasing sequence } i_1, i_2, \ldots, i_j)$$

for which $\mathbf{a}_{i_1}\mathbf{a}_{i_2} \ldots \mathbf{a}_{i_j} \in \mathrm{L}$, and $j < n$.

Proof. See the exercises.

Δ

Note that $\mathbf{a}_{i_1}\mathbf{a}_{i_2} \ldots \mathbf{a}_{i_j}$ represents a string formed by "removing" letters from perhaps several places in x, and that this new string has length less than n.

Theorem 2.7 can be applied in areas that do not initially seem to relate to DFAs. Consider an arbitrary right congruence R of (finite) rank n. It can be shown that each equivalence class of R is guaranteed to contain a representative of length less than n. For example, consider the relation R given by

$$[\lambda]_\mathrm{R} = \{\lambda\}$$
$$[\mathbf{11111}]_\mathrm{R} = \{y \mid |y| \text{ is odd, and } y \text{ ends with a } \mathbf{1}\}$$
$$[\mathbf{0101}]_\mathrm{R} = \{y \mid |y| \text{ is even and } |y| > 0\}$$
$$[\mathbf{00000}]_\mathrm{R} = \{y \mid |y| \text{ is odd, and } y \text{ ends with a } \mathbf{0}\}$$

In this relation, $rk(\mathrm{R}) = 4$, and appropriate representatives of length less than 4 are λ, **1**, **11**, and **100**, respectively. That is, $[\lambda]_\mathrm{R} = [\lambda]_\mathrm{R}$, $[\mathbf{1}]_\mathrm{R} = [\mathbf{11111}]_\mathrm{R}$, $[\mathbf{11}]_\mathrm{R} = [\mathbf{0101}]_\mathrm{R}$, and $[\mathbf{100}]_\mathrm{R} = [\mathbf{00000}]_\mathrm{R}$. By constructing a DFA based on the right congruence R, Theorem 2.7 can be used to prove that every equivalence class of R has a "short" representative (see the exercises).

We have seen that deterministic finite automata are limited in their cognitive powers, that is, there are languages that are too complex to be recognized by DFAs. When only a finite set of previous histories can be distinguished, the resulting languages must have a certain repetitious nature. Allowing automata to instead have an infinite number of states is uninteresting for several reasons. On the practical side, it would be inconvenient (to say the least) to physically construct such a machine. Infinite automata are also of little theoretical interest as they do not distinguish between simple and complex languages: any language can be accepted by the infinite analog of a DFA. With an infinite number of states available, the state transition diagrams can look like trees, with a unique state corresponding to each word in Σ^*. The states corresponding to desired words can simply be made final states.

More reasonable enhancements to automata will be explored later. Nondeterminism will be presented in Chapter 4, and machines with extended capabilities will be defined and investigated in Chapters 10 and 11.

EXERCISES

2.1 Let $\Sigma = \{\mathbf{a}, \mathbf{b}, \mathbf{c}\}$. Show that the relation $\Psi \subseteq \Sigma^* \times \Sigma^*$ defined by

$$x \Psi y \Leftrightarrow |x| - |y| \text{ is odd}$$

is *not* a right congruence. (Is it an equivalence relation?)

2.2. Let $\Sigma = \{\mathbf{a}, \mathbf{b}, \mathbf{c}\}$. Consider the relation $Q \subseteq \Sigma^* \times \Sigma^*$ defined by

$$x\,Q\,y \Leftrightarrow |x|_{\mathbf{a}} - |y|_{\mathbf{a}} \equiv 0 \bmod 3$$

(a) Show that Q is an equivalence relation.
(b) Assume that part (a) is true, and show that Q is a right congruence.

2.3. Let $\Sigma = \{\mathbf{a}, \mathbf{b}, \mathbf{c}\}$. Find all languages L such that $rk(R_L) = 1$. Justify your conclusions.

2.4. Let $P \subseteq \{\mathbf{0}, \mathbf{1}\}^* \times \{\mathbf{0}, \mathbf{1}\}^*$ be the equivalence relation with the following equivalence classes:

$$[\lambda]_P = \{\lambda\} = \{\mathbf{0}, \mathbf{1}\}^0$$

$$[\mathbf{1}]_P = \{\mathbf{0}, \mathbf{1}\} = \{\mathbf{0}, \mathbf{1}\}^1$$

$$[\mathbf{00}]_P = \{\mathbf{0}, \mathbf{1}\}^2 \cup \{\mathbf{0}, \mathbf{1}\}^3 \cup \{\mathbf{0}, \mathbf{1}\}^4 \cup \{\mathbf{0}, \mathbf{1}\}^5 \cup \ldots$$

Show that P is a right congruence.

2.5. For the relation P defined in Exercise 2.4, find all languages $L \ni R_L = P$.

2.6. For the relation Q defined in Exercise 2.2, find all languages $L \ni R_L = Q$.

2.7. Let $\Sigma = \{\mathbf{a}, \mathbf{b}\}$. Define the relation Q by $\lambda Q \lambda$, and $(\forall x \neq \lambda)(\lambda \not{Q} x)$, and

$$(\forall x \neq \lambda)(\forall y \neq \lambda)[x\,Q\,y \Leftrightarrow (|x| \text{ is even} \wedge |y| \text{ is even}) \vee (|x| \text{ is odd} \wedge |y| \text{ is odd})],$$

which implies that

$$(\forall x \neq \lambda)(\forall y \neq \lambda)[x \not{Q} y \Leftrightarrow (|x| \text{ is even} \wedge |y| \text{ is odd}) \vee (|x| \text{ is odd} \wedge |y| \text{ is even})].$$

(a) Show that Q is a right congruence, and list the equivalence classes.
(b) Define $L = [\lambda]_Q \cup [\mathbf{aa}]_Q$. Find a simple decription for L, and list the equivalence classes of R_L. (Note that Q does refine R_L.)
(c) Draw a machine with states corresponding to the equivalence classes of Q. Arrange the final states so that the machine accepts L (that is, find A_Q).
(d) Draw A_{R_L}.
(e) Consider the machine in part (c) above (A_Q). Does it look like A_{R_L}? Can you rearrange the final states in A_Q (producing a new langauge K) so that A_{R_K} looks like your new A_Q? Illustrate.
(f) Consider all eight languages found by taking unions of equivalence classes from Q, and see which ones would satisfy the criteria of part (e).

2.8. Let $\Sigma = \{\mathbf{a}\}$. Let I be the identity relation on Σ^*.
(a) Show that I is a right congruence.
(b) What do the equivalence classes of I look like?

2.9. Let $\Sigma = \{\mathbf{a}\}$, and let I be the identity relation on Σ^*. Let $L = \{\lambda\} \cup \{\mathbf{a}\} \cup \{\mathbf{aa}\}$, which is the union of three of the equivalence classes of I. I has infinite rank. Does Nerode's theorem imply that L is not FAD? Explain.

2.10. Define a machine $M = <\Sigma, S_M, s_0, \delta, F_M>$ for which $rk(R_{L(M)}) \neq \|S_M\|$.

2.11. Carefully show that F_{R_L} is a well-defined set; that is, show that the rule that assigns equivalence classes to F_{R_L} is unambiguous.

2.12. Carefully show that δ_{R_L} is well-defined, that is, that δ_{R_L} is a *function*.

2.13. Use induction to show that $(\forall x \in \Sigma^*)(\forall y \in \Sigma^*)(\bar{\delta}_{R_L}([x]_{R_L}, y) = [xy]_{R_L})$.

2.14. Consider the automaton P derived in Example 2.6, find R^P and notice that $R^P = R_L$.

2.15. Find R^A for each machine A you built in the exercises of Chapter 1; compare R^A to $R_{L(A)}$.

2.16. Prove by induction that, for the strings defined in the discussion of the pumping lemma, $(\forall i \in \mathbb{N})(\bar{\delta}(s, uv^i w) = f = \bar{\delta}(s, uvw))$.

2.17. Prove Theorem 2.1.

2.18. **(a)** Find a language that gives rise to the relation I defined in Exercise 2.8.
(b) Could such a language be FAD? Explain.

2.19. Starting with Theorem 2.3 as a given hypothesis, prove Theorem 2.4.

2.20. Prove Theorem 2.5 by constructing an argument similar to that given for Theorem 2.3.

2.21. Prove Theorem 2.6 by constructing an argument similar to that given for Theorem 2.3.

2.22. Prove Theorem 2.7.

2.23. Let $L = \{x \in \{\mathbf{a}, \mathbf{b}\}^* \mid |x|_\mathbf{a} < |x|_\mathbf{b}\}$. Show L is not FAD.

2.24. Let $G = \{x \in \{\mathbf{a}, \mathbf{b}\}^* \mid |x|_\mathbf{a} \geq |x|_\mathbf{b}\}$. Show G is not FAD.

2.25. Let $P = \{y \in \{\mathbf{d}\}^* \mid \exists \text{ prime } p \ni y = \mathbf{d}^p\} = \{\mathbf{dd}, \mathbf{ddd}, \mathbf{ddddd}, \mathbf{d}^7, \mathbf{d}^{11}, \mathbf{d}^{13}, \ldots\}$. Prove that P is not FAD.

2.26. Let $\Gamma = \{x \in \{\mathbf{0}, \mathbf{1}, \mathbf{2}\}^* \mid \exists w \in \{\mathbf{0}, \mathbf{1}\}^* \ni x = w \cdot \mathbf{2} \cdot w\} = \{\mathbf{2}, \mathbf{121}, \mathbf{020}, \mathbf{11211}, \mathbf{10210}, \ldots\}$. Prove that Γ is not FAD.

2.27. Let $\Psi = \{x \in \{\mathbf{0}, \mathbf{1}\}^* \mid \exists w \in \{\mathbf{0}, \mathbf{1}\}^* \ni x = w \cdot w\} = \{\lambda, \mathbf{00}, \mathbf{11}, \mathbf{0000}, \mathbf{1010}, \mathbf{1111}, \ldots\}$. Prove that Ψ is not FAD.

2.28. Define the reverse of a string w as follows: If $w = \mathbf{a}_1\mathbf{a}_2\mathbf{a}_3\mathbf{a}_4 \ldots \mathbf{a}_{n-1}\mathbf{a}_n$, then $w^r = \mathbf{a}_n\mathbf{a}_{n-1} \ldots \mathbf{a}_4\mathbf{a}_3\mathbf{a}_2\mathbf{a}_1$. Let $K = \{w \in \{\mathbf{0}, \mathbf{1}\}^* \mid w = w^r\} = \{\lambda, \mathbf{0}, \mathbf{1}, \mathbf{00}, \mathbf{11}, \mathbf{000}, \mathbf{010}, \mathbf{101}, \mathbf{111}, \mathbf{0000}, \mathbf{0110}, \ldots\}$. Prove K is not FAD.

2.29. Let $\Phi = \{x \in \{\mathbf{a}, \mathbf{b}, \mathbf{c}\}^* \mid \exists i, j, k \in \mathbb{N} \ni x = \mathbf{a}^j \mathbf{b}^k \mathbf{c}^m$, where $j \geq 3$ and $k = m\}$. Prove Φ is not FAD. *Hint:* The first version of the pumping lemma is hard to apply here (why?).

2.30. Let $C = \{y \in \{\mathbf{d}\}^* \mid \exists$ *non*prime $q \ni y = \mathbf{d}^q\} = \{\lambda, \mathbf{d}, \mathbf{d}^4, \mathbf{d}^6, \mathbf{d}^8, \mathbf{d}^9, \mathbf{d}^{10} \ldots\}$. Show C is not FAD. *Hint:* The first version of the pumping lemma is hard to apply here (why?).

2.31. Assume $\Sigma = \{\mathbf{a}, \mathbf{b}\}$ and L is a language for which R_L has the following three equivalence classes: $\{\lambda\}$, {all odd-length words}, {all even-length words except λ}.
(a) Why couldn't $L = \{x \mid |x| \text{ is odd}\}$? (*Hint:* Recompute $R_{\{x \mid |x| \text{ is odd}\}}$).
(b) List the languages L that *could* give rise to this R_L.

2.32. Let $\Sigma = \{\mathbf{a}, \mathbf{b}\}$ and let $\Psi = \{x \in \Sigma^* \mid x$ has an even number of **a**s and ends with (at least) one $\mathbf{b}\}$. Describe R_Ψ and draw a machine accepting Ψ.

2.33. Let $\Xi = \{x \in \{\mathbf{a}\}^* \mid \exists j \in \mathbb{N} \ni |x| = j^2\} = \{\lambda, \mathbf{a}, \mathbf{aaaa}, \mathbf{a}^9, \mathbf{a}^{16}, \mathbf{a}^{25}, \ldots\}$. Prove that Ξ is not FAD.

2.34. Let $\Phi = \{x \in \{\mathbf{b}\}^* \mid \exists j \in \mathbb{N} \ni |x| = 2^j\} = \{\mathbf{b}, \mathbf{bb}, \mathbf{bbbb}, \mathbf{b}^8, \mathbf{b}^{16}, \mathbf{b}^{32}, \ldots\}$. Prove that Φ is not FAD.

2.35. Let $\Sigma = \{\mathbf{a}, \mathbf{b}\}$. Assume R_L has the following five equivalence classes: $\{\lambda\}$, $\{\mathbf{a}\}$, $\{\mathbf{aa}\}$, $\{\mathbf{a}^3, \mathbf{a}^4, \mathbf{a}^5, \mathbf{a}^6, \ldots\}$, $\{x \mid x$ contains (at least) one $\mathbf{b}\}$. Also assume that L consists of exactly *one* of these equivalence classes.
(a) Which equivalence class is L?
(b) List the other languages L that *could* give rise to this R_L (and note that they might consist of several equivalence classes).

2.36. Let $\Omega = \{y \in \{\mathbf{0}, \mathbf{1}\}^* \mid (y$ contains exactly one $\mathbf{0}) \vee (y$ contains an even number of $\mathbf{1}$s$)\}$. Find R_Ω.

2.37. Let $\Sigma = \{\mathbf{a}, \mathbf{b}\}$ and $L_1 = \{x \in \Sigma^* \mid |x|_\mathbf{a} > |x|_\mathbf{b}\}$ and $L_2 = \{x \in \Sigma^* \mid |x|_\mathbf{a} < 3\}$. Which of the following are FAD? Support your answers.
(a) L_1 **(b)** L_2 **(c)** $L_1 \cap L_2$ **(d)** $\sim L_2$ **(e)** $L_1 \cup L_2$

2.38. Let $m \in \mathbb{N}$ and let R_m be defined by $x\ R_m\ y \Leftrightarrow |x| - |y|$ is a multiple of m.

(a) Prove that R_m is a right congruence.

(b) Show that $R_2 \cap R_3$ is R_6, and hence also a right congruence. (Note, for example, that $\langle \lambda, \mathbf{aaaaaa} \rangle \in R_6$ since $\langle \lambda, \mathbf{aaaaaa} \rangle \in R_3$ and $\langle \lambda, \mathbf{aaaaaa} \rangle \in R_2$; how do the equivalence classes of R_2 and R_6 compare?).

(c) Show that, in general, if R and S are right congruences, then so is $R \cap S$.

(d) Now consider $R_2 \cup R_3$, and show that this is not a right congruence because it is not even an equivalence relation.

(e) Prove that if R and S are right congruences and $R \cup S$ happens to be an equivalence relation then $R \cup S$ will be a right congruence, also.

2.39. Give an example of two right congruences R_1 and R_2 over Σ^* for which $R_1 \cup R_2$ is not a right congruence.

2.40. Let $\Sigma = \{\mathbf{a}, \mathbf{b}\}$ and let $\Gamma = \{\lambda, \mathbf{a}, \mathbf{ab}, \mathbf{ba}, \mathbf{bb}, \mathbf{bbb}\} \cup \{x \in \Sigma^* \mid |x| \geq 4\}$.

(a) Use the definition of R_Γ to show $\mathbf{ab}\ R_\Gamma\ \mathbf{ba}$.

(b) Use the definition of R_Γ to show **ab** is not related by R_Γ to **bb**.

(c) Show that the equivalence classes of R_Γ are $\{\lambda\}, \{\mathbf{a}\}, \{\mathbf{b}\}, \{\mathbf{aa}\}, \{\mathbf{bb}\}, \{\mathbf{ab}, \mathbf{ba}\}$, $\{x \mid x \neq \mathbf{bbb} \wedge |x| = 3\}, \{x \mid x = \mathbf{bbb} \vee |x| \geq 4\}$.

(d) Draw the minimal state DFA which accepts Γ.

2.41. Prove that the relation R^M given in Definition 2.4 is a right congruence.

2.42. We can view a text file as being one long "word," that is, a string of characters (including spaces, carriage returns, and so on). In this sense, each Pascal program can be considered to be a single word over the ASCII alphabet. We can define the *language* Pascal as the *set* of all valid Pascal programs (that is, the valid words are those text files that would compile with no compiler errors). Is this language FAD?

2.43. Define *"Short Pascal"* as the collection of valid Pascal programs that are composed of less than 1 million characters. Is Short Pascal FAD? Any volunteers for building the appropriate DFA?

2.44. Let $\Sigma = \{\mathbf{a}, \mathbf{b}, \mathbf{c}\}$, and define $L = \{\mathbf{a}^n \mathbf{b}^k \mathbf{c}^j \mid n < 3 \text{ or } (n \geq 3 \text{ and } k = j)\}$.

(a) Show that for this language the conclusion of Theorem 2.3 holds, but the hypothesis of Theorem 2.3 does *not* hold.

(b) Is the contrapositive of Theorem 2.3 true? Explain.

2.45. Carefully show that F_Q in Definition 2.5 is a well-defined set.

2.46. Carefully show that δ_Q in Definition 2.5 is well defined.

2.47. For δ_Q in Definition 2.5, use induction to show that

$$(\forall x \in \Sigma^*)(\forall y \in \Sigma^*)(\overline{\delta}_Q([x]_Q, y) = [xy]_Q).$$

2.48. For the L and Q in Definition 2.5, prove that $L(A_Q) = L$.

2.49. Given L and Q as in Definition 2.5, A_Q is a machine to which we can apply Definition 2.4. Prove or give a counterexample: $Q = R^{(A_Q)}$.

2.50. Given L and $Q = R_L$ as in Definition 2.5, A_{R_L} is a machine to which we can apply Definition 2.4. Prove or give a counterexample: $R_L = R^{(A_{R_L})}$.

2.51. Show that the converse of Theorem 2.3 is false (*Hint:* See Exercise 2.29 and let $L = \Phi$).

2.52. Let $L = \{x \in \{\mathbf{a}, \mathbf{b}\}^* \mid |x|_\mathbf{a} = 2|x|_\mathbf{b}\}$. Prove that L is not FAD.

2.53. Consider the language K defined in Exercise 2.28.

(a) Find $[\mathbf{110}]_{R_K}$; that is, find all strings y for which $y\ R_K\ \mathbf{110}$.

(b) Describe R_K.

2.54. Prove or give a counterexample: $R_{L_1} \cap R_{L_2} = R_{(L_1 \cap L_2)}$.

2.55. Given a right congruence R over Σ^* for which $rk(R) = n$. Prove that each equivalence class of R contains a representative whose length is less than n.

2.56. For the R given in Example 2.6, find all languages L for which $R_L = R^N$.

2.57. Consider the languages defined in Exercise 1.6. Find the right congruences induced by each of these four languages.

2.58. Assume $L \subseteq \{\mathbf{a}\}^*$ and $\lambda\, R_L\, \mathbf{a}$. List all possible choices for the language L.

2.59. Assume $L \subseteq \{\mathbf{a}\}^*$ and $\mathbf{a}\, R_L\, \mathbf{aa}$. List all possible choices for the language L.

2.60. Assume $L \subseteq \{\mathbf{a}\}^*$ and $\lambda\, R_L\, \mathbf{aa}$. List all possible choices for the language L.

2.61. **(a)** Give an example of a DFA M for which $R^M = R_{L(M)}$.
(b) Give an example of a DFA M for which $R^M \neq R_{L(M)}$.
(c) For every DFA M, show that R^M refines $R_{L(M)}$.

2.62. Find R^M and $R_{L(M)}$ for the machine M described in Example 1.5.

2.63. Is $A_{R_{L(A)}}$ always equivalent to A? Explain.

2.64. Consider $L_4 = \{y \in \{\mathbf{0}, \mathbf{1}\}^* \mid |y|_\mathbf{0} = |y|_\mathbf{1}\}$ as given in Example 2.11. Let n be given and consider $x = (\mathbf{01})^n = \mathbf{010101\ldots0101}$. Then $|x| = 2n > n$; but if $u = \mathbf{0101}$, $v = \mathbf{01}$, and $w = (\mathbf{01})^{n-3}$, $(\forall i \in \mathbb{N})uv^iw \in L_4$. Does this mean L_4 is FAD? Explain.

2.65. Consider $L_4 = \{y \in \{\mathbf{0}, \mathbf{1}\}^* \mid |y|_\mathbf{0} = |y|_\mathbf{1}\}$ as given in Example 2.11. Find R_{L_4}.

2.66. Show that the set of all postfix expressions over the alphabet $\{\mathbf{A}, \mathbf{B}, +, -\}$ is not FAD.

2.67. Show that the set of all parenthesized infix expressions over the alphabet $\{\mathbf{A}, \mathbf{B}, +, -, (,)\}$ is not FAD.

2.68. For a given language L, how does R_L compare to $R_{\sim L}$; that is, how does the right congruence generated by a language compare to the right congruence generated by its complement? Justify your statement.

2.69. Let $\Sigma = \{\mathbf{a}, \mathbf{b}\}$. Assume the right congruence Q has the following equivalence classes: $\{\lambda\}, \{\mathbf{a}\}, \{\mathbf{b}\}, \{x \mid |x| \geq 2\}$. Show that there is no language L such that $R_L = Q$.

2.70. Let Q be the equivalence relation with the two equivalence classes $\{\lambda, \mathbf{a}, \mathbf{aa}\}$ and $\{\mathbf{a}^3, \mathbf{a}^4, \mathbf{a}^5, \ldots\}$.
(a) Show that Q is *not* a right congruence.
(b) Attempt to build A_Q (ignoring F_Q for the moment), and describe any difficulties that you encounter.
(c) Explain how the failure in part (a) is related to the difficulties found in part (b).

2.71. Let $\Sigma = \{\mathbf{a}, \mathbf{b}, \mathbf{c}\}$. Show that $\{\mathbf{a}^i\mathbf{b}^j\mathbf{c}^k \mid i, j, k \in \mathbb{N} \text{ and } i + j = k\}$ is not FAD.

2.72. Let $Q \subseteq \{\mathbf{a}\}^* \times \{\mathbf{a}\}^*$ be the equivalence relation with the following equivalence classes:

$$[\lambda]_Q = \{\lambda\} = \{\mathbf{a}\}^0$$

$$[\mathbf{a}]_Q = \{\mathbf{a}\} = \{\mathbf{a}\}^1$$

$$[\mathbf{aa}]_Q = \{\mathbf{a}\}^2 \cup \{\mathbf{a}\}^3 \cup \{\mathbf{a}\}^4 \cup \{\mathbf{a}\}^5 \cup \cdots$$

Show that Q is a right congruence.

2.73. Let $\Sigma = \{\mathbf{a}, \mathbf{b}, \mathbf{c}\}$, and let R_2 be defined by $x\, R_2\, y \Leftrightarrow x$ and y end with the same letter.
(a) Show that R_2 is an equivalence relation.
(b) Assume that part (a) is true, and show that R_2 is a right congruence.

2.74. Let $\Sigma = \{\mathbf{a}, \mathbf{b}, \mathbf{c}\}$, and let R_3 be defined by $x\, R_3\, y \Leftrightarrow x$ and y begin with the same letter.

(a) Show that R_3 is an equivalence relation.
(b) Assume that part (a) is true, and show that R_3 is a right congruence.

2.75. Let $\Sigma = \{\mathbf{a}, \mathbf{b}\}$. Which of the following languages are FAD? (Support your answers.)
(a) L_1 = all words over Σ^* for which the last letter matches the first letter.
(b) L_2 = all odd-length words over Σ^* for which the first letter matches the center letter.
(c) L_3 = all words over Σ^* for which the last letter matches none of the other letters.
(d) L_4 = all even-length words over Σ^* for which the two center letters match.
(e) L_5 = all odd-length words over Σ^* for which the center letter matches none of the other letters.

2.76. In the proof of (2) $\Rightarrow$ (3) in Nerode's theorem:
(a) Complete the proof of case 1.
(b) Could case 1 actually be included under case 2?

2.77. Consider the right congruence property (RC) in Definition 2.1. Show that the implication could be replaced by an equivalence; that is, property (RC) could be rephrased as

$$(\forall x, y \in \Sigma^*)(x \mathrm{R} y \Leftrightarrow (\forall u \in \Sigma^*)(xu \mathrm{R} yu))$$

2.78. Given a DFA $\mathsf{M} = \langle \Sigma, S, s_0, \delta, F \rangle$, assume that $\bar{\delta}(s, u) = q$, and $\bar{\delta}(q, v) = q$. Use induction to show that $(\forall i \in \mathbb{N})(\bar{\delta}(s, uv^i) = q)$.

2.79. Let L be the set of all strings that agree with some initial part of the pattern $\mathbf{0}^1\mathbf{1}\mathbf{0}^2\mathbf{1}\mathbf{0}^3\mathbf{1}\mathbf{0}^4\mathbf{1}\ldots = \mathbf{0100100010000100000100}\ldots$. Thus, $L = \{\mathbf{0}, \mathbf{01}, \mathbf{010}, \mathbf{0100}, \mathbf{01001}, \mathbf{010010}, \mathbf{0100100}, \ldots\}$. Prove that L is not FAD.

2.80. Consider the following BNF over the three-symbol alphabet $\{\mathbf{a}, \mathbf{)}, \mathbf{(}\}$, and show that the resulting language is not FAD.

$$\langle \text{simple} \rangle ::= \mathbf{a} \mid \mathbf{(}\langle \text{simple} \rangle\mathbf{)}$$

2.81. (a) Let $\Sigma = \{\mathbf{0}, \mathbf{1}\}$. Let $L_2 = \{x \in \Sigma^* \mid$ the base 2 number represented by x is a power of 2$\}$. Show that L_2 is FAD.
(b) Let $\Sigma = \{\mathbf{0}, \mathbf{1}, \mathbf{2}, \mathbf{3}, \mathbf{4}, \mathbf{5}, \mathbf{6}, \mathbf{7}, \mathbf{8}, \mathbf{9}\}$.
Let $L_{10} = \{x \in \Sigma^* \mid$ the base 10 number represented by x is a power of 2$\}$. Prove that L_{10} is not FAD.

CHAPTER

3

MINIMIZATION of FINITE AUTOMATA

We have seen that there are many different automata that can be used to represent a given language. We would like to be able to find an automaton for a language L that is *minimal*, that is, a machine which can represent that language which has the fewest number of states possible.

Finding such an optimal DFA will involve transforming a given automaton into the most efficient equivalent machine. To effectively accomplish this transformation, we must have a set of clear, unequivocal directions specifying how to proceed. A *procedure* is a finite set of instructions that unambiguously defines deterministic, discrete steps for performing some task. As anyone who has programmed a computer knows, it is possible to generate procedures that will never halt for some inputs (or perhaps for *all* inputs if the program is seriously flawed). An *algorithm* is a procedure that is guaranteed to halt on all (legal) inputs. In this chapter we will specify a procedure for finding a minimal machine and then justify that this procedure is actually an algorithm. Thus, the theorems and definitions will show how to transform an inefficient DFA into an optimal automaton in a straightforward manner that can be easily programmed.

3.1 HOMOMORPHISMS AND ISOMORPHISMS

One of our goals for this chapter can be stated as follows: Given a language L, we wish to survey *all* the machines that recognize L and choose the machine (or machines) that is "smallest." It will be seen that there is indeed a *unique* smallest machine: A_{R_L}. The automaton A_{R_L} will be unique in the sense that any other optimal

DFA looks exactly like A_{R_L} except for a trivial relabeling of the state names. The concept of two automata "looking alike" will have to be formalized to provide a basis for our rigorous statements. Machines that "look alike" will be called *isomorphic*, and the relabeling specification will be called an *isomorphism*.

We have already learned some facts about A_{R_L}, which stem from the proof of Nerode's theorem. These are summarized below and show that A_{R_L} is indeed one of the optimal machines for the language L.

∇ **Corollary 3.1.** For any FAD language L, $L(A_{R_L}) = L$.

Proof. This was shown when (3) ⇒ (1) in Theorem 2.2 was proved.

Δ

Also, in the proof of (1) ⇒ (2) in Nerode's theorem, the relation R^M (defined by a given DFA $M = \langle \Sigma, S, s_0, \delta, F \rangle$ for which $L(M) = L$) was used to show $\|S\| \geq rk(R^M)$. Furthermore, in (2) ⇒ (3), right congruences such as R^M that satisfied property (2) must be refinements of R_L, and so $rk(R^M) \geq rk(R_L)$. Thus $\|S\| \geq rk(R^M) \geq rk(R_L) = \|S_{R_L}\|$, which leads immediately to the following corollary.

∇ **Corollary 3.2.** For any FAD language L, A_{R_L} is a minimal deterministic finite automaton that accepts L.

Proof. The proof follows from the definition of a minimal DFA (Definition 2.7); that is, if $M = \langle \Sigma, S, s_0, \delta, F \rangle$ is any machine that also accepts L, then $\|S\| \geq \|S_{R_L}\|$.

Δ

Besides being in some sense "the simplest," the minimal machine has some other nice properties. For example, if A is minimal, then the right congruence generated by A is identical to the right congruence generated by the language recognized by A; that is, $R^A = R_{L(A)}$ (see the exercises). Examples 3.1 and 3.2 illustrate the two basic ways a DFA can have superfluous states.

∇ **Definition 3.1.** A state s in a finite automaton $A = \langle \Sigma, S, s_0, \delta, F \rangle$ is called *accessible iff*

$$\exists x_s \in \Sigma^* \ni \overline{\delta}(s_0, x_s) = s$$

The automaton A is called *connected iff*

$$(\forall s \in S)(\exists x_s \in \Sigma^*)(\overline{\delta}(s_0, x_s) = s)$$

Δ

That is, a connected machine requires all states to be accessible; every state s of S must be "reachable" from s_0 by some string (x_s) in Σ^* (different states will require different strings, and hence it is convenient to associate an appropriate string x_s with the state s). States that are not accessible are sometimes called *disconnected*, *inaccessible*, or *unreachable*.

EXAMPLE 3.1

The machine defined in Figure 3.1 satisfies the definition of a deterministic finite automaton, but is disconnected since r cannot be reached by any string from the start state q. Note that x_q could be λ or **10**, while x_t might be **0** or **111**. There is no candidate for x_r. Furthermore, r could be "thrown away" without affecting the language that this machine accepts. This will be one of the techniques we will use to minimize finite automata: removing the inaccessible states.

There is a second way for an automaton to have superfluous states, as shown by the automata in the following examples. An overabundance of states may be present, recording nonessential information and consequently distinguishing between strings in ways that are unnecessary.

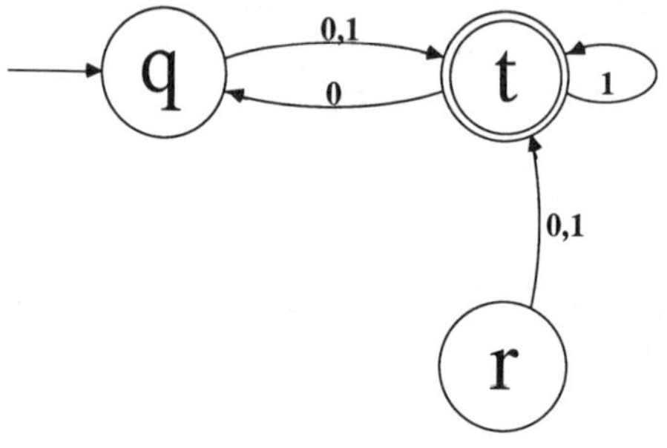

Figure 3.1 The automaton discussed in Example 3.1

EXAMPLE 3.2

Consider the four-state DFA over {**a**, **b**}* in which s_0 is the start and only final state, defined in Figure 3.2. This automaton is clearly connected, but it is still not optimal. This machine accepts all strings whose length is a multiple of 3, and s_1 and s_2 are really "remembering" the same information, that is, that we currently have read a string that is one more than a multiple of 3. The fact that some strings that end in **a** are sent to s_1, while those that end in **b** may be sent to s_2, is of no real importance; we do not have to "remember" what the last letter in the string actually was in order to correctly accept the given language. The states s_1 and s_2 are in some sense *equivalent*, since they are performing the same function. The careful reader may have noticed that this language could have been recognized with a three-state machine, in which a single state combines the functions of s_1 and s_2.

Now consider the automaton shown in Figure 3.3, in which there are three superfluous states. This automaton accepts the same language as the DFA in Figure 3.2, but this time not only are s_1 and s_2 performing the same function, but s_3 and s_4 are "equivalent," and s_0 and s_5 are both "remembering" that there has been a multiple of three letters seen so far. Note that it is not enough to check that s_1 and s_2 take you to exactly the same places (as was the case in the first example); in this

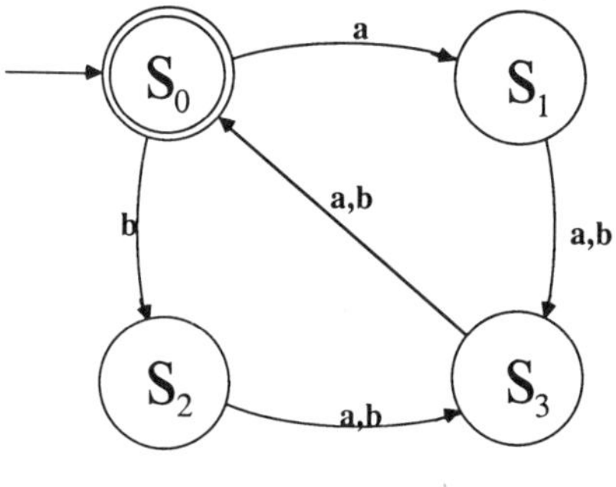

Figure 3.2 The first automaton discussed in Example 3.2

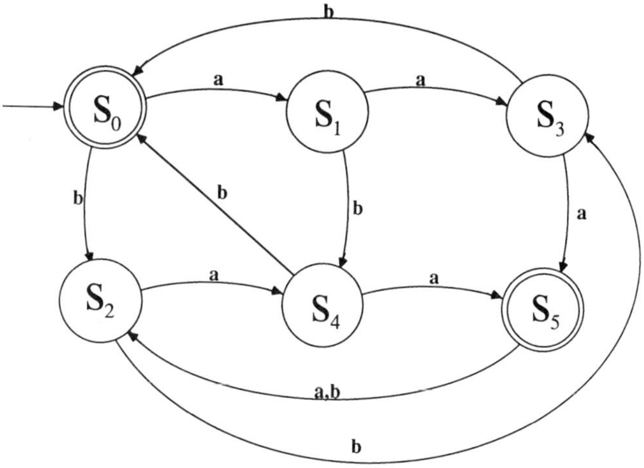

Figure 3.3 The second automaton discussed in Example 3.2

example, the arrows coming out of s_1 and s_2 do *not* point to the same places. The important thing is that, when leaving s_1 or s_2, when **a** is seen, we go to *equivalent* states, and when processing **b** from s_1 or s_2, we also go to *equivalent* states. However, deciding whether two states are equivalent or not is perhaps a little less straightforward than it may at first seem. This sets the stage for the appropriate definition of equivalence.

∇ **Definition 3.2.** Given a finite automaton $A = <\Sigma, S, s_0, \delta, F>$, there is a relation between the states of A called E_A, the *state equivalence relation* on A, defined by

$$(\forall s \in S)(\forall t \in S)(s \, E_A \, t \Leftrightarrow (\forall x \in \Sigma^*)(\overline{\delta}(s, x) \in F \Leftrightarrow \overline{\delta}(t, x) \in F))$$

Δ

In other words, we will relate s and t ***iff*** it is not possible to distinguish whether we are starting from state s or state t; each string $x \in \Sigma^*$ will *either* take x to a final state when starting from s and also take x to a final state from t, *or* neither s nor t will take x to a final state.

Another way of looking at this concept is to define new machines that "look like" A, but have different start states. Given a finite automaton $A = <\Sigma, S, s_0, \delta, F>$ and two states $s, t \in S$, define a new automaton $A^t = <\Sigma, S, t, \delta, F>$ that has t as a start state, and another automaton $A^s = <\Sigma, S, s, \delta, F>$ having s as a start state. Then $s E_A t \Leftrightarrow L(A^s) = L(A^t)$. (Why is this an equivalent definition?) These sets of words will be used in later chapters and are referred to as *terminal sets*. $T(A, t)$ will denote the set of all words that reach final states from t, and thus $T(A, t) = L(A_t) = \{x \mid \bar{\delta}(t, x) \in F\}$.

In terms of the black box model presented in Chapter 1, we see that we cannot distinguish between A^s and A^t by placing matching strings on the input tapes and observing the acceptance lights of the two machines. For any string, both A^s and A^t will accept, or both will reject; without looking inside the black boxes, there is no way to tell whether we are starting in state s or state t. This highlights the sense in which s and t are deemed equivalent: we cannot distinguish between s and t by the subsequent behavior of the automaton.

The modified automaton A^t, which gives rise to the terminal set $T(A, t)$, can be contrasted with the modified automaton $A_t = <\Sigma, S, s_0, \delta, \{t\}>$ from Chapter 2, which recognized the initial set $I(A, t) = \{x \mid \bar{\delta}(s_0, x) = t\}$. Notice that initial sets are comprised of strings that move from the start state to the distinguished state t, while terminal sets are made up of strings that go from t to a final state.

EXAMPLE 3.3

The automaton N discussed in Example 2.6 (Figure 3.4) has the following relations comprising E_N:

$$s_0 E_N s_0$$

$$s_1 E_N s_1,\ s_1 E_N s_2,\ s_1 E_N s_3$$

$$s_2 E_N s_1,\ s_2 E_N s_2,\ s_2 E_N s_3$$

$$s_3 E_N s_1,\ s_3 E_N s_2,\ s_3 E_N s_3$$

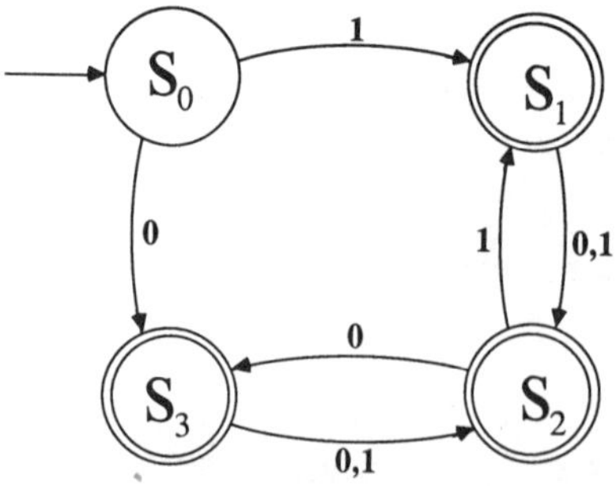

Figure 3.4 The automaton N discussed in Example 3.3

This can be succinctly described by listing the equivalence classes:

$$[s_0]_{E_N} = \{s_0\}$$

$$[s_1]_{E_N} = [s_2]_{E_N} = [s_3]_{E_N} = \{s_1, s_2, s_3\},$$

and we will abuse our notation slightly and blur the distinction between the relation E_N with the partition it generates by writing $E_N = \{\{s_0\}, \{s_1, s_2, s_3\}\}$.

Recall that Example 2.6 showed that the minimal machine that accepted $L(N)$ had two states; it will be seen that it is no coincidence that E_N has exactly the same number of equivalence classes.

∇ **Definition 3.3.** A finite automaton $A = <\Sigma, S, s_0, \delta, F>$ is called *reduced iff* $(\forall s, t \in S)(s\, E_A\, t \Leftrightarrow s = t)$.
Δ

In a reduced machine, E_A must be the identity relation on S, and in this case each equivalence class will contain only a single element.

EXAMPLE 3.4

The automaton N in Figure 3.4 is not reduced, since Example 3.3 shows that $[s_2]_{E_N}$ contains three states. On the other hand, the automaton A displayed in Figure 3.5a is reduced since $[s_0]_{E_A} = \{s_0\}$ and $[s_1]_{E_A} = \{s_1\}$. The concepts of homomorphism and isomorphism will play an integral part in justifying the correctness of the algorithms that produce the optimal DFA for a given language. We need to formalize what we mean when we say that two automata are "the same." The following examples illustrate the criteria that must exist between similar machines.

EXAMPLE 3.5

We now consider the automaton B shown in Figure 3.5b, which looks suspiciously like the DFA A given in Figure 3.5a. In fact, it is basically the "same" machine. While it has been oriented differently (which has no effect on the δ function), and the start state has been labeled q_0 rather than s_0, and the final state is called q_1 rather than s_1, A and B are otherwise "identical." For such a *relabeling* to truly reflect the same automaton structure, certain conditions must be met, as illustrated in the following examples.

EXAMPLE 3.6

Consider machine C, defined by the state transition diagram given in Figure 3.5c. This machine is identical to B, except for the position of the start state. However, it is not the same machine as B, since it behaves differently (and in fact accepts a different language). Thus we see that it is important for the start state of one machine to correspond to the start state of the other machine. Note that we cannot

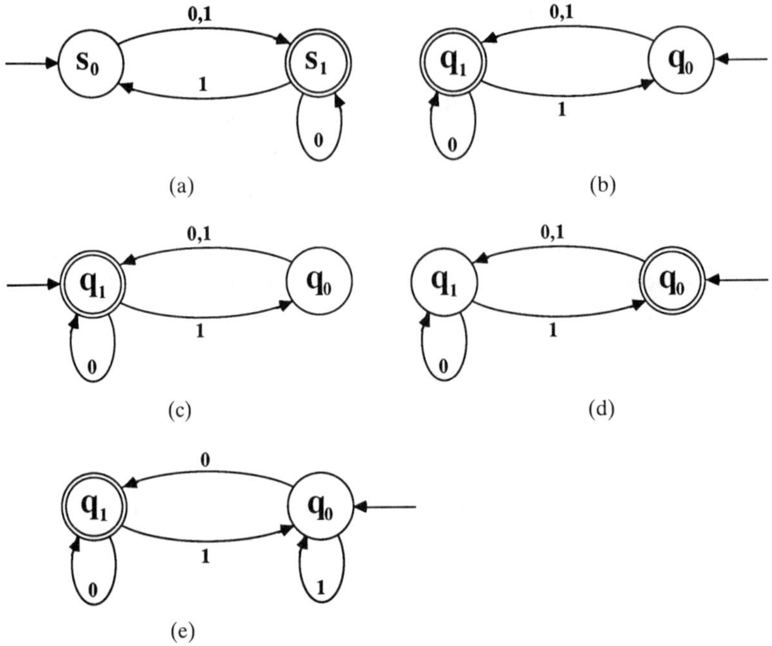

Figure 3.5 (a) The automaton A (b) The automaton B (c) The automaton C (d) The automaton D (e) The automaton E

circumvent this by letting q_0 correspond to s_1 and q_1 correspond to s_0, since other problems will develop, as shown next in Example 3.7.

EXAMPLE 3.7

Let machine D be defined by the state transition diagram given in Figure 3.5d. The automata B and D (Figures 3.5b and 3.5d) look much the same, with start states corresponding, but they are not the same (and will in fact accept different languages), because we cannot get the final states to correspond correctly. Even if we do get the start and final states to agree, we still have to make sure that the transitions correspond. This is illustrated in the next example.

EXAMPLE 3.8

Consider the machine E given in Figure 3.5e. In this automaton, when leaving the start state, we travel to a final state if we see **0**, and remain at the start state (which is nonfinal) if we see **1**; this is different from what happened in machine A, where we traveled to a final state regardless of whether we saw **0** or **1**. Thus it is seen that we not only have to find a correspondence (which can be thought of as a function μ) between the states of our two machines, but we must do this in a way that satisfies the above three conditions (or else we cannot claim the machines are "the same"). This is summed up in the following definition of a *homomorphism*.

∇ **Definition 3.4.** Given two finite automata, $A = \langle \Sigma, S_A, s_{0_A}, \delta_A, F_A \rangle$ and $B = \langle \Sigma, S_B, s_{0_B}, \delta_B, F_B \rangle$, and a function $\mu: S_A \to S_B$, μ is called a *finite automata homomorphism* from A to B ***iff*** the following three conditions hold:

i. $\mu(s_{0A}) = s_{0_B}$
ii. $(\forall s \in S_A)(s \in F_A \Rightarrow \mu(s) \in F_B)$
iii. $(\forall s \in S_A)(\forall \mathbf{a} \in \Sigma)(\mu(\delta_A(s, \mathbf{a})) = \delta_B(\mu(s), \mathbf{a}))$

Δ

Note that μ is called a homomorphism from A to B, but it is actually a function between state sets, that is, from S_A to S_B.

EXAMPLE 3.9

Machines A and B in Example 3.5 are homomorphic, since the homomorphism $\mu: \{s_0, s_1\} \to \{q_0, q_1\}$ defined by $\mu(s_0) = q_0$ and $\mu(s_1) = q_1$ satisfies the three conditions.

The following example shows that even if we can find a homomorphism that satisfies the 3 conditions the machines might not be the same.

EXAMPLE 3.10

Let $M = \langle \Sigma, \{s_0, s_1, s_2\}, s_0, \delta_M, \{s_1\} \rangle$ and $N = \langle \Sigma, \{q_0, q_1\}, q_0, \delta_N, \{q_1\} \rangle$ be given by the state transition diagrams in Figures 3.6a and 3.6b. Define a homomorphism $\psi: \{s_0, s_1, s_2\} \to \{q_0, q_1\}$ by $\psi(s_0) = q_0$, $\psi(s_1) = q_1$, and $\psi(s_2) = q_0$. Note that the start state maps to the start state, final states map to final states (and nonfinal states map to nonfinal states), and, furthermore, the transitions agree. Here is the statement that the **0** transition out of state s_0 is consistent:

$$\psi(\delta_M(s_0, \mathbf{0})) = \psi(s_1) = q_1 = \delta_N(q_0, \mathbf{0}) = \delta_N(\psi(s_0), \mathbf{0})$$

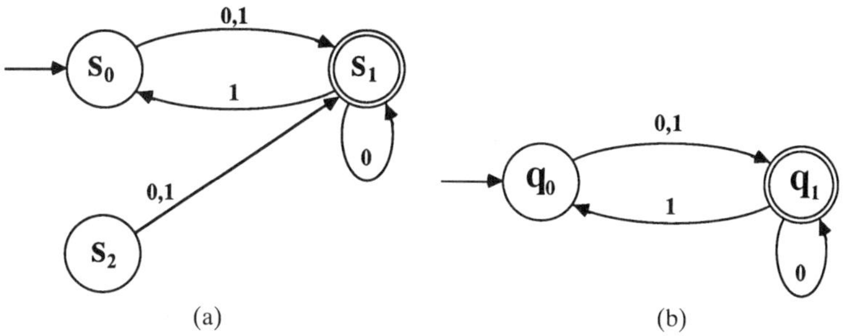

Figure 3.6 (a) The DFA M discussed in Example 3.10 (b) The DFA N discussed in Example 3.10

Note that this really *does* say that the transition labeled **0** leaving the start state conforms; s_0 has a **0**-transition pointing to s_1, and so the **0**-transition from $\psi(s_0)$ should point to $\psi(s_1)$ (that is, q_0 should point to q_1). But the transition taken from s_0 upon seeing a **0**, in our notation, is $\delta_M(s_0, \mathbf{0})$, and the place q_0 goes to is $\delta_N(q_0, \mathbf{0})$. We wish to make sure that the state in N corresponding to where the **0**-transition from s_0 points, denoted by $\psi(\delta_M(s_0, \mathbf{0}))$, agrees with the state to which q_0 points. Hence we require $\psi(\delta_M(s_0, \mathbf{0})) = \delta_N(q_0, \mathbf{0})$. In the last formula, q_0 was chosen because that was the state corresponding to s_0; that is, $\psi(s_0) = q_0$. Hence, in our formal notation, we were really checking $\psi(\delta_M(s_0, \mathbf{0})) = \delta_N(\psi(s_0), \mathbf{0})$. Hence, we see that rule (iii) requires us to check all transitions leading out of all states for all letters; that is, $(\forall s \in S_M)(\forall \mathbf{a} \in \Sigma)(\psi(\delta_M(s, \mathbf{a})) = \delta_N(\psi(s), \mathbf{a}))$. Applying this rule to each choice of letters **a** and states s, we have

$$\psi(\delta_M(s_0, \mathbf{0})) = \psi(s_1) = q_1 = \delta_N(q_0, \mathbf{0}) = \delta_N(\psi(s_0), \mathbf{0})$$

$$\psi(\delta_M(s_0, \mathbf{1})) = \psi(s_1) = q_1 = \delta_N(q_0, \mathbf{1}) = \delta_N(\psi(s_0), \mathbf{1})$$

$$\psi(\delta_M(s_1, \mathbf{0})) = \psi(s_1) = q_1 = \delta_N(q_1, \mathbf{0}) = \delta_N(\psi(s_1), \mathbf{0})$$

$$\psi(\delta_M(s_1, \mathbf{1})) = \psi(s_0) = q_0 = \delta_N(q_1, \mathbf{1}) = \delta_N(\psi(s_1), \mathbf{1})$$

$$\psi(\delta_M(s_2, \mathbf{0})) = \psi(s_1) = q_1 = \delta_N(q_0, \mathbf{0}) = \delta_N(\psi(s_2), \mathbf{0})$$

$$\psi(\delta_M(s_2, \mathbf{1})) = \psi(s_1) = q_1 = \delta_N(q_0, \mathbf{1}) = \delta_N(\psi(s_2), \mathbf{1})$$

Hence ψ *is* a homomorphism between M and N even though M has three states and N has two states. While the existence of a homomorphism is not enough to ensure that the machines are "the same," the exercises for this chapter indicate that the existence of a homomorphism *is* enough to ensure that the machines are equivalent. The extra condition we need to guarantee that the machines are identical (except for a trivial renaming of the states) is that ψ be a *bijection*.

∇ **Definition 3.5.** Given two finite automata $A = <\Sigma, S_A, s_{0_A}, \delta_A, F_A>$ and $B = <\Sigma, S_B, s_{0_B}, \delta_B, F_B>$, and a function μ: $S_A \rightarrow S_B$, μ is called a *finite automata isomorphism* from A to B *iff* the following five conditions hold:

i. $\mu(s_{0_A}) = s_{0_B}$.
ii. $(\forall s \in S_A)(s \in F_A \Leftrightarrow \mu(s) \in F_B)$.
iii. $(\forall s \in S_A)(\forall \mathbf{a} \in \Sigma)(\mu(\delta_A(s, \mathbf{a})) = \delta_B(\mu(s), \mathbf{a}))$.
iv. μ is a one-to-one function from S_A to S_B.
v. μ is onto S_B.

Δ

EXAMPLE 3.11

μ from Example 3.9 is an isomorphism. Example 3.5 illustrated that the automaton A was essentially "the same" as B except for the way the states were named. Note that μ can be thought of as the recipe for relabeling the states of A to form a machine that would then be in the very strictest sense absolutely *identical* to B. ψ from Example 3.10 is not an isomorphism because it is not one to one.

∇ **Definition 3.6.** Given two finite automata $A = <\Sigma, S_A, s_{0_A}, \delta_A, F_A>$ and $B = <\Sigma, S_B, s_{0_B}, \delta_B, F_B>$, A is said to be *isomorphic* to B *iff* there exists a finite automata isomorphism between A and B, and we will write $A \cong B$.
Δ

EXAMPLE 3.12

Machines A and B from Examples 3.4 and 3.5 are isomorphic. Machines M and N from Example 3.10 are not isomorphic (and not just because the particular function ψ fails to satisfy the conditions; we must actually prove that *no* function exists that qualifies as an isomorphism between M and N).

Now that we have rigorously defined the concept of two machines being "essentially identical," we can prove that, given a language L, any reduced and connected machine A accepting L must be *minimal*, that is, have as few states as possible for that particular language. We will prove this assertion by showing that any such A is isomorphic to A_{R_L}, which was shown in Corollary 3.2 to be the "smallest" possible machine for L.

∇ **Theorem 3.1.** Let L be any FAD language over an alphabet Σ, and let $A = <\Sigma, S, s_0, \delta, F>$ be any reduced and connected automaton that accepts L. Then $A \cong A_{R_L}$.

Proof. We must try to define a reasonable function μ from the states of A to the states of A_{R_L} (which you should recall corresponded to equivalence classes of R_L). A natural way to define μ (which happens to work!) is: For each $s \in S$, find a string $x_s \in \Sigma^* \ni \overline{\delta}(s_0, x_s) = s$. (Since A is connected, we are guaranteed to find such an x_s. In fact, there may be many strings that take us from s_0 to s; choose any one of them, and call it x_s.) We need to map s to some equivalence class of R_L; the logical choice is the class containing x_s. Thus we define

$$\mu(s) = [x_s]_{R_L}$$

An immediate question comes to mind: There may be several strings that we could use for x_s; does it matter which one we choose to find the equivalence class? It would not do if, say, R_L consisted of two equivalence classes, the even-length strings $= [\mathbf{11}]_{R_L}$ and the odd-length strings $= [\mathbf{0}]_{R_L}$, and both $\overline{\delta}(s_0, \mathbf{0})$ and $\overline{\delta}(s_0, \mathbf{11})$ equaled s. Then, on the one hand, $\mu(s)$ should be $[\mathbf{0}]_{R_L}$, and, on the other hand, it should be $[\mathbf{11}]_{R_L}$. μ must be a function; it cannot send s to two different equivalence classes. Note that there would be no problem if $\overline{\delta}(s_0, \mathbf{11}) = s$ and $\overline{\delta}(s_0 \mathbf{1111}) = s$, since $[\mathbf{11}]_{R_L} = [\mathbf{1111}]_{R_L}$, both of which represent the set of all even-length strings. Here x_s could be **11**, or it could be **1111**, and there is no inconsistency in the way in which $\mu(s)$ is defined; in either case, s is mapped by μ to the class of even-length strings. Thus we must first show:

1. μ is well-defined (which means it is defined everywhere, and the definitions are consistent; that is, if there are two choices for x_s, say, y and z, then $[y]_{R_L} = [z]_{R_L}$). Since A is connected, each state s can be reached by some string x_s; that is, $(\forall s \in S)(\exists x_s \in \Sigma^*)(\overline{\delta}(s_0, x_s) = s)$, and so there is indeed (at least) one equivalence class ($[x_s]_{R_L}$) to which s maps under μ. We therefore have $\mu(s) = [x_s]_{R_L}$. Thus μ is defined everywhere. We must still make sure that μ is not multiply defined: Let $x, y \in \Sigma^*$ and assume $\overline{\delta}(s_0, x) = \overline{\delta}(s_0, y)$. Then

$$\overline{\delta}(s_0, x) = \overline{\delta}(s_0, y) \Rightarrow \text{(by definition of =)}$$

$$(\forall u \in \Sigma^*)(\overline{\delta}(\overline{\delta}(s_0, x), u) \in F \Leftrightarrow \overline{\delta}(\overline{\delta}(s_0, y), u) \in F) \Rightarrow \text{(by Theorem 1.1)}$$

$$(\forall u \in \Sigma^*)(\overline{\delta}(s_0, xu) \in F \Leftrightarrow \overline{\delta}(s_0, yu) \in F) \Rightarrow \text{(by definition of } \boldsymbol{L}\text{)}$$

$$(\forall u \in \Sigma^*)(xu \in L \Leftrightarrow yu \in L) \Rightarrow \text{(by definition of } R_L\text{)}$$

$$x \, R_L \, y \Rightarrow \text{(by definition of [ ])}$$

$$[x]_{R_L} = [y]_{R_L}$$

Thus, if both x and y take us from s_0 to s, then it does not matter whether we let $\mu(s)$ equal $[x]_{R_L}$ or $[y]_{R_L}$, since they are identical. μ is therefore a bona fide function.

2. μ is onto S_{R_L}. Every equivalence class must be the image of some state in S, since $(\forall [x]_{R_L} \in S_{R_L})([x]_{R_L} = \mu(\overline{\delta}(s_0, x)))$, and so $\overline{\delta}(s_0, x)$ maps to $[x]_{R_L}$.

3. $\mu(s_0) = s_{0_{R_L}}$.

$$s_{0_{R_L}} = [\lambda]_{R_L} = \mu(\overline{\delta}(s_0, \lambda)) = \mu(s_0)$$

4. Final states map to final states; that is, $(\forall s \in S)(\mu(s) \in F_{R_L} \Leftrightarrow s \in F)$. Choose an $s \in F$ and pick a corresponding $x_s \in \Sigma^*$ such that $\overline{\delta}(s_0, x_s) = s$. Then

$$s \in F \Leftrightarrow \text{(by definition of } x_s, \boldsymbol{L}\text{)}$$

$$x_s \in \boldsymbol{L}(\mathsf{A}) \Leftrightarrow \text{(by definition of L)}$$

$$x_s \in L \Leftrightarrow \text{(by definition of } F_{R_L}\text{)}$$

$$[x_s] \in F_{R_L} \Leftrightarrow \text{(by definition of } \mu\text{)}$$

$$\mu(s) \in F_{R_L}$$

5. The transitions match up; that is, $(\forall s \in S)(\forall \mathbf{a} \in \Sigma)(\mu(\delta(s, \mathbf{a})) = \delta_{R_L}(\mu(s), \mathbf{a}))$. Choose an $s \in S$ and pick a corresponding $x_s \in \Sigma^*$ such that $\overline{\delta}(s_0, x_s) = s$. Note that this implies that $[x_s] = \mu(s) = \mu(\overline{\delta}(s_0, x_s))$. Then

$$\mu(\delta(s, \mathbf{a})) = \text{(by definition of } x_s\text{)}$$

$$\mu(\delta(\overline{\delta}(s_0, x_s), \mathbf{a})) = \text{(by Theorem 1.1)}$$

$$\mu(\overline{\delta}(s_0, x_s\mathbf{a})) = \text{(by definition of } \mu\text{)}$$

$$[x_s\mathbf{a}]_{R_L} = \text{(by definition of } \delta_{R_L})$$
$$\delta_{R_L}([x_s]_{R_L}, \mathbf{a}) = \text{(by definition of } \mu \text{ and } x_s)$$
$$\delta_{R_L}(\mu(s), \mathbf{a})$$

So far we have not needed the fact that A was reduced. In fact, we have now proved that μ is a homomorphism from A to A_{R_L} as long as A is merely connected. However, if A is reduced, we can show:

6. μ is one to one; that is, if $\mu(s) = \mu(t)$, then $s = t$. Let $s, t \in S$ and assume $\mu(s) = \mu(t)$.

$$\mu(s) = \mu(t) \Leftrightarrow \text{(by definition of =)}$$
$$(\forall u \in \Sigma^*)(\overline{\delta}_{R_L}(\mu(s), u) = \overline{\delta}_{R_L}(\mu(t), u)) \Leftrightarrow \text{[by property (5), induction]}$$
$$(\forall u \in \Sigma^*)(\mu(\overline{\delta}(s, u)) = \mu(\overline{\delta}(t, u))) \Rightarrow \text{(by definition of =)}$$
$$(\forall u \in \Sigma^*)(\mu(\overline{\delta}(s, u)) \in F_{R_L} \Leftrightarrow \mu(\overline{\delta}(t, u)) \in F_{R_L}) \Leftrightarrow \text{[by property (4) above]}$$
$$(\forall u \in \Sigma^*)(\overline{\delta}(s, u) \in F \Leftrightarrow \overline{\delta}(t, u) \in F) \Leftrightarrow \text{(by definition of } E_A)$$
$$s\, E_A\, t \Leftrightarrow \text{(since A is reduced)}$$
$$s = t$$

Thus, by results (1) through (6), μ is a well-defined homomorphism that is also a bijection; so μ is an isomorphism and therefore $A \cong A_{R_L}$.

Δ

∇ **Corollary 3.3.** Let A and B be reduced and connected finite automata. Under these conditions, A is equivalent to B *iff* $A \cong B$.

Proof. If $A \cong B$, it is easy to show that A is equivalent to B (as indicated in the exercises, this implication is true even if A and B are not reduced and connected). Now assume the hypothesis that A and B are reduced and connected does hold, and that A is equivalent to B. Since A is minimal, $A \cong A_{R_{L(A)}}$. Similarly, $B \cong A_{R_{L(B)}}$. Since $L(A) = L(B)$, $A_{R_{L(A)}} = A_{R_{L(B)}}$. Therefore, $A \cong A_{R_{L(A)}} = A_{R_{L(B)}} \cong B$.

Δ

3.2 MINIMIZATION ALGORITHMS

From the results in the previous section, it follows that a reduced and connected finite automaton must be minimal. This section demonstrates how to transform an existing DFA into an equivalent machine that is both reduced and connected and hence is the most efficient machine possible for the given language. The designer of an automaton can therefore focus solely on producing a machine that recognizes the correct set of strings (without regard for efficiency), knowing that the techniques presented in this section can later be employed to shrink the DFA to its optimal size.

The concepts explored in Chapters 4, 5, and 6 will provide further tools to aid in the design process and corresponding techniques to achieve optimality.

∇ **Corollary 3.4.** A reduced and connected deterministic finite automaton $A = <\Sigma, S, s_0, \delta, F>$ is minimal.

Proof. By Theorem 3.1, there is an isomorphism between A and A_{R_L}. Since an isomorphism is a bijection between the state sets, $\|S\| = \|S_{R_L}\|$. By Corollary 3.2, A_{R_L} has the smallest number of states, and therefore so does A.
Δ

Thus, if we had a machine for L that we could verify was reduced and connected, we would be able to state that we had found the minimal machine accepting L. We therefore would like some algorithms for determining if a machine M has these properties. We would also like to find a method for transforming a nonoptimal machine into one with the desired properties. The simplest transformation is from a disconnected machine to a connected machine: given any machine A, we will define a connected machine A^c that accepts the same language that A did; that is, $L(A) = L(A^c)$.

∇ **Definition 3.7.** Given a finite automaton $A = <\Sigma, S, s_0, \delta, F>$, define a new automaton $A^c = <\Sigma, S^c, s_0^c, \delta^c, F^c>$, called *A connected*, by

$$S^c = \{s \in S \mid \exists x \in \Sigma^* \ni \overline{\delta}(s_0, x) = s\}$$

$$s_0^c = s_0$$

$$F^c = F \cap S^c = \{f \in F \mid \exists x \in \Sigma^* \ni \overline{\delta}(s_0, x) = f\}$$

and δ^c is derived from the restriction of δ to $S^c \times \Sigma$:

$$(\forall a \in \Sigma)(\forall s \in S^c)(\delta^c(s, \mathbf{a}) = \delta(s, \mathbf{a}))$$

Δ

A^c is thus simply the machine A with the unreachable states "thrown away"; s_0 can be reached by $x = \lambda$, so it is a valid choice for the start state in A^c. F^c is simply the final states that can be reached from s_0, and δ^c is the collection of transitions that still come from (and consequently point to) states in the connected portion. Actually, δ^c was defined to be the transitions that merely come from states in S^c, with no mention of any restrictions on the range of δ^c. We must have, however, δ^c: $S^c \times \Sigma \to S^c$; in order for A^c to be well defined, δ^c must be shown to map into the proper range. It would not do to have a transition leading from a state in S^c to a state that is not in the new state set of A^c. The fact that δ^c does indeed have the desired properties is relegated to the exercises.

EXAMPLE 3.13

Let $M = <\{\mathbf{a}, \mathbf{b}\}, \{q_0, q_1, q_2, q_3\}, q_0, \delta, \{q_1, q_3\}>$, as illustrated in Figure 3.7a. By inspection, the only states that can be reached from the start state are q_0 and q_3.

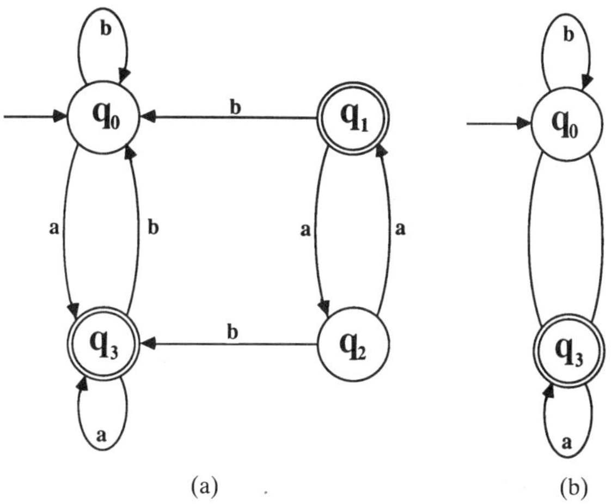

Figure 3.7 (a) The DFA M discussed in Example 3.13 (b) The DFA M^c discussed in Example 3.13

Hence $M^c = <\{\mathbf{a}, \mathbf{b}\}, \{q_0, q_3\}, q_0, \delta^c, \{q_3\}>$. The resulting automaton is shown in Figure 3.7b. An algorithm for effectively computing S^c will be presented later.

∇ **Theorem 3.2.** Given any finite automaton A, the new machine A^c is indeed connected.

Proof. This is an immediate consequence of the way S^c was defined.

Δ

Definition 3.7 and Theorem 3.2 would be of little consequence if it were not for the fact that A and A^c accept the same language. A^c is in fact equivalent to A, as proved in Theorem 3.3.

∇ **Theorem 3.3.** Given any finite automaton $A = <\Sigma, S, s_0, \delta, F>$, A and A^c are equivalent, that is, $L(A^c) = L(A)$.

Proof. Let $x \in \Sigma^*$. Then:

$$x \in L(A) \Leftrightarrow \text{(by definition of } L)$$
$$\exists s \in S \ni (\overline{\delta}(s_0, x) = s \wedge s \in F) \Leftrightarrow \text{(by definition of } S^c)$$
$$s \in S^c \wedge s \in F \Leftrightarrow \text{(by definition of } \cap)$$
$$s \in (S^c \cap F) \Leftrightarrow \text{(by definition of } F^c)$$
$$s \in F^c \Leftrightarrow \text{(by definition of s)}$$
$$\overline{\delta}(s_0, x) \in F^c \Leftrightarrow \text{(by definition of } \delta^c \text{ and induction)}$$
$$\overline{\delta}^c(s_0, x) \in F^c \Leftrightarrow \text{(by definition of } s_0^c)$$
$$\overline{\delta}^c(s_0^c, x) \in F^c \Leftrightarrow \text{(by definition of } L)$$
$$x \in L(A^c)$$

Δ

Thus, given any machine A, we can find an *equivalent* machine (that is, a machine that accepts the same language as A) that is connected. Furthermore, there is an algorithm that can be applied to find A^c (that is, we don't just know that such a machine exists, we actually have a method for calculating what it is). The definition of S^c implies that there is a *procedure* for finding S^c: one can begin enumerating the strings x in Σ^*, and by applying the transition function to each x, the new states that are reached can be included in S^c. This is not a very satisfactory process because there are an infinite number of strings in Σ^* to check. However, the indicated proof for Theorem 2.7 shows that, if a state can be reached by a "long" string, then it can be reached by a "short" string. Thus, we will only need to check the "short" strings. In particular,

$$S^c \equiv \bigcup_{x \in \Sigma^*} \bar{\delta}(s_0, x) = \bigcup_{x \in Q} \bar{\delta}(s_0, x)$$

where Q consists of the "short" strings: $Q = \{x \in \Sigma^* \mid |x| < \|S\|\}$. Thus, Q is the set of all strings of length less than the number of states in the DFA. Q is a finite set, and therefore we can check all strings x in Q in a finite amount of time; we therefore have an *algorithm* (that is, a procedure that is guaranteed to halt) for finding S^c, and consequently an algorithm for constructing A^c. Thus, given any machine, we can find an equivalent machine that is connected. The above method is not very efficient because many calculations are constantly repeated. A better algorithm based on Definition 3.10 will be presented later.

We now turn our attention to building a reduced machine from an arbitrary machine. The following definition gives a consistent way to combine the redundant states identified by the state equivalence relation E_A.

∇ **Definition 3.8.** Given a finite automaton $A = <\Sigma, S, s_0, \delta, F>$, define a new finite automaton A/E_A, called *A modulo its state equivalence relation*, by

$$A/E_A = <\Sigma, S_{E_A}, s_{0_{E_A}}, \delta_{E_A}, F_{E_A}>$$

where

$$S_{E_A} = \{[s]_{E_A} \mid s \in S\}$$

$$s_{0_{E_A}} = [s_0]_{E_A}$$

$$F_{E_A} = \{[s]_{E_A} \mid s \in F\}$$

and δ_{E_A} is defined by

$$(\forall \mathbf{a} \in \Sigma)(\forall [s] \in S_{E_A})(\delta_{E_A}([s]_{E_A}, \mathbf{a}) = [\delta(s, \mathbf{a})]_{E_A})$$

Δ

Thus, there is one state in A/E_A for each equivalence class in E_A, the new start state is the equivalence class containing s_0, and the final states are those equivalence classes that are made up of states from F. The transition function is also defined in a natural manner: Given an equivalence class $[t]_{E_A}$ and a letter $\mathbf{a}$, choose one state, say t, from the class and see what state the old transition specified ($\delta(t, \mathbf{a})$). The new transition function will choose the equivalence class containing this new state ($[\delta(t, \mathbf{a})]_{E_A}$). Once again, there may be several states in an equivalence class and thus several states from which to choose. We must make sure that the definition of δ_{E_A} does not depend on which state of $[t]_{E_A}$ we choose (that is, we must ascertain that δ_{E_A} is well defined.) Similarly, F_{E_A} should be shown to be well defined (see the exercises).

It stands to reason that if we coalesce all the states that performed the same function (that is, were related by E_A) into a single state the resulting machine should no longer have distinct states that perform the same function. We can indeed prove that this is the case, that is, that A/E_A is reduced.

∇ **Theorem 3.4.** Given a finite automaton $A = <\Sigma, S, s_0, \delta, F>$, A/E_A is reduced.

Proof. Note that the state equivalence relation for A/E_A is $E_{(A/E_A)}$, *not* E_A. We need to show that if two states of A/E_A are related by the state equivalence relation for A/E_A then those two states are identical; that is,

$$(\forall s, t \in S_{E_A})(s\, E_{(A/E_A)}\, t \Leftrightarrow s = t)$$

Assume $s, t \in S_{E_A}$. Then $\exists s', t' \in S \ni s = [s']_{E_A}$ and $t = [t']_{E_A}$; furthermore,

$$s\, E_{(A/E_A)}\, t \Leftrightarrow \text{(by definition of } s', t')$$
$$[s']_{E_A}\, E_{(A/E_A)}\, [t']_{E_A} \Leftrightarrow \text{(by definition of } E(_{A/E_A}))$$
$$(\forall x \in \Sigma^*)(\overline{\delta}_{E_A}([s'], x) \in F_{E_A} \Leftrightarrow \overline{\delta}_{E_A}([t'], x) \in F_{E_A}) \Leftrightarrow \text{(by } \delta_{E_A} \text{ and induction)}$$
$$(\forall x \in \Sigma^*)([\overline{\delta}(s', x)] \in F_{E_A} \Leftrightarrow [\overline{\delta}(t', x)] \in F_{E_A}) \Leftrightarrow \text{(by definition of } F_{E_A})$$
$$(\forall x \in \Sigma^*)(\overline{\delta}(s', x) \in F \Leftrightarrow \delta(t', x) \in F) \Leftrightarrow \text{(by definition of } E_A)$$
$$s'\, E_A\, t' \Leftrightarrow \text{(by definition of [ ])}$$
$$[s']_{E_A} = [t']_{E_A} \Leftrightarrow \text{(by definition of } s, t)$$
$$s = t$$

Δ

Since we ultimately want to first apply Definition 3.7 to find a connected DFA and then apply Definition 3.8 to reduce that DFA, we wish to show that this process of obtaining a reduced machine does not destroy connectedness. We can be assured that if Definition 3.8 is applied to a connected machine the result will then be both connected (Theorem 3.5) and reduced (Theorem 3.4).

∇ **Theorem 3.5.** If $A = <\Sigma, S, s_0, \delta, F>$ is connected, then A/E_A is connected.

Proof. We need to show that every state in A/E_A can be reached from the start state of A/E_A. Assume $s \in S_{E_A}$. Then $\exists s' \in S \ni s = [s']_{E_A}$; but A was connected, and so there exists an $x \in \Sigma^*$ such that $\overline{\delta}(s_0, x) = s'$; that is, there is a string that will take us from s_0 to s' in the original machine A. This same string will take us from $s_{0_{E_A}}$ to s in A/E_A since

$$\begin{aligned}\overline{\delta}(s_0, x) = s' &\Leftrightarrow (\text{by definition of } =)\\ [\overline{\delta}(s_0, x)]_{E_A} = [s']_{E_A} &\Leftrightarrow (\text{by definition of } \delta_{E_A} \text{ and induction})\\ \overline{\delta}_{E_A}([s_0]_{E_A}, x) = [s']_{E_A} &\Leftrightarrow (\text{by definition of } s_{0_{E_A}})\\ \overline{\delta}_{E_A}(s_{0_{E_A}}, x) = [s']_{E_A}&\end{aligned}$$

Therefore, every state $s \in S_{E_A}$ can be reached from the start state and A/E_A is thus connected.

Δ

Finally, we want to show that we do not change the language by reducing the machine. The following theorem proves that A/E_A and A are indeed equivalent.

∇ **Theorem 3.6.** Given a finite automaton $A = <\Sigma, S, s_0, \delta, F>$, then $L(A/E_A) = L(A)$.

Proof.

$$\begin{aligned}x \in L(A/E_A) &\Leftrightarrow (\text{by definition of } L)\\ \overline{\delta}_{E_A}(s_{0_{E_A}}, x) \in F_{E_A} &\Leftrightarrow (\text{by definition of } s_{0_{E_A}})\\ \overline{\delta}_{E_A}([s_0]_{E_A}, x) \in F_{E_A} &\Leftrightarrow (\text{by definition of } \delta_{E_A} \text{ and induction})\\ [\overline{\delta}(s_0, x)]_{E_A} \in F_{E_A} &\Leftrightarrow (\text{by definition of } F_{E_A})\\ \overline{\delta}(s_0, x) \in F &\Leftrightarrow (\text{by definition of } L)\\ x \in L(A)&\end{aligned}$$

Δ

∇ **Theorem 3.7.** Given a finite automaton definable language L and any finite automaton A that accepts L, then there exists an algorithm for constructing the *unique* (up to isomorphism) minimum-state finite automaton accepting L.

Proof. For the finite automaton A that accepts L, there is an algorithm for finding the set of connected states in A, and therefore there exists an algorithm for constructing A^c, which is a *connected* automaton with the property that $L(A^c) = L(A) = L$.

Furthermore, there exists an algorithm for computing E_{A^c}, the state equivalence relation on A^c; consequently, there is an algorithm for constructing A^c/E_{A^c}, which is a reduced, connected automaton with the property that $L(A^c/E_{A^c}) = L(A^c) = L(A) = L$.

From the main theorem on minimization (Theorem 3.1), we know that $A^c/E_{A^c} \cong A_{R_L}$, and A_{R_L} is the unique (up to isomorphism) minimum-state finite au-

tomaton accepting L. Consequently, the derived automaton A^c/E_{A^c} is likewise a minimum-state automaton.
Δ

The remainder of the chapter is devoted to developing the methods for computing S^c and E_A and justifying that the resulting algorithms are indeed correct.

Our formal definition of E_A requires that an infinite number of strings be checked before we can find the equivalence classes upon which A^c/E_{A^c} is based. If we could find an algorithm to generate E_A, we would then have an algorithm for building the minimal machine. This is the motivation for Definition 3.9.

∇ **Definition 3.9.** Given a finite automaton $A = <\Sigma, S, s_0, \delta, F>$ and an integer i, define the ith *partial state equivalence relation on A*, a relation between the states of A denoted by E_{iA}, by

$$(\forall s, t \in S)(sE_{iA}t \Leftrightarrow (\forall x \in \Sigma^* \ni |x| \leq i)(\overline{\delta}(s, x) \in F \Leftrightarrow \overline{\delta}(t, x) \in F))$$

Δ

Thus E_{iA} relates states that cannot be distinguished by strings of length i or less. Contrast this to the definition of E_A, which related states that could not be distinguished by any string of any length. E_{0A} denotes a relatively weak criterion that is progressively strengthened with successive E_{iA} relations. As illustrated by Example 3.14, these relations culminate in the relation we seek, E_A.

EXAMPLE 3.14

Let B be the DFA illustrated in Figure 3.8. Consider the relation E_{0B}. The empty string λ can differentiate between q_0 and the final states, but cannot differentiate between q_1, q_2, q_3, and q_4. Thus E_{0B} has two equivalence classes, $\{q_0\}$ and $\{q_1, q_2, q_3, q_4\}$.

In E_{1B}, λ still differentiates q_0 from the other states, but the string **1** can distinguish q_3 from q_1, q_2, and q_4 since $\overline{\delta}(q_3, \mathbf{1}) \notin F$, but $\overline{\delta}(q_i, \mathbf{1}) \in F$ for $i = 1$, 2, and 4. We still cannot distinguish between q_1, q_2, and q_4 with strings of length **0** or **1**, so these remain together and $E_{1B} = \{\{q_0\}, \{q_3\}, \{q_1, q_2, q_4\}\}$. Similarly, since $\overline{\delta}(q_1, \mathbf{11}) \in F$ but $\overline{\delta}(q_2, \mathbf{11}) \notin F$ and $\overline{\delta}(q_4, \mathbf{11}) \notin F$, $E_{2B} = \{\{q_0\}, \{q_3\}, \{q_1\}, \{q_2, q_4\}\}$. Further investigation shows $E_{2B} = E_{3B} = E_{4B} = E_{5B} = \cdots$, and indeed $E_B = E_{2B}$.

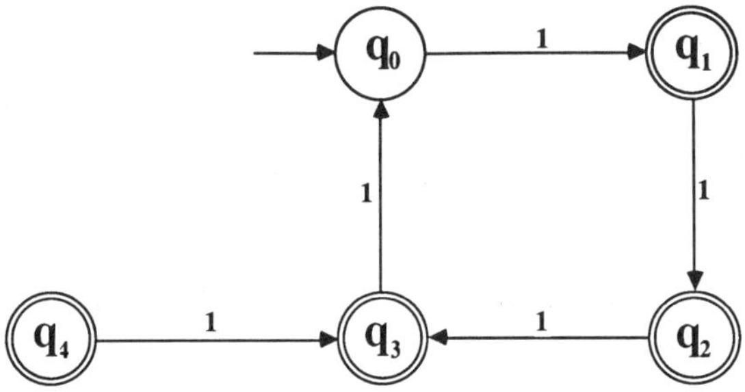

Figure 3.8 The DFA B discussed in Example 3.14

The ith state equivalence relation provides a convenient vehicle for computing E_A. The behavior exhibited by the relations in Example 3.14 follow a pattern that is similar for all deterministic finite automata. The following observations will culminate in a proof that the calculation of successive partial state equivalence relations is guaranteed to lead to the relation E_A.

Given an integer i and a finite alphabet Σ, there is clearly an *algorithm* for finding E_{iA} since there are only a finite number of strings in $\Sigma^0 \cup \Sigma^1 \cup \Sigma^2 \cup \cdots \cup \Sigma^i$. Furthermore, given every E_{iA}, there is an expression for E_A:

$$E_A = E_{0A} \cap E_{1A} \cap E_{2A} \cap E_{3A} \cap \cdots \cap E_{nA} \cap \cdots = \bigcap_{j=0}^{\infty} E_{jA}$$

The proof is relegated to the exercises and is related to the fact that

$$\Sigma^* = \Sigma^0 \cup \Sigma^1 \cup \Sigma^2 \cup \cdots \cup \Sigma^n \cup \cdots$$

Finally, it should be clear that if two states cannot be distinguished by strings of length 7 or less, they cannot be distinguished by strings of length 6 or less, which means E_{7A} is a refinement of E_{6A}. This principle generalizes, as formalized below.

∇ **Lemma 3.1.** Given a finite automaton $A = <\Sigma, S, s_0, \delta, F>$ and an integer m, E_{m+1A} is a refinement of E_{mA}, which means

$$(\forall s, t \in S)(s\, E_{m+1A}\, t \Rightarrow s\, E_{mA}\, t)$$

or

$$E_{m+1A} \subseteq E_{mA}$$

Proof. Scc the exercises.

Δ

Lemma 3.2 shows that each E_{mA} is related to the desired E_A. Lemma 3.1 thus shows that successive E_{mA} relations come closer to "looking like" E_A.

∇ **Lemma 3.2.** Given a finite automaton $A = <\Sigma, S, s_0, \delta, F>$ and an integer m, E_A is a refinement of E_{mA}, and so

$$(\forall s, t \in S)(s\, E_A\, t \Rightarrow s\, E_{mA}\, t)$$

That is,

$$E_A \subseteq E_{mA}$$

Proof. Let $s, t \in S$. Then

$$s\, E_A\, t \Rightarrow \text{(by definition of } E_A)$$
$$(\forall x \in \Sigma^*)(\overline{\delta}(s,x) \in F \Leftrightarrow \overline{\delta}(t,x) \in F) \Rightarrow \text{(true for all } x\text{, so it is true for all "short" } x)$$
$$(\forall x \in \Sigma^* \ni |x| \leq m)(\overline{\delta}(s,x) \in F \Leftrightarrow \overline{\delta}(t,x) \in F) \Rightarrow \text{(by definition of } E_{mA})$$
$$s\, E_{mA}\, t$$

Δ

While it is clearly possible to find a given E_{mA} by applying the definition to each of the strings in $\Sigma^0 \cup \Sigma^1 \cup \Sigma^2 \cup \cdots \cup \Sigma^m$, there is a much more efficient way if E_{m-1A} is already known, as outlined in Theorem 3.8. A starting point is provided by E_{0A}, which can be found very easily, as shown by Lemma 3.3. From E_{0A}, E_{1A} can then be found using Theorem 3.8, and then E_{2A}, and so on.

∇ **Lemma 3.3.** Given a finite automaton $A = <\Sigma, S, s_0, \delta, F>$, E_{0A} has two equivalence classes, F and S-F (unless either F or S-F is empty, in which case there is only one equivalence class, S).

Proof. The proof follows immediately from the definition of E_{0A}; the empty string λ differentiates between final and nonfinal states, producing the equivalence classes outlined above.

Δ

Given E_{0A} as a starting point, Theorem 3.8 shows how successive relations can be efficiently calculated.

∇ **Theorem 3.8.** Given a finite automaton $A = <\Sigma, S, s_0, \delta, F>$,

$$(\forall s \in S)(\forall t \in S)(\forall i \in \mathbb{N})(s\, E_{i+1A}\, t \Leftrightarrow s\, E_{iA}\, t \wedge (\forall \mathbf{a} \in \Sigma)(\delta(s, \mathbf{a})\, E_{iA}\, \delta(t, \mathbf{a})))$$

Proof. Let $s \in S$, $t \in S$. Then

$$\begin{aligned}
s\, E_{i+1A}\, t &\Leftrightarrow (\forall x \in \Sigma^* \ni |x| \le i+1)(\overline{\delta}(s, x) \in F \Leftrightarrow \overline{\delta}(t, x) \in F) \\
&\Leftrightarrow (\forall x \in \Sigma^* \ni |x| \le i)[\overline{\delta}(s, x) \in F \Leftrightarrow \overline{\delta}(t, x) \in F] \wedge \\
&\qquad (\forall y \in \Sigma^* \ni |y| = i+1)[\overline{\delta}(s, y) \in F \Leftrightarrow \overline{\delta}(t, y) \in F] \\
&\Leftrightarrow (\forall x \in \Sigma^* \ni |x| \le i)[\overline{\delta}(s, x) \in F \Leftrightarrow \overline{\delta}(t, x) \in F] \wedge \\
&\qquad (\forall y \in \Sigma^* \ni 1 \le |y| \le i+1)[\overline{\delta}(s, y) \in F \Leftrightarrow \overline{\delta}(t, y) \in F] \\
&\Leftrightarrow (\forall x \in \Sigma^* \ni |x| \le i)[\overline{\delta}(s, x) \in F \Leftrightarrow \overline{\delta}(t, x) \in F] \wedge \\
&\qquad (\forall \mathbf{a} \in \Sigma)(\forall x \in \Sigma^* \ni |x| \le i)[\overline{\delta}(s, \mathbf{a}x) \in F \Leftrightarrow \overline{\delta}(t, \mathbf{a}x) \in F] \\
&\Leftrightarrow s\, E_{iA}\, t \wedge \\
&\qquad (\forall \mathbf{a} \in \Sigma)(\forall x \in \Sigma^* \ni |x| \le i)(\overline{\delta}(s, \mathbf{a}x) \in F \Leftrightarrow \overline{\delta}(t, \mathbf{a}x) \in F) \\
&\Leftrightarrow s\, E_{iA}\, t \wedge \\
&\qquad (\forall \mathbf{a} \in \Sigma)(\forall x \in \Sigma^* \ni |x| \le i)(\overline{\delta}(\delta(s, \mathbf{a}), x) \in F \Leftrightarrow \overline{\delta}(\delta(t, \mathbf{a}), x) \in F) \\
&\Leftrightarrow s\, E_{iA}\, t \wedge (\forall \mathbf{a} \in \Sigma)(\delta(s, \mathbf{a})\, E_{iA}\, \delta(t, \mathbf{a}))
\end{aligned}$$

Δ

Note that Theorem 3.8 gives a far superior method for determining successive E_{jA} relations. The definition required the examination of many (long) *strings* using the $\overline{\delta}$ function; Theorem 3.8 allows us to simply check a few *letters* using the δ function. Theorems 3.9, 3.10, and 3.11 will assure us that E_A will eventually be found. The following theorem guarantees that the relations, should they ever begin to look alike, will continue to look alike as successive relations are computed.

∇ **Theorem 3.9.** Given a finite automaton $A = <\Sigma, S, s_0, \delta, F>$,

$$(\exists m \in \mathbb{N} \ni E_{mA} = E_{m+1A}) \Rightarrow (\forall k \in \mathbb{N})(E_{m+kA} = E_{mA})$$

Proof. By induction on k; see the exercises.

Δ

The result in Theorem 3.9 is essential to the proof of the next theorem, which guarantees that when successive relations look alike they are identical to E_A.

∇ **Theorem 3.10.** Given a finite automaton $A = <\Sigma, S, s_0, \delta, F>$,

$$(\exists m \in \mathbb{N} \ni E_{mA} = E_{m+1A}) \Rightarrow E_{mA} = E_A$$

Proof. Assume $\exists m \in \mathbb{N} \ni E_{mA} = E_{m+1A}$ and let $q, r \in S$:

1. By Lemma 3.2, $q\, E_A\, r \Rightarrow q\, E_{mA}\, r$.
2. Conversely, assume $q\, E_{mA}\, r$. Then

$$q\, E_{mA}\, r \Rightarrow \text{(by assumption)}$$
$$q\, E_{m+1A}\, r \Rightarrow \text{(by Theorem 3.9)}$$
$$(\forall j \geq m)(q\, E_{jA}\, r)$$

Furthermore, by Lemma 3.1, $(\forall j \leq m)(q\, E_{jA}\, r)$, and so $(\forall j \in \mathbb{N})(q\, E_{jA}\, r)$; but by definition or E_A, this implies $q\, E_A\, r$. We have just shown that $q\, E_{mA}\, r \Rightarrow q\, E_A\, r$.

3. Combining (1) and (2), we have $(\forall q, r \in S)(q\, E_{mA}\, r \Leftrightarrow q\, E_A\, r)$, and so $E_{mA} = E_A$.

Δ

The next theorem guarantees that these relations *will* eventually look alike (and so by Theorem 3.10, we are assured that successive computations of E_{iA} will yield an expression representing the relation E_A).

∇ **Theorem 3.11.** Given a finite automaton $A = <\Sigma, S, s_0, \delta, F>$,

$$(\exists m \in \mathbb{N} \ni m \leq \|S\| \wedge E_{mA} = E_{m+1A}).$$

Proof. Assume the conclusion is false; that is, that $E_{0A}, E_{1A}, \ldots, E_{\|S\|A}$ are all distinct. Since $E_{\|S\|A} \subseteq \cdots \subseteq E_{1A} \subseteq E_{0A}$, the only way for two successive relations to be different is for the number of equivalence classes to increase. Thus,

$$0 < rk(E_{0A}) < rk(E_{1A}) < rk(E_{2A}) < \cdots < rk(E_{\|S\|A}),$$

which means that $rk(E_{\|S\|A}) > \|S\|$, which is a contradiction (why?). Therefore,

not all these relations can be distinct, and so there is some index m for which $E_{mA} = E_{m+1A}$.
Δ

∇ **Corollary 3.5.** Given a DFA $A = <\Sigma, S, s_0, \delta, F>$, there is an *algorithm* for computing E_A.

Proof. E_A can be found by using Lemma 3.2 to find E_{0A}, and computing successive E_{iA} relations using Theorem 3.8 until $E_{iA} = E_{i+1A}$; this E_{iA} will equal E_A, and this will all happen before i reaches $\|S\|$, the number of states in S. The procedure is therefore guaranteed to halt.
Δ

Since E_A was the key to producing a reduced machine, we now have an algorithm for taking a DFA and finding an equivalent DFA that is reduced. The other necessary step needed to find the minimal machine was to produce a connected DFA from a given automaton. This construction hinged on the calculation of S^c, the set of connected states.

The algorithm suggested by the definition of S^c is by no means the most efficient; it involves checking long strings with the $\bar{\delta}$ function and hence massive duplication of effort. Furthermore, the definition seems to imply that all the strings in Σ^* must be checked, which certainly cannot be completed if it is done one string at a time. Theorem 2.7 can be used to justify that it is unnecessary to check any strings longer than $\|S\|$ (see the exercises). Thus $S^c = \{\bar{\delta}(s_0, x) \mid |x| < \|S\|\}$. While this set, being based on a finite number of words, justifies that there is an algorithm for finding S^c (and hence there exists an algorithm for constructing A^c), it is still a very inefficient way to calculate the set of accessible states.

As with the calculation of E_A, there is a way to avoid using $\bar{\delta}$ to process long strings when computing S^c. In this case, a better strategy is to begin with s_0 and find all the new states that can be reached from s_0 with just one transition. Note that this can be done by simply examining the row of the state transition table corresponding to s_0, and hence the computation can be accomplished quite fast. Each of these new states should then be examined in the same fashion to see if they lead to still more states, and this process can continue until all connected states are found. A sequence of state sets is thereby constructed, in a similar manner to the way successive partial state equivalence relations E_{iA} were built. This approach is reflected in Definition 3.10.

∇ **Definition 3.10.** Given a finite automaton $A = <\Sigma, S, s_0, \delta, F>$, the ith *partial state set* C_i is defined by the following rules: Let $C_0 = \{s_0\}$ and recursively define

$$C_{i+1} = C_i \cup \bigcup_{q \in C_i, \mathbf{a} \in \Sigma} \delta(q, \mathbf{a}).$$

Δ

$C_{\|S\|}$ must equal S^c (why?), and we will often arrive at the final answer long before $\|S\|$ iterations have been calculated (see the exercises and refer to the treatment of E_{iA}). It can also be proved (by induction) that C_i represents the set of all states that can be reached from s_0 by strings of length i or less (see the exercises).

Recall that the definition of S^c involved the extended state transition function $\overline{\delta}$. Definition 3.10 instead uses the information found in the previous iteration to avoid calculating paths for long strings. As suggested earlier, there is an even more efficient method of calculating C_{i+1} from C_i, since only paths from the newly added states need be explored anew.

EXAMPLE 3.15

Consider the DFA D given in Figure 3.9.

$$C_0 = \{s_0\}$$

and since $\delta(s_0, \mathbf{a}) = s_1$ and $\delta(s_0, \mathbf{b}) = s_3$,

$$C_1 = \{s_0, s_1, s_3\}$$

Note that there is no need to check s_0 again, but s_1 and s_3 generate

$$C_2 = \{s_0, s_1, s_3, s_2, s_4\}$$

Checking these two new states generates one more state, so

$$C_3 = \{s_0, s_1, s_3, s_2, s_4, s_5\}$$

and since s_5 leads to no new states, we have $C_4 = C_3$; as with E_{iA}, we will now find $C_3 = C_4 = C_5 = C_6 = \cdots = S^c$. The exercises will develop the parallels between the generation of the partial state sets C_i and the generation of the partial state equivalence relations E_{iA}.

The procedure for recursively calculating successive C_is to determine S^c pro-

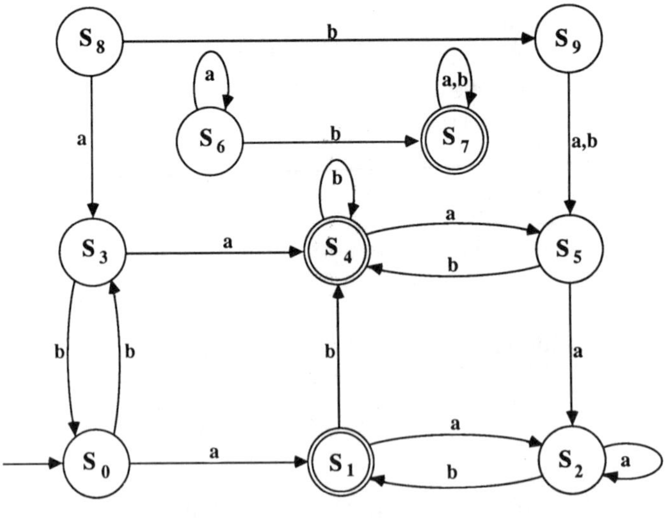

Figure 3.9 The DFA D discussed in Example 3.15

vides the final algorithm needed to efficiently find the minimal machine corresponding to a given automaton A. From A, we use the C_is to calculate S^c and thereby define A^c. Theorems 3.8 and related results suggest an efficient algorithm for computing E_{A^c}, from which we can construct A^c/E_{A^c}. A^c/E_{A^c} is indeed the minimal machine equivalent to A, as shown by the results in this chapter. Theorems 3.3 and 3.6 show that A^c/E_{A^c} is equivalent to A. By Theorems 3.2, 3.4, and 3.5, this automaton is reduced and connected, and Corollary 3.4 guarantees that A^c/E_{A^c} must therefore be minimal.

The proof of Theorem 3.7 suggests building a minimal equivalent determinstic finite automaton for A by first shrinking to a connected machine and then reducing modulo the state equivalence relation, that is, by finding A^c/E_{A^c}. Theorem 3.5 assures us that when we reduce a connected machine it will still be connected. An alternate strategy would be to first reduce modulo E_A and then shrink to a connected machine, that is, to find $(A/E_A)^c$. In this case, we would want to make sure that connecting a reduced machine will still leave us with a reduced machine. It can be shown that if A is reduced then A^c is reduced (see the exercises), and hence this method could also be used to find the minimal equivalent DFA.

Finding the minimal equivalent DFA by reducing A first and then eliminating the disconnected states is, however, less efficient than applying the algorithms in the opposite order. Finding the connected set of states is simpler than finding the state equivalence relation, so it is best to eliminate as many states as possible by finding S^c before embarking on the more complex search for the state equivalence relation.

It should be clear that the algorithms in this chapter are presented in sufficient detail to easily allow them to be programmed. As suggested in Chapter 1, the final states can be represented as a set and the transition function as a matrix. The minimization procedures would then return the minimized matrix and new final state set.

As a practical matter then, when generating an automaton to perform a given task, our concern can be limited to defining a machine that *works*. No further creative insight is then necessary to find the minimal machine. Once a machine that recognizes the desired language is found (however inefficient it may be), the minimization algorithms can then be applied to produce a machine that is both correct and efficient.

The proof that a reduced and connected machine is the most efficient was based on the properties of the automaton A_{R_L} obtained from the right congruence R_L. This can be proved without relying on the existence of A_{R_L}. We close this chapter with an outline of such a proof. The details are similar to the proofs given in Chapter 7 for finite-state transducers.

Theorem 3.3, which was not based in any way on R_L, implies that a minimal DFA must be connected. Similarly, an immediate corollary of Theorem 3.6 is that a minimal DFA must be reduced. Thus, a minimal machine is forced to be both reduced and connected. We now must justify that a reduced and connected machine is minimal. This result will follow from Corollary 3.3, which can also be proved without relying on A_{R_L}. The implication ($A \cong B \Rightarrow$ A is equivalent to B) is due solely to the properties of isomorphisms and is actually true irrespective of any other hypotheses (see the exercises). Conversely, if A is equivalent to B, then the fact that A and B are both reduced and connected allows an isomorphism to be defined from A to B (see the exercises).

Corollary 3.3 allows us to argue that any reduced and connected automaton A is isomorphic to a minimal automaton M, and hence A has as few states as M and is minimal. The argument would proceed as follows: Since M is minimal, we already know that Theorems 3.3 and 3.6 imply that M is reduced and connected. Thus, M and A are two reduced and connected equivalent automata, and Corollary 3.3 ensures that $A \cong M$. Thus, minimal machines are exactly those that are reduced and connected.

EXERCISES

3.1. Use induction to show $(\forall s \in S)(\forall x \in \Sigma^*)(\mu(\bar{\delta}(s,x)) = \bar{\delta}_{R_L}(\mu(s),x))$ for the mapping μ defined in Theorem 3.1. Do not appeal to the results of (5) in the proof of Theorem 3.1.

3.2. Consider the state transition function given in Definition 3.8 and use induction to show

$$(\forall x \in \Sigma^*)(\forall [s]_{E_A} \in S_{E_A})(\bar{\delta}_{E_A}([s]_{E_A}, x) = [\bar{\delta}(s,x)]_{E_A})$$

3.3. Prove that

$$E_A = E_{0A} \cap E_{1A} \cap E_{2A} \cap E_{3A} \cap \cdots \cap E_{nA} \cap \cdots = \bigcap_{j=0}^{\infty} E_{jA}$$

3.4. Given a finite automaton $A = \langle \Sigma, S, s_0, \delta, F \rangle$, show that the function δ_{E_A} given in Definition 3.8 is well defined.

3.5. Given a finite automaton $A = \langle \Sigma, S, s_0, \delta, F \rangle$, show that the set F_{E_A} given in Definition 3.8 is a well-defined set.

3.6. Show that the range of the function δ^c given in Definition 3.7 is contained in S^c.

3.7. Prove Lemma 3.1.

3.8. Prove Lemma 3.3.

3.9. Prove Theorem 3.9.

3.10. Given a homomorphism μ from the finite automaton $A = \langle \Sigma, S_A, s_{0_A}, \delta_A, F_A \rangle$ to the DFA $B = \langle \Sigma, S_B, s_{0_B}, \delta_B, F_B \rangle$, prove by induction that

$$(\forall s \in S_A)(\forall x \in \Sigma^*)(\mu(\bar{\delta}_A(s,x)) = \bar{\delta}_B(\mu(s),x))$$

3.11. Given a homomorphism μ from the finite automaton $A = \langle \Sigma, S_A, s_{0_A}, \delta_A, F_A \rangle$ to the DFA $B = \langle \Sigma, S_B, s_{0_B}, \delta_B, F_B \rangle$, prove that $L(A) = L(B)$. As long as it is explicitly cited, the result of Exercise 3.10 may be used without proof.

3.12. **(a)** Give an example of a DFA for which A is *not* connected and A/E_A is not connected.
(b) Give an example of a DFA for which A is *not* connected but A/E_A *is* connected.

3.13. Given a finite automaton $A = \langle \Sigma, S, s_0, \delta, F \rangle$ and the state equivalence relation E_A, show there exists a homomorphism from A to A/E_A.

3.14. Given a *connected* finite automaton $A = \langle \Sigma, S, s_0, \delta, F \rangle$, show there exists a homomorphism from A to $A_{R_{L(A)}}$ by:
(a) Define a mapping ψ from A to $A_{R_{L(A)}}$. (No justification need be given.)
(b) Prove that your ψ is well defined.
(c) Prove that ψ is a homomorphism.

3.15. Give an example to show that there may not exist a homomorphism from A to $A_{R_{L(A)}}$ if A is not connected (see Exercise 3.14).

3.16. Give an example to show that there may still exist a homomorphism from A to $A_{R_{L(A)}}$ even if A is not connected (see Exercise 3.14).

3.17. Give an example to show that, for the relations R and R_L given in Theorem 2.2, there need not exist a homomorphism from A_{R_L} to A_R.

3.18. $\cong$ is an equivalence relation; in Chapter 2 we saw some relations were also right congruences. Comment on the appropriateness of asking whether $\cong$ is a right congruence.

3.19. Is E_A a right congruence? Explain your answer.

3.20. Prove that if A is reduced then A^c is reduced.

3.21. For a homomorphism μ between two finite automata $A = <\Sigma, S_A, s_{0_A}, \delta_A, F_A>$ and $B = <\Sigma, S_B, s_{0_B}, \delta_B, F_B>$, prove $(\forall s, t \in S_A)(\mu(s)\, E_B\, \mu(t) \Leftrightarrow s\, E_A\, t)$.

3.22. Let M be a DFA, and let $L = L(M)$.
- **(a)** Define a mapping ψ from M^c to $A_{(R^M)}$. (No justification need be given.)
- **(b)** Prove that your ψ is well defined.
- **(c)** Prove that ψ is a homomorphism.
- **(d)** Prove that ψ is a bijection.
- **(e)** Argue that $M^c \cong A_{(R^M)}$.

3.23. For the machine A given in Figure 3.10a, find:
- **(a)** E_A (list each E_{iA})
- **(b)** $L(A)$
- **(c)** $A_{R_{L(A)}}$
- **(d)** $R_{L(A)}$
- **(e)** A/E_A

3.24. For the machine B given in Figure 3.10b, find:
- **(a)** E_B (list each E_{iB})
- **(b)** $L(B)$
- **(c)** $A_{R_{L(B)}}$
- **(d)** $R_{L(B)}$
- **(e)** B/E_B

Note that your answer to part (e) might contain some disconnected states.

3.25. For the machine C given in Figure 3.10c, find:
- **(a)** E_C (list each E_{iC})
- **(b)** $L(C)$
- **(c)** $A_{R_{L(C)}}$
- **(d)** $R_{L(C)}$
- **(e)** C/E_C

Note that your answer to part (e) might contain some disconnected states.

3.26. For the machine D given in Figure 3.10d, find:
- **(a)** E (list each E_i D)
- **(b)** $L(D)$
- **(c)** $A_{R_{L(D)}}$
- **(d)** $R_{L(D)}$
- **(e)** D/E_D

Note that your answer to part (e) might contain some disconnected states.

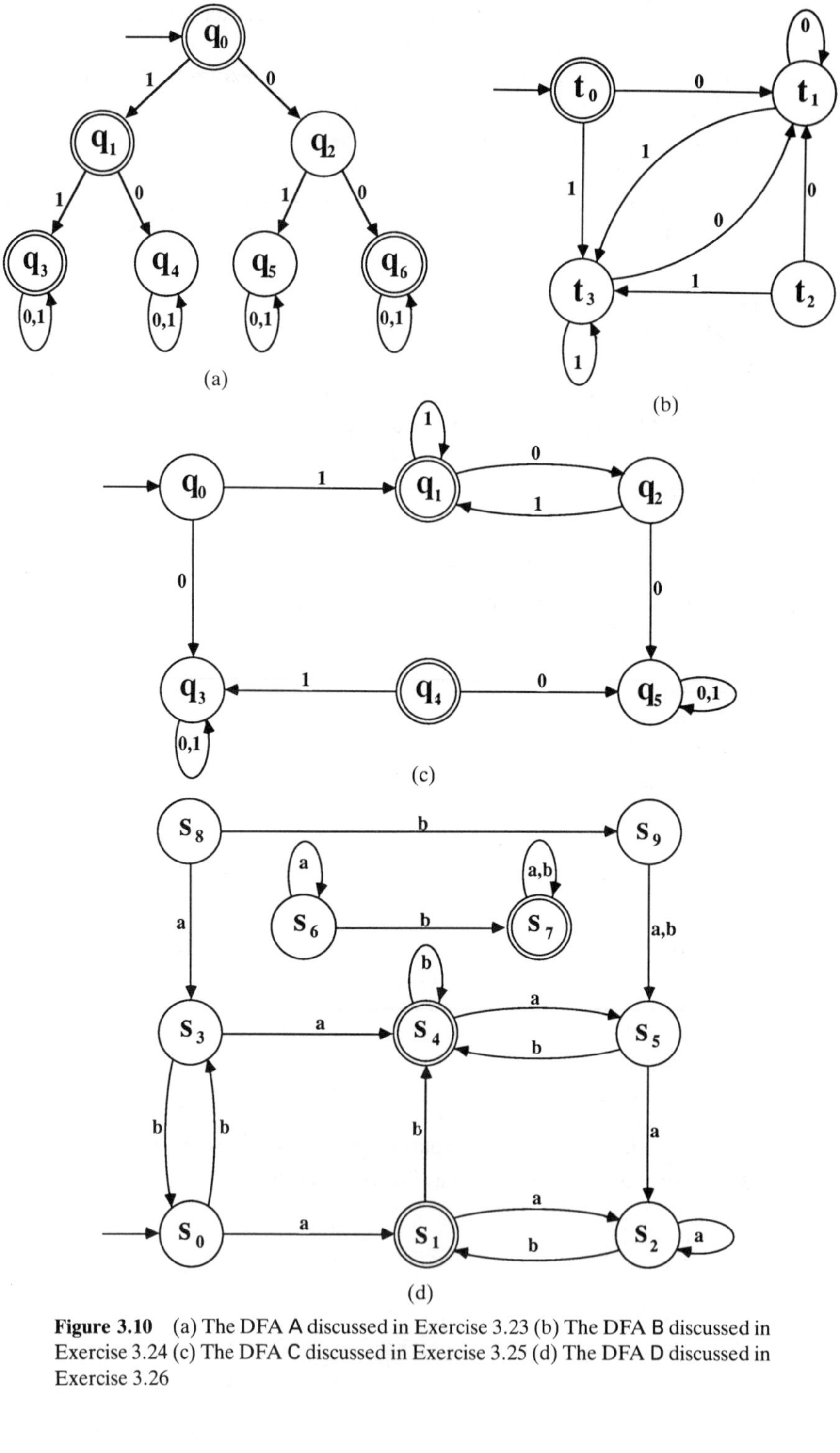

Figure 3.10 (a) The DFA A discussed in Exercise 3.23 (b) The DFA B discussed in Exercise 3.24 (c) The DFA C discussed in Exercise 3.25 (d) The DFA D discussed in Exercise 3.26

3.27. Without relying on A_{R_L}, prove that if A and B are both reduced and connected equivalent DFAs then $A \cong B$. Give the details for the following steps:

(a) Define an appropriate function ψ between the states of A and the states of B.

(b) Show that ψ is well defined.

(c) Show that ψ is a homomorphism.

(d) Show that ψ is a bijection.

3.28. In the proof of (6) in Theorem 3.1, one transition only involved $\Rightarrow$ rather than $\Leftrightarrow$. Show by means of an example that the two expressions involved in this transition are not equivalent.

3.29. Supply reasons for each of the equivalences in the proof of Theorem 3.8.

3.30. Minimize the machine defined in Figure 3.3.

3.31. **(a)** Give an example of a DFA for which A is *not* reduced and A^c is not reduced.

(b) Give an example of a DFA for which A is *not* reduced and A^c *is* reduced.

3.32. Note that $\cong$ relates some automata to other automata, and therefore $\cong$ is a relation over the set of all deterministic finite automata.

(a) For automata A, B, and C, show that if g is an isomorphism from A to B and f is an isomorphism from B to C, then $f \circ g$ is an isomorphism from A to C.

(b) Prove that $\cong$ is a symmetric relation; that is, formally justify that if there is an isomorphism from A to B then there is an isomorphism from B to A.

(c) Prove that $\cong$ is a reflexive relation.

(d) From the results in parts (a), (b), and (c), prove that $\cong$ is an equivalence relation over the set of all deterministic finite automata.

3.33. Show that homomorphism is *not* an equivalence relation over the set of all deterministic finite automata.

3.34. For the relations R and R_L given in Theorem 2.2, show that there exists a homomorphism from A_R to A_{R_L}.

3.35. Prove that if there is a homomorphism from A to B then R^A refines R^B.

3.36. Prove that if A is isomorphic to B then $R^A = R^B$

(a) By appealing to Exercise 3.35.

(b) Without appealing to Exercise 3.35.

3.37. Consider two deterministic finite automata for which A is not homomorphic to B, but $R^A = R^B$.

(a) Give an example of such automata for which $L(A) = L(B)$.

(b) Give an example of such automata for which $L(A) \neq L(B)$.

(c) Can such examples be found if both A and B are connected and $L(A) = L(B)$?

(d) Can such examples be found if both A and B are reduced and $L(A) = L(B)$?

3.38. Disprove that if A is homomorphic to B then $R^A = R^B$.

3.39. Prove or give a counterexample [assume $L = L(M)$].

(a) For any DFA M, there exists a homomorphism ψ from $A_{(R^M)}$ to M.

(b) For any DFA M, there exists an isomorphism ψ from $A_{(R^M)}$ to M.

(c) For any DFA M, there exists a homomorphism ψ from M to $A_{(R^M)}$.

3.40. Prove that if A is a minimal DFA then $R^A = R_{L(A)}$.

3.41. Give an example to show that Exercise 3.40 can be false if A is not minimal.

3.42. Give an example to show that Exercise 3.40 may still hold if A is not minimal.

3.43. Definition 3.8 takes an equivalence relation of the set of states S and defines a machine based on that relation. In general, we could choose a relation R in S and define a machine $A/_R$ (as we did when we defined $A/_{E_A}$ when the relation R was E_A).

(a) Consider $R = E_{0A}$. Is $A/_{E_{0A}}$ always well defined? Give an example to illustrate your answer.

(b) Assume R is a refinement of E_A. Is $A/_R$ always well defined? For the cases where it is well defined, consider the theorems that would correspond to Theorems 3.4, 3.5, and 3.6 if E_A were replaced by such a refinement R. Which of these theorems would still be true?

3.44. Given a DFA M, prove or give a counterexample.

(a) There exists a homomorphism from $M/_{E_M}$ to $A_{R_{L(M)}}$.

(b) There exists a homomorphism from $A_{R_{L(M)}}$ to $M/_{E_M}$.

3.45. Prove that the bound given for Theorem 3.11 can be sharpened: given a finite automaton $A = \langle \Sigma, S, s_0, \delta, F \rangle, (\exists m \in \mathbb{N} \ni m < \|S\| \wedge E_{mA} = E_{m+1A})$.

3.46. Prove or give a counterexample:

(a) If A and B are equivalent, then A and B are isomorphic.

(b) If A and B are isomorphic, then A and B are equivalent.

3.47. Given a finite automaton $A = \langle \Sigma, S, s_0, \delta, F \rangle$, prove that the C_is given in Definition 3.10 are nested: $(\forall i \in \mathbb{N})(C_i \subseteq C_{i+1})$.

3.48. Prove (by induction) that C_i does indeed represent the set of all states that can be reached from s_0 by strings of length i or less.

3.49. Prove that, given a finite automaton $A = \langle \Sigma, S, s_0, \delta, F \rangle$,

$$(\exists i \in \mathbb{N} \ni C_i = C_{i+1}) \Rightarrow (\forall k \in \mathbb{N})(C_i = C_{i+k}).$$

3.50. Prove that, given a DFA $A = \langle \Sigma, S, s_0, \delta, F \rangle$, $(\exists i \in \mathbb{N} \ni C_i = C_{i+1}) \Rightarrow (C_i = S^c)$.

3.51. Prove that, given a finite automaton $A = \langle \Sigma, S, s_0, \delta, F \rangle$, $\exists i \in \mathbb{N} \ni C_i = C_{i+1}$.

3.52. Prove that, given a DFA $A = \langle \Sigma, S, s_0, \delta, F \rangle$, $(\exists i \in \mathbb{N} \ni i \le \|S\| \wedge C_i = S^c)$.

3.53. Use the results of Exercises 3.47 through 3.52 to argue that the procedure for generating S^c from successive calculations of C_i is correct and is actually an algorithm.

3.54. Give an example of two DFAs A and B that simultaneously satisfy the following three criteria:

1. There is a homomorphism from A to B.
2. There is a homomorphism from B to A.
3. There does not exist any isomorphism between A and B.

3.55. Assume R and Q are both right congruences of finite rank, R refines Q, and L is a union of equivalence classes of Q.

(a) Show that L is also a union of equivalence classes of R.

(b) Show that there exists a homomorphism from A_R to A_Q. (*Hint:* Do *not* use the μ given in Theorem 3.1; there is a far more straightforward way to define a mapping.)

(c) Give an example to show that there need not be a homomorphism from A_Q to A_R.

3.56. Prove that A_Q must be connected.

3.57. Prove that if there is an isomorphism from A to B and A is connected then B must also be connected.

3.58. Prove that if there is an isomorphism from A to B and B is connected then A must also be connected.

3.59. Disprove that if there is a homomorphism from A to B and A is connected then B must also be connected.

3.60. Disprove that if there is a homomorphism from A to B and B is connected then A must also be connected.

3.61. Given a DFA A, recall the relation R^A on Σ^* induced by A. This relation gives rise to another DFA $A_{(R^A)}$ [with $Q = R^A$ and $L = L(A)$]. Consider also the connected version of A, A^c.

(a) Define an isomorphism ψ from $A_{(R^A)}$ to A^c. (No justification need be given.)
(b) Prove that your ψ is well defined.
(c) Prove that ψ is a homomorphism.
(d) Prove that ψ is an isomorphism.

3.62. Assume that A and B are connected DFAs. Assume that there exists an isomorphism ψ from A to B and an isomorphism μ from B to A. Prove that $\psi = \mu^{-1}$.

3.63. Assume that A and B are DFAs. Assume that there exists an isomorphism ψ from A to B and an isomorphism μ from B to A. Give an example for which $\psi \neq \mu^{-1}$.

3.64. Give an example of a three-state DFA for which E_{0A} has only one equivalence class. Is it possible for E_{0A} to be different from E_{1A} in such a machine? Explain.

3.65. Assume A and B are both reduced and connected. If ψ is a homomorphism from A to B, does ψ have to be an isomorphism? Justify your conclusions.

3.66. Prove Corollary 3.2.

3.67. Prove that $S^c = \{\bar{\delta}(s_0, x) \mid |x| \le \|S\|\}$.

3.68. Given a finite automaton $A = <\Sigma, S, s_0, \delta, F>$, two states $s, t \in S$, and the automata $A^t = <\Sigma, S, t, \delta, F>$ and $A^s = <\Sigma, S, s, \delta, F>$, prove that $s\, E_A\, t \Leftrightarrow L(A^s) = L(A^t)$.

3.69. Given a finite automaton $A = <\Sigma, S, s_0, \delta, F>$, consider the terminal sets $T(A, t) = \{x \mid \bar{\delta}(t, x) \in F\}$ and initial sets $I(A, t) = \{x \mid \bar{\delta}(s_0, x) = t\}$ for each $t \in S$.

(a) Prove that the initial sets of A must form a partition of Σ^*.
(b) Give an example to show that the terminal sets of A might not partition Σ^*.
(c) Give an example to show that the terminal sets of A might partition Σ^*.

CHAPTER

4

NONDETERMINISTIC FINITE AUTOMATA

A nondeterministic finite automaton, abbreviated NDFA, is a generalization of the deterministic machines that we have studied in previous chapters. Although nondeterministic machines lack some of the restrictions imposed on their deterministic cousins, the class of languages recognized by nondeterministic finite automata is exactly the same as the class of languages recognized by deterministic finite automata. In this sense, the recognition power of nondeterministic finite automata is equivalent to that of deterministic finite automata.

In this chapter we will show the correspondence of nondeterministic finite automata to deterministic finite automata, and we will prove that both types of machines accept the same class of languages. In a later section, we will again generalize our computational model to allow nondeterministic finite automata that make transitions spontaneously, without an input symbol being processed. It will be shown that the class of languages recognized by these new machines is exactly the same as the class of languages recognized by our first type of nondeterministic finite automata and is thus the same as the class of languages recognized by deterministic finite automata.

4.1 DEFINITIONS AND BASIC THEOREMS

Whereas deterministic finite automata are restricted to having exactly one transition from a state for each $\mathbf{a} \in \Sigma$, a nondeterministic finite automaton may have any number of transitions for a given input symbol, including zero transitions.

When processing an input string, if an NDFA comes to a state from which there is no transition arc labeled with the next input symbol, the path through the machine which is being followed is terminated. Termination can take the place of the "garbage state" (a permanent rejection state) found in many deterministic finite automata, which is used to reject some strings that are not in the language recognized by the automaton (the state s_7 played this role in Examples 1.11 and 1.9).

EXAMPLE 4.1

Let $L = \{w \in \{\mathbf{a}, \mathbf{b}, \mathbf{c}\}^* \mid \exists y \in \{\mathbf{b}\}^* \ni w = \mathbf{a}y\mathbf{c}\}$. We can easily build a nondeterministic finite automaton that accepts this set of words. One such automaton is displayed in Figure 4.1. In this example there are no transitions out of s_0 labeled with either **b** or **c**, nor are there any transitions from s_1 labeled with **a**. From state s_2 there are no transitions at all. This means that if either **b** or **c** is encountered in state s_0 or **a** is encountered in state s_1, or any input letter is encountered once we reach state s_2, the word on the input tape will not be able to follow this particular path through the machine. Thus, if a word is not fully processed by the NDFA, it will not be considered accepted (even if the state in which it was prematurely "stuck" was a final state).

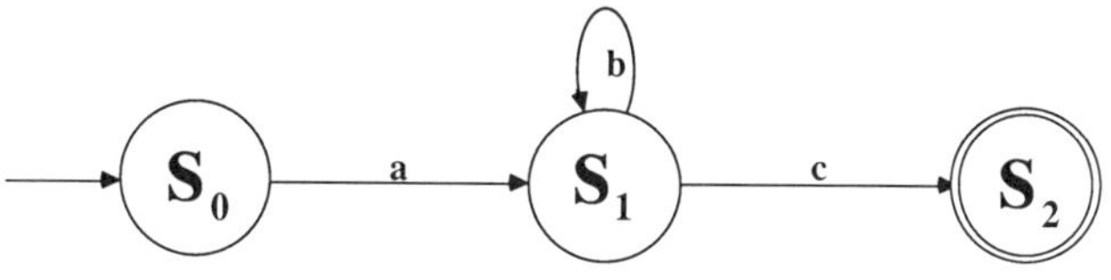

Figure 4.1 The NDFA described in Example 4.1

An equivalent, although more complicated, deterministic finite automaton is given in Figure 4.2. Note that this deterministic finite automaton requires the introduction of an extra state, a *dead state* or *garbage state*, to continue the processing of strings that are not in the language.

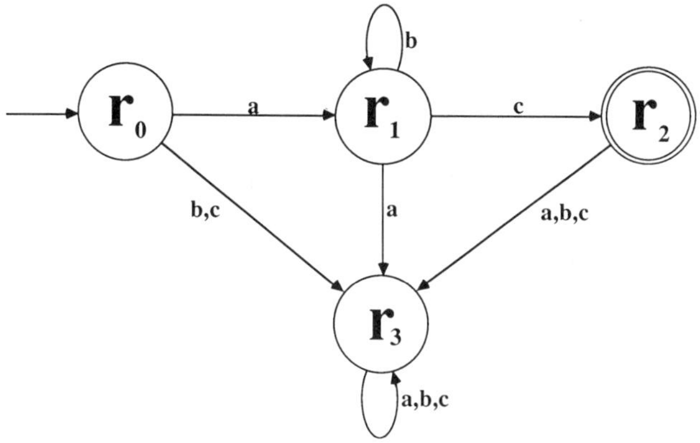

Figure 4.2 A deterministic version of the NDFA in Example 4.1

A nondeterministic finite automaton may also have *multiple* transitions from any state for a given input symbol. For example, consider the following construction of a nondeterministic acceptor for the language L, which consists of all even-length strings along with all strings whose number of **1**s is a multiple of 3. That is, $L = \{x \in \{\mathbf{0}, \mathbf{1}\}^* \mid |x| \equiv 0 \bmod 2 \vee |x|_{\mathbf{1}} \equiv 0 \bmod 3\}$.

EXAMPLE 4.2

In the NDFA given in Figure 4.3, there are multiple transitions from state s_0: processing the symbol **0** causes the machine to enter states s_1 and s_2, whereas processing a **1** causes the machine to enter both state s_3 and state s_2.

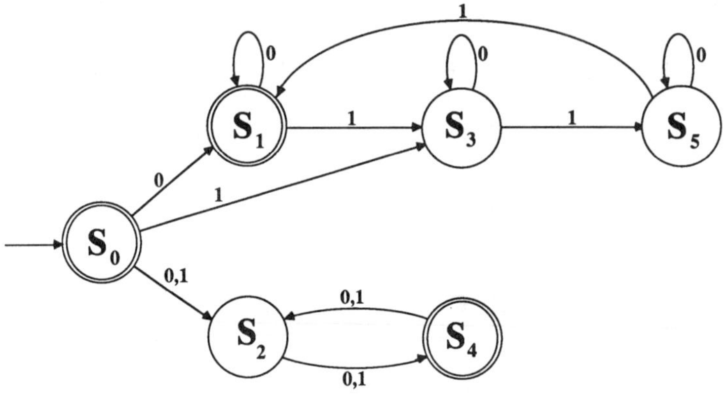

Figure 4.3 The NDFA discussed in Example 4.2

Within a nondeterministic finite automaton there can be multiple paths that are labeled with the components of a string. For example, if we let $w = \mathbf{01}$, then there are two paths labeled by the components of w: $(s_0 \to s_1 \to s_3)$ and $(s_0 \to s_2 \to s_4)$. The second path leads to a final state, s_4, while the first path does not. We will adopt the convention that this word w *is* accepted by the automaton since at least one of the paths *does* terminate in a final state. These concepts will be formalized later in Definition 4.3.

This ability to make multiple transitions from a given state can simplify the construction of the machine, but adds no more power to our computational model. The deterministic machine equivalent to Example 4.2 is substantially more complex, and its construction is left as an exercise for the reader.

Another restriction that is relaxed when we talk about nondeterministic finite automata is the number of initial states. While a deterministic machine is constrained to having exactly one start state, a nondeterministic finite automaton may have any number, other than zero, up to $\|S\|$. Indeed, some applications will be seen in which *all* the states are start states.

EXAMPLE 4.3

We can build a machine that will accept the same language as in Example 4.2, but in a slightly different way. Note that in Figure 4.4 the multiplicity of start states simplifies the construction considerably.

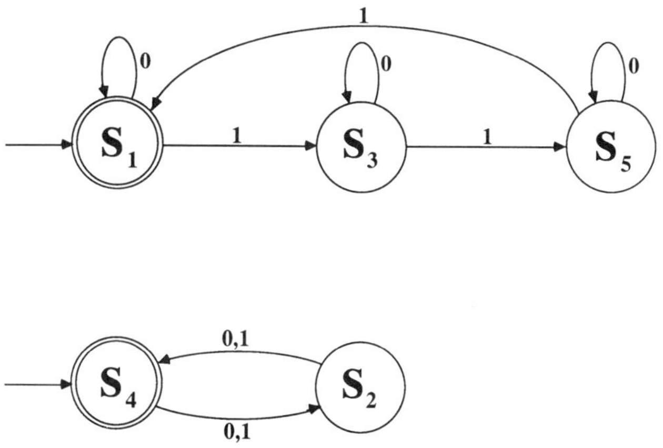

Figure 4.4 The NDFA discussed in Example 4.3

As before, the addition of multiple start states to our computational model facilitates machine construction but adds no more recognition power. We turn now to the formal definition of nondeterministic finite automata.

∇ **Definition 4.1.** A *nondeterministic finite automaton* (NDFA) is a quintuple $A = <\Sigma, S, S_0, \delta, F>$ where:

i. Σ is an alphabet.
ii. S is a finite nonempty set of states.
iii. S_0 is a *set* of initial states, a nonempty subset of S.
iv. $\delta: S \times \Sigma \rightarrow \rho(S)$ is the state transition function.
v. F is the set of accepting states, a (possibly empty) subset of S.

Δ

The input alphabet, the state space, and even the set of final states are the same as for deterministic finite automata. The important differences are contained in the definitions of the initial states and of the δ function.

The set of initial states can be any nonempty subset of the state space. These can be viewed as multiple entry points into the machine, with each start state beginning distinct, although not necessarily disjoint, paths through the machine.

The δ function for nondeterministic finite automata differs from the δ function of deterministic machines in that it maps a single state and a letter to a set of states. In some texts, one will find δ defined as simply a relation with range S and not as a function; without any loss of generality we define δ as a function with range $\rho(S)$, which makes the formal proofs of relevant theorems considerably easier.

EXAMPLE 4.4

Consider the machine $\mathsf{A} = <\Sigma, S, S_0, \delta, F>$, where

$$\Sigma = \{\mathbf{a}, \mathbf{b}\}$$

$$S = \{\mathrm{r}, \mathrm{s}, \mathrm{t}\}$$

$$S_0 = \{\mathrm{r}, \mathrm{s}\}$$

$$F = \{\mathrm{t}\}$$

and δ: $\{\mathrm{r}, \mathrm{s}, \mathrm{t}\} \times \{\mathbf{a}, \mathbf{b}\} \rightarrow \{\emptyset, \{\mathrm{r}\}, \{\mathrm{s}\}, \{\mathrm{t}\}, \{\mathrm{s}, \mathrm{t}\}, \{\mathrm{r}, \mathrm{s}\}, \{\mathrm{r}, \mathrm{t}\}, \{\mathrm{r}, \mathrm{s}, \mathrm{t}\}\}$ is given in Figure 4.5.

δ	**a**	**b**
r	{s}	$\emptyset$
s	$\emptyset$	{r, t}
t	$\emptyset$	{t}

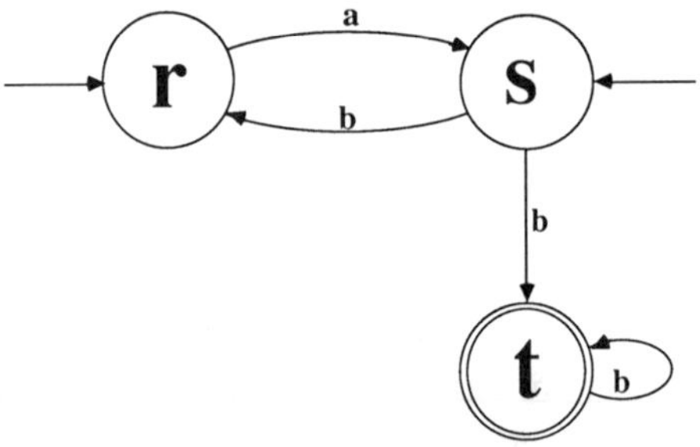

Figure 4.5 An NDFA state transition diagram corresponding to the formal definition given in Example 4.4

We will see later that this machine accepts strings that begin with alternating **a**s and **b**s and end with one or more consecutive **b**s.

∇ **Definition 4.2.** Given an NDFA $\mathsf{A} = <\Sigma, S, S_0, \delta, F>$, the *extended state transition function for* A is the function $\bar{\delta}$: $S \times \Sigma^* \rightarrow \rho(S)$ defined recursively as follows:

$$(\forall \mathrm{s} \in S)\ \bar{\delta}(\mathrm{s}, \lambda) = \{\mathrm{s}\}$$

$$(\forall \mathrm{s} \in S)(\forall \mathbf{a} \in \Sigma)(\forall x \in \Sigma^*)\ \bar{\delta}(\mathrm{s}, x\mathbf{a}) = \bigcup_{\mathrm{q} \in \bar{\delta}(\mathrm{s}, x)} \delta(\mathrm{q}, \mathbf{a})$$

Δ

Once again, $\overline{\delta}(s, x)$ is meant to represent where we arrive after starting at a state s and processing all the letters of the string x. In the case of nondeterministic finite automata, $\overline{\delta}$ does not map to a single state but to a set of states because of the multiplicity of paths.

EXAMPLE 4.5

Consider again the NDFA displayed in Example 4.4. To find all the places a string such as **bb** can reach from s, we would first determine what can be reached by the first **b**. The reachable states are r and t, since $\overline{\delta}(s, \mathbf{b}) = \{r, t\}$. From these states, we would then determine what could be reached by the second **b** (from r, no progress is possible, but from t, we can again reach t). These calculations are reflected in the recursive definition of $\overline{\delta}$:

$$\overline{\delta}(s, \mathbf{bb}) = \bigcup_{q \in \overline{\delta}(s, \mathbf{b})} \delta(q, \mathbf{b}) = \bigcup_{q \in \{r, t\}} \delta(q, \mathbf{b}) = \delta(r, \mathbf{b}) \cup \delta(t, \mathbf{b}) = \{\ \} \cup \{t\} = \{t\}$$

Because of the multiplicity of initial states and because the δ function is now set valued, it is possible for a nondeterministic finite automaton to be active in more than a single state at one time. Whereas in all deterministic finite automata there is a unique path through the machine labeled with components of w for each $w \in \Sigma^*$, this is not necessarily the case for nondeterministic finite automata. At any point in the processing of a string, the δ function maps the input symbol and the current state to a set of states. This implies that multiple paths through the machine are possible or that the machine can get "stuck" and be unable to process the remainder of the string if there is no transition from a state labeled with the appropriate letter. There is no more than one path for each word if there is exactly one start state and the δ function always maps to a singleton set (or $\emptyset$). If we were to further require that the δ function have a defined transition to another state for every input symbol, then the machine that we have would essentially be a deterministic finite automaton. Thus, all deterministic finite automata are simply a special class of nondeterministic finite automata; with some trivial changes in notation, any DFA can be thought of as an NDFA. Indeed, the state transition diagram of a DFA could be a picture of a well-behaved NDFA. Therefore, any language accepted by a DFA can be accepted by an NDFA.

EXAMPLE 4.6

Consider the machine given in Example 4.4 and let $x = \mathbf{b}$; the possible paths through the machine include (1) starting at s and proceeding to r, and (2) starting at s and proceeding to t. Note that it is not possible to start from t (since $t \notin S_0$), and there is no way to proceed with $x = \mathbf{b}$ by starting at r, the other start state.

Now let $x = \mathbf{ba}$ and consider the possibilities. The only path through the machine requires that we start at s, proceed to r, and return to s; starting at s and proceeding to t leaves no way to process the second letter of x. Starting from r is again hopeless (what types of strings are good candidates for starting at r?).

Now let $x = \mathbf{bab}$; the possible paths through the machine include (1) starting at s, proceeding to r, returning to s, and then moving again to r, and (2) starting at s, proceeding to r, returning to s, and then proceeding to t. Note that starting at s and moving immediately to t again leaves us with no way to process the remainder of the string. Both **b** and **bab** included paths that terminated at the final state t (among other places). These strings will be said to be *recognized* by this NDFA (compare with Definition 4.3). **ba** had no path that led to a final state, and as a consequence we will consider **ba** to be rejected by this machine.

There are a number of ways in which to conceptualize a nondeterministic finite automaton. Among the most useful are the following two schemes:

1. At each state where a multiple transition occurs, the machine replicates into identical copies of itself, with each copy following one of the possible paths.
2. Multiple states of the machine are allowed to be active, and each of the active states reacts to each input letter.

It happens that the second viewpoint is the most useful for our purposes. From a theoretical point of view, we use this as the basis for proving the equivalence of deterministic and nondeterministic finite automata. It is also a useful model upon which to base the circuits that implement NDFAs.

The concept of a language for nondeterministic finite automata is different from that for deterministic machines. Recall that the requirement for a word to be contained in the language accepted by a deterministic finite automaton was that the processing of a string would terminate in a final state. This is also the condition for belonging to the *language* accepted by a nondeterministic finite automaton; however, since the path through a nondeterministic finite automaton is not necessarily unique, only one of the many possible paths need terminate in a final state for the string to be accepted.

∇ **Definition 4.3.** Let $A = <\Sigma, S, S_0, \delta, F>$ be a nondeterministic finite automaton and w be a word in Σ^*. A *accepts w iff* $(\bigcup_{q \in S_0} \bar{\delta}(q, w)) \cap F \neq \emptyset$.
Δ

Again conforming with our previous usage, a word that is not accepted is *rejected*. The use of the symbol L will be consistent with its usage in previous chapters, although it does have a different formal definition. As before, $L(A)$ is used to designate all those strings that are accepted by a finite automaton A. Since the concept of *acceptance* must be modified for nondeterministic finite automata, the formal definition of L is necessarily different (contrast Definitions 4.3 and 1.12).

∇ **Definition 4.4.** Given an NDFA $A = <\Sigma, S, S_0, \delta, F>$, the language accepted by A, denoted $L(A)$, is $\{x \in \Sigma^* \mid (\bigcup_{q \in S_0} \bar{\delta}(q, x)) \cap F \neq \emptyset\}$.
Δ

Occasionally, it will be more convenient to express $L(\mathsf{A})$ in the following fashion: $L(\mathsf{A}) = \{x \in \Sigma^* \mid \exists t \in S_0 \ni \overline{\delta}(t, x) \cap F \neq \emptyset\}$. The concept of *equivalent* automata is unchanged: two machines are equivalent *iff* they accept the same language. Thus, if one or both of the machines happen to be nondeterministic, the definition still applies. For example, the NDFAs given in Figures 4.3 and 4.4 are equivalent.

The language recognized by a nondeterministic finite automaton is the set of all words where at least one of the paths through the machine labeled with components of that word ends in a final state. In other words, the set of terminal states at the ends of the paths labeled by components of a word w must have a state in common with the set of final states in order for w to belong to $L(\mathsf{A})$.

As a first example, refer to the NDFA defined in Example 4.4. As illustrated in Example 4.6, this machine accepts strings that begin with alternating **a**s and **b**s and end with one or more consecutive **b**s.

EXAMPLE 4.7

For a more concrete example, consider the problem of a ship attempting to transmit data to shore at random intervals. The receiver must continually listen, usually to noise, and recognize when an actual transmission starts so that it can record the data that follow. Let us assume that the start of a transmission is signaled by the string **010010** (in practice, such a signal string should be much longer to minimize the possibility of random noise triggering the recording mechanism). In essence, we wish to build an NDFA that will monitor a bit stream and move to a final state when the substring **010010** is detected (note that nonfinal states correspond to having the recording mechanism off, and final states signify that the current data should be recorded). The reader is encouraged to discover firsthand how hard it is to build a DFA that correctly implements this machine and contrast that solution to the NDFA T given in Figure 4.6.

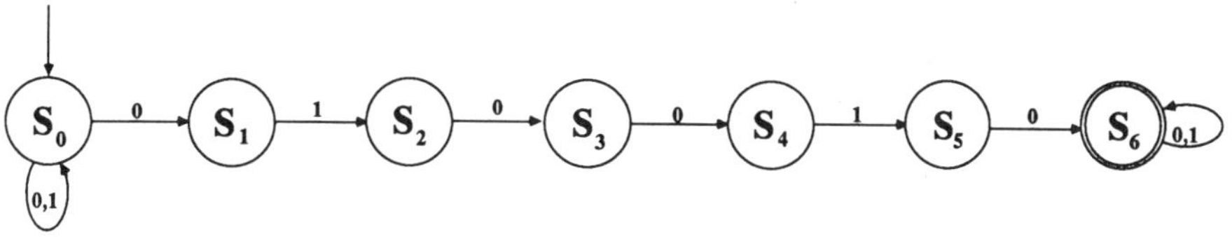

Figure 4.6 An NDFA for pattern recognition

Since the transitions leading to higher states are labeled by the symbols in **010010**, it is clear that the last state cannot be reached unless the sequence **010010** is actually scanned at some point during the processing of the input string. Thus, the NDFA clearly accepts no word that should be rejected. Conversely, since *all* possible legal paths are explored by an NDFA, valid strings *will* find a way to the final state. It is sometimes helpful to think of the NDFA as remaining in s_0 while the initial part of the input string is being processed and then "guessing" when it is the right time to move to s_1.

It is also possible to model an end-of-transmission signal that turns the recording device off (see the exercises). The device would remain in various final states until a valid end-of-transmission string was scanned, at which point it would return to the (nonfinal) start state.

While the NDFA given in Example 4.6 is very straightforward, it appears to be hard to simulate this nondeterminism in real time with a deterministic computer. It has not been difficult to keep track of the multiple paths in the simple machines seen so far. However, if each state has multiple transitions for a given symbol, the number of distinct paths a single word can take through an NDFA grows exponentially as the length of the word increases. For example, if each transition allowed a choice of three destination states, a word of length m would have 3^m possible paths from one single start state. An improvement can be made by calculating, as each letter is processed, the set of possible *destinations* (rather than recording all the *paths*). Still, in an n-state NDFA, there are potentially 2^n such combinations of states. This represents an improvement over the path set, since now the number of state combinations is independent of the length of the particular word being processed; it depends only on the number of states in the NDFA, which is fixed. We will see that keeping track of the set of possible destination states is indeed the best way to handle an NDFA in a deterministic manner.

Since we have seen in Chapter 1 that it is easy to implement a DFA, we now explore methods to convert an NDFA to an equivalent DFA. Suppose that we are given a nondeterministic finite automaton A and that we want to construct a corresponding deterministic finite automaton A^d. Using the concepts in Definitions 4.1 through 4.4, we can proceed in the following fashion. Our general strategy will be to keep track of all the states that can be reached by some string in the nondeterministic finite automaton. Since we can arbitrarily label the states of an automaton, we let the state space of A^d be the *power set* of S. Thus, $S^d = \rho(S)$, and each state in the new machine will be labeled by some subset of S. Furthermore, let the start state of A^d, denoted s_0^d, be labeled by the member of $\rho(S)$ containing those states that are initial states in A; that is, $s_0^d = S_0$.

Since our general strategy is to "remember" all the states that can be reached for some string, we can define the δ function in the following natural manner: For every letter in Σ, let the new state transition function, δ^d, map to the subset of $\rho(S)$ labeled by the union of all those states that are reached from some state contained in the current state name (according to the old state transition function δ).

According to Definition 4.4, for a word to be contained in the language accepted by some nondeterministic finite automaton, at least one of the terminal states was required to be contained in the set of final states. Thus, let the set of final states in the corresponding deterministic finite automaton be labeled by the subsets of S that contain at least one of the accepting states in the nondeterministic counterpart. The formal definition of our corresponding deterministic finite automaton is given in Definition 4.5.

∇ **Definition 4.5.** Given an NDFA $A = <\Sigma, S, S_0, \delta, F>$, the *corresponding deterministic finite automaton*, $A^d = <\Sigma, S^d, s_0^d, \delta^d, F^d>$, is defined as follows:

$$S^d = \rho(S)$$
$$s_0^d = S_0$$
$$F^d = \{Q \in S^d \mid Q \cap F \neq \emptyset\}$$

and δ^d is the state transition function, $\delta^d\colon S^d \times \Sigma \to S^d$, defined by

$$(\forall Q \in S^d)(\forall \mathbf{a} \in \Sigma)\ \delta^d(Q, \mathbf{a}) = \bigcup_{q \in Q} \delta(q, \mathbf{a})$$

δ^d extends to the function $\overline{\delta}^d\colon S^d \times \Sigma^* \to S^d$ as suggested by Theorem 1.1:

$$(\forall Q \in S^d) \qquad \overline{\delta}^d(Q, \lambda) = Q$$
$$(\forall Q \in S^d)(\forall \mathbf{a} \in \Sigma)(\forall x \in \Sigma^*)\ \overline{\delta}^d(Q, x\mathbf{a}) = \delta^d(\overline{\delta}^d(Q, x), \mathbf{a})$$

Δ

Definition 4.5 describes a deterministic finite automaton that observes the same restrictions as all other deterministic finite automata (a single start state, a finite state set, a well-defined transition function, and so on). The only peculiarity is the labeling of the states. Note that the definition implies that the state labeled by the empty set is *never* a final state and that all transitions from this state lead back to itself. This is the dead state, which is reached by strings that are always prematurely terminated in the corresponding nondeterministic machine.

EXAMPLE 4.8

Consider the NDFA B given in Figure 4.7. As specified by Definition 4.5, the corresponding DFA B^d would look like the machine shown in Figure 4.8. Note that all the states happen to be accessible in this particular example.

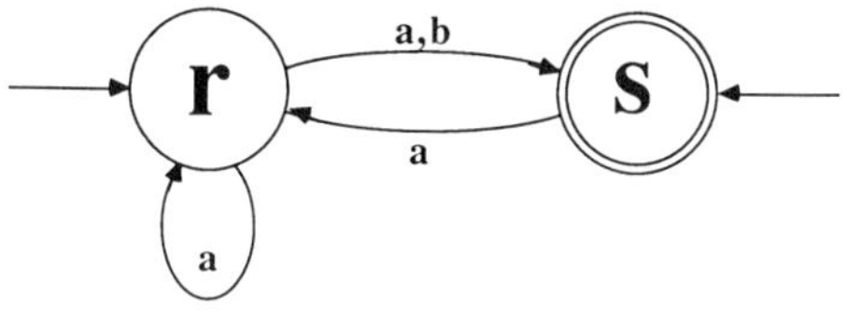

Figure 4.7 The NDFA B discussed in Example 4.8

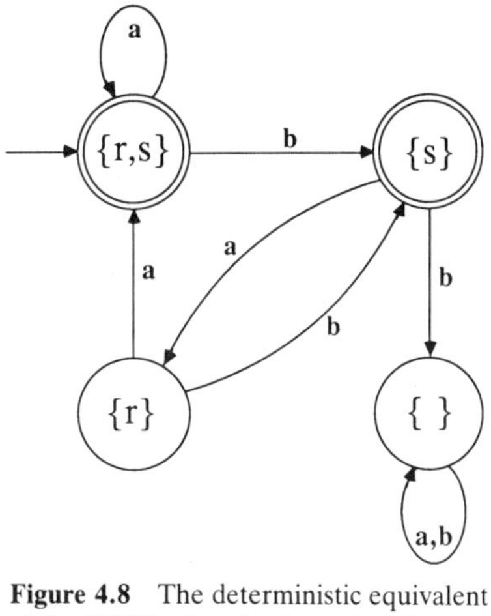

Figure 4.8 The deterministic equivalent of the NDFA given in Example 4.8

Since the construction of the corresponding deterministic machine involves $\rho(S)$, it should be obvious to the reader that the size of this deterministic finite automaton *can* grow exponentially larger as the number of states in the associated nondeterministic finite automaton increases. In general, however, there are often many inaccessible states. Thus, only the states that are found to be reachable during the construction process need to be included. The reader is encouraged to exploit this fact when constructing corresponding deterministic finite automata. The language accepted by the DFA A^d follows the definition given in Chapter 1.

To show that the deterministic finite automaton that we have just defined accepts the same language as the corresponding nondeterministic finite automaton, we must first show that the $\overline{\delta}^d$ function behaves in the same manner for strings as the δ^d function does for single letters. For any state $Q \in S^d$, the δ^d function maps this state and an input letter $\mathbf{a} \in \Sigma$, according to the mapping of the δ function for each $q \in Q$ and the letter $\mathbf{a}$. The following lemma establishes that $\overline{\delta}^d$ performs the corresponding mapping for strings.

∇ **Lemma 4.1.** Let $A = <\Sigma, S, S_0, \delta, F>$ be a nondeterministic finite automaton, and let $A^d = <\Sigma, S^d, s_0^d, \delta^d, F^d>$ represent the corresponding deterministic finite automaton. Then

$$(\forall Q \in S^d)(\forall x \in \Sigma^*)(\overline{\delta}^d(Q,x) = \bigcup_{q \in Q} \overline{\delta}(q,x))$$

Proof. By induction on $|x|$: Let P(k) be defined by

$$\text{P}(k)\text{: } (\forall Q \in S^d)(\forall x \in \Sigma^k)(\overline{\delta}^d(Q,x) = \bigcup_{q \in Q} \overline{\delta}(q,x))$$

Basis step: $|x| = 0 \Rightarrow x = \lambda$ and therefore

$$\overline{\delta}^d(Q,\lambda) = Q = \bigcup_{q \in Q} \{q\} = \bigcup_{q \in Q} \overline{\delta}(q,\lambda)$$

Inductive step: Suppose that the result holds for all $x \ni |x| = k$; that is, P(k) is true. Let $y \in \Sigma^{k+1}$. Then $\exists x \in \Sigma^k$ and $\exists \mathbf{a} \in \Sigma \ni y = x\mathbf{a}$. Then

$$\overline{\delta}^d(Q,y) = \text{(by definition of } y)$$

$$\overline{\delta}^d(Q,x\mathbf{a}) = \text{(by Theorem 1.1)}$$

$$\delta^d(\overline{\delta}^d(Q,x),\mathbf{a}) = \text{(by the induction hypothesis)}$$

$$\delta^d(\bigcup_{q \in Q} \overline{\delta}(q,x),\mathbf{a}) = (\forall A, B \in \rho(S))(\forall \mathbf{a} \in \Sigma)(\delta^d(A \cup B, \mathbf{a}) = \delta^d(A,\mathbf{a}) \cup \delta^d(B,\mathbf{a}))$$

$$\bigcup_{q \in Q} \delta^d(\overline{\delta}(q,x),\mathbf{a}) = \text{(by Definition 4.5)}$$

$$\bigcup_{q \in Q} (\bigcup_{p \in \overline{\delta}(q,x)} \delta(p,\mathbf{a})) = \text{(by Definition 4.2)}$$

$$\bigcup_{q \in Q} \overline{\delta}(q,x\mathbf{a}) = \text{(by definition of } y)$$

$$\bigcup_{q \in Q} \overline{\delta}(q,y)$$

Therefore, $\text{P}(k) \Rightarrow \text{P}(k+1)$ for all $k \geq 0$, and thus by the principle of mathematical induction we can say that the result holds for all $x \in \Sigma^*$.

Δ

Having established Lemma 4.1, proving that the language accepted by a nondeterministic finite automaton and the corresponding deterministic machine are the same language becomes a straightforward task. The equivalence of A and A^d is given in the following theorem.

∇ **Theorem 4.1.** Let $\mathsf{A} = <\Sigma, S, S_0, \delta, F>$ be a nondeterministic finite automaton, and let $\mathsf{A}^d = <\Sigma, S^d, s_0^d, \delta^d, F^d>$ represent its corresponding deterministic finite automaton. Then A and A^d are equivalent; that is, $\boldsymbol{L}(\mathsf{A}) = \boldsymbol{L}(\mathsf{A}^d)$.

Proof. Let $x \in \Sigma^*$. Then

$$\begin{aligned} x \in \boldsymbol{L}(\mathsf{A}) &\Leftrightarrow \text{(by Definition 4.4)} \\ \Big(\bigcup_{s \in S_0} \overline{\delta}(s, x)\Big) \cap F \neq \emptyset &\Leftrightarrow \text{(by Definition 4.5)} \\ \Big(\bigcup_{s \in S_0} \overline{\delta}(s, x)\Big) \in F^d &\Leftrightarrow \text{(by Lemma 4.1)} \\ \overline{\delta}^d(S_0, x) \in F^d &\Leftrightarrow \text{(by Definition 4.5)} \\ \overline{\delta}^d(s_0^d, x) \in F^d &\Leftrightarrow \text{(by Definition 1.15)} \\ x \in \boldsymbol{L}(\mathsf{A}^d) & \end{aligned}$$

Δ

Now that we have established that nondeterministic finite automata and deterministic finite automata are equal in computing power, the reader might wonder why we bother with nondeterministic finite automata. Even though nondeterministic finite automata cannot recognize any language that cannot be defined by a DFA, they are very useful both in theory and in machine construction (as illustrated by Example 4.7). The following examples further illustrate that NDFAs often yield more natural (and less complex) solutions to a given problem.

EXAMPLE 4.9

Recall the machine from Chapter 1 that accepted a subset of real constants in scientific notation according to the following BNF:

<sign> ::= **+** | **−**

<digit> ::= **0** | **1** | **2** | **3** | **4** | **5** | **6** | **7** | **8** | **9**

<natural> ::= <digit> | <digit><natural>

<integer> ::= <natural> | <sign><natural>

<real constant> ::= <integer> |
<integer>**.** |
<integer>**.**<natural> |
<integer>**.**<natural>**E**<integer>

By using nondeterministic finite automata, it is easy to construct a machine that will recognize this language (compare with the deterministic version given in Example 1.11). One such NDFA is shown in Figure 4.9.

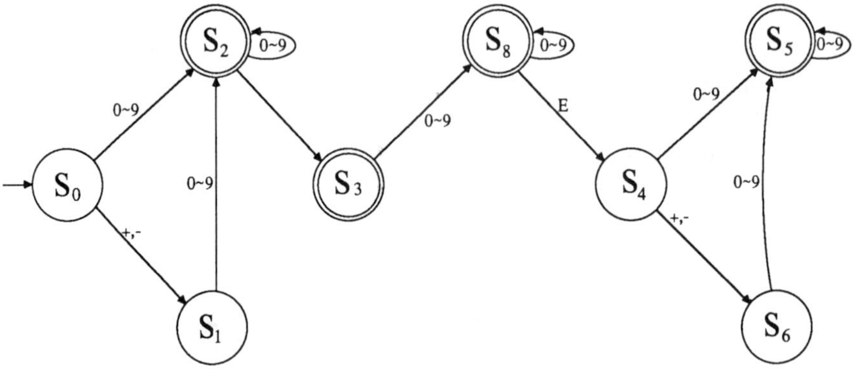

Figure 4.9 The NDFA discussed in Example 4.9

EXAMPLE 4.10

Let $L = \{x \in \{\mathbf{a}, \mathbf{b}\}^* \mid x$ begins with $\mathbf{a} \vee x$ contains **ba** as a substring$\}$. We can easily build a machine that will accept this language, as illustrated in Figure 4.10. Now suppose we wanted to construct a machine that would accept the *reverse* of this language, that is, to accept $L^r = \{x \in \{\mathbf{a}, \mathbf{b}\}^* \mid x$ ends with $\mathbf{a} \vee x$ contains $\mathbf{ab}\}$. The machine that will accept this language can be built using nondeterministic finite automata by simply exchanging the initial states and the final states and by reversing the arrows of the δ function. The automaton (definitely an NDFA in this case!) arising in this fashion is shown in Figure 4.11.

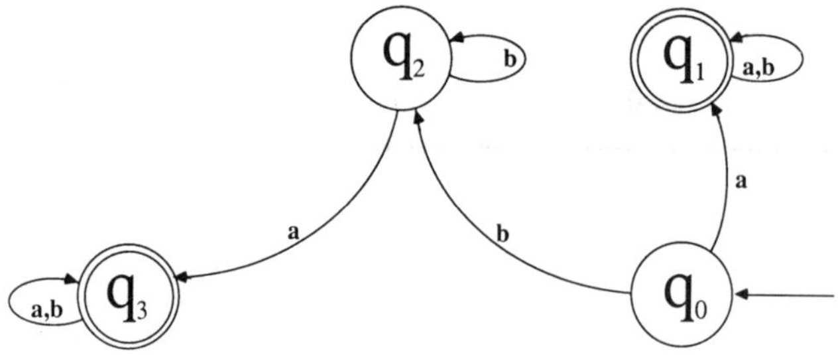

Figure 4.10 An NDFA accepting the language given in Example 4.10

It can be shown that the technique employed in Example 4.10, when applied to *any* automaton, will yield a new NDFA that is guaranteed to accept the *reverse* of the original language. The material in Chapter 5 will reveal many instances where the ability to define multiple start states and multiple transitions will be of great value.

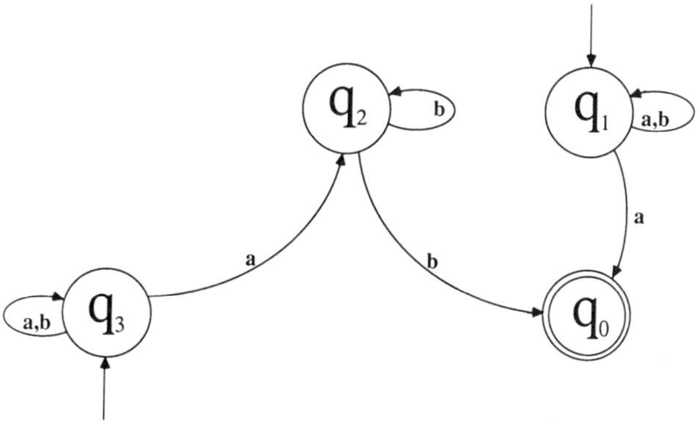

Figure 4.11 An NDFA representing the reverse of the language represented in Figure 4.10

EXAMPLE 4.11

Assume we wish to identify all words that contain at least one of the three strings **10110**, **1010**, or **01101** as substrings. Consequently, we let L be the set of all words that are made up of some characters, followed by one of our three target strings, followed by some other characters. That is,

$$L = \{w \in \{\mathbf{0},\mathbf{1}\}^* \mid w = xyz, x \in \{\mathbf{0},\mathbf{1}\}^*, y \in \{\mathbf{10110},\mathbf{1010},\mathbf{01101}\}, z \in \{\mathbf{0},\mathbf{1}\}^*\}$$

We can construct a nondeterministic finite automaton that will accept this language as follows. First construct three machines each of which will accept one of the candidates for y. Next, prepend a single state (s_0 in Figure 4.12) that loops on Σ^*; make this state an initial state and draw arrows from it which mimic the transitions from each of the other three initial states (as shown in Figure 4.12). Finally, append a single state machine (s_{18}) that accepts Σ^*; draw arrows from each of the final states to this state. The machine that accepts this language is given in Figure 4.12. The

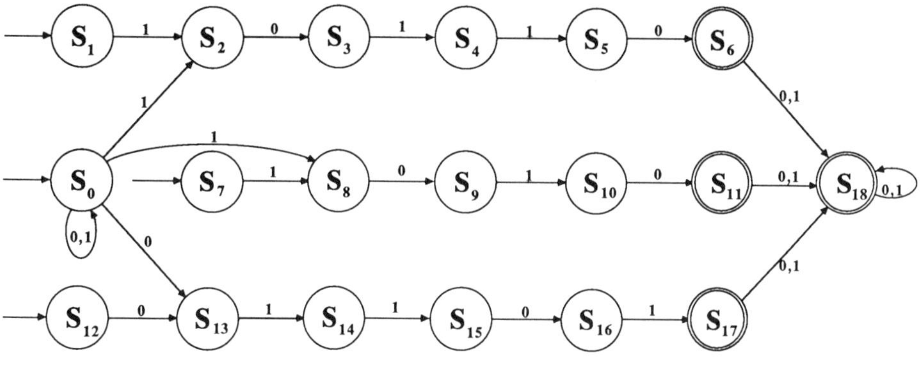

Figure 4.12 An NDFA for recognizing any of several substrings

reader is encouraged to try to construct a deterministic version of this machine in order to appreciate the simplicity of the above solution.

EXAMPLE 4.12

Recall the application in Chapter 1 involving string searching (Example 1.15). The construction of DFAs involved much thought, but there is an NDFA that solves the problem in an obvious and straightforward manner. For example, an automaton that recognizes all strings over the alphabet {**a**, **b**} containing the substring **aab** might look like the NDFA in Figure 4.13.

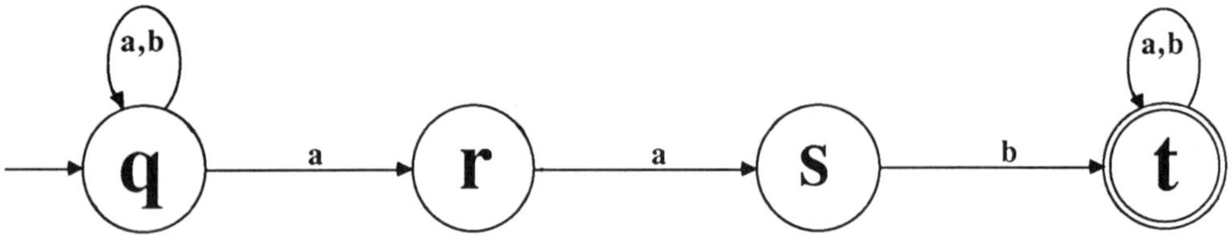

Figure 4.13 An automaton recognizing the substring **aab**

As is the case for this NDFA, it may be impossible for certain sets of states to all be active at once. These combinations can never be achieved during the normal operation of the NDFA. The DFA states corresponding to these combinations will not be in the connected part of A^d. Applying Definition 4.5 to find the entire deterministic version and then pruning it down to just the relevant portion is very inefficient. A better solution is to begin at the start state and "follow transitions" to new states until no further new states are uncovered. At this point, the relevant states and their transitions will have all been defined; the remainder of the machine can be safely ignored. For the NDFA in Figure 4.13, the connected portion of the equivalent DFA is shown in Figure 4.14. This automaton is still not reduced; the last

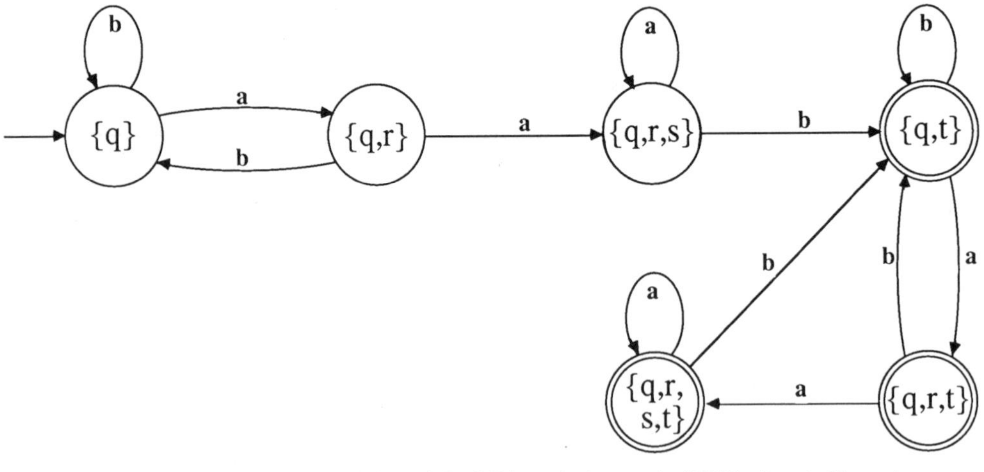

Figure 4.14 The connected portion of the DFA equivalent to the NDFA given in Example 4.12

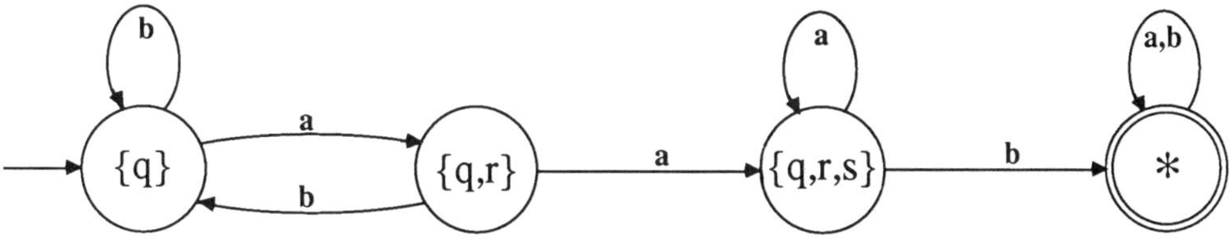

Figure 4.15 A reduced equivalent of the DFA given in Figure 4.14

three states are all equivalent and can be coalesced to form the minimal machine given in Figure 4.15.

The above process can be easily automated; an interesting but frustrating exercise might involve producing an appropriate set of rules for generating, given a specific string y, a DFA that will recognize all strings containing the substring y. Definition 4.5 can be used to generate the appropriate DFA from the obvious NDFA without subjecting the designer to such frustrations!

4.2 CIRCUIT IMPLEMENTATION OF NDFAs

As mentioned earlier, the presence of multiple paths within an NDFA for a single word characterizes the nondeterministic nature of these automata. The most profitable way to view the operation of an NDFA is to consider the automaton as having (potentially) several active states, with each of the active states reacting to the next letter to determine a new set of active states. In fact, by using one D flip-flop per state, this viewpoint can be directly translated into hardware. When a given state is active, the corresponding flip-flop will be on, and when it is inactive (that is, it cannot be reached by the substring that has been processed at this point), it will be off. As a new letter is processed, a state will be activated (that is, be placed in the new set of active states) if it can be reached from one of the previously active states. Thus, the state transition function will again determine the circuitry that feeds into each flip-flop.

Following the same conventions given for DFAs, the input tape will be assumed to be bounded by special start-of-string <SOS> and end-of-string <EOS> symbols. The <EOS> character is again used to activate the accept circuitry so that acceptance is not indicated until all letters on the tape have been processed. As before, the <SOS> symbol can be employed at the beginning of the string to ensure that the circuitry begins processing the string from the appropriate start state(s). Alternately, SR (set–reset) flip-flops can be used to initialize the configuration without relying on the <SOS> conventions.

EXAMPLE 4.13

Consider the NDFA D given in Figure 4.16. With the <SOS> and <EOS> transitions illustrated, the complete model would appear as in Figure 4.17.

Two bits of input data ($\mathbf{a}_1$ and $\mathbf{a}_2$) are required to represent the symbols

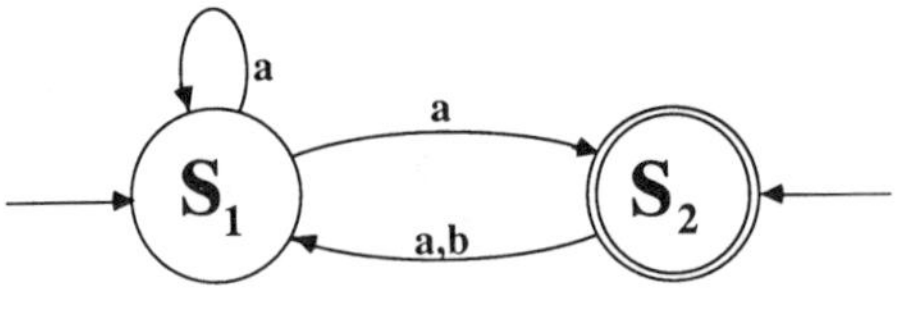

Figure 4.16 The NDFA discussed in Example 4.13

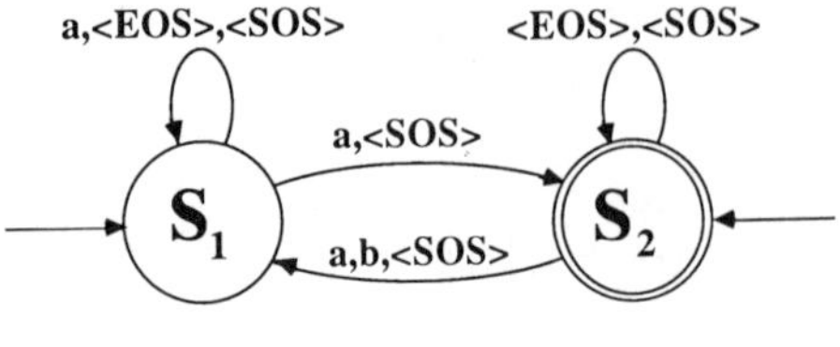

Figure 4.17 The expanded state transition diagram for the NDFA in Figure 4.16

<EOS>, **a**, **b**, and <SOS>. The standard encodings described in Chapter 1 would produce <EOS> = **00**, **a** = **01**, **b** = **10**, and <SOS> = **11**. If the flip-flop $\mathbf{t}_1$ is used to represent the activity of s_1, and $\mathbf{t}_2$ is used to record the status of s_2, then the subsequent activity of the two flip-flops can be determined from the current state activity and the current letter being scanned, as shown in Table 4.1.

TABLE 4.1

t_1	t_2	a_1	a_2	t'_1	t'_2	accept
0	0	0	0	0	0	0
0	0	0	1	0	0	0
0	0	1	0	0	0	0
0	0	1	1	1	1	0
0	1	0	0	0	1	1
0	1	0	1	1	0	0
0	1	1	0	1	0	0
0	1	1	1	1	1	0
1	0	0	0	1	0	0
1	0	0	1	1	1	0
1	0	1	0	0	0	0
1	0	1	1	1	1	0
1	1	0	0	1	1	1
1	1	0	1	1	1	0
1	1	1	0	1	0	0
1	1	1	1	1	1	0

The first four rows of Table 4.1 reflect the situation in which a string is hopelessly stuck, and no states are active. Processing subsequent symbols from Σ will not change this; both $\mathbf{t}'_1$ and $\mathbf{t}'_2$ remain **0**. The one exception is when the <SOS> symbol is scanned; in this case, each of the start states is activated ($\mathbf{t}'_1 = \mathbf{1}$ and $\mathbf{t}'_2 = \mathbf{1}$). This corrects the situation in which both flip-flops happen to initialize to **0** when power is first applied to the circuitry. Scanning the <SOS> symbol changes the state of the flip-flops to reflect the appropriate starting conditions (in this machine, both states are start states, and therefore both should be active as processing is begun). Note that each of the rows of Table 4.1 that correspond to scanning <SOS> show that $\mathbf{t}_1$ and $\mathbf{t}_2$ are reset in the same fashion.

Determining the circuit behavior for the symbols in Σ closely parallels the definition of δ^d in Definition 4.5. For example, when state s_1 is active but s_2 is inactive ($\mathbf{t}_1 = \mathbf{1}$ and $\mathbf{t}_2 = \mathbf{0}$) and **a** is scanned ($\mathbf{a}_1 = \mathbf{0}$ and $\mathbf{a}_2 = \mathbf{1}$), transitions from s_1 cause both states to next be active ($\mathbf{t}_1' = \mathbf{1}$ and $\mathbf{t}_2' = \mathbf{1}$). The other combinations are calculated similarly. Minimized expressions for the new values of each of the flip-flops and the accept circuitry are

$$\mathbf{t}_1' = (\mathbf{t}_1 \wedge \neg \mathbf{a}_1) \vee (\mathbf{t}_2 \wedge \mathbf{a}_2) \vee (\mathbf{t}_2 \wedge \mathbf{a}_1) \vee (\mathbf{a}_1 \wedge \mathbf{a}_2)$$

$$\mathbf{t}_2' = (\mathbf{t}_2 \wedge \neg \mathbf{a}_1 \wedge \neg \mathbf{a}_2) \vee (\mathbf{t}_1 \wedge \mathbf{a}_2) \vee (\mathbf{a}_1 \wedge \mathbf{a}_2)$$

$$\text{accept} = (\mathbf{t}_2 \wedge \neg \mathbf{a}_1 \wedge \neg \mathbf{a}_2)$$

Since similar terms appear in these expressions, these three subcircuits can "share" the common components, as shown in Figure 4.18.

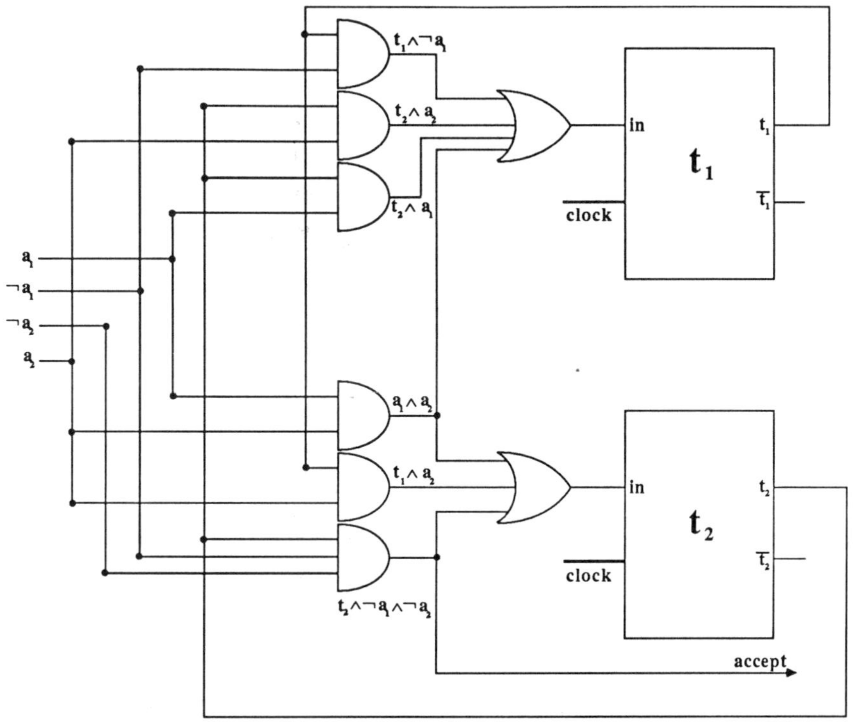

Figure 4.18 Circuitry for the automaton discussed in Example 4.13

Note that the accept circuitry reflects that a string should be recognized when some final state is active (s_2 in this example) and <EOS> is scanned. In more complex machines with several final states, lines leading from each of the flip-flops corresponding to final states would be joined by an OR gate before being ANDed with the <EOS> condition.

An interesting exercise involves converting the NDFA D given in Example 4.1 to the equivalent DFA D^d, which will have four states: $\emptyset$, $\{s_1\}$, $\{s_2\}$, and $\{s_1, s_2\}$. The deterministic automaton D^d can be realized by a circuit diagram as specified in Chapter 1. This four-state DFA will require 2 bits of state data. If the state encoding conventions $\emptyset = \mathbf{00}$, $\{s_1\} = \mathbf{10}$, $\{s_2\} = \mathbf{01}$, and $\{s_1, s_2\} = \mathbf{11}$ are used, the circuitry for the DFA D^d will be identical to that for the NDFA D.

For DFAs, m bits of state data $(\mathbf{t}_1, \mathbf{t}_2, \ldots, \mathbf{t}_m)$ can encode up to 2^m distinct states. With NDFAs, an n-state machine required a full n bits of state data (1 bit per state). This apparently "extravagant" use of state data is offset by the fact that an n-state NDFA may require 2^n states to form an equivalent DFA. This was the case in the preceding example, in which n and m were equal to 2; the two-state NDFA D required two flip-flops, and the equivalent four-state DFA also required two flip-flops; the savings induced by the DFA state encoding was exactly offset by the multiplicity of states needed by the NDFA.

A DFA may turn out to need less hardware than an equivalent NDFA, as illustrated by Example 4.12. The four-state NDFA C needs four flip-flops, and the (nonminimal, 16-state) DFA C^d would also need four. However, the minimal equivalent DFA derived in Example 4.12 has only four states and therefore can be encoded with just 2 bits of state data. Hence only two flip-flops are necessary to implement a recognizer for $L(\mathsf{C})$.

4.3 NDFAs WITH LAMBDA-TRANSITIONS

We now extend our computational model to include the nondeterministic finite automata that allow transitions between states to occur "spontaneously," without any input being processed. Transitions that occur without an input symbol being processed are called *λ-transitions* or *lambda-moves*. In texts that denote the empty string by the symbol ϵ, such transitions are usually referred to as *epsilon-moves*.

∇ **Definition 4.6.** A *nondeterministic finite automaton with λ-transitions* is a quintuple $\mathsf{A}_\lambda = \langle \Sigma, S, S_0, \delta_\lambda, F \rangle$, where

i. Σ is an alphabet.
ii. S is a finite nonempty set of states.
iii. S_0 is a set of initial states, a nonempty subset of S.
iv. $\delta_\lambda : (S \times (\Sigma \cup \{\lambda\})) \to \rho(S)$ is the state transition function.
v. F is the set of accepting states, a (possibly empty) subset of S.

Δ

A nondeterministic finite automaton *with* λ-transitions is very similar in structure to an NDFA that does not have λ-transitions. The only different aspect is the definition of the δ function. Instead of mapping state/letter pairs [from $S \times \Sigma$] to $\rho(S)$, it maps pairs consisting of a state and either a letter or the empty string [from $S \times (\Sigma \cup \{\lambda\})$ to $\rho(S)$]. From any state that has a λ-transition, we adopt the convention that the machine is capable of making a spontaneous transition to the new state specified by that λ-transition *without* processing an input symbol. However, the machine may also "choose" not to follow this path and instead remain in the original state. Before we can extend the δ_λ function to operate on strings from Σ^*, we need the very useful concept of *lambda-closure*.

∇ **Definition 4.7.** Given a nondeterministic finite automaton

$$A_\lambda = <\Sigma, S, S_0, \delta_\lambda, F>$$

with λ-transitions, the *λ-closure of a state* $t \in S$, denoted $\Lambda(t)$, is the set of all states that are reachable from t without processing any input symbols. The *λ-closure of a set of states T* is then $\Lambda(T) = \bigcup_{t \in T} \Lambda(t)$.
Δ

The λ-closure of a state is the set of all the states that can be reached from that state, including itself, by following λ-transitions only. Obviously, one can always reach the state currently occupied without having to move. Consequently, even if there are no explicit arcs labeled by λ going back to state t, t is always in the λ-closure of itself.

EXAMPLE 4.14

Consider the machine given in Figure 4.19, which contains λ-transitions from s_0 to s_1 and from s_1 to s_2. By Definition 4.7,

$$\Lambda(s_0) = \{s_0, s_1, s_2\}$$
$$\Lambda(s_1) = \{s_1, s_2\}$$
$$\Lambda(s_2) = \{s_2\}$$
$$\Lambda(s_3) = \{s_3\}$$

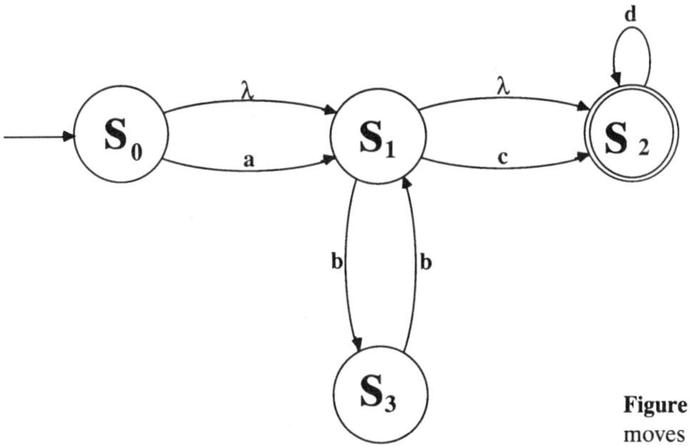

Figure 4.19 An NDFA with lambda-moves

∇ **Definition 4.8.** Given a nondeterministic finite automaton

$$A_\lambda = <\Sigma, S, S_0, \delta_\lambda, F>$$

with λ-transitions, the *extended state transition function for* A_λ is a function $\overline{\delta}_\lambda: S \times \Sigma^* \to \rho(S)$ defined as follows:

i. $(\forall s \in S)\ \overline{\delta}_\lambda(s, \lambda) = \Lambda(s)$

ii. $(\forall s \in S)(\forall \mathbf{a} \in \Sigma)\ \overline{\delta}_\lambda(s, \mathbf{a}) = \Lambda(\bigcup_{q \in \Lambda(s)} \delta_\lambda(q, \mathbf{a}))$

iii. $(\forall s \in S)(\forall x \in \Sigma^*)(\forall \mathbf{a} \in \Sigma)\ \overline{\delta}_\lambda(s, x\mathbf{a}) = \Lambda(\bigcup_{q \in \overline{\delta}_\lambda(s, x)} \delta_\lambda(q, \mathbf{a}))$

Δ

The $\overline{\delta}_\lambda$ function is *not* extended in the same way as for the nondeterministic finite automata given in Definition 4.2. Most importantly, due to the effects of the λ-closure, $\overline{\delta}_\lambda(s, \mathbf{a}) \neq \delta_\lambda(s, \mathbf{a})$. Thus, not only does the $\overline{\delta}_\lambda$ function map to a set of states based on a single letter, but it also includes the λ-closure of those states. This may seem strange for single letters (strings of length 1), but it is required for consistency when the $\overline{\delta}_\lambda$ function is presented with strings of length greater than 1, since at each state along the path there can be λ-transitions. Each λ-transition maps to a new state (which may have λ-transitions of its own) that must be included in this path and processed by the δ_λ function.

The nondeterministic finite automaton *without* λ-transitions that corresponds to a nondeterministic finite automaton *with* λ-transitions is given in Definition 4.9.

∇ **Definition 4.9.** Given a nondeterministic finite automaton *with* λ-transitions, $A_\lambda = <\Sigma, S, S_0, \delta_\lambda, F>$, the *corresponding nondeterministic finite automaton without λ-transitions*, $A_\lambda^\sigma = <\Sigma, S \cup \{q_0\}, S_0 \cup \{q_0\}, \delta_\lambda^\sigma, F^\sigma>$, is defined as follows:

$$F^\sigma = \begin{cases} F & \textit{iff}\quad \lambda \notin L(A_\lambda) \\ F \cup \{q_0\} & \textit{iff}\quad \lambda \in L(A_\lambda) \end{cases}$$

$$(\forall \mathbf{a} \in \Sigma)\delta_\lambda^\sigma(q_0, \mathbf{a}) = \emptyset$$

$$(\forall s \in S)(\forall \mathbf{a} \in \Sigma) \quad \delta_\lambda^\sigma(s, \mathbf{a}) = \overline{\delta}_\lambda(s, \mathbf{a}) = \Lambda(\bigcup_{q \in \Lambda(s)} \delta_\lambda(q, \mathbf{a}))$$

and which is extended in the "usual" way for nondeterministic finite automata to the function $\overline{\delta}_\lambda^\sigma: (S \cup \{q_0\}) \times \Sigma^* \to \rho(S \cup \{q_0\})$.

Δ

Note that from a state in A_λ several λ-transitions may be taken, then a single letter **a** may be processed, and then several more λ-moves may occur; all this activity can result from just a single symbol on the input tape being processed. The definition of δ_λ^σ reflects these types of transitions. The δ_λ^σ function is defined to be the same as the $\overline{\delta}_\lambda$ function for all single letters (strings of length 1), which adjusts for the λ-closure of A_λ. The δ_λ^σ function can then be extended in the usual nondeterministic manner.

To account for the case that λ might be in the language accepted by the automaton A_λ, we add an extra start state q_0 to the corresponding machine A_λ^σ, which is disconnected from the rest of the machine. If $\lambda \in L(A_\lambda)$, we also make q_0 a final state.

EXAMPLE 4.15

Let A_λ represent the NDFA given in Example 4.14. A_λ^σ would then be given by the NDFA shown in Figure 4.20. This new NDFA does indeed accept the same language as A_λ. To show in general that $L(A_\lambda) = L(A_\lambda^\sigma)$, we must first show that the respective extended state transition functions behave in similar fashions. However, these two functions can be equivalent only for strings of nonzero length (because of the effects of the λ-closure in the definition of δ_λ^σ). This result is established in Lemma 4.2.

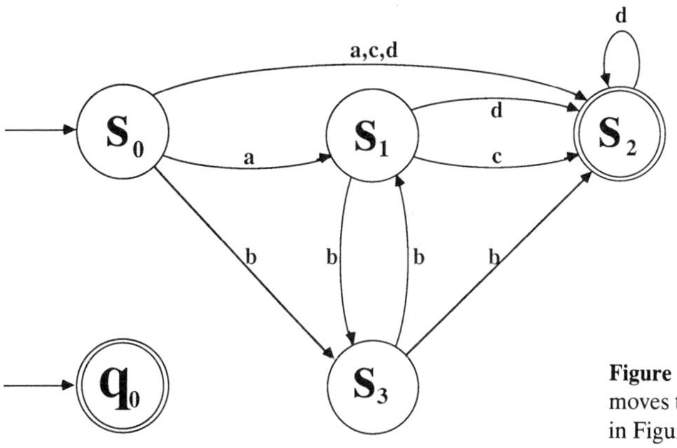

Figure 4.20 An NDFA without lambda-moves that is equivalent to the automaton in Figure 4.19

∇ **Lemma 4.2.** Given a nondeterministic finite automaton A_λ *with* λ-transitions and the corresponding nondeterministic finite automaton A_λ^σ *without* λ-transitions, then

$$(\forall s \in S)(\forall x \in \Sigma^+)(\overline{\delta}_\lambda^\sigma(s, x) = \overline{\delta}_\lambda(s, x))$$

Proof. The proof is by induction on $|x|$; see the exercises.

Δ

Once we have shown that the extended state transition functions behave (almost) identically, we can proceed to show that the languages accepted by these two machines are the same.

∇ **Theorem 4.2.** Given a nondeterministic finite automaton that contains λ-transitions, there exists an *equivalent* nondeterministic finite automaton that does not have λ-transitions.

Proof. Assume $A_\lambda = <\Sigma, S, S_0, \delta_\lambda, F>$ is an NDFA with λ-transitions. Construct the corresponding NDFA $A_\lambda^\sigma = <\Sigma, S \cup \{q_0\}, S_0 \cup \{q_0\}, \delta_\lambda^\sigma, F^\sigma>$, which has no

λ-transitions. We will show $L(A_\lambda) = L(A_\lambda^\sigma)$, and thereby prove that the two machines are equivalent. Because the way A_λ^σ was constructed limits the scope of Lemma 4.2, the proof is divided into two cases.

Case 1: If $x = \lambda$, then by Definition 4.9

$$(q_0 \in F^\sigma \textit{ iff } \lambda \in L(A_\lambda))$$

and so

$$(\lambda \in L(A_\lambda^\sigma) \Leftrightarrow \lambda \in L(A_\lambda))$$

Case 2: Assume $x \neq \lambda$. Since there are no transitions leaving q_0, it may be disregarded as one of the start states of A_λ^σ. Then

$$x \in L(A_\lambda^\sigma) \Rightarrow \text{(by definition of } L)$$

$$\left(\bigcup_{s_0 \in S_0} \bar{\delta}_\lambda^\sigma(s_0, x)\right) \cap F^\sigma \neq \emptyset \Rightarrow \text{(by Lemma 4.2)}$$

$$\left(\bigcup_{s_0 \in S_0} \bar{\delta}_\lambda(s_0, x)\right) \cap F^\sigma \neq \emptyset \Rightarrow \text{(since if } q_0 \text{ were the common element, then } x \text{ would have to be } \lambda \text{, which violates the assumption)}$$

$$\left(\bigcup_{s_0 \in S_0} \bar{\delta}_\lambda(s_0, x)\right) \cap F \neq \emptyset \Rightarrow \text{(by definition of } L)$$

$$x \in L(A_\lambda)$$

Conversely, and for many of the same reasons, we have

$$x \in L(A_\lambda) \Rightarrow \text{(by definition of } L)$$

$$\left(\bigcup_{s_0 \in S_0} \bar{\delta}_\lambda(s_0, x)\right) \cap F \neq \emptyset \Rightarrow \text{(by Lemma 4.2)}$$

$$\left(\bigcup_{s_0 \in S_0} \bar{\delta}_\lambda^\sigma(s_0, x)\right) \cap F \neq \emptyset \Rightarrow \text{(since } F \subseteq F^\sigma)$$

$$\left(\bigcup_{s_0 \in S_0} \bar{\delta}_\lambda^\sigma(s_0, x)\right) \cap F^\sigma \neq \emptyset \Rightarrow \text{(by definition of } L)$$

$$x \in L(A_\lambda^\sigma)$$

Consequently, $(\forall x \in \Sigma^*)(x \in L(A_\lambda^\sigma) \Leftrightarrow x \in L(A_\lambda))$.
Δ

Although nondeterministic finite automata *with* λ-transitions are no more powerful than nondeterministic finite automata *without* λ-transitions and consequently recognize the same class of languages as deterministic finite automata, they have their place in theory and machine construction. Because such machines can be constructed very easily from *regular expressions* (see Chapter 6), NDFAs are used by the UNIX™ text editor and by lexical analyzer generators such as LEX for pattern-matching applications. Example 4.16 involves the regular expression $(\mathbf{a} \cup \mathbf{c})^*\mathbf{bc}(\mathbf{a} \cup \mathbf{c})^*$, which describes the set of words composed of any number of **a**s and **c**s, followed by a single **b**, followed by a single **c**, followed by any number of **a**s and **c**s.

EXAMPLE 4.16

Suppose that we wanted to construct a machine that will accept the language $L = \{x \in \{\mathbf{a}, \mathbf{b}, \mathbf{c}\}^* \mid x$ contains exactly one **b**, which is immediately followed by **c**$\}$. A machine that accepts this language is given in Figure 4.21.

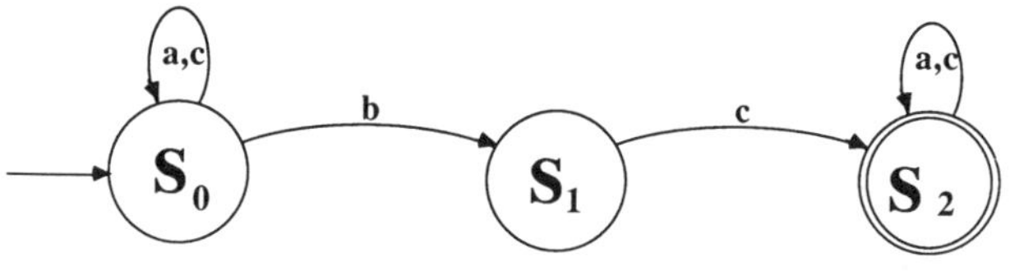

Figure 4.21 The NDFA described in Example 4.16

Suppose we now wish to build a machine that will accept any positive number of occurrences of various strings from this language concatenated together. In this case, the resulting language would include all strings (with at least one **b**) with the property that each and every **b** is immediately followed by **c**. By simply adding a λ-transition from every final state to the start state, we achieve our objective. The machine that accepts this new language is shown in Figure 4.22.

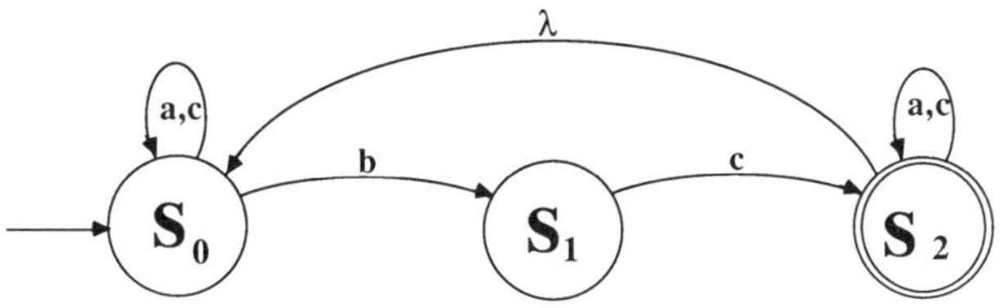

Figure 4.22 The modification of the NDFA in Figure 4.21

The previous section outlined how to implement nondeterministic finite automata *without* λ-transitions; accommodating λ-moves is in fact quite straightforward. A λ-transition from state s to state t indicates that state t should be considered active whenever state s is active. This can be assured by an obvious modification, as shown by the following example.

EXAMPLE 4.17

As an illustration of how circuitry can be defined for machines with λ-transitions, consider the DFA E given in Figure 4.23. This machine is similar to the NDFA D in Example 4.13, but a λ-transition has been added from s_1 to s_2; that is, $\delta(s_1, \lambda) = \{s_2\}$. This transition implies that s_2 should be considered active whenever s_1 is active. Consequently, the circuit diagram produced in Example 4.13 need only be slightly modified by establishing the extra connection indicated by the dotted line shown in Figure 4.24.

In general, the need for such "extra" connections leaving a given flip-flop input $\mathbf{t}_i$ is determined by examining $\delta(s_i, \lambda)$, the set of λ-transitions for s_i. Note that the propagation delay in this circuit has been increased; there are signals that must

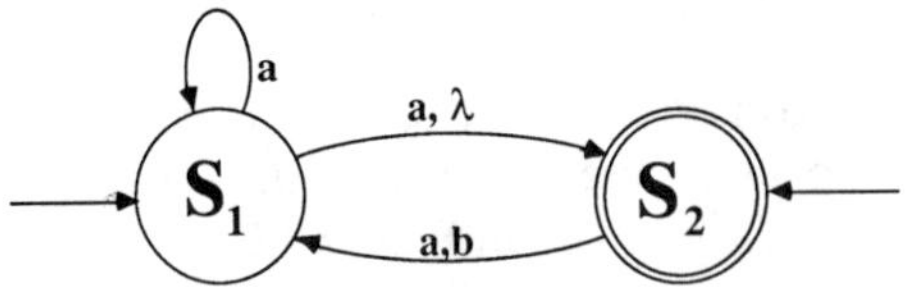

Figure 4.23 A simple NDFA with lambda moves

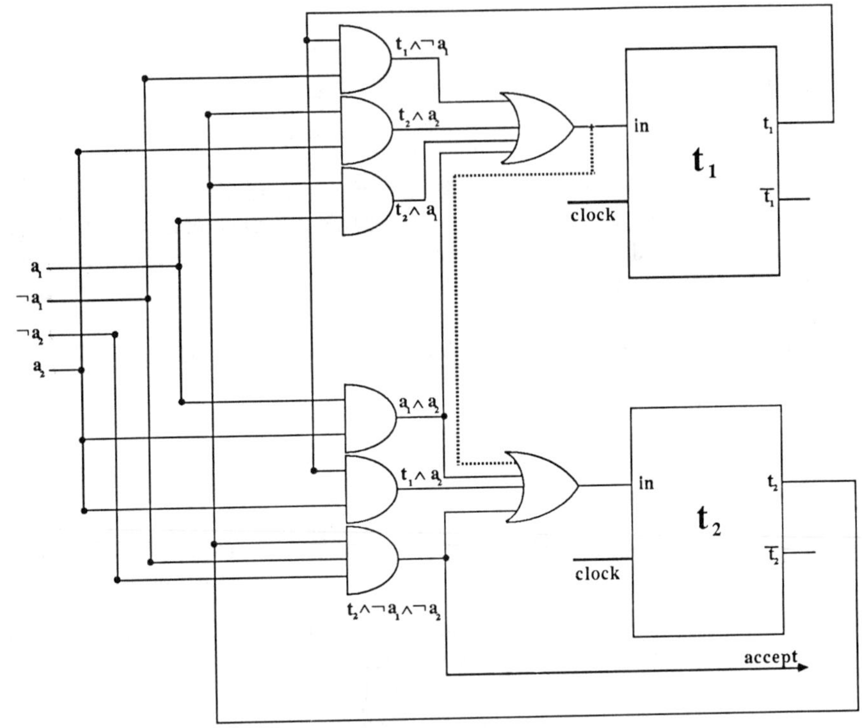

Figure 4.24 Circuitry for the automaton discussed in Example 4.17

now propagate through an extra gate during a single clock cycle. The delay will be exacerbated in automata that contain sequences of λ-transitions. In such cases, the length of the clock cycle may need to be increased to ensure proper operation. This problem can be minimized by adding all the connections indicated by $\Lambda(s_i)$, rather than just adding those implied by $\delta(s_i, \lambda)$.

EXERCISES

4.1. Draw the deterministic versions of each of the nondeterministic finite automata shown in Figure 4.25. In each part, assume $\Sigma = \{\mathbf{a}, \mathbf{b}, \mathbf{c}\}$.

4.2. Consider the automaton given in Example 4.17.

(a) Convert this automaton into an NDFA without λ-transitions using Definition 4.9.

(b) Convert this NDFA into a DFA using Definition 4.5.

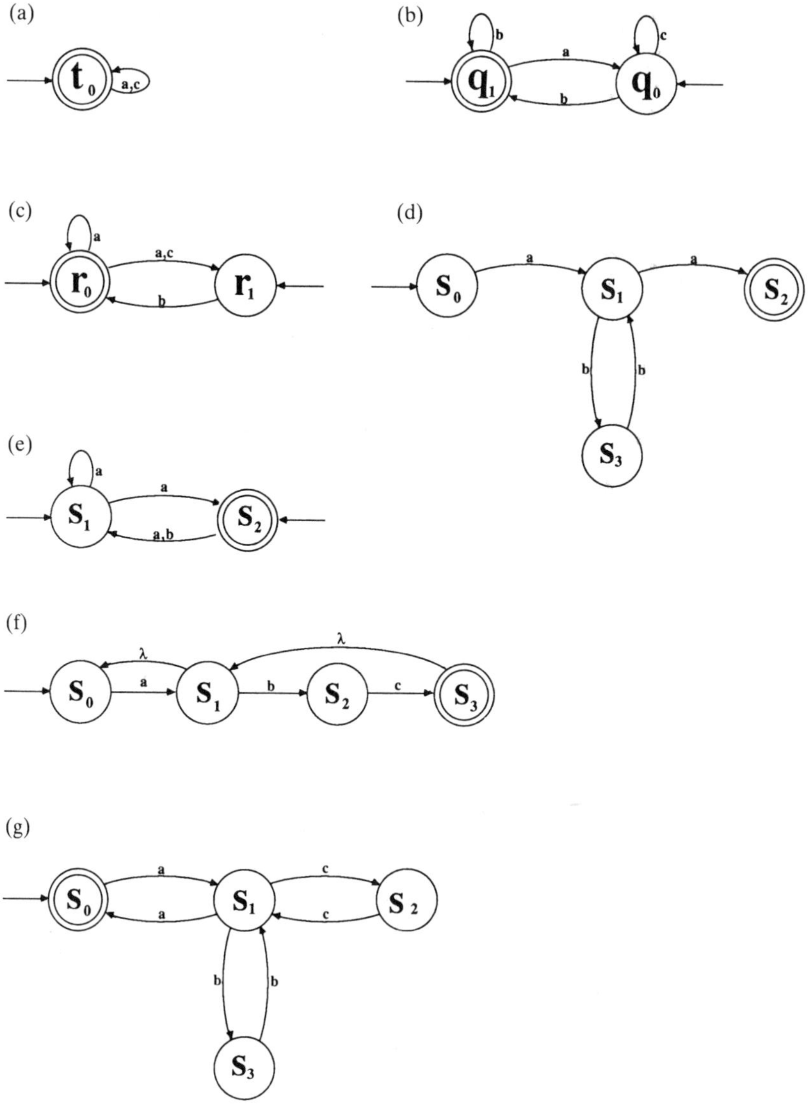

Figure 4.25 Automata for Exercise 4.1

4.3. Consider the automaton given in Example 4.4.

(a) Using the standard encodings, draw a circuit diagram for this NDFA (include neither <SOS> nor <EOS>).

(b) Using the standard encodings, draw a circuit diagram for this NDFA (include both <SOS> and <EOS>).

(c) Convert the NDFA into a DFA using Definition 4.5 (draw only the connected portion of the machine).

(d) Convert the NDFA into a DFA using Definition 4.5 (draw the entire machine, including the disconnected portion).

4.4. Consider the automaton given in Example 4.2.

(a) Using the standard encodings, draw a circuit diagram for this NDFA (include both <SOS> and <EOS>).

(b) Convert the NDFA into a DFA using Definition 4.5.

4.5. Consider the automaton given in Example 4.3.

(a) Using the standard encodings, draw a circuit diagram for this NDFA (include neither <SOS> nor <EOS>).

(b) Using the standard encodings, draw a circuit diagram for this NDFA (include both <SOS> and <EOS>).

(c) Convert the NDFA into a DFA using Definition 4.5 (draw only the connected portion of the machine).

(d) Is this DFA isomorphic to any of the automata constructed in Exercise 4.4?

4.6. Consider the automaton given in Example 4.14.

(a) Using the standard encodings, draw a circuit diagram for this NDFA (include neither <SOS> nor <EOS>).

(b) Using the standard encodings, draw a circuit diagram for the NDFA in part (b) (include neither <SOS> nor <EOS>).

4.7. Consider the automaton given in the second part of Example 4.16.

(a) Using the standard encodings, draw a circuit diagram for this NDFA (include <EOS> but not <SOS>).

(b) Build the equivalent automaton *without* λ-transitions using Definition 4.9.

(c) Using the standard encodings, draw a circuit diagram for the NDFA in part (b) (include <EOS> but not <SOS>).

(d) Convert the NDFA into a DFA using Definition 4.5 (draw only the connected portion of the machine).

4.8. It is possible to build a *deterministic finite automaton* $\overline{A}$ such that the language accepted by this machine is the *absolute complement* of the language accepted by a machine A [that is, $L(\overline{A}) = \Sigma^* - L(A)$] by simply complementing the set of final states (see Theorem 5.1). Can a similar thing be done for nondeterministic finite automata? If not, why not? Give an example to support your statements.

4.9. Given a nondeterministic finite automaton A *without* λ-transitions, show that it is possible to construct a nondeterministic finite automaton *with* λ-transitions A′ with the properties

(1) A′ has exactly *one* start state and exactly *one* final state and

(2) $L(A') = L(A)$.

4.10. Consider (ii) in Definition 4.8. Can this fact be deduced from parts (i) and (iii)? Justify your answer.

4.11. If we wanted another way to construct a nondeterministic finite automaton *without* λ-transitions corresponding to one that does have them, we could try the following: Let $S' = S$, $S'_0 = \Lambda(S_0)$, $F' = F$, and $\delta'(s, \mathbf{a}) = \overline{\delta}_\lambda(s, \mathbf{a})$ for all $\mathbf{a} \in \Sigma, s \in S$. Show that this works (or if it does not work, explain why not and give an example).

4.12. Using nondeterministic machines *with* λ-transitions, give an algorithm for constructing a λ-NDFA having *one* start state and *one* final state that will accept the *union* of two FAD languages.

4.13. Give an example of an NDFA A for which:

(a) A^d is not connected.

(b) A^d is not reduced.

(c) A^d is minimal.

4.14. Why was it necessary to include an "extra" state q_0 in the construction of A_λ^σ in Definition 4.9? Support your answer with an example.

4.15. **(a)** Using nondeterministic machines *without* λ-transitions, give an algorithm for constructing a machine that will accept the *union* of two languages.

(b) Is this easier or more difficult than using machines *with* λ-transitions?

(c) Is it possible to ensure that this machine *both* (i) has exactly *one* start state *and* (ii) has exactly *one* final state?

4.16. Consider the automaton A_λ^σ given in Example 4.15.

(a) Using the standard encodings, draw a circuit diagram for A_λ^σ (include neither <SOS> nor <EOS>).

(b) Convert A_λ^σ into $A_\lambda^{\sigma d}$ using Definition 4.5 (draw only the connected portion of the machine).

4.17. **(a)** Prove that for any NDFA *without* λ-transitions the definitions of $\bar{\delta}$ and δ agree for single letters; that is, $(\forall s \in S)(\forall \mathbf{a} \in \Sigma)(\bar{\delta}(s, \mathbf{a}) = \delta(s, \mathbf{a}))$.

(b) Give an example to show that this need not be true for an NDFA *with* λ-transitions.

4.18. Consider the NDFA that accepts the original language L in Example 4.10.

(a) Using the standard encodings, draw a circuit diagram for this NDFA (include neither <SOS> nor <EOS>).

(b) Convert the NDFA into a DFA using Definition 4.5 (draw only the connected portion of the machine).

4.19. Consider the NDFA which accepts the modified language L^r in Example 4.10.

(a) Using the standard encodings, draw a circuit diagram for this NDFA (include neither <SOS> nor <EOS>).

(b) Convert the NDFA into a DFA using Definition 4.5 (draw only the connected portion of the machine).

4.20. Consider the arguments leading up to the pumping lemma in Chapter 2. Are they still valid when applied to NDFAs?

4.21. Consider Theorem 2.7. Does the conclusion still hold if applied to an NDFA?

4.22. Given a nondeterministic finite automaton A (without λ-transitions) for which $\lambda \notin L(A)$, show that it is possible to construct a nondeterministic finite automaton (also without λ-transitions) A″ with the properties:

1. A″ has exactly *one* start state.
2. A″ has exactly *one* final state.
3. $L(A'') = L(A)$.

4.23. Give an example to show that if $\lambda \in L(A)$ it may not be possible to construct an NDFA without λ-transitions satisfying all three properties listed in Exercise 4.22.

4.24. Prove Lemma 4.2.

4.25. Given a DFA A, show that it can be thought of as an NDFA A^n and that, furthermore, $L(A^n) = L(A)$. *Hint:* Carefully define your "new" machine A^n, justify that it is indeed an NDFA, make the appropriate inductive statement, and argue that $L(A^n) = L(A)$.

4.26. Give an example to show that the domain of Lemma 4.2 cannot be expanded to include λ; that is, show that $\bar{\delta}^{\sigma}_{\lambda}(s, \lambda) \neq \bar{\delta}_{\lambda}(s, \lambda)$.

4.27. Refer to Definition 4.5 and prove the fact used in Lemma 4.1:

$$(\forall A \in \rho(S))(\forall B \in \rho(S))(\forall \mathbf{a} \in \Sigma)(\delta^d(A \cup B, \mathbf{a}) = \delta^d(A, \mathbf{a}) \cup \delta^d(B, \mathbf{a}))$$

4.28. Recall that if a word can reach several states in an NDFA, some of which are final and some nonfinal, Definition 4.4 requires us to accept that word.

(a) Change the definition of $L(\mathsf{A})$ so that a word is accepted only if *every* state the word can reach is final.

(b) Change the definition of A^d to produce a deterministic machine that accepts only those words specified in part (a).

4.29. Draw the connected part of T^d, the deterministic equivalent of the NDFA T in Example 4.7.

4.30. Refer to Example 4.7 and modify the NDFA T so that the machine reverts to a nonfinal state (that is, turns the recorder off) when the substring **000111** is detected. Note that **000111** functions as the EOT (end of transmission) signal.

4.31. Consider the automaton A given in Example 4.14.

(a) Draw a diagram of $\mathsf{A}^{\sigma}_{\lambda}$.

(c) Draw $\mathsf{A}^{\sigma d}_{\lambda}$ (draw only the connected portion of the machine).

4.32. What is wrong with the following "proof" of Lemma 4.2? Let P(k) be defined by P(k): $(\forall s \in S)(\forall x \in \Sigma^k)(\bar{\delta}^{\sigma}_{\lambda}(s, x) = \bar{\delta}_{\lambda}(s, x))$.

Basis step ($k = 1$): $(\forall s \in S)(\forall \mathbf{a} \in \Sigma)(\bar{\delta}^{\sigma}_{\lambda}(s, \mathbf{a}) = \delta^{\sigma}_{\lambda}(s, \mathbf{a}) = \bar{\delta}_{\lambda}(s, \mathbf{a}))$.

Inductive step: Suppose that the result holds for all $x \in \Sigma^k$ and let $y \in \Sigma^{k+1}$. Then $(\exists x \in \Sigma^k)(\exists \mathbf{a} \in \Sigma \ni y = x\mathbf{a})$. Then

$$\begin{aligned}
\bar{\delta}^{\sigma}_{\lambda}(s, y) &= \bar{\delta}^{\sigma}_{\lambda}(s, x\mathbf{a}) \\
&= \delta^{\sigma}_{\lambda}(\bar{\delta}^{\sigma}_{\lambda}(s, x), \mathbf{a}) \\
&= \bar{\delta}^{\sigma}_{\lambda}(\bar{\delta}_{\lambda}(s, x), \mathbf{a}) \\
&= \bar{\delta}_{\lambda}(\bar{\delta}_{\lambda}(s, x), \mathbf{a}) \\
&= \bar{\delta}_{\lambda}(s, x\mathbf{a}) \\
&= \bar{\delta}_{\lambda}(s, y)
\end{aligned}$$

Therefore, $P(k) \Rightarrow P(k+1)$ for all $k \geq 1$, and by the principle of mathematical induction, we are assured that the equation holds for all $x \in \Sigma^+$.

4.33. Consider the automaton given in Example 4.7.

(a) Using the standard encodings, draw a circuit diagram for this NDFA (include neither <SOS> nor <EOS>).

(b) Convert the NDFA into a DFA using Definition 4.5 (draw only the connected portion of the machine).

4.34. Consider the automaton given in Example 4.11.

(a) Using the standard encodings, draw a circuit diagram for this NDFA (include neither <SOS> nor <EOS>).

(b) Convert the NDFA into a DFA using Definition 4.5 (draw only the connected portion of the machine).

4.35. Consider the automaton B given in Example 4.8.

(a) Using the standard encodings, draw a circuit diagram for B (include neither <SOS> nor <EOS>).
(b) Using the standard encodings, draw a circuit diagram for B^d (include neither <SOS> nor <EOS>). Encode the states in such a way that your circuit is similar to the one found in part (a).

4.36. Draw a circuit diagram for each NDFA given in Exercise 4.1 (include neither <SOS> nor <EOS>). Use the standard encodings.

4.37. Draw a circuit diagram for each NDFA given in Exercise 4.1 (include both <SOS> and <EOS>). Use the standard encodings.

4.38. Definition 3.10 and the associated algorithms were used in Chapter 3 for finding the connected portion of a DFA.
(a) Adapt Definition 3.10 so that it applies to NDFAs.
(b) Prove that there is an algorithm for finding the connected portion of an NDFA.

CHAPTER

5

CLOSURE PROPERTIES

In this chapter we will look at ways to combine languages that are recognized by finite automata (that is, FAD languages) and consider whether the combinations result in other FAD languages. These results will provide insights into the construction of finite automata and will provide useful information that will have bearing on the topics covered in later chapters. After the properties of the collection of FAD languages have been fully explored, other classes of languages will be investigated. We begin with a review of the concept of *closure*.

5.1 FAD LANGUAGES AND BASIC CLOSURE THEOREMS

Notice that when many everyday operators combine objects of a given type they produce an object of the same type. In arithmetic, for example, the multiplication of any two whole numbers produces another whole number. Recall that this property is described by saying that the set of whole numbers is *closed* under the operation of multiplication. In contrast, the quotient of two whole numbers is likely to produce a fraction: the whole numbers are not closed under division. The formal definition of closure, both for operators that combine two other objects (binary operators) and those that modify only one object (unary operators) is given below.

∇ **Definition 5.1.** The *set K is closed under the (binary) operator* Θ ***iff*** $(\forall x, y \in K)(x \Theta y \in K)$.
Δ

∇ **Definition 5.2.** The *set* K *is closed under the (unary) operator* η *iff* $(\forall x \in K)(\eta(x) \in K)$.
Δ

EXAMPLE 5.1

$\mathbb{N}$ is closed under + since, if x and y are nonnegative integers, then $x + y$ is another nonnegative integer; that is, if $x, y \in \mathbb{N}$, then $x + y \in \mathbb{N}$.

EXAMPLE 5.2

$\mathbb{I}$ is closed under $|\ |$ (absolute value), since if x is an integer $|x|$ is also an integer.

EXAMPLE 5.3

Let $\rho = \{X \mid X$ is a *finite* subset of $\mathbb{N}\}$; then ρ is closed under $\cup$, since the union of two finite sets is still finite. (If Y and Z are subsets for which $\|Y\| = n < \infty$ and $\|Z\| = m < \infty$, then $\|Y \cup Z\| \le n + m < \infty$. Under what conditions would $\|Y \cup Z\| < n + m$?)

To show a set K is not closed under a binary operator Θ, we must show $\neg[(\forall x, y \in K)(x \Theta y \in K)]$, which means $\exists x, y \in K \ni x \Theta y \notin K$.

EXAMPLE 5.4

$\mathbb{N}$ is not closed under $-$ (subtraction) since $3 - 5 = -2 \notin \mathbb{N}$, even though both $3 \in \mathbb{N}$ and $5 \in \mathbb{N}$.

Notice that the set as well as the operator is important when discussing closure properties; unlike $\mathbb{N}$, the set of all integers $\mathbb{I}$ *is* closed under subtraction. As with the binary operator in Example 5.4, a single counterexample is sufficient to show that a given set is not closed under a unary operator.

EXAMPLE 5.5

$\mathbb{N}$ is not closed under $\sqrt{\ }$ (square root) since $7 \in \mathbb{N}$ but $\sqrt{7} \notin \mathbb{N}$.

We will not be concerned so much with sets of numbers as with sets of languages. As in Example 5.3, the collection will be a set of sets. Of prime concern are those languages that are related to automata.

∇ **Definition 5.3.** Let Σ be an alphabet. The symbol $\mathfrak{D}_\Sigma$ is used to denote the set of all FAD languages over Σ; that is,

$$\mathfrak{D}_\Sigma = \{L \subseteq \Sigma^* \mid \exists \text{ deterministic finite automaton } M \ni L(M) = L\}$$

Δ

$\mathscr{D}_\Sigma$ is the set of all languages that can be recognized by finite automata. In this chapter, it is this set whose closure properties with respect to various operations in Σ^* we are most interested in investigating. For example, if there exists a machine that accepts a language K, then there is also a machine that accepts the complement of K. That is, if K is FAD, then $\sim$K is FAD: $\mathscr{D}_\Sigma$ is closed under $\sim$.

∇ **Theorem 5.1.** For any alphabet Σ, $\mathscr{D}_\Sigma$ is closed under $\sim$ (complementation).

Proof. Let $K \in \mathscr{D}_\Sigma$. We must show $\sim K \in \mathscr{D}_\Sigma$ also; that is, there is a machine that recognizes $\sim$K. But $K \in \mathscr{D}_\Sigma$, and thus there is a deterministic finite automaton that recognizes K: Let $A = <\Sigma, S, s_0, \delta, F>$ and $L(A) = K$. Define a new machine $A^\sim$ as follows: $A^\sim = <\Sigma, S^\sim, s_0^\sim, \delta^\sim, F^\sim> = <\Sigma, S, s_0, \delta, S\text{-}F>$, which looks just like A except that the final and nonfinal states have been interchanged. We claim that $L(A^\sim) = \sim K$. To show this, let x be an arbitrary element of Σ^*. Then

$$
\begin{aligned}
x \in L(A^\sim) &\Leftrightarrow \text{(by definition of } L\text{)}\\
\bar{\delta}^\sim(s_0^\sim, x) \in F^\sim &\Leftrightarrow \text{(by induction and the fact that } \delta = \delta^\sim\text{)}\\
\bar{\delta}(s_0^\sim, x) \in F^\sim &\Leftrightarrow \text{(by definition of } s_0^\sim\text{)}\\
\bar{\delta}(s_0, x) \in F^\sim &\Leftrightarrow \text{(by definition of } F^\sim\text{)}\\
\bar{\delta}(s_0, x) \in S\text{-}F &\Leftrightarrow \text{(by definition of complement)}\\
\bar{\delta}(s_0, x) \notin F &\Leftrightarrow \text{(by definition of } L\text{)}\\
x \notin L(A) &\Leftrightarrow \text{(by definition of K)}\\
x \notin K &\Leftrightarrow \text{(by definition of complement)}\\
x \in \sim K &
\end{aligned}
$$

Thus $L(A^\sim) = \sim K$ as claimed, and therefore the complement of a FAD language can also be recognized by a machine and is consequently also FAD. Thus $\mathscr{D}_\Sigma$ is closed under complementation.
Δ

It turns out that $\mathscr{D}_\Sigma$ is closed under all the common set operators. Notice that the definition of $\mathscr{D}_\Sigma$ implies that we are working with only one alphabet; if we combine two machines in some way, it is understood that both automata use exactly the same input alphabet. This turns out to be not much of a restriction, however, for if we wish to consider two machines that use different alphabets Σ_1 and Σ_2, we can simply modify each machine so that it is able to process the new common alphabet $\Sigma = \Sigma_1 \cup \Sigma_2$. It should be clear that this can be done in such a way as not to affect the language accepted by either machine (see the exercises).

We will now prove that the union of two FAD languages is also FAD. This can be shown by demonstrating that, given two automata M_1 and M_2, it is possible to construct another automaton that recognizes the union of the languages accepted by M_1 and M_2.

EXAMPLE 5.6

Consider the two machines M_1 and M_2 displayed in Figure 5.1. These two machines can easily be employed to construct a *non*deterministic finite automaton that clearly accepts the appropriate union. We simply need to combine them into a single machine, which in this case will have two start states, as shown in Figure 5.2.

The structure inside the dotted box should be viewed as a single NDFA with two start states. Any string that would be accepted by M_1 will reach a final state if it starts in the "upper half" of the new machine, while strings that are recognized by M_2 will be accepted by the "lower half" of the machine. Recall that the definition of acceptance by a nondeterministic finite automaton implies that the NDFA in Figure 5.2 will accept a string if *any* path leads to a final state. This new NDFA will therefore accept all the strings that M_1 accepted and all the strings that M_2 accepted. Furthermore, these are the *only* strings that will be accepted. This trick is the basis of the following proof, which demonstrates the convenience of using the NDFA concept; a proof involving only DFAs would be both longer and less obvious (see the exercises).

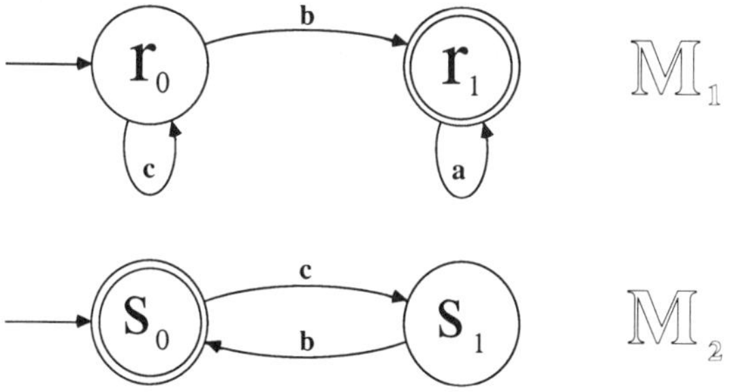

Figure 5.1 The two automata discussed in Example 5.6

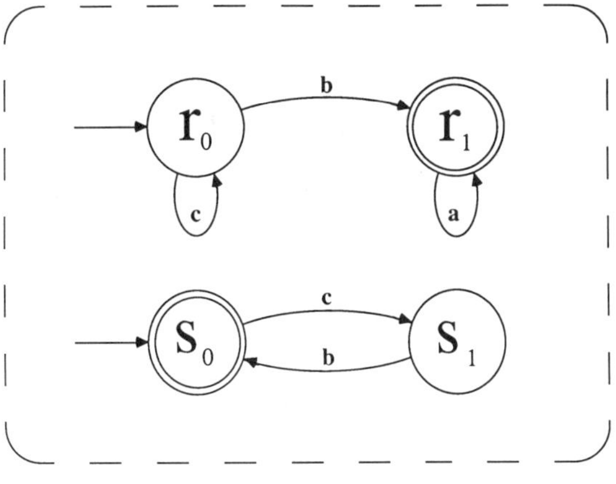

Figure 5.2 The resulting automaton in Example 5.6

∇ **Theorem 5.2.** For any alphabet Σ, $\mathfrak{D}_\Sigma$ is closed under $\cup$.

Proof. Let L_1 and L_2 belong to $\mathfrak{D}_\Sigma$. Then there are *non*deterministic finite automata $A_1 = <\Sigma, S_1, S_{0_1}, \delta_1, F_1>$ and $A_2 = <\Sigma, S_2, S_{0_2}, \delta_2, F_2>$ such that $L(A_1) = L_1$ and $L(A_2) = L_2$ (why?). Define $A^\cup = <\Sigma, S^\cup, S_0^\cup, \delta^\cup, F^\cup>$, where

$$S^\cup = S_1 \cup S_2 \quad \text{(without loss of generality, we can assume } S_1 \cap S_2 = \emptyset)$$

$$S_0^\cup = S_{0_1} \cup S_{0_2}$$

$$F^\cup = F_1 \cup F_2$$

and $\delta^\cup: (S_1 \cup S_2) \times \Sigma \to \wp(S_1 \cup S_2)$ is defined by

$$\delta^\cup(s, \mathbf{a}) = \begin{cases} \delta_1(s, \mathbf{a}) & \text{if } s \in S_1 \\ \delta_2(s, \mathbf{a}) & \text{if } s \in S_2 \end{cases}, \qquad \forall s \in S_1 \cup S_2, \quad \forall \mathbf{a} \in \Sigma$$

We claim that $L(A^\cup) = L(A_1) \cup L(A_2) = L_1 \cup L_2$. This must be proved using the definition of L from Chapter 4, since A_1, A_2, and $A^\cup$ are all NDFAs.

$$x \in L(A^\cup) \Leftrightarrow \text{(from Definition 4.4)}$$

$$(\exists s \in S_0^\cup)[\overline{\delta}^\cup(s, x) \cap F^\cup \neq \emptyset] \Leftrightarrow \text{(by definition of } S_0^\cup)$$

$$(\exists s \in S_{0_1} \cup S_{0_2})[\overline{\delta}^\cup(s, x) \cap F^\cup \neq \emptyset] \Leftrightarrow \text{(by definition of } \cup)$$

$$(\exists s \in S_{0_1})[\overline{\delta}^\cup(s, x) \cap F^\cup \neq \emptyset] \vee (\exists s \in S_{0_2})[\overline{\delta}^\cup(s, x) \cap F^\cup \neq \emptyset] \Leftrightarrow \text{(by definition of } \delta^\cup \text{ and induction)}$$

$$(\exists s \in S_{0_1})[\overline{\delta}_1(s, x) \cap F^\cup \neq \emptyset] \vee (\exists s \in S_{0_2})[\overline{\delta}_2(s, x) \cap F^\cup \neq \emptyset] \Leftrightarrow \text{(by definition of } F^\cup)$$

$$(\exists s \in S_{0_1})[\overline{\delta}_1(s, x) \cap F_1 \neq \emptyset] \vee (\exists s \in S_{0_2})[\overline{\delta}_2(s, x) \cap F_2 \neq \emptyset] \Leftrightarrow \text{(from Definition 4.4)}$$

$$x \in L(A_1) \vee x \in L(A_2) \Leftrightarrow \text{(by definition of } \cup)$$

$$x \in (L(A_1) \cup L(A_2)) \Leftrightarrow \text{(by definition of } L_1, L_2)$$

$$x \in L_1 \cup L_2$$

Δ

The above "proof" is actually incomplete; the transition from line 4 to line 5 actually depends on the assumed properties of $\overline{\delta}^\cup$, and not the known properties of $\delta^\cup$. A rigorous justification should include an inductive proof of (or at least a reference to) the fact that $\overline{\delta}^\cup$ reflects the same sort of behavior that $\delta^\cup$ does; that is,

$$\overline{\delta}^\cup(s, x) = \begin{cases} \overline{\delta}_1(s, x) & \text{if } s \in S_1 \\ \overline{\delta}_2(s, x) & \text{if } s \in S_2 \end{cases}, \qquad \forall s \in S_1 \cup S_2, \quad \forall x \in \Sigma^*$$

The above rule essentially states that the definition that applies to the single letter **a** also applies to the string x, and it is easy to prove by induction on the length of x (see the exercises).

The following theorem, which states that $\mathfrak{D}_\Sigma$ is closed under $\cap$, will be justified in two separate ways. The first proof will argue that the closure property must hold due to previous results; no new DFA need be constructed. The drawback to this type of proof is that we have no suitable guide for actually combining two existing DFAs into a new machine that will recognize the appropriate intersection (although, as outlined in the exercises, in this case a construction based on the first proof is fairly easy to generate).

Some operators are so bizarre that a nonconstructive proof of closure is the best we can hope for; intersection is definitely *not* that strange, however. In a second proof of the closure of $\mathfrak{D}_\Sigma$ under $\cap$, Lemma 5.1 will explicitly outline how an intersection machine could be built. When such constructions can be demonstrated, we will say that $\mathfrak{D}_\Sigma$ is *effectively* closed under the operator in question (see Theorem 5.12 for a discussion of an operator that is not effectively closed).

∇ **Theorem 5.3.** For any alphabet Σ, $\mathfrak{D}_\Sigma$ is closed under $\cap$.

Proof. Let L_1 and L_2 belong to $\mathfrak{D}_\Sigma$. Then by Theorem 5.1, $\sim L_1$ and $\sim L_2$ are also FAD. By Theorem 5.2, $\sim L_1 \cup \sim L_2$ is also FAD. By Theorem 5.1 again, $\sim(\sim L \cup \sim L_2)$ is also FAD. By De Morgan's law, this last expression is equivalent to $L_1 \cap L_2$, so $L_1 \cap L_2$ is FAD, and thus $L_1 \cap L_2 \in \mathfrak{D}_\Sigma$.
Δ

Note that the above argument could be made to apply to *any* collection C of sets that were known to be closed under union and complementation. A second proof of Theorem 5.3 might rely on the following lemma, using the "dircct" method of constructing a deterministic machine that accepts $L_1 \cap L_2$. This would show that $\mathfrak{D}_\Sigma$ is *effectively* closed under the intersection operator.

∇ **Lemma 5.1.** Given *deterministic* finite automata $A_1 = <\Sigma, S_1, s_{0_1}, \delta_1, F_1>$ and $A_2 = <\Sigma, S_2, s_{0_2}, \delta_2, F_2>$ such that $L(A_1) = L_1$ and $L(A_2) = L_2$, define a new DFA $A^\cap = <\Sigma, S^\cap, s_0^\cap, \delta^\cap, F^\cap>$, where

$$S^\cap = S_1 \times S_2$$

$$s_0^\cap = \langle s_{0_1}, s_{0_2} \rangle$$

$$F^\cap = F_1 \times F_2,$$

and $\delta^\cap: (S_1 \times S_2) \times \Sigma \to S_1 \times S_2$ is defined by

$$\delta^\cap(\langle s, t \rangle, \mathbf{a}) = \langle \delta_1(s, \mathbf{a}), \delta_2(t, \mathbf{a}) \rangle \quad \forall s \in S_1, \forall t \in S_2, \forall \mathbf{a} \in \Sigma$$

Then $L(A^\cap) = L_1 \cap L_2$.

Proof. As usual, the key is to show that $x \in L(A^\cap) \Leftrightarrow x \in L_1 \cap L_2$. The proof hinges on the inductive statement that $\overline{\delta}^\cap$ obeys the same rule that defines $\delta^\cap$; that is, $(\forall s \in S_1)(\forall t \in S_2)(\forall x \in \Sigma^*)(\overline{\delta}^\cap(\langle s, t \rangle, x) = \langle \overline{\delta}_1(s, x), \overline{\delta}_2(t, x) \rangle)$. The details are left for the reader (see the exercises).
Δ

The idea behind the above construction is to build a machine that "remembers" the state changes that both A_1 and A_2 make as they each process the same string, and hence the state set consists of all possible pairs of states from A_1 and A_2. The goal was to design the transition function $\delta^\cap$ so that being in state $\langle s, t\rangle$ in $A^\cap$ indicates that A_1 would currently be in state s and A_2 would be in state t. This goal also motivates the definition of the new start state; we want to begin in the start states of A_1 and A_2, and hence $s_0^\cap = \langle s_{0_1}, s_{0_2}\rangle$. We only wish to accept strings that are common to both languages, which means that the terminating state in A_1 belongs to F_1 and the last state reached in A_2 is likewise a final state. This requirement naturally leads to the definition of $F^\cap$, where $\langle s, t\rangle$ is a final state if and only if both s and t were final states in their respective machines.

EXAMPLE 5.7

Consider the two machines A_1 and A_2 displayed in Figure 5.3. Note that A_2 "remembers" whether there have been an even or an odd number of **b**s, while A_1 "counts" the number of letters (mod 3). We now demonstrate how the definition in Lemma 5.1 can be applied to form a deterministic machine that accepts the intersection of $L(A_1)$ and $L(A_2)$. The structure of $A^\cap$ would in this case look like the automaton shown in Figure 5.4. Note that $A^\cap$ does indeed keep track of the criteria that both A_1 and A_2 use to accept or reject strings. We will be in a state on the right side of $A^\cap$ if

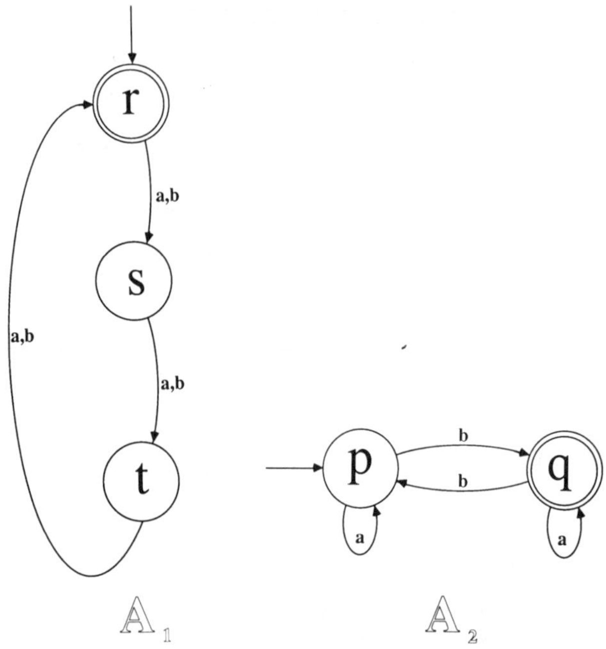

(a) (b)

Figure 5.3 The automata discussed in Example 5.7

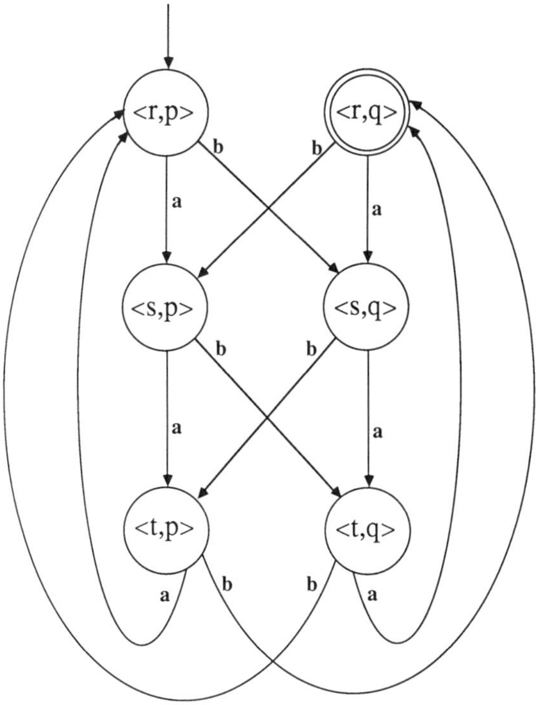

Figure 5.4 The resulting DFA for Example 5.7

an odd number of **b**s have been seen and on the left side when an even number of **b**s have been processed. At the same time, we will be in the upper, middle, or lower row of states depending on the total number of letters (mod 3) that have been processed. There is but one final state, corresponding to the situation where we have both an odd number of **b**s and the letter count is 0 (mod 3).

The operations used in the previous three theorems are common to set theory. We now present some new operators that are special to string algebra. We have defined concatenation (·) for individual strings, but there is a natural extension of the definition to languages, as indicated by the next definition.

∇ **Definition 5.4.** Let L_1 and L_2 be languages. The *concatenation* of L_1 with L_2, written $L_1 \cdot L_2$, is defined by

$$L_1 \cdot L_2 = \{x \cdot y \mid x \in L_1 \wedge y \in L_2\}$$

Δ

EXAMPLE 5.8

If $L_1 = \{\lambda, \mathbf{b}, \mathbf{cc}\}$ and $L_2 = \{\lambda, \mathbf{aa}, \mathbf{baa}\}$, then

$$L_1 \cdot L_2 = \{\lambda, \mathbf{b}, \mathbf{cc}, \mathbf{aa}, \mathbf{baa}, \mathbf{ccaa}, \mathbf{bbaa}, \mathbf{ccbaa}\}.$$

Note that **baa** qualifies to be in $L_1 \cdot L_2$ for two reasons: **baa** $= \lambda \cdot$**baa** and **baa** $=$ **b**$\cdot$**aa**. Thus we see that the concatenation contains only eight words rather than the expected 9 ($= 3 \cdot 3$). In general, $L_1 \cdot L_2$ consists of all words that can be formed by the concatenation of a word from L_1 with a word from L_2; for finite sets, concatenating an n word set with an m word set results in no more than $n \cdot m$ words. As shown in this example, the number of words can actually be less than $n \cdot m$. Larger languages can be concatenated, also. For example, $\Sigma^* \cdot \Sigma = \Sigma^+$.

The concatenation of two FAD languages is also FAD, as can easily be seen by employing NDFAs with λ-transitions.

EXAMPLE 5.9

Figure 5.5 illustrates two nondeterministic finite automata B_1 and B_2 that accept the languages L_1 and L_2 given in Example 5.8. Combining these two machines and linking the final states of B_1 to the start states of B_2 with λ-transitions yields a new NDFA that accepts $L_1 \cdot L_2$, as shown in Figure 5.6.

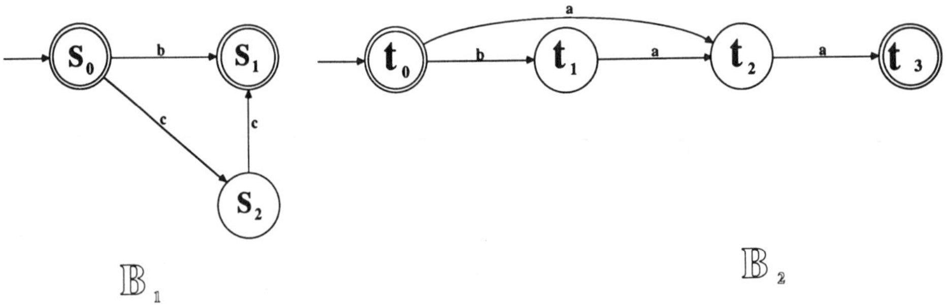

Figure 5.5 Two candidates for concatenation

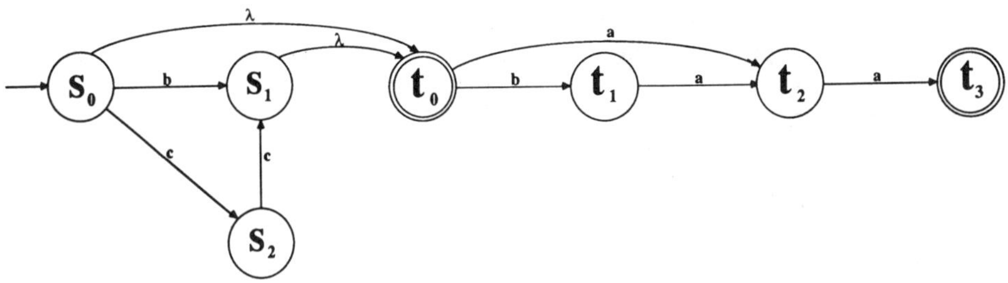

Figure 5.6 An NDFA which accepts the concatenation of the machines discussed in Example 5.9

EXAMPLE 5.10

Consider the *deterministic* finite automata A_1 and A_2 displayed in Figure 5.7. These can similarly be linked together to form an NDFA that accepts the concatenation of the languages accepted by A_1 and A_2, as shown in Figure 5.8.

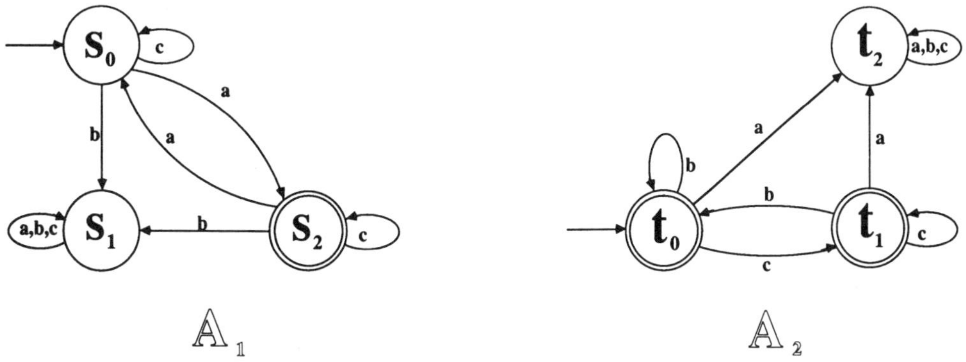

Figure 5.7 A pair of candidates for concatenation

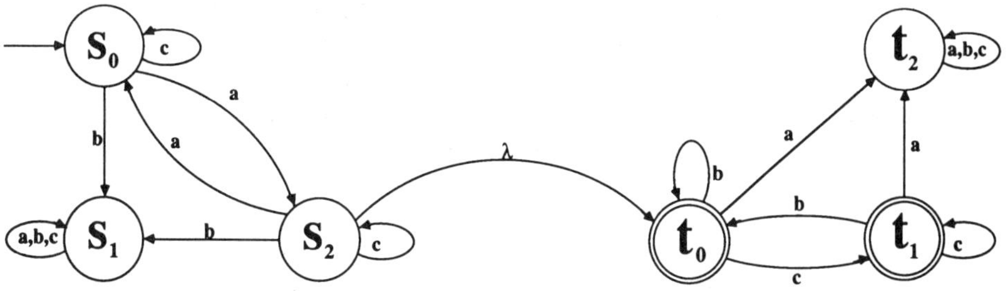

Figure 5.8 Concatenation of the machines in Example 5.10 via lambda-moves

It is also possible to directly build a machine for concatenation without using any λ-transitions, although the penalty for limiting our attention to less exotic machines is a loss of clarity in the construction. While the proof of the following theorem does not depend on λ-transitions, the resulting machine is still nondeterministic.

∇ **Theorem 5.4.** For any alphabet Σ, $\mathfrak{D}_\Sigma$ is closed under $\cdot$ (concatenation).

Proof. Let L_1 and L_2 belong to $\mathfrak{D}_\Sigma$. Then there are deterministic finite automata $A_1 = <\Sigma, S_1, s_{0_1}, \delta_1, F_1>$ and $A_2 = <\Sigma, S_2, s_{0_2}, \delta_2, F_2>$ such that $L(A_1) = L_1$ and $L(A_2) = L_2$. Without loss of generality, assume $S_1 \cap S_2 \neq \emptyset$. Define a nondeterministic machine $A^\bullet = <\Sigma, S^\bullet, S_0^\bullet, \delta^\bullet, F^\bullet>$, where

$$S^\bullet = S_1 \cup S_2 \quad \text{(without loss of generality, assume } S_1 \cap S_2 = \emptyset)$$

$$S_0^\bullet = \{s_{0_1}\}$$

$$F^\bullet = \begin{cases} F_2 & \text{if } \lambda \notin L_2 \\ F_1 \cup F_2 & \text{if } \lambda \in L_2 \end{cases}$$

and $\delta^\bullet: (S_1 \cup S_2) \times \Sigma \to \rho(S_1 \cup S_2)$ is defined by

$$\delta^{\bullet}(s, \mathbf{a}) = \begin{cases} \{\delta_1(s, \mathbf{a})\} & \text{if } s \in S_1 - F_1 \\ \{\delta_1(s, \mathbf{a}), \delta_2(s_{0_2}, \mathbf{a})\} & \text{if } s \in F_1 \\ \{\delta_2(s, \mathbf{a})\} & \text{if } s \in S_2 \end{cases}$$

It can be shown that $L(A^{\bullet}) = L(A_1) \cdot L(A_2) = L_1 \cdot L_2$ (see the exercises).
Δ

EXAMPLE 5.11

Conside the deterministic finite automata A_1 and A_2 in Example 5.10. These can be linked together to form the NDFA $A^{\bullet}$, and the reader can indeed verify that the machine illustrated in Figure 5.9 accepts the concatenation of the languages accepted by A_1 and A_2. Notice that the new transitions from the final states of A_1 mimic the transitions out of the start state of A_2.

Thus we see that avoiding λ-transitions while defining a concatenation machine is relatively simple. Unfortunately, avoiding the nondeterministic aspects of the construction is relatively impractical and would basically entail re-creating the construction in Definition 4.5 (which outlined the method for converting an NDFA into a DFA). Whereas it was merely convenient (rather than necessary) to employ NDFAs to demonstrate that $\mathfrak{D}_\Sigma$ is closed under union, the use of nondeterminism is essential to the proof of closure under concatenation.

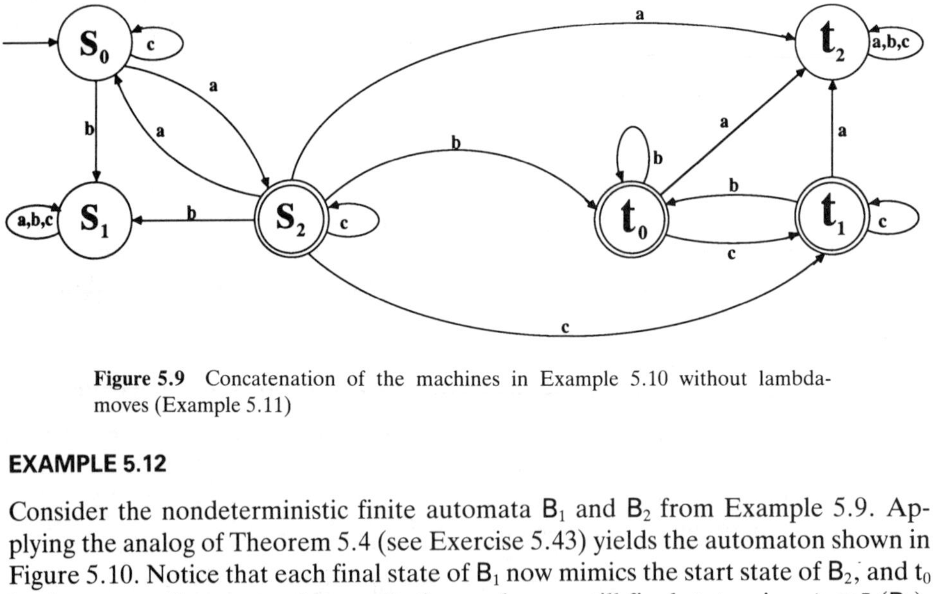

Figure 5.9 Concatenation of the machines in Example 5.10 without lambda-moves (Example 5.11)

EXAMPLE 5.12

Consider the nondeterministic finite automata B_1 and B_2 from Example 5.9. Applying the analog of Theorem 5.4 (see Exercise 5.43) yields the automaton shown in Figure 5.10. Notice that each final state of B_1 now mimics the start state of B_2, and t_0 has become a disconnected state. Both s_0 and s_1 are still final states since $\lambda \in L(B_2)$.

EXAMPLE 5.13

Consider the nondeterministic finite automata B_1 and B_3 shown in Figure 5.11, where B_1 is the same as that given in Example 5.9, while B_3 differs just slightly from B_2 (t_0 is no longer a final state). Note that $L(B_3) = \{\mathbf{aa}, \mathbf{baa}\}$, and $\lambda \notin L(B_3)$. Apply-

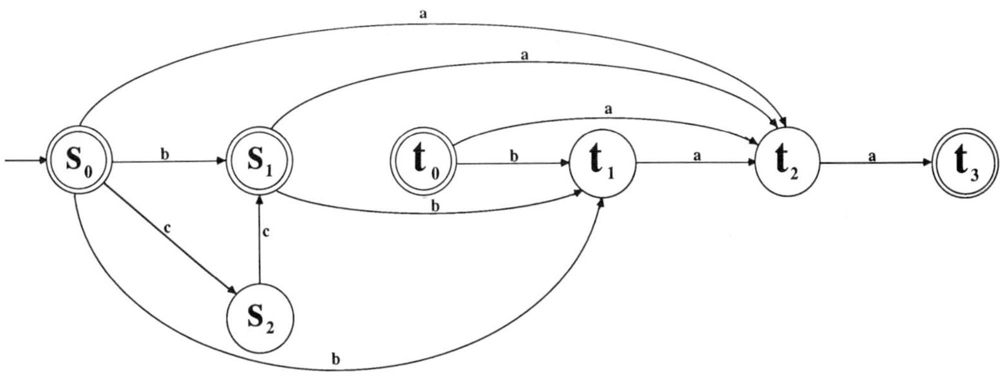

Figure 5.10 An NDFA without lambda-moves which accepts the concatenation of the languages discussed in Example 5.8

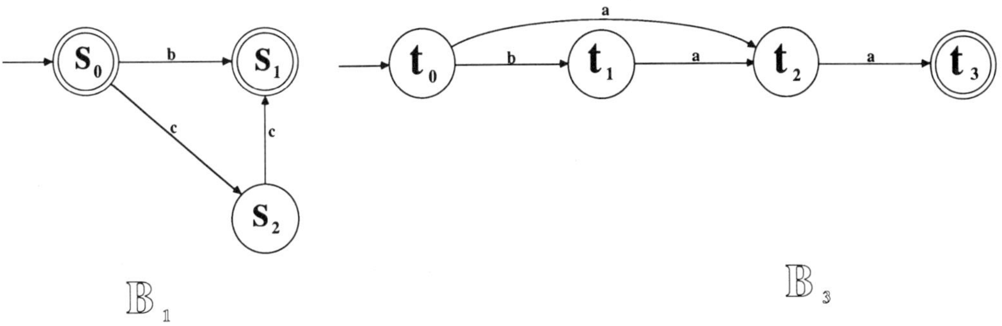

Figure 5.11 Candidates for concatenation in which the second machine does not accept λ (Example 5.13)

ing Theorem 5.4 in this case yields the automaton shown in Figure 5.12. In this construction, s_0 and s_1 are no longer final states since the definition of F' must follow a different rule when $\lambda \notin L(B_3)$. By examining the resulting machine, the reader can verify that having t_3 as the only final state is indeed the correct strategy for this case.

Besides concatenation, string algebra allows other new operators on lan-

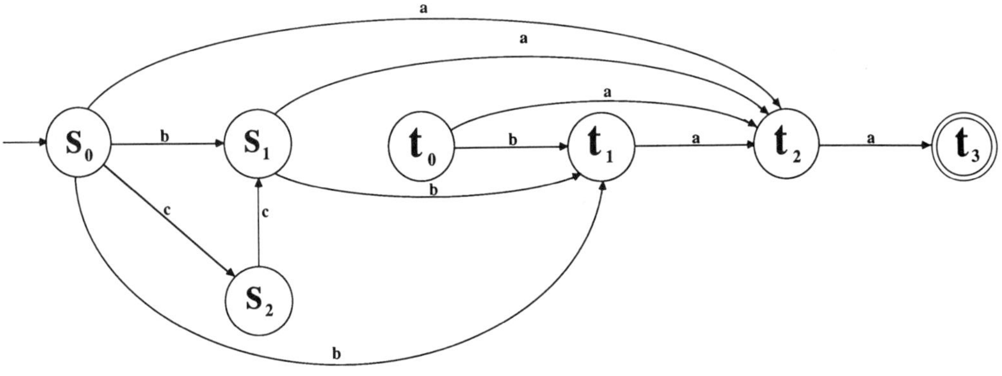

Figure 5.12 The concatenation of the NDFAs in Example 5.13

guages. The operators * and $^+$, which have at this point only been defined for alphabets, likewise have natural extensions to languages. Loosely, we would expect L^* to consist of all words that can be formed by the concatenation of several words from L.

∇ **Definition 5.5.** Let L be a language over some alphabet Σ. Define

$$\begin{aligned} L^0 &= \{\lambda\} \\ L^1 &= L \\ L^2 &= L\cdot L \\ L^3 &= L\cdot L^2 = L\cdot L\cdot L \end{aligned}$$

and in general

$$L^n = L\cdot L^{n-1}, \qquad \text{for } n = 1, 2, 3, \ldots$$

$$L^* = \bigcup_{i=0}^{\infty} L^i = L^0 \cup L^1 \cup L^2 \cup \cdots = \{\lambda\} \cup L \cup L\cdot L \cup L\cdot L\cdot L \cup \ldots$$

$$L^+ = \bigcup_{i=1}^{\infty} L^i = L^1 \cup L^2 \cup L^3 \cup \cdots = L \cup L\cdot L \cup L\cdot L\cdot L \cup \ldots$$

L^* is called the *Kleene closure* of the language L.
Δ

EXAMPLE 5.14

If $L = \{\mathbf{aa}, \mathbf{c}\}$, then $L^* = \{\lambda, \mathbf{aa}, \mathbf{c}, \mathbf{aac}, \mathbf{caa}, \mathbf{aaaa}, \mathbf{cc}, \mathbf{aaaaaa}, \mathbf{aaaac}, \mathbf{aacaa}, \ldots\}$.

EXAMPLE 5.15

If $K = \{\mathbf{db}, \mathbf{b}, \mathbf{c}\}$, then K^* consists of all words (over $\{\mathbf{b}, \mathbf{c}, \mathbf{d}\}$) for which each occurrence of **d** is immediately followed by (at least) one **b**.

$\mathfrak{D}_\Sigma$ is closed under both * and +. The technique for Kleene closure is outlined in Theorem 5.5. The construction for L^+ is similar (see the exercises).

∇ **Theorem 5.5.** For any alphabet Σ, $\mathfrak{D}_\Sigma$ is closed under * (Kleene closure).

Proof. Let L belong to $\mathfrak{D}_\Sigma$. Then there is a nondeterministic finite automaton $A = <\Sigma, S, S_0, \delta, F>$ such that $L(A) = L$. Define a nondeterministic machine $A_* = <\Sigma, S_*, S_{0*}, \delta_*, F_*>$, where

$$S_* = S \cup \{q_0\} \quad \text{(where } q_0 \text{ is some new element; } q_0 \notin S\text{)}$$

$$S_{0*} = S_0 \cup \{q_0\}$$

$$F_* = F \cup \{q_0\}$$

and $\delta_* : (S \cup \{q_0\} \times \Sigma \to \rho(S \cup \{q_0\})$ is defined by

$$\delta_*(s, \mathbf{a}) = \begin{cases} \delta(s, \mathbf{a}) & \text{if } s \notin F \cup \{q_0\} \\ \delta(s, \mathbf{a}) \cup \left(\bigcup_{t \in S_0} \delta(t, \mathbf{a}) \right) & \text{if } s \in F \\ \emptyset & \text{if } s = q_0 \end{cases}$$

We claim that $L(A_*) = L(A)^* = L^*$ (see the exercises).
Δ

EXAMPLE 5.16

Consider the *non*deterministic finite automaton B displayed in Figure 5.13, which accepts all words that contain exactly two (consecutive) **b**s. Using the modifications described above, the new NDFA B_* would look like the automaton shown in Figure 5.14. Notice that the new automaton does indeed accept $L(B)^*$, the set of all words in which the **b**s always occur in side-by-side pairs. This example also demonstrates the need for the special extra start (and final) state q_0 (see the exercises).

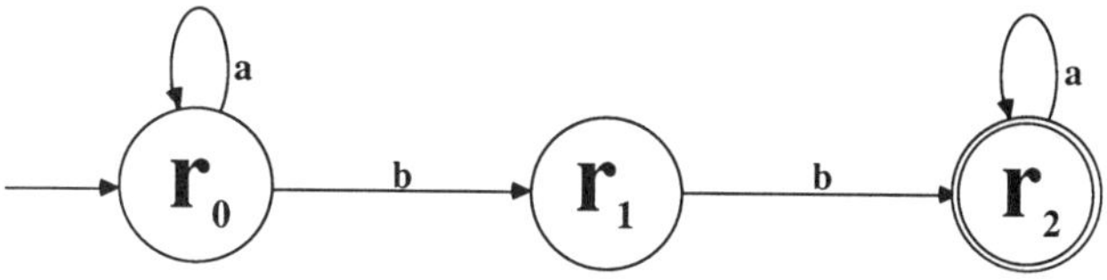

Figure 5.13 The NDFA B in Example 5.16.

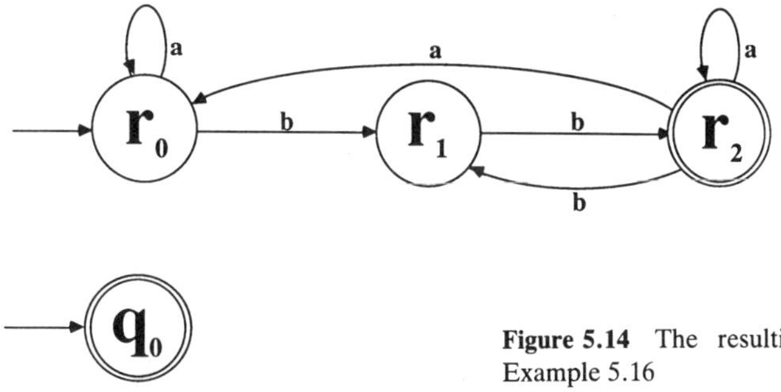

Figure 5.14 The resulting NDFA for Example 5.16

It is instructive to compare the different approaches taken in the proofs of Theorems 5.4 and 5.5. In both cases, nondeterministic automata were built, but Theorem 5.4 began with deterministic machines, while Theorem 5.5 assumed that a NDFA was provided. Note that, in the construction of $\delta^{\bullet}$ in Theorem 5.4, δ_1 was a deterministic transition function and as such produced a single state, whereas $\delta^{\bullet}$, on the other hand, must adhere to the nondeterministic definition and produce a *set* of states. As a consequence, the definition of $\delta^{\bullet}$ involved expressions like $\{\delta_1(s, \mathbf{a})\}$, which indicated that the single state given by $\delta_1(s, \mathbf{a})$ should be viewed as a singleton set.

By contrast, Theorem 5.5 specified the nondeterministic transition function δ_* in terms of δ, which was also assumed to be nondeterministic. This gave rise to definitions of the form $\delta_*(s, \mathbf{a}) = \delta(s, \mathbf{a})$. In this case, no set brackets { } were necessary since $\delta(s, \mathbf{a})$ by assumption already represented a set (rather than just a single element as in the deterministic case).

The definition of the new set of start states S_0 is also affected by the type of machine from which the new NDFA is formed. In reviewing Theorems 5.4 and 5.5, the reader should be able to see the parallel between the differences in the specifications of the δ function and the differences in the definitions of $S_0^{\bullet}$ and S_{0^*}. It is also instructive to compare and contrast the proof of Theorem 5.2 to those discussed above.

5.2 FURTHER CLOSURE PROPERTIES

The operators discussed in this section, while not as fundamental as those presented earlier, illustrate some useful techniques for constructing modified automata. Also explored are techniques that provide existence proofs rather than constructive proofs.

∇ **Theorem 5.6.** For any alphabet Σ, $\mathfrak{D}_\Sigma$ is closed under the operator Z, where Z is defined by

$$Z(\mathrm{L}) = \{x \mid x \text{ is formed by deleting zero or more letters from a word in L}\}.$$

Proof. See the exercises and the following example.

Δ

EXAMPLE 5.17

Consider the deterministic finite automaton C displayed in Figure 5.15, which accepts the language $\{\mathbf{a}^n\mathbf{b}^m \mid n \geq 1, m \geq 1\}$. $Z(\boldsymbol{L}(\mathrm{C}))$ would then be

$$\{\mathbf{a}^n\mathbf{b}^m \mid n \geq 0, m \geq 0\}$$

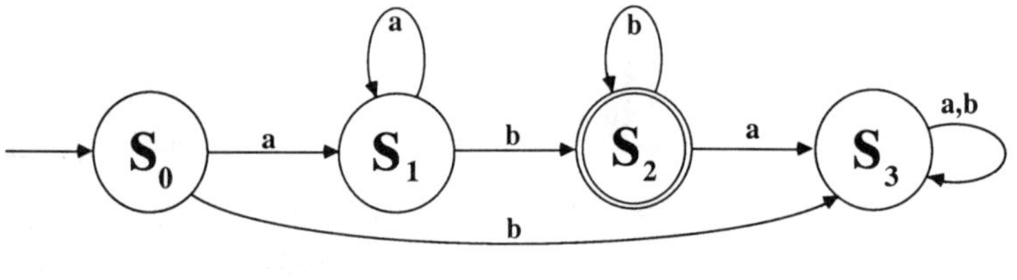

Figure 5.15 The automaton C discussed in Example 5.17

and can be accepted by modifying C so that every transition in the diagram has a corresponding λ-move (allowing that particular letter to be skipped), as shown in Figure 5.16.

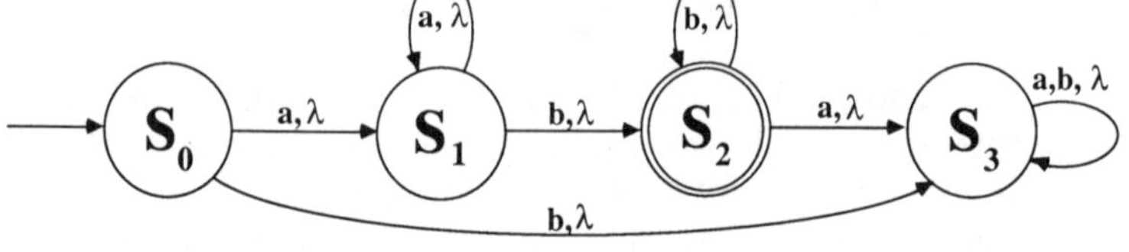

Figure 5.16 An automaton accepting Z(C) in Example 5.17

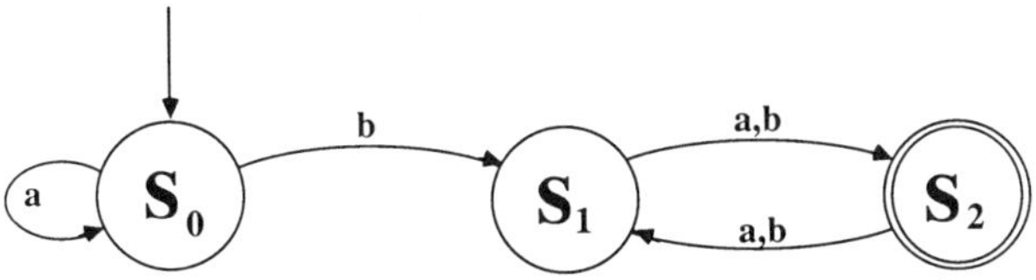

Figure 5.17 The automaton D discussed in Example 5.18

∇ **Theorem 5.7.** For any alphabet Σ, $\mathfrak{D}_\Sigma$ is closed under the operator Y, where Y is defined by

$$Y(L) = \{x \mid x \text{ is formed by deleting exactly one letter from a word in } L\}.$$

Proof. See the exercises and the following example.

Δ

EXAMPLE 5.18

We need a way to skip a letter as was done in Example 5.17, but we must now skip one and only one letter. The technique for accomplishing this involves using *copies* of the original machine. Consider the deterministic finite automaton D displayed in Figure 5.17. We will use λ-moves to mimic normal transitions, but in this case we will move from one copy of the machine to an appropriate state in a second copy. Being in the first copy of the machine will indicate that we have yet to skip a letter, and being in the second copy will signify that we have followed exactly one λ-move and have thus skipped exactly one letter. Hence the second copy will be the only one in which states are deemed final, and the first copy will contain the only start state. The modified machine for this example might look like the NDFA shown in Figure 5.18. The string **aba**, which is accepted by the original machine, should cause **ab**, **aa**, and **ba** to be accepted by the new machine. Each of these three are indeed accepted, by following the correct λ-move at the appropriate time. A similar technique, with the state transition function slightly redefined, could be used to accept words in which every other letter was deleted. If one wished only to acknowledge every third letter, three copies of the machine could be suitably connected together to achieve the desired result (see the exercises).

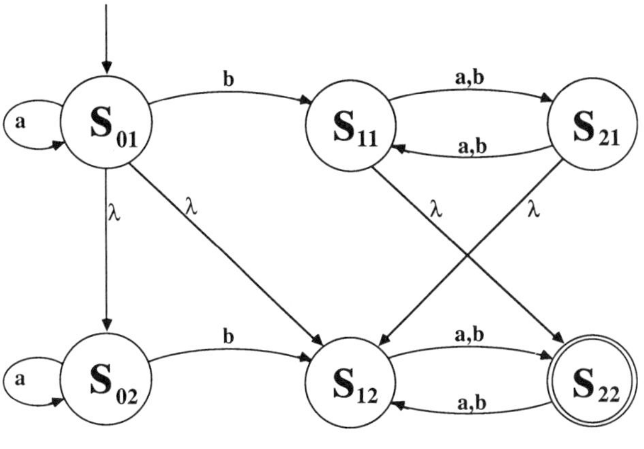

Figure 5.18 The modified machine in Example 5.18

While $\mathscr{D}_\Sigma$ is certainly the most important class of languages we have seen so far, we will now consider some other classes whose properties can be investigated. The closure properties of other collections of languages will be considered in the exercises and in later chapters.

∇ **Definition 5.6.** Let Σ be an alphabet. Then $\mathscr{W}_\Sigma$ is defined to be the set of all languages over Σ recognized by NDFAs; that is,

$$\mathscr{W}_\Sigma = \{L \subseteq \Sigma^* \mid \exists \text{ NDFA } N \ni \boldsymbol{L}(N) = L\}.$$

Δ

∇ **Lemma 5.2.** Let Σ be an alphabet. Then $\mathscr{W}_\Sigma = \mathscr{D}_\Sigma$.

Proof. The proof follows immediately from Theorem 4.1 and Exercise 4.25.

Δ

The reader should note that Lemma 5.2 simply restates in new terms the conclusion reached in Chapter 4, where it was proved that NDFAs were exactly as powerful as DFAs. More specifically, it was shown that any language that could be recognized by a NDFA could also be recognized by a DFA, and conversely. While every subset of Σ^* represents a language, those in $\mathscr{D}_\Sigma$ have exhibited many nice properties owing to the convenient representation afforded by finite automata. We now focus our attention on "the other languages," that is, those that are *not* in $\mathscr{D}_\Sigma$.

∇ **Definition 5.7.** Let Σ be an alphabet. Then $\mathscr{N}_\Sigma$ is defined to be the set of all *non*-FAD languages over Σ; that is,

$$\mathscr{N}_\Sigma = \{L \subseteq \Sigma^* \mid \text{there does } \textit{not} \text{ exist } \textit{any} \text{ finite automaton } M \ni \boldsymbol{L}(M) = L\}.$$

Δ

$\mathscr{N}_\Sigma$ is all the "complicated" languages (subsets) that can be formed from Σ^*; that is, $\mathscr{N}_\Sigma = \rho(\Sigma^*) - \mathscr{D}_\Sigma$. Be careful not to confuse $\mathscr{N}_\Sigma$ with the set of languages that can be recognized by NDFAs ($\mathscr{W}_\Sigma$ in Definition 5.6).

∇ **Theorem 5.8.** Let Σ be an alphabet. Then $\mathscr{N}_\Sigma$ is closed under ~ (complementation).

Proof. (by contradiction): Assume the lemma is not true, which means that there exists a language K for which

$$\begin{aligned} K \in \mathscr{N}_\Sigma \wedge {\sim}K \notin \mathscr{N}_\Sigma &\Rightarrow (\text{by definition of } \mathscr{N}_\Sigma) \\ {\sim}K \in \mathscr{D}_\Sigma &\Rightarrow (\text{by Theorem 5.1}) \\ {\sim}({\sim}K) \in \mathscr{D}_\Sigma &\Rightarrow (\text{since } {\sim}({\sim}K) = K) \\ K \in \mathscr{D}_\Sigma &\Rightarrow (\text{by definition of } \mathscr{N}_\Sigma) \\ K \notin \mathscr{N}_\Sigma & \end{aligned}$$

which contradicts the assumption. Thus the lemma must be true.
Δ

∇ **Lemma 5.3.** $\mathcal{N}_{\{\mathbf{a},\mathbf{b}\}}$ is *not* closed under $\cap$.

Proof. Let $L_1 = \{\mathbf{a}^p \mid p \text{ is prime}\}$ and let $L_2 = \{\mathbf{b}^p \mid p \text{ is prime}\}$. Then $L_1 \in \mathcal{N}_{\{\mathbf{a},\mathbf{b}\}}$, $L_2 \in \mathcal{N}_{\{\mathbf{a},\mathbf{b}\}}$, but $L_1 \cap L_2 = \emptyset \notin \mathcal{N}_{\{\mathbf{a},\mathbf{b}\}}$ (why?).

Δ

As another useful example of closure, we consider the transformation of one language to another via a *language homomorphism*, which represents the process of consistently replacing each single letter $\mathbf{a}_i$ by a word w_i. Such transformations are commonplace in computer science; some applications expect lines in a text file to be delimited with a carriage return/line feed pair, while other applications expect only a carriage return. Stripping away the unwanted line feeds is tantamount to applying a homomorphism that replaces most ASCII characters by the same symbol, but replaces line feeds by λ. Converting all lowercase letters in a file to uppercase is another common transformation that can be defined by a language homomorphism.

∇ **Definition 5.8.** Let $\Sigma = \{\mathbf{a}_1, \mathbf{a}_2, \ldots, \mathbf{a}_m\}$ be an alphabet and let Γ be a second alphabet. Given words $w_1, w_2, \ldots, w_m$ over Γ^*, define a *language homomorphism* $\psi: \Sigma \to \Gamma^*$ by $\psi(\mathbf{a}_i) = w_i$ for each i, which can be extended to $\overline{\psi}: \Sigma^* \to \Gamma^*$ by:

$$\overline{\psi}(\lambda) = \lambda$$

$$(\forall \mathbf{a} \in \Sigma)(\forall x \in \Sigma^*)(\overline{\psi}(\mathbf{a} \cdot x) = \psi(\mathbf{a}) \cdot (\overline{\psi}(x)))$$

$\overline{\psi}$ can be further extended to operate on a language L by defining

$$\overline{\psi}(L) = \{\overline{\psi}(z) \in \Gamma^* \mid z \in L\}$$

In this context, $\overline{\psi}: \rho(\Sigma^*) \to \rho(\Gamma^*)$.
Δ

EXAMPLE 5.19

Let $\Sigma = \{\mathbf{a}, \mathbf{b}\}$ and $\Gamma = \{\mathbf{c}, \mathbf{d}\}$, and define ψ by $\psi(\mathbf{a}) = \mathbf{cd}$ and $\psi(\mathbf{b}) = \mathbf{d}$. For $K = \{\lambda, \mathbf{ab}, \mathbf{bb}\}$, $\overline{\psi}(K) = \{\lambda, \mathbf{cdd}, \mathbf{dd}\}$, while for $L = \{\mathbf{a}, \mathbf{b}\}^*$, $\overline{\psi}(L)$ represents all words over $\{\mathbf{c}, \mathbf{d}\}$ in which every $\mathbf{c}$ is immediately followed by $\mathbf{d}$.

EXAMPLE 5.20

As a second example, let $\Sigma = \{), (\}$ and let Γ be the ASCII alphabet. If μ is defined by $\mu(() = $ **begin** and $\mu()) = $ **end**, then the set M of all strings of matched parentheses maps to K, the set of all matched **begin**–**end** pairs.

A general homomorphism ψ maps a language over Σ to a language over Γ. However, to consider the closure of $\mathcal{D}_\Sigma$, we will restrict our attention for the moment to homomorphisms for which $\Gamma = \Sigma$. It is more generally true, though, that even for language homomorphisms between two different alphabets, if L is FAD, the homomorphic image of L is also FAD (see the exercises).

∇ **Theorem 5.9.** Let Σ be an alphabet, and let $\psi: \Sigma \to \Sigma^*$ be a language homomorphism. Then $\mathcal{D}_\Sigma$ is closed under $\overline{\psi}$.

Proof. See the exercises and the following examples. A much more concise way to handle this transformation will be seen in Chapter 6 when substitutions are explored.
Δ

If the homomorphism is *length preserving*, that is, if it always maps letters to single letters, it is relatively easy to define a new automaton from the old one. Indeed, the state transition diagram hardly changes at all; all transitions marked **b** are simply relabeled with $\psi(\mathbf{b})$. For more complex homomorphisms, extra states must be added to accommodate the processing of the surplus letters. The following two examples illustrate the appropriate transformation of the state transition function and suggest a convenient labeling for the new states.

EXAMPLE 5.21

Consider the DFA B displayed in Figure 5.19a. For the homomorphism μ defined by $\xi(\mathbf{a}) = \mathbf{a}$ and $\xi(\mathbf{b}) = \mathbf{a}$, the automaton that will accept $\mu(L(\mathrm{B}))$ is shown in Figure 5.19b. Note that even in simple examples like this one the resulting automaton can be nondeterministic.

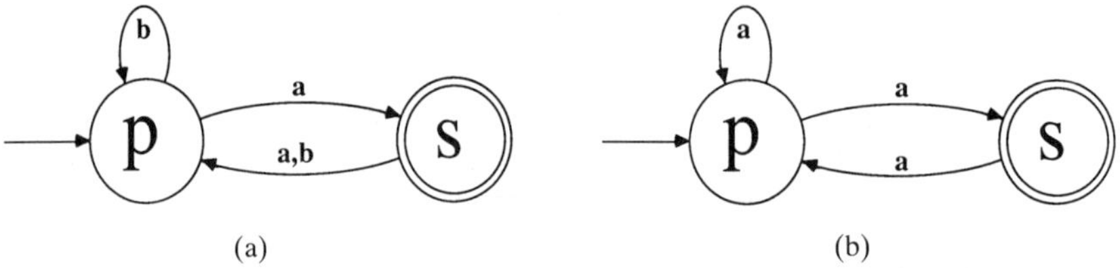

Figure 5.19 (a) The automaton discussed in Example 5.21 (b) The resulting automaton for Example 5.21

EXAMPLE 5.22

For the NDFA C displayed in Figure 5.20a and the homomorphism μ defined by $\mu(\mathbf{a}) = \mathbf{cc}$ and $\mu(\mathbf{b}) = \mathbf{a}$, the automaton that will accept $\mu(L(\mathrm{C}))$ is shown in Figure 5.20b. Note that each state of C requires an extra state to accommodate the **cc** transition.

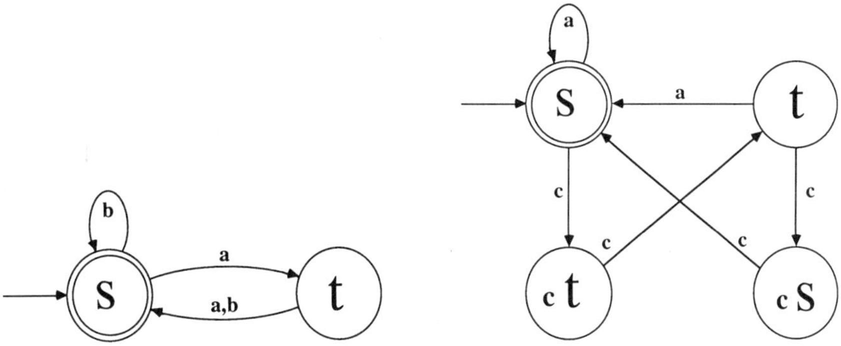

(a) (b)

Figure 5.20 (a) The automaton discussed in Example 5.22 (b) The resulting automaton for Example 5.22

EXAMPLE 5.23

Consider the *identity* homomorphism $\mu: \Sigma \to \Sigma^*$ defined by $(\forall \mathbf{a} \in \Sigma)(\mu(\mathbf{a}) = \mathbf{a})$. Since $\overline{\mu}(\mathrm{L}) = \mathrm{L}$, *any* collection of languages, including $\mathcal{N}_\Sigma$, is clearly closed under this homomorphism. Unlike $\mathfrak{D}_\Sigma$, though, there are many homomorphisms under which $\mathcal{N}_\Sigma$ is not closed.

∇ **Lemma 5.4.** Let $\Sigma = \{\mathbf{a}, \mathbf{b}\}$, and let $\xi: \Sigma \to \Sigma^*$ be defined by $\xi(\mathbf{a}) = \mathbf{a}$ and $\xi(\mathbf{b}) = \mathbf{a}$. Then $\mathcal{N}_\Sigma$ is *not* closed under $\overline{\xi}$.

Proof. Consider the set L of all strings that have the same number of **a**s as **b**s. This language is in $\mathcal{N}_\Sigma$, but $\overline{\xi}(\mathrm{L})$ is the set of all even-length strings of **a**s, which is clearly not in $\mathcal{N}_\Sigma$.
Δ

A rather trivial example involves the homomorphism defined by $\psi(\mathbf{a}) = \lambda$ for every letter $\mathbf{a} \in \Sigma$. Then for all languages L, whether or not $\mathrm{L} \in \mathcal{N}_\Sigma$, $\overline{\psi}(\mathrm{L}) = \{\lambda\}$, which is definitely not in $\mathcal{N}_\Sigma$.

∇ **Definition 5.9.** Let $\psi: \Sigma \to \Gamma^*$ be a language homomorphism and consider $z \in \Gamma^*$. The *inverse homomorphic image of z under* $\overline{\psi}$ is then

$$\overline{\psi}^{-1}(z) = \{x \in \Sigma^* \mid \overline{\psi}(x) = z\}$$

For a language $\mathrm{L} \subseteq \Gamma^*$, the *inverse homomorphic image of L under* $\overline{\psi}$ is defined by

$$\overline{\psi}^{-1}(\mathrm{L}) = \{x \in \Sigma^* \mid \overline{\psi}(x) \in \mathrm{L}\}$$

Δ

Thus, $x \in \overline{\psi}^{-1}(\mathrm{L}) \Leftrightarrow \overline{\psi}(x) \in \mathrm{L}$. While the image of a string under a homomorphism is a single word, note that the inverse image of a single string may be an entire set of words.

EXAMPLE 5.24

Consider $\bar{\xi}$ from Lemma 5.4 in which $\xi: \Sigma \to \Sigma^*$ was defined by $\xi(\mathbf{a}) = \mathbf{a}$ and $\xi(\mathbf{b}) = \mathbf{a}$. Let $z = \mathbf{aa}$. Since $\bar{\xi}(\mathbf{bb}) = \bar{\xi}(\mathbf{ba}) = \bar{\xi}(\mathbf{ab}) = \bar{\xi}(\mathbf{aa}) = \mathbf{aa}$,

$$\bar{\xi}^{-1}(\mathbf{aa}) = \{\mathbf{bb}, \mathbf{ba}, \mathbf{ab}, \mathbf{aa}\}. \text{ Note that } \bar{\xi}^{-1}(\mathbf{ba}) = \emptyset.$$

For $\mathrm{L} = \{x \in \{\mathbf{a}\}^* \mid |x| \equiv 0 \bmod 3\}$, $\bar{\xi}^{-1}(\mathrm{L}) = \{x \in \{\mathbf{a}, \mathbf{b}\}^* \mid |x| \equiv 0 \bmod 3\}$. Note that this second set is definitely larger, since it also contains words with **b**s in them.

It can be shown that $\mathfrak{D}_\Sigma$ is closed under inverse homomorphism. The trick is to make the state transition function of the new automaton *simulate*, for a given letter **a**, the action the old automaton would have taken for the entire string $\psi(\mathbf{a})$. As the following proof will illustrate, the only change that need take place is in the δ function; the newly constructed machine is even deterministic!

∇ **Theorem 5.10.** Let Σ be an alphabet, and let $\psi: \Sigma \to \Sigma^*$ be a language homomorphism. Then $\mathfrak{D}_\Sigma$ is closed under $\bar{\psi}^{-1}$.

Proof. Let $\mathrm{L} \in \mathfrak{D}_\Sigma$. Then there exists a DFA $\mathsf{A} = <\Sigma, S, s_0, \delta, F>$ such that $L(\mathsf{A}) = \mathrm{L}$. Define a new DFA $\mathsf{A}^\psi = <\Sigma, S^\psi, s_0^\psi, \delta^\psi, F^\psi>$ by

$$S^\psi = S$$

$$s_0^\psi = s_0$$

$$F^\psi = F$$

and δ^ψ is defined by

$$\delta^\psi(s, \mathbf{a}) = \bar{\delta}(s, \psi(\mathbf{a})) \; \forall s \in S, \forall \mathbf{a} \in \Sigma$$

Induction can be used to show $\bar{\delta}^\psi(s, x) = \bar{\delta}(s, \bar{\psi}(x)) \; \forall s \in S, \forall x \in \Sigma^*$, and in particular $\bar{\delta}^\psi(s_0, x) = \bar{\delta}(s_0, \bar{\psi}(x)) \; \forall x \in \Sigma^*$. Hence $L(\mathsf{A}^\psi) = \bar{\psi}^{-1}(L(\mathsf{A}))$.
Δ

This theorem makes it possible to extend the range of the pumping lemma (Theorem 2.3) to many otherwise unpleasant problems. The set M given in Example 5.20 can easily be shown to violate Theorem 2.3 and is therefore not FAD. The set K given in Example 5.20 is just as clearly not FAD, but this is quite tedious to formally prove by the pumping lemma (the number of choices for u, v, and w is prohibitively large to thoroughly cover). An argument might proceed as follows: Assume K were FAD. Then M, being the inverse homomorphic image of a FAD language, must also be FAD. Since M is known (by an easy pumping lemma proof) to be definitely not FAD, the assumption that K is FAD must be incorrect. Thus, $\mathrm{K} \in \mathcal{N}_\Sigma$.

∇ **Lemma 5.5.** Let $\Sigma = \{\mathbf{a}, \mathbf{b}\}$, and let $\xi: \Sigma \to \Sigma^*$ be defined by $\xi(\mathbf{a}) = \mathbf{a}$ and $\xi(\mathbf{b}) = \mathbf{a}$. Then $\mathcal{N}_\Sigma$ is *not* closed under $\bar{\xi}^{-1}$.

Proof. Consider the set L of all strings that have the same number of **a**s as **b**s. This language is in $\mathcal{N}_\Sigma$, but $\bar{\xi}^{-1}(\mathrm{L})$ is $\{\lambda\}$, which is clearly not in $\mathcal{N}_\Sigma$.
Δ

We close this chapter by considering two operators for which it is definitely not convenient to modify the structure of an existing automaton to construct a new automaton with which to demonstrate closure.

∇ **Theorem 5.11.** Let Σ be an alphabet. Define the operator b by

$$\mathrm{L}^b = \{x \mid \exists y \in \Sigma^* \ni (xy \in \mathrm{L} \wedge |x| = |y|)\}$$

Then $\mathfrak{D}_\Sigma$ is closed under the operator b.

Proof. L^b represents the first halves of all the words in L. For example, if $\mathrm{K} = \{\mathbf{ad}, \mathbf{abaa}, \mathbf{ccccc}\}$, then $\mathrm{K}^b = \{\mathbf{a}, \mathbf{ab}\}$. Assume that L is FAD. Then there exists a DFA $\mathsf{A} = \langle \Sigma, S, s_0, \delta, F \rangle$ that accepts L. The proof consists of identifying those states q that are "midway" between the start state and a final state; specifically, we need to identify the set of *strings* for which q is the midpoint. The previous closure results for union, intersection, homomorphism, and inverse homomorphism will be used to construct the language representing L^b. Define the *length* homomorphism $\psi: \Sigma \to \{\mathbf{1}\}^*$ by $\psi(\mathbf{a}) = \mathbf{1}$ for all $\mathbf{a} \in \Sigma$. Note that $\bar{\psi}$ effectively counts the number of letters in a word:

$$\bar{\psi}(x) = \mathbf{1}^{|x|}$$

The following argument can be applied to each state q to determine the set of strings that use it as a "midway" state.

Consider the initial set for q, $I(\mathsf{A}, \mathrm{q}) = \{x \mid \bar{\delta}(s_0, x) = \mathrm{q}\}$ and the terminal set for q, $T(\mathsf{A}, \mathrm{q}) = \{x \mid \bar{\delta}(\mathrm{q}, x) \in F\}$. We are interested in finding those words in $I(\mathsf{A}, \mathrm{q})$ that are the same length as words in $T(\mathsf{A}, \mathrm{q})$. $\bar{\psi}(I(\mathsf{A}, \mathrm{q}))$ represents strings of **1**s whose lengths are the same as words in $I(\mathsf{A}, \mathrm{q})$. A similar interpretation can be given for $\bar{\psi}(T(\mathsf{A}, \mathrm{q}))$. Therefore, $\bar{\psi}(I(\mathsf{A}, \mathrm{q})) \cap \bar{\psi}(T(\mathsf{A}, \mathrm{q}))$ will reflect those lengths that are common to both the initial set and the terminal set. The inverse image under $\bar{\psi}$ for this set will then reflect only those strings in Σ^* that are of the correct length to reach q from s_0. This set is $\bar{\psi}^{-1}(\bar{\psi}(I(\mathsf{A}, \mathrm{q})) \cap \bar{\psi}(T(\mathsf{A}, \mathrm{q})))$. Not all strings of a given length are likely to reach q, though, so this set must be intersected with $I(\mathsf{A}, \mathrm{q})$ to correctly describe those strings that are both of the proper length and that reach q from the start state. This set, $I(\mathsf{A}, \mathrm{q}) \cap \bar{\psi}^{-1}(\bar{\psi}(I(\mathsf{A}, \mathrm{q})) \cap \bar{\psi}(T(\mathsf{A}, \mathrm{q})))$, is thus the first halves of all words that have q as their midpoint. This process can be repeated for each of the (finite) number of states in the automaton A, and the union of the resulting sets will form all the first halves of words that are accepted by A; that is, the union will equal L^b.

Note that by moving the start state of A and forming the automaton $\mathsf{A}^{\mathrm{q}} = \langle \Sigma, S, \mathrm{q}, \delta, F \rangle$, each of the initial sets $I(\mathsf{A}, \mathrm{q})$ can be shown to be FAD. Similarly, the automaton $\mathsf{A}_{\mathrm{q}} = \langle \Sigma, S, s_0, \delta, \{\mathrm{q}\} \rangle$ illustrates that each terminal set $T(\mathsf{A}, \mathrm{q})$ must be FAD, also. Since L^b has now been shown to be formed from these

basic FAD sets by applying homomorphisms, intersections, inverse homomorphisms, and unions, L^b must be FAD since $\mathcal{D}_\Sigma$ is closed under each of these types of operations.
Δ

EXAMPLE 5.25

Consider the automaton A displayed in Figure 5.21. For the state highlighted as q, the quantities discussed in Theorem 5.11 would be as follows:

$$I(\mathsf{A}, q) = \{\mathbf{abc}, \mathbf{abcabc}, \mathbf{abcabcabc}, \mathbf{abcabcabcabc}, \dots\}$$

$$T(\mathsf{A}, q) = \{\mathbf{aa}, \mathbf{aaaa}, \mathbf{aaaaaa}, \mathbf{aaaaaaaa}, \dots\} = \{\mathbf{a}^2, \mathbf{a}^4, \mathbf{a}^6, \mathbf{a}^8, \mathbf{a}^{10}, \mathbf{a}^{12}, \dots\}$$

$$\overline{\psi}(I(\mathsf{A}, q)) = \{\mathbf{1}^3, \mathbf{1}^6, \mathbf{1}^9, \mathbf{1}^{12}, \mathbf{1}^{15}, \dots\}$$

$$\overline{\psi}(T(\mathsf{A}, q)) = \{\mathbf{1}^2, \mathbf{1}^4, \mathbf{1}^6, \mathbf{1}^8, \mathbf{1}^{10}, \mathbf{1}^{12}, \dots\}$$

$$\overline{\psi}(I(\mathsf{A}, q)) \cap \overline{\psi}(T(\mathsf{A}, q)) = \{\mathbf{1}^6, \mathbf{1}^{12}, \mathbf{1}^{18}, \dots\} = \{x \in \{\mathbf{1}\}^+ \mid |x| \equiv 0 \bmod 6\}$$

$$\overline{\psi}^{-1}(\overline{\psi}(I(\mathsf{A}, q)) \cap \overline{\psi}(T(\mathsf{A}, q))) = \{x \in \{\mathbf{a}, \mathbf{b}, \mathbf{c}\}^+ \mid |x| \equiv 0 \bmod 6\} = \{\mathbf{aaaaaa}, \mathbf{aaaaab}, \mathbf{aaaaac}, \mathbf{aaaaba}, \mathbf{aaaabb}, \dots\}$$

$$\mathrm{I}(\mathsf{A}, q) \cap \overline{\psi}^{-1}(\overline{\psi}(I(\mathsf{A}, q)) \cap \overline{\psi}(T(\mathsf{A}, q))) = \{\mathbf{abcabc}, \mathbf{abcabcabcabc}, \dots\}$$

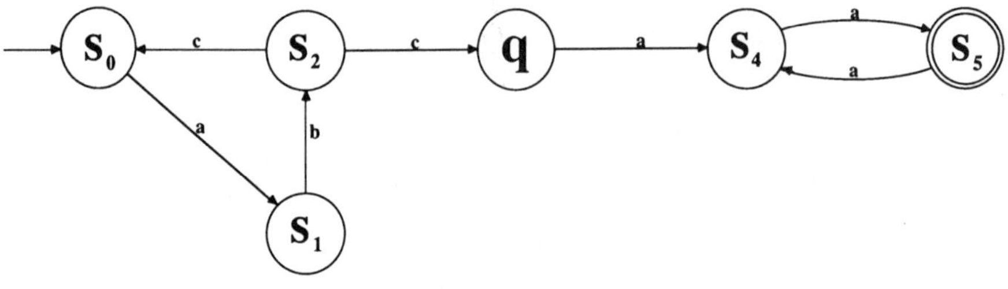

Figure 5.21 The automaton discussed in Example 5.25

Similar calculations would have to be done for each of the other states of A.

Once again, $\mathcal{N}_\Sigma$ does not enjoy the same closure properties that $\mathcal{D}_\Sigma$ does.

∇ **Lemma 5.6.** Let Σ be an alphabet. Then $\mathcal{N}_\Sigma$ is not closed under the operator *b*.

Proof. Let $L = \{\mathbf{a}^n\mathbf{b}^n \mid n \geq 0\} \in \mathcal{N}_\Sigma$. Then $L^b = \{\mathbf{a}^n \mid n \geq 0\} \notin \mathcal{N}_\Sigma$.

Δ

Other examples that show $\mathcal{N}_\Sigma$ is not closed under the operator b abound. If $K = \{x \in \{\mathbf{a}, \mathbf{b}\}^* \mid |x|_{\mathbf{a}} = |x|_{\mathbf{b}}\}$, then $K^b = \{\mathbf{a}, \mathbf{b}\}^*$. The last operator we will cover in this chapter is useful for illustrating closures that may not be *effective*, that is, for which there may not exist an algorithm for constructing the desired entity.

∇ **Definition 5.10.** Let L_1 and L_2 be languages. The *quotient* of L_1 with L_2, written L_1/L_2, is defined by $L_1/L_2 = \{x \mid \exists y \in \Sigma^* \ni y \in L_2 \wedge xy \in L_1\}$
Δ

Roughly speaking, the quotient consists of the beginnings of those words in L_1 that terminate in a word from L_2.

EXAMPLE 5.26

Let $\Sigma = \{\mathbf{a}, \mathbf{b}\}^*$. $\{\mathbf{b}^2, \mathbf{b}^4, \mathbf{b}^6, \mathbf{b}^8, \mathbf{b}^{10}, \mathbf{b}^{12}, \ldots\}/\{\mathbf{b}\} = \{\mathbf{b}^1, \mathbf{b}^3, \mathbf{b}^5, \mathbf{b}^7, \mathbf{b}^{19}, \mathbf{b}^{11}, \ldots\}$. Note that $\{\mathbf{b}^2, \mathbf{b}^4, \mathbf{b}^6, \mathbf{b}^8, \mathbf{b}^{10}, \mathbf{b}^{12}, \ldots\}/\{\mathbf{a}\} = \{\ \}$.

∇ **Theorem 5.12.** For any alphabet Σ, $\mathcal{D}_\Sigma$ is closed under quotient.

Proof. Let L_1 and L_2 belong to $\mathcal{D}_\Sigma$. Then there is a deterministic finite automaton $A_1 = \langle\Sigma, S_1, s_{0_1}, \delta_1, F_1\rangle$ such that $L(A_1) = L_1$. An automaton that accepts L_1/L_2 can be defined by $A' = \langle\Sigma, S_1, s_{0_1}, \delta_1, F'\rangle$, where F' is defined to be the set of all states t for which there is a word in L_2 that reaches a final state from t. That is, $F' = \{t \mid \exists y \in \Sigma^* \ni (y \in L_2 \wedge \delta_1(t, y) \in F)\}$. It can be shown that A' does indeed accept L_1/L_2, and hence $\mathcal{D}_\Sigma$ is closed under quotient (see the exercises).
Δ

Note that the above proof did not mention the automaton associated with the second language L_2. Indeed, the definition given for F' is sufficient to argue that the new automaton does recognize the quotient of the two languages. It was not actually necessary to deal with an automaton for L_2 in order to argue that there must exist a DFA that recognizes L_1/L_2. The proof of Theorem 5.12 is thus an *existence* proof, but does not indicate whether $\mathcal{D}_\Sigma$ is *effectively* closed under quotient. Indeed, Theorem 5.12 actually proves that the quotient of a FAD language with *any* other language (including those in $\mathcal{N}_\Sigma$) will always be FAD. However, if it is hard to determine just which strings in the other language may have the properties we need to define F'; we may not really know which subset of states F' should actually be [after all, we could hardly check the property $\overline{\delta}_1(q, y) \in F$, one string at a time, for each of an infinite number of strings y in L_2 in a finite amount of time]. Fortunately, it is not necessary to know F' exactly, since there are only a finite number of ways to choose a set of final states in the automaton A', and the proof of Theorem 5.12 assures us that one of those ways must be the correct one that admits the conclusion $L(A') = L_1/L_2$.

It would, however, be quite convenient to know what F' actually is so that we could construct the automaton that actually accepts the quotient; this seems much more satisfying that just knowing that such a machine must exist! If L_2 is FAD, the existence of an automaton $A_2 = <\Sigma, S_2, s_{0_2}, \delta_2, F_2>$ for which $L(A_2) = L_2$ does make it possible to calculate F' exactly (see the exercises). Thus, $\mathfrak{D}_\Sigma$ *is* effectively closed under quotient. In later chapters, languages that may make it impossible to determine F' will be studied. We defer the details of such problems until then.

∇ **Lemma 5.7.** Let $\Sigma = \{\mathbf{a}, \mathbf{b}\}$. $\mathcal{N}_\Sigma$ is *not* closed under quotient.

Proof. Consider the set L of all strings that have a different number of **a**s than **b**s. This language is in $\mathcal{N}_\Sigma$, but $L/L = \Sigma^*$ (why?).

Δ

From the exercises it will become clear that $\mathcal{N}_\Sigma$ is not closed over most of the usual (or unusual!) operators. Note that $\mathfrak{D}_\Sigma$ is by contrast a very special set, in that it appears to be closed over every reasonable unary and binary operation that we might consider. The question of closure will again arise as more complex classes of machines and languages are presented in later chapters.

EXERCISES

5.1. Let Σ be an alphabet. Define $\mathbf{F}_\Sigma$ to be the collection of all finite languages over Σ. Prove or give counterexamples to the following:

(a) $\mathbf{F}_\Sigma$ is closed under complementation.
(b) $\mathbf{F}_\Sigma$ is closed under union.
(c) $\mathbf{F}_\Sigma$ is closed under intersection.
(d) $\mathbf{F}_\Sigma$ is closed under concatenation.
(e) $\mathbf{F}_\Sigma$ is closed under Kleene closure.
(f) $\mathbf{F}_\Sigma$ is closed under relative complement.

5.2. Let Σ be an alphabet. Define $\mathbf{C}_\Sigma$ to be the collection of all *cofinite* languages over Σ (a language is cofinite if it is the complement of a finite language). Prove or give counterexamples to the following:

(a) $\mathbf{C}_\Sigma$ is closed under complementation.
(b) $\mathbf{C}_\Sigma$ is closed under union.
(c) $\mathbf{C}_\Sigma$ is closed under intersection.
(d) $\mathbf{C}_\Sigma$ is closed under concatenation.
(e) $\mathbf{C}_\Sigma$ is closed under Kleene closure.
(f) $\mathbf{C}_\Sigma$ is closed under relative complement.

5.3. Let Σ be an alphabet. Define $\mathbf{B}_\Sigma = \mathbf{F}_\Sigma \cup \mathbf{C}_\Sigma$ (see Exercises 5.1 and 5.2). Prove or give counterexamples to the following:

(a) $\mathbf{B}_\Sigma$ is closed under complementation.
(b) $\mathbf{B}_\Sigma$ is closed under union.
(c) $\mathbf{B}_\Sigma$ is closed under intersection.
(d) $\mathbf{B}_\Sigma$ is closed under concatenation.
(e) $\mathbf{B}_\Sigma$ is closed under Kleene closure.
(f) $\mathbf{B}_\Sigma$ is closed under relative complement.

5.4. Let Σ be an alphabet. Define $\mathbf{I}_\Sigma$ to be the collection of all infinite languages over Σ. Note that $\mathbf{I}_\Sigma = \rho(\Sigma^*) - \mathbf{F}_\Sigma$ (see Exercise 5.1). Prove or give counterexamples to the following:
(a) $\mathbf{I}_\Sigma$ is closed under complementation.
(b) $\mathbf{I}_\Sigma$ is closed under union.
(c) $\mathbf{I}_\Sigma$ is closed under intersection.
(d) $\mathbf{I}_\Sigma$ is closed under concatenation.
(e) $\mathbf{I}_\Sigma$ is closed under Kleene closure.
(f) $\mathbf{I}_\Sigma$ is closed under relative complement.

5.5. Let Σ be an alphabet. Define $\mathbf{J}_\Sigma$ to be the collection of all languages over Σ that have infinite complements. Note that $\mathbf{J}_\Sigma = \rho(\Sigma^*) - \mathbf{C}_\Sigma$ (see Exercise 5.2). Prove or give counterexamples to the following:
(a) $\mathbf{J}_\Sigma$ is closed under complementation.
(b) $\mathbf{J}_\Sigma$ is closed under union.
(c) $\mathbf{J}_\Sigma$ is closed under intersection.
(d) $\mathbf{J}_\Sigma$ is closed under concatenation.
(e) $\mathbf{J}_\Sigma$ is closed under Kleene closure.
(f) $\mathbf{J}_\Sigma$ is closed under relative complement.

5.6. Let Σ be an alphabet. Define **E** to be the collection of all languages over $\{\mathbf{a}, \mathbf{b}\}$ that contain the word **abba**. Prove or give counterexamples to the following:
(a) **E** is closed under complementation.
(b) **E** is closed under union.
(c) **E** is closed under intersection.
(d) **E** is closed under concatenation.
(e) **E** is closed under Kleene closure.
(f) **E** is closed under relative complement.

5.7. If a collection of languages is closed under intersection, does it have to be closed under union? Prove or give a counterexamaple.

5.8. If a collection of languages is closed under intersection and complement, does it have to be closed under union? Prove or give a counterexample.

5.9. Show that if a collection of languages is closed under concatenation it is not necessarily closed under Kleene closure.

5.10. Show that if a collection of languages is closed under Kleene closure it is not necessarily closed under concatenation.

5.11. Show that if a collection of languages is closed under complementation it is not necessarily closed under relative complement.

5.12. Give a finite set of numbers that is closed under $\sqrt{\ }$.

5.13. Give an infinite set of numbers that is closed under $\sqrt{\ }$.

5.14. Given deterministic machines A_1 and A_2, use the definition of $\mathsf{A}^\cup$ and Definition 4.5 to describe an algorithm for building a *deterministic* automaton $\mathsf{A}^\cup$ that will accept $L(\mathsf{A}_1) \cup L(\mathsf{A}_2)$.

5.15. Given deterministic machines A_1 and A_2, and without relying on the construction used in Theorem 5.2:
(a) Build a *deterministic* automaton A^u that will accept $L(\mathsf{A}_1) \cup L(\mathsf{A}_2)$.
(b) Prove that your construction behaves as advertised.
(c) If *no* minimization is performed in Exercise 5.14, how do the number of states in

A^{U}, $\mathsf{A}^{\cup}$, and A^{u} compare? (Assume A_1 has n states and A_2 has m states, and give expressions based on these variables.)

5.16. Let Σ be an alphabet. Define the (unary) operator P by

$$P(\mathrm{L}) = \{x \mid \exists y \in \Sigma^* \ni xy \in \mathrm{L}\} \text{ (for any collection of words L)}$$

$P(\mathrm{L})$ then represents all the *prefixes* of words in L. For example, if $\mathrm{K} = \{\mathbf{a}, \mathbf{bbc}, \mathbf{dd}\}$, then $P(\mathrm{K}) = \{\lambda, \mathbf{a}, \mathbf{b}, \mathbf{bb}, \mathbf{bbc}, \mathbf{d}, \mathbf{dd}\}$. Prove that $\mathscr{D}_\Sigma$ is closed under the operator P.

5.17. Let Σ be an alphabet. Define the (unary) operator S by

$$S(\mathrm{L}) = \{x \mid \exists y \in \Sigma^* \ni yx \in \mathrm{L}\} \text{ (for any collection of words L)}$$

$S(\mathrm{L})$ then represents all the *suffixes* of words in L. For example, if $\mathrm{K} = \{\mathbf{a}, \mathbf{bbc}, \mathbf{dd}\}$, then $S(\mathrm{K}) = \{\lambda, \mathbf{a}, \mathbf{c}, \mathbf{bc}, \mathbf{bbc}, \mathbf{d}, \mathbf{dd}\}$.

(a) Given an automaton accepting L, describe how to modify it to produce an automaton accepting $S(\mathrm{L})$.

(b) Prove that your construction behaves as advertised.

(c) Argue that $\mathscr{D}_\Sigma$ is closed under the operator S.

5.18. Let Σ be an alphabet. Define the (unary) operator C by

$$C(\mathrm{L}) = \{x \mid \exists y, z \in \Sigma^* \ni yxz \in \mathrm{L}\} \text{ (for any collection of words L)}$$

$C(\mathrm{L})$ then represents all the *centers* of words in L. For example, if $\mathrm{K} = \{\mathbf{a}, \mathbf{bbc}, \mathbf{dd}\}$, then $C(\mathrm{K}) = \{\lambda, \mathbf{a}, \mathbf{c}, \mathbf{bc}, \mathbf{bbc}, \mathbf{b}, \mathbf{bb}, \mathbf{d}, \mathbf{dd}\}$.

(a) Given an automaton accepting L, describe how to modify it to produce an automaton accepting $C(\mathrm{L})$.

(b) Prove that your construction behaves as advertised.

(c) Argue that $\mathscr{D}_\Sigma$ is closed under the operator C.

5.19. Let Σ be an alphabet. Define the (unary) operator F by

$$F(\mathrm{L}) = \{x \mid x \in \mathrm{L} \wedge (\text{if } \exists y \in \Sigma^* \ni xy \in \mathrm{L}, \text{ then } y = \lambda)\}$$

$F(\mathrm{L})$ then represents all the words in L that are *not* the beginnings of other words in L. For example, if $\mathrm{K} = \{\mathbf{ad}, \mathbf{ab}, \mathbf{abbad}\}$, then $F(\mathrm{K}) = \{\mathbf{ad}, \mathbf{abbad}\}$. Prove that $\mathscr{D}_\Sigma$ is closed under the operator F.

5.20. Let Σ be an alphabet, and $x = \mathbf{a}_1\mathbf{a}_2 \ldots \mathbf{a}_{n-1}\mathbf{a}_n \in \Sigma^*$; define $x^{\mathrm{r}} = \mathbf{a}_n\mathbf{a}_{n-1} \ldots \mathbf{a}_2\mathbf{a}_1$. For a language L over Σ, define $\mathrm{L}^{\mathrm{r}} = \{x^{\mathrm{r}} \mid x \in \mathrm{L}\}$. Note that the (unary) reversal operator r is thus defined by $\mathrm{L}^{\mathrm{r}} = \{\mathbf{a}_n\mathbf{a}_{n-1} \ldots \mathbf{a}_3\mathbf{a}_2\mathbf{a}_1 \mid \mathbf{a}_1\mathbf{a}_2\mathbf{a}_3 \ldots \mathbf{a}_{n-1}\mathbf{a}_n \in \mathrm{L}\}$, and L^{r} therefore represents all the words in L written backward. For example, if $\mathrm{K} = \{\lambda, \mathbf{ad}, \mathbf{bbc}, \mathbf{bbad}\}$, then $\mathrm{K}^{\mathrm{r}} = \{\lambda, \mathbf{da}, \mathbf{cbb}, \mathbf{dabb}\}$.

(a) Given an automaton accepting L, describe how to modify it to produce an automaton accepting L^{r}.

(b) Prove that your construction behaves as advertised.

(c) Argue that $\mathscr{D}_\Sigma$ is closed under the operator r.

5.21. Let $\Sigma = \{\mathbf{a}, \mathbf{b}, \mathbf{c}, \mathbf{d}\}$. Define the (unary) operator G by

$$\begin{aligned} G(\mathrm{L}) &= \{\mathbf{a}_n\mathbf{a}_{n-1} \ldots \mathbf{a}_3\mathbf{a}_2\mathbf{a}_1\mathbf{a}_1\mathbf{a}_2\mathbf{a}_3 \ldots \mathbf{a}_{n-1}\mathbf{a}_n \mid \mathbf{a}_1\mathbf{a}_2\mathbf{a}_3 \ldots \mathbf{a}_{n-1}\mathbf{a}_n \in \mathrm{L}\} \\ &= \{w^{\mathrm{r}} \cdot w \mid w \in \mathrm{L}\} \end{aligned}$$

(see the definition of w^{r} in Exercise 5.20). As an example, if $\mathrm{K} = \{\lambda, \mathbf{ad}, \mathbf{bbc}, \mathbf{bbad}\}$, then $G(\mathrm{K}) = \{\lambda, \mathbf{daad}, \mathbf{cbbbbc}, \mathbf{dabbbbad}\}$.

(a) Prove that $\mathcal{D}_\Sigma$ is *not* closed under the operator G.
(b) Prove that $\mathcal{N}_\Sigma$ is closed under the operator b.

5.22. Prove that $\mathcal{N}_\Sigma$ *is* closed under the operator r (see Exercise 5.20).

5.23. Prove that $\mathcal{N}_\Sigma$ is *not* closed under the operator P (see Exercise 5.16).

5.24. Prove that $\mathcal{N}_\Sigma$ is *not* closed under the operator S (see Exercise 5.17).

5.25. Prove that $\mathcal{N}_\Sigma$ is *not* closed under the operator C (see Exercise 5.18).

5.26. Prove that $\mathcal{N}_\Sigma$ is *not* closed under the operator F (see Exercise 5.19).

5.27. Consider the following alternate "proof" of Theorem 5.1: Let A be an NDFA and define $A^\sim$ as suggested in Theorem 5.1. Give an example to show that $L(A)$ might not be equal to $\sim L(A)$.

5.28. Complete the proof of Lemma 5.7.

5.29. Give an example of a collection of languages that is closed under union, concatenation, and Kleene closure, but is not closed under intersection.

5.30. If a collection of languages is closed under union, does it have to be closed under intersection? Prove or give a counterexample.

5.31. Refer to the construction in Theorem 5.4 and prove that $L(A^\cdot) = L_1 \cdot L_2$. Warning! This involves a *lot* of tedious details.

5.32. Refer to the construction in Theorem 5.5 and prove that $L(A_*) = L^*$. Warning! This involves a *lot* of tedious details.

5.33. Amplify the explanations for each of the equivalences in the proof of Theorem 5.2.

5.34. Given a DFA $A = \langle\Sigma, S, s_0, \delta, F\rangle$, define an NDFA that will accept $L(A)^+$.

5.35. Given a NDFA $A = \langle\Sigma, S, S_0, \delta, F\rangle$, define a NDFA that will accept $L(A)^+$.

5.36. If L is FAD, is it necessarily true that all subsets of L are FAD? Prove or give a counterexample.

5.37. If $L \in \mathcal{D}_\Sigma$, is it necessarily true that all supersets of L are in $\mathcal{D}_\Sigma$? Prove or give a counterexample.

5.38. If $L \in \mathcal{N}_\Sigma$, is it necessarily true that all subsets of L are in $\mathcal{N}_\Sigma$? Prove or give a counterexample.

5.39. If $L \in \mathcal{N}_\Sigma$, is it necessarily true that all supersets of L are in $\mathcal{N}_\Sigma$? Prove or give a counterexample.

5.40. Explain the purpose of the new start state q_0 in the proof of Theorem 5.5.

5.41. Redesign the construction in the proof of Theorem 5.4, making use of λ-transitions where appropriate.

5.42. Redesign the construction in the proof of Theorem 5.5, making use of λ-transitions where appropriate. Do this in such a way as to make the "extra" start state q_0 unnecessary.

5.43. Redesign the construction in the proof of Theorem 5.4, assuming that A_1 and A_2 are NDFAs.

5.44. Redesign the construction in the proof of Theorem 5.5, assuming that A is a DFA.

5.45. How does the right congruence generated by a language L compare to the right congruence generated by the complement of L? *Hint:* It may be helpful to consider the construction of $A^\sim$ given in Theorem 5.1 when A is a minimal machine accepting L.

5.46. (a) Give examples of languages L_1 and L_2 for which $R_{(L_1 \cap L_2)} = R_{L_1} \cap R_{L_2}$.

(b) Give examples of languages L_1 and L_2 for which $R_{(L_1 \cap L_2)} \neq R_{L_1} \cap R_{L_2}$. *Hint:* It may be helpful to consider the construction of $A^\cap$ given in Lemma 5.1 to direct your thinking.

5.47. Consider the following assertion: $\mathscr{D}_\Sigma$ is closed under *relative complement;* that is, if L_1 and L_2 are FAD, then $L_1 - L_2$ is also FAD.

(a) Prove this by appealing to existing theorems.

(b) Define an appropriate "new" machine.

(c) Prove that the machine constructed in part (b) behaves as advertised.

5.48. Define $\mathscr{L}_\Sigma$ to be the set of all languages recognized by NDFAs with λ-transitions. What sort of closure properties does $\mathscr{L}_\Sigma$ have? How does $\mathscr{L}_\Sigma$ compare to $\mathscr{D}_\Sigma$?

5.49. **(a)** Give an example of a language L for which $\lambda \in L^+$.

(b) Give three examples of languages L for which $L^+ = L$.

5.50. Recall that $\delta^\cup: (S_1 \cup S_2) \times \Sigma \to \wp(S_1 \cup S_2)$ was defined by

$$\delta^\cup(s, \mathbf{a}) = \begin{cases} \delta_1(s, \mathbf{a}) & \text{if } s \in S_1 \\ \delta_2(s, \mathbf{a}) & \text{if } s \in S_2 \end{cases}, \qquad \forall s \in S_1 \cup S_2, \quad \forall \mathbf{a} \in \Sigma$$

(a) Prove (by induction) that $\overline{\delta}^\cup$ conforms to a similar formula:

$$\overline{\delta}^\cup(s, x) = \begin{cases} \overline{\delta}_1(s, x) & \text{if } s \in S_1 \\ \overline{\delta}_2(s, x) & \text{if } s \in S_2 \end{cases}, \qquad \forall s \in S_1 \cup S_2, \quad \forall x \in \Sigma^*$$

(b) Was this fact used in the proof of Theorem 5.2?

5.51. Let Σ be an alphabet. Prove or give counterexamples to the following:

(a) $\mathscr{N}_\Sigma$ is closed under relative complement.

(b) $\mathscr{N}_\Sigma$ is closed under union.

(c) $\mathscr{N}_\Sigma$ is closed under concatenation.

(d) $\mathscr{N}_\Sigma$ is closed under Kleene closure.

(g) If $L \in \mathscr{N}_\Sigma$, then $L^+ \in \mathscr{N}_\Sigma$.

5.52. Why was it necessary to require that $S_1 \cap S_2 = \emptyset$ in the proof of Theorem 5.4? Would any step of the proof be invalid without this assumption? Explain.

5.53. Let Σ be an alphabet. Define $E(L) = \{z \mid (\exists y \in \Sigma^+)(\exists x \in L)(z = yx)\}$.

(a) Given an automaton accepting L, describe how to modify it to produce an automaton accepting $E(L)$.

(b) Prove that your construction behaves as advertised.

(c) Argue that $\mathscr{D}_\Sigma$ is closed under the operator E.

5.54. Let Σ be an alphabet. Define $B(L) = \{z \mid (\exists x \in L)(\exists y \in \Sigma^*)(z = xy)\}$.

(a) Given an automaton accepting L, describe how to modify it to produce an automaton accepting $B(L)$.

(b) Prove that your construction behaves as advertised.

(c) Argue that $\mathscr{D}_\Sigma$ is closed under the operator B.

5.55. Let Σ be an alphabet. Define $M(L) = \{z \mid (\exists x \in L)(\exists y \in \Sigma^+)(z = xy)\}$.

(a) Given an automaton accepting L, describe how to modify it to produce an automaton accepting $M(L)$.

(b) Prove that your construction behaves as advertised.

(c) Argue that $\mathscr{D}_\Sigma$ is closed under the operator M.

5.56. Refer to the definitions given in Lemma 5.1 and use induction to show that

$$(\forall s \in S_1)(\forall t \in S_2)(\forall x \in \Sigma^*)(\bar{\delta}^{\cap}(\langle s, t\rangle, x) = \langle \bar{\delta}_1(s, x), \bar{\delta}_2(t, x)\rangle)$$

5.57. Refer to Lemma 5.1 and prove that $L(A^{\cap}) = L_1 \cap L_2$. As long as the reference is explicitly stated, the result in Exercise 5.56 can be used without proof.

5.58. Prove Theorem 5.6.

5.59. Prove Theorem 5.7.

5.60. **(a)** Cleverly define a machine modification that does not use any λ-moves that could be used to prove Theorem 5.7 (your new machine is still likely to be nondeterministic, however).
(b) Prove that your modified machine behaves as advertised.

5.61. Let $W(L) = \{x \mid x$ is formed by deleting one or more letters from a word in $L\}$.
(a) Given an automaton accepting L, describe how to modify it to produce an automaton accepting $W(L)$.
(b) Prove that your construction behaves as advertised.
(c) Argue that $\mathfrak{D}_\Sigma$ is closed under the operator W.

5.62. Let $V(L) = \{x \mid x$ is formed by deleting the odd-positioned letters from a word in $L\}$. [*Note:* This refers to the first, third, fifth, and so on, letters in a word. For example, if **abcdef** $\in$ L, then **bdf** $\in V(L)$.]
(a) Given an automaton accepting L, describe how to modify it to produce an automaton accepting $V(L)$.
(b) Prove that your construction behaves as advertised.
(c) Argue that $\mathfrak{D}_\Sigma$ is closed under the operator V.

5.63. Let $U(L) = \{x \mid x$ is formed by deleting the even-positioned letters from a word in $L\}$. [*Note:* This refers to the second, fourth, sixth, and so on, letters in a word. For example, if **abcdefg** $\in$ L, then **aceg** $\in U(L)$.]
(a) Given an automaton accepting L, describe how to modify it to produce an automaton accepting $U(L)$.
(b) Prove that your construction behaves as advertised.
(c) Argue that $\mathfrak{D}_\Sigma$ is closed under the operator U.

5.64. Let $T(L) = \{x \mid x$ is formed by deleting every third, sixth, ninth, and so on, letters from a word in $L\}$. [*Note:* This refers to those letters in a word whose index position is congruent to $0 \bmod 3$. For example, if **abcdefg** $\in$ L, then **abdeg** $\in T(L)$.]
(a) Given an automaton accepting L, describe how to modify it to produce an automaton accepting $T(L)$.
(b) Prove that your construction behaves as advertised.
(c) Argue that $\mathfrak{D}_\Sigma$ is closed under the operator T.

5.65. Let $P = \{x \mid |x| \text{ is prime}\}$ and let $I(L)$ be defined by $I(L) = L \cap P$.
(a) Show that $\mathfrak{D}_\Sigma$ is not closed under I.
(b) Show that $\mathbf{F}_\Sigma$ is closed under I (see Exercise 5.1).
(c) Prove or disprove: $\mathbf{C}_\Sigma$ is closed under I (see Exercise 5.2).
(d) Prove or disprove: $\mathbf{B}_\Sigma$ is closed under I (see Exercise 5.3).
(e) Prove or disprove: $\mathbf{I}_\Sigma$ is closed under I (see Exercise 5.4).
(f) Prove or disprove: $\mathbf{J}_\Sigma$ is closed under I (see Exercise 5.5).
(g) Prove or disprove: $\mathbf{E}$ is closed under I (see Exercise 5.6).
(h) Prove or disprove: $\mathcal{N}_\Sigma$ is closed under I.

5.66. Define **C** to be the collection of all languages over $\{\mathbf{a}, \mathbf{b}\}$ that do not contain λ. Prove or give counterexamples to the following:

(a) **C** is closed under complementation.
(b) **C** is closed under union.
(c) **C** is closed under intersection.
(d) **C** is closed under concatenation.
(e) **C** is closed under Kleene closure.
(f) **C** is closed under relative complement.
(g) If $L \in \mathbf{C}$, then $L^+ \in \mathbf{C}$.

5.67. **(a)** Consider the statement that $\mathcal{D}_\Sigma$ is closed under finite union:
(i) Prove by existing theorems and induction.
(ii) Prove by construction.

(b) Prove or disprove that $\mathcal{D}_\Sigma$ is closed under infinite union. Justify your assertions.

5.68. Let $\Sigma = \{\mathbf{a}, \mathbf{b}\}$.

(a) Give examples of three homomorphisms under which $\mathcal{N}_\Sigma$ is not closed.
(b) Give examples of three homomorphisms under which $\mathcal{N}_\Sigma$ is closed.

5.69. Let $\Sigma = \{\mathbf{a}\}$. Can you find two different homomorphisms under which $\mathcal{N}_\Sigma$ is not closed? Justify your conclusions.

5.70. Refer to the construction given in Theorem 5.10.

(a) Prove $\bar{\delta}^{\psi}(s, x) = \bar{\delta}(s, \bar{\psi}(x))\ \forall s \in S, \forall x \in \Sigma^*$.
(b) Complete the proof of Theorem 5.10.

5.71. Consider the homomorphism ξ given in Lemma 5.4 and the set L of all strings that have the same number of **a**s as **b**s.

(a) $\mathcal{D}_\Sigma$ is closed under inverse homomorphism, but $\xi(L)$ is the set of all even-length strings of **a**s, and it appears that under $\bar{\xi}^{-1}$ the DFA language $\xi(L)$ maps to the non-FAD language L. Explain the apparent contradiction. *Hint:* First compute $\bar{\xi}^{-1}(\xi(L))$.
(b) Give an example of a homomorphism for which $\bar{\psi}(\bar{\psi}^{-1}(L)) \neq L$.
(c) Give an example of a homomorphism for which $\bar{\psi}^{-1}(\bar{\psi}(L)) \neq L$.
(d) Prove $\bar{\psi}(\bar{\psi}^{-1}(L)) \subseteq L$.
(e) Prove $L \subseteq \bar{\psi}^{-1}(\bar{\psi}(L))$.

5.72. Let Σ be an alphabet. Define the (unary) operator e by

$$L^e = \{x \mid \exists y \in \Sigma^* \ni (yx \in L \wedge |x| = |y|)\}$$

L^e then represents the last halves of all the words in L. For example, if

$$K = \{\mathbf{ad}, \mathbf{abaa}, \mathbf{ccccc}\},$$

then $K^e = \{\mathbf{d}, \mathbf{aa}\}$. Prove that $\mathcal{D}_\Sigma$ is closed under the operator e.

5.73. Refer to the proof of Theorem 5.11 and show that there exists an automaton A for which it would be incorrect to try to accept L^b by redefining the set of final states to be the set of "midway" states.

5.74. Consider the sets M and K in Example 5.20. Assume that we have used the pumping lemma to show that M is not FAD. What would be wrong with arguing that, since M was not FAD, its homomorphic image cannot be FAD either, and hence K is therefore not FAD.

5.75. Prove Theorem 5.9.

5.76. Let Σ be the ASCII alphabet. Define a homomorphism that will capitalize all lowercase letters (and does not change punctuation, spelling, and the like).

5.77. Consider the proof of Theorem 5.12.

(a) Show that for A' defined by $\mathsf{A}' = <\Sigma, S_1, s_{0_1}, \delta_1, F'>$, where

$$F' = \{t \mid \exists y \in \Sigma^* \ni (y \in L_2 \land \overline{\delta}_1(t, y) \in F)\}, \boldsymbol{L}(\mathsf{A}') = L_1/L_2.$$

(b) Given deterministic finite automata $\mathsf{A}_1 = <\Sigma, S_1, s_{0_1}, \delta_1, F_1>$ such that $\boldsymbol{L}(\mathsf{A}_1) = L_1$ and $\mathsf{A}_2 = <\Sigma, S_2, s_{0_2}, \delta_2, F_2>$ for which $\boldsymbol{L}(\mathsf{A}_2) = L_2$, give an algorithm for computing $F' = \{t \mid \exists y \in \Sigma^* \ni (y \in L_2 \land \overline{\delta}_1(t, y) \in F)\}$.

5.78. Given two alphabets Σ_1 and Σ_2 and a DFA $\mathsf{A} = <\Sigma_1, S, s_0, \delta, F>$:

(a) Define a new automaton $\mathsf{A}' = <\Sigma_1 \cup \Sigma_2, S', s_0', \delta', F'>$ for which $\boldsymbol{L}(\mathsf{A}') = \boldsymbol{L}(\mathsf{A})$.

(b) Prove that A' behaves as advertised.

5.79. Let **S** be a collection of languages that is closed under union, concatenation, and Kleene closure. Prove or disprove: If **S** contains an infinite number of languages, every language in **S** must be FAD.

5.80. Let **S** be a collection of languages that is closed under union, concatenation, and Kleene clsoure. Prove or disprove: If **S** is a finite collection, every language in **S** must be FAD.

5.81. Let u be a unary language operator that, when composed with itself, yields the identity function. Prove that $\mathcal{N}_\Sigma$ must be closed under u.

CHAPTER

6

REGULAR EXPRESSIONS

In this chapter we will develop a standard notation for denoting FAD languages and thus explore yet another characterization of these languages. The specification of a language by an automaton unfortunately does not provide a convenient summary of those strings that are accepted; it is straightforward to check whether any particular word belongs to the language, but it is often difficult to get an overall sense of the set of accepted words. Were the language finite, the individual words could simply be explicitly listed. The delineation of an infinite set in this manner is clearly impossible.

Up to this point, we have relied on English descriptions of the languages under consideration. Natural languages are unfortunately imprecise, and even small machines can have impossibly complex descriptions. the concept of regular expressions provides a clear and concise vehicle for denoting many of the languages we have studied in the previous chapters.

6.1 ALGEBRA OF REGULAR EXPRESSIONS

The definition of set union and the concepts of language concatenation (Definition 5.4) and Kleene closure (Definition 5.5) afford a convenient and powerful method for building new languages from existing ones. The expression $(\{\mathbf{a}, \mathbf{b}\} \cdot \{\mathbf{c}\})^* \cdot \{\mathbf{d}\}$ is an infinite set built from simple alphabets and the operators presented in Chapter 5. We will see that this type of representation is quite suitable for our purposes and is intimately related to the finite automaton definable languages.

∇ **Definition 6.1.** Let $\Sigma = \{\mathbf{a}_1, \mathbf{a}_2, \ldots, \mathbf{a}_m\}$ be an alphabet. A *regular set over* Σ is any set that can be formed by a sequence of applications of the following rules:

i. $\{\mathbf{a}_1\}, \{\mathbf{a}_2\}, \ldots, \{\mathbf{a}_m\}$ are regular sets.
ii. $\{\ \}$ (the empty set of words) is a regular set.
iii. $\{\lambda\}$ (the set containing only the empty *word*) is a regular set.
iv. If L_1 and L_2 are regular sets, then so is $L_1 \cdot L_2$.
v. If L_1 and L_2 are regular sets, then so is $L_1 \cup L_2$.
vi. If L_1 is a regular set, then so is L_1^*.

Δ

EXAMPLE 6.1

Let $\Sigma = \{\mathbf{a}, \mathbf{b}, \mathbf{c}\}$. Each of the following languages are regular sets:

$\{\lambda\}$	$\{\mathbf{b}\} \cup \{\mathbf{c}\}$	$\{\mathbf{a}\}\cdot(\{\mathbf{b}\} \cup \{\mathbf{c}\})$	$\{\mathbf{b}\cdot\lambda\}$
$\{\mathbf{a}\}^*$	$(\{\mathbf{a}\} \cup \{\lambda\})\cdot(\{\mathbf{b}\}^*)$	$\{\ \}^*$	$\{\mathbf{c}\}\cdot\{\ \}$

The multitude of set brackets in these expressions is somewhat undesirable; we now present a common shorthand notation to represent such sets. Expressions like $\{\mathbf{a}\}^*$ will simply be written as $\mathbf{a}^*$, and $\{\mathbf{a}\}\cdot\{\mathbf{b}\}$ will be shortened to **ab**. The notation we wish to use can be formally defined in the following recursive manner.

∇ **Definition 6.2.** Let $\Sigma = \{\mathbf{a}_1, \mathbf{a}_2, \ldots, \mathbf{a}_m\}$ be an alphabet. A *regular expression over* Σ is a sequence of symbols formed by repeated application of the following rules:

i. $\mathbf{a}_1, \mathbf{a}_2, \ldots, \mathbf{a}_m$ are all regular expressions, representing the regular sets $\{\mathbf{a}_1\}, \{\mathbf{a}_2\}, \ldots, \{\mathbf{a}_m\}$, respectively.
ii. $\emptyset$ is a regular expression representing $\{\ \}$.
iii. ϵ is a regular expression representing $\{\lambda\}$.
iv. If R_1 and R_2 are regular expressions corresponding to the sets L_1 and L_2, then $(R_1 \cdot R_2)$ is a regular expression representing the set $L_1 \cdot L_2$.
v. If R_1 and R_2 are regular expressions corresponding to the sets L_1 and L_2, then $(R_1 \cup R_2)$ is a regular expression representing the set $L_1 \cup L_2$.
vi. If R_1 is a regular expression corresponding to the set L_1, then $(R_1)^*$ is a regular expression representing the set L_1^*.

Δ

EXAMPLE 6.2

Let $\Sigma = \{\mathbf{a}, \mathbf{b}, \mathbf{c}\}$. The regular sets in Example 6.1 can be represented by the following regular expressions:

ϵ	$(\mathbf{b} \cup \mathbf{c})$	$(\mathbf{a}\cdot(\mathbf{b} \cup \mathbf{c}))$	$(\mathbf{b}\cdot\epsilon)$
$(\mathbf{a})^*$	$((\mathbf{a} \cup \epsilon)\cdot(\mathbf{b})^*)$	$(\emptyset)^*$	$(\mathbf{c}\cdot\emptyset)$

Note that each expression consists of the "basic building blocks" given by 6.2i through 6.2iii and are connected by the operators $\cup$, $\cdot$ and * according to rules 6.2iv through 6.2vi. Each expression is intended to denote a particular language over Σ. Such representations of languages are by no means unique. For example, $(\mathbf{a}\cdot(\mathbf{b}\cup\mathbf{c}))$ and $((\mathbf{a}\cdot\mathbf{b})\cup(\mathbf{a}\cdot\mathbf{c}))$ both represent the same set, $\{\mathbf{ab}, \mathbf{ac}\}$. Similarly, $(\mathbf{b}\cdot\epsilon)$ and $\mathbf{b}$ both represent $\{\mathbf{b}\}$.

The intention of the parentheses is to prevent ambiguity; $\mathbf{a}\cdot\mathbf{b}\cup\mathbf{c}$ could mean $(\mathbf{a}\cdot(\mathbf{b}\cup\mathbf{c}))$ or $((\mathbf{a}\cdot\mathbf{b})\cup\mathbf{c})$, and the difference is important: the first expression represents $\{\mathbf{ab}, \mathbf{ac}\}$, while the second represents $\{\mathbf{ab}, \mathbf{c}\}$, which are obviously different languages. To ease the burden of all these parentheses, we will adopt the following simplifying conventions.

Notational Convention: The precedence of the operators, from highest to lowest, shall be *, $\cdot$, $\cup$. When writing a regular expression, parentheses that conform to this hierarchy may be omitted. In particular, the outermost set of parentheses can always be omitted. Juxtaposition may be used in place of the concatenation symbol $(\cdot)$.

EXAMPLE 6.3

Thus, $\mathbf{a}\cdot\mathbf{b}\cup\mathbf{c}$ will be taken to mean $((\mathbf{a}\cdot\mathbf{b})\cup\mathbf{c})$, not $(\mathbf{a}\cdot(\mathbf{b}\cup\mathbf{c}))$, since $\cdot$ has precedence over $\cup$. Redundant parentheses that are implied by the precedence rules can be eliminated, and thus $(((\mathbf{a}\cdot\mathbf{b})\cup\mathbf{c})\cdot\mathbf{d})$ can be written as $(\mathbf{ab}\cup\mathbf{c})\mathbf{d}$. Notice that $\mathbf{b}\cup\mathbf{c}^*$ represents $(\mathbf{b}\cup(\mathbf{c}^*))$, not $(\mathbf{b}\cup\mathbf{c})^*$. Kleene closure therefore behaves much like exponentiation does in ordinary algebraic expressions in that it is given precedence over the other operators. Concatenation and union behave much like the algebraic operators multiplication and addition, respectively. Indeed, some texts use $+$ instead of $\cup$ for union; the symbol for concatenation already agrees with that for multiplication $(\cdot)$, and we will likewise allow the symbol to be omitted in favor of juxtaposition. The constants $\emptyset$ and ϵ behave much like the numbers 0 and 1 do in algebra. The common identities $x+0=x$, $x\cdot 1=x$ and $x\cdot 0=0$ have parallels in language theory (see Lemma 6.1). Indeed, $\emptyset$ is the *identity* for union and ϵ is the identity for concatenation.

Thus far we have been very careful to distinguish between the name of an object and the object itself. In algebra, we are used to saying that the symbol **4** *equals* the string of symbols (that is, the word) $20 \div 5$; we really mean that both names refer to the same object, the concept we generally call the number ***four***. (You should be able to think of many more strings that are commonly used as a name for this number, for example, ||||, IV, and 100_2. We will be equally inexact here, writing $\mathbf{a}\cdot(\mathbf{b}\cup\mathbf{c}) = (\mathbf{a}\cdot\mathbf{b})\cup(\mathbf{a}\cdot\mathbf{c})$. This will be taken to mean that the *sets represented* by the two expressions are equal (as is the case here; both equal $\{\mathbf{ab}, \mathbf{ac}\}$) and will not be construed to mean that the two *expressions themselves* are identical (which is clearly not the case here; the right-hand side has more **a**s, more parentheses, and more concatenation symbols).

∇ **Definition 6.3.** Let R be a regular expression. The language represented by R is formally denoted by $\boldsymbol{L}(\mathrm{R})$. Two regular expressions R_1 and R_2 will be said to be *equivalent* if the sets represented by the two expressions are equal, and we will write $R_1 = R_2$.
Δ

Thus, R_1 and R_2 are equivalent if $\boldsymbol{L}(R_1) = \boldsymbol{L}(R_2)$, but this is commonly abbreviated $R_1 = R_2$. The word "equivalent" has been seen in three different contexts so far: there are equivalent DFAs, equivalent NDFAs, and now equivalent regular expressions. In each case, the intent has been to equate constructs that are associated with the same language. Now that the idea of equality (equivalence) has been established, some general identities can be outlined. The properties given in Lemma 6.1 follow directly from the definitions of the operators.

∇ **Lemma 6.1.** Let Σ be an alphabet, and let R_1, R_2, and R_3 be regular expressions. Then:

(a) $R_1 \cup \emptyset = R_1$
(b) $R_1 \cdot \epsilon = R_1 = \epsilon \cdot R_1$
(c) $R_1 \cdot \emptyset = \emptyset = \emptyset \cdot R_1$
(d) $R_1 \cup R_2 = R_2 \cup R_1$
(e) $R_1 \cup R_1 = R_1$
(f) $R_1 \cup (R_2 \cup R_3) = (R_1 \cup R_2) \cup R_3$
(g) $R_1 \cdot (R_2 \cdot R_3) = (R_1 \cdot R_2) \cdot R_3$
(h) $R_1 \cdot (R_2 \cup R_3) = (R_1 \cdot R_2) \cup (R_1 \cdot R_3)$
(i) $\epsilon^* = \epsilon$
(j) $\emptyset^* = \epsilon$
(k) $(R_1 \cup R_2)^* = (R_1^* \cup R_2^*)^*$
(l) $(R_1 \cup R_2)^* = (R_1^* \cdot R_2^*)^*$
(m) $(R_1^*)^* = R_1^*$
(n) $(R_1)^* \cdot (R_1^*) = R_1^*$

Furthermore, there are examples of sets for which:

(b′) $R_1 \cup \epsilon \neq R_1$
(d′) $R_1 \cdot R_2 \neq R_2 \cdot R_1$
(e′) $R_1 \cdot R_1 \neq R_1$
(h′) $R_1 \cup (R_2 \cdot R_3) \neq (R_1 \cup R_2) \cdot (R_1 \cup R_3)$
(k′) $(R_1 \cdot R_2)^* \neq (R_1^* \cdot R_2^*)^*$
(l′) $(R_1 \cdot R_2)^* \neq (R_1^* \cup R_2^*)^*$

Proof. Property (h) will be proved here. The remainder are left as exercises.

$$w \in R_1 \cdot (R_2 \cup R_3) \Leftrightarrow \text{(by definition of } \cdot)$$

$$(\exists x, y)(y \in (R_2 \cup R_3) \wedge x \in R_1 \wedge w = x \cdot y) \Leftrightarrow \text{(by definition of } \cup)$$

$$(\exists x, y)((y \in R_2 \vee y \in R_3) \wedge (x \in R_1 \wedge w = x \cdot y)) \Leftrightarrow \text{(by the distributive law)}$$

$$(\exists x, y)(((y \in R_2) \wedge (x \in R_1 \wedge w = x \cdot y))$$

$$\vee ((y \in R_3) \wedge (x \in R_1 \wedge w = x \cdot y))) \Leftrightarrow \text{(by definition of } \cdot)$$

$$(\exists x, y)((w = x \cdot y \in R_1 \cdot R_2) \vee (w = x \cdot y \in R_1 \cdot R_3)) \Leftrightarrow \text{(by definition of } \cup)$$

$$w \in (R_1 \cdot R_2) \cup (R_1 \cdot R_3)$$

Δ

Note that identity (c) in Lemma 6.1 implies that $\{\mathbf{a}, \mathbf{b}\} \cdot \emptyset = \emptyset$, which follows immediately from the definition of concatenation. If $w \in \{\mathbf{a}, \mathbf{b}\} \cdot \emptyset$, then w would have to be of the form $x \cdot y$, where $x \in \{\mathbf{a}, \mathbf{b}\}$ and $y \in \emptyset$; there are clearly no valid choices for y, so $\{\mathbf{a}, \mathbf{b}\} \cdot \emptyset$ is empty.

6.2 REGULAR SETS AS FAD LANGUAGES

Armed with the constructs and properties discussed in the first section, we will now consider what types of languages can actually be defined by regular expressions. How general is this method of expressing sets of words? Can the FAD languages be represented by regular expressions? (Yes). Can all programming languages be represented by regular expressions? (No). Are regular sets always finite automaton definable languages? (Yes). We begin by addressing this last question.

∇ **Definition 6.4.** Let Σ be an alphabet. $\mathcal{R}_\Sigma$ is defined to be the set of all regular sets over Σ.
Δ

The first question to be considered is, Can every regular set be recognized by a DFA? That is, is $\mathcal{R}_\Sigma \subseteq \mathcal{D}_\Sigma$? It is clear that the "basic building blocks" are recognizable. Figure 6.1 shows three NDFAs that accept { }, $\{\lambda\}$, and $\{\mathbf{c}\}$, respectively. Recalling the constructions outlined in Chapter 5, it is easy to see how to combine these "basic machines" into machines that will accept expressions involving the operators $\cup$, $\cdot$, and $*$.

EXAMPLE 6.4

An NDFA that accepts $\mathbf{a} \cup \mathbf{b}$ (as suggested by the proof of Theorem 5.2) is shown in Figure 6.2. Note that it is composed of the basic building blocks for the letters $\mathbf{a}$ and $\mathbf{b}$, as suggested by the constructions in Figure 6.1.

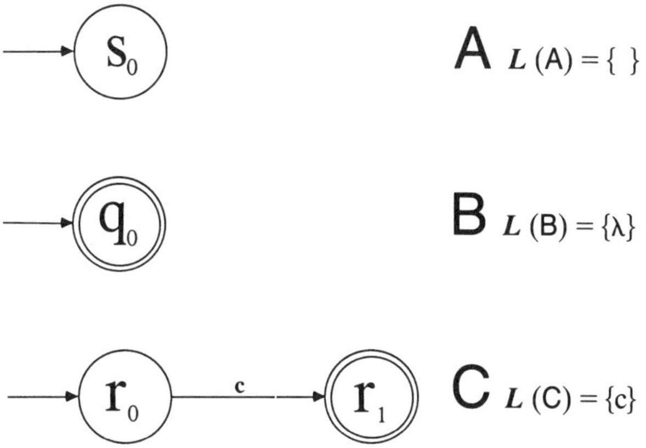

Figure 6.1 NDFAs which recognize regular expressions with zero operators

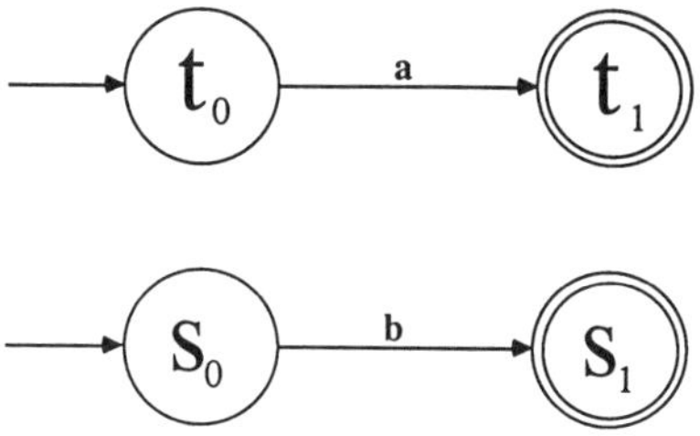

Figure 6.2 The NDFA discussed in Example 6.4

EXAMPLE 6.5

An NDFA that accepts $(\mathbf{a} \cup \mathbf{b})^*$ is shown in Figure 6.3. The automaton given in Figure 6.2 for $(\mathbf{a} \cup \mathbf{b})$ is modified as suggested by the proof of Theorem 5.5 to produce the Kleene closure of $(\mathbf{a} \cup \mathbf{b})$. Recall that the "extra" state q_0 was added to ensure that λ is accepted by the new machine.

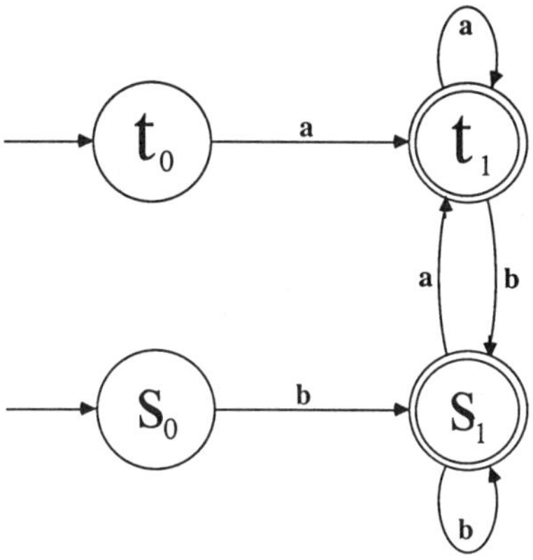

Figure 6.3 The NDFA discussed in Example 6.5

EXAMPLE 6.6

An NDFA that accepts $\mathbf{c}\cdot(\mathbf{a} \cup \mathbf{b})^*$ (as suggested by the proof of Theorem 5.4) is shown in Figure 6.4.

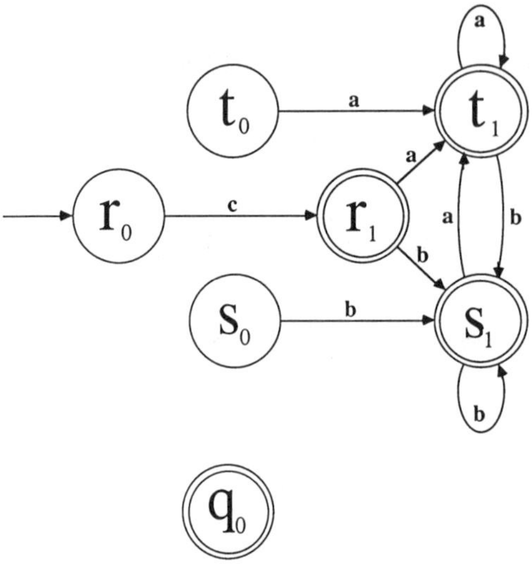

Figure 6.4 The NDFA discussed in Example 6.6

Note that in this last example q_0, t_0, and s_0 are disconnected states, and r_1, s_1, and t_1 could be coalesced into a single state. The resulting machines are not advertised to be *efficient*; the main point is that they can be built. The techniques illustrated above are used to prove the following lemma.

∇ **Lemma 6.2.** Let Σ be an alphabet and let R be a regular set over Σ. Then there is a DFA that accepts R.

Proof. The proof is by induction on the number of operators in the regular expression describing R (see the exercises). Note that Figure 6.1 effectively illustrates the basis step: Those regular expressions with *zero* operators $(\emptyset, \epsilon, \mathbf{a}_1, \mathbf{a}_2, \ldots, \mathbf{a}_m)$ do indeed correspond to FAD languages. This covers sets generated by rules i, ii, and iii of Definition 6.2. For sets corresponding to regular expressions with a positive number of operators, the outermost operator can be identified, and it will be either $\cdot$, $\cup$, or *, corresponding to an application of rule iv, v, or vi. The induction assumption will guarantee that the subexpressions used by the outermost operator have corresponding DFAs. Theorems 5.2, 5.4, and 5.5 can then be invoked to argue that the entire expression has a corresponding DFA.
Δ

∇ **Corollary 6.1.** Let Σ be an alphabet. then $\mathscr{R}_\Sigma \subseteq \mathscr{D}_\Sigma$.

Proof. The proof follows immediately from Lemma 6.2.

Δ

Since we are assured that every regular set can be accepted by a finite automaton, the collection of regular sets is clearly contained in the set of FAD languages. This also means that those languages that cannot be represented by a DFA (that is, those contained in $\mathcal{N}_\Sigma$) have no chance of being represented by a regular expression.

6.3 LANGUAGE EQUATIONS

The next question we will address is whether $\mathcal{D}_\Sigma \subseteq \mathcal{R}_\Sigma$, that is, whether every FAD language can be represented by a regular expression. The reader is invited to take a sample DFA and try to express the language it accepts by a regular expression. You will probably be able to do it, but only by guesswork and trial and error. Our first question appears to have a much more methodical solution: Given a regular expression, it was a relatively straightforward task to draw a NDFA (and then a DFA); in fact, we have a set of *algorithms* for doing just that, and we could program a computer to do the task for us. This second question does not seem to have an obvious algorithm connected with it, and we will have to attack the problem using a new concept: *language equations*.

In algebra, we are used to algebraic equations such as $3x + 7 = 19$. Recall that a *solution* to this equation is a numerical value for x that will make the equation *true*, that is, make both sides equal. In the above example, there is only one choice for x, the unique solution 4. Equations can have two different solutions, like $x^2 = 9$, no solutions, like $x^2 = -9$, or an *infinite* number of solutions, like $2(x + 3) = x + 6 + x$. In a similar way, set equations can be solved, such as $\{\mathbf{a}, \mathbf{b}, \mathbf{c}\} = \{\mathbf{a}, \mathbf{b}\} \cup \mathrm{X}$. Here X represents a *set*, and we are again looking for a value for X that will make the equation true; an obvious choice is $\mathrm{X} = \{\mathbf{c}\}$, but there are other choices, like $\mathrm{X} = \{\mathbf{b}, \mathbf{c}\}$ (since $\{\mathbf{a}, \mathbf{b}, \mathbf{c}\} = \{\mathbf{a}, \mathbf{b}\} \cup \{\mathbf{b}, \mathbf{c}\}$). Such equations may likewise have no solutions, like $\mathrm{X} \cup \{\mathbf{b}\} = \{\mathbf{a}, \mathbf{c}\}$, or an infinite number of solutions, such as $\mathrm{X} \cup \{\mathbf{b}\} = \mathrm{X}$ (what sorts of sets satisfy this last equation?). We wish to look at set equations where the sets are actually sets of strings, that is, *language* equations. The type of equation in which we are most interested has one and only one solution, as outlined in the next theorem. It is very similar in form and spirit to the theorem in algebra that says "For any numbers a and b, where $a \neq 0$, the equation $ax = b$ has a unique solution given by $x = b \div a$."

∇ **Theorem 6.1.** Let Σ be an alphabet. Let E and A be any subsets of Σ^*. Then the language equation $\mathrm{X} = \mathrm{E} \cup \mathrm{A} \cdot \mathrm{X}$ admits the solution $\mathrm{X} = \mathrm{A}^* \cdot \mathrm{E}$. Any other solution Y must contain $\mathrm{A}^* \cdot \mathrm{E}$. Furthermore, if $\lambda \notin \mathrm{A}$, $\mathrm{X} = \mathrm{A}^* \cdot \mathrm{E}$ is the unique solution.

Proof. First note that the set $\mathrm{A}^*\mathrm{E}$ is indeed a solution to this equation, since $\mathrm{A}^*\mathrm{E} = \mathrm{E} \cup \mathrm{A} \cdot (\mathrm{A}^*\mathrm{E})$ (see the exercises). Now assume that some set Y is a solution to this equation, and let us investigate some of the properties that Y must have: If Y is a solution, then

$$Y = E \cup A \cdot Y \Rightarrow \text{(by definition of } \cup)$$
$$E \subseteq Y \wedge A \cdot Y \subseteq Y \Rightarrow \text{(if } E \subseteq Y\text{, then } A \cdot E \subseteq A \cdot Y)$$
$$A \cdot E \subseteq A \cdot Y \subseteq Y \Rightarrow \text{(by substitution)}$$
$$A \cdot A \cdot E \subseteq A \cdot A \cdot Y \subseteq A \cdot Y \subseteq Y \Rightarrow \text{(by induction)}$$
$$(\forall n \in \mathbb{N})(A^n \cdot E \subseteq Y) \Rightarrow \text{(by definition of } A^*)$$
$$A^* \cdot E \subseteq Y$$

Thus, every solution must contain all of A^*E, and A^*E is in this sense the smallest solution. This is true regardless of whether or not λ belongs to A.

Now let us assume that $\lambda \notin A$ and that we have a solution W that is actually "bigger" than A^*E; we will show that this is a contradiction, and thus all solutions must look *exactly* like A^*E. If W is a solution, $W \neq A^*E$, then there must be some elements in the set $W - A^*E$; choose a string of *minimal length* from among these elements and call it z. Thus $z \in W$ and $z \notin A^*E$, and since $E \subseteq A^*E$ (why?), $z \notin E$. Since W is a solution, we have

$$W = E \cup A \cdot W \Rightarrow \text{(since } z \in W \text{ and it cannot be in the E part)}$$
$$z \in A \cdot W \Rightarrow \text{(by definition of } \cdot)$$
$$(\exists x \in A, \exists y \in W) \ni z = x \cdot y \Rightarrow \text{(by definition of } |\ |)$$
$$|z| = |x| + |y| \Rightarrow \text{(since } \lambda \notin A \text{ and } x \in A\text{, so } x \neq \lambda \text{ and } |x| > 0)$$
$$|y| < |z|$$

Note that y cannot belong to A^*E (if $y \in A^*E$, then, since $x \in A$, $z(= x \cdot y) \in A \cdot (A^*E) \subseteq A^*E$, which means that $z \in A^*E$, and we started by assuming that $z \notin A^*E$); since $y \in W$, we have $y \in W - A^*E$, and we have produced a string shorter than z, which belongs to $W - A^*E$. This is the contradiction we were looking for, and we can conclude that it is impossible for a solution W to be larger than A^*E. Since we have already shown that no solution can be smaller than A^*E, we now know that the only solution is *exactly* A^*E.

Δ

EXAMPLE 6.7

$X = \{\mathbf{b}, \mathbf{c}\} \cup \{\mathbf{a}\} \cdot X$ does indeed have a solution; X can equal $\{\mathbf{a}\}^* \cdot \{\mathbf{b}, \mathbf{c}\}$. Note also that this is the only solution (verify, for example, that $X = \{\mathbf{a}\}^* \cdot \{\mathbf{c}\}$ is *not* a solution). The equation $Z = \{\mathbf{b}, \mathbf{c}\} \cup \{\mathbf{a}, \lambda\} \cdot Z$ has several solutions; among them are $Z = \{\mathbf{a}\}^* \cdot \{\mathbf{b}, \mathbf{c}\}$ and $Z = \{\mathbf{a}, \mathbf{b}, \mathbf{c}\}^*$.

It is instructive to explicitly list the first few elements of $\{\mathbf{a}\}^* \cdot \{\mathbf{b}, \mathbf{c}\}$ and begin to check the validity of the solution to the first equation. If Y is a solution, then the two sides of the equation $Y = \{\mathbf{b}, \mathbf{c}\} \cup \{\mathbf{a}\} \cdot Y$ must be equal. Since both **b** and **c** appear on the right-hand side they must also be on the left-hand side, which clearly means that they have to be in Y. Once **b** is known to be in Y, it will give rise to a term on the right-hand side due to the presence of {**a**}·Y. Thus, **a**·**b** must also be found on the left-hand side and therefore is in Y, and so on. The resulting sequence of implications parallels the first part of the proof of Theorem 6.1.

To see intuitively why no string other than those found in {**a**}*·{**b**, **c**} may belong to a solution for X = {**b**, **c**} ∪ {**a**}·X, consider a string such as **aa**. If this were to belong to X, then it would appear on the left-hand side and therefore would have to appear on the right-hand side as well if the two sides were to indeed be equal. On the right-hand side are just the two components, {**b**, **c**} and {**a**}·X. **aa** is clearly not in {**b**, **c**}, so it must be in {**a**}·X, which does seem plausible; all that is necessary is for **a** to be in X, and then **aa** will belong to {**a**}·X. If **a** is in X, though, it must also appear on the left-hand side, and so **a** must be on the right-hand side as well. Again, **a** is not in {**b**, **c**}, so it must be in {**a**}·X. This can happen only if λ belongs to X so that **a**·λ will belong to {**a**}·X. This implies that λ must now show up on both sides, and this leads to a contradiction: λ cannot be on the right-hand side since λ clearly is not in {**b**, **c**}, and it cannot belong to {**a**}·X either, since all these words begin with an **a**. This contradiction shows why **aa** cannot be part of any solution X.

This example illustrates the basic nature of these types of equations: for words that are not in {**a**}*·{**b**, **c**}, the inclusion of that word in the solution leads to the inclusion of shorter and shorter strings, which eventually leads to a contradiction. This property was exploited in the second half of the proof of Theorem 6.1. Rather than finding shorter and shorter strings, though, it was assumed we already had the shortest, and we showed that there had to be a still shorter one; this led to the desired contradiction more directly.

Our main goal will be to solve *systems* of language equations, since the relationships between the *terminal sets* of an automaton can be described by such a system. Systems of language equations are similar in form and spirit to systems of algebraic equations, such as

$$3x_1 + x_2 = 10$$
$$x_1 - x_2 = 2$$

which has the unique solution $x_1 = 3, x_2 = 1$. We will look at systems of language equations such as

$$\mathrm{X}_1 = \epsilon \cup \mathbf{a}\cdot\mathrm{X}_1 \cup \mathbf{b}\cdot\mathrm{X}_2$$
$$\mathrm{X}_2 = \emptyset \cup \mathbf{b}\cdot\mathrm{X}_1 \cup \emptyset\cdot\mathrm{X}_2$$

which has the (unique) solution $\mathrm{X}_1 = (\mathbf{a} \cup \mathbf{bb})^*, \mathrm{X}_2 = \mathbf{b}\cdot(\mathbf{a} \cup \mathbf{bb})^*$. Checking that this is a solution entails verifying that both equations are satisifed if these expressions are substituted for the variables X_1 and X_2.

The solution of such systems parallels the solution of algebraic equations. For example, the system

$$3x_1 + x_2 = 10$$

$$x_1 - x_2 = 2$$

can be solved by treating the second statement as an equation in just the variable x_2 and solving as indicated by the algebraic theorem "For any numbers a and b, where $a \neq 0$, the equation $ax = b$ has a unique solution given by $x = b \div a$." The second statement can be written as $(-1)x_2 = 2 - x_2$, which then admits the solution $x_2 = (2 - x_1) \div (-1)$ or $x_2 = x_1 - 2$. This solution can be inserted into the first equation to eliminate x_2 and form an equation solely in x_1. Terms can be regrouped and the algebraic theorem can be applied to find x_1. We would have

$$3x_1 + x_2 = 10$$

which becomes

$$3x_1 + x_1 - 2 = 10$$

or

$$4x_1 - 2 = 10$$

or

$$4x_1 = 12$$

or

$$x_1 = 12 \div 4$$

yielding

$$x_1 = 3$$

This value of x_1 can be back-substituted to find the unique solution for x_2: $x_2 = x_1 - 2 = 3 - 2 = 1$.

Essentially, the same technique can be applied to any two equations in two unknowns, and formulas can be developed that predict the coefficients for the reduced set of equations. Consider the generalized system of algebraic equations with unknowns x_1 and x_2, constant terms E_1 and E_2, and coefficients A_{11}, A_{12}, A_{21}, and A_{22}:

$$A_{11}x_1 + A_{12}x_2 = E_1$$

$$A_{21}x_1 + A_{22}x_2 = E_2$$

Recall that the appropriate formulas for reducing this to a single equation of the form $\hat{A}_{11}x_1 = \hat{E}_1$, where the new coefficients $\hat{A}_{11}$ and $\hat{E}_1$ can be calculated as

$$\hat{E}_1 = E_1A_{22} - E_2A_{12}$$

$$\hat{A}_{11} = A_{11}A_{22} - A_{12}A_{21}$$

A similar technique can be used to eliminate variables when there is a larger number of equations in the system. The following theorem makes similar predictions of the new coefficients for language equations.

∇ **Theorem 6.2.** Let $n \geq 2$ and consider the system of equations in the unknowns $X_1, X_2, \ldots, X_n$ given by

$$X_1 = E_1 \cup A_{11}X_1 \cup A_{12}X_2 \cup \cdots \cup A_{1(n-1)}X_{n-1} \cup A_{1n}X_n$$
$$X_2 = E_2 \cup A_{21}X_1 \cup A_{22}X_2 \cup \cdots \cup A_{2(n-1)}X_{n-1} \cup A_{2n}X_n$$
$$\vdots$$
$$X_{n-1} = E_{n-1} \cup A_{(n-1)1}X_1 \cup A_{(n-1)2}X_2 \cup \cdots \cup A_{(n-1)(n-1)}X_{n-1} \cup A_{(n-1)n}X_n$$
$$X_n = E_n \cup A_{n1}X_1 \cup A_{n2}X_2 \cup \cdots \cup A_{n(n-1)}X_{n-1} \cup A_{nn}X_n$$

in which $(\forall i, j \in \{1, 2, \ldots, n\})(\lambda \notin A_{ij})$.

a. This system has a unique solution.

b. Define $\hat{E}_i = E_i \cup (A_{in} \cdot A_{nn}^* \cdot E_n)$ for all $i = 1, 2, \ldots, n-1$

and

$$\hat{A}_{ij} = A_{ij} \cup (A_{in} \cdot A_{nn}^* \cdot A_{nj}) \text{ for all } i, j = 1, 2, \ldots, n-1.$$

The solution of the original set of equations will agree with the solution of the following set of $n-1$ equations in the unknowns $X_1, X_2, \ldots, X_{n-1}$:

$$X_1 = \hat{E}_1 \cup \hat{A}_{11}X_1 \cup \hat{A}_{12}X_2 \cup \cdots \cup \hat{A}_{1(n-1)}X_{n-1}$$
$$X_2 = \hat{E}_2 \cup \hat{A}_{21}X_1 \cup \hat{A}_{22}X_2 \cup \cdots \cup \hat{A}_{2(n-1)}X_{n-1}$$
$$\vdots$$
$$X_{n-1} = \hat{E}_{n-1} \cup \hat{A}_{(n-1)1}X_1 \cup \hat{A}_{(n-1)2}X_2 \cup \cdots \cup \hat{A}_{(n-1)(n-1)}X_{n-1}$$

c. Once the solution to the above $n-1$ equations in (b) is known, that solution can be used to find the remaining unknown:

$$X_n = A_{nn}^* \cdot (E_n \cup A_{n1}X_1 \cup A_{n2}X_2 \cup \cdots \cup A_{n(n-1)}X_{n-1})$$

Proof. The proof hinges on the repeated application of Theorem 6.1. The last of the n equations, $X_n = E_n \cup A_{n1}X_1 \cup A_{n2}X_2 \cup \cdots \cup A_{n(n-1)}X_{n-1} \cup A_{nn}X_n$ can be thought of as an equation in the one unknown X_n with a coefficient of A_{nn} for X_n, and the remainder of the expression a "constant" term not involving X_n. The following parenthetical grouping illustrates this viewpoint:

$$X_n = (E_n \cup A_{n1}X_1 \cup A_{n2}X_2 \cup \cdots \cup A_{n(n-1)}X_{n-1}) \cup A_{nn}X_n$$

Note that for any subscript k, if A_{nk} does not contain λ, neither will $A_{nk}X_k$. Theorem 6.1 can therefore be applied, to the one equation in the one unknown X_n, with coefficients

$$E = (E_n \cup A_{n1}X_1 \cup A_{n2}X_2 \cup \cdots \cup A_{n(n-1)}X_{n-1})$$

and $A = A_{nn}$. The solution, A^*E, is exactly as given by part (c) above:

$$X_n = A_{nn}^* \cdot (E_n \cup A_{n1}X_1 \cup A_{n2}X_2 \cup \cdots \cup A_{n(n-1)}X_{n-1})$$

or

$$X_n = A_{nn}^* \cdot E_n \cup A_{nn}^* \cdot A_{n1}X_1 \cup A_{nn}^* \cdot A_{n2}X_2 \cup \cdots \cup A_{nn}^* \cdot A_{n(n-1)}X_{n-1})$$

If there was a unique solution for the terms X_1 through X_{n-1}, then Theorem 6.1 would guarantee a unique solution for X_n, too.

The solution for X_n can be substituted for X_n in each of the other $n-1$ equations. If the kth equation is represented by

$$X_k = E_k \cup A_{k1}X_1 \cup A_{k2}X_2 \cup \cdots \cup A_{kn}X_n$$

then the substitution will yield

$$X_k = E_k \cup A_{k1}X_1 \cup A_{k2}X_2 \cup \cdots \\ \cup (A_{kn} \cdot (A_{nn}^* \cdot E_n \cup A_{nn}^* \cdot A_{n1}X_1 \cup A_{nn}^* \cdot A_{n2}X_2 \cup \cdots \cup A_{nn}^* \cdot A_{n(n-1)}X_{n-1}))$$

By using the distributive law, this becomes

$$X_k = E_k \cup A_{k1}X_1 \cup A_{k2}X_2 \cup \cdots \\ \cup(A_{kn} \cdot A_{nn}^* \cdot E_n \cup A_{kn} \cdot A_{nn}^* \cdot A_{n1}X_1 \cup A_{kn} \cdot A_{nn}^* \cdot A_{n2}X_2 \cup \cdots \cup A_{kn} \cdot A_{nn}^* \cdot A_{n(n-1)}X_{n-1})$$

Collecting like terms yields

$$X_k = (E_k \cup A_{kn} \cdot A_{nn}^* \cdot E_n) \cup (A_{k1}X_1 \cup A_{kn} \cdot A_{nn}^* \cdot A_{n1}X_1) \\ \cup (A_{k2}X_2 \cup A_{kn} \cdot A_{nn}^* \cdot A_{n2}X_2) \cup \cdots \cup (A_{k(n-1)}X_{n-1} \cup A_{kn} \cdot A_{nn}^* \cdot A_{n(n-1)}X_{n-1})$$

or

$$X_k = (E_k \cup A_{kn} \cdot A_{nn}^* \cdot E_n) \cup (A_{k1} \cup A_{kn} \cdot A_{nn}^* \cdot A_{n1})X_1 \\ \cup (A_{k2} \cup A_{kn} \cdot A_{nn}^* \cdot A_{n2})X_2 \cup \cdots \cup (A_{k(n-1)} \cup A_{kn} \cdot A_{nn}^* \cdot A_{n(n-1)})X_{n-1}$$

The constant term in this equation is $(E_k \cup A_{kn} \cdot A_{nn}^* \cdot E_n)$, which is exactly the formula given for $\hat{E}_k$ in part (b). The coefficient for X_1 is seen to be

$$(A_{k1} \cup A_{kn} \cdot A_{nn}^* \cdot A_{n1}),$$

while the coefficient for X_2 is $(A_{k2} \cup A_{kn} \cdot A_{nn}^* \cdot A_{n2})$, and so on. The coefficient for X_j would then be $\hat{A}_{kj} = A_{kj} \cup (A_{kn} \cdot A_{nn}^* \cdot A_{nj})$, which also agrees with the formula given in part (b). This is why the solution of the original set of equations agrees with the solution of the set of $n-1$ equations given in part (b).

Part (a) is proved by induction on n: the method outlined above can be repeated on the new set of $n-1$ equations to eliminate X_{n-1}, and so on, until one equation in the one unknown X_1 is obtained. Theorem 6.1 will guarantee a unique solution for X_1, and part (c) can then be used to find the unique solution for X_2, and so on.

Δ

EXAMPLE 6.8

Consider the system defined before, where

$$X_1 = \epsilon \cup \mathbf{a}\cdot X_1 \cup \mathbf{b}\cdot X_2$$

$$X_2 = \emptyset \cup \mathbf{b}\cdot X_1 \cup \emptyset\cdot X_2$$

The proof of Theorem 6.2 implies the solution for X_1 will agree with the solution to the one-variable equation $X_1 = \hat{E}_1 \cup \hat{A}_{11}X_1$, where

$$\hat{E}_1 = E_1 \cup (A_{12}\cdot A_{22}^*\cdot E_2) = \epsilon \cup (\mathbf{b}\cdot\emptyset^*\cdot\emptyset) = \epsilon \cup (\mathbf{b}\cdot\epsilon\cdot\emptyset) = \epsilon \cup \emptyset = \epsilon,$$

and

$$\hat{A}_{11} = A_{11} \cup (A_{12}\cdot A_{22}^*\cdot A_{21}) = \mathbf{a} \cup (\mathbf{b}\cdot\emptyset^*\cdot\mathbf{b}) = \mathbf{a} \cup (\mathbf{b}\cdot\epsilon\cdot\mathbf{b}) = \mathbf{a} \cup \mathbf{bb}.$$

Thus we have $X_1 = \epsilon \cup (\mathbf{a} \cup \mathbf{bb}).\ X_1$, which by Theorem 6.1 has the (unique) solution $X_1 = \hat{A}_{11}^*\hat{E}_1 = (\mathbf{a} \cup \mathbf{bb})^*\cdot\epsilon$. Substituting this into the second equation yields $X_2 = \emptyset \cup \mathbf{b}\cdot(\mathbf{a} \cup \mathbf{bb})^* \cup \emptyset\cdot X_2$, which by Theorem 6.1 has the (unique) solution $X_2 = \emptyset^*\cdot(\mathbf{b}\cdot(\mathbf{a} \cup \mathbf{bb})^*) = \mathbf{b}\cdot(\mathbf{a} \cup \mathbf{bb})^*$. Note that this expression for X_2 could also be found by applying the back-substitution formula given in the proof of Theorem 6.2.

We will now see that the language accepted by a DFA can be equated with the solution of a set of language equations, which will allow us to prove the following important theorem.

∇ **Theorem 6.3.** Let Σ be an alphabet and let L be an FAD language over Σ. Then L is a regular set over Σ.

Proof. If L is FAD, then there exists an $n > 0$ and a deterministic finite automaton $A = <\Sigma, \{s_1, s_2, \ldots, s_n\}, s_1, \delta, F>$ such that $L(A) = L$. For each $i = 1, 2, \ldots, n$, define $X_i = \{z \in \Sigma^* \mid \overline{\delta}(s_i, z) \in F\}$; that is, X_i is the set of all strings that, *when starting at state* s_i, reach a final state in A. Each X_i then represents the terminal set $T(A, s_i)$ defined in Chapter 3. Since s_1 is the start state of this machine, it should be clear that $X_1 = L(A) = L$. Define

$$E_i = \begin{cases} \emptyset & \text{if } s_i \notin F \\ \varepsilon & \text{if } s_i \in F \end{cases} \qquad \text{for } i = 1, 2, \ldots, n$$

and

$$A_{ij} = \bigcup_{\mathbf{a} \in \Sigma \wedge \delta(s_i, \mathbf{a}) = s_j} \mathbf{a} \qquad \text{for } i, j = 1, 2, \ldots, n$$

That is, A_{ij} represents the set of all letters that cause a transition from state s_i to state s_j. Notice that since $\lambda \notin \Sigma$ none of the sets A_{ij} contain the empty string, and therefore by Theorem 6.2, there is a unique solution to the system:

$$X_1 = E_1 \cup A_{11}X_1 \cup A_{12}X_2 \cup \cdots \cup A_{1n}X_n$$
$$X_2 = E_2 \cup A_{21}X_1 \cup A_{22}X_2 \cup \cdots \cup A_{2n}X_n$$
$$\vdots$$
$$X_n = E_n \cup A_{n1}X_1 \cup A_{n2}X_2 \cup \cdots \cup A_{nn}X_n$$

However, these equations exactly describe the relationships between the terminal sets denoted by $X_1, X_2, \ldots, X_n$ at the beginning of this proof (compare with Example 6.11), and hence the solution will represent exactly those quantities. In particular, the solution for X_1 will be a regular expression for $L(A)$, that is, for L.
Δ

EXAMPLE 6.9

Consider the DFA B given by the diagram in Figure 6.5, which accepts all strings with an odd number of **b**s over {**a**, **b**}. This machine generates the following system of language equations:

$$X_1 = \emptyset \cup \mathbf{a}X_1 \cup \mathbf{b}X_2$$
$$X_2 = \epsilon \cup \mathbf{b}X_1 \cup \mathbf{a}X_2$$

which will have the same solution for X_1 as the equation

$$X_1 = \hat{E}_1 \cup \hat{A}_{11}X_1$$

where

$$\hat{E}_1 = E_1 \cup (A_{12} \cdot A_{22}^* \cdot E_2) = \emptyset \cup (\mathbf{b} \cdot \mathbf{a}^* \cdot \epsilon) = \mathbf{b} \cdot \mathbf{a}^*$$

and

$$\hat{A}_{11} = A_{11} \cup (A_{12} \cdot A_{22}^* \cdot A_{21}) = \mathbf{a} \cup (\mathbf{b} \cdot \mathbf{a}^* \cdot \mathbf{b})$$

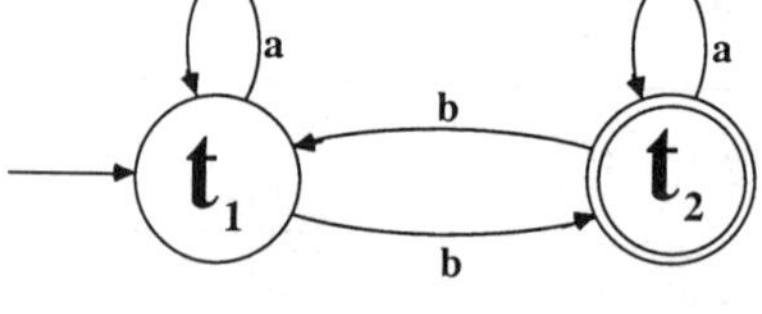

Figure 6.5 The DFA discussed in Example 6.9

Theorem 6.1 predicts the solution for X_1 to be $(\mathbf{a} \cup (\mathbf{b} \cdot \mathbf{a}^* \cdot \mathbf{b}))^* \cdot \mathbf{b} \cdot \mathbf{a}^*$. It can be verified that this solution describes all those strings with an odd number of **b**s. X_1 is indeed the terminal set for s_1, that is, $T(B, s_1)$. Likewise, finding X_2 yields all strings with an even number of **b**s, which is the terminal set for s_2, $T(B, s_2)$.

Nondeterministic finite automata can likewise be represented by language equations, and without the intermediate step of applying Definition 4.5 to acquire a deterministic equivalent. The sets E_i and A_{ij} retain essentially the same definitions as before: E_i is ϵ or $\emptyset$, depending on whether or not s_i is a final state, and A_{ij} again represents exactly the set of all letters that cause a transition from state s_i to state s_j. This definition requires a minor cosmetic change for NDFAs, since the state transition function is slightly different:

$$A_{ij} = \bigcup_{\mathbf{a} \in \Sigma \wedge s_j \in \delta(s_i, \mathbf{a})} \mathbf{a} \qquad \text{for } i, j = 1, 2, \ldots, n$$

An n-state NDFA therefore gives rise to n equation in n unknowns, which can be solved as outlined by Theorems 6.2 and 6.1. While Definition 4.5 need not be used as a conversion step, an NDFA with λ-moves will have to be transformed into an equivalent NDFA without λ-moves. An appropriate definition for A_{ij} *could* be given for the original NDFA, and while the resulting equations would describe the relation between the terminal sets, some A_{ij} set might then contain λ as a member. There are systems of equations arising in this manner that do not have unique solutions (see the exercises). For an NDFA with λ-moves, Definition 4.9 could be applied to find an equivalent NDFA without λ-moves, since Theorems 6.2 and 6.1 specifically prohibit the empty string as a part of a coefficient. However, if the ambiguous equations generated from a machine with λ-moves were solved as suggested in Theorems 6.1 and 6.2, a "minimal" solution would be obtained that would correspond to the desired answer.

EXAMPLE 6.10

Consider again the system described in Example 6.8. This can be thought of as the set of language equations corresponding to the NDFA called B, illustrated in Figure 6.6a. Note that L(B) is indeed the given solution: $L(\mathrm{B}) = X_1 = (\mathbf{a} \cup \mathbf{bb})^*$. Notice the

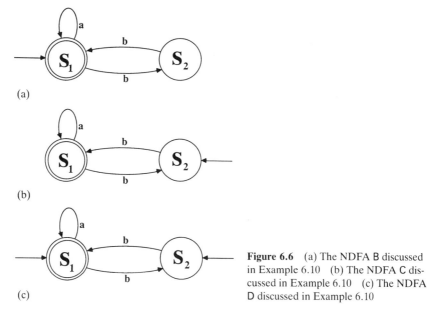

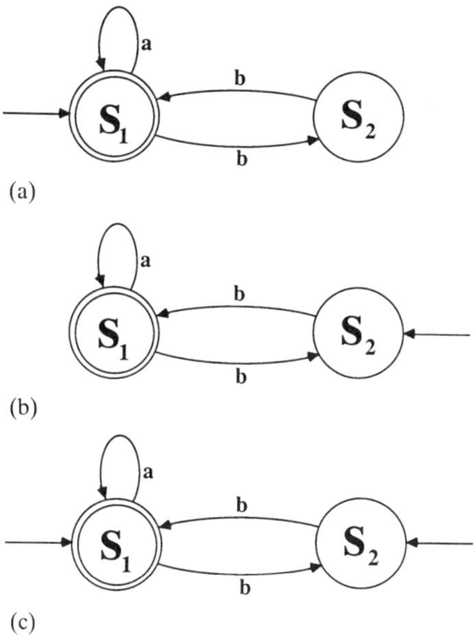

Figure 6.6 (a) The NDFA B discussed in Example 6.10 (b) The NDFA C discussed in Example 6.10 (c) The NDFA D discussed in Example 6.10

similarity between B and the machine C shown in Figure 6.6b, which has s_2 as the start state. Note that $L(C)$ is given by $X_2 = \mathbf{b}\cdot(\mathbf{a} \cup \mathbf{bb})^*$, where X_2 was the other part of the solution given in Example 6.8 (verify this). Finally, consider a similar machine D in Figure 6.6c with both s_1 and s_2 as start states. Can you quickly write a regular expression that describes the language accepted by D?

EXAMPLE 6.11

Regular expressions for machines with more than two states can be found by repeated application of the technique described in Theorem 6.2. For example, consider the three-state DFA given in Figure 6.7. The solution for this three-state machine will be explored shortly. We begin by illustrating the natural relationships between the terminal sets described in Theorem 6.3. First let us note that the language accepted by this machine includes:

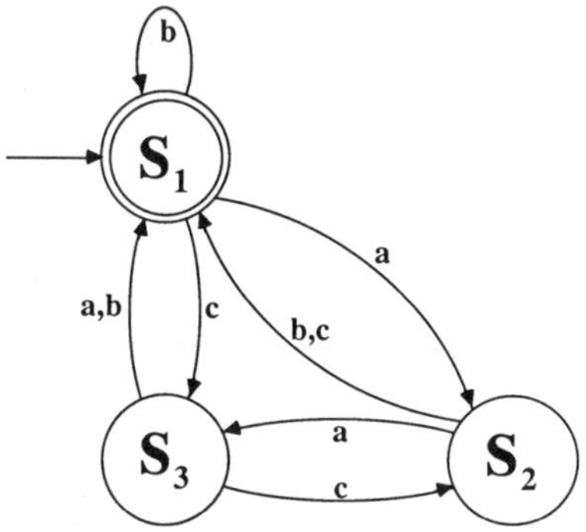

Figure 6.7 The DFA discussed in Example 6.11

1. All strings that end with **b**.
2. Strings that contain no **b**s, but for which $|x|_{\mathbf{a}} - |x|_{\mathbf{c}}$ is a multiple of 3.
3. Strings that are concatenations of type (1) and type (2) strings.

According to Theorem 6.3, the equations for this machine are

$$X_1 = \epsilon \cup \mathbf{b}X_1 \cup \mathbf{a}X_2 \cup \mathbf{c}X_3$$
$$X_2 = \emptyset \cup (\mathbf{b} \cup \mathbf{c})X_1 \cup \emptyset X_2 \cup \mathbf{a}X_3$$
$$X_3 = \emptyset \cup (\mathbf{a} \cup \mathbf{b})X_1 \cup \mathbf{c}X_2 \cup \emptyset X_3$$

which can be simplified to

$$X_1 = \epsilon \cup \mathbf{b}X_1 \cup \mathbf{a}X_2 \cup \mathbf{c}X_3$$
$$X_2 = (\mathbf{b} \cup \mathbf{c})X_1 \cup \mathbf{a}X_3$$
$$X_3 = (\mathbf{a} \cup \mathbf{b})X_1 \cup \mathbf{c}X_2$$

and rewritten as

$$X_1 = \epsilon \cup \mathbf{b}X_1 \cup \mathbf{a}X_2 \cup \mathbf{c}X_3$$

$$X_2 = \mathbf{b}X_1 \cup \mathbf{c}X_1 \cup \mathbf{a}X_3$$

$$X_3 = \mathbf{a}X_1 \cup \mathbf{b}X_1 \cup \mathbf{c}X_2$$

The equation for X_1 admits the following interpretation; recalling that X_1 represents all the strings that reach a final state when starting from s_1, we see that these can be broken up into four distinct classes:

1. Strings of length 0: (ϵ).
2. Strings that start with **a** (and note that **a** moves the current state from s_1 to s_2) and then proceed (from s_2) to a final state: ($\mathbf{a}X_2$).
3. Strings that start with **b** and then proceed to a final state: ($\mathbf{b}X_1$).
4. Strings that start with **c** and then proceed to a final state: ($\mathbf{c}X_3$).

The union of these four classes should equal X_1, which is exactly what the first equation states.

$X_2 = \mathbf{b}X_1 \cup \mathbf{c}X_1 \cup \mathbf{a}X_3$ can be interpreted similarly; ϵ does not appear in this equation because there is *no* way to reach a final state from s_2 if no letters are processed. If at least one letter is processed, then that first letter is an **a**, **b**, or **c**. If it is **a**, then we move from state s_2 to s_3, and the remainder of the string must take us to a final state from s_3 (that is, the remainder must belong to X_3). Strings that begin with an **a** and are followed by a string from X_3 can easily be described by $\mathbf{a}\cdot X_3$. Similarly, strings that start with **b** or **c** must move from s_2 to s_1, and then be followed by a string from X_1. These strings are described by $\mathbf{b}\cdot X_1$ and $\mathbf{c}\cdot X_1$. The three cases for reaching a final state from s_2 that have just been described are exhaustive (and mutually exclusive), and so their union should equal all of X_2. This is exactly the relation expressed by the second equation, $X_2 = \mathbf{b}X_1 \cup \mathbf{c}X_1 \cup \mathbf{a}X_3$. The last equation admits a similar interpretation.

None of the above observations are necessary to actually solve the system! The preceding discussion is intended to illustrate that the natural relationships between the terminal sets described by Theorem 6.3 and the correspondences we have so laboriously developed here are succinctly predicted by the language equations. Once the equations are written down, we can simply apply Theorem 6.2 and reduce to a system with only two unknowns. We have

$$E_1 = \epsilon, \qquad E_2 = \emptyset, \qquad E_3 = \emptyset$$

$$A_{11} = \mathbf{b}, \qquad A_{12} = \mathbf{a}, \qquad A_{13} = \mathbf{c}$$

$$A_{21} = \mathbf{b} \cup \mathbf{c}, \qquad A_{22} = \emptyset, \qquad A_{23} = \mathbf{a}$$

$$A_{31} = \mathbf{a} \cup \mathbf{b}, \qquad A_{32} = \mathbf{c}, \qquad A_{33} = \emptyset$$

from which we can compute

$\hat{E}_1 = E_1 \cup A_{13}A_{33}^*E_3 = \epsilon \cup \mathbf{c}\emptyset^*\emptyset = \epsilon,$ $\qquad \hat{E}_2 = \emptyset$

$\hat{A}_{11} = A_{11} \cup A_{13}A_{33}^*A_{31} = \mathbf{b} \cup \mathbf{c}\emptyset^*(\mathbf{a} \cup \mathbf{b}) = \mathbf{b} \cup \mathbf{c}(\mathbf{a} \cup \mathbf{b}),$ $\qquad \hat{A}_{12} = \mathbf{a} \cup \mathbf{c}\emptyset^*\mathbf{c} = \mathbf{a} \cup \mathbf{cc}$

$\hat{A}_{21} = \mathbf{b} \cup \mathbf{c} \cup \mathbf{a}\emptyset^*(\mathbf{a} \cup \mathbf{b}) = \mathbf{b} \cup \mathbf{c} \cup \mathbf{a}(\mathbf{a} \cup \mathbf{b}),$ $\qquad \hat{A}_{22} = \emptyset \cup \mathbf{a}\emptyset^*\mathbf{c} = \mathbf{ac}$

which gives the following system of equations:

$$X_1 = \epsilon \cup (\mathbf{b} \cup \mathbf{c}(\mathbf{a} \cup \mathbf{b}))X_1 \cup (\mathbf{a} \cup \mathbf{cc})X_2$$

$$X_2 = \emptyset \cup ((\mathbf{b} \cup \mathbf{c}) \cup \mathbf{a}(\mathbf{a} \cup \mathbf{b}))X_1 \cup \mathbf{ac}X_2$$

These two equations can be reduced to a single equation by applying Theorem 6.2 again:

$$\hat{\hat{E}}_1 = \hat{E}_1 \cup \hat{A}_{12}(\hat{A}_{22})^*\hat{E}_2 = \epsilon \cup (\mathbf{a} \cup \mathbf{cc})\cdot(\mathbf{ac})^*\cdot\emptyset = \epsilon$$

$$\hat{\hat{A}}_{11} = \hat{A}_{11} \cup \hat{A}_{12}(\hat{A}_{22})^*\hat{A}_{21} = \mathbf{b} \cup \mathbf{c}(\mathbf{a} \cup \mathbf{b}) \cup (\mathbf{a} \cup \mathbf{cc})(\mathbf{ac})^*((\mathbf{b} \cup \mathbf{c}) \cup \mathbf{a}(\mathbf{a} \cup \mathbf{b}))$$

which yields one equation in one unknown whose solution is

$$X_1 = (\hat{\hat{A}}_{11})^*\hat{\hat{E}}_1 = (\mathbf{b} \cup \mathbf{c}(\mathbf{a} \cup \mathbf{b}) \cup (\mathbf{a} \cup \mathbf{cc})(\mathbf{ac})^*((\mathbf{b} \cup \mathbf{c}) \cup \mathbf{a}(\mathbf{a} \cup \mathbf{b})))^*\cdot\epsilon$$

Since s_1 was the only start state, the regular expression given by X_1 should describe the language accepted by the original three-state automaton.

Returning to our observations above, this expression can be reconciled with our intuitive notion of what the solution "should" look like. $\hat{\hat{A}}_{11}$ can be expanded to yield the following form:

$$\hat{\hat{A}}_{11} = \mathbf{b} \cup \mathbf{ca} \cup \mathbf{cb} \cup \mathbf{a(ac)^*b} \cup \mathbf{a(ac)^*c} \cup \mathbf{a(ac)^*ab} \cup \mathbf{a(ac)^*aa}$$
$$\cup\, \mathbf{cc(ac)^*b} \cup \mathbf{cc(ac)^*c} \cup \mathbf{cc(ac)^*ab} \cup \mathbf{cc(ac)^*aa}$$

Observe that each of the 11 subexpressions consists of strings that (1) end with **b**, or (2) contain no **b**s, but for which $|x|_\mathbf{a} - |x|_\mathbf{c}$ is a multiple of 3. Hence the Kleene closure of this expression, which represents the language accepted by this machine, does indeed agree with our notion of what X_1 should describe.

Since s_1 is also the only final state in this example, it is interesting to note that each of the subexpressions of $\hat{\hat{A}}_{11}$ describes strings that, when starting at s_1 in the automaton, return you to s_1 again *for the first time* (examine the diagram and verify this).

EXAMPLE 6.12

Consider the automaton shown in Figure 6.8. It is similar to the one in Example 6.11, but it now gives rise to four equations in four unknowns. As these equations are solved, the final $\hat{\hat{\hat{A}}}_{11}$ coefficient for X_1 will again describe strings that, when starting at s_1 in the automaton, return you to s_1 again for the first time; it will agree with $\hat{\hat{A}}_{11}$ in Example 6.11. The final constant term associated with X_1 (that is, $\hat{\hat{\hat{E}}}_1$), will represent all those strings that deposit you in a final state from s_1 without ever returning to s_1. In this automaton, this will be given by $\hat{\hat{\hat{E}}}_1 = \mathbf{de}^*$. $\hat{\hat{\hat{A}}}{}_{11}^*\hat{\hat{\hat{E}}}_1$ therefore represents strings that go from s_1 back to s_1 any number of times, followed by a string that leaves s_1 (for the last time) for a final state.

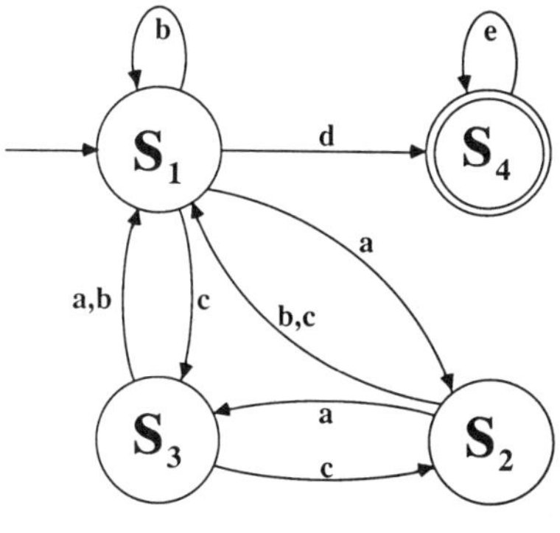

Figure 6.8 The DFA discussed in Example 6.12

In general, the final coefficient and constant terms can always be interpreted in this manner. In Example 6.11, the only way to reach a final state from s_1 and avoid having to return again to s_1 was to not leave in the first place; this was reflected by the fact that $\hat{\hat{E}}_1 = \epsilon$.

EXAMPLE 6.13

Consider the automaton illustrated in Figure 6.9, which is identical to the DFA in Example 6.11 except for the placement of the final state. Even though the initial system of three equations is now different, we can expect $\hat{\hat{A}}_{11}$ to compute to the same expression as before. Since $\hat{\hat{E}}_1$ is supposed to represent all those strings that deposit you in a final state from s_1 without ever returning to s_1, one should be able to predict that the new final constant term will look like $\hat{\hat{E}}_1 = \mathbf{a}(\mathbf{ac})^* \cup \mathbf{c}(\mathbf{ca})^*\mathbf{c}$. An expression for the language recognized by this automaton would then be given by

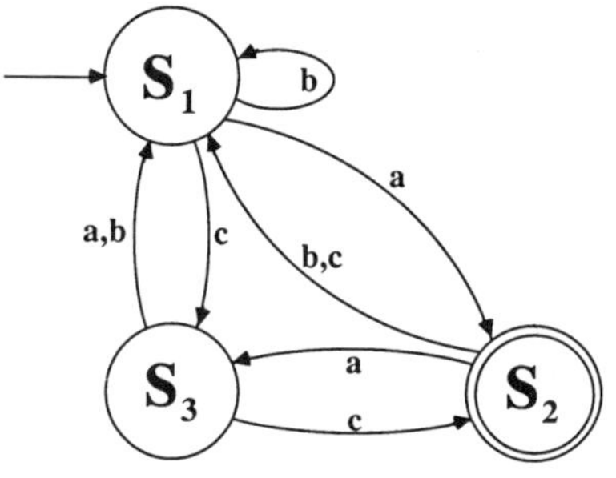

Figure 6.9 The DFA discussed in Example 6.13

$$\begin{aligned} X_1 &= (\hat{\hat{A}}_{11})^*\hat{\hat{E}}_1 \\ &= (\mathbf{b} \cup \mathbf{c}(\mathbf{a} \cup \mathbf{b}) \cup (\mathbf{a} \cup \mathbf{cc})(\mathbf{ac})^*((\mathbf{b} \cup \mathbf{c}) \cup \mathbf{a}(\mathbf{a} \cup \mathbf{b})))^* \cdot (\mathbf{a}(\mathbf{ac})^* \cup \mathbf{c}(\mathbf{ca})^*\mathbf{c}) \end{aligned}$$

It may often be convenient to eliminate a variable other than the one that is numerically last. This can be accomplished by appropriately renumbering the unknowns and applying Theorem 6.2 to the new set of equations. For convenience, we state an analog of Theorem 6.2 that allows the elimination of the mth unknown from a set of n equations in n unknowns. The following lemma agrees with Theorem 6.2 if $m = n$.

∇ **Lemma 6.3.** Let n and m be positive integers and let $m \le n$. Consider the system of $n \ge 2$ equations in the unknowns $X_1, X_2, \ldots, X_n$ given by

$$X_k = E_k \cup A_{k1}X_1 \cup A_{k2}X_2 \cup \cdots \cup A_{kn}X_n, \qquad \text{for } k = 1, 2, \ldots, n$$

in which $(\forall i, j)(\lambda \notin A_{ij})$.

The unknown X_m can be eliminated from this system to form the following $n - 1$ equations in the unknowns $X_1, X_2, \ldots, X_{m-1}, X_{m+1}, \ldots, X_n$.

$$X_k = \hat{E}_k \cup \hat{A}_{k1}X_1 \cup \hat{A}_{k2}X_2 \cup \cdots \cup \hat{A}_{k(m-1)}X_{m-1} \cup \hat{A}_{k(m+1)}X_{m+1} \cup \ldots \cup \hat{A}_{kn}X_n,$$

$$\text{for } k = 1, 2, \ldots, m-1, m+1, \ldots, n$$

where

$$\hat{E}_i = E_i \cup (A_{im} \cdot A_{mm}^* \cdot E_m), \qquad \text{for all } i = 1, 2, \ldots, m-1, m+1, \ldots, n$$

and

$$\hat{A}_{ij} = A_{ij} \cup (A_{im} \cdot A_{mm}^* \cdot A_{mj}), \qquad \text{for all } i, j = 1, 2, \ldots, m - 1, m+1, \ldots, n$$

Furthermore, once the solution to the above $n - 1$ equations is known, that solution can be used to find the remaining unknown:

$$X_m = A_{mm}^* \cdot (E_m \cup A_{m1}X_1 \cup A_{m2}X_2 \cup \cdots \cup A_{m(m-1)}X_{m-1}$$
$$\cup A_{m(m+1)}X_{m+1} \cup \ldots \cup A_{mn}X_n)$$

Proof. The proof follows from a renumbering of the equations given in Theorem 6.2.
Δ

A significant reduction in the size of the expressions representing the solutions can often be achieved by carefully choosing the order in which to eliminate the unknowns. This situation can easily arise when solving language equations that correspond to finite automata. For example, consider the DFA illustrated in Figure 6.10. The equations for this machine are given by

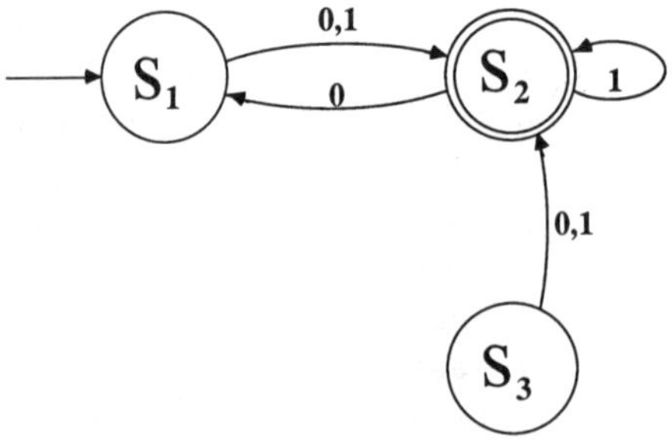

Figure 6.10 The DFA discussed in Exercise 6.19

$$X_1 = \emptyset \cup \emptyset X_1 \cup (\mathbf{0} \cup \mathbf{1})X_2 \cup \emptyset X_3$$

$$X_2 = \epsilon \cup \mathbf{0}X_1 \cup \mathbf{1}X_2 \cup \emptyset X_3$$

$$X_3 = \emptyset \cup \emptyset X_1 \cup (\mathbf{0} \cup \mathbf{1})X_2 \cup \emptyset X_3$$

Using Theorem 6.2 to methodically solve for X_1, X_2, and X_3 involves eliminating X_3 and then eliminating X_2. Theorem 6.1 can then be used to solve for X_1, and then the back-substitution rules can be employed to find X_2 and X_3. The regular expressions found in this manner are quite complex. A striking simplification can be made by eliminating X_3 and then eliminating X_1 (instead of X_2). The solution for X_2 is quite concise, which leads to simple expressions for X_1 and X_3 during the back-substitution phase (see Exercise 6.19).

Let $A = <\Sigma, \{s_1, s_2, \ldots, s_n\}, s_1, \delta, F>$ be a deterministic finite automaton. We have seen that the relationships between the terminal sets $T(A, s_i)$ described in Chapter 3 give rise to a system of equations. Similarly, the initial sets $I(A, s_i)$ defined in Chapter 2 are also interrelated. Recall that, for a state s_i, $I(A, s_i)$ is comprised of strings that, when starting in the start state, lead to the state s_i. That is, $I(A, s_i) = \{x \mid \overline{\delta}(s_1, x) = s_i\}$. The equations we have discussed to this point have been *right linear*; that is, the unknowns X_i appear to the right of their coefficients. The initial sets for an automaton are also related by a system of equations, but these equations are *left linear*; the unknowns Y_i appear to the left of their coefficients. The solution for sets of left-linear equations parallels that of right-linear systems.

∇ **Theorem 6.4.** Let n and m be positive integers and let $m \leq n$. Consider the system of $n \geq 2$ equations in the unknowns $Y_1, Y_2, \ldots, Y_n$ given by

$$Y_k = I_k \cup Y_1 B_{k1} \cup Y_2 B_{k2} \cup \cdots \cup Y_n B_{kn}, \qquad \text{for } k = 1, 2, \ldots, n$$

in which $(\forall i, j)(\lambda \notin B_{ij})$.

a. The unknown Y_m can be eliminated from this system to form the following $n - 1$ equations in the unknowns $Y_1, Y_2, \ldots, Y_{m-1}, Y_{m+1}, \ldots, Y_n$.

$$Y_k = \hat{I}_k \cup Y_1 \hat{B}_{k1} \cup Y_2 \hat{B}_{k2} \cup \cdots \cup Y_{m-1} \hat{B}_{k(m-1)} \cup Y_{m+1} \hat{B}_{k(m+1)} \cup \ldots \cup Y_n \hat{B}_{kn},$$

for $k = 1, 2, \ldots, m - 1, m + 1, \ldots, n$

where

$$\hat{I}_i = I_i \cup (I_m \cdot B_{mm}^* \cdot B_{im}), \qquad \text{for all } i = 1, 2, \ldots, m - 1, m + 1, \ldots, n$$

and

$$\hat{B}_{ij} = B_{ij} \cup (B_{mj} \cdot B_{mm}^* \cdot B_{im}), \qquad \text{for all } i, j = 1, 2, \ldots, m - 1, m + 1, \ldots, n$$

b. Once the solution to the above $n - 1$ equations is known, that solution can be used to find the remaining unknown:

$$Y_m = (I_m \cup Y_1 B_{m1} \cup Y_2 B_{m2} \cup \cdots \cup Y_{m-1} B_{m(m-1)}$$
$$\cup Y_{m+1} B_{m(m+1)} \cup \ldots \cup Y_n B_{mn}) \cdot B_{mm}^*$$

c. A single equation $Y_1 = I_1 \cup Y_1B_{11}$ has the unique solution $Y_1 = I_1B_{11}^*$.

Proof. The proof is essentially a mirror image of the proofs given in Theorems 6.1 and 6.2.

Δ

∇ **Lemma 6.4.** Let $A = <\Sigma, \{s_1, s_2, \ldots, s_n\}, S_0, \delta, F>$ be an NDFA. For each $i = 1, 2, \ldots, n$, let the initial set $I(A, s_i) = \{x \mid \bar{\delta}(s_1, x) = s_i\}$ be denoted by Y_i. The unknowns $Y_1, Y_2, \ldots, Y_n$ satisfy a system of n left-linear equations of the form

$$Y_k = I_k \cup Y_1B_{k1} \cup Y_2B_{k2} \cup \cdots \cup Y_nB_{kn}, \qquad \text{for } k = 1, 2, \ldots, n$$

where the coefficients are given by

$$I_i = \begin{cases} \emptyset & \text{if } s_i \notin S_0 \\ \epsilon & \text{if } s_i \in S_0 \end{cases} \qquad \text{for } i = 1, 2, \ldots, n$$

and

$$B_{ij} = \bigcup_{a \in \Sigma \wedge s_i \in \delta(s_j, a)} \mathbf{a} \qquad \text{for } i, j = 1, 2, \ldots, n$$

Proof. See the exercises.

Δ

In contrast to Theorem 6.3, where A_{ij} represented the set of all letters that causes a transition from state s_i to state s_j, B_{ij} represents the set of all letters that causes a transition from state s_j to state s_i. That is, $B_{ij} = A_{ji}$. In the definition in Theorem 6.3, E_i represented the set of all strings of length zero that can reach final states from s_i. Compare this with the definition of I_i above, which represents the set of all strings of length zero that can reach s_i from a start state.

6.4 FAD LANGUAGES AS REGULAR SETS; CLOSURE PROPERTIES

The technique outlined by Theorems 6.1, 6.2, and 6.3 provide the second half of the correspondence between regular sets and FAD languages. As a consequence, regular expressions and automata characterize exactly the same class of languages.

∇ **Corollary 6.2.** Let Σ be an alphabet. Then $\mathfrak{D}_\Sigma \subseteq \mathfrak{R}_\Sigma$.

Proof. The proof follows immediately from Theorem 6.3.

Δ

∇ **Theorem 6.5: Kleene's Theorem.** Let Σ be an alphabet. Then $\mathfrak{R}_\Sigma = \mathfrak{D}_\Sigma$.

Proof. The proof follows immediately from Corollaries 6.1 and 6.2.

Δ

Thus the terms *FAD language* and *regular set* can be used interchangeably, since languages accepted by finite automata can be described by regular expressions, and vice versa. Such languages are often referred to as *regular languages*. The correspondence will allow, for example, the pumping lemma to be invoked to justify that certain languages cannot be represented by any regular expression.

$\mathscr{R}_\Sigma$ is therefore closed under every operator for which $\mathscr{D}_\Sigma$ is closed. We have now seen two representations for FAD languages, and a third will be presented in Chapter 8. Since there are effective algorithms for switching from one representation to another, we may use whichever vehicle is most convenient to describe a language or prove properties about regular languages. For example, we may use whichever concept best lends itself to the proof of closure properties. The justification that $\mathscr{R}_\Sigma$ is closed under union follows immediately from Definition 6.1; much more effort was required in Chapter 5 to prove that the union of two languages represented by DFAs could be represented by another DFA. On the other hand, attempting to justify closure under complementation by using regular expressions is an exercise in frustration. We will now see that closure under *substitution* is conveniently proved via regular expressions.

A substitution is similar to a language homomorphism (Definition 5.8), in which letters were replaced by single words. Substitutions will denote the methodical replacement of the individual letters within a regular expression with *sets* of words. The only restriction on these sets is that they must also be regular expressions, though not necessarily over the same alphabet.

∇ **Definition 6.5.** Let $\Sigma = \{\mathbf{a}_1, \mathbf{a}_2, \ldots, \mathbf{a}_m\}$ be an alphabet and let Γ be a second alphabet. Given regular expressions $R_1, R_2, \ldots, R_m$ over Γ, define a *regular set substitution* s: $\Sigma \to \rho(\Gamma^*)$ by $s(\mathbf{a}_i) = R_i$ for each $i = 1, 2, \ldots, m$, which can be extended to $\bar{s}$: $\Sigma^* \to \rho(\Gamma^*)$ by

$$\bar{s}(\lambda) = \epsilon$$

and

$$(\forall \mathbf{a} \in \Sigma)(\forall x \in \Sigma^*)(\bar{s}(\mathbf{a} \cdot x) = s(\mathbf{a}) \cdot \bar{s}(x))$$

$\bar{s}$ can be further extended to operate on a language $L \subseteq \Sigma^*$ by defining

$$\bar{s}(L) = \bigcup_{z \in L} \bar{s}(z)$$

In this context, $\bar{s}$: $\rho(\Sigma^*) \to \rho(\Gamma^*)$.
Δ

EXAMPLE 6.14

Let $\Sigma = \{\mathbf{0}\}$ and $\Gamma = \{\mathbf{a}, \mathbf{b}\}$. Define $s(\mathbf{0}) = (\mathbf{a} \cup \mathbf{b}) \cdot (\mathbf{a} \cup \mathbf{b})$. From the recursive definition, $\bar{s}(\mathbf{00}) = (\mathbf{a} \cup \mathbf{b}) \cdot (\mathbf{a} \cup \mathbf{b}) \cdot (\mathbf{a} \cup \mathbf{b}) \cdot (\mathbf{a} \cup \mathbf{b})$. Furthermore, the language $\bar{s}(\mathbf{0}^*)$ represents all even-length strings over $\{\mathbf{a}, \mathbf{b}\}$.

The definition of $\bar{s}(L)$ for a language L allows the domain of the substitution to be extended all the way to $\bar{s}$: $\rho(\Sigma^*) \to \rho(\Gamma^*)$. It can be proven that the image of $\mathscr{R}_\Sigma$

under $\bar{s}$ is contained in $\mathcal{R}_\Gamma$ (see the exercises); however, the image of $\mathcal{N}_\Sigma$ under $\bar{s}$ is not completely contained in $\mathcal{N}_\Gamma$.

In Example 6.14, the language $\mathbf{0}^*$ was regular and so was its image under $\bar{s}$. Neither of the sets described in the second example were regular. It is possible to start with a nonregular set and define a substitution that produces a regular set (see Lemma 6.5), but it is impossible for the image of a regular set to avoid being regular, as shown by the next theorem.

∇ **Theorem 6.6.** Let Σ be an alphabet, and let s: $\Sigma \to \wp(\Sigma^*)$ be a substitution. Then $\mathcal{R}_\Sigma$ is closed under $\bar{s}$.

Proof. Choose an arbitrary regular expression R over Σ. We must show that $\bar{s}$(R) represents a regular set. R is an expression made up of the letters in Σ and the characters (,), $\cdot$, $\cup$, and *. Form the new expression R′ by replacing each letter **a** by s(**a**). R′ is then clearly another regular expression over Σ. In fact, it can be shown that R′ represents exactly the words in $\bar{s}$(R); this is formally accomplished by inducting on the number of operators in the expression R. To prove this, one must argue that this substitution correspondence is preserved by each of the six rules defining regular expressions. The basis step of the induction involves all regular expressions with zero operators, that is, those defined by the first three rules for generating a regular expression.

- **i.** The substitution corresponding to any single letter $\mathbf{a}_i$ is a regular expression corresponding to $\bar{s}(\mathbf{a}_i)$, since, by definition of $\bar{s}$, $\bar{s}(\mathbf{a}_i) = s(\mathbf{a}_i)$.
- **ii.** The substitution corresponding to $\emptyset$ is a regular expression corresponding to $\bar{s}(\emptyset)$, since, by definition of $\bar{s}$, $\bar{s}(\emptyset) = \emptyset$.
- **iii.** The substitution corresponding to ϵ is a regular expression corresponding to $\bar{s}(\lambda)$, since, by definition of $\bar{s}$, $\bar{s}(\lambda) = \epsilon$.

The inductive step requires an argument that the correspondence is preserved whenever another of the three operators is introduced to form a more complex expression. These assertions involve the final three rules for generating regular expressions.

- **iv.** If R_1 and R_2 are regular expressions, then the substitution corresponding to $(R_1 \cdot R_2)$ is a regular expression representing the concatenation of the two corresponding substitutions. That is, $\bar{s}(R_1 \cdot R_2) = \bar{s}(R_1) \cdot \bar{s}(R_2)$.
- **v.** If R_1 and R_2 are regular expressions, then the substitution corresponding to $(R_1 \cup R_2)$ is a regular expression representing $\bar{s}(R_1) \cup \bar{s}(R_2)$.
- **vi.** If R_1 is a regular expression, then the substitution corresponding to $(R_1)^*$ is a regular expression representing $(\bar{s}(R_1))^*$.

Each of these three assertions follows immmediately from the definition of substitution and is left as an exercise. The inductive step guarantees that the substitution correspondence is preserved in any regular expression R, regardless of the number of operators in R. Consequently, R′ is indeed a regular expression denoting $\bar{s}(\mathrm{R})$, and $\mathscr{R}_\Sigma$ is therefore closed under $\bar{s}$.
Δ

The analogous result does *not* always hold for the nonregular sets.

∇ **Lemma 6.5.** Let Σ be an alphabet.

a. There are examples of regular set substitutions $s: \Sigma \to \rho(\Sigma^*)$ for which $\mathscr{N}_\Sigma$ is not closed under $\bar{s}$.

b. There are examples of regular set substitutions $t: \Sigma \to \rho(\Sigma^*)$ for which $\mathscr{N}_\Sigma$ is closed under $\bar{t}$.

Proof. (a) $\mathscr{N}_\Sigma$ is *not* closed under some substitutions. Let $\Sigma = \{\mathbf{a}, \mathbf{b}\}$ and define $s(\mathbf{a}) = (\mathbf{a} \cup \mathbf{b})$ and $s(\mathbf{b}) = (\mathbf{a} \cup \mathbf{b})$. The image of the nonregular set

$$\mathrm{L} = \{x \mid |x|_{\mathbf{a}} = |x|_{\mathbf{b}}\}$$

is the set of even-length words, which *is* regular. Thus $\mathrm{L} \in \mathscr{N}_\Sigma$ but $\bar{s}(\mathrm{L}) \notin \mathscr{N}_\Sigma$.

(b) $\mathscr{N}_\Sigma$ *is* closed under some substitutions. Some substitutions do preserve nonregularity (such as the identity substitution i, since for any language L, $\bar{i}(\mathrm{L}) = \mathrm{L}$). In this case, $(\forall \mathrm{L})(\mathrm{L} \in \mathscr{N}_\Sigma \Rightarrow \bar{i}(\mathrm{L}) \in \mathscr{N}_\Sigma)$ and therefore $\mathscr{N}_\Sigma$ is closed under $\bar{i}$.
Δ

Note that a substitution in which each R_i is a single string then conforms to Definition 5.8 and represents a language homomorphism.

∇ **Corollary 6.3.** Let Σ be an alphabet, and let $\psi: \Sigma \to \Sigma^*$ be a language homomorphism. Then $\mathscr{R}_\Sigma$ is closed under $\bar{\psi}$.

Proof. The proof follows immediately from Theorem 6.6, since a language homomorphism is a special type of substitution.
Δ

As in Chapter 5, this result can also be proved by successfully modifying an appropriate DFA, showing that $\mathscr{D}_\Sigma$ $(= \mathscr{R}_\Sigma)$ is closed under language homomorphism. It is likewise possible to use machine constructs to show that $\mathscr{D}_\Sigma$ is closed under substitution, but this becomes much more complex than the argument given for Theorem 6.6. A third characterization of regular languages will be presented in Chapter 8, affording a choice of three distinct avenues for proving closure properties of $\mathscr{R}_\Sigma$.

EXERCISES

6.1. Let $\Sigma = \{\mathbf{a}, \mathbf{b}\}$. Give (if possible) a regular expression that describes the set of all even-length words in Σ^*.

6.2. Let $\Sigma = \{\mathbf{a}, \mathbf{b}\}$. Give (if possible) a regular expression that describes the set of all words x in Σ^* for which $|x| \geq 2$.

6.3. Let $\Sigma = \{\mathbf{a}, \mathbf{b}\}$. Give (if possible) a regular expression that describes the set of all words x in Σ^* for which $|x|_{\mathbf{a}} = |x|_{\mathbf{b}}$.

6.4. Let $\Sigma = \{\mathbf{a}, \mathbf{b}, \mathbf{c}\}$. Give a regular expression that describes the set of all odd-length words in Σ^* that do not end in **b**.

6.5. Let $\Sigma = \{\mathbf{a}, \mathbf{b}, \mathbf{c}\}$. Give a regular expression that describes the set of all words in Σ^* that do *not* contain two consecutive **c**s.

6.6. Let $\Sigma = \{\mathbf{a}, \mathbf{b}, \mathbf{c}\}$. Give a regular expression that describes the set of all words in Σ^* that *do* contain two consecutive **c**s.

6.7. Let $\Sigma = \{\mathbf{a}, \mathbf{b}, \mathbf{c}\}$. Give a regular expression that describes the set of all words in Σ^* that do *not* contain *any* **c**s.

6.8. Let $\Sigma = \{\mathbf{0}, \mathbf{1}\}$. Give, if possible, regular expressions that will describe each of the following languages. Try to write these directly from the descriptions (that is, avoid relying on the nature of the corresponding automata).

(a) $L_1 = \{x \mid |x| \bmod 3 = 2\}$

(b) $L_2 = \Sigma^* - \{w \mid \exists n \geq 1 \ni w = a_1 \cdots a_n \wedge a_n = \mathbf{1}\}$

(c) $L_3 = \{y \mid |y|_0 > |y|_1\}$

6.9. Let $\Sigma = \{\mathbf{a}, \mathbf{b}, \mathbf{c}\}$. Give, if possible, regular expressions that will describe each of the following languages. Try to write these directly from the descriptions (that is, avoid relying on the nature of the corresponding automata).

(a) $L_1 = \{x \mid (|x|_{\mathbf{a}} \text{ is odd}) \wedge (|x|_{\mathbf{b}} \text{ is even})\}$

(b) $L_2 = \{y \mid (|y|_{\mathbf{c}} \text{ is even}) \vee (|y|_{\mathbf{b}} \text{ is odd})\}$

(c) $L_3 = \{z \mid (|z|_{\mathbf{a}} \text{ is even})\}$

(d) $L_4 = \{z \mid |z|_{\mathbf{c}} \text{ is a prime number}\}$

(e) $L_5 = \{x \mid \mathbf{abc} \text{ is a substring of } x\}$

(f) $L_6 = \{x \mid \mathbf{acaba} \text{ is a substring of } x\}$

(g) $L_7 = \{x \in \{\mathbf{a}, \mathbf{b}, \mathbf{c}\}^* \mid |x|_{\mathbf{a}} \equiv 0 \bmod 3\}$

6.10. Let $\Sigma = \{\mathbf{a}, \mathbf{b}, \mathbf{d}\}$. Give a regular expression that will describe

$$\Psi = \{x \in \Sigma^* \mid (x \text{ begins with } \mathbf{d}) \vee (x \text{ contains two consecutive } \mathbf{b}\text{s})\}.$$

6.11. Let $\Sigma = \{\mathbf{a}, \mathbf{b}, \mathbf{c}\}$. Give a regular expression that will describe

$$\Phi = \{x \in \Sigma^* \mid \text{every } \mathbf{b} \text{ in } x \text{ is immediately followed by } \mathbf{c}\}.$$

6.12. Let $\Sigma = \{\mathbf{0}, \mathbf{1}, \mathbf{2}, \mathbf{3}, \mathbf{4}, \mathbf{5}, \mathbf{6}, \mathbf{7}, \mathbf{8}, \mathbf{9}\}$. Give a regular expression that will describe

$$\Gamma = \{x \in \Sigma^* \mid \text{the number represented by } x \text{ is evenly divisible by } 3\}$$

$$= \{\lambda, \mathbf{0}, \mathbf{00}, \mathbf{000}, \ldots, \mathbf{3}, \mathbf{03}, \mathbf{003}, \ldots, \mathbf{6}, \mathbf{9}, \mathbf{12}, \mathbf{15}, \ldots\}.$$

6.13. Let $\Sigma = \{\mathbf{0}, \mathbf{1}, \mathbf{2}, \mathbf{3}, \mathbf{4}, \mathbf{5}, \mathbf{6}, \mathbf{7}, \mathbf{8}, \mathbf{9}\}$. Give a regular expression that will describe

$$K = \{x \in \Sigma^* \mid \text{the number represented by } x \text{ is evenly divisible by } 5\}.$$

6.14. Use the *exact* constructs given in the theorems of Chapter 5 to build a NDFA that accepts $\mathbf{b} \cup \mathbf{a}^*\mathbf{c}$ (refer to Examples 6.4, 6.5, and 6.6). Do *not* simplify your answer.

6.15. Give examples of sets that demonstrate the following inequalities listed in Lemma 6.1:

(a) $R_1 \cup \epsilon \neq R_1$

(b) $R_1 \cdot R_2 \neq R_2 \cdot R_1$

(c) $R_1 \cdot R_1 \neq R_1$

(d) $R_1 \cup (R_2 \cdot R_3) \neq (R_1 \cup R_2) \cdot (R_1 \cup R_3)$

(e) $(R_1 \cdot R_2)^* \neq (R_1^* \cdot R_2^*)^*$

(f) $(R_1 \cdot R_2)^* \neq (R_1^* \cup R_2^*)^*$

Find other examples of sets that show the following expressions may be equal under some conditions:

(g) $R_1 \cup \epsilon = R_1$

(h) $R_1 \cdot R_2 = R_2 \cdot R_1$ (even if $R_1 \neq R_2$)

(i) $R_1 \cdot R_1 = R_1$

(j) $R_1 \cup (R_2 \cdot R_3) = (R_1 \cup R_2) \cdot (R_1 \cup R_3)$ (even if $R_1 \neq R_2 \neq R_3 \neq R_1$)

(k) $(R_1 \cdot R_2)^* = (R_1^* \cdot R_2^*)^*$ (even if $R_1 \neq R_2$)

(l) $(R_1 \cdot R_2)^* = (R_1^* \cup R_2^*)^*$ (even if $R_1 \neq R_2$)

6.16. Prove the equalities listed in Lemma 6.1.

6.17. **(a)** Consider Theorem 6.1. Find examples of sets A and E that will show that $A^* \cdot E$ is not a unique solution if $\lambda \in A$.

(b) Find examples of sets A and E that will show that $A^* \cdot E$ can be the unique solution even if $\lambda \in A$.

6.18. Solve the following set of language equations for X_0 *and* X_1 over $\{\mathbf{0}, \mathbf{1}\}^*$:

$$X_0 = (\mathbf{0} \cup \mathbf{1})X_1$$

$$X_1 = \epsilon \cup \mathbf{1}X_0 \cup \mathbf{0}X_1$$

Do you see any relation between these equations and the DFA A in Example 3.4?

6.19. **(a)** Solve the following set of language equations for X_1, X_2, *and* X_3 by eliminating X_3 and then eliminating X_2. Solve for X_1 and then back-substitute to find X_2 and X_3. Note that these equations arise from the automaton in Figure 6.10.

$$X_1 = \emptyset \cup \emptyset X_1 \cup (\mathbf{0} \cup \mathbf{1})X_2 \cup \emptyset X_3$$

$$X_2 = \epsilon \cup \mathbf{0}X_1 \cup \mathbf{1}X_2 \qquad \cup \emptyset X_3$$

$$X_3 = \emptyset \cup \emptyset X_1 \cup (\mathbf{0} \cup \mathbf{1})X_2 \cup \emptyset X_3$$

(b) Rework part (a) by eliminating X_3 and then eliminating X_1 (instead of X_2).

(c) How does the solution in part (b) compare to the solution in part (a)? Is one more concise? Are they equivalent?

6.20. Prove Lemma 6.2. [*Hint:* Let P(m) be the statement that "Every regular expression R with m or fewer operators represents a regular set that is FAD," and induct on m.]

6.21. Let $\Sigma = \{\mathbf{a}, \mathbf{b}, \mathbf{c}\}$. Find all solutions to the language equation $X = X \cup \{\mathbf{b}\}$.

6.22. Prove that, for any languages A and E, $A^*E = E \cup A \cdot (A^*E)$.

6.23. Give a regular expression that will describe the *intersection* of the regular sets $(\mathbf{ab} \cup \mathbf{b})^*\mathbf{a}$ and $(\mathbf{ba} \cup \mathbf{a})^*$.

6.24. Develop an algorithm that, when applied to two regular expressions, will generate an expression describing their intersection.

6.25. Verify by direct substitution that $X_1 = (\mathbf{a} \cup \mathbf{bb})^*$ and $X_2 = \mathbf{b} \cdot (\mathbf{a} \cup \mathbf{bb})^*$ is a solution to

$$X_1 = \epsilon \cup \mathbf{a} \cdot X_1 \cup \mathbf{b} \cdot X_2$$

$$X_2 = \emptyset \cup \mathbf{b} \cdot X_1 \cup \emptyset \cdot X_2$$

6.26. **(a)** Find $L(\mathsf{D})$ for the machine D described in Example 6.10.

(b) Generalize your technique: For a machine A with start states $s_{i_1}, s_{i_2}, \ldots, s_{i_m}$, $L(\mathsf{A})$ is given by __________?

6.27. Let $\Sigma = \{\mathbf{a}, \mathbf{b}\}$. Give a regular expression that will describe the *complement* of the regular set $(\mathbf{ab} \cup \mathbf{b})^*\mathbf{a}$.

6.28. Develop an algorithm that, when applied to a regular expression, will generate an expression describing the complement.

6.29. Let $\Sigma = \{\mathbf{a}, \mathbf{b}, \mathbf{c}\}$. Define $E(\mathrm{L}) = \{z \mid (\exists y \in \Sigma^+)(\exists x \in \mathrm{L}) z = yx\}$. Use the regular expression concepts given in this chapter to argue that $\mathfrak{R}_\Sigma$ is closed under the operator E (that is, don't build a new automaton; build a new regular expression from the old expression).

6.30. Let $\Sigma = \{\mathbf{a}, \mathbf{b}, \mathbf{c}\}$. Define $B(\mathrm{L}) = \{z \mid (\exists x \in \mathrm{L})(\exists y \in \Sigma^*) z = xy\}$. Use the regular expression concepts given in this chapter to argue that $\mathfrak{R}_\Sigma$ is closed under the operator B (that is, don't build a new automaton; build a new regular expression from the old expression).

6.31. Let $\Sigma = \{\mathbf{a}, \mathbf{b}, \mathbf{c}\}$. Define $M(\mathrm{L}) = \{z \mid (\exists x \in \mathrm{L})(\exists y \in \Sigma^+) z = xy\}$. Use the regular expression concepts given in this chapter to argue that $\mathfrak{R}_\Sigma$ is closed under the operator M (that is, don't build a new automaton; build a new regular expression from the old expression).

6.32. **(a)** Let $\Sigma = \{\mathbf{a}, \mathbf{b}, \mathbf{c}\}$. Show that there does *not* exist a *unique* solution to the following set of language equations:

$$X_1 = \mathbf{b} \cup \epsilon \cdot X_1 \cup \mathbf{a} \cdot X_2$$

$$X_2 = \mathbf{c} \cup \emptyset \cdot X_1 \cup \epsilon \cdot X_2$$

(b) Does this contradict Theorem 6.2? Explain.

6.33. Solve the following set of language equations for X_0 *and* X_1 over $\{\mathbf{0}, \mathbf{1}\}^*$:

$$\begin{aligned} X_0 &= \mathbf{0}^*\mathbf{1} \cup (\mathbf{10})^* X_0 \cup \mathbf{0}(\mathbf{0} \cup \mathbf{1}) X_1 \\ X_1 &= \epsilon \quad \cup \mathbf{1}^*\mathbf{01}\, X_0 \cup \quad \mathbf{0} X_1 \end{aligned}$$

6.34. Let $\Sigma = \{\mathbf{a}, \mathbf{b}, \mathbf{c}\}$.

(a) Give a regular expression that describes the set of all words in Σ^* that end with **c** and for which **aa**, **bb**, and **cc** never appear as substrings.

(b) Give a regular expression that describes the set of all words in Σ^* that begin with **c** and for which **aa**, **bb**, and **cc** never appear as substrings.

6.35. Let $\Sigma = \{\mathbf{a}, \mathbf{b}, \mathbf{c}\}$.

(a) Give a regular expression that describes the set of all words in Σ^* that contain no more than two **c**s.

(b) Give a regular expression that describes the set of all words in Σ^* that do not have exactly one **c**.

6.36. Recall that the reverse of a word x, written x^r, is the word written backward. The reverse of a language is likewise given by $\mathrm{L}^r = \{x^r \mid x \in \mathrm{L}\}$. Let $\Sigma = \{\mathbf{a}, \mathbf{b}, \mathbf{c}\}$.

(a) Note that $(R_1 \cup R_2)^r = (R_1^r \cup R_2^r)$ for any regular sets R_1 and R_2. Give similar equivalences for each of the rules in Definition 6.1.

(b) If L were represented by a regular expression, explain how to generate a regular expression representing L^r (compare with the technique used in the proof of Theorem 6.6).

(c) Prove part (b) by inducting on the number of operators in the expression.

(d) Use parts (a), (b), and (c) to argue that $\mathfrak{R}_\Sigma$ is closed under the operator r.

6.37. Complete the details of the proof of Theorem 6.4.

6.38. Let $\Sigma = \{\mathbf{a}, \mathbf{b}, \mathbf{c}\}$.

(a) Give a regular expression that describes the set of all words in Σ^* for which no **b** is immediately preceded by **a**.

(b) Give a regular expression that describes the set of all words in Σ^* that contain exactly two **c**s and for which no **b** is immediately preceded by **a**.

6.39. Let $\Sigma = \{\mathbf{a}, \mathbf{b}, \mathbf{c}\}$.

(a) Give a regular expression that describes the set of all words in Σ^* for which no **b** is immediately preceded by **c**.

(b) Give a regular expression that describes the set of all words in Σ^* that contain exactly one **c** and for which no **b** is immediately preceded by **c**.

6.40. (a) Use Theorem 6.3 to write the two right-linear equations in two unknowns corresponding to the NDFA given in Figure 6.11.

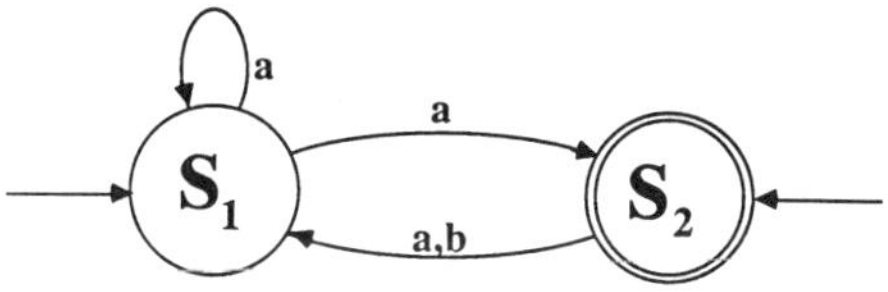

Figure 6.11 The NDFA for Exercise 6.40

(b) Solve these equations for both unknowns.

(c) Give a regular expression that corresponds to the language accepted by this NDFA.

(d) Rework the problem with two left-linear equations.

6.41. (a) Use Theorem 6.3 to write the four right-linear equations in four unknowns corresponding to the NDFA given in Figure 6.12.

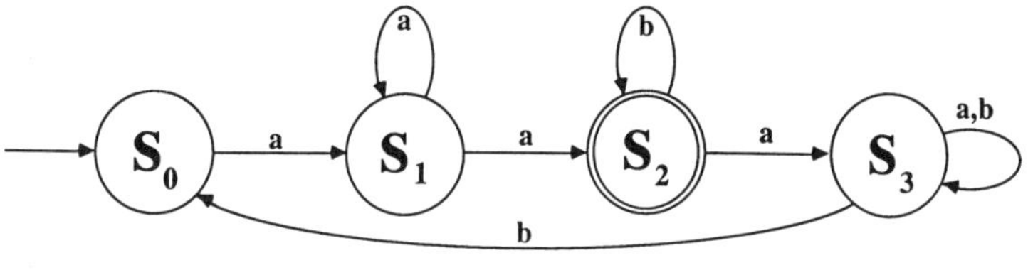

Figure 6.12 The automaton for Exercise 6.41

(b) Solve these equations for all four unknowns.

(c) Give a regular expression that corresponds to the language accepted by this NDFA.

(d) Rework the problem with four left-linear equations.

6.42. **(a)** Use Theorem 6.3 to write the seven right-linear equations in seven unknowns corresponding to the NDFA given in Figure 6.13.

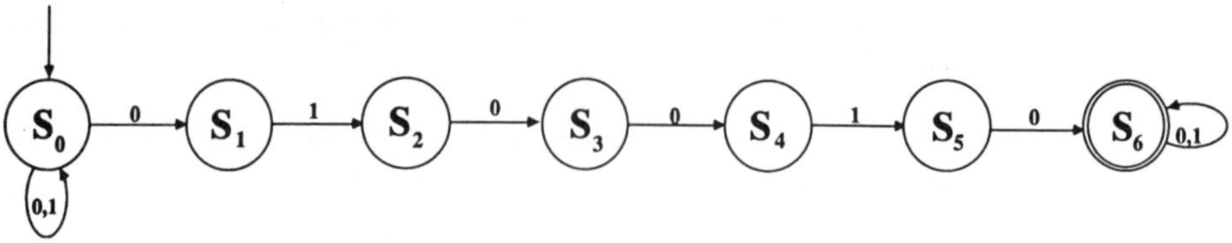

Figure 6.13 The NDFA for Exercise 6.42

(b) Solve these equations for all seven unknowns. *Hint:* Make use of the simple nature of these equations to eliminate variables without appealing to Theorem 6.2.

(c) Give a regular expression that corresponds to the language accepted by this NDFA.

(d) Rework the problem with seven left-linear equations.

6.43. Prove that for *any* languages A, E, and Y, if $E \subseteq Y$, then $A \cdot E \subseteq A \cdot Y$.

6.44. Let Σ be an alphabet, and let $s: \Sigma \to \Gamma^*$ be a substitution.

(a) Prove that the image of $\mathfrak{R}_\Sigma$ under $\bar{s}$ is contained in $\mathfrak{R}_\Gamma$.

(b) Give an example to show that the image of $\mathcal{N}_\Sigma$ under $\bar{s}$ need not be completely contained in $\mathcal{N}_\Gamma$.

6.45. Give a detailed proof of Lemma 6.3.

6.46. Let $\Sigma = \{\mathbf{a}, \mathbf{b}\}$ and $\Xi = \{x \in \Sigma^* \mid x$ contains (at least) two consecutive **b**s $\wedge$ x does *not* contain two consecutive **a**s$\}$. Draw a machine that will accept Ξ.

6.47. Let $\Sigma = \{\mathbf{a}, \mathbf{b}, \mathbf{c}\}$. Give regular expressions that will describe:

(a) $\{x \in \{\mathbf{a}, \mathbf{b}, \mathbf{c}\}^* \mid$ every **b** in x is eventually followed by **c**$\}$; that is, x might look like **baabacaa**, or **bcacc**, and so on.

(b) $\{x \in \{\mathbf{a}, \mathbf{b}, \mathbf{c}\}^* \mid$ every **b** in x is immediately followed by **c**$\}$.

6.48. Let $\Sigma = \{\mathbf{a}, \mathbf{b}\}$. Give, if possible, regular expressions that will describe each of the following languages. Try to write these directly from the descriptions (that is, avoid relying on the nature of the corresponding automata).

(a) The language consisting of all words that have neither consecutive **a**s nor consecutive **b**s.

(b) The language consisting of all words that begin and end with different letters.

(c) The language consisting of all words for which the last two letters match.

(d) The language consisting of all words for which the first two letters match.

(e) The language consisting of all words for which the first and last letters match.

6.49. The set of all valid regular *expressions* over $\{\mathbf{a}, \mathbf{b}\}$ is a language over the alphabet $\{\mathbf{a}, \mathbf{b}, (,), \cup, \bullet, *, \emptyset, \epsilon\}$. Show that this language is not FAD.

6.50. Give regular expressions corresponding to the languages accepted by each of the NDFAs listed in Figure 6.14.

6.51. Complete the details of the proof of Theorem 6.6.

6.52. Prove Lemma 6.4.

6.53. Corollary 6.3 followed immediately from Theorem 6.6. Show that Theorems 5.2, 5.4, and 5.5 are also corollaries of Theorem 6.6.

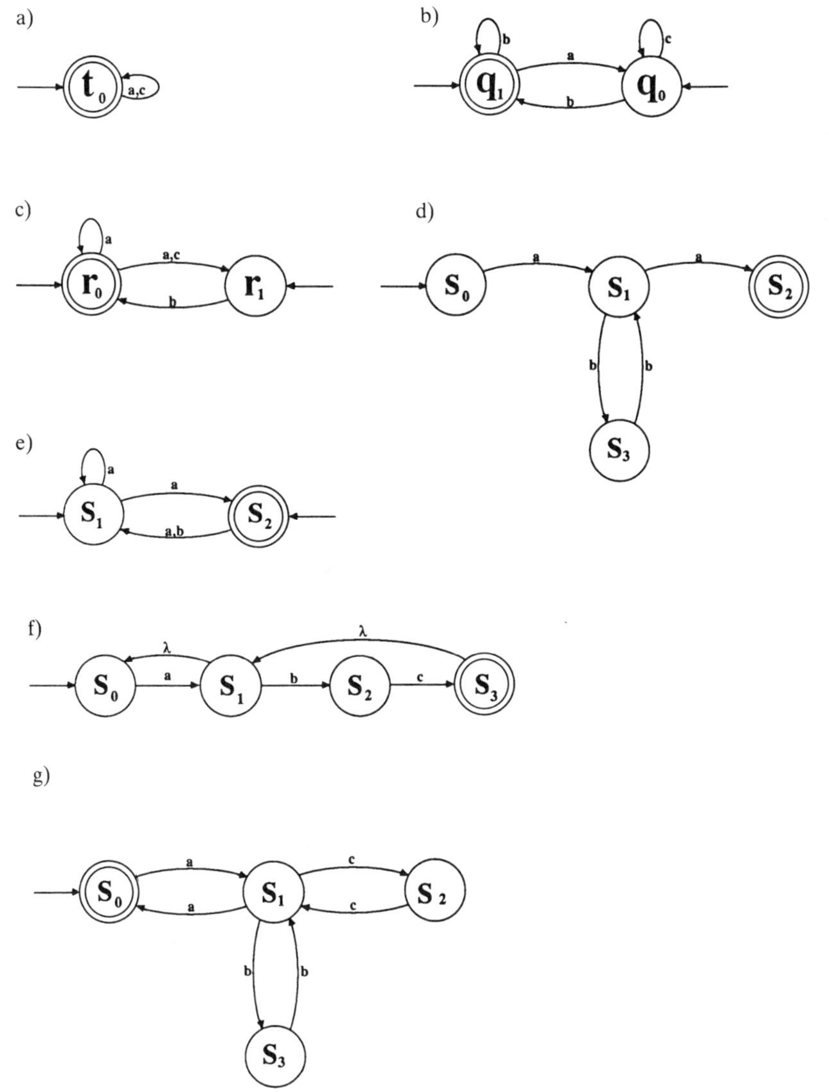

Figure 6.14 The automata for Exercise 6.50

6.54. Let **F** be the collection of languages that can be formed by repeated application of the following five rules:

i. $\{\mathbf{a}\} \in \mathbf{F}$ and $\{\mathbf{b}\} \in \mathbf{F}$

ii. $\{\ \} \in \mathbf{F}$

iii. $\{\lambda\} \in \mathbf{F}$

iv. If $F_1 \in \mathbf{F}$ and $F_2 \in \mathbf{F}$, then $F_1 \cdot F_2 \in \mathbf{F}$

v. If $F_1 \in \mathbf{F}$ and $F_2 \in \mathbf{F}$, then $F_1 \cup F_2 \in \mathbf{F}$

Describe the class of languages generated by these five rules.

CHAPTER 7

FINITE-STATE TRANSDUCERS

We have seen that finite-state acceptors are by no means robust enough to accept standard computer languages like Pascal. Furthermore, even if a DFA could reliably recognize valid Pascal programs, a machine that only indicates "Yes, this is a valid program" or "No, this is not a valid program" is certainly not all we expect from a compiler. To emulate a compiler, it is necessary to have a mechanism that will produce some *output* other than a simple yes or no: in this case, we would expect the corresponding machine language code (if the program compiled successfully) or some hint as to the location and nature of the syntax errors (if the program was invalid).

A machine that accepts input strings and *translates* them into output strings is called a *sequential machine* or *transducer*. Our conceptual picture of such a device is only slightly different from the model of a DFA shown in Figure 7.1a. We still have a finite-state control and an input tape with a read head, but the accept/reject indicator is replaced by an output tape and writing device, as shown in Figure 7.1b.

These machines do not have the power to model useful compilers, but they can be employed in many other areas. Applications of sequential machine concepts are by no means limited to the computer world or even to the normal connotations associated with "read" and "write." A vending machine is essentially a transducer that interprets inserted coins and button presses as valid inputs and returns candy bars and change as output. Elevators, traffic lights, and many other common devices that monitor and react to limited stimuli can be modeled by finite-state transducers.

The vending machine analogy illustrates that the types of input to a device (coins) may be very different from the types of output (candy bars). In terms of our

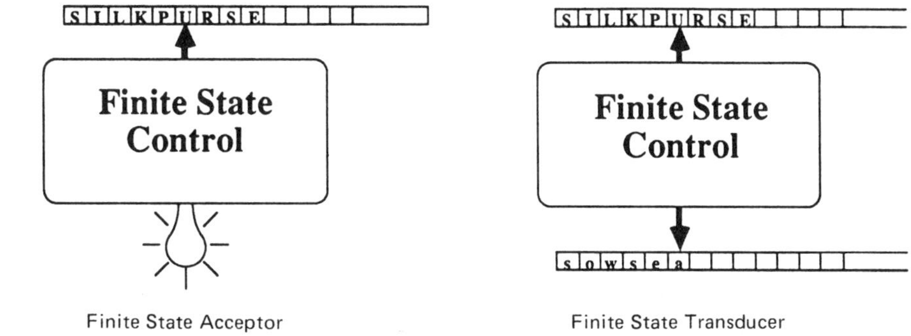

Figure 7.1 The difference between an acceptor and a transducer

conceptual model, the read head may be capable of recognizing symbols that are different from those that the output head can print. Thus we will have an *output alphabet* Γ that is not necessarily the same as our *input alphabet* Σ.

Also essential to our model is a rule that governs what characters are printed. For our first type of transducer, this rule will depend on both the current internal state of the machine and the current symbol being scanned by the read head and will be represented by the function ω. Finally, since we are dealing with translation rather than acceptance/rejection, there is no need to single out accepting states: the concept of final states can be dispensed with entirely.

7.1 BASIC DEFINITIONS

∇ **Definition 7.1.** A *finite-state transducer* (FST) or *Mealy sequential machine* with a distinguished start state is a sextuple $<\Sigma, \Gamma, S, s_0, \delta, \omega>$, where:

i. Σ denotes the input alphabet.
ii. Γ denotes the output alphabet.
iii. S denotes the set of states, a finite nonempty set.
iv. s_0 denotes the start (or initial) state; $s_0 \in S$.
v. δ denotes the state transition function; $\delta: S \times \Sigma \to S$.
vi. ω denotes the output function; $\omega: S \times \Sigma \to \Gamma$.

Δ

The familiar state transition diagram needs to be slightly modified to represent these new types of machines. Since there is one labeled arrow for each ordered pair in the domain of the state transition function and there is also one output symbol for each ordered pair, we will place the appropriate output symbol by its corresponding arrow, and separate it from the associated input symbol by a slash, /.

EXAMPLE 7.1

Let $V = \langle\{\mathbf{n}, \mathbf{d}, \mathbf{q}, \mathbf{b}\}, \{\varphi, \mathbf{n}', \mathbf{d}', \mathbf{q}', \mathbf{c}_0, \mathbf{c}_1, \mathbf{c}_2, \mathbf{c}_3, \mathbf{c}_4\}, S, s_0, \delta, \omega\rangle$ be the FST illustrated in Figure 7.2. V describes the action of a candy machine that dispenses 30¢ Chocolate Explosions. $\mathbf{n}, \mathbf{d}, \mathbf{q}$ denote inputs of nickels, dimes, and quarters (respectively), and **b** denotes the act of pushing the button to select a candy bar. $\varphi, \mathbf{n}', \mathbf{d}', \mathbf{q}', \mathbf{c}_0, \mathbf{c}_1, \mathbf{c}_2, \mathbf{c}_3, \mathbf{c}_4$ represent the vending machine's response to these inputs: it may do nothing, return the nickel that was just inserted, return the dime, return the quarter, or dispense a candy bar with 0, 1, 2, 3, or 4 nickels as change, respectively. Note that the transitions agree with the vending machine model presented in Chapter 1; the new model now specifies the action corresponding to the given input. It is relatively simple to modify the above machine to include a new input **r** that signifies that the coin return has been activated and a new output **a** representing the release of all coins that have been inserted (see the exercises).

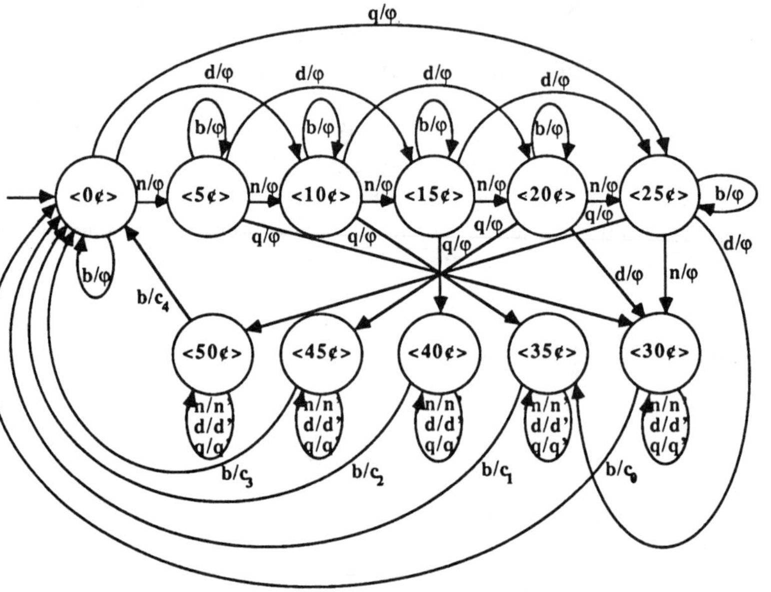

Figure 7.2 A finite-state transducer model of the vending machine discussed in Example 7.1

Various modern appliances can be modeled by FSTs. Many microwave ovens accept input through the door latch mechanism and an array of keypad sensors, and typical outputs include the control lines to the microwave generator, the elements of a digital display, an interior light, and an audible buzzer. The physical circuitry needed to implement these common machines will be discussed in a later section. We now examine the ramifications of Definition 7.1 by concentrating on the details of a very simple finite-state transducer.

EXAMPLE 7.2

Let B = $<\Sigma, \Gamma, S, s_0, \delta, \omega>$ be given by

$$\Sigma = \{\mathbf{a}, \mathbf{b}\}$$
$$\Gamma = \{\mathbf{0}, \mathbf{1}\}$$
$$S = \{s_0, s_1\}$$
$$s_0 = s_0$$

The state transition function is defined in Table 7.1a.

TABLE 7.1a

δ	**a**	**b**
s_0	s_0	s_1
s_1	s_0	s_1

It can be more succinctly specified by $(\forall s \in S)[\delta(s, \mathbf{a}) = s_0$ and $\delta(s, \mathbf{b}) = s_1]$. Finally, Table 7.1b displays the output function, which can be summarized by

$$(\forall \mathbf{c} \in \Sigma)[\omega(s_0, \mathbf{c}) = \mathbf{0} \quad \text{and} \quad \omega(s_1, \mathbf{c}) = \mathbf{1}]$$

TABLE 7.1b

ω	**a**	**b**
s_0	**0**	**0**
s_1	**1**	**1**

All the information about B is contained in the diagram displayed in Figure 7.3. Consider the input sequence z = **abaabbaa**. From s_0, the first letter of z, that is, **a**, causes a **0** to be printed, since $\omega(s_0, \mathbf{a}) = \mathbf{0}$, and since $\delta(s_0, \mathbf{a}) = s_0$, the machine remains in state s_0. The second letter **b** causes a second **0** to be printed since $\omega(s_0, \mathbf{b}) = \mathbf{0}$, but the machine now switches to state s_1 $[\delta(s_0, \mathbf{b}) = s_1]$. The third input letter causes a **1** to be printed $[\omega(s_1, \mathbf{a}) = \mathbf{1}]$, and so on. The entire output string will be **00100110**, and the machine, after starting in state s_0, will successively assume the state $s_0, s_1, s_0, s_0, s_1, s_1, s_0, s_0$ as the input string is processed. We are not currently interested in the terminating state for a given string (s_0 in this case), but rather in the resulting output string, **00100110**.

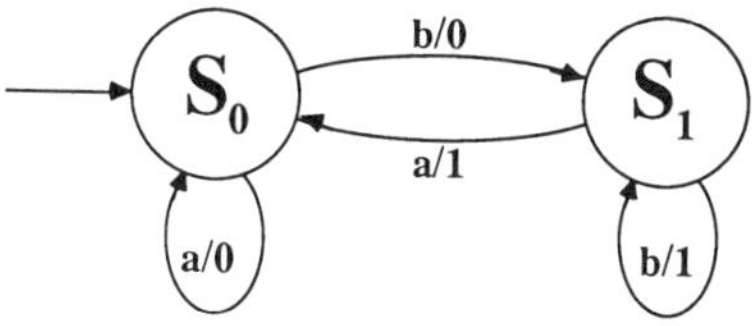

Figure 7.3 The state transition diagram for the transducer discussed in Example 7.2

It should be clear that the above discussion illustrates a very awkward way of describing translations. While ω describes the way in which single *letters* are translated, the study of finite-state transducers will involve descriptions of how entire *strings* are translated. This situation is reminiscent of the modification of the state transition function δ, which likewise operated on single *letters*, to the extended state transition function $\bar{\delta}$ (which was defined for *strings*). Indeed, what is called for is an extension of ω to $\bar{\omega}$, which will encompass the translation of entire strings. The translation cited in the last example could then be succinctly stated as $\bar{\omega}(s_0, \mathbf{abaabbaa}) = \mathbf{00100110}$. That is, the notation $\bar{\omega}(t, y)$ is intended to represent the output string produced by a transducer (beginning from state t) in response to the input string y.

The formal recursive definition of $\bar{\omega}$ will depend not only on ω but also on the state transition function δ (and its extension $\bar{\delta}$). $\bar{\delta}$ retains the same conceptual meaning it had for finite-state acceptors: $\bar{\delta}(s, x)$ denotes the state reached when starting from s and processing, in sequence, the individual letters of the string x. Furthermore, the conclusion stated in Theorem 1.1 still holds:

$$(\forall x \in \Sigma^*)(\forall y \in \Sigma^*)(\forall s \in S)(\bar{\delta}(s, yx) = \bar{\delta}(\bar{\delta}(s, y), x))$$

A similar statement can be made about $\bar{\omega}$ once it has been rigorously defined.

∇ **Definition 7.2.** Given a FST $A = <\Sigma, \Gamma, S, s_0, \delta, \omega>$, the *extended output function* for A, denoted by $\bar{\omega}$, is a function $\bar{\omega}: S \times \Sigma^* \to \Gamma^*$ defined recursively as follows:

i. $(\forall t \in S) \qquad \bar{\omega}(t, \lambda) = \lambda$
ii. $(\forall t \in S)(\forall x \in \Sigma^*)(\forall \mathbf{a} \in \Sigma)(\bar{\omega}(t, \mathbf{a}x) = \omega(t, \mathbf{a}) \cdot \bar{\omega}(\delta(t, \mathbf{a}), x))$

Δ

EXAMPLE 7.3

Let $B = <\Sigma, \Gamma, S, s_0, \delta, \omega>$ be the FST given in Example 7.2. Then

$$\bar{\omega}(s_1, \mathbf{baa}) = \omega(s_1, \mathbf{b}) \cdot \bar{\omega}(\delta(s_1, \mathbf{b}), \mathbf{aa}) = 1 \cdot \bar{\omega}(s_1, \mathbf{aa})$$
$$= \mathbf{1} \cdot \omega(s_1, \mathbf{a}) \cdot \bar{\omega}(\delta(s_1, \mathbf{a}), \mathbf{a}) = \mathbf{11} \cdot \bar{\omega}(s_0, \mathbf{a}) = \mathbf{110}$$

Note that a three-letter input sequence gives rise to exactly three output symbols: $\bar{\omega}$ is *length preserving*, in the sense that $(\forall t \in S)(\forall x \in \Sigma^*)(|\bar{\omega}(t, x)| = |x|)$.

The $\bar{\omega}$ function extends the ω function from single letters to words. Whereas the ω function maps a state and a *letter* to a single symbol from Γ, the $\bar{\omega}$ function maps a state and a *word* to an entire *string* from Γ^*. It can be deduced from (i) and (ii) (see the exercises) that (iii) $(\forall t \in S)(\forall \mathbf{a} \in \Sigma)(\bar{\omega}(t, \mathbf{a}) = \omega(t, \mathbf{a}))$, which is the observation that ω and $\bar{\omega}$ treat single letters the same. The extended output function $\bar{\omega}$ has properties similar to those of $\bar{\delta}$, in that the single letter **a** found in the recursive definition of $\overline{\omega}$ can be replaced by an entire word y. The analog of Theorem 1.1 is given below.

∇ **Theorem 7.1.** Let A = $<\Sigma, \Gamma, S, s_0, \delta, \omega>$ be a FST. Then:

$$(\forall x \in \Sigma^*)(\forall y \in \Sigma^*)(\forall t \in S)(\overline{\omega}(t, yx) = \overline{\omega}(t, y) \cdot \overline{\omega}(\overline{\delta}(t, y), x))$$

and

$$(\forall x \in \Sigma^*)(\forall y \in \Sigma^*)(\forall s \in S)(\overline{\delta}(s, yx) = \overline{\delta}(\overline{\delta}(s, y), x))$$

Proof. The proof is by induction on $|y|$ (see the exercises and compare with Theorem 1.1).
Δ

EXAMPLE 7.4

Let B = $<\Sigma, \Gamma, S, s_0, \delta, \omega>$ be the FST given in Example 7.2. Consider the string $z = \mathbf{abaabbaa} = yx$, where $y = \mathbf{abaab}$ and $x = \mathbf{baa}$. To apply Theorem 7.1 with $t = s_0$, we first calculate $\overline{\omega}(s_0, y) = \overline{\omega}(s_0, \mathbf{abaab}) = \mathbf{00100}$, and $\overline{\delta}(s_0, y) = s_1$. From Example 7.3, $\overline{\omega}(s_1, \mathbf{baa}) = \mathbf{110}$, and hence, as required by Theorem 7.1,

$$\mathbf{00100110} = \overline{\omega}(s_0, \mathbf{abaabbaa}) = \overline{\omega}(s_0, yx) = \overline{\omega}(s_0, y) \cdot \overline{\omega}(\overline{\delta}(t, y), x) = \mathbf{00100} \cdot \mathbf{110}$$

For a given FST A with a specified start state, the deterministic nature of finite-state transducers requires that each input string be translated into a *unique* output string; that is, the relation f_A that associates input strings with their corresponding output strings is a *function*.

∇ **Definition 7.3.** Given a FST M = $<\Sigma, \Gamma, S, s_0, \delta, \omega>$, the *translation function* for M, denoted by f_M, is the function $f_M: \Sigma^* \to \Gamma^*$ defined by $f_M(x) = \overline{\omega}(s_0, x)$.
Δ

Note that f_M, like $\overline{\omega}$, is *length preserving:* $(\forall x \in \Sigma^*)(|f_M(x)| = |x|)$. Consequently, for any $n \in \mathbb{N}$, if the domain of f_M were restricted to Σ^n, then the range of f_M would likewise be contained in Γ^n.

EXAMPLE 7.5

Let B = $<\Sigma, \Gamma, S, s_0, \delta, \omega>$ be the finite-state transducer given in Figure 7.3. Since $\overline{\omega}(s_0, \mathbf{abaab}) = (\mathbf{00100})$, $f_B(\mathbf{abaab}) = \mathbf{00100}$. Similarly, $f_B(\lambda) = \lambda$, $f_B(\mathbf{a}) = \mathbf{0}$, $f_B(\mathbf{b}) = \mathbf{0}$, $f_B(\mathbf{aa}) = \mathbf{00}$, $f_B(\mathbf{ab}) = \mathbf{00}$, $f_B(\mathbf{ba}) = \mathbf{01}$, $f_B(\mathbf{bb}) = \mathbf{01}$. Coupled with these seven base definitions, this particular f_B could be recursively defined by

$$(\forall x \in \Sigma^*) f_B(x\mathbf{aa}) = f_B(x\mathbf{a}) \cdot \mathbf{0}$$
$$f_B(x\mathbf{ab}) = f_B(x\mathbf{a}) \cdot \mathbf{0}$$
$$f_B(x\mathbf{ba}) = f_B(x\mathbf{b}) \cdot \mathbf{1}$$

and

$$f_B(x\mathbf{bb}) = f_B(x\mathbf{b}) \cdot \mathbf{1}$$

f_B in essence replaces **a**s with **0**s and **b**s with **1**s, and "delays" the output by one letter. More specifically, the translation function for B takes an entire string and substitutes **0**s and **1**s for **a**s and **b**s (respectively), deletes the last letter of the string, and appends a **0** to the front of the resulting string. The purpose of the two states s_0 and s_1 in the FST B is to remember whether the previous symbol was an **a** or a **b** (respectively) and output the appropriate replacement letter. Note that **1**s are always printed on transitions from s_1, and **0**s are printed as we leave s_0.

EXAMPLE 7.6

Let $C = <\{\mathbf{a}, \mathbf{b}\}, \{\mathbf{0}, \mathbf{1}\}, \{t_0, t_1, t_2, t_3\}, t_0, \delta_C, \omega_C>$ be the FST shown in Figure 7.4. C *flags* occurrences of the string **aab** by printing a **1** on the output tape only when the substring **aab** appears in the input stream.

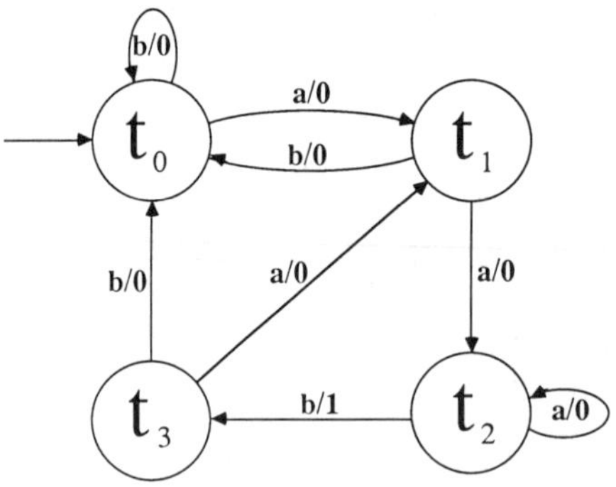

Figure 7.4 The state transition diagram for the Mealy machine C in Example 7.6

Clearly, not all functions from Σ^* to Γ^* can be represented by finite-state transducers; we have already observed that functions that are not length preserving cannot possibly qualify. As the function discussed later in Example 7.7 shows, not all length-preserving functions qualify, either.

∇ **Definition 7.4.** Given a function f: $\Sigma^* \to \Gamma^*$, f is *finite transducer definable* (FTD) ***iff*** there exists a transducer A such that $f = f_A$.
Δ

Due to the deterministic nature of transducers, any two strings that "begin the same" must start being "translated the same." This observation is the basis for the following theorem.

∇ **Theorem 7.2.** Assume f is FTD. Then

$(\forall n \in \mathbb{N})(\forall x \in \Sigma^n)(\forall y \in \Sigma^*)(\forall z \in \Sigma^*)$ (the first n letters of $f(xy)$ must agree with the first n letters of $f(xz)$)

Proof. See the exercises.

Δ

EXAMPLE 7.7

Consider the function g: $\{\mathbf{a},\mathbf{b},\mathbf{c}\}^* \to \{\mathbf{0},\mathbf{1}\}^*$, which replaces input symbols by **0** unless the next letter is **c**, in which case **1** is used instead. Thus,

$$g(\mathbf{abcaaccb}) = \mathbf{01001100} \quad \text{and} \quad g(\mathbf{abb}) = \mathbf{000}.$$

With $n = 2$, choosing $x = \mathbf{ab}$, $y = \mathbf{caaccb}$, and $z = \mathbf{b}$ shows that g violates Theorem 7.2, so g cannot be FTD.

The necessary condition outlined in the previous theorem is by no means sufficient to guarantee that a function is FTD; other properties such as a pumping lemma-style repetitiousness of the translation must also be present (see the exercises).

7.2 MINIMIZATION OF FINITE-STATE TRANSDUCERS

Two transducers that perform exactly the same translation over the entire range of input strings from Σ^* will be called *equivalent* transducers. This is in spirit similar to the way equivalence was defined for deterministic finite automata.

∇ **Definition 7.5.** Given transducers

$$\mathsf{A} = <\Sigma, \Gamma, S_\mathsf{A}, s_{0_\mathsf{A}}, \delta_\mathsf{A}, \omega_\mathsf{A}> \quad \text{and} \quad \mathsf{B} = <\Sigma, \Gamma, S_\mathsf{B}, s_{0_\mathsf{B}}, \delta_\mathsf{B}, \omega_\mathsf{B}>,$$

A is said to be *equivalent* to B ***iff*** $f_\mathsf{A} = f_\mathsf{B}$.

Δ

Just as with finite automata, a reasonable goal when constructing a transducer is to produce an efficient machine, and, as before, this will be equated with the size of the finite-state control; given a translation function f, a minimal machine for f is a FST that has the minimum number of states necessary to perform the required translation.

∇ **Definition 7.6.** Given a finite-state transducer $\mathsf{A} = <\Sigma, \Gamma, S_\mathsf{A}, s_{0_\mathsf{A}}, \delta_\mathsf{A}, \omega_\mathsf{A}>$, A is the *minimal Mealy machine for the translation* f_A ***iff*** for all finite-state transducers $\mathsf{B} = <\Sigma, \Gamma, S_\mathsf{B}, s_{0_\mathsf{B}}, \delta_\mathsf{B}, \omega_\mathsf{B}>$ for which $f_\mathsf{A} = f_\mathsf{B}$, $\|S_\mathsf{A}\| \leq \|S_\mathsf{B}\|$.

Δ

Thus, A is minimal if there is no equivalent machine with fewer states.

EXAMPLE 7.8

The FST $\mathsf{C} = <\{\mathbf{a},\mathbf{b}\}, \{\mathbf{0},\mathbf{1}\}, \{t_0, t_1, t_2, t_3\}, t_0, \delta_\mathsf{C}, \omega_\mathsf{C}>$ given in Figure 7.4 is *not* minimal. The FST $\mathsf{D} = <\{\mathbf{a},\mathbf{b}\}, \{\mathbf{0},\mathbf{1}\}, \{q_0, q_1, q_2\}, q_0, \delta_\mathsf{D}, \omega_\mathsf{D}>$ given in Figure 7.5 performs the same translation, but has only three states.

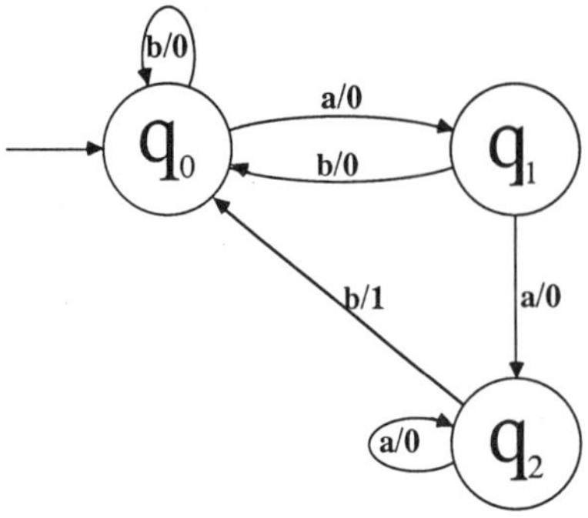

Figure 7.5 The state transition diagram for the Mealy machine D in Example 7.8

The concept of two transducers being essentially the same except for a trivial renaming of the states will again be formalized through the definition of *isomorphism* (and *homomorphism*). As before, it will be important to match the respective start states and state transitions; but rather than matching up final states (which do not exist in the FST model), we must instead ensure that the output function is preserved by the relabeling process.

∇ **Definition 7.7.** Given two FSTs

$$\mathsf{A} = <\Sigma, \Gamma, S_\mathsf{A}, s_{0_\mathsf{A}}, \delta_\mathsf{A}, \omega_\mathsf{A}> \quad \text{and} \quad \mathsf{B} = <\Sigma, \Gamma, S_\mathsf{B}, s_{0_\mathsf{B}}, \delta_\mathsf{B}, \omega_\mathsf{B}>,$$

and a function $\mu: S_\mathsf{A} \to S_\mathsf{B}$, μ is called a *Mealy machine homomorphism* from A to B *iff* the following three conditions hold:

i. $\mu(s_{0_\mathsf{A}}) = s_{0_\mathsf{B}}$.
ii. $(\forall s \in S_\mathsf{A})(\forall \mathbf{a} \in \Sigma)(\mu(\delta_\mathsf{A}(s, \mathbf{a})) = \delta_\mathsf{B}(\mu(s), \mathbf{a}))$.
iii. $(\forall s \in S_\mathsf{A})(\forall \mathbf{a} \in \Sigma)(\omega_\mathsf{A}(s, \mathbf{a}) = \omega_\mathsf{B}(\mu(s), \mathbf{a}))$.

Δ

As in Chapter 3, a bijective homomorphism will be called an isomorphism and will signify that the isomorphic machines are essentially the same (except perhaps for the names of the states). The isomorphism is essentially a recipe for renaming the states of one machine to produce identical transducers.

∇ **Definition 7.8.** Given two FSTs

$$\mathsf{A} = <\Sigma, \Gamma, S_\mathsf{A}, s_{0_\mathsf{A}}, \delta_\mathsf{A}, \omega_\mathsf{A}> \quad \text{and} \quad \mathsf{B} = <\Sigma, \Gamma, S_\mathsf{B}, s_{0_\mathsf{B}}, \delta_\mathsf{B}, \omega_\mathsf{B}>,$$

and a function $\mu: S_\mathsf{A} \to S_\mathsf{B}$, μ is called a *Mealy machine isomorphism* from A to B *iff* the following five conditions hold:

i. $\mu(s_{0_\mathsf{A}}) = s_{0_\mathsf{B}}$.
ii. $(\forall s \in S_\mathsf{A})(\forall \mathbf{a} \in \Sigma)(\mu(\delta_\mathsf{A}(s, \mathbf{a})) = \delta_\mathsf{B}(\mu(s), \mathbf{a}))$.
iii. $(\forall s \in S_\mathsf{A})(\forall \mathbf{a} \in \Sigma)(\omega_\mathsf{A}(s, \mathbf{a}) = \omega_\mathsf{B}(\mu(s), \mathbf{a}))$.

iv. μ is a one-to-one function from S_A to S_B.

v. μ is onto S_B.

Δ

∇ **Definition 7.9.** If μ: $S_A \to S_B$ is an isomorphism between two transducers $A = <\Sigma, \Gamma, S_A, s_{0_A}, \delta_A, \omega_A>$ and $B = <\Sigma, \Gamma, S_B, s_{0_B}, \delta_B, \omega_B>$, then A is said to be *isomorphic* to B, and we will write $A \cong B$.
Δ

EXAMPLE 7.9

Consider the two FSTs $C = <\{\mathbf{a}, \mathbf{b}\}, \{\mathbf{0}, \mathbf{1}\}, \{t_0, t_1, t_2, t_3\}, t_0, \delta_C, \omega_C>$, given in Figure 7.4, and $D = <\{\mathbf{a}, \mathbf{b}\}, \{\mathbf{0}, \mathbf{1}\}, \{q_0, q_1, q_2\}, q_0, \delta_D, \omega_D>$, displayed in Figure 7.5. The function μ: $\{t_0, t_1, t_2, t_3\} \to \{q_0, q_1, q_2\}$, defined by $\mu(t_0) = q_0$, $\mu(t_1) = q_1$, $\mu(t_2) = q_2$, and $\mu(t_3) = q_0$ is a homomorphism between C and D. Conditions (i) and (ii) are exactly the same criteria used for finite automata homomorphisms and have exactly the same interpretation: the start states must correspond and the transitions must match. The third condition is present to ensure that the properties of the ω function are respected; for example, since t_2 causes **1** to be printed when **b** is processed, so should the corresponding state in the D machine, which is $q_2 = \mu(t_2)$ in this example. Indeed, $\omega_C(t_2, \mathbf{b}) = \mathbf{1} = \omega_D(\mu(t_2), \mathbf{b})$. Such similarities extend to full strings also: note that $\overline{\omega}_C(t_0, \mathbf{aab}) = \mathbf{001} = \overline{\omega}_D(\mu(t_0), \mathbf{aab})$ in this example. The results can be generalized as presented in the next lemma.

∇ **Lemma 7.1.** If μ: $S_A \to S_B$ is a homomorphism between two FSTs

$$A = <\Sigma, \Gamma, S_A, s_{0_A}, \delta_A, \omega_A> \text{ and } B = <\Sigma, \Gamma, S_B, s_{0_B}, \delta_B, \omega_B>,$$

then

$$(\forall s \in S_A)(\forall x \in \Sigma^*)(\mu(\overline{\delta}_A(s, x)) = \overline{\delta}_B(\mu(s), x))$$

and

$$(\forall s \in S_A)(\forall x \in \Sigma^*)(\overline{\omega}_A(s, x) = \overline{\omega}_B(\mu(s), x))).$$

Proof. The proof is by induction on $|x|$ (see the exercises).

Δ

∇ **Corollary 7.1.** If μ: $S_A \to S_B$ is a homomorphism between two FSTs $A = <\Sigma, \Gamma, S_A, s_{0_A}, \delta_A, \omega_A>$ and $B = <\Sigma, \Gamma, S_B, s_{0_B}, \delta_B, \omega_B>$, then A is equivalent to B; that is, $f_A = f_B$.

Proof. The proof follows immediately from Lemma 7.1 and the definition of f_M.
Δ

In a manner very reminiscent of the approach taken to minimize deterministic finite automata, notions of state equivalence relations, reduced machines, and connectedness can be defined. As was the case in Chapter 3, a reduced and connected machine will be isomorphic to every other equivalent minimal machine. The definition for connectedness is essentially unchanged.

∇ **Definition 7.10.** A state s in a transducer $\mathsf{M} = <\Sigma, \Gamma, S, s_0, \delta, \omega>$ is called *accessible iff*

$$(\exists x_s \in \Sigma^*) \ni \bar{\delta}(s_0, x_s) = s$$

The transducer $\mathsf{M} = <\Sigma, \Gamma, S, s_0, \delta, \omega>$ is called *connected iff*

$$(\forall s \in S)(\exists x_s \in \Sigma^*) \ni \bar{\delta}(s_0, x_s) = s$$

Δ

That is, every state s of S can be reached by some string (x_s) in Σ^*; once again, the choice of the state s will have a bearing on which particular string is used as a representative. States that are not accessible do not affect the translation performed by the transducer; such states can be safely deleted to form a connected version of the machine.

∇ **Definition 7.11.** Given a FST $\mathsf{M} = <\Sigma, \Gamma, S, s_0, \delta, \omega>$, define the transducer $\mathsf{M}^c = <\Sigma, \Gamma, S^c, s_0^c, \delta^c, \omega^c>$, called *M connected*, by

$$S^c = \{s \in S \mid \exists x \in \Sigma^* \ni \bar{\delta}(s_0, x) = s\}$$

$$s_0^c = s_0$$

δ^c is essentially the restriction of δ to $S^c \times \Sigma$: $(\forall \mathbf{a} \in \Sigma)(\forall s \in S^c)(\delta^c(s, \mathbf{a}) = \delta(s, \mathbf{a}))$, and ω^c is the restriction of ω to $S^c \times \Sigma$: $(\forall \mathbf{a} \in \Sigma)(\forall s \in S^c)(\omega^c(s, \mathbf{a}) = \omega(s, \mathbf{a}))$.
Δ

M^c is, as in Chapter 3, the machine M with the unreachable states "thrown away." As with DFAs, trimming a machine in this fashion has no effect on the operation of the transducer. To formally prove this, the following lemma is needed.

∇ **Lemma 7.2.** Given transducers

$$\mathsf{M} = <\Sigma, \Gamma, S, s_0, \delta, \omega> \quad \text{and} \quad \mathsf{M}^c = <\Sigma, \Gamma, S^c, s_0^c, \delta^c, \omega^c>,$$

the restriction of $\bar{\omega}$ to $S^c \times \Sigma^*$ is $\bar{\omega}^c$.

Proof. We must show that $(\forall y \in \Sigma^*)(\forall t \in S^c)(\bar{\omega}^c(t, y) = \bar{\omega}(t, y))$. This can be done with a straightforward induction on $|y|$. Let P(n) be defined by

$$(\forall y \in \Sigma^n)(\forall t \in S^c)(\bar{\omega}^c(t, y) = \bar{\omega}(t, y)).$$

The basis step is trivial, since $\bar{\omega}^c(t, \lambda) = \lambda = \bar{\omega}(t, \lambda)$. For the inductive step, assume $(\forall y \in \Sigma^m)(\forall t \in S^c)(\bar{\omega}^c(t, y) = \bar{\omega}(t, y))$, and let $t \in S^c$ and $z \in \Sigma^{m+1}$ be given. Then $\exists x \in \Sigma^m$, $\exists \mathbf{a} \in \Sigma$ for which $z = \mathbf{a}x$, and therefore

$$\begin{aligned}
\overline{\omega}^c(\mathrm{t}, \mathrm{z}) &= \text{(by definition of } z\text{)}\\
\overline{\omega}^c(\mathrm{t}, \mathbf{a}x) &= \text{(by Definition 7.2ii)}\\
\omega^c(\mathrm{t}, \mathbf{a})\cdot\overline{\omega}^c(\delta^c(\mathrm{t}, \mathbf{a}), x) &= \text{(by definition of } \delta^c\text{)}\\
\omega^c(\mathrm{t}, \mathbf{a})\cdot\overline{\omega}^c(\delta(\mathrm{t}, \mathbf{a}), x) &= \text{(by the induction assumption)}\\
\omega^c(\mathrm{t}, \mathbf{a})\cdot\overline{\omega}(\delta(\mathrm{t}, \mathbf{a}), x) &= \text{(by definition of } \omega^c\text{)}\\
\omega(\mathrm{t}, \mathbf{a})\cdot\overline{\omega}(\delta(\mathrm{t}, \mathbf{a}), x) &= \text{(by Definition 7.2ii)}\\
\overline{\omega}(\mathrm{t}, \mathbf{a}x) &= \text{(by definition of } z\text{)}\\
\overline{\omega}(\mathrm{t}, z)
\end{aligned}$$

Since z was an arbitrary element of Σ^{m+1}, and t was an arbitrary state in S^c,

$$(\forall y \in \Sigma^{m+1})(\forall \mathrm{t} \in S^c)(\overline{\omega}^c(\mathrm{t}, z) = \overline{\omega}(\mathrm{t}, z)),$$

which proves P($m + 1$). Hence, P(m)$\Rightarrow$P($m + 1$), and, since m was arbitrary, $(\forall m \in \mathbb{N})(\mathrm{P}(m) \Rightarrow \mathrm{P}(m + 1))$. By the principle of mathematical induction, P(n) is therefore true for all n, and the lemma is proved.
Δ

Since $\overline{\omega}^c = \overline{\omega}$, it immediately follows that $f_{\mathsf{M}} = f_{\mathsf{M}^c}$, and we are therefore assured that the operation of any transducer is indistinguishable from the operation of its connected counterpart.

∇ **Theorem 7.3.** Given transducers

$$\mathsf{M} = <\Sigma, \Gamma, S, \mathrm{s}_0, \delta, \omega> \quad \text{and} \quad \mathsf{M}^c = <\Sigma, \Gamma, S^c, \mathrm{s}_0^c, \delta^c, \omega^c>,$$

M is equivalent to M^c.

Proof. $f_{\mathsf{M}^c}(x) = \overline{\omega}^c(\mathrm{s}_0^c, x) = \overline{\omega}^c(\mathrm{s}_0, x) = \overline{\omega}(\mathrm{s}_0, x) = f_{\mathsf{M}}(x)$, and hence by the definition of equivalence of transducers, M is equivalent to M^c.
Δ

∇ **Corollary 7.2.** Given a FTD function f, the minimal machine corresponding to f must be connected.

Proof. (by contradiction): Assume the minimal machine M is not connected; then, by Theorem 7.3, $f_{\mathsf{M}^c} = f_{\mathsf{M}} = f$, and clearly $\|S^c\| < \|S\|$, and hence M could not be minimal.
Δ

While connectedness is a necessary condition for minimality, it is not sufficient, as evidenced by the machine C in Figure 7.4: C was connected, but the FST D in Figure 7.5 was an equivalent but smaller transducer.

As was the case with finite automata in Chapter 3, connectedness is just one of the two major requirements for minimality. The other requirement is that no two states behave identically. For DFAs, this translated into statements about acceptance and rejection. For FSTs, this will instead involve the behavior of the output function. The analog to Definition 3.2 is given next.

∇ **Definition 7.12.** Given a transducer $\mathsf{M} = <\Sigma, \Gamma, S, s_0, \delta, \omega>$, the *state equivalence relation* on M, E_M, is defined by

$$(\forall s \in S)(\forall t \in S)(s\, E_\mathsf{M}\, t \Leftrightarrow (\forall x \in \Sigma^*)(\overline{\omega}(s, x) = \overline{\omega}(t, x)))$$

Δ

In other words, we will relate states s and t if and only if it is not possible to determine, by only observing the output, whether we are starting from state s or state t (no matter what input string is used). The more efficient machines will not have such duplication of states, and, as with DFAs, will be said to be *reduced*.

∇ **Definition 7.13.** A transducer $\mathsf{M} = <\Sigma, \Gamma, S, s_0, \delta, \omega>$ is called *reduced iff* $(\forall s, t \in S)(s\, E_\mathsf{M}\, t \Leftrightarrow s = t)$.

Δ

As before, if M is reduced, E_M must be the identity relation on the set of states S, and each equivalence class must contain only a single element. We defer for the moment the discussion of how E_M can be efficiently calculated. Once the state equivalence relation is known, in a manner that is also analogous to the treatment of finite automata, states related by E_M can be coalesced to form a machine that is reduced.

∇ **Definition 7.14.** Given a FST $\mathsf{M} = <\Sigma, \Gamma, S, s_0, \delta, \omega>$, defined *M modulo its state equivalence relation*, M/E_M, by $\mathsf{M}/E_\mathsf{M} = <\Sigma, \Gamma, S_{E_\mathsf{M}}, s_{0_{E_\mathsf{M}}}, \delta_{E_\mathsf{M}}, \omega_{E_\mathsf{M}}>$, where

$$S_{E_\mathsf{M}} = \{[s]_{E_\mathsf{M}} \mid s \in S\}$$

$$s_{0_{E_\mathsf{M}}} = [s_0]_{E_\mathsf{M}}$$

δ_{E_M} is defined by

$$(\forall \mathbf{a} \in \Sigma)(\forall [s]_{E_\mathsf{M}} \in S_{E_\mathsf{M}})(\delta_{E_\mathsf{M}}([s]_{E_\mathsf{M}}, \mathbf{a}) = [\delta(s, \mathbf{a})]_{E_\mathsf{M}}),$$

and ω_{E_M} is defined by

$$(\forall \mathbf{a} \in \Sigma)(\forall [s]_{E_\mathsf{M}} \in S_{E_\mathsf{M}})(\omega_{E_\mathsf{M}}([s]_{E_\mathsf{M}}, \mathbf{a}) = \omega(s, \mathbf{a})).$$

Δ

The proof that δ_{E_M} is well defined is similar to that found in Chapter 3. In an analogous fashion, ω_{E_M} must be shown to be well defined (see the exercises).

All the properties that one would expect of M/E_M are present, as outlined in the following theorem.

∇ **Theorem 7.4.** Given a FST $\mathsf{M} = <\Sigma, \Gamma, S, s_0, \delta, \omega>$,

$$\mathsf{M}/E_M = <\Sigma, \Gamma, S_{E_M}, s_{0_{E_M}}, \delta_{E_M}, \omega_{E_M}>$$

is equivalent to M and is reduced. Furthermore, if M is connected, so is M/E_M.

Proof. The proof that connectedness is preserved is identical to that given for Theorem 3.5; showing that M/E_M is reduced is very similar to the proof of Theorem 3.4. The proof of the fact that the two machines are equivalent requires the inductive argument that $(\forall y \in \Sigma^*)(\forall t \in S)(\overline{\omega}(t, y) = \overline{\omega}_{E_M}([t]_{E_M}, y))$ and is indeed very similar to the proofs of Lemma 7.2 and Theorem 7.3.
Δ

An argument similar to that given for Corollary 7.2 shows that a reduced FST is also a requirement for minimality.

∇ **Corollary 7.3.** Given a FTD function *f*, the minimal machine corresponding to *f* must be reduced.

Proof. The proof is by contradiction; see the exercises.
Δ

Being reduced, like connectedness, is a necessary condition for a machine to be minimal, but it is also not sufficient (see the exercises). One would hope that the combination of being reduced and connected *would* be sufficient to guarantee that the given machine is minimal. This is indeed the case, and one more important result, proved next in Theorem 7.5, is needed to complete the argument: Two reduced and connected FSTs are equivalent ***iff*** they are isomorphic. Armed with this result, we can also show that a minimal transducer can be obtained from any FST M by reducing and connecting it. As in Chapter 3, connecting and reducing an arbitrary machine M will therefore be guaranteed to produce the most efficient possible machine for that particular function.

∇ **Theorem 7.5.** Two reduced and connected FSTs, $\mathsf{M}_1 = <\Sigma, \Gamma, S_1, s_{0_1}, \delta_1, \omega_1>$ and $\mathsf{M}_2 = <\Sigma, \Gamma, S_2, s_{0_2}, \delta_2, \omega_2>$, are equivalent ***iff*** $\mathsf{M}_1 \cong \mathsf{M}_2$.

Proof. By Corollary 7.1, if $\mathsf{M}_1 \cong \mathsf{M}_2$, then M_1 is equivalent to M_2. The converse half of the proof is very reminiscent of that given for Theorem 3.1. We must assume M_1 and M_2 are equivalent and then prove that an isomorphism can be exhibited between M_1 and M_2. A natural way to define such an isomorphism is as follows: Given a state s in M_1, choose a string x_s such that $\overline{\delta}_1(s_{0_1}, x_s) = s$. Let $\mu(s) = \overline{\delta}_2(s_{0_2}, x_s)$. At least one such string x_s must exist for each state of M_1, since M_1 was assumed to be connected. There may be several choices for x_s for a given state s, but all will yield the same value for $\overline{\delta}_2(s_{0_2}, x_s)$, and so μ is well defined (see the exercises). The function μ satisfies the three properties of a homomorphism and turns out to be a bijection (see the exercises). Thus $\mathsf{M}_1 \cong \mathsf{M}_2$. As will be clear from

the exercises, the hypothesis that M_1 and M_2 are reduced and connected is crucial to the proof of this part of the theorem.
Δ

Note that Theorem 7.5 implies that, as long as we are dealing with reduced and connected machines, $f_{M_1} = f_{M_2}$ *iff* $M_1 \cong M_2$. The conclusions discussed earlier now follow immediately from Theorem 7.5.

∇ **Corollary 7.4.** Given a FST M, a necessary and sufficient condition for M to be minimal is that M is both reduced and connected.

Proof. See the exercises.
Δ

∇ **Corollary 7.5.** Given a FST M, M^c/E_{M^c} is minimal.

Proof. Let M be a FST and let A be a minimal machine that is equivalent to M. By Corollaries 7.2 and 7.3, A must be both reduced and connected. By Theorems 7.3 and 7.4, M^c/E_{M^c} is also reduced, connected, and equivalent to M (and hence to A). Theorem 7.5 would then guarantee that A and M^c/E_{M^c} are isomorphic, and therefore they have the same number of states. Since A was assumed to have the minimum possible number of states, M^c/E_{M^c} also has that property and is thus minimal.
Δ

The minimal machine can therefore be found as long as M^c/E_{M^c} can be computed. Finding S^c (and from that M^c) is accomplished in exactly the same manner as described in Chapter 3. The strategy for generating E_M is likewise quite similar, and again uses the *i*th *state equivalence relation*, as outlined below.

∇ **Definition 7.15.** Given a transducer $M = <\Sigma, \Gamma, S, s_0, \delta, \omega>$ and a nonnegative integer i, define a relation between the states of M called E_{iM}, the *i*th *state equivalence relation* on M, by

$$(\forall s, t \in S)(s\, E_{iM}\, t \Leftrightarrow (\forall x \in \Sigma^* \ni |x| \leq i)(\overline{\omega}(s, x) = \overline{\omega}(t, x)))$$
Δ

Thus E_{iM} relates states that cannot be distinguished by strings of length i or less, whereas E_M relates states that cannot be distinguished by any string of any length. All the properties attributable to the analogous relations for finite automata (E_{iA}) carry over, with essentially the same proofs, to the relations for finite-state transducers (E_{iM}).

∇ **Lemma 7.3.** Given a transducer $M = <\Sigma, \Gamma, S, s_0, \delta, \omega>$:

a. E_{m+1M} is a refinement of E_{mM}; that is, $(\forall s, t \in S)(s\, E_{m+1M}\, t \Rightarrow s\, E_{mM}\, t)$.

b. E_M is a refinement of E_{mM}; that is, $(\forall s, t \in S)(s\, E_M\, t \Rightarrow s\, E_{mM}\, t)$; hence, $E_M \subseteq E_{mM}$.

c. $(\exists m \in \mathbb{N} \ni E_{mM} = E_{m+1M}) \Rightarrow (\forall k \in \mathbb{N})(E_{m+kM} = E_{mM})$.

d. $(\exists m \in \mathbb{N} \ni m \leq \|S\| \wedge E_{mM} = E_{m+1M})$.

e. $(\exists m \in \mathbb{N} \ni E_{mM} = E_{m+1M}) \Rightarrow E_{mM} = E_M$.

Proof. The proof is similar to the proofs given in Chapter 3 for E_{iA} (see the exercises).
Δ

∇ **Lemma 7.4.** Given a FST $M = <\Sigma, \Gamma, S, s_0, \delta, \omega>$:

a. E_{0M} has just one equivalence classes, which consists of all of S.

b. E_{1M} is defined by $s\, E_{1M}\, t \Leftrightarrow (\forall \mathbf{a} \in \Sigma)(\omega(s, \mathbf{a}) = \omega(t, \mathbf{a}))$.

c. For $i \geq 1$, E_{i+1M} can be computed from E_{iM} as follows:

$$(\forall s \in S)(\forall t \in S)(\forall i \geq 1)(s\, E_{i+1M}\, t \Leftrightarrow s\, E_{iM}\, t \wedge (\forall \mathbf{a} \in \Sigma)(\delta(s, \mathbf{a})\, E_{iM}\, \delta(t, \mathbf{a}))).$$

Proof. The proof is similar to the proofs given in Chapter 3 for E_{iA} (see the exercises).
Δ

∇ **Corollary 7.6.** Given a FST $M = <\Sigma, \Gamma, S, s_0, \delta, \omega>$, there is an *algorithm* for computing E_M.

Proof. Use Lemma 7.4 to compute successive E_{iM} relations from E_{1M} until $E_{iM} = E_{i+1M}$; by Lemma 7.3, this E_{iM} will equal E_M, and this will all happen before i reaches $\|S\|$, the number of states in S. Thus the procedure is guaranteed to halt.
Δ

∇ **Corollary 7.7.** Given a FST $M = <\Sigma, \Gamma, S, s_0, \delta, \omega>$, there is an *algorithm* for computing the minimal machine equivalent to M.

Proof. Using the algorithm for computing the set of connected states, M^c can be found. The output function is used to find E_{1M^c}, and the state transition function is then used to calculate successive relations until E_{M^c} is found. M^c/E_{M^c} can then be defined and will be the minimal machine equivalent to M.
Δ

7.3 MOORE SEQUENTIAL MACHINES

Moore machines form another class of transducer that is equivalent in power to Mealy machines. They use a less complex output function, but often require more states than an equivalent Mealy machine to perform the same translation. An illustration of the convenience and utility of Moore machines can be found in

Example 7.16, which demonstrates that traffic signal controllers can most naturally be modeled by the transducers discussed in this section.

∇ **Definition 7.16.** A *Moore sequential machine* (MSM) with a distinguished start state is a sextuple $<\Sigma, \Gamma, S, s_0, \delta, \omega>$, where:

i. Σ denotes the input alphabet.
ii. Γ denotes the output alphabet.
iii. S denotes the set of states, a finite nonempty set.
iv. s_0 denotes the start (or initial) state; $s_0 \in S$.
v. δ denotes the state transition function; $\delta: S \times \Sigma \to S$.
vi. ω denotes the output function; $\omega: S \to \Gamma$.

Δ

Note that the only change from Definition 7.1 is the specification of the domain of ω. Conceptually, we will envision the machine printing an output symbol as a new state is reached (rather than during the transition, as was the case for Mealy machines). Note that the output symbol can no longer depend (directly) on the current symbol being scanned; it is solely a function of the current state of the machine. Consequently, the state transition diagrams will list the output function next to the state name, separated by a slash, /. We will adopt the convention that no symbol will be printed until the first character is read and a transition is made (an alternate view, not adopted here, is to decree that the machine print the symbol associated with s_0 when the machine is first turned on; in this case, an output string would be one character longer than its corresponding input string).

EXAMPLE 7.10

Let $C = <\Sigma, \Gamma, S, r_0, \delta, \omega>$ be given by

$$\Sigma = \{\mathbf{a}, \mathbf{b}\}$$

$$\Gamma = \{\mathbf{0}, \mathbf{1}\}$$

$$S = \{r_0, r_1, r_2, r_3\}$$

$$s_0 = r_0$$

The state transition table is shown in Table 7.2.

TABLE 7.2

δ	**a**	**b**
r_0	r_0	r_2
r_1	r_0	r_2
r_2	r_1	r_3
r_3	r_1	r_3

Finally, the output function is given by $\omega(r_0) = \mathbf{0}$, $\omega(r_1) = \mathbf{1}$, $\omega(r_2) = \mathbf{0}$, and $\omega(r_3) = \mathbf{1}$, or, more succinctly, $[\omega(r_i) = \boldsymbol{i} \bmod 2]$ for $i = 0, 1, 2, 3$. All the above information about C is contained in Figure 7.6. This Moore machine performs the same translation as the Mealy machine B in Example 7.2.

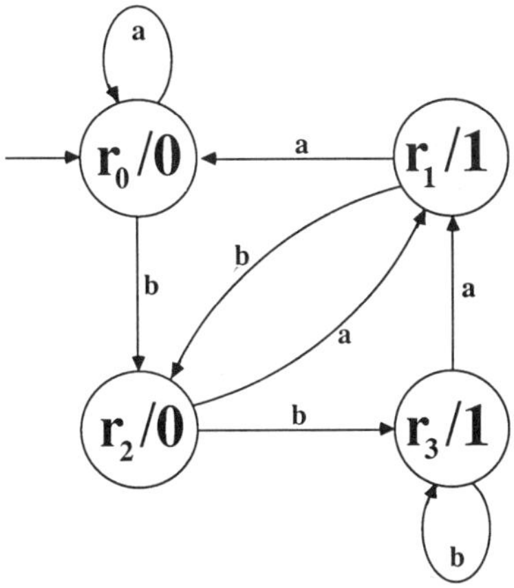

Figure 7.6 The state transition diagram for the transducer discussed in Example 7.10

Results that were targeted toward a FST in the previous sections were specific to Mealy machines. When the descriptor "transducer" appears in the theorems and definitions presented earlier, the concept or result applies unchanged to both FSTs and MSMs. Most of these results are alluded to but not restated in this section. For example, $\overline{\delta}$ is defined like and behaves like the extended state transition functions for DFAs and FSTs. On the other hand, because of the drastic change in the domain of ω, $\overline{\omega}$ must be modified as outlined below in order for $\overline{\omega}(s, x)$ to represent the output string produced when starting at s and processing x.

∇ **Definition 7.17.** Given a MSM $A = <\Sigma, \Gamma, S, s_0, \delta, \omega>$, the *extended output function* for A, denoted again by $\overline{\omega}$, is a function $\overline{\omega}: S \times \Sigma^* \to \Gamma^*$ defined recursively by:

i. $(\forall t \in S)$ $\qquad \overline{\omega}(t, \lambda) = \lambda$

ii. $(\forall t \in S)(\forall x \in \Sigma^*)(\forall \mathbf{a} \in \Sigma)(\overline{\omega}(t, \mathbf{a}x) = \omega(\delta(t, \mathbf{a})) \cdot \overline{\omega}(\delta(t, \mathbf{a}), x))$

Δ

Note that the domain of the function ω has been extended further than usual: in all previous cases, the domain was enlarged from $S \times \Sigma$ to $S \times \Sigma^*$; in this instance, we are beginning with a domain of only S and still extending it to $S \times \Sigma^*$. The above definition allows the following analog of Theorem 7.1 to remain essentially unchanged.

∇ **Theorem 7.6.** Let Σ be an alphabet and $A = <\Sigma, \Gamma, S, s_0, \delta, \omega>$ be a Moore sequential machine. Then

$$(\forall x \in \Sigma^*)(\forall y \in \Sigma^*)(\forall \mathrm{t} \in S)(\overline{\omega}(\mathrm{t}, yx) = \overline{\omega}(\mathrm{t}, y) \cdot \overline{\omega}(\overline{\delta}(\mathrm{t}, y), x))$$

Proof. The proof is by induction on $|y|$ (see the exercises and compare with Theorem 1.1).
Δ

As before, the essence of a Moore machine is captured in the translation function that the machine describes.

∇ **Definition 7.18.** Given a MSM $\mathsf{M} = <\Sigma, \Gamma, S, \mathrm{s}_0, \delta, \omega>$, the *translation function* for M, denoted by f_{M}, is the function $f_{\mathsf{M}}: \Sigma^* \to \Gamma^*$ defined by $f_{\mathsf{M}}(x) = \overline{\omega}(\mathrm{s}_0, x)$.
Δ

Definition 7.5 applies to Moore machines; two MSMs are equivalent if they define the same translation. Indeed, it is possible for a Mealy machine to be equivalent to a Moore machine, as shown by the transducers in Figures 7.2 and 7.6.

It is easy to turn a Moore machine $\mathsf{A} = <\Sigma, \Gamma, S, \mathrm{s}_0, \delta, \omega>$ into an equivalent Mealy machine $\mathsf{M} = <\Sigma, \Gamma, S, \mathrm{s}_0, \delta, \omega'>$. The first five parts of the transducer are unchanged. Only the sixth component (the output function) must be redefined, as outlined below.

∇ **Definition 7.19.** Given a Moore machine $\mathsf{A} = <\Sigma, \Gamma, S, \mathrm{s}_0, \delta, \omega>$, the corresponding Mealy machine M is given by $\mathsf{M} = <\Sigma, \Gamma, S, \mathrm{s}_0, \delta, \omega'>$, where ω' is defined by

$$(\forall \mathbf{a} \in \Sigma)(\forall \mathrm{s} \in S)(\omega'(\mathrm{s}, \mathbf{a}) = \omega(\delta(\mathrm{s}, \mathbf{a})))$$

Δ

Pictorially, all arrows that lead into a given state in the Moore machine should be labeled in the corresponding Mealy machine with the output symbol for that particular state. It follows easily from the definition that the corresponding machines perform the same translation.

∇ **Theorem 7.7.** Given a Moore machine $\mathsf{A} = <\Sigma, \Gamma, S, \mathrm{s}_0, \delta, \omega>$, the corresponding Mealy machine $\mathsf{M} = <\Sigma, \Gamma, S, \mathrm{s}_0, \delta, \omega'>$ is equivalent to A; that is, $(\forall x \in \Sigma^*)(f_{\mathsf{M}}(x) = f_{\mathsf{A}}(x))$.

Proof. The proof is by induction on $|x|$ (see the exercises).
Δ

EXAMPLE 7.11

Let $\mathsf{A} = <\Sigma, \Gamma, S, \mathrm{r}_0, \delta, \omega>$ be the Moore machine given in Figure 7.6. The corresponding Mealy machine $\mathsf{M} = <\Sigma, \Gamma, S, \mathrm{s}_0, \delta, \omega'>$ is then given by

$$\Sigma = \{\mathbf{a}, \mathbf{b}\}, \qquad \Gamma = \{\mathbf{0}, \mathbf{1}\}, \qquad S = \{\mathrm{r}_0, \mathrm{r}_1, \mathrm{r}_2, \mathrm{r}_3\}, \qquad \mathrm{s}_0 = \mathrm{r}_0$$

and the state transition table and the output function table are specified as in Tables 7.3a and 7.3b.

TABLE 7.3A

δ	a	b
r_0	r_0	r_2
r_1	r_0	r_2
r_2	r_1	r_3
r_3	r_1	r_3

TABLE 7.3B

ω'	a	b
r_0	**0**	**0**
r_1	**0**	**0**
r_2	**1**	**1**
r_3	**1**	**1**

The new Mealy machine is shown in Figure 7.7. Note that the arrow labeled **a** leaving r_1 now has a **0** associated with it, since the state at which the arrow pointed (r_0/**0**) originally output a **0**.

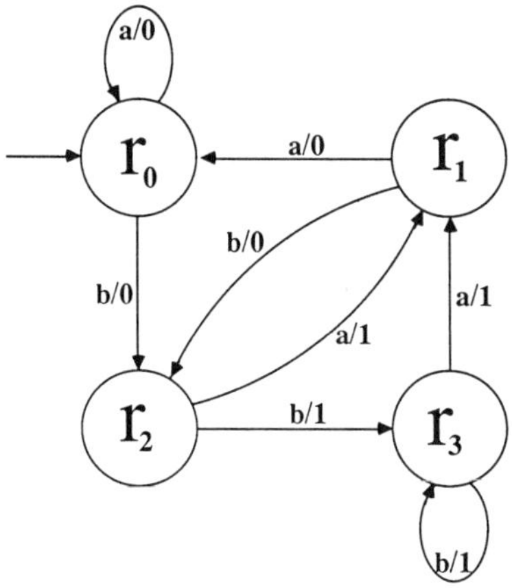

Figure 7.7 The state transition diagram for the Mealy machine M in Example 7.11

In a similar fashion, an equivalent Moore machine can be defined that corresponds to a given Mealy machine. However, due to the more restricted nature of the output function of the Moore constructs, the new machine will generally need more states to perform the same translation.

The idea behind the construct is to break each state in the Mealy machine up into a group of several similar states in the Moore machine, each of which prints a different output symbol. The new transition function mimics the old one; if state r maps to state t in the Moore machine, then any state in the group corresponding to r will map to one particular state in the group of states corresponding to t. The particular state within the group is chosen in a manner that will guarantee that the appropriate output symbol will be printed. This construct is implemented in the following definition.

∇ **Definition 7.20.** Given a Mealy machine M $= <\Sigma, \Gamma, S, s_0, \delta, \omega>$, the *corresponding Moore machine* A is given by A $= <\Sigma, \Gamma, S \times \Gamma, \langle s_0, \alpha\rangle, \delta', \omega'>$, where α is an (arbitrary) member of Γ,

$$\delta' \text{ is defined by } (\forall s \in S)(\forall \mathbf{b} \in \Gamma)(\forall \mathbf{a} \in \Sigma)(\delta'(\langle s, \mathbf{b}\rangle, \mathbf{a}) = \langle \delta(s, \mathbf{a}), \omega(s, \mathbf{a})\rangle)$$

and

$$\omega' \text{ is defined by } (\forall s \in S)(\forall \mathbf{b} \in \Gamma)(\omega'(\langle s, \mathbf{b}\rangle) = \mathbf{b}).$$

Δ

∇ **Theorem 7.8.** Given a Mealy machine $\mathsf{M} = <\Sigma, \Gamma, S, s_0, \delta, \omega>$, the corresponding Moore machine $\mathsf{A} = <\Sigma, \Gamma, S, s_0, \delta', \omega'>$ is equivalent to M; that is, $(\forall x \in \Sigma^*)(f_{\mathsf{A}}(x) = f_{\mathsf{M}}(x))$.

Proof. The proof is by induction on $|x|$ (see the exercises).

Δ

Since every Mealy machine has an equivalent Moore machine and every Moore machine has an equivalent Mealy machine, either construct can be used as a basis of what was meant by a translation *f* being finite transducer definable.

∇ **Corollary 7.8.** A translation *f* is FTD ***iff*** *f* can be defined by a FST M ***iff*** *f* can be defined by a MSM A.

Proof. The proof is immediate from the definition of FTD and Theorems 7.7 and 7.8.

Δ

EXAMPLE 7.12

Consider the Mealy machine B from Figure 7.3. The corresponding Moore machine $\mathsf{A} = <\Sigma, \Gamma, S, q_0, \delta, \omega>$ is given by

$$\Sigma = \{\mathbf{a}, \mathbf{b}\}$$

$$\Gamma = \{\mathbf{0}, \mathbf{1}\}$$

$$S = \{\langle s_0, \mathbf{0}\rangle, \langle s_0, \mathbf{1}\rangle, \langle s_1, \mathbf{0}\rangle, \langle s_1, \mathbf{1}\rangle\}$$

$$q_0 = \langle s_0, \mathbf{1}\rangle$$

$$\omega(\langle s_0, \mathbf{0}\rangle) = \mathbf{0}, \quad \omega(\langle s_0, \mathbf{1}\rangle) = \mathbf{1}, \quad \omega(\langle s_1, \mathbf{0}\rangle) = \mathbf{0}, \quad \omega(\langle s_1, \mathbf{1}\rangle) = \mathbf{1}$$

and the state transition table is specified as in Table 7.4.

TABLE 7.4

δ	a	b
$\langle s_0, \mathbf{0}\rangle$	$\langle s_0, \mathbf{0}\rangle$	$\langle s_1, \mathbf{0}\rangle$
$\langle s_0, \mathbf{1}\rangle$	$\langle s_0, \mathbf{0}\rangle$	$\langle s_1, \mathbf{0}\rangle$
$\langle s_1, \mathbf{0}\rangle$	$\langle s_0, \mathbf{1}\rangle$	$\langle s_1, \mathbf{1}\rangle$
$\langle s_1, \mathbf{1}\rangle$	$\langle s_0, \mathbf{1}\rangle$	$\langle s_1, \mathbf{1}\rangle$

Figure 7.8 displays this new Moore machine. Note that this transducer A, except for the placement of the start state, looks very much like the Moore machine

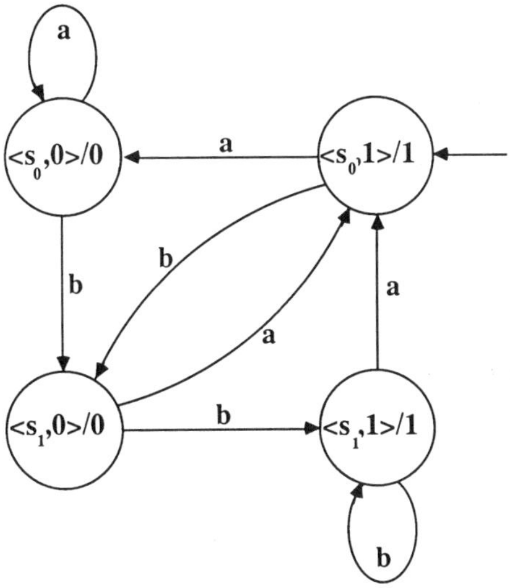

Figure 7.8 The state transition diagram for the Moore machine A in Example 7.12

C given in Figure 7.4. Indeed, any ordered pair that is labeled with the original start state would be an acceptable choice for the new start state in the corresponding Moore machine. For example, the automaton A′, which is similar to A but utilizes $\langle s_0, \mathbf{0} \rangle$ as the new start state, is another Moore machine that is equivalent to the original Mealy machine B. The transition diagram for A′ is shown in Figure 7.9. In fact, by appropriately recasting the definition of isomorphism so that it applies to Moore sequential machines, it can be shown that A′ and C are isomorphic. The definition of isomorphic again guarantees that a renaming of the states can be found that preserves start states, transition functions, and output functions. Indeed, the definition of isomorphism agrees with that of Mealy machines (and of DFAs, for

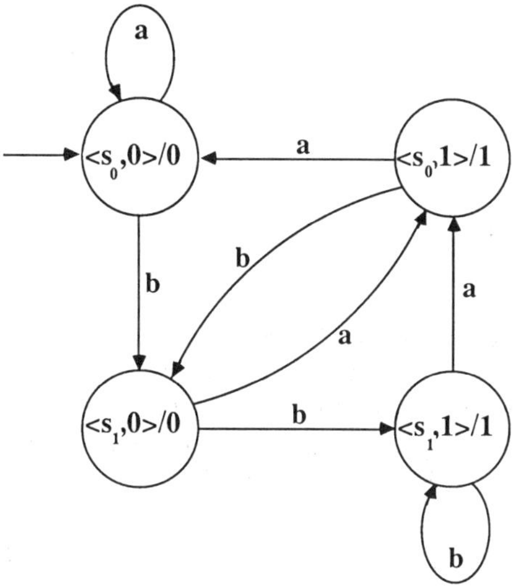

Figure 7.9 The state transition diagram for the Moore machine A′ in Example 7.12

that matter) except in the specification of the correspondence between output functions. The formal definition is given below.

∇ **Definition 7.21.** Given two MSMs

$$A = <\Sigma, \Gamma, S_A, s_{0_A}, \delta_A, \omega_A> \quad \text{and} \quad B = <\Sigma, \Gamma, S_B, s_{0_B}, \delta_B, \omega_B>,$$

and a function $\mu: S_A \to S_B$, μ is called a *Moore machine isomorphism* from A to B ***iff*** the following five conditions hold:

i. $\mu(s_{0_A}) = s_{0_B}$.
ii. $(\forall s \in S_A)(\forall \mathbf{a} \in \Sigma)(\mu(\delta_A(s, \mathbf{a})) = \delta_B(\mu(s), \mathbf{a})$.
iii. $(\forall s \in S_A)(\omega_A(s) = \omega_B(\mu(s)))$.
iv. μ is a one-to-one function between S_A and S_B.
v. μ is onto S_B.

Δ

EXAMPLE 7.13

The two Moore machines A′ in Figure 7.9 and C in Figure 7.6 are indeed isomorphic. There is a function μ from the states of A′ to the states of C that satisfies all five properties of an isomorphism. This correspondence is given by $\mu(\langle s_0, \mathbf{0}\rangle) = r_0$, $\mu(\langle s_0, \mathbf{1}\rangle) = r_1$, $\mu(\langle s_1, \mathbf{0}\rangle) = r_2$, and $\mu(\langle s_1, \mathbf{1}\rangle) = r_3$, succinctly defined by $\mu(\langle s_i, j\rangle) = r_{2i+j}$ for $i, j \in \{0, 1\}$. As before, a homomorphism is meant to represent a correspondence between states that preserves the algebraic structure of the transducer without necessarily being a bijection.

∇ **Definition 7.22.** Given two MSMs

$$A = <\Sigma, \Gamma, S_A, s_{0_A}, \delta_A, \omega_A> \quad \text{and} \quad B = <\Sigma, \Gamma, S_B, s_{0_B}, \delta_B, \omega_B>,$$

and a function $\mu: S_A \to S_B$, μ is called a *Moore machine homomorphism* from A to B ***iff*** the following three conditions hold:

i. $\mu(s_{0_A}) = s_{0_B}$
ii. $(\forall s \in S_A)(\forall \mathbf{a} \in \Sigma)(\mu(\delta_A(s, \mathbf{a})) = \delta_B(\mu(s), \mathbf{a}))$
iii. $(\forall s \in S_A)(\omega_A(s) = \omega_B(\mu(s)))$

Δ

The isomorphism μ discussed in Example 7.13 is also a homomorphism. Preserving the algebraic structure of the transducer guarantees that the translation is also preserved: if A and B are homomorphic, then they are equivalent. The homomorphism criterion that applies to single letters once again extends to similar statements about strings, as outlined in Lemma 7.5.

∇ **Lemma 7.5.** If $\mu: S_A \to S_B$ is a homomorphism between two MSMs

$$\mathsf{A} = <\Sigma, \Gamma, S_{\mathsf{A}}, s_{0_{\mathsf{A}}}, \delta_{\mathsf{A}}, \omega_{\mathsf{A}}> \text{ and } \mathsf{B} = <\Sigma, \Gamma, S_{\mathsf{B}}, s_{0_{\mathsf{B}}}, \delta_{\mathsf{B}}, \omega_{\mathsf{B}}>,$$

then

$$(\forall s \in S_{\mathsf{A}})(\forall x \in \Sigma^*)(\mu(\overline{\delta}_{\mathsf{A}}(s, x)) = \overline{\delta}_{\mathsf{B}}(\mu(s), x))$$

and

$$(\forall s \in S_{\mathsf{A}})(\forall x \in \Sigma^*)(\overline{\omega}_{\mathsf{A}}(s, x) = \overline{\omega}_{\mathsf{B}}(\mu(s), x))).$$

Proof. The proof is by induction on $|x|$ (see the exercises).

Δ

∇ **Corollary 7.9.** If $\mu: S_{\mathsf{A}} \rightarrow S_{\mathsf{B}}$ is a homomorphism between two MSMs $\mathsf{A} = <\Sigma, \Gamma, S_{\mathsf{A}}, s_{0_{\mathsf{A}}}, \delta_{\mathsf{A}}, \omega_{\mathsf{A}}>$ and $\mathsf{B} = <\Sigma, \Gamma, S_{\mathsf{B}}, s_{0_{\mathsf{B}}}, \delta_{\mathsf{B}}, \omega_{\mathsf{B}}>$, then A is equivalent to B; that is, $f_{\mathsf{A}} = f_{\mathsf{B}}$.

Proof. The proof follows immediately from Lemma 7.5 and the definition of f_{M}.

Δ

It is interesting to note that the MSMs A in Figure 7.8 and A′ in Figure 7.9 are *not* isomorphic. In fact, there does not even exist a homomorphism (in either direction) between A and A′ since the start states print different symbols, and rules (i) and (iii) therefore conflict. The absence of an isomorphism in this instance illustrates that an analog to Theorem 7.5 cannot be asserted under the definition of Moore sequential machines presented here. Observe that A and A′ are equivalent and they are both minimal (four states are necessary in a Moore machine to perform this translation), yet they are not isomorphic. The reader should contrast this failure with the analogous statement about Mealy machines in Theorem 7.5.

Producing a result comparable to Theorem 7.5 is not possible without a fundamental adjustment of at least one of the definitions. One possibility is to drop the distinguished start state from the definition of the Moore machine. This removes condition (i) from the isomorphism definition and thereby resolves the conflict between (i) and (iii). We have already noted that many applications do not require a distinguished start state (such as elevators and traffic signal controls), which makes this adjustment not altogether unreasonable.

A more common alternative is to decree that a Moore sequential machine first print the character specified by the start state upon being turned on (before any of the input tape is read) and then proceed as before. This results in output strings that are always one symbol longer than the corresponding input strings, and the length-preserving property of transducers is thereby lost. A more substantial drawback results from the less natural correspondence between Mealy and Moore machines: no FST can be truly equivalent to any MSM since translations would not even be of the same length.

The advantage of this decree is that machines like A and A′ (from Figures 7.8 and 7.9) would no longer be equivalent, and hence they would not be expected to be isomorphic. Note that equivalence is lost since, under the new decree for translations, they would produce different output when presented with, say, λ as input: A would print **1** while A′ would produce **0**. Our definition of a MSM (Definition 7.16) was chosen to remain compatible with the translations obtained from Mealy machines and to preserve a distinguished state as the start state; these advantages were obtained at the expense of a convenient analog to Theorem 7.5.

A third, and perhaps the best, alternative is to modify what we mean by a MSM isomorphism. Definition 7.21 can be rephrased to relax the condition that the start states of the two machines must print the same character.

As with Mealy machines, Moore machines can also be minimized, and a reduced and connected MSM is guaranteed to be the smallest MSM which performs that translation. Note that Definitions 7.4 (FTD), 7.5 (equivalence), 7.9 (isomorphic), 7.10 (connected), 7.12 (state equivalence relation), 7.13 (reduced), and 7.15 (*i*th relation) have been phrased to encompass both forms of transducers. Minor changes (generally involving the domain of the output function) are all that is necessary to make the remaining definitions and results conform to the Moore constructs. We begin with a formal definition of minimality, which is in essence the same as the definitions presented for DFAs and FSTs (Definitions 2.7 and 7.6).

∇ **Definition 7.23.** Given a MSM $A = <\Sigma, \Gamma, S_A, s_{0_A}, \delta_A, \omega_A>$, A is the *minimal Moore machine for the translation* f_A ***iff*** for all MSMs $B = <\Sigma, \Gamma, S_B, s_{0_B}, \delta_B, \omega_B>$ for which $f_A = f_B$, $\|S_A\| \le \|S_B\|$.
Δ

A connected Moore machine is essential to minimality. The previous definition of connectedness (Definition 7.10) suffices for both FSTs and MSMs and was therefore phrased to apply to all transducers, rather than to one specific type of transducer. For an arbitrary Moore machine, the algorithm for finding the set of accessible states is unchanged; transitions are followed from the start state until no further new states are found. The connected version of a MSM is again obtained by paring down the state set to encompass only the connected states and restricting the δ and ω functions to the smaller domain.

∇ **Definition 7.24.** Given a MSM $M = <\Sigma, \Gamma, S, s_0, \delta, \omega>$, define the transducer $M^c = <\Sigma, \Gamma, S^c, s_0^c, \delta^c, \omega^c>$, called *M connected*, by

$$S^c = \{s \in S \mid \exists x \in \Sigma^* \ni \overline{\delta}(s_0, x) = s\}$$

$$s_0^c = s_0$$

δ^c is essentially the restriction of δ to $S^c \times \Sigma$: $(\forall \mathbf{a} \in \Sigma)(\forall s \in S^c)(\delta^c(s, \mathbf{a}) = \delta(s, \mathbf{a}))$, and ω^c is the restriction of ω to $S^c \times \Sigma$: $(\forall s \in S^c)(\omega^c(s) = \omega(s))$.
Δ

The concept of a reduced Moore machine and the definition of the state equivalence relation are identical in spirit and in form to those presented for Mealy machines (Definitions 7.12 and 7.13). The definition that outlines how to reduce a Moore machine by coalescing states differs from that given for FSTs (Definition 7.14) only in the specification of the output function. In both Definition 7.14 and the following Moore machine analog, the value ω takes for an equivalence class is determined by the value given for a representative of that equivalence class. As before, this natural definition for the output function can be shown to be well defined (see the exercises).

∇ **Definition 7.25.** Given a MSM $M = <\Sigma, \Gamma, S, s_0, \delta, \omega>$, define M/E_M, *M modulo its state equivalence relation*, by $M/E_M = <\Sigma, \Gamma, S_{E_M}, s_{0_{E_M}}, \delta_{E_M}, \omega_{E_M}>$, where

$$S_{E_M} = \{[s]_{E_M} \mid s \in S\}$$

$$s_{0_{E_M}} = [s_0]_{E_M}$$

δ_{E_M} is defined by

$$(\forall \mathbf{a} \in \Sigma)(\forall [s] \in S_{E_M})(\delta_{E_M}([s]_{E_M}, \mathbf{a}) = [\delta(s, \mathbf{a})]_{E_M}),$$

and ω_{E_M} is defined by

$$(\forall [s] \in S_{E_M})(\omega_{E_M}([s]_{E_M}) = \omega(s))$$

Δ

The Moore machine M/E_M has all the properties attributed to the Mealy version. Without changing the nature of the translation, it is guaranteed to produce a MSM which is reduced.

∇ **Theorem 7.9.** Given a MSM $M = <\Sigma, \Gamma, S, s_0, \delta, \omega>$:

a. $M/E_M = <\Sigma, \Gamma, S_{E_M}, s_{0_{E_M}}, \delta_{E_M}, \omega_{E_M}>$ is equivalent to M.
b. M/E_M is reduced.
c. If M is conected, so is M/E_M.
d. Given a FTD function *f*, the minimal Moore machine corresponding to *f* must be reduced.

Proof. The proof is similar to Theorem 7.4 (see the exercises).

Δ

As mentioned earlier, the definition of a MSM chosen here denies a convenient analog to Theorem 7.5. However, a reduced and connected Moore machine must be minimal.

∇ **Theorem 7.10**

(a) Given a MSM M, a necessary and sufficient condition for M to be minimal is that M is both reduced and connected.

(b) Given a MSM M, M^c/E_{M^c} is minimal.

Proof. See the exercises.

Δ

The minimal Moore machine corresponding to a MSM M can thus be obtained if the connected state set and the state equivalence relation can be computed. The algorithm for calculating the accessible states is the same as before, and computing the state equivalence relation will again be accomplished using the concept of the *i*th state equivalence relation (Definition 7.15). All the results proved previously in Lemma 7.3 still hold, showing that successive calculations are guaranteed to halt and produce E_M. All that remains is to specify both a starting point and a way to find the next relation from the current E_{iM}.

With Mealy machines, E_{0M} consisted of one single equivalence class, since λ could not distinguish between states. All states were therefore related to each other under E_{0M}. With Moore machines, different states cause different letters to be printed. E_{0M} can therefore be thought of as grouping together states that print the same symbol.

∇ **Lemma 7.6.** Given a MSM $M = <\Sigma, \Gamma, S, s_0, \delta, \omega>$:

(a) E_{0M} is defined by $s\, E_{0M}\, t \Leftrightarrow (\omega(s) = \omega(t))$.

(b) For $i \geq 0$, E_{i+1M} can be computed from E_{iM} as follows:

$$(\forall s \in S)(\forall t \in S)(\forall i \geq 0)(s\, E_{i+1M}\, t \Leftrightarrow s\, E_{iM}\, t \wedge (\forall \mathbf{a} \in \Sigma)(\delta(s, \mathbf{a})\, E_{iM}\, \delta(t, \mathbf{a}))).$$

Proof. The proof is essentially the same as in Chapter 3 (see Theorem 3.8).

Δ

∇ **Corollary 7.10.** Given a MSM $M = <\Sigma, \Gamma, S, s_0, \delta, \omega>$, there is an *algorithm* for computing E_M.

Proof. See the exercises.

Δ

E_{0M} will generally have one equivalence class for each symbol in Γ; $rk(E_{0M})$ could be less than $\|\Gamma\|$ if some output symbols are not printed by any state (remember that equivalence classes are by definition nonempty). The rule for computing E_{i+1M} from E_{iM} is identical to that given for Mealy machines (and DFAs); only the starting point, E_{0M}, had to be redefined for Moore machines (compare with Lemma 7.4). Lemmas 7.3 and 7.6 imply that there is an algorithm for finding E_M for any Moore machine M; this was the final computation needed to produce M^c/E_{M^c}, which will be the minimal Moore machine equivalent to the MSM M.

∇ **Corollary 7.11.** Given a MSM $M = <\Sigma, \Gamma, S, s_0, \delta, \omega>$, there is an *algorithm* for computing the minimal machine equivalent to M.

Proof. See the exercises.

Δ

7.4 TRANSDUCER APPLICATIONS AND CIRCUIT IMPLEMENTATION

The vending machine example that began this chapter showed that the transducer was capable of modeling many of the machines we deal with in everyday life. This section gives examples of several types of applications and then shows how to form the circuitry that will implement such transducers. Transducers can be used not only to model physical machinery, but can also form the basis for computational algorithms. The following example can be best thought of not as a model of a machine that receives files, but as a model of the behavior of the computer algorithm that specifies how such files are to be received.

EXAMPLE 7.14

The transducer metaphor is often used to succinctly describe the structure of many algorithms commonly used in computer applications, most notably in network communications. *Kermit* is a popular means of transferring files between mainframes and microcomputers. A transfer is accomplished by the send portion of Kermit on the source host exchanging information with the receive portion of Kermit on the destination host. The two processes communicate by exchanging *packets* of information; these packets comprise the input alphabet of our model. When the Kermit protocol was examined in Chapter 1 (Example 1.16), it was noted that a full description of the algorithm must also describe the action taken upon receipt of an incoming packet; these actions comprise the output alphabet of our model. During a file transfer, the states of the receiving portion of Kermit on the destination host are R (awaiting a transfer request), RF (awaiting the name of the file to be transferred), RD (awaiting more data to be placed in the new file), and A (abort due to an unrecoverable error). The set of states will again be {A, R, RD, RF}.

Expected inputs are represented by **S** (an initialization packet, indicating that a transfer is requested), **H** (a header packet, containing the name of one of the files to be created and opened), **D** (a data packet), **Z** (an end of file marker, signaling that no more data need be placed in the currently opened file), and **B** (break, signaling the end of transmission). Unexpected input, representing a garbled transmission, is denoted by **X**. The input alphabet is therefore $\Sigma = \{\mathbf{B}, \mathbf{D}, \mathbf{H}, \mathbf{S}, \mathbf{X}, \mathbf{Z}\}$.

When Kermit receives a recognizable packet, it sends an acknowledgment (ACK) back to the other host. This action will be represented in the output alphabet by the symbol **Y**. When the receiver expects and gets a valid header packet, it opens the appropriate file and also acknowledges the packet. This pair of actions is represented by the output symbol **O**. **W** will denote the writing of the packet contents to the opened file and acknowledgment of the packet, and φ will denote that no action is taken. **C** will indicate that the currently opened file is closed. **N** will represent the transmission of a NAK (negative acknowledgment), which is used to alert the sender that a garbled packet was detected. The output alphabet is therefore $\Gamma = \{\mathbf{N}, \mathbf{O}, \mathbf{W}, \mathbf{Y}, \varphi\}$. The complete algorithm is summed up in the state transition diagram given in Figure 7.10.

Hardware as well as software can be profitably modeled by finite-state transducers. The column-by-column addition of two binary numbers is quite naturally

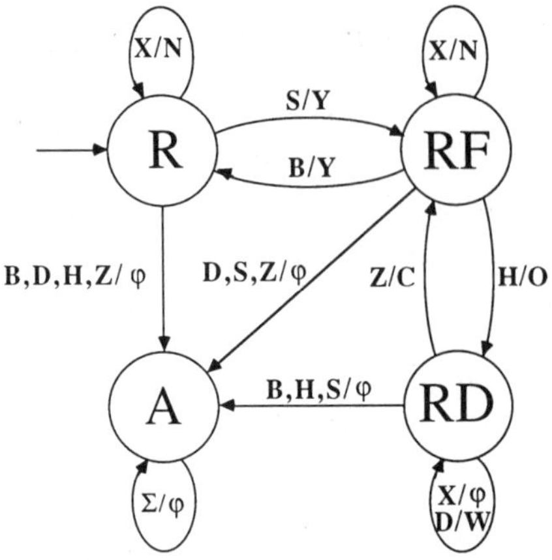

Figure 7.10 The state transition diagram for the receive portion of Kermit, as discussed in Example 7.14

modeled by a simple two-state FST, since the carry bit is the only piece of previous history needed by the transducer to correctly sum the current column. This discussion will focus on binary numbers in order to keep the alphabets small, but trivial extensions will make the two-state machine apply to addition in any base system.

EXAMPLE 7.15

A computation such as the one shown in Figure 7.11a would be divided up into columns and presented to the FST as indicated in Figure 7.11b (shown in mid-computation). A digit from the first number and the corresponding digit from the second number are presented to the transducer as a single input symbol. With the column pairs represented by standard ordered pairs, the corresponding input tape

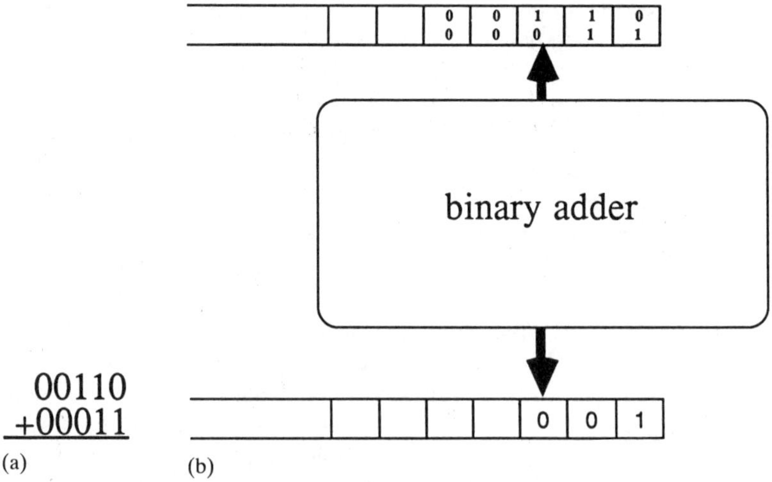

Figure 7.11 (a) The addition problem discussed in Example 7.15 (b) Conceptual model of the binary adder discussed in Example 7.15

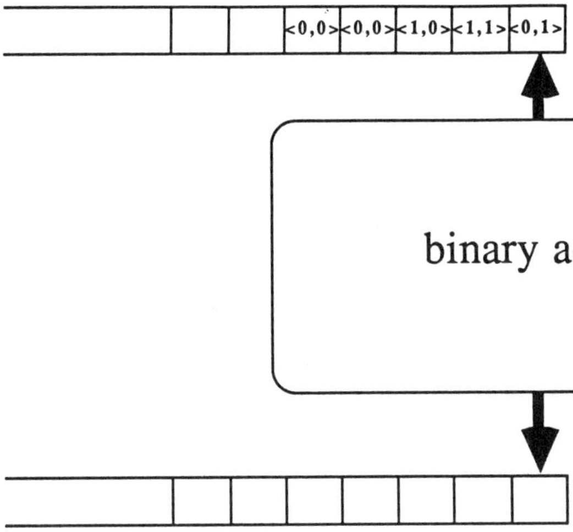

Figure 7.12 The binary adder discussed in Example 7.15

might appear as in Figure 7.12 (shown at the start of computation). As illustrated by the orientation of the tape, this FST must be set up to process strings *in reverse*, that is, from right to left, since computations must start with the low-order bits to ensure that the correct answer is always (deterministically) computed. With states C (representing carry) and N (no carry), input alphabet $\Sigma = \{\langle 0,0\rangle, \langle 0,1\rangle, \langle 1,0\rangle, \langle 1,1\rangle\}$ and output alphabet $\Gamma = \{\mathbf{0}, \mathbf{1}\}$, this binary adder behaves as shown in the state transition diagram given for B in Figure 7.13. For the problem displayed in Figure 7.11a, the output produced by B would be **01001** (9 in binary), which is the appropriate translation of the addition problem given (6 + 3).

Unfortunately, addition is not truly length preserving; adding the three-digit numbers **110** and **011** produces a binary answer that is four digits long. The adder B defined in Example 7.15 cannot correctly reflect a carry out of the most significant binary position. While the concept of final states is not present in our formal definition of transducers, this FST B provides an example in which it is natural to both produce continuous output and track the terminal state: if a computation ends in state C, then we know that an overflow condition has occurred. B clearly operates correctly on all strings that have been padded with $\langle 0,0\rangle$ as the last (leftmost) symbol; employing such padding is reminiscent of the use of the <EOS> symbol when building circuits for DFAs. Indeed, it might be profitable to specifically

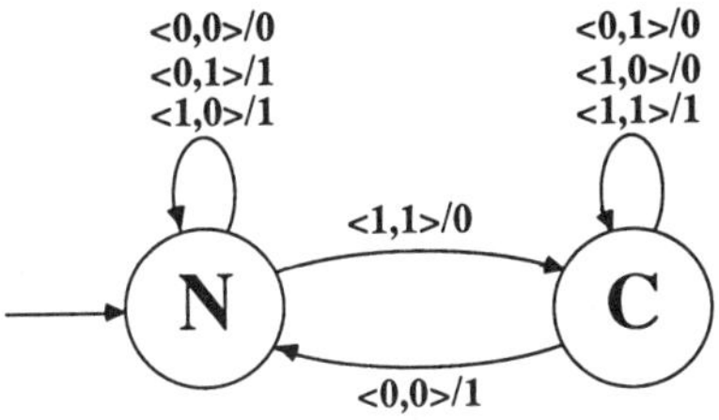

Figure 7.13 The state transition diagram for a binary adder modeled as a Mealy machine, as discussed in Example 7.15

include an <EOS> symbol and have the transducer react to <EOS> by printing a **y** or **n** to indicate whether or not there was overflow.

While the binary adder is only one small component of a computer, finite-state transducers can be profitably used to model complete systems; one such application involves traffic lights. The controller for a large intersection may handle eight banks of traffic signals for the various straight-ahead and left-turn lanes, as well as four sets of walk lights (see the exercises). Input about the intersection conditions is often fed to the controller from pedestrian walk buttons and metal detectors embedded in the roadway. For simplicity, we will choose a simplified intersection to illustrate how to model a traffic controller by a transducer. The simplified example nevertheless incorporates all the essential features of the more intricate intersections. A full-blown model would only require larger alphabets and more states.

EXAMPLE 7.16

Consider a small north–south street that terminates as it meets a large east–west avenue, as shown in Figure 7.14. Due to the heavy traffic along the avenue, the westbound traffic attempting to turn left is governed by a left-turn signal (signal 2 in Figure 7.14). Traffic continuing west is controlled by signal 1, while signal 3 governs eastbound traffic. Vehicles entering the intersection from the south rely on signal 4. The red, yellow, and green lights of these four signals represent the output of the transducer. Protecting westbound traffic while turning left is accomplished by an output configuration of $\langle G, G, R, R\rangle$, which is meant to indicate that the first two signals are green while the eastbound and northbound lanes have red lights. The output alphabet can thus be represented by ordered foursomes of R, Y, and G (red, yellow, and green). We can succinctly define

$$\Gamma = \{R, Y, G\} \times \{R, Y, G\} \times \{R, Y, G\} \times \{R, Y, G\},$$

though there will be some combinations (like $\langle G, G, G, G\rangle$) that are not expected to appear in the model.

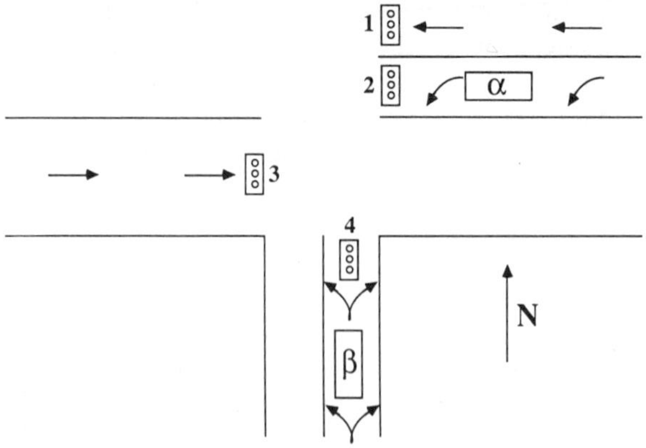

Figure 7.14 The intersection discussed in Example 7.16

The most prevalent output configuration is expected to be ⟨G, R, G, R⟩, which allows unrestricted flow of the east–west traffic on the avenue. Due to the relatively small amount of traffic on the north–south street, the designers of the intersection chose to embed the sensors α in the left-turn lane and β in the northbound lane and only depart from the ⟨G, R, G, R⟩ configuration when a vehicle is sensed by these detectors. There is therefore a pair of inputs to our transducer, indicating the status of sensor α and sensor β. The four combinations will be represented by ⟨0, 0⟩, (no traffic above either sensor), ⟨1, 0⟩ (sensor α active), ⟨0, 1⟩ (sensor β active), and ⟨1, 1⟩ (both detectors have currently sensed vehicles).

The controller is most naturally modeled by a Moore machine, since the state of the system is so intimately tied to the status of the four lights. From the configuration ⟨G, R, G, R⟩, activation of the β sensor signifies that all traffic should be stopped except that governed by signal 4. The output should therefore move through the pattern ⟨Y, R, Y, R⟩ to ⟨R, R, R, G⟩ and remain in that state until the β sensor is deactivated. This and the other transitions are illustrated in Figure 7.15.

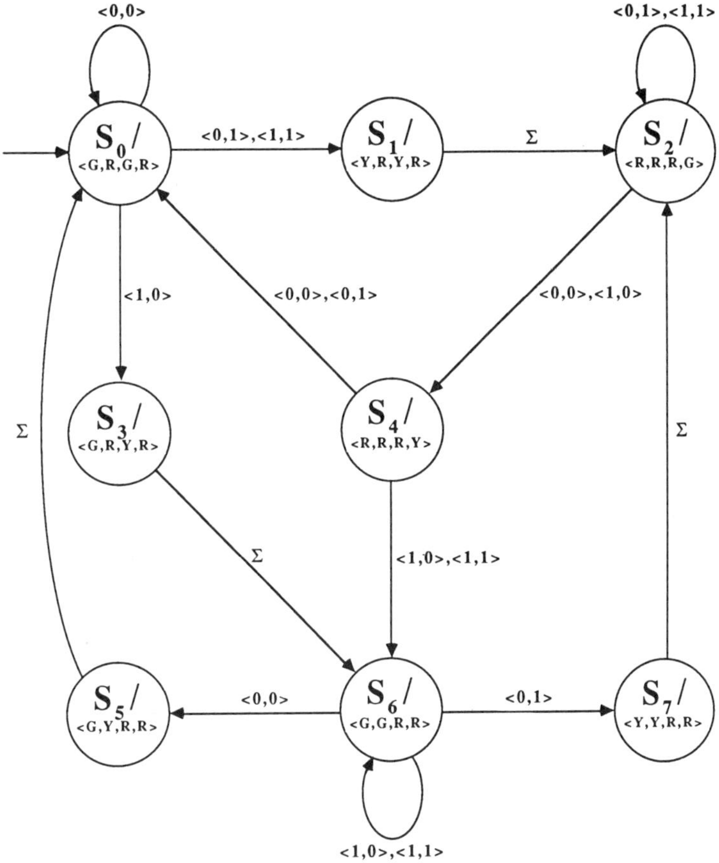

Figure 7.15 The state transition diagram for a stoplight modeled as a Moore machine, as discussed in Example 7.16

In actuality, the duration of patterns incorporating the yellow caution light is shorter than others. With the addition of extra states, a clock cycle length on the order of 5 seconds (commensurate with the typical length of a yellow light) could be used to govern the length of the different output configurations. For example, incorporating s_8 as shown in Figure 7.16 guarantees that the output ⟨R, R, R, G⟩ will persist for at least two cycles (10 seconds). From an engineering standpoint, complicating the finite-state control in this manner can be avoided by varying the clock cycle length.

We now discuss some of the hardware that comprise the heart of traffic controllers and vending machines. As was done with deterministic finite automata in Chapter 1 and nondeterministic finite automata in Chapter 4, finite-state transducers can be implemented with digital logic circuits. We again use a clock pulse, D flip-flops, and an encoding for the states. Besides needing an encoding for the input alphabet, it is now necessary to have an encoding for the output alphabet, which will

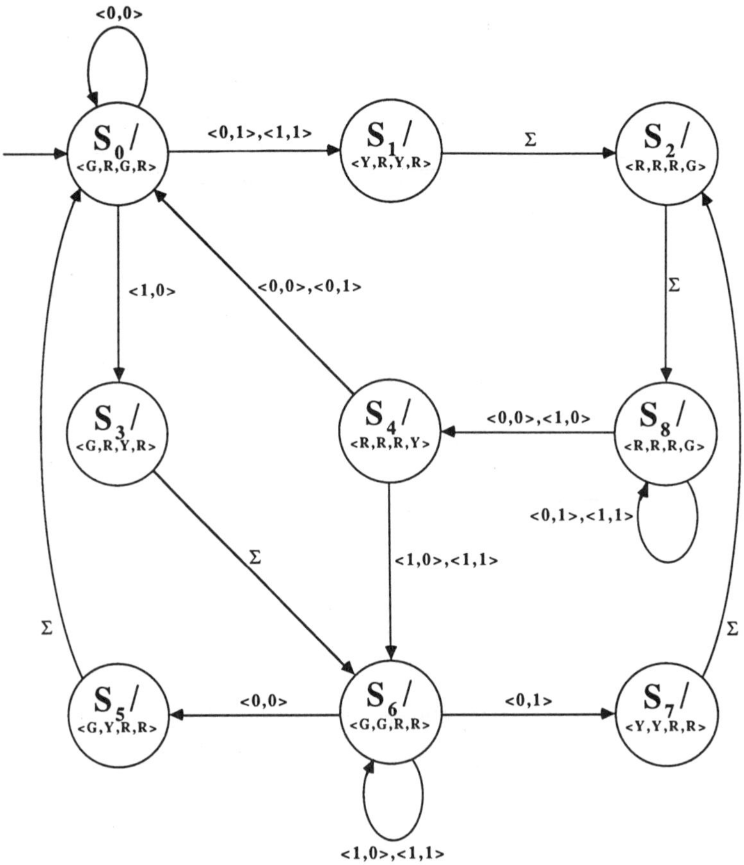

Figure 7.16 The modified controller discussed in Example 7.16

be represented by the bits $\mathbf{w}_1, \mathbf{w}_2, \mathbf{w}_3 \ldots$. We again suggest (solely for simplicity and standardization in the exercises) ordering the symbols in Γ alphabetically and assigning binary codes in ascending order, as was recommended earlier for Σ. We must construct a circuit for generating each $\mathbf{w}_j$, in the same manner as we built circuits implementing the accept function for finite automata.

Many practical applications of FSTs (such as traffic signals) operate continuously, rather than starting and stopping for one small string. In such cases, an <EOS> symbol is not necessary; the circuit operates until power is shut off. Similarly, an <SOS> symbol is not essential for a traffic signal complex; upon resuming operation after a power failure, it is usually immaterial whether east–west traffic first gets a green light or whether it gets a red light in deference to the north–south traffic. In contrast, it *is* important for vending machines to initialize to the proper state or some interesting discounts could be obtained by playing with the power cord.

EXAMPLE 7.17

Consider the FST displayed in Figure 7.17. If <EOS> and <SOS> is unnecessary, then the input alphabet can be represented by a single bit $\mathbf{a}_1$, with $\mathbf{a}_1 = \mathbf{0}$ representing **c** and $\mathbf{a}_1 = \mathbf{1}$ representing **d**. Similarly, the output alphabet can be represented by a single bit $\mathbf{w}_1$, with $\mathbf{w}_1 = \mathbf{0}$ representing **a** and $\mathbf{w}_1 = \mathbf{1}$ representing **b**. The states can

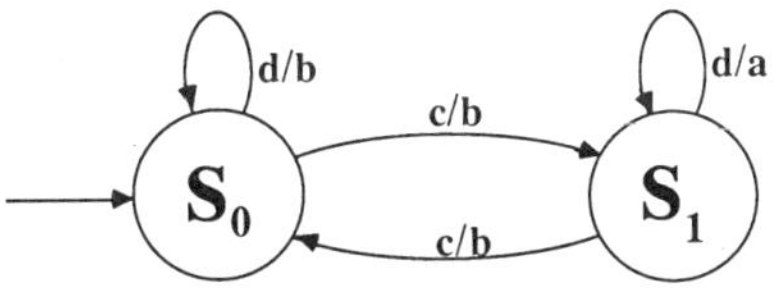

Figure 7.17 The state transition diagram for the Mealy machine in Example 7.17

likewise be represented by a single bit $\mathbf{t}_1$, with $\mathbf{t}_1 = \mathbf{0}$ representing s_0 and $\mathbf{t}_1 = \mathbf{1}$ representing s_1. As before, we can construct a truth table to represent the state transition function, defining $\mathbf{t}_1'$ in terms of $\mathbf{t}_1$ and $\mathbf{a}_1$. The complete table is given in Table 7.5a.

TABLE 7.5a

$\mathbf{t}_1$	$\mathbf{a}_1$	$\mathbf{t}_1'$
1	1	1
0	1	0
1	0	0
0	0	1

The principal disjunctive normal form for the transition function is therefore seen to be $\mathbf{t}_1' = (\mathbf{t}_1 \wedge \mathbf{a}_1) \vee (\neg \mathbf{t}_1 \wedge \neg \mathbf{a}_1)$. The output function can be found in a similar manner, as shown in Table 7.5b.

Thus, $\mathbf{w}_1 = (\mathbf{t}_1 \uparrow \mathbf{a}_1)$. As in Example 1.12, the circuit for $\mathbf{t}_1$ will be fed back into the D flip-flop(s); the circuit for $\mathbf{w}_1$ will form the output for the machine (replacing the acceptance circuit used in DFAs). The complete network is shown in Figure

TABLE 7.5b

t_1	a_1	w_1
1	1	0
0	1	1
1	0	1
0	0	1

7.18. Note that we would want the output device to print on the rising edge of the clock cycle, before the new value of $\mathbf{t}_1$ propagates through the circuitry.

A larger output alphabet would require an encoding of several bits; each $\mathbf{w}_i$ would have its own network of gates, and the complete circuit would then simultaneously generate several bits of output information. As in Chapter 1, additional states or input symbols will add bits to the other encoding schemes and add to the number of rows in the truth tables for δ and ω. Each additional state bit will also require its own D flip-flop and a new truth table for its feedback loop. Each additional state bit doubles the number of states that can be represented, which means that, as was the case with deterministic finite automata, the number of flip-flops grows as the logarithm of the number of states.

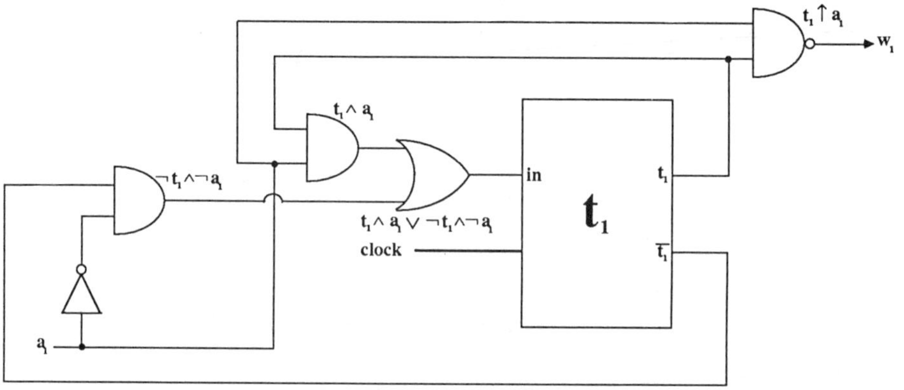

Figure 7.18 Circuit diagram for Example 7.17

EXERCISES

7.1. Let $A = <\Sigma, \Gamma, S, s_0, \delta, \omega>$ be a Mealy machine. Prove the following statements from Theorem 7.1:

(a) $(\forall x \in \Sigma^*)(\forall y \in \Sigma^*)(\forall t \in S)(\overline{\omega}(t, yx) = \overline{\omega}(t, y)\cdot\overline{\omega}(\overline{\delta}(t, y), x))$

(b) $(\forall x \in \Sigma^*)(\forall y \in \Sigma^*)(\forall s \in S)(\overline{\delta}(s, yx) = \overline{\delta}(\overline{\delta}(s, y), x))$

7.2. Refer to Lemma 7.1 and prove:

(a) $(\forall s \in S_A)(\forall x \in \Sigma^*)((\mu(\overline{\delta}_A(s, x)) = \overline{\delta}_B(\mu(s), x))$

(b) $(\forall s \in S_A)(\forall x \Sigma^*)(\overline{\omega}_A(s, x) = \overline{\omega}_B(\mu(s), x)))$

7.3. Prove Corollary 7.3.

7.4. Prove Corollary 7.4 by showing that a necessary and sufficient condition for a Mealy machine M to be minimal is that M is both reduced and connected.

7.5. Show that any FTD function f must satisfy a "pumping lemma."

(a) Devise the statement of a theorem that shows that the way any sufficiently long string is translated determines how an entire sequence of longer strings are translated.

(b) Prove the statement made in part (a).

7.6. In each of the following parts, you may assume the results in the preceding parts; for example, you may assume parts (a) and (b) when proving (c).

(a) Prove Lemma 7.3a.

(b) Prove Lemma 7.3b.

(c) Prove Lemma 7.3c.

(d) Prove Lemma 7.3d.

(e) Prove Lemma 7.3e.

7.7. Given a FST $M = <\Sigma, \Gamma, S, s_0, \delta, \omega>$, prove the following statements from Lemma 7.4:

(a) E_{0M} has just one equivalence classes, which consists of all of S.

(b) E_{1M} is defined by $s\, E_{1M}\, t \Leftrightarrow (\forall \mathbf{a} \in \Sigma)(\omega(s, \mathbf{a}) = \omega(t, \mathbf{a}))$.

(c) $(\forall s \in S)(\forall t \in S)(\forall i \geq 1)(s\, E_{i+1M}\, t \Leftrightarrow s\, E_{iM}\, t \wedge (\forall \mathbf{a} \in \Sigma)(\delta(s, \mathbf{a})\, E_{iM}\, \delta(t, \mathbf{a})))$.

7.8. Prove Theorem 7.6 by showing that if $A = <\Sigma, \Gamma, S, s_0, \delta, \omega>$ is a Moore machine then $(\forall x \in \Sigma^*)(\forall y \in \Sigma^*)(\forall t \in S)(\overline{\omega}(t, yx) = \overline{\omega}(t, y) \cdot \overline{\omega}(\overline{\delta}(t, y), x))$.

7.9. Prove Theorem 7.7.

7.10. Prove Theorem 7.8.

7.11. Use Lemma 7.6 to find E_C in Example 7.10.

7.12. Show that there is a homomorphism from the machine M in Example 7.11 to the machine B in Example 7.2.

7.13. Prove that, in a FST $M = <\Sigma, \Gamma, S, s_0, \delta, \omega>$, $(\forall t \in S)(\forall \mathbf{a} \in \Sigma)(\overline{\omega}(t, \mathbf{a}) = \omega(t, \mathbf{a}))$.

7.14. Modify the vending machine in Example 7.1 so that it can return all the coins that have been inserted. Let **r** denote a new input that represents activating the coin return, and let **a** represent a new output corresponding to the vending machine releasing all the coins in its temporary holding area.

7.15. Given a FST $M = <\Sigma, \Gamma, S, s_0, \delta, \omega>$ and $M/E_M = <\Sigma, \Gamma, S_{E_M}, s_{0_{E_M}}, \delta_{E_M}, \omega_{E_M}>$, show that δ_{E_M} is well defined.

7.16. Given a FST $M = <\Sigma, \Gamma, S, s_0, \delta, \omega>$ and $M/E_M = <\Sigma, \Gamma, S_{E_M}, s_{0_{E_M}}, \delta_{E_M}, \omega_{E_M}>$, show that ω_{E_M} is well defined.

7.17. Give an example that shows that requiring a FST M to be reduced is not a sufficient condition to ensure that M is minimal.

7.18. Show that the function μ defined in the proof of Theorem 7.5 is well defined.

7.19. Given the function μ defined in the proof of Theorem 7.5, prove that μ is really an isomorphism; that is:

(a) $\mu(s_{0_1}) = s_{0_2}$.

(b) $(\forall s \in S_1)(\forall \mathbf{a} \in \Sigma)(\mu(\delta_1(s, \mathbf{a})) = \delta_2(\mu(s), \mathbf{a}))$

(c) $(\forall s \in S_1)(\forall \mathbf{a} \in \Sigma)(\omega_1(s, \mathbf{a}) = \omega_2(\mu(s), \mathbf{a}))$

(d) μ is a one-to-one function between S_1 and S_2.

(e) μ is onto S_2.

7.20. Consider a transducer that implements a "one-unit delay" over the alphabets $\Sigma = \{\mathbf{a}, \mathbf{b}\}$

and $\Gamma = \{\mathbf{a}, \mathbf{b}, \mathbf{x}\}$. The first letter of the output string should be **x**, and the nth letter of the output string should be the $n-1$st letter of the input string (for $n > 1$). Thus, $\overline{\omega}(\mathbf{abbab}) = \mathbf{xabba}$, and so on.

(a) Define a sextuple for a Mealy machine that will perform this translation.
(b) Draw a Mealy machine that will perform this translation.
(c) Define a sextuple for a Moore machine that will perform this translation.
(d) Draw a Moore machine that will perform this translation.

7.21. Consider the circuit diagram that would correspond to the vending machine in Example 7.1.

(a) Does there appear to be any reason to use an <EOS> symbol in the input alphabet? Explain.
(b) Does there appear to be any reason to use an <SOS> symbol in the input alphabet? Explain.
(c) How many encoding bits are needed for the input alphabet? Define an appropriate encoding scheme.
(d) How many encoding bits are needed for the output alphabet? Define an appropriate encoding scheme.
(e) How many encoding bits are needed for the state names? Define an appropriate encoding scheme.
(f) Write the truth table and corresponding (minimized) Boolean function for $\mathbf{t}_2$. Try to make the best possible use of the don't-care combinations.
(g) Write the truth table and corresponding (minimized) Boolean function for $\mathbf{w}_2$. Try to make the best possible use of the don't-care combinations.
(h) Define the other functions and draw the complete circuit for the vending machine.

7.22. Consider the vending machine described in Exercise 7.14.

(a) Does there appear to be any reason to use an <EOS> symbol in the input alphabet? Explain.
(b) How many encoding bits are needed for the input alphabet? Define an appropriate encoding scheme.
(c) How many encoding bits are needed for the output alphabet? Define an appropriate encoding scheme.
(d) How many encoding bits are needed for the state names? Define an appropriate encoding scheme.
(e) Write the truth table and corresponding (minimized) Boolean function for $\mathbf{t}_3$. Try to make the best possible use of the don't-care combinations.
(f) Write the truth table and corresponding (minimized) Boolean function for $\mathbf{w}_3$. Try to make the best possible use of the don't-care combinations.
(g) Define the other functions and draw the complete circuit for the vending machine.

7.23. Use the standard encoding conventions to draw the circuit corresponding to the FST defined in Example 7.2.

7.24. Use the standard encoding conventions to draw the circuit corresponding to the FST defined in Example 7.6.

7.25. Use the standard encoding conventions to draw the circuit corresponding to the FST D defined in Example 7.8.

7.26. Give an example that shows that requiring a FST M to be connected is not a sufficient condition to ensure that M is minimal.

7.27. Consider a transducer that implements a "two-unit delay" over the alphabets $\Sigma = \{\mathbf{a}, \mathbf{b}\}$

and $\Gamma = \{\mathbf{a}, \mathbf{b}, \mathbf{x}\}$. The first two letters of the output string should be **xx**, and the nth letter of the output string should be the $n-2$nd letter of the input string (for $n > 2$). Thus, $\overline{\omega}(\mathbf{abbaba}) = \mathbf{xxabba}$, and so on.

(a) Define a sextuple for a Mealy machine that will perform this translation.
(b) Draw a Mealy machine that will perform this translation.
(c) Define a sextuple for a Moore machine that will perform this translation.
(d) Draw a Moore machine that will perform this translation.

7.28. **(a)** Give an example that shows that the conclusion of Theorem 7.5 can be false if M_1 is not reduced.
(b) What essential property of the proposed isomorphism μ is now absent?

7.29. **(a)** Give an example that shows that the conclusion of Theorem 7.5 can be false if M_1 is not connected.
(b) What essential property of the proposed isomorphism μ is now absent?

7.30. **(a)** Give an example that shows that the conclusion of Theorem 7.5 can be false if M_2 is not reduced.
(b) What essential property of the proposed isomorphism μ is now absent?

7.31. **(a)** Give an example that shows that the conclusion of Theorem 7.5 can be false if M_2 is not connected.
(b) What essential property of the proposed isomorphism μ is now absent?

7.32. **(a)** Give an example of a FST A for which A is *not* reduced and A^c is not reduced.
(b) Give an example of a FST A for which A is *not* reduced and A^c *is* reduced.

7.33. Complete the proof of Theorem 7.4 by showing:
(a) $(\forall y \in \Sigma^*)(\forall \mathrm{t} \in S)(\overline{\omega}(\mathrm{t}, y) = \overline{\omega}_{\mathsf{E_M}}([\mathrm{t}]_{\mathsf{E_M}}, y))$.
(b) $\mathsf{M}/\mathsf{E_M}$ is equivalent to M.
(c) $\mathsf{M}/\mathsf{E_M}$ is reduced.
(d) If M is connected, then $\mathsf{M}/\mathsf{E_M}$ is connected.

7.34. Let $\Sigma = \{\mathbf{0}, \mathbf{1}\}$ and $\Gamma = \{\mathbf{y}, \mathbf{n}\}$.
(a) Define $f_1(\mathbf{a}_1\mathbf{a}_2\ldots\mathbf{a}_m) = \mathbf{y}^m$ if $\mathbf{a}_1 = \mathbf{1}$, and let $f_1(\mathbf{a}_1\mathbf{a}_2\ldots\mathbf{a}_m) = \mathbf{n}^m$ otherwise. Thus, $f_1(\mathbf{10}) = \mathbf{yy}$ and $f_1(\mathbf{0101}) = \mathbf{nnnn}$. Demonstrate that f_1 is FTD.
(b) Define $f_2(\mathbf{a}_1\mathbf{a}_2\ldots\mathbf{a}_m) = \mathbf{y}^m$ if $\mathbf{a}_m = \mathbf{1}$, and let $f_2(\mathbf{a}_1\mathbf{a}_2\ldots\mathbf{a}_m) = \mathbf{n}^m$ otherwise. Thus, $f_2(\mathbf{10}) = \mathbf{nn}$ and $f_2(\mathbf{0101}) = \mathbf{yyyy}$. Prove that f_2 is *not* FTD.

7.35. Let $\Sigma = \{\mathbf{a}, \mathbf{b}\}$ and $\Gamma = \{\mathbf{0}, \mathbf{1}\}$. Define $f_3(\mathbf{a}_1\mathbf{a}_2\ldots\mathbf{a}_m)$ to be the first m letters of the infinite sequence $\mathbf{010010001000010^5 10^6 10^7 10^8 1}\ldots$. Thus, $f_3(\mathbf{ababababab}) = \mathbf{0100100010}$ and $f_3(\mathbf{abbaa}) = \mathbf{01001}$. Argue that f_3 is *not* FTD.

7.36. Assume f is FTD. Prove that $(\forall x \in \Sigma^n)(\forall y \in \Sigma^*)(\forall z \in \Sigma^*)$ (the first n letters of $f(xy)$ must agree with the first n letters of $f(xz)$).

7.37. Consider an elevator in a building with two floors. Floor 1 has an up button **u** on the wall, floor two has a down button **d**, and there are buttons labeled **1** and **2** inside the elevator itself. The four actions taken by the elevator are close the doors, open the doors, go to floor 1, and go to floor 2. Assume that an inactive elevator will attempt to close the doors. For simplicity, assume that the model is not to incorporate sensors to test for improperly closed doors, nor are there buttons to hold the doors open, and the like. Also assume that when the elevator arrives on a given floor the call button for that floor is automatically deactivated, rather than modeling the shutoff as a component of the output.
(a) Define the input alphabet for this transducer (compare with Example 7.16).

(b) Define the output alphabet for this transducer.
(c) Define the Mealy sextuple that will model this elevator.
(d) Draw a Mealy machine that will model this elevator.
(e) Define the Moore sextuple that will model this elevator.
(f) Draw a Moore machine that will model this elevator.
(g) Without using <EOS> or <SOS>, draw a circuit that will implement the transducer defined in part (d).

7.38. Build a Mealy machine that will serve as a traffic signal controller for the intersection described in Example 7.16.

7.39. Consider the intersection described in Example 7.16 with walk signals added to the north–south crosswalks (only). As shown in Figure 7.19, there is an additional input sensor γ corresponding to the pedestrian walk button and an additional component of the output that will always be in one of two states (**W** for walk and **D** for don't walk). There are walk buttons at each of the corners, but they all trip the same single input sensor; similarly, the output for the walk light is displayed on each corner, but they all change at once and can be modeled as a single component. Assume that if the walk button is activated all traffic but that on the side street is stopped, and the walk lights change from **D** to **W**. Further assume that the walk lights revert to **D** and **W** before the side street light turns to yellow.

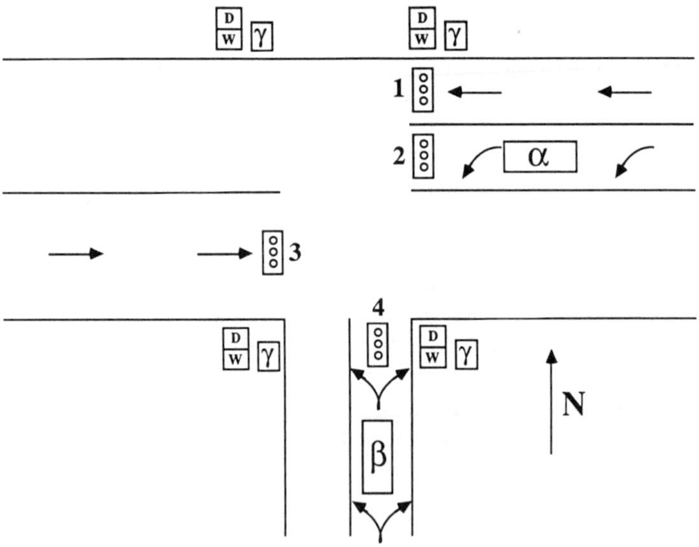

Figure 7.19 The intersection discussed in Exercise 7.39

(a) Define the new input and output alphabets.
(b) Draw a Moore machine that implements this scenario.
(c) Draw a Mealy machine that implements this scenario.

7.40. Consider an intersection similar to that described in Example 7.16, as shown in Figure 7.20. There are now four left-turn signals in addition to the four straight-ahead signals and additional input sensors γ and δ for the other left-turn lanes. Assume that a normal

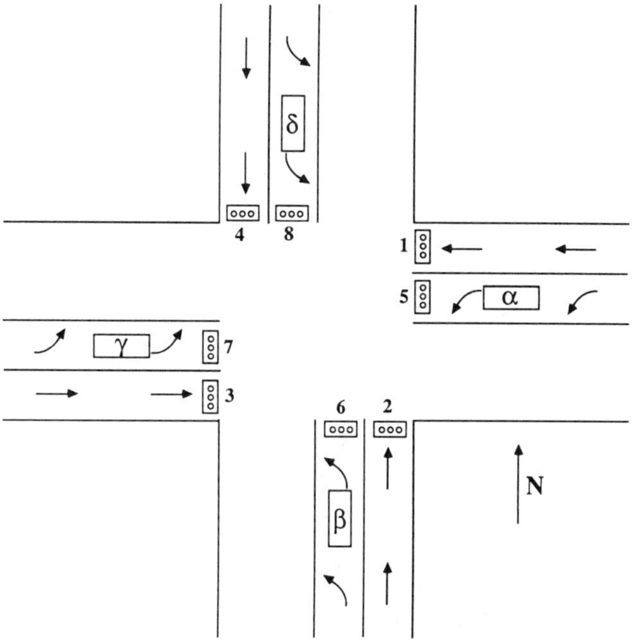

Figure 7.20 The intersection discussed in Exercise 7.40

alternation of straight-ahead traffic is carried out, with no left turns indicated unless the corresponding sensor is activated. Further assume that left-turn traffic will be allowed to precede the opposing traffic.

(a) Define the new input and output alphabets.

(b) Draw a Moore machine that implements this scenario.

(c) Draw a Mealy machine that implements this scenario.

7.41. Consider an adder similar to the one in Example 7.15, but which instead models addition in base 3.

(a) Define the input and output alphabets.

(b) Draw a Mealy machine that performs this addition.

(c) Draw a Moore machine that performs this addition.

(d) Draw a circuit that will implement the transducer built in part (b); use both <EOS> and <SOS>.

7.42. Consider an adder similar to the one in Example 7.15, but which models addition in base 10.

(a) Define the input and output alphabets.

(b) Define the sextuple of a Mealy machine that performs this addition (by indicating the output and transitions by concise formulas, rather than writing out the 200 entries in the tables).

(c) Define the sextuple of a Moore machine that performs this addition.

(d) Draw a circuit that will implement the transducer built in part (b); use both <EOS> and <SOS>.

7.43. Consider a function f_4 implementing addition in a manner similar to the function described by the transducer in Example 7.15, but that scans the characters (that is, columns of digits) from left to right (rather than right to left as in Example 7.15). Argue that f_4 is not FTD.

7.44. Given a MSM M, prove the following statements from Theorem 7.9:

(a) M/E_M is equivalent to M.

(b) M/E_M is reduced.

(c) If M is connected, so is M/E_M.

7.45. Given a FTD function f, prove that the minimal Moore machine corresponding to f must be reduced.

7.46. Given a MSM M, prove the following statements from Theorem 7.10:

(a) A necessary and sufficient condition for M to be minimal is that M is both reduced and connected.

(b) M^c/E_{M^c} is minimal.

7.47. Given MSMs $A = <\Sigma, \Gamma, S_A, s_{0_A}, \delta_A, \omega_A>$ and $B = <\Sigma, \Gamma, S_B, s_{0_B}, \delta_B, \omega_B>$, and a homomorphism μ: $S_A \rightarrow S_B$, prove the following statements from Lemma 7.5 and Corollary 7.9:

(a) $(\forall s \in S_A)(\forall x \in \Sigma^*)(\mu(\overline{\delta}_A(s, x)) = \overline{\delta}_B(\mu(s), x))$.

(b) $(\forall s \in S_A)(\forall x \in \Sigma^*)(\overline{\omega}_A(s, x) = \overline{\omega}_B(\mu(s), x)))$.

(c) A is equivalent to B; that is, $f_A = f_B$.

7.48. Prove Corollary 7.10.

7.49. Prove Corollary 7.11.

7.50. Given a FST $M = <\Sigma, \Gamma, S, s_0, \delta, \omega>$ and $M/E_M = <\Sigma, \Gamma, S_{E_M}, s_{0_{E_M}}, \delta_{E_M}, \omega_{E_M}>$ defined by

$$S_{E_M} = \{[s]_{E_M} \mid s \in S\}$$
$$s_{0_{E_M}} = [s_0]_{E_M}$$

δ_{E_M} is defined by

$$(\forall \mathbf{a} \in \Sigma)(\forall [s]_{E_M} \in S_{E_M})(\delta_{E_M}([s]_{E_M}, \mathbf{a}) = [\delta(s, \mathbf{a})]_{E_M})$$

and ω_{E_M} is defined by

$$(\forall \mathbf{a} \in \Sigma)(\forall [s]_{E_M} \in S_{E_M})(\omega_{E_M}([s]_{E_M}, \mathbf{a}) = \omega(s, \mathbf{a}))$$

(a) Show that δ_{E_M} is well defined.

(b) Show that ω_{E_M} is well defined.

7.51. Given a MSM $M = <\Sigma, \Gamma, S, s_0, \delta, \omega>$ and $M/E_M = <\Sigma, \Gamma, S_{E_M}, s_{0_{E_M}}, \delta_{E_M}, \omega_{E_M}>$ defined by

$$S_{E_M} = \{[s]_{E_M} \mid s \in S\}$$
$$s_{0_{E_M}} = [s_0]_{E_M}$$

δ_{E_M} is defined by

$$(\forall \mathbf{a} \in \Sigma)(\forall [s]_{E_M} \in S_{E_M})(\delta_{E_M}([s]_{E_M}, \mathbf{a}) = [\delta(s, \mathbf{a})]_{E_M})$$

and ω_{E_M} is defined by

$$(\forall [s]_{E_M} \in S_{E_M})(\omega_{E_M}([s]_{E_M}) = \omega(s))$$

(a) Show that δ_{E_M} is well defined.

(b) Show that ω_{E_M} is well defined.

7.52. Consider the following assertion: If there is an isomorphism from A to B and A is connected, then B must also be connected.

(a) Prove that this is true for isomorphisms between Mealy machines.

(b) Prove that this is true for isomorphisms between Moore machines.

7.53. Consider the following assertion: If there is an isomorphism from A to B and B is connected, then A must also be connected.

(a) Prove that this is true for isomorphisms between Mealy machines.

(b) Prove that this is true for isomorphisms between Moore machines.

7.54. Consider the following assertion: If there is a homomorphism from A to B and A is connected, then B must also be connected.

(a) Give an example of two Mealy machines for which this assertion is false.

(b) Give an example of two Moore machines for which this assertion is false.

7.55. Consider the following assertion: If there is a homomorphism from A to B and B is connected, then A must also be connected.

(a) Give an example of two Mealy machines for which this assertion is false.

(b) Give an example of two Moore machines for which this assertion is false.

7.56. Assume A and B are connected FSTs and that there exists an isomorphism ψ from A to B and an isomorphism μ from B to A. Prove that $\psi = \mu^{-1}$.

7.57. Assume A and B are FSTs and there exists an isomorphism ψ from A to B and an isomorphism μ from B to A. Give an example for which $\psi \neq \mu^{-1}$.

7.58. Give an example of a three-state MSM for which E_{0A} has only one equivalence class. Is it possible for E_{0A} to be different from E_{1A} in such a machine? Explain.

7.59. **(a)** Give an example of a Mealy machine for which M is *not* connected and M/E_M is not connected.

(b) Give an example of a Mealy machine for which M is *not* connected but M/E_M *is* connected.

7.60. **(a)** Give an example of a Moore machine for which M is *not* connected and M/E_M is not connected.

(b) Give an example of a Moore machine for which M is *not* connected but M/E_M *is* connected.

7.61. For a homomorphism $\mu: S_A \to S_B$ between two Mealy machines

$$A = <\Sigma, \Gamma, S_A, s_{0_A}, \delta_A, \omega_A> \quad \text{and} \quad B = <\Sigma, \Gamma, S_B, s_{0_B}, \delta_B, \omega_B>,$$

prove $(\forall s, t \in S_A)(\mu(s)\, E_B\, \mu(t) \Leftrightarrow s\, E_A\, t)$.

7.62. For a homomorphism $\mu: S_A \to S_B$ between two Moore machines

$$A = <\Sigma, \Gamma, S_A, s_{0_A}, \delta_A, \omega_A> \quad \text{and} \quad B = <\Sigma, \Gamma, S_B, s_{0_B}, \delta_B, \omega_B>,$$

prove $(\forall s, t \in S_A)(\mu(s)\, E_B\, \mu(t) \Leftrightarrow s\, E_A\, t)$.

7.63. **(a)** Give an example of a FST for which A is *not* reduced and A^c is not reduced.

(b) Give an example of a FST for which A is *not* reduced and A^c *is* reduced.

7.64. **(a)** Give an example of a MSM for which A is *not* reduced and A^c is not reduced.

(b) Give an example of a MSM for which A is *not* reduced and A^c *is* reduced.

7.65. Isomorphism ($\cong$) is a relation in the set of all Mealy machines.

(a) Prove that $\cong$ is a symmetric relation; that is, formally justify that if there is an isomorphism from A to B then there is an isomorphism from B to A.

(b) Prove that $\cong$ is a reflexive relation.

(c) Show that if f and g are isomorphisms, then $f \circ g$ is also an isomorphism (whenever $f \circ g$ is defined).

(d) From the results of parts (a), (b), and (c) given above, prove that $\cong$ is an equivalence relation over the set of all Mealy machines.

(e) Show that homomorphism is *not* an equivalence relation over the set of all Mealy machines.

7.66. **(a)** Prove that $\cong$ is an equivalence relation in the set of all Moore machines.

(b) Show that homomorphism is *not* an equivalence relation over the set of all Moore machines.

7.67. Given a Mealy machine $M = <\Sigma, \Gamma, S, s_0, \delta, \omega>$, prove that there exists a homomorphism μ from M to M/E_M.

7.68. Given a Moore machine $M = <\Sigma, \Gamma, S, s_0, \delta, \omega>$, prove that there exists a homomorphism μ from M to M/E_M.

7.69. Consider the intersection presented in Example 7.16 and note that the construction presented in Figure 7.15 prevents the transducer from leaving s_2 or s_6 while the appropriate sensor is active. The length of time spent in each output configuration can be limited by replacing s_2 with a sequence of states that ensures that the output configuration will change within, say, three clock cycles (this is similar to the spirit in which s_8 was added). A similar expansion can be made with regard to s_6. While this would not be a likely problem if the side street were not heavily traveled, higher traffic situations would require a different solution than that shown in Figure 7.15.

(a) Modify Figure 7.15 so that the output configuration can, if necessary, remain at $\langle R, R, R, G \rangle$ for three clock cycles, but not for four clock cycles.

(b) Starting with the larger transducer found in part (a), make a similar expansion to s_6.

(c) Starting with the larger transducer found in part (a), make an expansion to s_6 in such a way that the left-turn signal is guaranteed to be green for a minimum of two clock cycles and a maximum of four clock cycles.

7.70. Consider the intersection presented in Example 7.16 and note that the construction presented in Figure 7.15 prevents the transducer from returning to s_0 while either of the sensors is active. Thus, even if the length of time spent in each output configuration was limited (see Exercise 7.69), left-turn and northbound traffic could perpetually alternate without ever allowing the east–west traffic to resume. This would not be a likely problem if the side street were not heavily traveled, but higher traffic situations would require a different solution than the one presented in Example 7.16.

(a) Without adding any states to Figure 7.15, modify the state transition diagram so that east–west traffic will receive a green light occasionally.

(b) By adding new states to Figure 7.15 (to remember the last lanes that had the right of way), implement a controller that will ensure that no lane will get a second green light if any other lane that has an active sensor has yet to receive a green light. (It may be helpful to think of the east–west traffic as having an implicit sensor that is always actively demanding service).

7.71. Prove that if two Moore machines are homomorphic then they are equivalent.

7.72. Show that, for any FTD function f: $\Sigma^* \to \Sigma^*$, $\mathfrak{D}_\Sigma$ is closed under f.

CHAPTER

8

REGULAR GRAMMARS

In the preceding chapters, we have seen several ways to characterize the set of FAD languages: via DFAs, NDFAs, right congruences, and regular expressions. In this chapter we will look at still another way to represent this class, using the concept of *grammars*. This construct is very powerful, and many restrictions must be placed on the general definition of a grammar in order to limit the scope to FAD languages. The very restrictive *regular* grammars will be explored in full detail in this chapter. The more robust classes of grammars introduced here will be discussed at length in later chapters.

8.1 OVERVIEW OF THE GRAMMAR HIERARCHY

Much like the rules given in Backus–Naur Form (BNF) in Chapters 0 and 1, the language-defining power of a grammar stems from the generation of strings through the successive replacement of symbols in a partially constructed string. These replacement rules form the foundation for the definition of programming languages and are used in compiler construction not only to determine correct syntax, but also to help determine the *meaning* of the statements and thereby guide the translation of a program into machine language.

EXAMPLE 8.1

A BNF that describes the set of all valid FORTRAN identifiers is given below. Recall that such identifiers must begin with a letter and be followed by no more than five other letters and numerals. These criteria can be specified by the following set of rules.

$$S ::= \mathbf{a}S_1 | \mathbf{b}S_1 | \ldots | \mathbf{z}S_1 | \mathbf{a} | \mathbf{b} | \ldots | \mathbf{z}$$

$$S_1 ::= \mathbf{a}S_2 | \mathbf{b}S_2 | \ldots | \mathbf{z}S_2 | \mathbf{a} | \mathbf{b} | \ldots | \mathbf{z} | \mathbf{0}S_2 | \mathbf{1}S_2 | \mathbf{2}S_2 | \ldots | \mathbf{9}S_2 | \mathbf{0} | \mathbf{1} | \mathbf{2} | \ldots | \mathbf{9}$$

$$S_2 ::= \mathbf{a}S_3 | \mathbf{b}S_3 | \ldots | \mathbf{z}S_3 | \mathbf{a} | \mathbf{b} | \ldots | \mathbf{z} | \mathbf{0}S_3 | \mathbf{1}S_3 | \mathbf{2}S_3 | \ldots | \mathbf{9}S_3 | \mathbf{0} | \mathbf{1} | \mathbf{2} | \ldots | \mathbf{9}$$

$$S_3 ::= \mathbf{a}S_4 | \mathbf{b}S_4 | \ldots | \mathbf{z}S_4 | \mathbf{a} | \mathbf{b} | \ldots | \mathbf{z} | \mathbf{0}S_4 | \mathbf{1}S_4 | \mathbf{2}S_4 | \ldots | \mathbf{9}S_4 | \mathbf{0} | \mathbf{1} | \mathbf{2} | \ldots | \mathbf{9}$$

$$S_4 ::= \mathbf{a}S_5 | \mathbf{b}S_5 | \ldots | \mathbf{z}S_5 | \mathbf{a} | \mathbf{b} | \ldots | \mathbf{z} | \mathbf{0}S_5 | \mathbf{1}S_5 | \mathbf{2}S_5 | \ldots | \mathbf{9}S_5 | \mathbf{0} | \mathbf{1} | \mathbf{2} | \ldots | \mathbf{9}$$

$$S_5 ::= \mathbf{a} | \mathbf{b} | \ldots | \mathbf{z} | \mathbf{0} | \mathbf{1} | \mathbf{2} | \ldots | \mathbf{9}$$

The first rule specifies that S can be replaced by any of the 26 letters of the Roman alphabet or any such letter followed by the token S_1. These *productions* (rules) do indeed define the variable names found in FORTRAN programs. Starting with S, a derivation might proceed as $S \Rightarrow \mathbf{s}S_1 \Rightarrow \mathbf{su}S_2 \Rightarrow \mathbf{sum}$, indicating that **sum** is a valid FORTRAN identifier. Invalid identifiers, such as **2a**, cannot be derived from these productions by starting with S.

EXAMPLE 8.2

The strings used to represent regular sets (see Chapter 6) could have been succinctly specified using BNF. Recall that regular languages over, say, {**a**, **b**, **c**} are described by regular expressions. These regular expressions were strings over the alphabet {**∅**, **ϵ**, **a**, **b**, **c**, ∪, •, *,), (}, and the formal definition was quite complex. A regular expression over {**a**, **b**, **c**} was defined to be a sequence of symbols formed by repeated application of the following rules:

- **i.** **a**, **b**, **c** are each regular expressions.
- **ii.** ∅ is a regular expression.
- **iii.** ϵ is a regular expression.
- **iv.** If R_1 and R_2 are regular expressions, then so is $(R_1 \cdot R_2)$.
- **v.** If R_1 and R_2 are regular expressions, then so is $(R_1 \cup R_2)$.
- **vi.** If R_1 is a regular expression, then so is R_1^*.

The conditions set forth above could have instead been succinctly specified by the BNF shown below.

$$R ::= \mathbf{a} | \mathbf{b} | \mathbf{c} | \boldsymbol{\epsilon} | \boldsymbol{\emptyset} | \mathbf{(}R\mathbf{\cdot}R\mathbf{)} | \mathbf{(}R\mathbf{\cup}R\mathbf{)} | R\mathbf{*}$$

The following is a typical derivation, culminating in the regular expression **(a•(c∪ϵ))***.

$$\begin{aligned} R &\Rightarrow R\mathbf{*} \\ &\Rightarrow \mathbf{(}R\mathbf{\cdot}R\mathbf{)*} \\ &\Rightarrow \mathbf{(a\cdot}R\mathbf{)*} \\ &\Rightarrow \mathbf{(a\cdot(}R\mathbf{\cup}R\mathbf{))*} \end{aligned}$$

$$\Rightarrow (\mathbf{a}\bullet(\mathbf{c}\cup R))^*$$

$$\Rightarrow (\mathbf{a}\bullet(\mathbf{c}\cup\epsilon))^*$$

Note that in the intermediate steps of the derivation we do not wish to consider strings such as **(a•**R**)*** to be valid regular expressions. **(a•**R**)*** is not a string over the alphabet {**∅, ϵ, a, b, c, ∪, •, *,), (**}, and it does not represent a regular language over {**a, b, c**}. To generate a valid regular expression, the derivation *must* proceed until all occurrences of R are removed. To differentiate between the symbols that may remain and those that must be replaced, grammars divide the tokens into *terminal* symbols and *nonterminal* symbols, respectively.

The following notational conventions will be used throughout the remainder of the text. Members of Σ will be represented by lowercase roman letters such as **a**, **b**, **c**, **d** and will be referred to as *terminal symbols*. A new alphabet Ω will be introduced, and its members will be represented by uppercase roman letters such as A, B, C, and S, and these will be called *nonterminal symbols*. S will often denote a special nonterminal, called the *start* symbol. The specification of the production rules will be somewhat different from the BNF examples given above. The common grammatical notation for rules such as $S ::= \mathbf{a}S_1$ and $S ::= \mathbf{b}S_1$ is $S \to \mathbf{a}S_1$ and $S \to \mathbf{b}S_1$. As with BNF, a convenient shorthand notation for a group of productions involves the use of the | (*or*) symbol. The productions Z→**aa**B, Z→**ac**, Z→**cb**T, which all denote replacements for Z, could be succinctly represented by Z→**aa**B|**ac**|**cb**T.

A production can be thought of as a replacement rule; that is, A→**cdba** indicates that occurrences of the (nonterminal) A can be replaced by the string **cdba**. For example, the string **ab**B<u>A</u>**d**B**c** can be transformed into the string **ab**B<u>**cdba**</u>**d**B**c** by applying the production A→**cdba**; we will write

abBA**d**B**c**⇒**ab**B**cdbad**B**c**,

and say that **ab**B**cdbad**B**c** was derived (in one step) from **ab**BA**d**B**c**. Productions may be applied in succession; for example, if both A→**cdba** and B→**ef**B were available, then the following modifications of the string **ab**BA**d**B**c** would be possible: **ab**BA**d**B**c**⇒**ab**B**cdbad**B**c**⇒**abef**B**cdbad**B**c**⇒**abefef**B**cdbad**B**c**, and we might write **ab**BA**d**B**c**$\overline{\Rightarrow}$**abefef**B**cdbad**B**c** to indicate that **ab**BA**d**B**c** can produce **abefef**B**cdbad**B**c** in zero or more steps (three steps in this case). Note that the distinction between ⇒ and $\overline{\Rightarrow}$ is reminiscent of the difference between the state transition functions δ and $\overline{\delta}$. As with the distinction between the transducer output functions ω and $\overline{\omega}$, the overbar is meant to indicate the result of successive applications of the underlying operation. The symbol $\overset{*}{\Rightarrow}$ is often used in place of $\overline{\Rightarrow}$.

As illustrated by Example 8.1, several nonterminals may be used in the grammar. The set of nonterminals in the grammar given for FORTRAN identifiers was comprised of $\{S, S_1, S_2, S_3, S_4, S_5\}$. The start symbol designates which of these nonterminals should always be used to begin derivations.

The previous examples discussed in this section have illustrated all the essential components of a grammar. A grammar must specify the terminal alphabet, the set of intermediary nonterminal symbols, and the designated start symbol, and it must also enumerate the set of rules for replacing phrases within a derivation with other phrases. In the above examples, the productions have all involved the replacement of single nonterminals with other strings. In an unrestricted grammar, a general replacement rule may allow an entire string α to be replaced by another string β. Thus, **aBcD** $\rightarrow$ **beA** would be a legal production, and thus whenever the sequence **aBcD** is found within a derivation it can be replaced by the shorter string **beA**.

∇ **Definition 8.1.** An *unrestricted* or *type 0 grammar* over an alphabet Σ is a quadruple $G = \langle \Omega, \Sigma, S, P \rangle$, where:

Ω is a (nonempty) set of *nonterminals*.

Σ is a (nonempty) set of *terminal symbols* (and $\Omega \cap \Sigma = \emptyset$).

S is the designated *start symbol* (and $S \in \Omega$).

P is a set of *productions* of the form $\alpha \rightarrow \beta$, where $\alpha \in (\Omega \cup \Sigma)^+$, $\beta \in (\Omega \cup \Sigma)^*$.

Δ

EXAMPLE 8.3

Consider the grammar

$$G'' = \langle \{A, B, S, T\}, \{\mathbf{a}, \mathbf{b}, \mathbf{c}\}, S, \{S \rightarrow \mathbf{a}S B\mathbf{c}, S \rightarrow T, T \rightarrow \lambda, TB \rightarrow \mathbf{b}T, \mathbf{c}B \rightarrow B\mathbf{c}\} \rangle$$

A typical derivation, starting from the start state S, would be:

$$\begin{aligned}
S &\Rightarrow \text{(by applying } S \rightarrow \mathbf{a}SB\mathbf{c}) \\
\mathbf{a}SB\mathbf{c} &\Rightarrow \text{(by applying } S \rightarrow \mathbf{a}SB\mathbf{c}) \\
\mathbf{aa}SB\mathbf{c}B\mathbf{c} &\Rightarrow \text{(by applying } S \rightarrow T) \\
\mathbf{aa}TB\mathbf{c}B\mathbf{c} &\Rightarrow \text{(by applying } TB \rightarrow \mathbf{b}T) \\
\mathbf{aab}T\mathbf{c}B\mathbf{c} &\Rightarrow \text{(by applying } \mathbf{c}B \rightarrow B\mathbf{c}) \\
\mathbf{aab}TB\mathbf{cc} &\Rightarrow \text{(by applying } TB \rightarrow \mathbf{b}T) \\
\mathbf{aabb}T\mathbf{cc} &\Rightarrow \text{(by applying } T \rightarrow \lambda) \\
&\mathbf{aabbcc}
\end{aligned}$$

Depending on how many times the production $S \rightarrow \mathbf{a}SB\mathbf{c}$ is used, this grammar will generate strings such as λ, **abc**, **aabbcc**, and **aaabbbccc**. The set of strings that can be generated by this particular grammar is $\{\mathbf{a}^i\mathbf{b}^i\mathbf{c}^i \mid i \geq 0\}$. In this sense, each grammar defines a *language*. Specifically, we require that derivations start with the designated start symbol and proceed until only members of Σ remain in the resulting string.

∇ **Definition 8.2.** Given a grammar $G = <\Omega, \Sigma, S, P>$, the *language generated by* G, denoted by $L(G)$, is given by $L(G) = \{x \mid x \in \Sigma^* \wedge S \overset{*}{\Rightarrow} x\}$.
Δ

A language that can be defined by a type 0 grammar is called a *type 0 language*. Thus, as shown by the grammar G″ given in Example 8.3, $L(G'') = \{\mathbf{a}^i\mathbf{b}^i\mathbf{c}^i \mid i \geq 0\}$ is a type 0 language.

The way grammars define languages is fundamentally different from the way automata define languages. An automaton is a *cognitive* device, in that it is used to directly decide whether a given string should be accepted into the language. In contrast, a grammar is a *generative* device: the productions specify how to generate all the words in the language represented by the grammar, but do not provide an obvious means of determining whether a given string can be generated by those rules. There are many applications in which it is important to be able to determine whether a given string can be generated by a particular grammar, and the task of obtaining cognitive answers from a generative construct will be addressed at several points later in the text. The reverse transformation, that is, producing an automaton that recognizes exactly those strings that are generated by a given grammar, is addressed in the next section.

The distinction between generative and cognitive approaches to representing languages has been explored previously, when regular expressions were considered in Chapter 6. Regular expressions are also a generative construct, in the sense that a regular expression can be used to begin to enumerate the words in the corresponding regular set. As is the case with grammars, it is inconvenient to use regular expressions in a cognitive fashion: it may be difficult to tell whether a given string is among those represented by a particular regular expression. Chapter 6 therefore explored ways to transform a regular expression into a corresponding automaton. It is likewise feasible to define corresponding automata for certain grammars (see Lemma 8.2). However, Example 8.3 illustrated that some grammars produce non-FAD languages and therefore cannot possibly be represented by deterministic finite automata. The translation from a mechanical representation of a language to a grammatical representation is always successful, in that every automaton has a corresponding grammar (Lemma 8.1). This result is similar to Theorem 6.3, which showed that every automaton has a corresponding regular expression.

Note that in Example 8.3 the only production that specified that a string be replaced by a shorter string was $T \to \lambda$. Consequently, the length of the derived string either increased or remained constant except where this last production was applied. Rules such as $\mathbf{a}B\mathbf{c}D \to \mathbf{be}A$, in which four symbols are replaced by only three, will at least momentarily decrease the length of the string. Such productions are called *contracting* productions. Grammars that satisfy the added requirement that no production may decrease the length of the derivation are called *context sensitive*. Such grammars cannot generate as many languages as the unrestricted grammars, but they have the added advantage of allowing derivations to proceed in a more predictable manner. Programming languages are explicitly designed to ensure that they can be represented by grammars that are context sensitive.

∇ **Definition 8.3.** A *pure context-sensitive grammar* over an alphabet Σ is a quadruple $G = <\Omega, \Sigma, S, P>$, where:

> Ω is a (nonempty) set of *nonterminals*.
> Σ is a (nonempty) set of *terminal symbols* (and $\Omega \cap \Sigma = \emptyset$).
> S is the designated *start symbol* (and $S \in \Omega$).
> P is a set of *productions* of the form $\alpha \to \beta$, where $\alpha \in (\Omega \cup \Sigma)^+$, $\beta \in (\Omega \cup \Sigma)^+$, and $|\alpha| \leq |\beta|$.

Δ

In a derivation in a context-sensitive grammar, if $S \Rightarrow x_1 \Rightarrow x_2 \Rightarrow \cdots \Rightarrow x_n$, then we are assured that $1 = |S| \leq |x_1| \leq |x_2| \leq \cdots \leq |x_n|$. Unfortunately, this means that in a pure context-sensitive grammar it is impossible to begin with the start symbol (which has length 1) and derive the empty string (which is of length 0).

EXAMPLE 8.4

Languages that contain λ, such as $\{\mathbf{a}^i\mathbf{b}^i\mathbf{c}^i \mid i \geq 0\}$ generated in Example 8.3 by the unrestricted grammar G″, cannot possibly be represented by a pure context-sensitive grammar. However, the empty string is actually the only impediment to finding an alternative collection of productions that all satisfy the condition $|\alpha| \leq |\beta|$. The language $\{\mathbf{a}^i\mathbf{b}^i\mathbf{c}^i \mid i \geq 1\}$ can be represented by a pure context-sensitive grammar, as illustrated by the following grammar. Let G be given by

$$G = <\{A, B, S, T\}, \{\mathbf{a}, \mathbf{b}, \mathbf{c}\}, S, \{S \to \mathbf{a}S\mathrm{B}\mathbf{c}, S \to \mathbf{a}T\mathbf{c}, T \to \mathbf{b}, TB \to \mathbf{b}T, \mathbf{c}B \to B\mathbf{c}\}>$$

The derivation to produce **aabbcc** would now be

$$S \Rightarrow \text{(by applying } S \to \mathbf{a}S\mathrm{B}\mathbf{c})$$
$$\mathbf{a}S\mathrm{B}\mathbf{c} \Rightarrow \text{(by applying } S \to \mathbf{a}T\mathbf{c})$$
$$\mathbf{aa}T\mathbf{c}B\mathbf{c} \Rightarrow \text{(by applying } \mathbf{c}B \to B\mathbf{c})$$
$$\mathbf{aa}TB\mathbf{cc} \Rightarrow \text{(by applying } TB \to \mathbf{b}T)$$
$$\mathbf{aab}T\mathbf{cc} \Rightarrow \text{(by applying } T \to \mathbf{b})$$
$$\mathbf{aabbcc}$$

The shortest string derivable by G is $S \Rightarrow \mathbf{a}T\mathbf{c} \Rightarrow \mathbf{abc}$. In Example 8.3, the shortest derivation was $S \Rightarrow T \Rightarrow \lambda$.

Any pure context-sensitive grammar can be modified to include λ by adding a new start state Z and two new productions $Z \to \lambda$ and $Z \to S$, where S was the original start state. Such grammars and their resulting languages are generally referred to as *type 1* or *context sensitive.*

∇ **Definition 8.4.** A *context-sensitive* or *type 1 grammar* over an alphabet Σ is either a pure context-sensitive grammar or a quadruple

$$G' = <\Omega \cup \{Z\}, \Sigma, Z, P \cup \{Z \to \lambda, A \to S\}>,$$

where $G = <\Omega, \Sigma, S, P>$ is a pure context-sensitive grammar and $Z \notin \Omega \cup \Sigma$.
Δ

The only production $\alpha \to \beta$ that violates the condition $|\alpha| \leq |\beta|$ is $Z \to \lambda$, and this production cannot play a part in any derivation other than $Z \Rightarrow \lambda$. From the start symbol Z, the application $Z \to \lambda$ immediately ends the derivation (producing λ), while the application of $Z \to S$ will provide no further opportunity to use $Z \to \lambda$, since the requirement that $Z \notin \Omega \cup \Sigma$ means that the other productions will never allow Z to reappear in the derivation. Thus, G′ enhances the generating power of G only to the extent that G′ can produce λ. Every string in $L(G)$ can be derived from the productions of G′, and G′ generates no new strings besides λ. This argument essentially proves that $L(G') = L(G) \cup \{\lambda\}$ (see the exercises).

EXAMPLE 8.5

The language generated by G″ in Example 8.3 was $L(G'') = \{\mathbf{a}^i\mathbf{b}^i\mathbf{c}^i \mid i \geq 0\}$. Since $L(G'')$ is $\{\mathbf{a}^i\mathbf{b}^i\mathbf{c}^i \mid i \geq 1\} \cup \{\lambda\}$, it can therefore be represented by a context-sensitive grammar by modifying the pure context-sensitive grammar in Example 8.4. Let G′ be given by

$$G' = <\{A, B, S, T, Z\}, \{\mathbf{a}, \mathbf{b}, \mathbf{c}\}, Z, \{S \to \mathbf{a}S B\mathbf{c}, S \to \mathbf{a}T\mathbf{c}, T \to \mathbf{b}, TB \to \mathbf{b}T, \mathbf{c}B \to B\mathbf{c}, Z \to \lambda, Z \to S\}>$$

The derivation to produce **aabbcc** would now be

$$\begin{aligned} Z &\Rightarrow \text{(by applying } Z \to S) \\ S &\Rightarrow \text{(by applying } S \to \mathbf{a}S B\mathbf{c}) \\ \mathbf{a}SB\mathbf{c} &\Rightarrow \text{(by applying } S \to \mathbf{a}T\mathbf{c}) \\ \mathbf{aa}T\mathbf{c}B\mathbf{c} &\Rightarrow \text{(by applying } \mathbf{c}B \to B\mathbf{c}) \\ \mathbf{aa}TB\mathbf{cc} &\Rightarrow \text{(by applying } TB \to \mathbf{b}T) \\ \mathbf{aab}T\mathbf{cc} &\Rightarrow \text{(by applying } T \to \mathbf{b}) \\ \mathbf{aabbcc} & \end{aligned}$$

This grammar does produce λ, and all other derivations are strictly length-increasing. Note that this was not the case in the grammar G″ in Example 8.3. The last step of the derivation shown there transformed a string of length 7 into a string of length 6. G″ does not satisfy the definition of a context-sensitive grammar; even though only T could produce λ, T could occur later in the derivation. The presence of T at later steps destroys the desirable property of having all other derivations strictly length-increasing at each step. Definition 8.4 is constructed to ensure that the start symbol Z can never appear in a later derivation step.

The restriction of productions to nondecreasing length reduces the number of languages that can be generated; as discussed in later chapters, there exist type 0 languages that cannot be generated by any type 1 grammar. The restriction also allows arguments about the derivation process to proceed by induction on the number of symbols in the resulting terminal string and is crucial to the development of *normal forms* for context-sensitive grammars.

We have already seen examples of different grammars generating the same set of words, as in the grammars G″ and G′ from Examples 8.3 and 8.5. The term context sensitive comes from the fact that context-sensitive languages (that is, type 1 languages) can be represented by grammars in which the productions are all of the form $\alpha B\gamma \to \alpha\beta\gamma$, where a single nonterminal B is replaced by the string β in the *context* of the strings α on the left and γ on the right. Specialized grammars such as these, in which there are restrictions on the form of the productions, are examples of *normal forms* and are discussed later in the text.

If the productions in a grammar all imply that single nonterminals can be replaced without regard to the context, then the grammar is called *context free*. In essence, this means that all productions are of the form $A \to \beta$, where the left side is just a single nonterminal and the right side is an arbitrary string. The resulting languages are also called *type 2* or *context free*.

∇ **Definition 8.5.** A *pure context-free grammar* over an alphabet Σ is a quadruple $G = \langle \Omega, \Sigma, S, P \rangle$, where:

Ω is a (nonempty) set of *nonterminals*.

Σ is a (nonempty) set of *terminal symbols* (and $\Omega \cap \Sigma = \emptyset$).

S is the designated *start symbol* (and $S \in \Omega$).

P is a set of *productions* of the form $A \to \beta$, where $A \in \Omega$, $\beta \in (\Omega \cup \Sigma)^+$.

Δ

Note that since the length of the left side of a context-free production is 1 and the right side cannot be empty, pure context-free grammars have no contracting productions and are therefore pure context-sensitive grammars. As with pure context-sensitive grammars, pure context-free grammars cannot generate languages that contain the empty string.

∇ **Definition 8.6.** A *context-free* or *type 2 grammar* over an alphabet Σ is either a pure context-free grammar or a quadruple

$$G' = \langle \Omega \cup \{Z\}, \Sigma, Z, P \cup \{Z \to \lambda, Z \to S\} \rangle,$$

where $G = <\Omega, \Sigma, S, P>$ is a pure context-free grammar and $Z \notin \Omega \cup \Sigma$.
Δ

Productions of the form $C \to \beta$ are called *C-rules*. As was done with context-sensitive grammars, this definition uses a new start state Z to avoid all such length-decreasing productions except for a single one of the form $Z \to \lambda$, which is used only for generating the empty string. Type 2 languages will therefore always be type 1 languages. Note that the definition ensures that the only production that can decrease the length of a derivation must be the Z-rule $Z \to \lambda$.

The grammar corresponding to the BNF given in Example 8.2 would be a context-free grammar, and thus the collection of all regular expressions is a type 2 language. The grammar given in Example 8.4 is not context free due to the presence of the production $\mathbf{c}B \to B\mathbf{c}$, but this does not yield sufficient evidence to claim that the resulting language $\{\mathbf{a}^i\mathbf{b}^i\mathbf{c}^i \mid i \geq 1\}$ is not a context-free language. To support this claim, it must be shown that *no* type 2 grammar can generate this language. A pumping lemma for context-free languages will be presented in Chapter 10 to provide a tool for measuring the complexity of such languages. Just as there are type 1 languages that are not type 2, there are type 0 languages that are not type 1.

Note that even these very restrictive type 2 grammars can produce languages that are not FAD. As shown in Example 8.2, the language consisting of the collection of all strings representing regular expressions is context free. However, this collection is *not* FAD, since it is clear that the pumping lemma (Theorem 2.3) would show that a DFA could not hope to correctly match up unlimited pairs of parentheses.

Consequently, even more severe restrictions must be placed on grammars if they are to have generative powers similar to the cognitive powers of a deterministic finite automaton. The type 3 grammars explored in the next section are precisely what is required. It will follow from the definitions that all type 3 languages are type 2. It is likewise clear that all type 2 languages must be type 1, and every type 1 language is type 0. Thus, a *hierarchy* of languages is formed, from the most restrictive type 3 languages to the most robust type 0 languages. The four classes of languages are distinct; there are type 2 languages that are not type 3 (for example, Example 8.2), type 1 languages that are not type 2 (see Chapter 9), and type 0 languages that are not type 1 (see Chapter 12).

8.2 RIGHT-LINEAR GRAMMARS AND AUTOMATA

The grammatical classes described in Section 8.1 are each capable of generating all the FAD languages; indeed, they even generate languages that cannot be recognized by finite automata. This section will explore a class of grammars that generate the class of regular languages: every FAD language can be generated by one of the right-linear grammars defined below, and yet no right-linear grammar can generate a non-FAD language.

∇ **Definition 8.7.** A *right-linear grammar* over an alphabet Σ is a quadruple $G = <\Omega, \Sigma, S, P>$, where

Ω is a (nonempty) set of *nonterminals*.

Σ is a (nonempty) set of *terminal symbols* (and $\Omega \cap \Sigma = \emptyset$).

S is the designated *start symbol* (and $S \in \Omega$).

P is a set of *productions* of the form $A \to xB$, where $A \in \Omega$, $B \in (\Omega \cup \lambda)$, and $x \in \Sigma^*$.

Δ

Right-linear grammars belong to the class of type 3 grammars and generate all the type 3 languages. Grammars that are right linear are very restrictive; only one nonterminal can appear, and it must appear at the very end of the expression. Consequently, in the course of a derivation, new terminals appear only on the right end of the developing string, and the only time the string might shrink in size is when a (final) production of the form $A \to \lambda$ is applied. A right-linear grammar may have several contracting productions that produce λ and may not strictly conform with the definition of a context-free grammar. However, Corollary 8.3 will show that every type 3 language is a type 2 language.

Right-linear grammars generate words in the same fashion as the grammars defined in Section 8.1. The following definition of *derivation* is tailored to right-linear grammars, but it can easily be generalized to less restrictive grammars (see Chapter 9).

∇ **Definition 8.8.** Let $G = <\Omega, \Sigma, S, P>$ be a right-linear grammar, $y \in \Sigma^*$, and $A \to xB$ be a production in P. We will say that yxB can be *directly derived* from yA by applying the production $A \to xB$, and write $yA \Rightarrow yxB$. Furthermore, if

$$(x_1A_1 \Rightarrow x_2A_2) \wedge (x_2A_2 \Rightarrow x_3A_3) \wedge \cdots \wedge (x_{n-1}A_{n-1} \Rightarrow x_nA_n),$$

where $x_i \in \Sigma^*$ for $i = 1, 2, \ldots, n$, $A_i \in \Omega$ for $i = 1, 2, \ldots, n-1$, and $A_n \in (\Omega \cup \lambda)$, then we will say that x_1A_1 *derives* x_nA_n, and write $x_1A_1 \overset{*}{\Rightarrow} x_nA_n$.

Δ

While the symbol $\overline{\Rightarrow}$ might be more consistent with our previous extension notations, $\overset{*}{\Rightarrow}$ is most commonly used in the literature.

EXAMPLE 8.6

Let $G_1 = <\{T, S\}, \{\mathbf{a}, \mathbf{b}\}, S, \{S \to \mathbf{a}S, S \to \mathbf{b}T, T \to \mathbf{aa}\}>$. Then $S \overset{*}{\Rightarrow} \mathbf{aabaa}$, since by Definition 8.2, with $x_1 = \lambda$, $x_2 = \mathbf{a}$, $x_3 = \mathbf{aa}$, $x_4 = \mathbf{aab}$, $x_5 = \mathbf{aabaa}$, $A_1 = A_2 = A_3 = S$, $A_4 = T$, and $A_5 = \lambda$.

$$S \Rightarrow \mathbf{a}S \text{(by applying } S \to \mathbf{a}S)$$

$$\Rightarrow \mathbf{aa}S \text{(by applying } S \to \mathbf{a}S)$$

$$\Rightarrow \mathbf{aab}\mathrm{T}(\text{by applying } \mathrm{S} \to \mathbf{b}\mathrm{T})$$

$$\Rightarrow \mathbf{aabaa}(\text{by applying } \mathrm{T} \to \mathbf{aa})$$

Derivations similar to Example 8.1, which begin with only the start symbol S and end with a string with symbols entirely from Σ (that is, which do not contain *any* nonterminals) will be the main ones in which we are interested. As formally stated in Definition 8.2, the set of all strings (in Σ^*) that can be derived from the start symbol form the language generated by the grammar G and will be represented by $L(\mathrm{G})$. In symbols, $L(\mathrm{G}) = \{x \mid x \in \Sigma^* \wedge \mathrm{S} \overset{*}{\Rightarrow} x\}$.

EXAMPLE 8.7

As in Example 8.6, consider $\mathrm{G}_1 = <\{\mathrm{T}, \mathrm{S}\}, \{\mathbf{a}, \mathbf{b}\}, \mathrm{S}, \{\mathrm{S} \to \mathbf{a}\mathrm{S}, \mathrm{S} \to \mathbf{b}\mathrm{T}, \mathrm{T} \to \mathbf{aa}\}>$. Then $L(\mathrm{G}_1) = \mathbf{a}^*\mathbf{baa} = \{\mathbf{baa}, \mathbf{abaa}, \mathbf{aabaa}, \ldots\}$. Note that each of these words can certainly be produced by G_1; the number of **a**s at the front of the string is entirely determined by how many times the production $\mathrm{S} \to \mathbf{a}\mathrm{S}$ is used in the derivation. Furthermore, no other words *in* Σ^* can be derived from G_1; beginning from S, the production $\mathrm{S} \to \mathbf{a}\mathrm{S}$ may be used several times, but if no other production is used, a string of the form $\mathbf{a}^n\mathrm{S}$ will be produced, and since $\mathrm{S} \notin \Sigma$, this is not a valid string of terminals. The only way to remove the S is to apply the production $\mathrm{S} \to \mathbf{b}\mathrm{T}$, which will leave a string of the form $\mathbf{a}^n\mathbf{b}\mathrm{T}$, which is also not in Σ^*. The only production that can be applied at this point is $\mathrm{T} \to \mathbf{aa}$, deriving a string of the form $\mathbf{a}^n\mathbf{baa}$. A proof involving induction on n would be required to formally prove that $L(\mathrm{G}_1) = \{\mathbf{a}^n\mathbf{baa} \mid n \in \mathbb{N}\} = \mathbf{a}^*\mathbf{baa}$. If G contains many productions, such inductive proofs can be truly unpleasant.

EXAMPLE 8.8

Consider the grammar $\mathrm{Q} = <\{\mathrm{I}, \mathrm{F}\}, \{\mathbf{0}, \mathbf{1}, .\}, \mathrm{I}, \{\mathrm{I} \to \mathbf{0}\mathrm{I} \mid \mathbf{1}\mathrm{I} \mid \mathbf{0}.\mathrm{F} \mid \mathbf{1}.\mathrm{F}, \mathrm{F} \to \lambda \mid \mathbf{0}\mathrm{F} \mid \mathbf{1}\mathrm{F}\}>$. $L(\mathrm{Q})$ generates the set of all (terminating) binary numbers including **101.11**, **011.**, **10.0**, **0.010**, and so on.

In a manner similar to that used for automata and regular expressions, we will consider two grammars to be similar in some fundamental sense if they generate the same language. The following definition formalizes this notion.

∇ **Definition 8.9.** Two grammars $\mathrm{G}_1 = <\Omega_1, \Sigma, \mathrm{S}_1, P_1>$ and $\mathrm{G}_2 = <\Omega_2, \Sigma, \mathrm{S}_2, P_2>$ are called *equivalent iff* $L(\mathrm{G}_1) = L(\mathrm{G}_2)$, and we will write $\mathrm{G}_2 \simeq \mathrm{G}_1$.
Δ

EXAMPLE 8.9

Consider G_1 from Examples 8.6 and 8.7, and define the right-linear grammar $\mathrm{G}_8 = <\{\mathrm{Z}\}, \{\mathbf{a}, \mathbf{b}\}, \mathrm{Z}, \{\mathrm{Z} \to \mathbf{a}\mathrm{Z}, \mathrm{Z} \to \mathbf{baa}\}>$. Then $L(\mathrm{G}_8) = \mathbf{a}^*\mathbf{baa} = L(\mathrm{G}_1)$, and therefore $\mathrm{G}_8 \simeq \mathrm{G}_1$. The concept of equivalence applies to all types of grammars, whether or not they are right linear, and hence the grammars G″ and G′ from Examples 8.3 and 8.5 are likewise equivalent.

Definition 8.9 marks the fourth distinct use of the operator $\boldsymbol{L}$ and the concept of equivalence. It has previously been used to denote the language recognized by a DFA, the language recognized by an NDFA, and the language represented by a regular expression [although the more precise notation $\boldsymbol{L}(\mathrm{R})$, which is the regular set represented by the regular expression R, has generally been eschewed in favor of the more common convention of denoting both the set and the expression by the same symbol R]. In the larger sense, then, a representation X of a language, regardless of whether X is a grammar, DFA, NDFA, or regular expression, is *equivalent* to another representation Y *iff* $\boldsymbol{L}(\mathsf{X}) = \boldsymbol{L}(\mathsf{Y})$.

Our first goal in this section is to demonstrate that a cognitive representation of a language (via a DFA) can be replaced by a generative representation (via a right-linear grammar). In the broader sense of equivalence of representations discussed above, Lemma 8.1 shows that any language defined by a DFA has an *equivalent* representation as a right-linear grammar. We begin with a definition of the class of all type 3 languages.

∇ **Definition 8.10.** Given an alphabet Σ, $\mathcal{G}_\Sigma$ is defined to be the collection of all languages generated by right-linear grammars over Σ.
Δ

The language generated by G_1 in Example 8.7 turned out to be FAD. We will now prove that every language in $\mathcal{G}_\Sigma$ is FAD, and, conversely, every FAD language L has (at least one) right-linear grammar that generates L. This will show that $\mathcal{G}_\Sigma = \mathcal{D}_\Sigma$. We begin by showing that a mechanical representation A of a language is equivalent to a grammatical representation (denoted by $\mathsf{G_A}$ in Lemma 8.1).

∇ **Lemma 8.1.** Given any alphabet Σ and a DFA $\mathsf{A} = <\Sigma, Q, \mathrm{q}_0, \delta, F>$, there exists a right-linear grammar $\mathsf{G_A}$ for which $\boldsymbol{L}(\mathsf{A}) = \boldsymbol{L}(\mathsf{G_A})$.

Proof. Without loss of generality, assume $Q = \{\mathrm{q}_0, \mathrm{q}_1, \mathrm{q}_2, \ldots, \mathrm{q}_m\}$. Define $\mathsf{G_A} = <Q, \Sigma, \mathrm{q}_0, P_\mathsf{A}>$, where $P_\mathsf{A} = \{\mathrm{q} \to \mathbf{a}\cdot\delta(\mathrm{q}, \mathbf{a}) \mid \mathrm{q} \in Q, \mathbf{a} \in \Sigma\} \cup \{\mathrm{q} \to \lambda \mid \mathrm{q} \in F\}$. There is one production of the form $\mathrm{s} \to \mathbf{bt}$ for each transition in the DFA, and one production of the form $\mathrm{s} \to \lambda$ for each final state s in F. (It may be helpful to look over Example 8.10 to get a firmer grasp of the nature of P_A before proceeding with this proof.) Note that the set of nonterminals Ω is made up of the names of the states in A, and the start symbol S is the name of the start state of A.

The heart of this proof is an inductive argument, which will show that for any string $x = \mathbf{a}_1\mathbf{a}_2 \cdots \mathbf{a}_n \in \Sigma^*$,

$$\mathrm{q}_0 \Rightarrow \mathbf{a}_1\cdot(\overline{\delta}(\mathrm{q}_0, \mathbf{a}_1))$$
$$\Rightarrow \mathbf{a}_1\cdot\mathbf{a}_2\cdot(\overline{\delta}(\mathrm{q}_0, \mathbf{a}_1\mathbf{a}_2))$$

$$\stackrel{*}{\Rightarrow} \mathbf{a}_1 \cdot \mathbf{a}_2 \cdots \mathbf{a}_{n-1} \cdot (\overline{\delta}(q_0, \mathbf{a}_1\mathbf{a}_2 \ldots \mathbf{a}_{n-1}))$$

$$\Rightarrow \mathbf{a}_1 \cdot \mathbf{a}_2 \cdots \mathbf{a}_n \cdot (\overline{\delta}(q_0, \mathbf{a}_1\mathbf{a}_2 \ldots \mathbf{a}_n))$$

from which it follows that, if $\overline{\delta}(q_0, \mathbf{a}_1\mathbf{a}_2 \ldots \mathbf{a}_n) \in F$, then

$$q_0 \stackrel{*}{\Rightarrow} \mathbf{a}_1\mathbf{a}_2 \cdots \mathbf{a}_n \cdot \overline{\delta}(q_0, \mathbf{a}_1\mathbf{a}_2 \ldots \mathbf{a}_n) \Rightarrow \mathbf{a}_1\mathbf{a}_2 \cdots \mathbf{a}_n$$

The actual inductive statement and proof is left as an exercise; given this fact, if $x \in \boldsymbol{L}(\mathsf{A})$, then $\overline{\delta}(q_0, x) \in F$ and there is a corresponding derivation $q_0 \stackrel{*}{\Rightarrow} x$, and so $x \in \boldsymbol{L}(\mathsf{G_A})$. Thus $\boldsymbol{L}(\mathsf{A}) \subseteq \boldsymbol{L}(\mathsf{G_A})$. A similarly tedious inductive argument will show that if, for some sequence of integers $i_1, i_2, \ldots, i_n$,

$$q_{i_0} \Rightarrow \mathbf{a}_1 q_{i_1} \Rightarrow \mathbf{a}_1\mathbf{a}_2 q_{i_2} \Rightarrow \cdots \Rightarrow \mathbf{a}_1\mathbf{a}_2 \cdots \mathbf{a}_n q_{i_n},$$

then the string $\mathbf{a}_1\mathbf{a}_2 \cdots \mathbf{a}_n$ will cause the DFA (when starting in state q_{i_0}) to visit the states $q_{i_1}, q_{i_2}, \ldots, q_{i_n}$. Furthermore, if $q_{i_n} \in F$, then, by applying the production $q_{i_n} \to \lambda$, $q_0 \stackrel{*}{\Rightarrow} \mathbf{a}_1\mathbf{a}_2 \cdots \mathbf{a}_n q_{i_n} \Rightarrow \mathbf{a}_1\mathbf{a}_2 \cdots \mathbf{a}_n$. This will show that valid derivations correspond to strings reaching final states in A, and so $\boldsymbol{L}(\mathsf{G_A}) \subseteq \boldsymbol{L}(\mathsf{A})$ (see the exercises). Thus $\boldsymbol{L}(\mathsf{G_A}) = \boldsymbol{L}(\mathsf{A})$.

Δ

EXAMPLE 8.10

Let

$$\mathsf{B} = <\{\mathbf{a}, \mathbf{b}\}, \{S, T\}, S, \delta, \{T\}>$$

where

$$\delta(S, \mathbf{a}) = T, \ \delta(S, \mathbf{b}) = T$$

$$\delta(T, \mathbf{a}) = S, \ \delta(T, \mathbf{b}) = S$$

This automaton is shown in Figure 8.1. Applying the construction in Lemma 8.1, we have $\Omega = \{S, T\}$, $\Sigma = \{\mathbf{a}, \mathbf{b}\}$, $S = S$, and

$$P_{\mathsf{B}} = \{S \to \mathbf{a}T, S \to \mathbf{b}T, T \to \mathbf{a}S, T \to \mathbf{b}S, T \to \lambda\}.$$

Note that the derivation $S \Rightarrow \mathbf{b}T \Rightarrow \mathbf{ba}S \Rightarrow \mathbf{bab}T \Rightarrow \mathbf{bab}$ mirrors the action of the DFA as it processes the string **bab**, recording at each step of the derivation the string that has been processed so far, followed by the current state of B. Conversely, in trying to duplicate the action of B as it processes the string **ab**, we have $S \Rightarrow \mathbf{a}T \Rightarrow \mathbf{ab}S$, which cannot be transformed into a string of only **a**s and **b**s without processing at least one more letter, and hence $\mathbf{ab} \notin \boldsymbol{L}(\mathsf{G_B})$. Since S is not a final state, it cannot be removed from the derivation, corresponding to the rejection of any string that brings us to a nonfinal state. Those strings that are accepted by B are exactly those that end in the state T, and for which we will have the opportunity to use the production $T \to \lambda$ in the corresponding derivation in $\mathsf{G_B}$, which will leave us with a terminal string of only **a**s and **b**s.

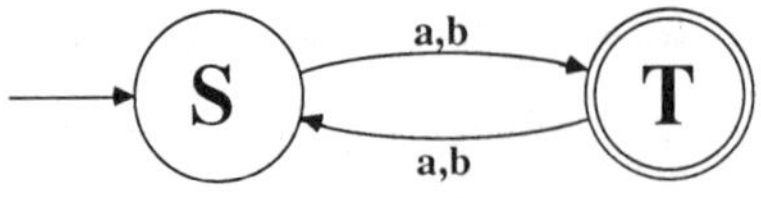

Figure 8.1 The automaton discussed in Example 8.10

Lemma 8.1 showed that a cognitive representation of a finite automaton definable language can be expressed in an appropriate generative form (via a right-linear grammar). There are many practical applications in which it is necessary to test whether certain strings can be generated by a particular grammar. For unrestricted grammars, the answers to such questions can be far from obvious. In contrast, the specialized right-linear grammars discussed in this section can always be transformed into a simple cognitive representation: every right-linear grammar has a corresponding equivalent NDFA.

∇ **Lemma 8.2.** Let Σ be any alphabet and $\mathsf{G} = <\Omega, \Sigma, S, P>$ be a right-linear grammar, then there exists an NDFA A_G (with λ-transitions) for which $\boldsymbol{L}(\mathsf{G}) = \boldsymbol{L}(\mathsf{A}_\mathsf{G})$.

Proof. Define $\mathsf{A}_\mathsf{G} = <\Sigma, Q_\mathsf{G}, q_{0_\mathsf{G}}, \delta_\mathsf{G}, F_\mathsf{G}>$, where

$$Q_\mathsf{G} = \{<z> \mid z = \lambda \vee z \in \Omega \vee \exists y \in \Sigma^* \text{ and } \exists B \in \Omega \text{ such that } B \rightarrow yz \text{ is a production in } P\}$$

$$q_{0_\mathsf{G}} = \{<S>\}$$

$$F_\mathsf{G} = \{<\lambda>\},$$

and δ_G is comprised of (normal) transitions of the form

$$\delta_\mathsf{G}(<w>, \mathbf{a}) = \{<x> \mid \exists y \in (\Omega \cup \Sigma)^*, \exists B \in \Omega \ni w = \mathbf{a}x \wedge B \rightarrow yw \text{ is a production in } P\}$$

δ_G also contains some λ-transitions of the form

$$\delta_\mathsf{G}(<B>, \lambda) = \{<v> \mid B \rightarrow v \text{ is a production in } P\}$$

As in the proof of Lemma 8.1, there is a one-to-one correspondence between paths through the machine and derivations in the grammar. Inductive statements will be the basis from which it will follow that $\boldsymbol{L}(\mathsf{A}_\mathsf{G}) = \boldsymbol{L}(\mathsf{G})$ (see the exercises).
Δ

The following example may be helpful in providing a firmer grasp of the nature of A_G.

EXAMPLE 8.11

Let $\mathsf{G}_1 = <\{T, S\}, \{\mathbf{a}, \mathbf{b}\}, S, \{S \rightarrow \mathbf{a}S, S \rightarrow \mathbf{b}T, T \rightarrow \mathbf{aa}\}>$. Then

$\mathsf{A}_{\mathsf{G}_1} = <\{\mathbf{a}, \mathbf{b}\}, \{<\mathbf{a}S>, <S>, <\mathbf{b}T>, <T>, <\mathbf{aa}>, <\mathbf{a}>, <\lambda>\}, \{<S>\}, \delta_{\mathsf{G}_1}, \{<\lambda>\}>$,

where δ_{G_1} is given by

$$\delta_{G_1}(<S>, \lambda) = \{<\mathbf{a}S>, <\mathbf{b}T>\} \qquad \delta_{G_1}(<T>, \lambda) = \{<\mathbf{aa}>\}$$

$$\delta_{G_1}(<\mathbf{a}S>, \mathbf{a}) = \{<S>\} \qquad \delta_{G_1}(<\mathbf{b}T>, \mathbf{b}) = \{<T>\}$$

$$\delta_{G_1}(<\mathbf{aa}>, \mathbf{a}) = \{<\mathbf{a}>\} \qquad \delta_{G_1}(<\mathbf{a}>, \mathbf{a}) = \{<\lambda>\}$$

and all other transitions are empty [for example, $\delta_{G_1}(<S>, \mathbf{a}) = \emptyset$]. This automaton is shown in Figure 8.2. Note that **abaa** is accepted by this machine by visiting the states $<S>$, $<\mathbf{a}S>$, $<S>$, $<\mathbf{b}T>$, $<T>$, $<\mathbf{aa}>$, $<\mathbf{a}>$, $<\lambda>$, and that the corresponding derivation in G_1 is $S \Rightarrow \mathbf{a}S \Rightarrow \mathbf{ab}T \Rightarrow \mathbf{abaa}$.

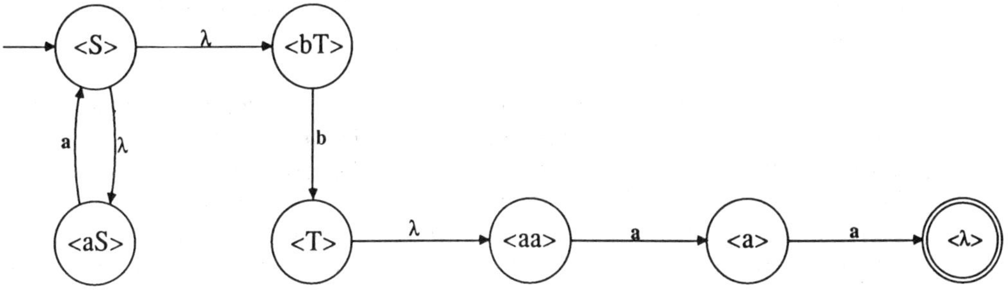

Figure 8.2 The automaton corresponding to the grammar G_1

∇ **Theorem 8.1.** Given any alphabet Σ, $\mathcal{G}_\Sigma = \mathcal{D}_\Sigma$.

Proof. Lemma 8.1 guaranteed that every DFA has a corresponding grammar, and so $\mathcal{D}_\Sigma \subseteq \mathcal{G}_\Sigma$. By Lemma 8.2, every grammar has a corresponding NDFA, and so $\mathcal{G}_\Sigma \subseteq \mathcal{W}_\Sigma = \mathcal{D}_\Sigma$. Thus $\mathcal{G}_\Sigma = \mathcal{D}_\Sigma$.

Δ

8.3 REGULAR GRAMMARS AND REGULAR EXPRESSIONS

The grammars we have considered so far are called *right* linear because productions are constrained to have the resulting nonterminal appear to the right of the terminal symbols. We next consider the class of grammars that arises by forcing the lone nonterminal to appear to the left of the terminal symbols.

∇ **Definition 8.11.** A *left-linear grammar* over an alphabet Σ is a quadruple $G = <\Omega, \Sigma, S, P>$, where:

Ω is a (nonempty) set of *nonterminals*.

Σ is a (nonempty) set of *terminal symbols* (and $\Omega \cap \Sigma = \emptyset$).

S is the designated *start symbol* (and $S \in \Omega$).

P is a set of *productions* of the form $A \to Bx$, where $A \in \Omega$, $B \in (\Omega \cup \lambda)$, and $x \in \Sigma^*$.

Δ

Note that a typical production might now look like $A \to B\mathbf{cd}$, where the nonterminal B occurs to the left of the terminal string **cd**.

EXAMPLE 8.12

Let $G_2 = <\{A, S\}, \{\mathbf{a}, \mathbf{b}\}, S, \{S \to A\mathbf{baa}, A \to A\mathbf{a}, A \to \lambda\}>$. Then

$$L(G_2) = \mathbf{a}^*\mathbf{baa} = \{\mathbf{baa}, \mathbf{abaa}, \mathbf{aabaa}, \ldots\} = L(G_1),$$

and so $G_2 \simeq G_1$ (compare with Example 8.7). Note that there does not seem to be an obvious way to transform the right-linear grammar G_1 discussed in Example 8.7 into an equivalent left-linear grammar such as G_2 (see the exercises).

As was done for right-linear grammars in the last section, we *could* show that these left-linear grammars also generate the set of regular languages by constructing corresponding mac'iines and grammars (see the exercises). However, we will instead prove that left-linear grammars are equivalent in power to right-linear grammars by applying known results from previous chapters. The key to this strategy is the reverse operator r (compare with Example 4.10 and Exercises 5.20 and 6.36).

∇ **Definition 8.12.** For an alphabet Σ, and $x = \mathbf{a}_1\mathbf{a}_2 \cdots \mathbf{a}_{n-1}\mathbf{a}_n \in \Sigma^*$; define $x^r = \mathbf{a}_n\mathbf{a}_{n-1} \cdots \mathbf{a}_2\mathbf{a}_1$. For a language L over Σ, define $L^r = \{x^r \mid x \in L\}$. For a grammar $G = <\Omega, \Sigma, S, P>$, define $G^r = <\Omega, \Sigma, S, P'>$, where P' is given by $P' = \{A \to x^r \mid A \to x \text{ was a production in } P\}$.
Δ

∇ **Lemma 8.3.** Let G be a right-linear grammar. Then G^r is a left-linear grammar, and $L(G^r) = L(G)^r$. Similarly, if G is a left-linear grammar, then G^r is a right-linear grammar, and again $L(G^r) = L(G)^r$.

Proof. A straightforward induction on the number of productions used to produce a given terminal string (see the exercises). It can be shown that $S \overset{*}{\Rightarrow} Bx$ by applying n productions from G *iff* $S \overset{*}{\Rightarrow} x^r B$ by applying n corresponding productions from G^r.
Δ

EXAMPLE 8.13

Consider

$$G_3 = <\{T, S\}, \{\mathbf{a}, \mathbf{b}, \mathbf{c}, \mathbf{d}\}, S, \{S \to \mathbf{ab}S, S \to \mathbf{cd}T, T \to \mathbf{b}T, T \to \mathbf{b}\}>.$$

Then

$$G_3^r = <\{T, S\}, \{\mathbf{a}, \mathbf{b}, \mathbf{c}, \mathbf{d}\}, S, \{S \to S\mathbf{ba}, S \to T\mathbf{dc}, T \to T\mathbf{b}, T \to \mathbf{b}\}>,$$

$$L(G_3) = (\mathbf{ab})^*\mathbf{cdbb}^*, \ L(G_3^r) = \mathbf{b}^*\mathbf{bdc}(\mathbf{ba})^*,$$

and

$$\boldsymbol{L}(\mathrm{G}_3^r) = \boldsymbol{L}(\mathrm{G}_3)^r \text{ [and } \boldsymbol{L}(\mathrm{G}_3) = \boldsymbol{L}(\mathrm{G}_3^r)^r\text{]}.$$

∇ **Theorem 8.2.** Let Σ be an alphabet. Then the class of languages generated by the set of all left-linear grammars over Σ is the same as the class of languages generated by the set of all right-linear grammars over Σ.

Proof. Let G be a left-linear grammar. G^r is then a right-linear grammar, and $\boldsymbol{L}(\mathrm{G}^r)$ is therefore FAD by Theorem 8.1. Since $\mathcal{D}_\Sigma$ is closed under the reverse operator r (see Exercise 5.20), $\boldsymbol{L}(\mathrm{G}^r)^r$ is also FAD. But, by Lemma 8.3, $\boldsymbol{L}(\mathrm{G}^r)^r = \boldsymbol{L}(\mathrm{G})$, and so $\boldsymbol{L}(\mathrm{G})$ is FAD. Hence every left-linear grammar generates a member of $\mathcal{D}_\Sigma$ and therefore has a corresponding right-linear grammar.

Conversely, if L is generated by a right-linear grammar, then L is a language in $\mathcal{D}_\Sigma$, and so is L^r (as shown by Exercise 5.20 or 6.36). Since $\mathcal{D}_\Sigma = \mathcal{G}_\Sigma$, there is a right-linear grammar G that generates L^r, and hence G^r is a left-linear grammar that generates L (why?). Thus every right-linear grammar has a corresponding left-linear grammar.

Δ

∇ **Definition 8.13.** A *regular* or *type 3 grammar* is a grammar that is either right-linear or left-linear.

Δ

Thus, the languages generated by left-linear (and hence regular) grammars are referred to as type 3 languages. The class of type 3 languages is exactly $\mathcal{G}_\Sigma$.

∇ **Corollary 8.1.** The class of languages generated by regular grammars is equal to $\mathcal{G}_\Sigma$.

Proof. The proof follows immediately from Theorem 8.2.

Δ

With the correspondences developed between the grammatical descriptors and the mechanical constructs, it is possible to transform a regular expression into an equivalent grammar by first transforming the representation of the language into an automaton (as described in Chapter 6) and then applying Lemma 8.1 to the resulting machine. Conversely, the grammar G_1 in Example 8.11 gives rise to the seven-state NDFA $\mathrm{A}_{\mathrm{G}_1}$ (using Lemma 8.2), which could in turn be used to generate seven equations in seven unknowns. These could then be solved for a regular expression representing $\boldsymbol{L}(\mathrm{G}_1)$ via Theorems 6.1 and 6.2. A much more efficient method, which generates equations directly from the productions themselves, is outlined in the following theorem.

∇ **Theorem 8.3.** Let $\mathrm{G} = <\{\mathrm{S}_1, \mathrm{S}_2, \ldots, \mathrm{S}_n\}, \Sigma, \mathrm{S}_1, P>$ be a right-linear grammar, and for each nonterminal S_i define $\mathrm{X}_{\mathrm{S}_i}$ to be the set of all terminal strings that can be derived from S_i by using the productions in P. X_{S_1} then represents $L(G)$, and these sets satisfy the language equations

$$X_{S_k} = E_k \cup A_{k1}X_{S_1} \cup A_{k2}X_{S_2} \cup \cdots \cup A_{kn}X_{S_n}, \qquad \text{for } k = 1, 2, \ldots, n$$

where E_i is the union of all terminal strings x that appear in productions of the form $S_i \to x$, and A_{ij} is the union of all terminal strings x that appear in productions of the form $S_i \to xS_j$.

Proof. Since S_1 is the start symbol, X_{S_1} is by definition the set of all words that can be derived from the start symbol, and hence $X_{S_1} = L(G)$. The relationships between the variables X_{S_i} essentially embody the relationships enforced by the productions in P.
Δ

EXAMPLE 8.14

Consider G_1 from Example 8.11, in which

$$G_1 = \langle\{T, S\}, \{\mathbf{a}, \mathbf{b}\}, S, \{S \to \mathbf{a}S, S \to \mathbf{b}T, T \to \mathbf{aa}\}\rangle.$$

The corresponding equations are

$$X_S = \emptyset \cup \mathbf{a}X_S \cup \mathbf{b}X_T$$

$$X_T = \mathbf{aa} \cup \emptyset X_S \cup \emptyset X_T$$

Eliminating X_T via Theorem 6.2 yields $X_S = \mathbf{baa} \cup \mathbf{a}X_S$. Theorem 6.1 can be applied to this equation to yield $X_S = L(G_1) = \mathbf{a}^*\mathbf{baa}$. Solving these two equations is indeed preferable to appealing the resulting NDFA from Example 8.11 and solving the corresponding seven equations.

EXAMPLE 8.15

Let $\Sigma = \{\mathbf{a}, \mathbf{b}, \mathbf{c}\}$,and consider the set of all words that end in **b** and for which every **c** is immediately followed by **a**. This can be succinctly described by the grammar $G = \langle\{S\}, \{\mathbf{a}, \mathbf{b}, \mathbf{c}\}, S, \{S \to \mathbf{a}S, S \to \mathbf{b}S, S \to \mathbf{ca}S, S \to \mathbf{b}\}\rangle$. The resulting one equation in the single unknown X_S is $X_S = \mathbf{b} \cup (\mathbf{a} \cup \mathbf{b} \cup \mathbf{ca})X_S$, and Theorem 6.1 can be applied to yield a regular expression for this language; that is, $X_S = (\mathbf{a} \cup \mathbf{b} \cup \mathbf{ca})^*\mathbf{b}$.

Unfortunately, another grammar that generates this same language is

$$G' = \langle\{S\}, \{\mathbf{a}, \mathbf{b}, \mathbf{c}\}, S, \{S \to \lambda S, S \to \mathbf{a}S, S \to \mathbf{b}S, S \to \mathbf{ca}S, S \to \mathbf{b}\}\rangle.$$

In this case, however, the resulting one equation in the single unknown X_S is $X_S = \mathbf{b} \cup (\lambda \cup \mathbf{a} \cup \mathbf{b} \cup \mathbf{ca})X_S$, and Theorem 6.1 explicitly prohibits λ from appearing as a coefficient of an unknown. The equation no longer has a unique solution; other solutions are now possible, such as $X_S = \Sigma^*$. Nevertheless, the reduction described by Theorem 6.1 still predicts the correct expression for this language; that is, $X_S = (\lambda \cup \mathbf{a} \cup \mathbf{b} \cup \mathbf{ca})^*\mathbf{b}$. For equations arising from grammatical constructs, the desired solution will *always* be the minimal solution predicted by the technique used in Theorem 6.1. The condition prohibiting λ from appearing in the set A in the equation $X = E \cup AX$ was required to guarantee a unique solution. Regardless of the nature of the set A, A^*E is guaranteed to be a solution, and it will be contained in any other solution, as restated in Lemma 8.4.

∇ **Lemma 8.4.** Let E and A be any two sets, and consider the language equation $X = E \cup AX$. A^*E is always a solution for X, and any other solution Y must satisfy the property $A^*E \subseteq Y$.

Proof. Follows immediately from Theorem 6.1.

Δ

Consider again the grammar

$$G' = \langle\{S\}, \{\mathbf{a}, \mathbf{b}, \mathbf{c}\}, S, \{S \to \lambda S, S \to \mathbf{a}S, S \to \mathbf{b}S, S \to \mathbf{ca}S, S \to \mathbf{b}\}\rangle,$$

which generates the language $(\lambda \cup \mathbf{a} \cup \mathbf{b} \cup \mathbf{ca})^*\mathbf{b}$. The corresponding equation was $X = E \cup AX$, where $E = \mathbf{b}$, and $A = (\lambda \cup \mathbf{a} \cup \mathbf{b} \cup \mathbf{ca})$. Note that E represents the set of terminal strings that can be generated from S using exactly one production, while $A \cdot E = (\lambda \cup \mathbf{a} \cup \mathbf{b} \cup \mathbf{ca})\mathbf{b}$ is the set of all strings that can be generated from S using exactly two productions. Similarly, $A \cdot A \cdot E$ represents all terminal strings that can be generated from S using exactly three productions. By induction, it can be shown that $A^{n-1} \cdot E$ is the set of all strings that can be generated from S using exactly n productions. From this it follows that the minimal solution A^*E is indeed the language generated by the grammar.

Clearly, a useless production of the form $S \to \lambda S$ in a grammar can simply be removed from the production set without affecting the language that is generated. In the above example, it was the production $S \to \lambda S$ that was responsible for λ appearing in the coefficient set A. It is only the *nongenerative* productions, which do not produce any terminal symbols, that can give rise to a nonunique solution. However, the removal of productions of the form $V \to \lambda T$ will require the addition of other productions when T is a different nonterminal than V. Theorem 9.4, developed later, will show that these grammars can be transformed into equivalent grammars that do not contain productions of the form $V \to \lambda T$. Theorem 8.4 shows that it is not necessary to perform such transformations before producing equations that will provide equivalent regular expressions: the techniques outlined in Theorem 6.2 can indeed be used to solve systems of equations, even if the coefficients contain the empty word. Indeed, the minimal solution found in this manner will be the regular expression sought. This robustness is similar to that found in Theorem 6.3, which was stated for deterministic finite automata. Regular expressions for nondeterministic finite automata can be generated by transforming the NDFA into a DFA and then applying Theorem 6.3, but it was seen that it is both possible and more efficient to apply the method directly to the NDFA without performing the transformation. The following theorem justifies that a transformation to a well-behaved grammar is an unnecessary step in the algorithm for finding a regular expression describing the language generated by a right-linear grammar.

∇ **Lemma 8.5.** Consider the system of equations in the unknowns $X_1, X_2, \ldots, X_n$ given by

$$X_1 = E_1 \cup A_{11}X_1 \cup A_{12}X_2 \cup \cdots \cup A_{1(n-1)}X_{n-1} \cup A_{1n}X_n$$

$$X_2 = E_2 \cup A_{21}X_1 \cup A_{22}X_2 \cup \cdots \cup A_{2(n-1)}X_{n-1} \cup A_{2n}X_n$$

$$\vdots$$

$$X_{n-1} = E_{n-1} \cup A_{(n-1)1}X_1 \cup A_{(n-1)2}X_2 \cup \cdots \cup A_{(n-1)(n-1)}X_{n-1} \cup A_{(n-1)n}X_n$$

$$X_n = E_n \cup A_{n1}X_1 \cup A_{n2}X_2 \cup \cdots \cup A_{n(n-1)}X_{n-1} \cup A_{nn}X_n$$

a. Define $\hat{E}_i = E_i \cup (A_{in} \cdot A_{nn}^* \cdot E_n)$ for all $i = 1, 2, \ldots, n-1$ and

$$\hat{A}_{ij} = A_{ij} \cup (A_{in} \cdot A_{nn}^* \cdot A_{nj}) \text{ for all } i, j = 1, 2, \ldots, n-1.$$

Any solution of the original set of equations will agree with a solution of the following set of $n-1$ equations in the unknowns $X_1, X_2, \ldots, X_{n-1}$:

$$X_1 = \hat{E}_1 \cup \hat{A}_{11}X_1 \cup \hat{A}_{12}X_2 \cup \cdots \cup \hat{A}_{1(n-1)}X_{n-1}$$

$$X_2 = \hat{E}_2 \cup \hat{A}_{21}X_1 \cup \hat{A}_{22}X_2 \cup \cdots \cup \hat{A}_{2(n-1)}X_{n-1}$$

$$\vdots$$

$$X_{n-1} = \hat{E}_{n-1} \cup \hat{A}_{(n-1)1}X_1 \cup \hat{A}_{(n-1)2}X_2 \cup \cdots \cup \hat{A}_{(n-1)(n-1)}X_{n-1}$$

b. Given a solution to the above $n-1$ equations in (a), that solution can be used to find a compatible expression for the remaining unknown:

$$X_n = A_{nn}^* \cdot (E_n \cup A_{n1}X_1 \cup A_{n2}X_2 \cup \cdots \cup A_{n(n-1)}X_{n-1})$$

c. This system has a unique *minimal* solution in the following sense: Let $W_1, W_2, \ldots, W_n$ denote the solution found by eliminating variables and back-substituting as specified in (a) and (b). If $Y_1, Y_2, \ldots, Y_n$ is any other solution to the original n equations in n unknowns, then $W_1 \subseteq Y_1$, $W_2 \subseteq Y_2, \ldots,$ and $W_n \subseteq Y_n$.

Proof. This proof is by induction on the number of equations. Lemma 8.4 proved the basis step for $n = 1$. As in Theorem 6.2, the inductive step is proved by considering the last of the n equations,

$$X_n = (E_n \cup A_{n1}X_1 \cup A_{n2}X_2 \cup \cdots \cup A_{n(n-1)}X_{n-1}) \cup A_{nn}X_n$$

This can be thought of as an equation in the one unknown X_n with a coefficient of A_{nn} for X_n, and the remainder of the expression a "constant" term not involving X_n.

For a given solution for X_1 through X_{n-1}, Lemma 8.4 can therefore be applied to the above equation in the one unknown X_n, with coefficients

$$E = (E_n \cup A_{n1}X_1 \cup A_{n2}X_2 \cup \cdots \cup A_{n(n-1)}X_{n-1})$$

and $A = A_{nn}$ to find a minimal solution for X_n for the corresponding values of X_1 through X_{n-1}. This is exactly as given by part (b) above:

$$X_n = A_{nn}^* \cdot (E_n \cup A_{n1}X_1 \cup A_{n2}X_2 \cup \cdots \cup A_{n(n-1)}X_{n-1})$$

or

$$X_n = A_{nn}^* \cdot E_n \cup A_{nn}^* \cdot A_{n1}X_1 \cup A_{nn}^* \cdot A_{n2}X_2 \cup \cdots \cup A_{nn}^* \cdot A_{n(n-1)}X_{n-1})$$

Specifically, if X_1 through X_{n-1} are represented by a minimal solution W_1 through W_{n-1}, then Lemma 8.4 implies that the inclusion of W_n, given by

$$W_n = A_{nn}^* \cdot E_n \cup A_{nn}^* \cdot A_{n1}W_1 \cup A_{nn}^* \cdot A_{n2}W_2 \cup \cdots \cup A_{nn}^* \cdot A_{n(n-1)}W_{n-1})$$

will yield a minimal solution W_1 through W_n of the original n equations in n unknowns.

The minimal solution for the $n-1$ equations in the unknowns $X_1, X_2, \ldots, X_{n-1}$, denoted by W_1 through W_{n-1}, can be found by substituting this particular solution W_n for X_n in each of the other $n-1$ equations. If the kth equation is represented by

$$X_k = E_k \cup A_{k1}X_1 \cup A_{k2}X_2 \cup \cdots \cup A_{kn}X_n$$

then the substitution will yield

$$X_k = E_k \cup A_{k1}X_1 \cup A_{k2}X_2 \cup \cdots$$
$$\cup (A_{kn} \cdot (A_{nn}^* \cdot E_n \cup A_{nn}^* \cdot A_{n1}X_1 \cup A_{nn}^* \cdot A_{n2}X_2 \cup \cdots \cup A_{nn}^* \cdot A_{n(n-1)}X_{n-1}))$$

Due to the nature of union and concatenation, no other solution for X_n can possibly allow a smaller solution for $X_1, X_2, \ldots, X_{n-1}$ to be found. Specifically, if Y_n is a solution satisfying the nth equation, then Lemma 8.4 guarantees that $W_n \subseteq Y_n$, and consequently

$$X_k = E_k \cup A_{k1}X_1 \cup A_{k2}X_2 \cup \cdots \cup A_{kn}W_n \subseteq E_k \cup A_{k1}X_1 \cup A_{k2}X_2 \cup \cdots \cup A_{kn}Y_n$$

Thus, the minimal value for each X_k is compatible with the substitution of W_n defined earlier. Hence, by using the distributive law, the revised equation becomes

$$X_k = E_k \cup A_{k1}X_1 \cup A_{k2}X_2 \cup \cdots \cup (A_{kn} \cdot A_{nn}^* \cdot E_n \cup A_{kn} \cdot A_{nn}^* \cdot A_{n1}X_1$$
$$\cup A_{kn} \cdot A_{nn}^* \cdot A_{n2}X_2 \cup \cdots \cup A_{kn} \cdot A_{nn}^* \cdot A_{n(n-1)}X_{n-1})$$

Collecting like terms yields

$$X_k = (E_k \cup A_{kn} \cdot A_{nn}^* \cdot E_n) \cup (A_{k1}X_1 \cup A_{kn} \cdot A_{nn}^* \cdot A_{n1}X_1)$$
$$\cup (A_{k2}X_2 \cup A_{kn} \cdot A_{nn}^* \cdot A_{n2}X_2) \cup \cdots \cup (A_{k(n-1)}X_{n-1} \cup A_{kn} \cdot A_{nn}^* \cdot A_{n(n-1)}X_{n-1}),$$

or

$$X_k = (E_k \cup A_{kn} \cdot A_{nn}^* \cdot E_n) \cup (A_{k1} \cup A_{kn} \cdot A_{nn}^* \cdot A_{n1})X_1$$
$$\cup (A_{k2} \cup A_{kn} \cdot A_{nn}^* \cdot A_{n2})X_2 \cup \cdots \cup (A_{k(n-1)} \cup A_{kn} \cdot A_{nn}^* \cdot A_{n(n-1)})X_{n-1}$$

The constant term in this equation is $(E_k \cup A_{kn} \cdot A_{nn}^* \cdot E_n)$, and the coefficient for X_j is $\hat{A}_{kj} = A_{kj} \cup (A_{kn} \cdot A_{nn}^* \cdot A_{nj})$, which agrees with the formula given in (a). The substitution of X_n was shown to yield a minimal set of $n-1$ equations in the unknowns X_1 through X_{n-1}, and the induction assumption guarantees that the elimination and back-substitution method yields a minimal solution for W_1 through W_{n-1}. Lemma 8.4 then guarantees that the solution for

$$W_n = A_{nn}^* \cdot E_n \cup A_{nn}^* \cdot A_{n1} W_1 \cup A_{nn}^* \cdot A_{n2} W_2 \cup \cdots \cup A_{nn}^* \cdot A_{n(n-1)} W_{n-1})$$

is minimal, which completes the minimal solution for the original system of n equations.

Δ

As with Lemma 8.4, the minimal expressions thus generated describe exactly those terminal strings that can be produced by a right-linear grammar. In an analogous fashion, left-linear grammars give rise to a set of left-linear equations, which can be solved as indicated in Theorem 6.4.

The above discussion describes the transformation of regular grammars into regular expressions. Generating grammars from regular expressions hinges on the interpretation of the six building blocks of regular expressions, as described in Definition 6.2. Since $\mathcal{G}_\Sigma$ is the same as $\mathfrak{D}_\Sigma$, all the closure properties known about $\mathfrak{D}_\Sigma$ must also apply to $\mathcal{G}_\Sigma$, but it can be instructive to reprove these theorems using grammatical constructions. Such proofs will also provide guidelines for directly transforming a regular expression into a grammar without first constructing a corresponding automaton.

∇ **Theorem 8.4.** Let Σ be an alphabet. Then $\mathcal{G}_\Sigma$ is effectively closed under union.

Proof. Let $G_1 = <\Omega_1, \Sigma, S_1, P_1>$ and $G_2 = <\Omega_2, \Sigma, S_2, P_2>$ be two right-linear grammars, and without loss of generality assume that $\Omega_1 \cap \Omega_2 = \emptyset$. Choose a new nonterminal Z such that $Z \notin \Omega_1 \cup \Omega_2$, and consider the new grammar $G^\cup$ defined by $G^\cup = <\Omega_1 \cup \Omega_2 \cup \{Z\}, \Sigma, Z, P_1 \cup P_2 \cup \{Z \to S_1, Z \to S_2\}>$. It is straightforward to show that $L(G^\cup) = L(G_1) \cup L(G_2)$ (see the exercises). From the start symbol Z there are only two productions that can be applied; if $Z \to S_1$ is chosen, then the derivation will have to continue with productions from P_1 and produce a word from $L(G_1)$ (why can't productions from P_2 be applied?). Similarly, if $Z \to S_2$ is chosen instead, the only result can be a word from $L(G_2)$.

Δ

In an analogous fashion, effective closure of $\mathcal{G}_\Sigma$ can be demonstrated for the operators Kleene closure and concatenation. The proof for Kleene closure is outlined below. The construction for concatenation is left for the exercises; the technique is illustrated in Example 8.18.

∇ **Theorem 8.5.** Let Σ be an alphabet. Then $\mathcal{G}_\Sigma$ is effectively closed under Kleene closure.

Proof. Let $G = <\Omega, \Sigma, S, P>$ be a right-linear grammar. Choose a new nonterminal Z such that $Z \notin \Omega$, and consider the new grammar G_* defined by

$$G_* = <\Omega \cup \{Z\}, \Sigma, Z, P_*>,$$

where

$$P_* = <\{Z \to \lambda, Z \to S\}$$
$$\cup \{A \to xB \mid (x \in \Sigma^*) \wedge (A, B \in \Omega) \wedge (A \to xB \in P)\}$$
$$\cup \{A \to xZ \mid (x \in \Sigma^*) \wedge (A \in \Omega) \wedge (A \to x \in P)\}.$$

That is, all productions in P that end in a nonterminal are retained, while all other productions in P are appended with the new symbol Z, and the two new productions $Z \to \lambda$ and $Z \to S$ are added. A straightforward induction argument will show that the derivations that use n applications of productions of the form $A \to xZ$ generate exactly the words in $\boldsymbol{L}(G)^n$. Consequently, $\boldsymbol{L}(G_*) = \boldsymbol{L}(G)^*$.
Δ

∇ **Theorem 8.6.** Let Σ be an alphabet. Then $\mathcal{G}_\Sigma$ is effectively closed under concatenation.

Proof. See the exercises.
Δ

∇ **Corollary 8.2.** Every regular expression has a corresponding right-linear grammar.

Proof. While this follows immediately from the fact that $\mathcal{G}_\Sigma = \mathcal{D}_\Sigma$ and Theorem 6.1, the previous theorems outline an effective procedure for transforming a regular expression into a right-linear grammar. This can be proved by induction on the number of operators in the regular expression. The basis step consists of the observation that expressions with zero operators, which must be of the form $\emptyset$, λ, or **a**, can be represented by the right-linear grammars $<\{S\}, \Sigma, S, \{S \to S\}>$, $<\{S\}, \Sigma, S, \{S \to \lambda\}>$, and $<\{S\}, \Sigma, S, \{S \to \mathbf{a}\}>$, respectively.

To prove the inductive step, choose an arbitrary regular expression R with $m + 1$ operators, and identify the outermost operator. R must be of the form $R_1 \cup R_2$ or $R_1 \cdot R_2$ or R_1^*, where R_1 (and R_2) have m or fewer operators. By the induction hypothesis, R_1 (and R_2) can be represented as right-linear grammars, and therefore by Theorem 8.4, 8.5, or 8.6, R can also be represented by a right-linear grammar. Any regular expression can thus be methodically transformed into an equivalent right-linear grammar.
Δ

EXAMPLE 8.16

Let $\Sigma = \{\mathbf{a}, \mathbf{b}, \mathbf{c}\}$, and consider the regular expression $(\mathbf{a} \cup \mathbf{b})$. The grammars $G_1 = <\{R\}, \{\mathbf{a}, \mathbf{b}, \mathbf{c}\}, R, \{R \to \mathbf{a}\}>$ and $G_2 = <\{T\}, \{\mathbf{a}, \mathbf{b}, \mathbf{c}\}, T, \{T \to \mathbf{b}\}>$ can be combined as suggested in Theorem 8.4 (with A playing the role of Z) to form $G = <\{T, R, A\}, \{\mathbf{a}, \mathbf{b}, \mathbf{c}\}, A, \{A \to R, A \to T, R \to \mathbf{a}, T \to \mathbf{b}\}>$.

EXAMPLE 8.17

Consider the regular expression $(\mathbf{a} \cup \mathbf{b})^*$. The grammar

$$G = \langle\{T, R, A\}, \{\mathbf{a}, \mathbf{b}, \mathbf{c}\}, A, \{A \to R, A \to T, R \to \mathbf{a}, T \to \mathbf{b}\}\rangle$$

can be modified as suggested in Theorem 8.5 to form
$G_* = \langle\{T, R, A, Z\}, \{\mathbf{a}, \mathbf{b}, \mathbf{c}\}, Z, \{Z \to \lambda, Z \to A, A \to R, A \to T, R \to \mathbf{a}Z, T \to \mathbf{b}Z\}\rangle$.
G_* generates $(\mathbf{a} \cup \mathbf{b})^*$.

EXAMPLE 8.18

Consider the regular expression $(\mathbf{a} \cup \mathbf{b})^*\mathbf{c}$. The grammars

$$G_* = \langle\{T, R, A, Z\}, \{\mathbf{a}, \mathbf{b}, \mathbf{c}\}, Z, \{Z \to \lambda, Z \to A, A \to R, A \to T, R \to \mathbf{a}Z, T \to \mathbf{b}Z\rangle$$

and

$$G_3 = \langle\{V\}, \{\mathbf{a}, \mathbf{b}, \mathbf{c}\}, V, \{V \to \mathbf{c}\}\rangle$$

can be combined with modified productions to form

$$\begin{aligned} G' = \langle&\{T, R, A, Z, V, S\}, \{\mathbf{a}, \mathbf{b}, \mathbf{c}\}, S, \\ &\{S \to Z, Z \to \lambda V, Z \to A, A \to R, A \to T, R \to \mathbf{a}Z, T \to \mathbf{b}Z, V \to \mathbf{c}\}\rangle. \end{aligned}$$

G' generates $(\mathbf{a} \cup \mathbf{b})^*\mathbf{c}$.

The previous examples illustrate the manner in which regular expressions can be systematically translated into right-linear grammars. Constructions corresponding to those given in Theorems 8.4, 8.5, and 8.6 can similarly be found for left-linear grammars (see the exercises).

Normal forms for grammars are quite useful in many contexts. A standard representation can be especially useful in proving theorems about grammars. For example, the construction given in Lemma 8.2 would have been more concise and easier to investigate if complex productions such as $S \to \mathbf{bcaa}T$ could be avoided. Indeed, if all productions in the grammar G had been of the form $A \to \mathbf{a}B$ or $A \to \lambda$, both the state set and the state transition function of A_G could have been defined more easily. Other constructions and proofs may also be able to make use of the simpler types of productions in grammars that conform to such normal forms. The following theorem guarantees that a given right-linear grammar has a corresponding equivalent grammar containing only productions that conform to the above standard.

∇ **Theorem 8.7.** Every right-linear grammar G has an equivalent right-linear grammar G^1 in which all productions are of the form $A \to \mathbf{a}B$ or $A \to \lambda$.

Proof. Let G be a right-linear grammar. By Lemma 8.2, there exists an NDFA A_G that is equivalent to G. From Chapter 4, A_G^d is an equivalent deterministic finite automaton, and Lemma 8.1 can be applied to A_G^d to form an equivalent

right-linear grammar. By the construction given in Lemma 8.1, all the productions in this grammar are indeed of the form $A \rightarrow \mathbf{a}B$ or $A \rightarrow \lambda$.
Δ

Note that the proof given is a constructive proof: rather than simply arguing the existence of such a grammar, a method for obtaining G^1 is outlined. The above theorem could have been proved without relying on automata constructs. Basically, "long" productions like $T \rightarrow \mathbf{abc}R$ would be replaced by a series of productions involving newly introduced nonterminals, for example, $T \rightarrow \mathbf{a}X, X \rightarrow \mathbf{b}Y, Y \rightarrow \mathbf{c}R$. Similarly, a production like $T \rightarrow \mathbf{aa}$ might be replaced by the sequence $T \rightarrow \mathbf{a}B$, $B \rightarrow \mathbf{a}C, C \rightarrow \lambda$. If the existence of such a normal form had been available for the proof of Lemma 8.2, the construction of A_G could have been simplified and the complexity of the proof drastically curtailed. Indeed, the resulting machine would have contained no λ-moves. Only one state per nonterminal would have been necessary, with final states corresponding to nonterminals that had productions of the form $A \rightarrow \lambda$. Productions of the form $A \rightarrow \mathbf{a}B$ would imply that $B \in \delta(A, \mathbf{a})$.

EXAMPLE 8.19

$G = <\{S, T, B, C\}, \{\mathbf{a}, \mathbf{b}\}, S, \{S \rightarrow \mathbf{a}S, S \rightarrow \mathbf{b}T, T \rightarrow \mathbf{a}B, B \rightarrow \mathbf{a}C, C \rightarrow \lambda\}>$ can be represented by the NDFA shown in Figure 8.3.

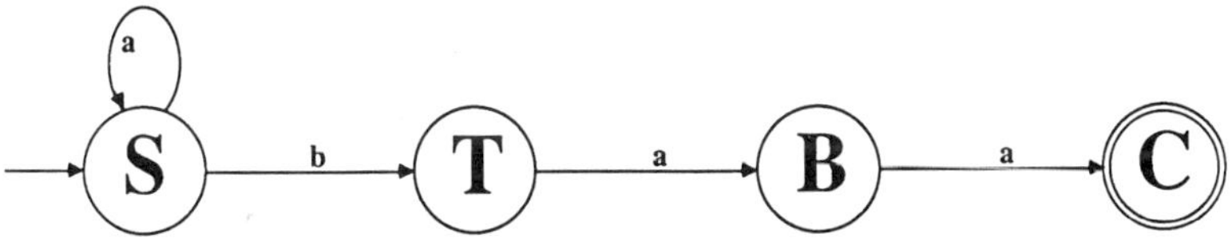

Figure 8.3 An automaton corresponding to a grammar in normal form

In practice, given an arbitrary right-linear grammar G, the work associated with finding the complex machine defined in Lemma 8.2 has simply been replaced by the effort needed to transform G into the appropriate normal form. Nevertheless, the guarantee that regular languages have grammars that conform to the above normal form is useful in many proofs, as illustrated above and in Theorem 8.8 below.

As with context-free and context-sensitive languages, the contracting productions can be limited to $Z \rightarrow \lambda$, where Z is the start symbol. This is only necessary if $\lambda \in L$; if $\lambda \notin L$, there need be no contracting productions at all. We wish to show how to produce a grammar with no more than one contracting production. By relying on the existence of the normal form described in Theorem 8.7, this can be done without dealing with right-linear grammars in their full generality.

∇ **Theorem 8.8.** Every right-linear grammar G has an equivalent right-linear grammar G^0 in which the start symbol Z never appears on the right in any production, and the only length-contracting production that may appear is $Z \rightarrow \lambda$. Furthermore, all other productions are of the form $A \rightarrow \mathbf{a}B$ or $A \rightarrow \mathbf{a}$.

Proof. Let $G = \langle \Omega, \Sigma, S, P \rangle$ be a right-linear grammar. Without loss of generality, assume that G is of the form specified by Theorem 8.7. (If G were not of the proper form, Theorem 8.7 guarantees that an equivalent grammar that *is* in the proper form could be found and used in place of G.) Choose a new nonterminal Z such that $Z \notin \Omega$, and consider the new grammar G^0 defined by $G^0 = \langle \Omega \cup \{Z\}, \Sigma, Z, P^0 \rangle$, where P^0 contains $Z \to S$, and all productions from P of the form $A \to xB$, where $x \in \Sigma^*$ and $A, B \in \Omega$. P^0 also contains the productions in the set $\{A \to \mathbf{a} \mid (\exists B \in \Omega)(A \to \mathbf{a}B \in P \wedge B \to \lambda \in P)\}$. Finally, if $S \to \lambda$ was a production in P, then $Z \to \lambda$ is included in P^0. Note that no other productions of the form $B \to \lambda$ are part of P^0. Other productions have been added to compensate for this loss. Derivations using the productions in P^0 typically start with $Z \to S$, then proceed with productions of the form $A \to xB$, and terminate with one production of the form $A \to \mathbf{a}$. The corresponding derivation in the original grammar G would be very similar, but would start with the old start symbol S and therefore avoid the $Z \to S$ application used in G^0. The productions of the form $A \to xB$ are common to both grammars, and the final step in G^0 that uses $A \to \mathbf{a}$ would be handled by two productions in G: $A \to \mathbf{a}B$ and $B \to \lambda$. An induction argument on the number of productions in a derivation will show that every derivation from G^0 has a corresponding derivation in G that produces the same terminal string, and vice versa. Thus, $\boldsymbol{L}(G^0) = \boldsymbol{L}(G)$, which justifies that G^0 is equivalent to G. G^0 was constructed to conform to the conditions specified by the theorem, and thus the proof is complete.
Δ

∇ **Corollary 8.3.** Every type 3 language is also a type 2 language.

Proof. Let L be a type 3 language. Then there exists a right-linear grammar G that generates L. By Theorem 8.8, there is an equivalent right-linear grammar G^0 that satisfies the definition of a context-free grammar. Thus, L is context free.
Δ

Section 8.1 explored several generalizations of the definition of a regular grammar, and, unlike the generalization from DFAs to NDFAs, new and larger classes of languages result from these generalizations. These new types of grammars will be explored in the following chapters, and the corresponding generalized machines will be developed.

EXERCISES

8.1. Can strings like **abBAdBc** (where B and A are nonterminals) ever be derived from the start symbol S in a right-linear grammar? Explain.

8.2. Given A and G_A as defined in Lemma 8.1, let P(n) be the statement that $(\forall x \in \Sigma^n)(\exists j \in N)$ [if $t_0 \overset{*}{\Rightarrow} xt_j$ then $\overline{\delta}_A(t_0, x) = t_j$]. Prove that P($n$) is true for all $n \in \mathbb{N}$.

8.3. Give regular expressions that describe the language generated by:

(a) $G_4 = <\{S, A, B, C, V, W, X\}, \{\mathbf{a}, \mathbf{b}, \mathbf{c}\}, S, \{S \to \mathbf{ab}A \mid \mathbf{bb}B \mid \mathbf{cc}V, A \to \mathbf{b}C \mid \mathbf{c}X, B \to \mathbf{ab}, C \to \lambda \mid \mathbf{c}S, V \to \mathbf{a}V \mid \mathbf{c}X, W \to \mathbf{aa} \mid \mathbf{a}W, X \to \mathbf{b}V \mid \mathbf{aa}X\}>$
(b) $G_5 = <\{S_0, S_1, S_2\}, \{\mathbf{0}, \mathbf{1}\}, S_0, \{S_0 \to \lambda \mid \mathbf{0}S_2 \mid \mathbf{1}S_1, S_1 \to \mathbf{0}S_1 \mid \mathbf{1}S_2, S_2 \to \mathbf{0}S_2 \mid \mathbf{1}S_0>$
(c) $G_6 = <\{T, Z\}, \{\mathbf{a}, \mathbf{b}\}, Z, \{Z \to \mathbf{a}Z, Z \to \mathbf{b}T, T \to \mathbf{a}Z\}>$
(d) $G_7 = <\{S, B, C\}, \{\mathbf{a}, \mathbf{b}, \mathbf{c}\}, S, \{S \to \mathbf{a}S \mid \mathbf{ab}B \mid \mathbf{c}C, B \to \mathbf{ab}B \mid \lambda, C \to \mathbf{c}C \mid \mathbf{ca}\}>$

8.4. Use the inductive fact proved in Exercise 8.2 to formally prove Lemma 8.1.

8.5. Draw the automata corresponding to the grammars given in Exercise 8.3.

8.6. Give, if possible, right-linear grammars that will generate:
(a) All words in $\{\mathbf{a}, \mathbf{b}, \mathbf{c}\}^*$ that do *not* contain two consecutive **b**s.
(b) All words in $\{\mathbf{a}, \mathbf{b}, \mathbf{c}\}^*$ that *do* contain two consecutive **b**s.
(c) All words in $\{\mathbf{a}, \mathbf{b}, \mathbf{c}\}^*$ that have the same number of **a**s as **b**s.
(d) All words in $\{\mathbf{a}, \mathbf{b}, \mathbf{c}\}^*$ that have an even number of **a**s.
(e) All words in $\{\mathbf{a}, \mathbf{b}, \mathbf{c}\}^*$ that do *not* end in the letter **b**.
(f) All words in $\{\mathbf{a}, \mathbf{b}, \mathbf{c}\}^*$ that do *not* contain any **c**s.

8.7. Give left-linear grammars that will generate the languages described in Exercise 8.6.

8.8. Complete the inductive portion of the proof of Theorem 8.8.

8.9. Complete the inductive portion of the proof of Theorem 8.5.

8.10. Use the more efficient algorithm indicated in Theorem 8.3 to find regular expressions to describe $L(G_5)$, $L(G_6)$, and $L(G_7)$ in Exercise 8.3.

8.11. (a) Restate Theorem 8.3 so that it generates valid language equations for left-linear grammars.
(b) Restate Lemmas 8.4 and 8.5 for these new types of equations.
(c) Use your new methods to find a regular expression for $L(G_2)$ in Example 8.12.

8.12. Consider the grammar $Q = <\{I, F\}, \{\mathbf{0}, \mathbf{1}, \mathbf{.}\}, I, \{I \to \mathbf{0}I \mid \mathbf{1}I \mid \mathbf{0.}F \mid \mathbf{1.}F, F \to \lambda \mid \mathbf{0}F \mid \mathbf{1}F\}>$. $L(Q)$ generates the set of all (terminating) binary numbers including **101.11**, **011.**, **10.0**, **0.010**, and so on.
(a) Find the corresponding NDFA for this grammar.
(b) Write the right-linear equations corresponding to this grammar.
(c) Solve the equations found in part (b) for both unknowns.

8.13. Find right-linear grammars for:
(a) $(\mathbf{a} \cup \mathbf{b})\mathbf{c}^*(\mathbf{d} \cup (\mathbf{ab})^*)$
(b) $(\mathbf{a} \cup \mathbf{b})^*\mathbf{a}(\mathbf{a} \cup \mathbf{b})^*$

8.14. Find left-linear grammars for:
(a) $(\mathbf{a} \cup \mathbf{b})\mathbf{c}^*(\mathbf{d} \cup (\mathbf{ab})^*)$
(b) $(\mathbf{a} \cup \mathbf{b})^*\mathbf{a}(\mathbf{a} \cup \mathbf{b})^*$

8.15. (a) Describe an *efficient* algorithm that will convert a right-linear grammar into a left-linear grammar.
(b) Apply your algorithm to

$$G_4 = <\{S, A, B, C, V, W, X\}, \{\mathbf{a}, \mathbf{b}, \mathbf{c}\}, S, \{S \to \mathbf{ab}A \mid \mathbf{bb}B \mid \mathbf{cc}V, A \to \mathbf{b}C \mid \mathbf{c}X, B \to \mathbf{ab},$$
$$C \to \lambda \mid \mathbf{c}S, V \to \mathbf{a}V \mid \mathbf{c}X, W \to \mathbf{aa} \mid \mathbf{a}W, X \to \mathbf{b}V \mid \mathbf{aa}X\}>$$

8.16. Describe an algorithm that will convert a given regular grammar G into another regular grammar G′ that generates the complement of $L(G)$.

8.17. Without appealing to results from Chapter 12, outline an algorithm that will determine whether the language generated by a given regular grammar G is empty.

8.18. Without appealing to results from Chapter 12, outline an algorithm that will determine whether the language generated by a given regular grammar G is infinite.

8.19. Without appealing to results from Chapter 12, outline an algorithm that will determine whether two right-linear grammars G_1 and G_2 generate the same language.

8.20. Consider the grammar

$$H = \langle\{A, B, S\}, \{\mathbf{a}, \mathbf{b}, \mathbf{c}\}, S, \{S \to \mathbf{a}S B\mathbf{c}, S \to \lambda, SB \to \mathbf{b}S, \mathbf{c}B \to B\mathbf{c}\}\rangle$$

Determine $\boldsymbol{L}(H)$.

8.21. What is wrong with proving that $\mathcal{G}_\Sigma$ is closed under concatenation by using the following construction? Let $G_1 = \langle\Omega_1, \Sigma, S_1, P_1\rangle$ and $G_2 = \langle\Omega_2, \Sigma, S_2, P_2\rangle$ be two right-linear grammars, and, without loss of generality, assume that $\Omega_1 \cap \Omega_2 = \emptyset$. Choose a new nonterminal Z such that $Z \notin \Omega_1 \cup \Omega_2$, and define a new grammar $G^\bullet = \langle\Omega_1 \cup \Omega_2 \cup \{Z\}, \Sigma, Z, P_1 \cup P_2 \cup \{Z \to S_1 \cdot S_2\}\rangle$. *Note:* It *is* straightforward to show that $\boldsymbol{L}(G^\bullet) = \boldsymbol{L}(G_1) \cdot \boldsymbol{L}(G_2)$ (see Chapter 9).

8.22. Prove that $\mathcal{G}_\Sigma$ is closed under concatenation by:

(a) Constructing a new grammar $G^\bullet$ with the property that $\boldsymbol{L}(G^\bullet) = \boldsymbol{L}(G_1) \cdot \boldsymbol{L}(G_2)$.

(b) Proving that $\boldsymbol{L}(G^\bullet) = \boldsymbol{L}(G_1) \cdot \boldsymbol{L}(G_2)$.

8.23. Use the constructs presented in this chapter to solve the following problem from Chapter 4: Given a nondeterministic finite automaton A *without* λ-transitions, show that it is possible to construct a nondeterministic finite automaton *with* λ-transitions A′ with the properties (1) A′ has exactly *one* start state and exactly *one* final state, and (2) $\boldsymbol{L}(A') = \boldsymbol{L}(A)$.

8.24. Complete the proof of Lemma 8.2 by:

(a) Defining an appropriate inductive statement.

(b) Proving the statement defined in part (a).

8.25. Complete the proof of Lemma 8.3 by:

(a) Defining an appropriate inductive statement.

(b) Proving the statement defined in part (a).

8.26. Fill in the details in the second half of the proof of Theorem 8.2 by providing reasons for each of the assertions that were made.

8.27. **(a)** Refer to Example 8.7 and use induction to formally prove that $\boldsymbol{L}(G_1) = \{\mathbf{a}^n\mathbf{baa} \mid n \in \mathbb{N}\}$.

(b) Refer to Example 8.9 and use induction to formally prove that $\boldsymbol{L}(G_8) = \{\mathbf{a}^n\mathbf{baa} \mid n \in \mathbb{N}\}$.

8.28. Notice that regular grammars are defined to have production sets that contain *only* right-linear-type productions or *only* left-linear-type productions. Consider the following grammar C, which contains both types of productions:

$$C = \langle\{S, A, B\}, \{\mathbf{0}, \mathbf{1}\}, S, \{S \to \mathbf{0}A \mid \mathbf{1}B \mid \mathbf{0} \mid \mathbf{1} \mid \lambda, A \to S\mathbf{0}, B \to S\mathbf{1}\}\rangle.$$

Note that $S \Rightarrow \mathbf{0}A \Rightarrow \mathbf{0}S\mathbf{0} \Rightarrow \mathbf{01}B\mathbf{0} \Rightarrow \mathbf{01}S\mathbf{10} \Rightarrow \mathbf{0110}$.

(a) Find $\boldsymbol{L}(C)$.

(b) Is $\boldsymbol{L}(C)$ FAD?

(c) Should the definition of regular grammars be expanded to include grammars like this one? Explain.

8.29. **(a)** Why was it important to assume that $\Omega_1 \cap \Omega_2 = \emptyset$ in the proof of Theorem 8.4? Give an example.

(b) Why was it *possible* to assume that $\Omega_1 \cap \Omega_2 = \emptyset$ in the proof of Theorem 8.4? Give a justification.

8.30. Consider the NDFA A_G defined in Lemma 8.2. If A_G is disconnected, what does this say about the grammar G?

8.31. Apply Lemma 8.1 to the automata in Figure 8.4.

8.32. **(a)** Restate Lemma 8.1 so that it directly applies to NDFAs.

(b) Prove this new lemma.

(c) Assume $\Sigma = \{\mathbf{a}, \mathbf{b}, \mathbf{c}\}$ and apply this new lemma to the automata in Figure 8.5.

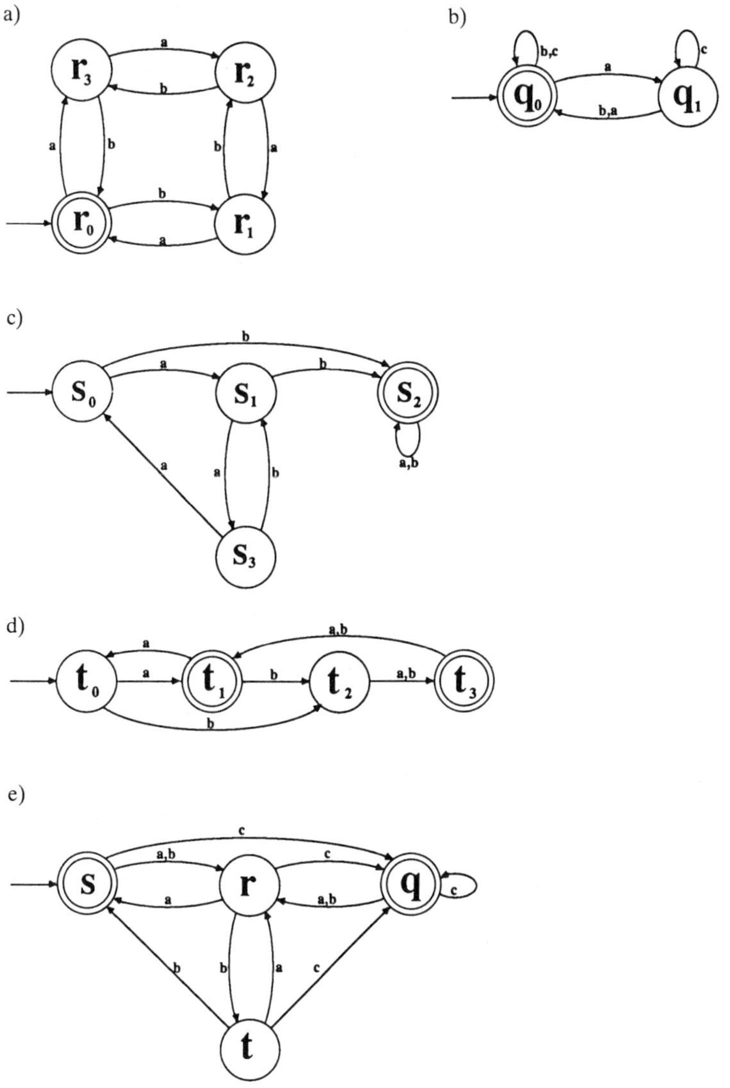

Figure 8.4 Automata for Exercise 8.31

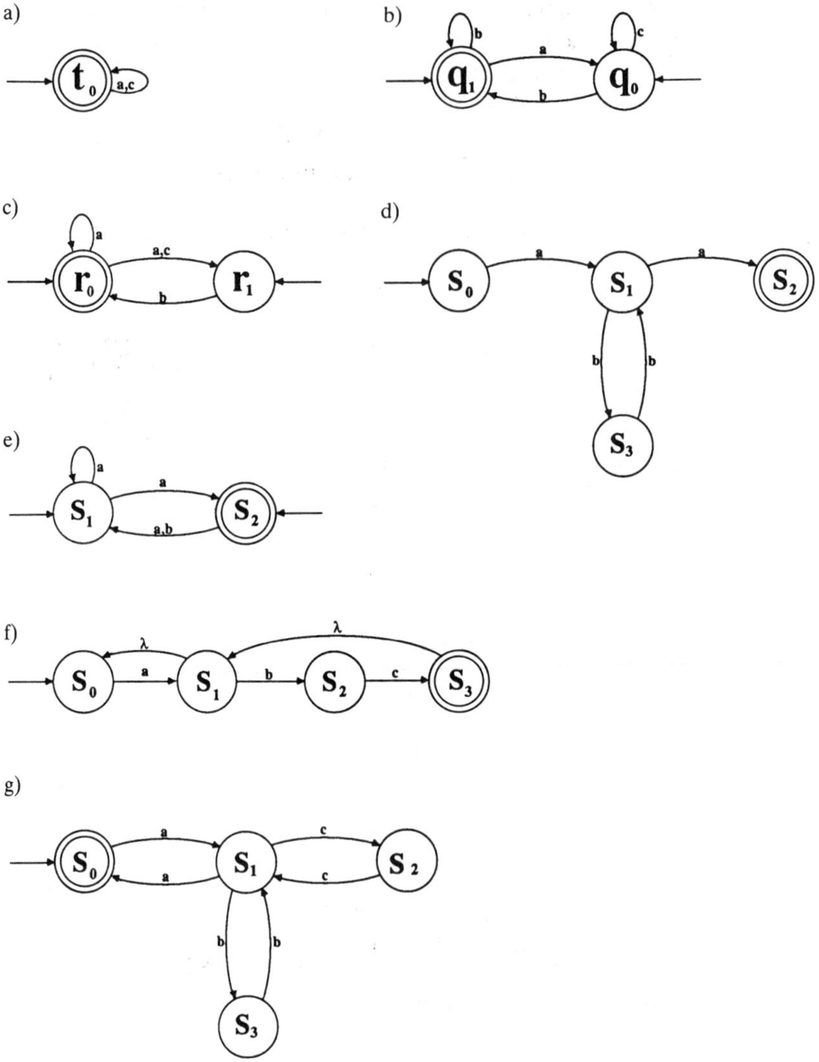

Figure 8.5 Automata for Exercise 8.32

8.33. Define context-free grammars for the following languages:

(a) L_1 = all words over Σ^* for which the last letter matches the first letter.

(b) L_2 = all odd-length words over Σ^* for which the first letter matches the center letter.

(c) L_3 = all words over Σ^* for which the last letter matches none of the other letters.

(d) L_4 = all even-length words over Σ^* for which the two center letters match.

(e) L_5 = all odd-length words over Σ^* for which the center letter matches none of the other letters.

(f) Which of the above languages are regular?

8.34. Define context-free grammars for the following languages:

(a) $L = \{x \in \{\mathbf{a},\mathbf{b}\}^* \mid |x|_{\mathbf{a}} < |x|_{\mathbf{b}}\}$

(b) $G = \{x \in \{\mathbf{a},\mathbf{b}\}^* \mid |x|_{\mathbf{a}} \geq |x|_{\mathbf{b}}\}$

(c) $K = \{w \in \{\mathbf{0},\mathbf{1}\}^* \mid w = w^r\}$

(d) $\Phi = \{x \in \{\mathbf{a},\mathbf{b},\mathbf{c}\}^* \mid \exists i,j,k \in \mathbb{N} \ni x = \mathbf{a}^j\mathbf{b}^k\mathbf{c}^m$, where $j \geq 3$ and $k = m\}$

8.35. Define context-free grammars for the following languages:

(a) $L_1 = \{x \in \{\mathbf{a},\mathbf{b}\}^* \mid |x|_{\mathbf{a}} = 2|x|_{\mathbf{b}}\}$

(b) $L_2 = \{x \in \{\mathbf{a},\mathbf{b}\}^* \mid |x|_{\mathbf{a}} \neq |x|_{\mathbf{b}}\}$

(c) The set of all postfix expressions over the alphabet $\{\mathbf{A},\mathbf{B},+,-\}$

(d) The set of all parenthesized infix expressions over the alphabet $\{\mathbf{A},\mathbf{B},+,-,(,)\}$

8.36. Define context-sensitive grammars for the following languages:

(a) $\Gamma = \{x \in \{\mathbf{0},\mathbf{1},\mathbf{2}\}^* \mid \exists w \in \{\mathbf{0},\mathbf{1}\}^* \ni x = w \cdot \mathbf{2} \cdot w\} = \{\mathbf{2},\mathbf{121},\mathbf{020},\mathbf{11211},\mathbf{10210},\ldots\}$

(b) $\Phi = \{x \in \{\mathbf{b}\}^* \mid \exists j \in \mathbb{N} \ni |x| = 2^j\} = \{\mathbf{b},\mathbf{bb},\mathbf{bbbb},\mathbf{b}^8,\mathbf{b}^{16},\mathbf{b}^{32},\ldots\}$

8.37. Consider the grammar

$$G = \langle\{A,B,S\},\{\mathbf{a},\mathbf{b},\mathbf{c}\},S,\{S\rightarrow\mathbf{a}S\mathrm{B}\mathbf{c}, S\rightarrow\lambda, S\mathrm{B}\rightarrow\mathbf{b}S, \mathbf{c}\mathrm{B}\rightarrow\mathrm{B}\mathbf{c}\}\rangle$$

Show that this context-sensitive grammar is *not* equivalent to G″ given in Example 8.3, where

$$G'' = \langle\{A,B,S,T\},\{\mathbf{a},\mathbf{b},\mathbf{c}\},S,\{S\rightarrow\mathbf{a}S\mathrm{B}\mathbf{c}, S\rightarrow T, T\rightarrow\lambda, T\mathrm{B}\rightarrow\mathbf{b}T, \mathbf{c}\mathrm{B}\rightarrow\mathrm{B}\mathbf{c}\}\rangle$$

8.38. Design context-free grammars that accept:

(a) $L_1 = \mathbf{a}^*(\mathbf{b} \cup \mathbf{c})^* \cap \{x \in \{\mathbf{a},\mathbf{b},\mathbf{c}\}^* \mid |x|_{\mathbf{a}} = |x|_{\mathbf{b}} + |x|_{\mathbf{c}}\}$

(b) $L_2 = \{x \in \{\mathbf{a},\mathbf{b},\mathbf{c}\}^* \mid \exists i,j,k \in \mathbb{N} \ni x = \mathbf{a}^i\mathbf{b}^j\mathbf{c}^k$, where $i + j = k\}$

(c) $L_3 = \{x \in \{\mathbf{a},\mathbf{b},\mathbf{c}\}^* \mid |x|_{\mathbf{a}} + |x|_{\mathbf{b}} = |x|_{\mathbf{c}}\}$

8.39. Refer to Definition 8.4 and prove that $L(G') = L(G) \cup \{\lambda\}$.

8.40. Refer to Definition 8.6 and prove that $L(G') = L(G) \cup \{\lambda\}$.

8.41. **(a)** Show that if G is in the form specified in Theorem 8.8 so is G_* in Theorem 8.5.

(b) Give an example that shows that, even if G_1 and G_2 are in the form specified in Theorem 8.8, the grammar $G^{\cup}$ described in Theorem 8.4 may not be.

(c) Is your construction for $G^{\bullet}$ in Example 8.22 normal form preserving?

8.42. Given two left-linear grammars G_1 and G_2, give a set of rules to find a new left-linear grammar that will generate:

(a) $L(G_1) \cup L(G_2)$

(b) $L(G_1) \cdot L(G_2)$

(c) $L(G_1)^*$

CHAPTER

9

CONTEXT-FREE GRAMMARS

The preceding chapter explored the properties of the type 3 grammars. The next class of grammars in the language hierarchy, the *type 2* or *context-free* grammars, are central to the linguistic aspects of computer science. Context-free grammars were originally used to help specify natural languages and are thus well-suited for defining computer languages. These context-free grammars represent a much wider class of languages than did the regular grammars. Due to the need for balancing parentheses and matched begin–end pairs (among other things), the language Pascal cannot be specified by a regular grammar, but it can be defined with a context-free grammar. Programming languages are specifically designed to be representable by context-free grammars in order to take advantage of the desirable properties inherent in type 2 grammars. These properties are explored in this chapter, while Chapter 10 investigates the generalized automata corresponding to context-free languages.

9.1 PARSE TREES

Derivations in a context-free grammar are similar to those of regular grammars, and the definition of derivation given below is compatible with that given in Definition 8.8.

∇ **Definition 9.1.** Let Σ be any alphabet, $G = \langle\Omega, \Sigma, S, P\rangle$ be a right-linear grammar, $\alpha A \gamma \in (\Sigma \cup \Omega)^*$, and $A \rightarrow \beta$ be a production in P. We will say that $\alpha\beta\gamma$

can be *directly derived* from $\alpha A\gamma$ by applying the production $A \to \beta$, and write $\alpha A\gamma \Rightarrow \alpha\beta\gamma$. Furthermore, if $(\alpha_1 \Rightarrow \alpha_2) \wedge (\alpha_2 \Rightarrow \alpha_3) \wedge \cdots \wedge (\alpha_{n-1} \Rightarrow \alpha_n)$, then we will say that α_1 *derives* α_n and write $\alpha_1 \stackrel{*}{\Rightarrow} \alpha_n$.
Δ

As with Definition 8.8, $\alpha_1 \stackrel{*}{\Rightarrow} \alpha_1$ in zero steps. In generating a particular string, regular grammars typically allowed only a single sequence of applicable productions. Context-free grammars are generally more robust, as shown by Example 9.4, which illustrates several derivations for a single string.

The special nature of the productions in a context-free grammar, which replace a single nonterminal with a string of symbols, allow derivations to be diagrammed in a treelike structure, much as sentences are diagrammed in English. For example, the rules of English specify that a sentence is composed of a subject followed by a predicate, which is reflected in the production

<sentence> → <subject><predicate>

Other rules include

<noun phrase> → <modifier><noun>

and

<predicate> → <verb><prepositional phrase>

A specific sequential application of these and other rules to form an English sentence might be diagrammed as shown in Figure 9.1. Such diagrams are called *parse trees* or *derivation trees*.

∇ **Definition 9.2.** A *parse tree* or *derivation tree* for a regular or context-free grammar $G = <\Omega, \Sigma, S, P>$ is a labeled, ordered tree in which the root node is labeled S, and the n subtrees of a node labeled A are labeled α_1 through α_n only if $A \to \alpha_1 \cdot \alpha_2 \cdots \alpha_n$ is a production in P, and each $\alpha_i \in (\Omega \cup \Sigma)$. However, if $B \to \lambda$ is a production in P, then a node labeled B may instead have a single subtree labeled λ. The parse tree is called *complete* if no leaf is labeled with a nonterminal.
Δ

Recall that for context-free grammars only the start symbol Z can have a production of the form $B \to \lambda$; regular grammars are allowed to have several such rules.

EXAMPLE 9.1

As illustrated in Figure 9.1, a parse tree shows a particular sequence of substitutions allowed by a given grammar. A left-to-right rendering of the leaves of this complete parse tree yields the terminal string "the check is in the mail."

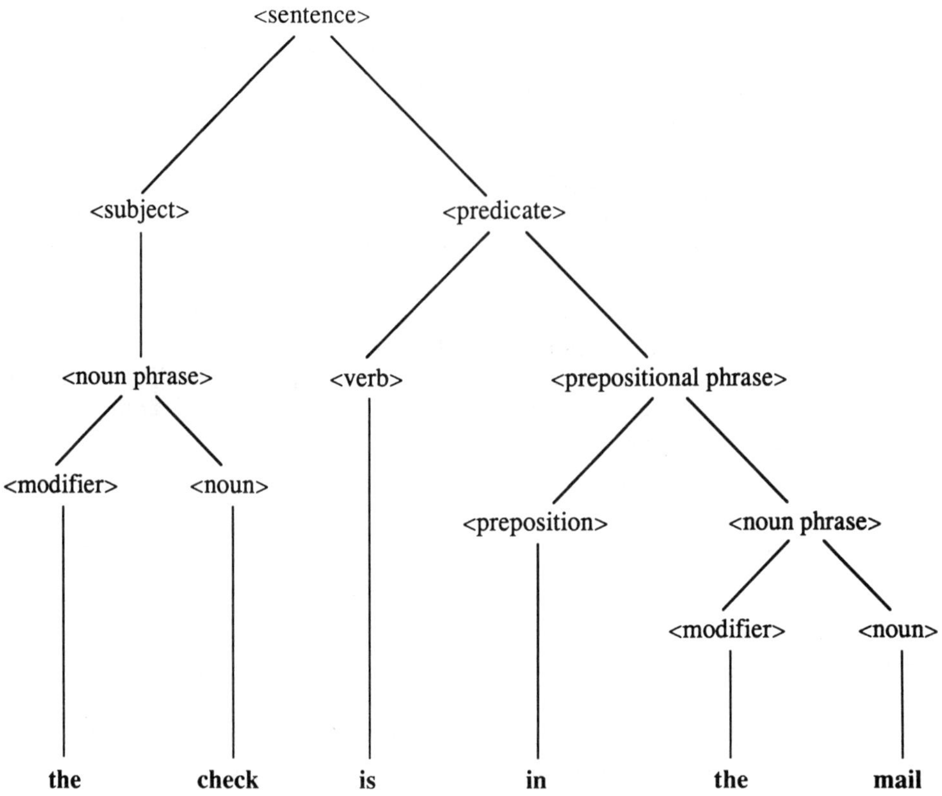

Figure 9.1 A parse tree for the English grammar

EXAMPLE 9.2

Regular grammars form parse trees that are much more restrictive; at any given level in the tree, only one node can be labeled with a nonterminal. Figure 9.2 shows the parse tree for the word **aaabaa** from the grammar

$$G_1 = <\{T, S\}, \{\mathbf{a}, \mathbf{b}\}, S, \{S \to \mathbf{a}S, S \to \mathbf{b}T, T \to \mathbf{aa}\}>.$$

In general, since productions in a right-linear grammar allow only the rightmost symbol to be a nonterminal, parse trees for right-linear grammars will only allow the rightmost child of a node to have a nontrivial subtree.

EXAMPLE 9.3

Given a context-free grammar G, a common task required of compilers is to scan a proposed terminal string x belonging to $L(G)$ and build a parse tree corresponding

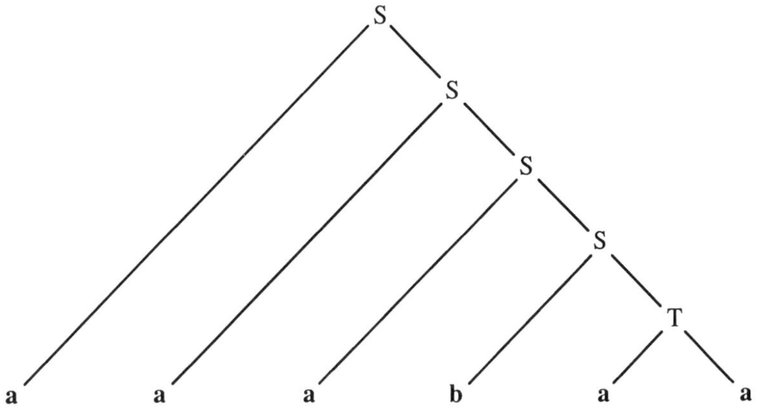

Figure 9.2 The parse tree discussed in Example 9.2

to x. If G is the "regular expression" grammar defined in Example 8.2, G = <{R}, {**a**, **b**, **c**, **(**, **)**, **ϵ**, **∅**, ∪, •, *}, R, {R → **a**|**b**|**c**|**ϵ**|**∅**|(R•R)|(R∪R)|R*}> and x is **((a∪b)*•c)**, the desired result would be a representation of the tree shown in Figure 9.3.

In a perfect world of perfect programmers, it might be appropriate to assume that x can definitely be generated by the productions in G. In our world, however, compilers must unfortunately perform the added task of determining whether it is possible to generate the proposed terminal string x, that is, whether the file presented represents a syntactically correct program. This is typically done as the parse trees are being built, and discrepancies are reported to the user. For the "regular expression" grammar used in Example 9.3, there is an algorithm for scanning the symbols of proposed strings such as **((a∪b)*•c)** to determine whether a parse tree can be constructed. In the case of a string like **((a∪•b)**, no such parse tree exists, and the string therefore cannot be generated by the grammar. If the productions of a grammar follow certain guidelines, the task of finding the correct scanning algorithm is greatly simplified. The desired properties that should be inherent in a programming language grammar are investigated later in the text.

In a separate phase, after the parse trees are found, the compiler then uses the trees and other constructs to infer meaning to the program, that is, to generate appropriate machine code that reflects the advertised meaning (that is, the semantics) of the program statements. For example, the parse tree for **((a∪b)*•c)** in Figure 9.3 clearly shows both the order in which the operators ∪, •, and * should be applied and the expressions to which they should be applied.

Given a particular complete parse tree for a string x, there may be some freedom in the *order* in which the associated productions are applied.

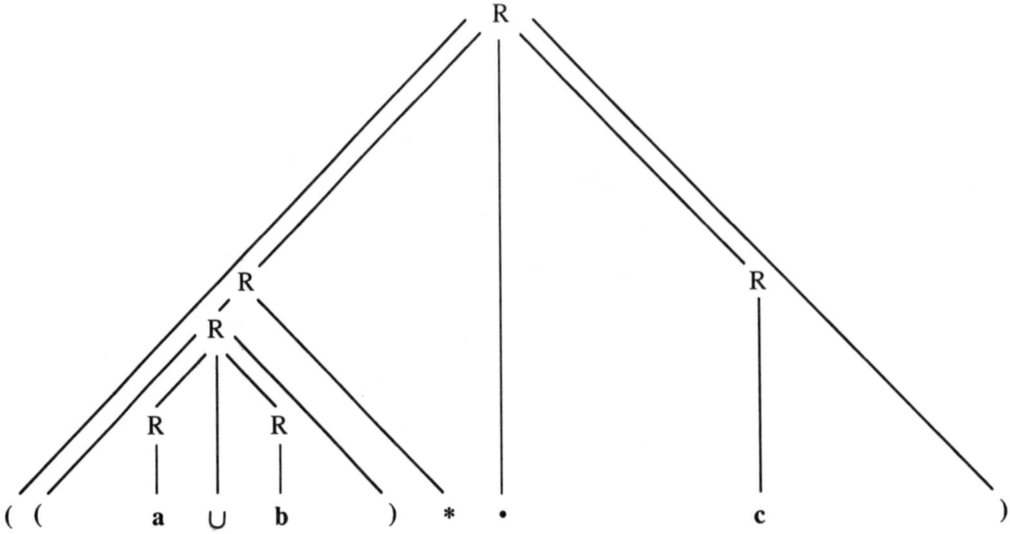

Figure 9.3 The parse tree discussed in Example 9.3

EXAMPLE 9.4

For the grammar

$$G = \langle \{R\}, \{\mathbf{a}, \mathbf{b}, \mathbf{c}, \mathbf{(}, \mathbf{)}, \boldsymbol{\epsilon}, \boldsymbol{\emptyset}, \cup, \cdot, {}^{*}\}, R, \{R \to \mathbf{a} \mid \mathbf{b} \mid \mathbf{c} \mid \boldsymbol{\epsilon} \mid \boldsymbol{\emptyset} \mid \mathbf{(}R\cdot R\mathbf{)} \mid \mathbf{(}R\cup R\mathbf{)} \mid R^{*}\}\rangle,$$

each of the following are valid derivations of the string $x =$ **((a∪b)*•c)**.

Derivation 1:

$$\begin{aligned} R &\Rightarrow (R\cdot R) \\ &\Rightarrow (R^{*}\cdot R) \\ &\Rightarrow ((R\cup R)^{*}\cdot R) \\ &\Rightarrow ((\mathbf{a}\cup R)^{*}\cdot R) \\ &\Rightarrow ((\mathbf{a}\cup \mathbf{b})^{*}\cdot R) \\ &\Rightarrow ((\mathbf{a}\cup \mathbf{b})^{*}\cdot \mathbf{c}) \end{aligned}$$

Derivation 2:

$$\begin{aligned} R &\Rightarrow (R\cdot R) \\ &\Rightarrow (R^{*}\cdot R) \\ &\Rightarrow ((R\cup R)^{*}\cdot R) \\ &\Rightarrow ((R\cup R)^{*}\cdot \mathbf{c}) \\ &\Rightarrow ((R\cup \mathbf{b})^{*}\cdot \mathbf{c}) \\ &\Rightarrow ((\mathbf{a}\cup \mathbf{b})^{*}\cdot \mathbf{c}) \end{aligned}$$

Derivation 3:

$$\begin{aligned} R &\Rightarrow (R \cdot R) \\ &\Rightarrow (R \cdot c) \\ &\Rightarrow (R^* \cdot c) \\ &\Rightarrow ((R \cup R)^* \cdot c) \\ &\Rightarrow ((a \cup R)^* \cdot c) \\ &\Rightarrow ((a \cup b)^* \cdot c) \end{aligned}$$

Derivation 4:

$$\begin{aligned} R &\Rightarrow (R \cdot R) \\ &\Rightarrow (R \cdot c) \\ &\Rightarrow (R^* \cdot c) \\ &\Rightarrow ((R \cup R)^* \cdot c) \\ &\Rightarrow ((R \cup b)^* \cdot c) \\ &\Rightarrow ((a \cup b)^* \cdot c) \end{aligned}$$

∇ **Definition 9.3.** A derivation sequence is called a *leftmost* derivation if at each step in the sequence the leftmost nonterminal is next expanded to produce the following step. A derivation sequence is called a *rightmost* derivation if at each step in the sequence the rightmost nonterminal is next expanded to produce the following step.
Δ

The first of the derivations given in Example 9.4 is a *leftmost* derivation since at each step it is always the leftmost nonterminal that is expanded to arrive at the next step. Similarly, the last of these, derivation 4, is a *rightmost* derivation. There are many other possible derivations, such as derivations 2 and 3, which are neither leftmost nor rightmost.

The restrictions on regular grammars ensure that there is never more than one nonterminal present at any point during a derivation. This *linear* nature of regular grammars ensures that all derivations of a parse tree follow exactly the same sequence, since there is never a choice of nonterminals to expand. Thus, the rightmost derivation of a parse tree in a regular grammar is always the same as its leftmost derivation.

Parse trees in context-free grammars are generally more robust, allowing several different derivation sequences to correspond to the same tree. For a given parse tree, though, there is only one leftmost derivation. In Figure 9.4, the nodes in the parse tree for $((a \cup b)^* \cdot c)$ are numbered to show the order in which they would

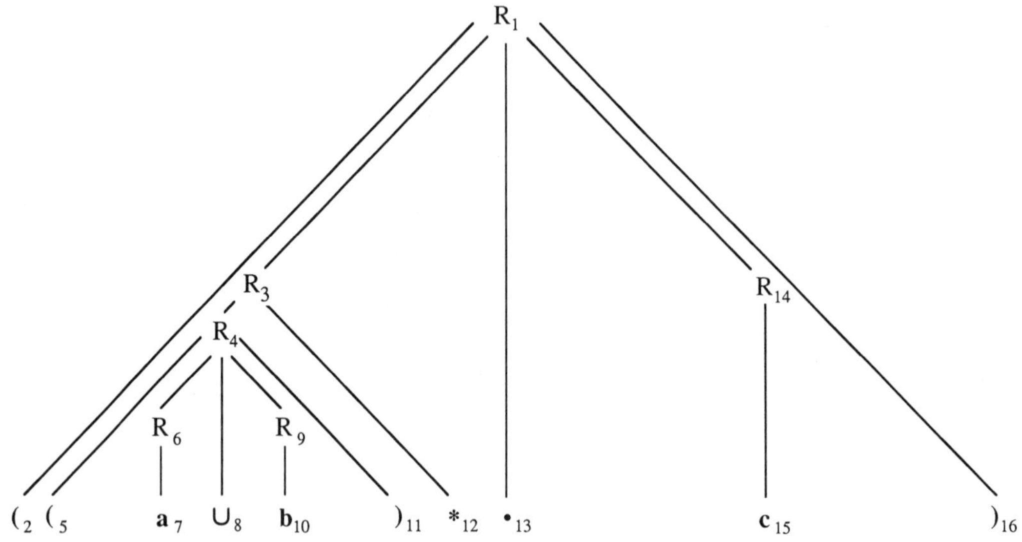

Figure 9.4 The preorder traversal of the parse tree

be visited by a preorder traversal. Note that the sequence in which the *non*terminals would be expanded in a leftmost derivation corresponds to the order in which they appear in the preorder traversal.

9.2 AMBIGUITY

Whereas each tree corresponds to a unique leftmost derivation, it is possible for a terminal string to have more than one leftmost derivation. This will happen whenever a string x corresponds to more than one parse tree, that is, whenever there are truly distinct ways of applying the productions of the grammar to form x. Grammars for which this can happen are called *ambiguous*.

∇ **Definition 9.4.** A grammar $G = <\Omega, \Sigma, S, P>$ is called *ambiguous* if there exists a string $x \in \Sigma^*$ that corresponds to two distinct parse trees. A grammar that is not ambiguous is called *unambiguous*.
Δ

EXAMPLE 9.5

Consider the grammar $G_2 = <\{S, A\}, \{\mathbf{a}\}, S, \{S \to AA, A \to \mathbf{a}S\mathbf{a}, A \to \mathbf{a}\}>$. Figure 9.5 shows the two distinct parse trees associated with the word **aaaaa**. Note that the leftmost derivations corresponding to these trees are indeed different:

$$\begin{aligned} S &\Rightarrow AA \\ &\Rightarrow \mathbf{a}S\mathbf{a}A \\ &\Rightarrow \mathbf{a}AA\mathbf{a}A \\ &\Rightarrow \mathbf{aa}A\mathbf{a}A \\ &\Rightarrow \mathbf{aaaa}A \\ &\Rightarrow \mathbf{aaaaa} \end{aligned}$$

is the sequence indicated by the parse tree in Figure 9.5a, while

$$\begin{aligned} S &\Rightarrow AA \\ &\Rightarrow \mathbf{a}A \\ &\Rightarrow \mathbf{aa}S\mathbf{a} \\ &\Rightarrow \mathbf{aa}AA\mathbf{a} \\ &\Rightarrow \mathbf{aaa}A\mathbf{a} \\ &\Rightarrow \mathbf{aaaaa} \end{aligned}$$

corresponds to Figure 9.5b.

Recall that context-free grammars are used to inspect statements within a computer program and determine corresponding parse trees. Such ambiguity is undesirable in a grammar that describes a programming language, since it would be unclear which of the trees should be used to infer the meaning of the string. Indeed, this ambiguity would be intolerable if a statement could give rise to two trees that implied different meanings, as illustrated in Example 9.6 below. It is therefore of practical importance to avoid descriptions of languages that entail this sort of ambiguity.

The language defined by the grammar G_2 in Example 9.5 is actually quite simple. Even though G_2 is not a regular grammar, it can easily be shown that $L(G_2)$ is the regular set $\{\mathbf{a}^2, \mathbf{a}^5, \mathbf{a}^8, \mathbf{a}^{11}, \mathbf{a}^{14}, \ldots\}$. The ambiguity is therefore not inherent in the language, but is rather a consequence of the needlessly complex grammar used to describe the language. A much simpler context-free grammar is given by $G_3 = \langle\{T\}, \{\mathbf{a}\}, T, \{T \to \mathbf{aaa}T, T \to \mathbf{aa}\}\rangle$. This grammar happens to be right linear and is definitely not ambiguous.

EXAMPLE 9.6

The following sampling from a potential programming language grammar illustrates the semantic problems that can be caused by ambiguity. Consider the grammar $G_s = \langle\{\langle\text{expression}\rangle, \langle\text{identifier}\rangle\}, \{\mathbf{a}, \mathbf{b}, \mathbf{c}, \mathbf{d}, -\}, \langle\text{expression}\rangle, P\rangle$, where P consists of the productions

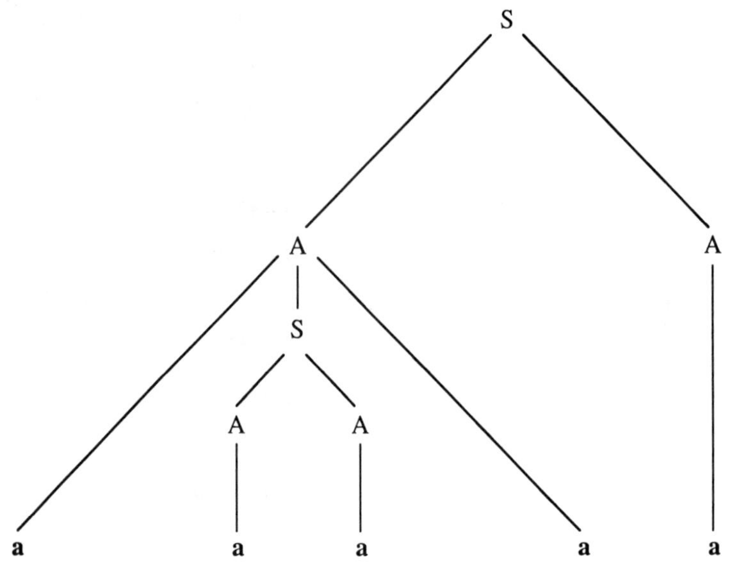

(a)

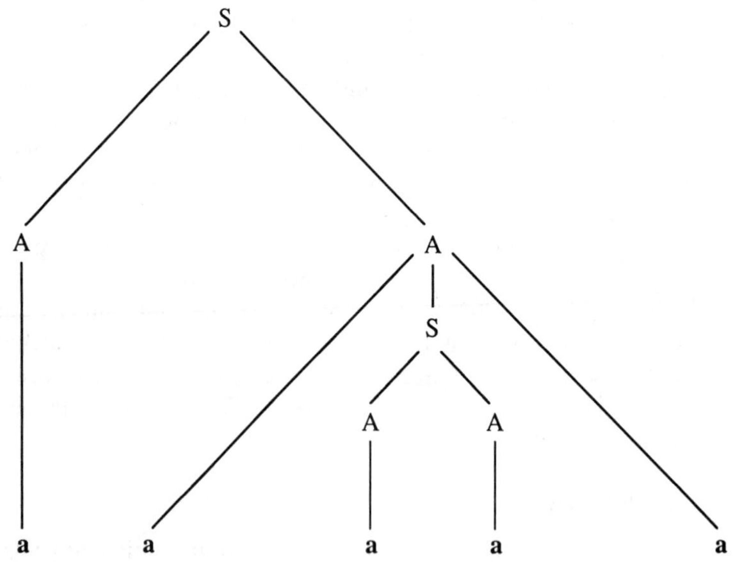

(b)

Figure 9.5 (a) A parse tree for **aaaaa** in Example 9.5 (b) An alternate parse tree for **aaaaa**

<expression> → <identifier>
<expression> → <identifier> − <expression>
<expression> → <expression> − <identifier>
<identifier> → **a**
<identifier> → **b**
<identifier> → **c**
<identifier> → **d**

$L(G_s)$ then contains the string **a − b − d**, which can be generated by two distinct parse trees, as shown in Figure 9.6. Figure 9.6a corresponds to the following leftmost derivation.

<expression> ⇒ <expression> − <identifier>
⇒ <identifier> − <expression> − <identifier>
⇒ **a** − <expression> − <identifier>
⇒ **a** − <identifier> − <identifier>
⇒ **a − b** − <identifier>
⇒ **a − b − d**

Figure 9.6b corresponds to a different leftmost derivation, as shown below.

<expression> ⇒ <identifier> − <expression>
⇒ **a** − <expression>
⇒ **a** − <identifier> − <expression>
⇒ **a − b** − <expression>
⇒ **a − b** − <identifier>
⇒ **a − b − d**

If the productions of G_s were part of a grammatical description of a programming language, there are obvious semantics associated with the productions involving the − operator. The productions

<expression> → <identifier> − <expression>

and

<expression> → <expression> − <identifier>

indicate that two values should be combined using the subtraction operator to form a new value. The compiler would be responsible for generating code that carried out the appropriate subtraction. Unfortunately, the two parse trees give rise to functionally different code. For the parse tree in Figure 9.6a, the subtraction will be performed left to right, while in the parse tree in Figure 9.6b the ordering of the operators is right to left. Subtraction is *not* a commutative operation, and the expression (a − b) − d will usually produce a different value than a − (b − d). Ambiguity can thus be a fatal flaw in a grammar describing a programming language.

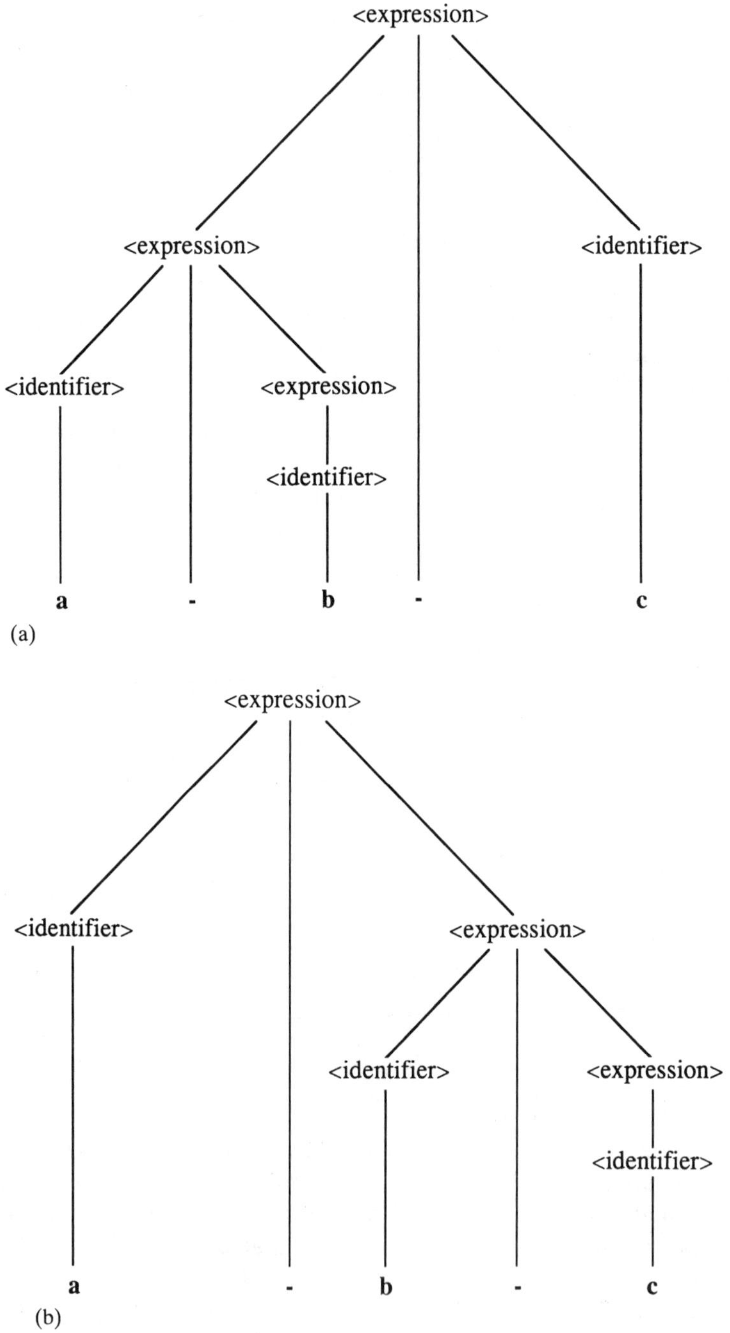

Figure 9.6 (a) A parse tree for **a-b-d** in Example 9.6 (b) An alternate parse tree for **a-b-d**

In the language $L(G_s)$ discussed in Example 9.6, the ambiguity is again not inherent in the language itself, but is rather a consequence of the specific productions in the grammar G_s describing the language. In most programming languages, the expression **a − b − d** is allowed and has a well-defined meaning. Most languages decree that such expressions be evaluated from left to right, and hence **a − b − d** would be interpreted as (a − b) − d. This interpretation can be enforced by simply removing the production

<expression> → <identifier> − <expression>

from G_s to form the new grammar

G_m = <{<expression>, <identifier>}, {**a**, **b**, **c**, **d**, **−**}, <expression>, P′>

where P′ consists of the productions

<expression> → <identifier>
<expression> → <expression> − <identifier>
<identifier> → **a**
<identifier> → **b**
<identifier> → **c**
<identifier> → **d**

It should be clear that G_s and G_m are equivalent, and both generate the regular language **((a∪b∪c∪d)•−)*•(a∪b∪c∪d)**. G_m gives rise to unique parse trees and is therefore unambiguous. It should be noted that the language could have been defined with a single nonterminal; a simpler grammar equivalent to G_m is G_t = <{T}, {**a**, **b**, **c**, **d**, **−**}, T, {T → **a**|**b**|**c**|**d**|T − T}>. However, since G_t is ambiguous, it is much more difficult to work with than G_m. The pair of nonterminals <expression> and <identifier> are used to circumvent the ambiguity problem in this language. For the grammar G_m, the production

<expression> → <expression> − <identifier>

contains the nonterminal <expression> to the left of the subtraction token and <identifier> to the right of the **−**. Since <identifier> can only be replaced by a terminal representing a single variable, the resulting parse tree will ensure that the entire expression to the left of the **−** will be evaluated before the operation corresponding to this current subtraction token is performed. In this fashion, the distinction between the two nonterminals forces a left-to-right evaluation sequence. In fact, a more robust language with other operators like × and ÷ will require more nonterminals to enforce the default precedence among these operators.

Most modern programming languages employ a solution to the ambiguity problem that is different from the one just described. Programmers generally do not want to be constrained by operators that can only be evaluated from left to right, and hence matched parentheses are used to indicate an order of evaluation that may differ from the default. Thus, unambiguous grammars that correctly reflect the meaning of expressions like d − (b − c) or even (a) − ((c − (d))) are sought.

EXAMPLE 9.7

The following grammar G_p allows expressions with parentheses, minus signs, and single-letter identifiers to be uniquely parsed.

G_p = <{<expression>, <identifier>}, {**a**, **b**, **c**, **d**, **−**, **(**, **)**}, <expression>, P''>

where P'' consists of the productions

<expression> → **(**<expression>**)**
<expression> → <expression> **−** **(**<expression>**)**
<expression> → <identifier>
<expression> → <expression> **−** <identifier>
<identifier> → **a**
<identifier> → **b**
<identifier> → **c**
<identifier> → **d**

The first two productions in P'', which were not present in P', are designed to handle the balancing of parentheses. The first rule allows superfluous sets of parentheses to be correctly recognized. The second rule ensures that an expression that is surrounded by parentheses is evaluated before the operator outside those parentheses is evaluated. In the absence of parentheses, the left-to-right ordering of the operators is maintained. Figure 9.7 illustrates the unique parse tree for the expression (a) − ((c − (d))).

G_p is a context-free language that is too complex to be regular; the pumping lemma for regular sets (Theorem 2.3) can be used to show that is impossible for a DFA to maintain an unlimited number of corresponding balanced parentheses. This language, and the others discussed so far, can all be expressed by unambiguous grammars. It should be clear that *every* language generated by grammars has ambiguous grammars that also generate it, since an unambiguous grammar can always be modified to become ambiguous. What is not immediately clear is whether there are languages that can *only* be generated by ambiguous grammars.

∇ **Definition 9.5.** A context-free language L is called *inherently ambiguous* if every grammar that generates L is ambiguous. A context-free language that is not inherently ambiguous is called unambiguous.
Δ

∇ **Definition 9.6.** Let the class of context-free language L over the alphabet Σ be denoted by $\mathcal{C}_\Sigma$. Let the class of unambiguous context-free languages be denoted by $\mathcal{U}_\Sigma$.
Δ

∇ **Theorem 9.1.** There are context-free languages that are inherently ambiguous; that is, $\mathcal{U}_\Sigma$ is properly contained in $\mathcal{C}_\Sigma$.

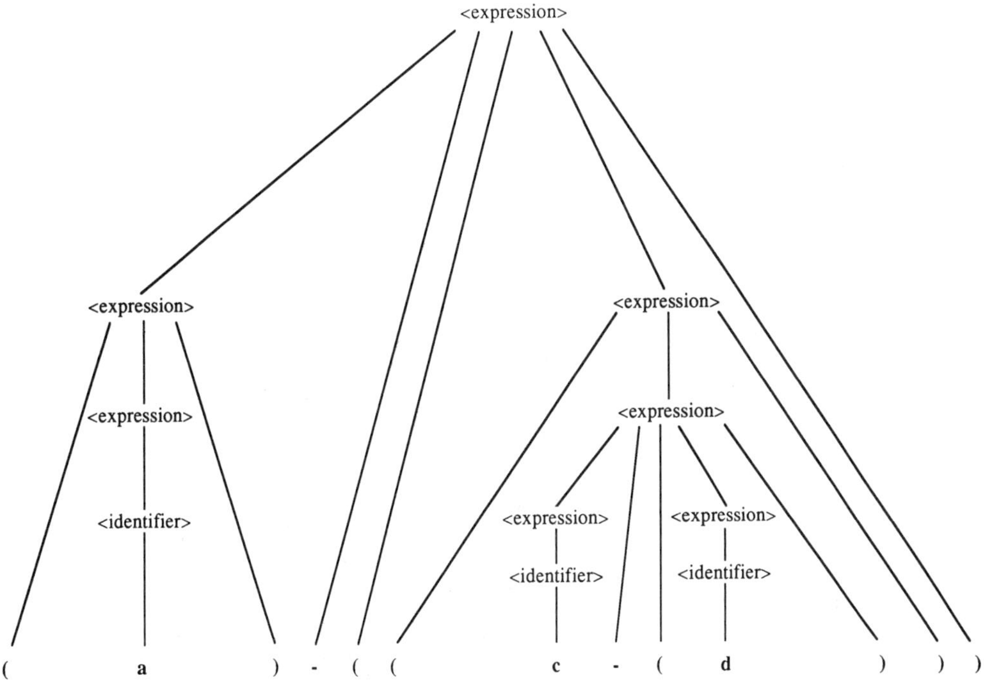

Figure 9.7 The parse tree discussed in Example 9.7

Proof. The language $L = \{\mathbf{a}^n\mathbf{b}^n\mathbf{c}^m\mathbf{d}^m \mid n, m \in \mathbb{N}\} \cup \{\mathbf{a}^i\mathbf{b}^j\mathbf{c}^j\mathbf{d}^i \mid i, j \in \mathbb{N}\}$ is a context-free language (see the exercises). L is also inherently ambiguous, since there must exist two parse trees for some of the strings in the intersection of the two sets $\{\mathbf{a}^n\mathbf{b}^n\mathbf{c}^m\mathbf{d}^m \mid n, m \in \mathbb{N}\}$ and $\{\mathbf{a}^i\mathbf{b}^j\mathbf{c}^j\mathbf{d}^i \mid i, j \in \mathbb{N}\}$. The proof of this last statement is tedious to formalize; the interested reader is referred to [HOPC].
Δ

Theorem 9.1 states that there exist inherently ambiguous type 2 languages. No type 3 language is inherently ambiguous. Even though there are regular grammars that are ambiguous, every regular grammar has an equivalent grammar that is unambiguous. This assertion is supported by the following examples and results.

EXAMPLE 9.8

Consider the following right-linear grammar G_r:

$$G_r = <\{S, A, C\}, \{\mathbf{a}, \mathbf{b}, \mathbf{c}\}, S, \{S \to A\mathbf{bc}, S \to \mathbf{ab}C, A \to \mathbf{a}, C \to \mathbf{c}\}>$$

Only one terminal string can be derived from G_r, but this word has two distinct derivation trees, as shown in Figure 9.8. Thus, there are regular grammars that are ambiguous.

∇ **Theorem 9.2.** Given any right-linear grammar $G = <\Omega, \Sigma, S, P>$, there exists an equivalent right-linear grammar that is unambiguous.

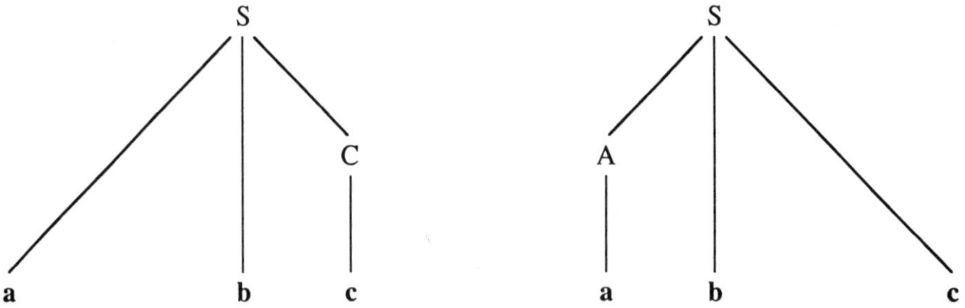

Figure 9.8   The parse trees discussed in Example 9.8

Proof. Let $G' = G_{(A_G^{\sigma d})}$. That is, beginning with the right-linear grammar G, use the construction outlined in Lemma 8.2 to find the corresponding automaton A_G. Use Definition 4.9 to remove the lambda-transitions and Definition 4.5 to produce a deterministic machine, and then apply the construction outlined in Lemma 8.1 to form the new right-linear grammar G'. By Lemma 8.2, Theorem 4.2, Theorem 4.1, and Lemma 8.1, the language defined by each of these constructs is unchanged, so G' is equivalent to G. Due to the deterministic nature of the machine from which this new grammar was built, the resulting parse tree for a given string must be unique, since only one production is applicable at any point in the derivation. A formal inductive statement of this property is left as an exercise.
Δ

∇ **Corollary 9.1.**   The class $\mathcal{G}_\Sigma$ of languages generated by regular grammars is properly contained in $\mathcal{U}_\Sigma$.

Proof. Containment follows immediately from Theorem 9.2. Proper containment is demonstrated by the language and grammar discussed in Example 9.3.
Δ

EXAMPLE 9.9

The right-linear grammar

$$G_r = \langle \{S, B, C\}, \{a, b, c\}, S, \{S \to aB, S \to abC, B \to bc, C \to c\} \rangle$$

in Example 9.8 can be transformed, as outlined in Theorem 9.2, into an unambiguous grammar. The automaton corresponding to G_r, found by applying the technique given in Lemma 8.2 is shown in Figure 9.9a. The version of this automaton without lambda-moves (with the inaccessible states not shown) is illustrated in Figure 9.9b. The deterministic version, with the disconnected states again removed, is given in Figure 9.9c. For simplicity, the states are relabeled in Figure 9.9d. The corresponding grammar specified by Lemma 8.1 is

$$G' = \langle \{S_0, S_1, S_2, S_3, S_4\}, \{a, b, c\}, S_0, \{S_0 \to aS_1 | bS_4 | cS_4, \ S_1 \to aS_4 | bS_2 | cS_4,$$

$$S_2 \to aS_4 | bS_4 | cS_3, \ S_3 \to \lambda | aS_4 | bS_4 | cS_4, \ S_4 \to aS_4 | bS_4 | cS_4 \} \rangle$$

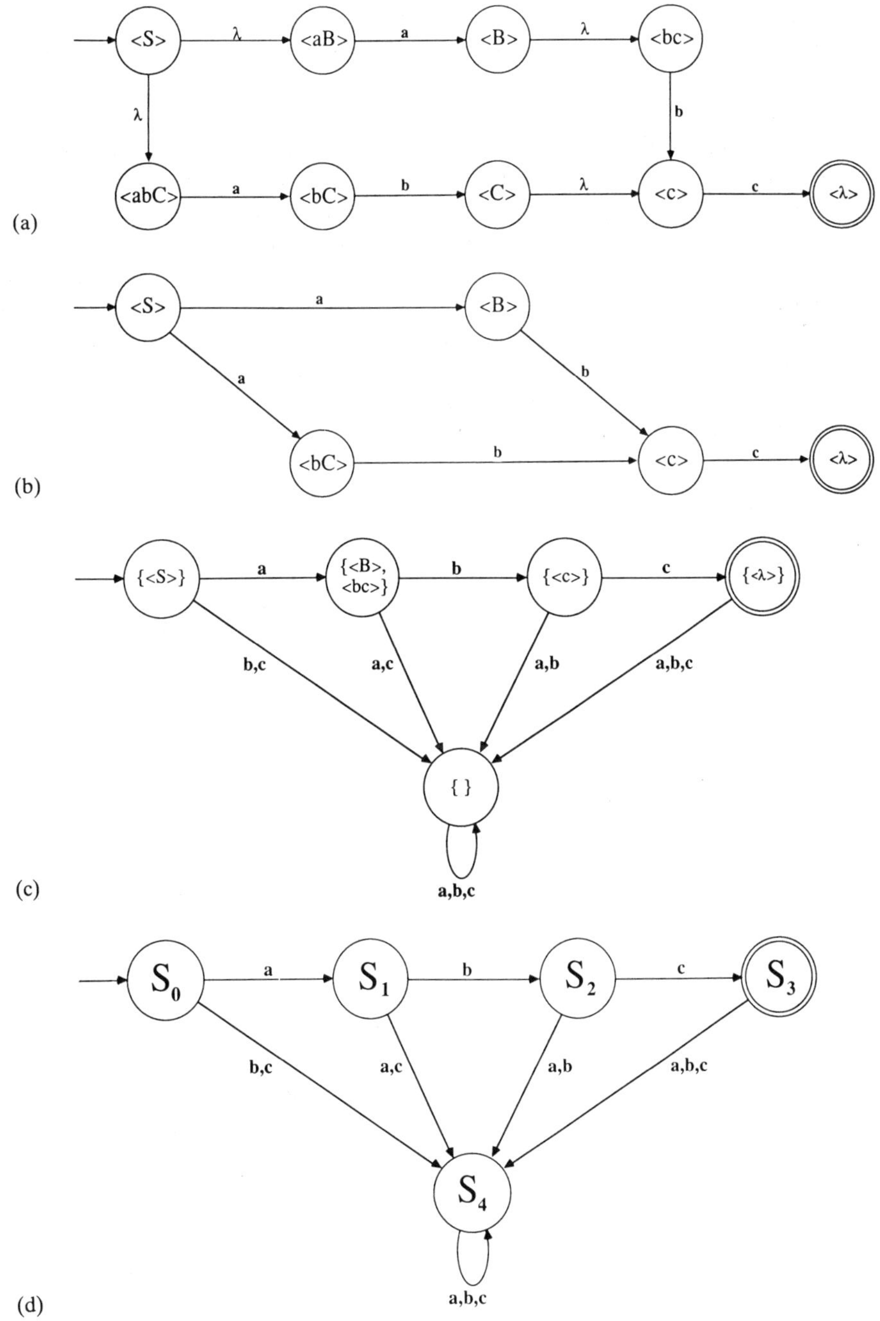

Figure 9.9 (a) The automaton discussed in Example 9.9 (b) The simplified automaton discussed in Example 9.9 (c) The deterministic automaton discussed in Example 9.9 (d) The final automaton discussed in Example 9.9

The orderly nature of this resulting type of grammar easily admits the specification of an algorithm that scans a proposed terminal string and builds the corresponding parse tree. The partial parse tree for a string such as **abb** would be as pictured in Figure 9.10a. This would clearly be an invalid string since S_4 cannot be replaced by λ. By contrast, the tree for the word **abc** would produce a complete parse tree, and it is instructive to step through the process by which it is built. The root of the tree must be labeled S_0, and scanning the first letter of the word **abc** is sufficient to determine that the first production to be applied is $S_0 \rightarrow \mathbf{a}S_1$ (since no other S_0-rule immediately produces an **a**). Scanning the next letter provides enough information to determine that the next S_1 rule that is used must be $S_1 \rightarrow \mathbf{b}S_2$, and the third letter admits the production $S_2 \rightarrow \mathbf{c}S_3$ and no other. Recognizing the end of the string causes a check for whether the current nonterminal can produce the empty string. Since $S_3 \rightarrow \lambda$ is in the grammar, the string **abc** is a valid terminal string, and corresponds to the parse tree shown in Figure 9.10b.

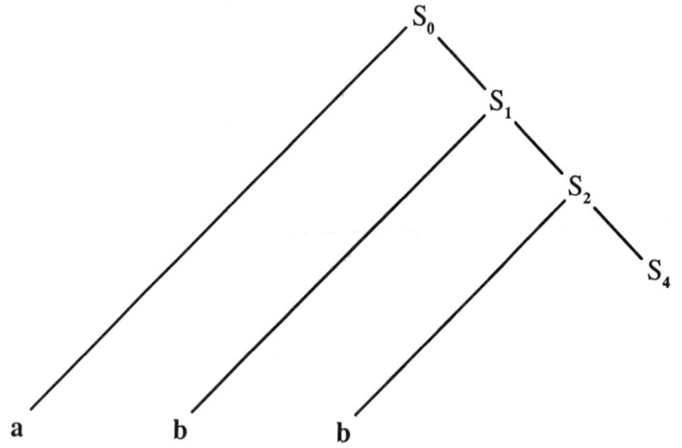

(a)

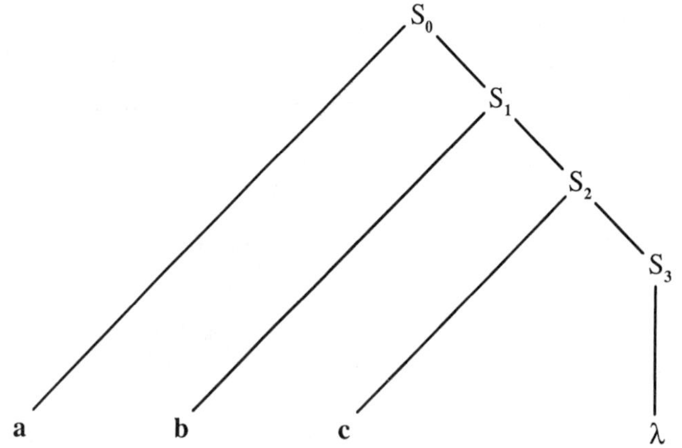

(b)

Figure 9.10 (a) The partial parse tree for the string **abb** (b) The parse tree for the string **abc**

Grammars that admit scanning algorithms like the one outlined above are called LL0 grammars since the parse tree can be deduced using a left-to-right scan of the proposed string while looking ahead 0 symbols to produce a leftmost derivation. That is, the production that produces a given symbol can be immediately determined without regard to the symbols that follow.

Note that the grammar $G_3 = <\{T\}, \{\mathbf{a}\}, T, \{T \to \mathbf{aaa}T, T \to \mathbf{aa}\}>$ is LL2; that is, upon seeing **a**, the scanner must look ahead two symbols to see if the end-of-string marker is imminent. In this grammar, **a** may be produced by either of the two T-rules; the letters following this symbol in the proposed string are an important factor in determining which production must be applied. The language described by G_3 is simple enough to be defined by a grammar that *is* LL0, since every regular grammar can be transformed as suggested by the proof of Theorem 9.2.

The deterministic orderliness of LL0 grammars may be generally unattainable, but it represents a desirable goal that a compiler designer would strive to approximate when specifying a grammatical model of a programming language. When a grammar is being defined to serve as a guide to construct a compiler, an LL0 grammar is clearly the grammar of choice. Indeed, if even a portion of a context-free grammar conforms to the LL0 property, this is of considerable benefit. Whereas the technique outlined in Theorem 9.2 could be applied to any regular language to find a hospitable LL0 grammar, programming languages are generally more complex than regular languages, and these languages are unlikely to have LL0 models. For context-free languages, it is much more likely that it will not be possible to determine which production (or sequence of productions) will produce the symbol currently being scanned. In such cases, it will be necessary to look ahead to successive symbols to make this determination.

A classic example of the need to look ahead in parsing programming languages is reflected in the following FORTRAN statement:

```
DO 77 I = 1.5
```

Since FORTRAN allows blanks within identifiers, this is a valid statement and should cause the variable `DO77I` to be assigned the value 1.5. On the other hand, the statement

```
DO 77 I = 1,5
```

specifies a "do" loop, and has an entirely different meaning. A lexical analyzer that sees the three characters '`DO `' cannot immediately determine whether this represents a token for a do loop, or is instead part of a variable identifier. It may have to wait until well after the equal sign is scanned to correctly identify the tokens.

9.3 CANONICAL FORMS

The definition of a context-free grammar was quite broad, and it is desirable to establish canonical forms that will restrict the type of productions that can be employed. Unrestricted context-free grammars do not admit very precise relationships between the strings generated by the grammar and the production sequences generating those strings. In particular, the length of a terminal string may bear very little relation to the number of productions needed to generate that string.

EXAMPLE 9.10

A string of length 18 can be generated with only three applications of productions from the grammar

$$\langle\{S\}, \{\mathbf{a}, \mathbf{b}, \mathbf{c}\}, S, \{S \to \mathbf{abcabc}S, S \to \mathbf{abcabc}\}\rangle$$

A string of length 1 can be generated by no less than five productions in the grammar

$$\langle\{S_1, S_2, S_3, S_4, S_5\}, \{\mathbf{a}, \mathbf{b}, \mathbf{c}\}, S_1, \{S_1 \to S_2, S_2 \to S_3, S_3 \to S_4, S_4 \to S_5, S_5 \to \mathbf{a}\}\rangle$$

It should be clear that even more extreme examples can be defined, in which the number of terminal symbols markedly dominates the number of productions, and vice versa.

The pumping theorem for context-free grammars (Theorem 9.7) and other theorems hinge on a more precise relationship between the number of terminal symbols produced and the number of productions used to produce those symbols. Grammars whose production sets satisfy more rigorous constraints are needed if such relationships are to be guaranteed. The constraints should not be so severe that some context-free languages cannot be generated by a set of productions that conform to the restrictions. In other words, some well-behaved *normal forms* are sought.

A practical step toward that goal is the abolition of productions that cannot participate in valid derivations. The algorithm for identifying such productions constitutes an application of the algorithms developed previously for finite automata. The following definition formally identifies productions that cannot participate in valid derivations.

∇ **Definition 9.7.** A production $A \to \beta$ in a context-free grammar $G = \langle \Omega, \Sigma, S, P\rangle$ is *useful* if it is part of a derivation beginning with the start symbol and ending with a terminal string. That is, the A-rule $A \to \beta$ is useful if there is a derivation $S \overset{*}{\Rightarrow} \alpha A \omega \Rightarrow \alpha\beta\omega \overset{*}{\Rightarrow} x$, where $x \in \Sigma^*$.

A production that is not useful is called *useless*.

A nonterminal that does not appear in any useful production is called *useless*.

A nonterminal that is not useless is called *useful*.

Δ

EXAMPLE 9.11

Consider the grammar with productions

$$
\begin{aligned}
&S \to \mathbf{g}A\mathbf{e}, S \to \mathbf{a}YB, S \to CY \\
&A \to \mathbf{b}BY, A \to \mathbf{oo}C \\
&B \to \mathbf{dd}, B \to D \\
&C \to \mathbf{j}VB, C \to \mathbf{gi} \\
&D \to \mathbf{n} \\
&U \to \mathbf{k}W \\
&V \to \mathbf{ba}XXX, V \to \mathbf{o}V \\
&W \to \mathbf{c} \\
&X \to \mathbf{f}V \\
&Y \to Y\mathbf{hm}
\end{aligned}
$$

This grammar illustrates the three basic ways a nonterminal can qualify as useless.

1. For the nonterminal W above, it is impossible to find a derivation from the start symbol S that produces a sentential form containing W. U also lacks this quality.
2. No derivation containing the nonterminal Y can produce a *terminal* string. X and V are likewise useless for the same reason.
3. B is only produced in conjunction with useless nonterminals, and it is therefore useless also. Once B is judged useless, D is seen to be useless for similar reasons.

∇ **Theorem 9.3.** Every nonempty context-free language L can be generated by a context-free grammar that contains no useless productions and no useless nonterminals.

Proof. Note that if L were empty the conclusion would be impossible to attain: the start symbol would be useless, and every grammar by definition must have a start symbol. Assume that L is a nonempty context-free language. By Definition 8.6, there is a context-free grammar $G = <\Omega, \Sigma, S, P>$ that generates L. The desired grammar G^u can be formed from G, with the useless productions removed from P and the useless nonterminals removed from Ω. The new grammar G^u will be equivalent to G, since the lost items were by definition unable to participate in significant derivations. G^u will then obviously contain no useless productions and no useless nonterminals.

A grammar with the desired properties must therefore exist, but the outlined argument does not indicate *how* to identify the items that must be removed. The following algorithm, based on the procedures used to investigate finite automata, shows how to effectively transform a context-free grammar G into an equivalent context-free grammar G^u with no useless items.

Several nondeterministic finite automata over the (unrelated) alphabet $\{\mathbf{1}\}$ will be considered, each identical except for the placement of the start state. The states of the NDFA correspond to nonterminals of the grammar, and one extra state, denoted by ω, is added to serve as the only final state. A transition from A to C will arise if a production in P allows A to be replaced by a string containing the nonterminal C. States corresponding to nonterminals that directly produce terminal strings will also have transitions to the sole final state ω. Formally, for the grammar $G = <\Omega, \Sigma, S, P>$ and any nonterminal $B \in \Omega$, define the NDFA $A^B = <\{\mathbf{1}\}, \Omega \cup \{\omega\}, B, \delta, \{\omega\}>$, where δ is defined by $\delta(\omega, \mathbf{1}) = \emptyset$, and for each $A \in \Omega$, let

$$\delta(A, \mathbf{1}) = \{C \mid (C \in \Omega \wedge (\exists \alpha, \gamma \in (\Omega \cup \Sigma)^*)(A \to \alpha C \gamma \in P))\} \cup \{\omega\}$$

if $(\exists \alpha \in \Sigma^*)(A \to \alpha \in P)$, and

$$\delta(A, \mathbf{1}) = \{C \mid (C \in \Omega \wedge (\exists \alpha, \gamma \in (\Omega \cup \Sigma)^*)(A \to \alpha C \gamma \in P))\}$$

otherwise.

Note that, for any two nonterminals R and Q in Ω, A^R and A^Q are identical except for the specification of the start state. The previously presented algorithms for determining the set of connected states in an automaton can be applied to these new automata to identify the useless nonterminals. As noted before, there are three basic ways a nonterminal can qualify as useless. The inaccessible states in the NDFA A^S correspond to nonterminals of the first type and can be eliminated from both the grammar and the automata. For each remaining nonterminal B, if the final state ω is not accessible in A^B, then B is a useless nonterminal of the second type and can be eliminated from further consideration in both the grammar and the automata. Checking for disconnected states in the pared-down version of A^S will identify useless nonterminals of the third type. The process can be repeated until no further disconnected states are found.

Δ

EXAMPLE 9.12

Consider again the grammar introduced in Example 9.11. The structure of each of the automata is similar to that of A^S, shown in Figure 9.11a. Note that the disconnected states are indeed W and U, which can be eliminated from the state transition table. Checking the accessibility of ω in A^S, A^A, A^B, A^C, and A^D result in no changes, but V, X, and Y are eliminated when A^V, A^X, and A^Y are examined, resulting in the automaton displayed in Figure 9.11b. Eliminating transitions associated with the corresponding useless productions yields the automaton shown in Figure 9.11c. Checking for disconnected states in this machine reveals the remaining inaccessible states. Thus, the equivalent grammar G^u with no useless nonterminals contains only the productions $S \to \mathbf{g}A\mathbf{e}$, $A \to \mathbf{oo}C$, and $C \to \mathbf{gi}$.

Note that the actual language described by the NDFA A^S is of no consequence, nor may any finite automaton be capable of producing the context-free language in question. However, the above method illustrates that the tools developed for automata can be brought to bear in areas that do not directly apply to FAD languages. A more efficient algorithm for identifying useless nonterminals can be

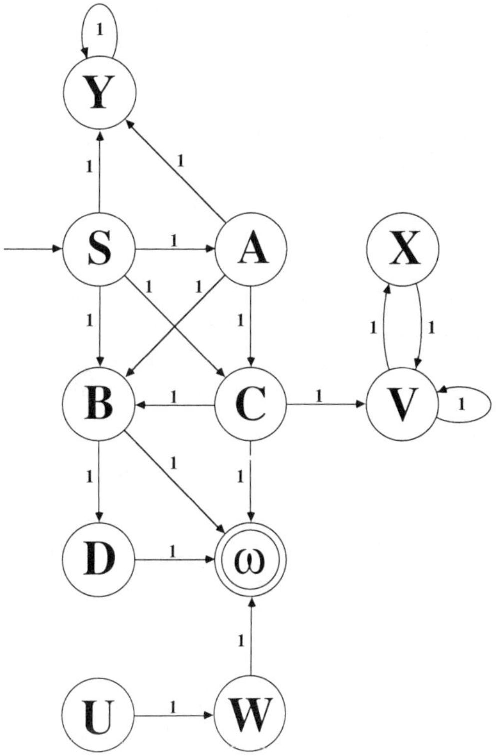

(a)

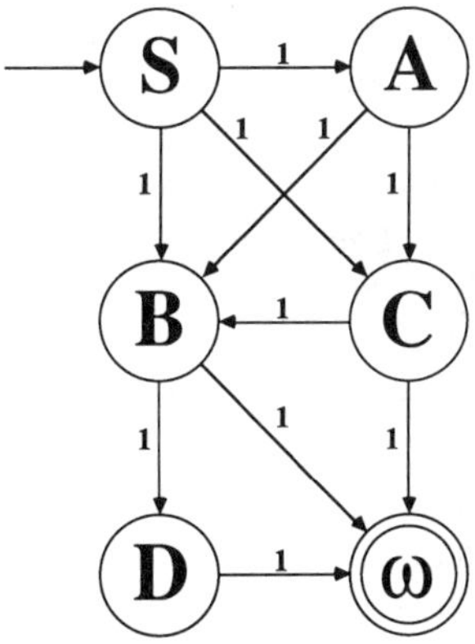

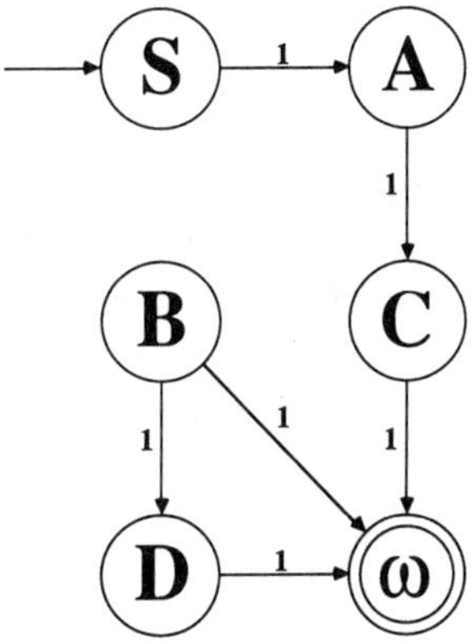

(b) (c)

Figure 9.11 (a) The automaton discussed in Example 9.12 (b) The simplified automaton discussed in Example 9.12 (c) The final automaton discussed in Example 9.12

found in [HOPC]. If computerized, such a tailored algorithm would consume less CPU time than if the automata modules described above were employed. In terms of the programming effort required, though, it is often more advantageous to adhere to the "toolbox approach" and adapt existing tools to new situations.

Note that the algorithm developed in Theorem 9.3 relied on connectedness, and hence the specification of the final states was unimportant in this approach. With ω as the lone final state, some of the decision algorithms developed in Chapter 12 could have been used in place of the connectivity and accessibility checks.

Example 9.12 illustrates the simplification that can be attained by the elimination of useless productions. Further convenience is afforded by the elimination of nongenerative A-rules of the form $A \rightarrow B$. Recall that in the grammar $<\{S_1, S_2, S_3, S_4, S_5\}, \{\mathbf{a}, \mathbf{b}, \mathbf{c}\}, S_1, \{S_1 \rightarrow S_2, S_2 \rightarrow S_3, S_3 \rightarrow S_4, S_4 \rightarrow S_5, S_5 \rightarrow \mathbf{a}\}>$, all the nonterminals were useful, but the production set was still needlessly complex.

∇ **Definition 9.8.** A production of the form $A \rightarrow B$, where $A, B \in \Omega$, is called a *unit* production or a *nongenerative* production.
Δ

As with the elimination of useless nonterminals, unit productions can be removed with the help of automata constructs. The interested reader is referred to [DENN] for the constructive proof. The proof given below indicates the general algorithmic approach.

∇ **Theorem 9.4.** Every pure context-free language L can be generated by a pure context-free grammar which contains no useless non-terminals and no unit productions. Every context-free language L′ can be generated by a context-free grammar which contains no useless non-terminals and no unit productions except perhaps the Z-rule $Z \rightarrow S$, where Z is the new start symbol.

Proof. If the first statement of the theorem is proved, the second will follow immediately from Definition 8.6. If L is a pure context-free language, then by Definition 8.5 there is a pure context-free grammar $G = <\Omega, \Sigma, S, P>$ that generates L. Divide the production set up into P^u and P^n, the set of unit productions and the set of nonunit productions, respectively. For each nonterminal B found in P^u, find $B^u = \{C \mid B \overset{*}{\Rightarrow} C\}$, the *unit closure* of B. The derivations sought must all come from the (finite) set P^u, and there is clearly an algorithm that correctly calculates B^u. In fact, B^u is represented by the set of accessible states in a suitably defined automaton (see the exercises). Define a new grammar $G' = <\Omega, \Sigma, S, P'>$, where $P' = P^n \cup \{B \rightarrow \alpha \mid B \text{ is a nonterminal in } P^u \wedge C \in B^u \wedge C \rightarrow \alpha \in P^n\}$. A straightforward induction argument shows that G′ is equivalent to G, and G′ contains no unit productions. Note that if G is pure, so is G′.

G′ is likely to contain useless nonterminals, even if all the productions in G were useful (see Example 9.13). However, the algorithm from Theorem 9.3 can now be applied to G′ to eliminate useless nonterminals. Since that algorithm creates no new productions, the resulting grammar will still be free of unit productions.
Δ

EXAMPLE 9.13

Consider again the pure context-free grammar

$$<\{S_1, S_2, S_3, S_4, S_5\}, \{\mathbf{a}, \mathbf{b}, \mathbf{c}\}, S_1, \{S_1 \to S_2, S_2 \to S_3, S_3 \to S_4, S_4 \to S_5, S_5 \to \mathbf{a}\}>$$

The production set is split into $P^n = \{S_5 \to \mathbf{a}\}$ and

$$P^u = \{S_1 \to S_2, S_2 \to S_3, S_3 \to S_4, S_4 \to S_5\}.$$

The unit-closure sets are

$$S_1^u = \{S_1, S_2, S_3, S_4, S_5\}$$

$$S_2^u = \{S_2, S_3, S_4, S_5\}$$

$$S_3^u = \{S_3, S_4, S_5\}$$

$$S_4^u = \{S_4, S_5\}$$

$$S_5^u = \{S_5\}$$

Since $S_5 \to \mathbf{a}$ and $S_5 \in S_3^u$, the production $S_3 \to \mathbf{a}$ is added to P'. The full set of productions is $P' = \{S_1 \to \mathbf{a}, S_2 \to \mathbf{a}, S_3 \to \mathbf{a}, S_4 \to \mathbf{a}, S_5 \to \mathbf{a}\}$. The elimination of useless nonterminals and productions results in the grammar $<\{S_1\}, \{\mathbf{a}, \mathbf{b}, \mathbf{c}\}, S_1, \{S_1 \to \mathbf{a}\}>$.

EXAMPLE 9.14

Consider the context-free grammar with productions

$$Z \to S, Z \to \lambda$$

$$S \to C B \mathbf{h}, S \to D$$

$$A \to \mathbf{aa} C$$

$$B \to S\mathbf{f}, B \to \mathbf{ggg}$$

$$C \to \mathbf{c}A, C \to \mathbf{d}, C \to C$$

$$D \to E, D \to SABC$$

$$E \to \mathbf{be}$$

The unit closures of each of the appropriate nonterminals and the new productions they imply are shown below. Note that $Z \to S$ is not considered and that the productions suggested by $C \to C$ are already present.

$S \stackrel{*}{\Rightarrow} D$	$S \to SABC$
$S \stackrel{*}{\Rightarrow} E$	$S \to \mathbf{be}$
$D \stackrel{*}{\Rightarrow} E$	$D \to \mathbf{be}$
$C \stackrel{*}{\Rightarrow} C$	$C \to \mathbf{c}A, C \to \mathbf{d}$

The new set of productions is therefore

$$Z \rightarrow S, Z \rightarrow \lambda$$

$$S \rightarrow SABC, S \rightarrow \mathbf{be}, S \rightarrow CB\mathbf{h}$$

$$A \rightarrow \mathbf{aa}C$$

$$B \rightarrow S\mathbf{f}, B \rightarrow \mathbf{ggg}$$

$$C \rightarrow \mathbf{c}A, C \rightarrow \mathbf{d}$$

$$D \rightarrow \mathbf{be}, D \rightarrow SABC$$

Note that D is now useless and can be eliminated.

The assurance that every context-free grammar corresponds to an equivalent grammar with no unit productions is helpful in many situations. In particular, it is instrumental to the proof showing that the following restrictive type of grammar is indeed a canonical form for context-free languages.

∇ **Definition 9.9.** A pure context-free grammar $G = <\Omega, \Sigma, S, P>$ is in *pure Chomsky normal form* (PCNF) if P contains only productions of the form $A \rightarrow BC$ and $A \rightarrow \mathbf{d}$, where B and C are nonterminals and $\mathbf{d} \in \Sigma$.

A context-free grammar $G = <\Omega, \Sigma, Z, P>$ is in *Chomsky normal form* (CNF) if the Z-rules $Z \rightarrow S$ and $Z \rightarrow \lambda$ are the only allowable productions involving the start symbol Z, and all other productions are of the form $A \rightarrow BC$ and $A \rightarrow \mathbf{d}$, where B and C are nonterminals and $\mathbf{d} \in \Sigma$.

Δ

Thus, in PCNF the grammatical rules are limited to producing exactly two nonterminals or one terminal symbol. Few of the grammars discussed so far have met the restricted criteria required by Chomsky normal form. However, every context-free grammar can be transformed into an equivalent CNF grammar, as indicated in the following proof. The basic strategy will be to add new nonterminals and replace undesired productions such as $A \rightarrow JK\mathbf{cb}$ by a set of equivalent productions in the proper form, such as $A \rightarrow JY_{11}$, $Y_{11} \rightarrow KY_{12}$, $Y_{12} \rightarrow X_{\mathbf{c}}X_{\mathbf{b}}$, $X_{\mathbf{c}} \rightarrow \mathbf{c}$, $X_{\mathbf{b}} \rightarrow \mathbf{b}$, where Y_{11}, Y_{12}, $X_{\mathbf{b}}$, and $X_{\mathbf{c}}$ are new nonterminals.

∇ **Theorem 9.5.**

Every pure context-free language L can be generated by a pure Chomsky normal form grammar.

Every context-free language L′ can be generated by a Chomsky normal form grammar.

Proof. Again, if the first statement of the theorem is proved, the second will follow immediately from Definition 8.6. If L is a pure context-free language, then by Definition 8.5 there is a pure context-free grammar $G = <\Omega, \Sigma, S, P>$ that generates L. Theorem 9.4 shows that without loss of generality we may assume that P contains no unit productions. We construct a new grammar $G' = <\Omega, \Sigma, S, P'>$ in the following manner. Number the productions in P, and consider each production in turn. If the right side of the kth production consists of only a single symbol, then it must be a terminal symbol, since there are no unit productions. No modifications are necessary in this case, and the production is retained for use in the new set of productions P'. The same is true if the kth production consists of two symbols and they are both nonterminals. If one or both of the symbols is a terminal, then the rule must be modified by replacing any terminal symbol **a** with a new nonterminal $X_{\mathbf{a}}$. Whenever such a replacement is done, a production of the form $X_{\mathbf{a}} \rightarrow \mathbf{a}$ must also be included in the new set of productions P'. If the kth production is $A \rightarrow \alpha_1\alpha_2\alpha_3 \cdots \alpha_n$, where the number of (terminal and nonterminal) symbols is $n > 2$, then new nonterminals $Y_{k1}, Y_{k2}, \ldots, Y_{kn-2}$ must be introduced and the rule must be replaced by the set of productions $A \rightarrow \alpha_1 Y_{k1}, Y_{k1} \rightarrow \alpha_2 Y_{k2}, Y_{k2} \rightarrow \alpha_3 Y_{k3}, \ldots, Y_{kn-2} \rightarrow \alpha_{n-1}\alpha_n$. Again, if any α_i is a terminal symbol such as **a**, it must be replaced as indicated earlier by the nonterminal $X_{\mathbf{a}}$.

Each new set of rules is clearly capable of producing the same effect as the rule that was replaced. Each nonterminal Y_{ki} is used in only one such replacement set to ensure that the new rules do not combine in unexpected new ways. Tedious but straightforward inductive proofs will justify that $L(G) = L(G')$.
Δ

EXAMPLE 9.15

The grammar discussed in Example 9.14 can be transformed into CNF by the algorithm given in Theorem 9.5. After elimination of the unit productions and the consequent useless productions, the productions (suitably numbered) that must be examined are

1. $S \rightarrow SABC$	**5.** $B \rightarrow S\mathbf{f}$
2. $S \rightarrow \mathbf{be}$	**6.** $B \rightarrow \mathbf{ggg}$
3. $S \rightarrow CB\mathbf{h}$	**7.** $C \rightarrow \mathbf{c}A$
4. $A \rightarrow \mathbf{aa}C$	**8.** $C \rightarrow \mathbf{d}$

In the corresponding lists given below, notice that only production 8 is retained; the others are replaced by

$$S \rightarrow SY_{11}, Y_{11} \rightarrow AY_{12}, Y_{12} \rightarrow BC$$

$$S \rightarrow X_{\mathbf{b}}X_{\mathbf{e}}$$

$$S \rightarrow CY_{31}, Y_{31} \rightarrow BX_{\mathbf{h}}$$

$$A \rightarrow X_{\mathbf{a}}Y_{41}, Y_{41} \rightarrow X_{\mathbf{a}}C$$

$$B \rightarrow SX_{\mathbf{f}}$$

$$B \rightarrow X_{\mathbf{g}}Y_{61}, Y_{61} \rightarrow X_{\mathbf{g}}X_{\mathbf{g}}$$

$$C \rightarrow X_{\mathbf{c}}A$$

$$C \rightarrow \mathbf{d}$$

and the terminal productions $X_b \to \mathbf{b}$, $X_e \to \mathbf{e}$, $X_h \to \mathbf{h}$, $X_a \to \mathbf{a}$, $X_f \to \mathbf{f}$, $X_g \to \mathbf{g}$. Since **d** did not appear as part of a two-symbol production, the rule $X_d \to \mathbf{d}$ was not needed. The above rules, with S as the start symbol, form a pure Chomsky normal form grammar. The new start symbol Z and productions $Z \to S$ and $Z \to \lambda$ would be added to this pure context-free grammar to obtain the required CNF.

Grammars in Chomsky normal form allow an exact correspondence to be made between the length of a terminal string and the length of the derivation sequence that produces that string. If the empty string can be derived, the production sequence will consist of exactly one rule application ($Z \to \lambda$). A simple inductive argument shows that, if a string of length $n > 0$ can be derived, the derivation sequence must contain exactly $2n$ steps. In the grammar derived in Example 9.15, for example, the following terminal string of length 5 is generated in exactly ten productions:

$$Z \Rightarrow S \Rightarrow CY_{31} \Rightarrow \mathbf{d}Y_{31} \Rightarrow \mathbf{d}BX_h \Rightarrow \mathbf{d}SX_fX_h \Rightarrow \mathbf{d}X_bX_eX_fX_h \Rightarrow \mathbf{db}X_eX_fX_h$$

$$\Rightarrow \mathbf{dbe}X_fX_h \Rightarrow \mathbf{dbef}X_h \Rightarrow \mathbf{dbefh}$$

Other useful properties are also assured for grammars in Chomsky normal form. When a grammar is in CNF, all parse trees can be represented by binary trees, and upper and lower bounds on the depth of a parse tree for a string of length n can be found (see the exercises). The derivational relationship between the number of production steps used and the number of terminals produced implies that CNF grammars generate an average of one terminal every two productions. The following canonical form requires every production to contain at least one terminal symbol, and grammars in this form must produce strings of length $n (> 0)$ in no more than n steps.

∇ **Definition 9.10.** A pure context-free grammar $G = \langle \Omega, \Sigma, S, P \rangle$ is in *pure Greibach normal form* (PGNF) if P contains only productions of the form $A \to \mathbf{d}\alpha$, where $\alpha \in (\Omega \cup \Sigma)^*$ and $\mathbf{d} \in \Sigma$.

A context-free grammar $G = \langle \Omega, \Sigma, Z, P \rangle$ is in *Greibach normal form* (GNF) if the Z-rules $Z \to S$ and $Z \to \lambda$ are the only allowable productions involving the start symbol Z, and all other productions are of the form $A \to \mathbf{d}\alpha$, where $\alpha \in (\Omega \cup \Sigma)^*$ and $\mathbf{d} \in \Sigma$.

Δ

In pure Greibach normal form, the grammatical rules are limited to producing at least one terminal symbol as the first symbol. The original grammar in Example 9.9 is a PGNF grammar, but few of the other grammars presented in this chapter meet the seemingly mild restrictions required for Greibach normal form. The main obstacle to obtaining a GNF grammar is the possible presence of *left recursion*. A nonterminal A is called *left recursive* if there is a sequence of one or more productions for which $A \stackrel{*}{\Rightarrow} A\beta$ for some string β. Greibach normal form disallows such occurrences since no production may produce a string starting with a nonterminal.

Replacing productions involved with left recursion is complex, but every context-free grammar can be transformed into an equivalent GNF grammar, as shown by Theorem 9.6. Two techniques will be needed to transform the productions into the appropriate form, and the following lemmas ensure that the grammatical transformations leave the language unchanged. The first indicates how to remove an X-rule that begins with an undesired nonterminal; Lemma 9.1 specifies a new set of productions that compensate for the loss.

∇ **Lemma 9.1.** Let $G = <\Omega, \Sigma, S, P>$ be a context-free grammar, and assume there is a string α and nonterminals X and B for which $X \to B\alpha \in P$. Further assume that the set of all B-rules is given by $\{B \to \beta_1, B \to \beta_2, \ldots, B \to \beta_m\}$ and let $G' = <\Omega, \Sigma, S, P'>$, where

$$P' = P \cup \{X \to \beta_1\alpha, X \to \beta_2\alpha, \ldots, X \to \beta_m\alpha\} - \{X \to B\alpha\}.$$

Then $\boldsymbol{L}(G) = \boldsymbol{L}(G')$.

Proof. Let each nonterminal A be associated with the set of sentential form X_A that A can produce. That is, let $A = X_A = \{x \in (\Sigma \cup \Omega)^* \mid A \stackrel{*}{\Rightarrow} x\}$. The nonterminals then denote variables in a set of language equations that reflect the productions in P. These equations will generally not be linear; several variables may be concatenated together within a single term. Since the set of all B-rules were $B \to \beta_1, B \to \beta_2, \ldots, B \to \beta_m$, X_B satisfies the equation

$$X_B = \beta_1 \cup \beta_2 \cup \cdots \cup \beta_m$$

Similarly, if the X-rules other than $X \to B\alpha$ are $X \to \gamma_1, X \to \gamma_2, \ldots, X \to \gamma_n$, then X satisfies the equation

$$X_X = \gamma_1 \cup \gamma_2 \cup \cdots \cup \gamma_n \cup X_B\alpha$$

Substituting for X_B in the X_X equation yields

$$X_X = \gamma_1 \cup \gamma_2 \cup \cdots \cup \gamma_n \cup (\beta_1 \cup \beta_2 \cup \cdots \cup \beta_m)\alpha$$

which by the distributive law becomes

$$X_X = \gamma_1 \cup \gamma_2 \cup \cdots \cup \gamma_n \cup \beta_1\alpha \cup \beta_2\alpha \cup \cdots \cup \beta_m\alpha$$

This shows why the productions $X \to \beta_1\alpha, X \to \beta_2\alpha, \ldots, X \to \beta_m\alpha$ can replace the rule $X \to B\alpha$.

Δ

The type of replacement justified by Lemma 9.1 will not eliminate left recursion. The following lemma indicates a way to remove all the left-recursive X-rules by introducing a new right-recursive nonterminal.

∇ **Lemma 9.2.** Let $G = <\Omega, \Sigma, S, P>$ be a context-free grammar, and choose a nonterminal $X \in \Omega$. Denote the set of all recursive X-rules by $X^r = \{X \to X\alpha_1, X \to X\alpha_2, \ldots, X \to X\alpha_m\}$ and the set of all nonrecursive X-rules by

$X^r = \{X \to \gamma_1, X \to \gamma_2, \ldots, X \to \gamma_n\}$. Choose a new nonterminal $Y \notin \Omega$ and let $G'' = <\Omega \cup \{Y\}, \Sigma, S, P''>$, where $P'' = P \cup \{X \to \gamma_1 Y, X \to \gamma_2 Y, \ldots, X \to \gamma_n Y\} \cup \{Y \to \alpha_1, Y \to \alpha_2, \ldots, Y \to \alpha_m\} \cup \{Y \to \alpha_1 Y, Y \to \alpha_2 Y, \ldots, Y \to \alpha_m Y\} - X^r$. Then $L(G) = L(G'')$.

Proof. As in Lemma 9.1, let each nonterminal A be associated with the set of sentential forms X_A that A can produce, and consider the set of language equations generated by P. The X_X equation is

$$X_X = \gamma_1 \cup \gamma_2 \cup \cdots \cup \gamma_n \cup X_X\alpha_1 \cup X_X\alpha_2 \cup \cdots \cup X_X\alpha_m$$

Solving by the method indicated in Theorem 6.4c for an equivalent expression for X_X shows that

$$X_X = (\gamma_1 \cup \gamma_2 \cup \cdots \cup \gamma_n)(\alpha_1 \cup \alpha_2 \cup \cdots \cup \alpha_m)^*$$

In the new set of productions P″, the equations of interest are

$$X_X = \gamma_1 \cup \gamma_2 \cup \cdots \cup \gamma_n \cup \gamma_1 X_Y \cup \gamma_2 X_Y \cup \cdots \cup \gamma_n X_Y$$

$$X_Y = \alpha_1 \cup \alpha_2 \cup \cdots \cup \alpha_m \cup \alpha_1 X_Y \cup \alpha_2 X_Y \cup \cdots \cup \alpha_m X_Y$$

Factoring each equation produces

$$X_X = \gamma_1 \cup \gamma_2 \cup \cdots \cup \gamma_n \cup (\gamma_1 \cup \gamma_2 \cup \cdots \cup \gamma_n)X_Y$$

$$X_Y = \alpha_1 \cup \alpha_2 \cup \cdots \cup \alpha_m \cup (\alpha_1 \cup \alpha_2 \cup \cdots \cup \alpha_m)X_Y$$

and the second can also be solved for an equivalent expression for X_Y, yielding

$$X_Y = (\alpha_1 \cup \alpha_2 \cup \cdots \cup \alpha_m)^*(\alpha_1 \cup \alpha_2 \cup \cdots \cup \alpha_m)$$

Substituting this expression for X_Y in the X_X equation produces

$$X_X = \gamma_1 \cup \gamma_2 \cup \cdots \cup \gamma_n \cup (\gamma_1 \cup \gamma_2 \cup \cdots \cup \gamma_n)(\alpha_1 \cup \alpha_2 \cup \cdots \cup \alpha_m)^*(\alpha_1 \cup \alpha_2 \cup \cdots \cup \alpha_m)$$

which by the distributive law becomes

$$X_X = (\gamma_1 \cup \gamma_2 \cup \cdots \cup \gamma_n)(\lambda \cup (\alpha_1 \cup \alpha_2 \cup \cdots \cup \alpha_m)^*(\alpha_1 \cup \alpha_2 \cup \cdots \cup \alpha_m))$$

Using the fact that $\lambda \cup B^*B = B^*$, this simplifies to

$$X_X = (\gamma_1 \cup \gamma_2 \cup \cdots \cup \gamma_n)(\alpha_1 \cup \alpha_2 \cup \cdots \cup \alpha_m)^*$$

Therefore, when X_Y is eliminated from the sentential forms, X_X produces exactly the same strings as before. This indicates why the productions in the sets

$$\{X \to \gamma_1 Y, X \to \gamma_2 Y, \ldots, X \to \gamma_n Y\} \cup \{Y \to \alpha_1, Y \to \alpha_2, \ldots, Y \to \alpha_m\} \cup$$
$$\{Y \to \alpha_1 Y, Y \to \alpha_2 Y, \ldots, Y \to \alpha_m Y\}$$

can replace the recursive X-rules $X \to \gamma_1, X \to \gamma_2, \ldots, X \to \gamma_n$.
Δ

Note that the new production set eliminates all recursive X-rules and does not introduce any new recursive productions. The techniques discussed in Lemmas 9.1

and 9.2, when applied in the proper order, will transform any context-free grammar into one that is in Greibach normal form. The appropriate sequence is given in the next theorem.

∇ **Theorem 9.6.**

Every pure context-free language L can be generated by a pure Greibach normal form grammar.

Every context-free Language L′ can be generated by a Greibach normal form grammar.

Proof. Because of Definition 8.6, the second statement will follow immediately from the first. If L is a pure context-free language, then by Definition 8.5 there is a pure context-free grammar $G = <\{S_1, S_2, \ldots, S_r\}, \Sigma, S_1, P>$ that generates L. We construct a new grammar by applying the transformations discussed in the previous lemmas.

Phase 1: The replacements suggested by Lemmas 9.1 and 9.2 will be used to ensure that the *increasing condition* is met: if $S_i \rightarrow S_j\alpha$ belongs to the new grammar, then $i > j$. We transform the S_k rules for $k = r, r-1, \ldots, 2, 1$ (in that order), considering the productions for each nonterminal in turn. At the end of the ith iteration, the top i nonterminals will conform to the increasing condition. After the final step, all nonterminals (including any newly introduced ones) will conform, all left recursion will be eliminated, and we can proceed to phase 2.

The procedure for the ith iteration is: If an S_i-rule of the form $S_i \rightarrow S_j\alpha$ is found where $i < j$. eliminate it as specified in Lemma 9.1. This may introduce other rules of the form $S_i \rightarrow S_{j'}\alpha'$, in which i is still less than j'. Such new rules will likewise have to be eliminated via Lemma 9.1, but since the offending subscript will decrease each time, this process will eventually terminate. S_i-rules of the form $S_i \rightarrow S_j\alpha$ where $i = j$ can then be eliminated according to Lemma 9.2. This will introduce some new nonterminals, which can be given new, higher-numbered subscripts. Lemma 9.2 is designed so that the new rules will automatically satisfy the increasing condition specified earlier. The remaining S_i-rules must then conform to the increasing condition. The process continues with lower-numbered rules until all the rules in the new production set conform to the increasing condition.

Phase 2: At this point, S_1 conforms to the increasing condition, and since there are no nonterminals with subscripts that are less than 1, all the S_1-rules must begin with terminal symbols, as required by GNF. The only S_2-rules that may not conform to GNF are those of the form $S_2 \rightarrow S_1\alpha$, and Lemma 9.1 can eliminate such rules by replacing them with the S_1-rules. Since all the S_1-rules now begin with terminal symbols, all the new S_2-rules will have the same property. This process is applied to S_k-rules for increasing k until the entire production set conforms to GNF.

The resulting context-free grammar is in GNF, and since all modifications were of the type allowed by Lemmas 9.1 and 9.2, the new grammar is equivalent to the original.

Δ

EXAMPLE 9.16

Consider the pure context-free grammar

$$<\{S_1, S_2, S_3\}, \{\mathbf{a}, \mathbf{b}, \mathbf{c}, \mathbf{d}, \mathbf{e}\}, S_1, \{S_1 \rightarrow S_1S_2\mathbf{c}, S_1 \rightarrow S_3\mathbf{b}S_3, S_2 \rightarrow S_1S_1, S_2 \rightarrow \mathbf{d}, S_3 \rightarrow S_2\mathbf{e}\}>$$

If the given subscript ordering is not the most convenient, the nonterminals can be renumbered. The current ordering will minimize the number of transformations needed to produce Greibach normal form, since the only production that does not conform to the increasing condition is $S_1 \rightarrow S_3\mathbf{b}S_3$. Thus, the first and second steps of phase 1 are trivially completed; no substitutions are necessary. In the third step, Lemma 9.1 allows the offending production

$$S_1 \rightarrow S_3\mathbf{b}S_3$$

to be replaced by

$$S_1 \rightarrow S_2\mathbf{eb}S_3$$

The new production produces the smaller-subscripted nonterminal S_2, but the new rule still does not satisfy the increasing condition. Replacing $S_1 \rightarrow S_2\mathbf{eb}S_3$ as indicated by Lemma 9.1 yields the two productions

$$S_1 \rightarrow S_1S_1\mathbf{eb}S_3 \quad \text{and} \quad S_1 \rightarrow \mathbf{deb}S_3$$

At this point, the grammar contains the productions

$$S_1 \rightarrow S_1S_2\mathbf{c}, \quad S_1 \rightarrow S_1S_1\mathbf{eb}S_3, \quad S_1 \rightarrow \mathbf{deb}S_3, \quad S_2 \rightarrow S_1S_1, \quad S_2 \rightarrow \mathbf{d}, \quad S_3 \rightarrow S_2\mathbf{e}$$

The first nonterminal has a left-recursive rule that must be eliminated by introducing the new nonterminal S_4. In the notation of Lemma 9.2, $n = 1, m = 2, \gamma_1 = \mathbf{deb}S_3$, $\alpha_1 = S_2\mathbf{c}$, and $\alpha_2 = S_1\mathbf{eb}S_3$. Eliminating $S_1 \rightarrow S_1S_2\mathbf{c}$ and $S_1 \rightarrow S_1S_1\mathbf{eb}S_3$ introduces the new nonterminal $Y = S_4$ and the productions

$$S_1 \rightarrow \mathbf{deb}S_3S_4, \quad S_4 \rightarrow S_2\mathbf{c}, \quad S_4 \rightarrow S_1\mathbf{eb}S_3, \quad S_4 \rightarrow S_2\mathbf{c}S_4, \quad S_4 \rightarrow S_1\mathbf{eb}S_3S_4$$

Phase 1 is now complete. All left-recursion has been eliminated and the grammar now contains the productions

$$S_1 \rightarrow \mathbf{deb}S_3S_4, \quad S_1 \rightarrow \mathbf{deb}S_3$$

$$S_2 \rightarrow S_1S_1, \quad S_2 \rightarrow \mathbf{d}$$

$$S_3 \rightarrow S_2\mathbf{e}$$

$$S_4 \rightarrow S_2\mathbf{c}, \quad S_4 \rightarrow S_1\mathbf{eb}S_3, \quad S_4 \rightarrow S_2\mathbf{c}S_4, \quad S_4 \rightarrow S_1\mathbf{eb}S_3S_4$$

all of which satisfy the increasing condition. The grammar is now set up for phase 2, in which substitutions specified by Lemma 9.1 will ensure that every rule begins with a nonterminal.

The S_1-rules are in acceptable form, as is the S_2-rule $S_2 \rightarrow \mathbf{d}$. The other S_2-rule, $S_2 \rightarrow S_1S_1$, is replaced via Lemma 9.1 with $S_2 \rightarrow \mathbf{deb}S_3S_4S_1$ and $S_2 \rightarrow \mathbf{deb}S_3S_1$. Replacement of the S_3-rule then yields $S_3 \rightarrow \mathbf{deb}S_3S_4S_1\mathbf{e}$, $S_3 \rightarrow \mathbf{deb}S_3S_1\mathbf{e}$ and $S_3 \rightarrow \mathbf{de}$.

The S_4 rules are treated similarly. The final set of productions at the completion of phase 2 contains

$S_1 \to \mathbf{deb}S_3S_4, \quad S_1 \to \mathbf{deb}S_3$

$S_2 \to \mathbf{deb}S_3S_4S_1, \quad S_2 \to \mathbf{deb}S_3S_1, \quad S_2 \to \mathbf{d}$

$S_3 \to \mathbf{deb}S_3S_4S_1\mathbf{e}, \quad S_3 \to \mathbf{deb}S_3S_1\mathbf{e}, \quad S_3 \to \mathbf{de}$

$S_4 \to \mathbf{dc}, \quad S_4 \to \mathbf{deb}S_3S_4S_1\mathbf{c}, \quad S_4 \to \mathbf{deb}S_3S_1\mathbf{c}, \quad S_4 \to \mathbf{deb}S_3S_4\mathbf{eb}S_3, \quad S_4 \to \mathbf{deb}S_3\mathbf{eb}S_3,$

$S_4 \to \mathbf{deb}S_3S_4S_1\mathbf{c}S_4,$

$S_4 \to \mathbf{dc}S_4, \quad S_4 \to \mathbf{deb}S_3S_1\mathbf{c}S_4, \quad S_4 \to \mathbf{deb}S_3S_4\mathbf{eb}S_3S_4, \quad S_4 \to \mathbf{deb}S_3\mathbf{eb}S_3S_4$

In this grammar, S_2 is now useless and can be eliminated.

Greibach normal form is sometimes considered to require all productions to be of the form $A \to \mathbf{d}\alpha$, where $\alpha \in \Omega^*$ and $\mathbf{d} \in \Sigma$. Such rules must produce exactly one leading terminal symbol; the rest of the string must be exclusively nonterminals. It should be clear that this extra restriction can always be enforced by a technique similar to the one employed for Chomsky normal form. The above conversion process would be extended to *phase 3*, in which unwanted terminals such as $\mathbf{e}$ are replaced by a new nonterminal $X_\mathbf{e}$, and new productions such as $X_\mathbf{e} \to \mathbf{e}$ are introduced. For the grammar in Example 9.16, the first production might look like $S_1 \to \mathbf{d}X_\mathbf{e}X_\mathbf{b}S_3S_4$.

9.4 PUMPING THEOREM

As was the case with type 3 languages, some languages are too complex to be defined by a context-free grammar. To prove a language L is context-free, one need only define a grammar that generates L. By contrast, to prove L is not context free, one must effectively argue that no context-free grammar can possibly generate L. The pumping lemma for deterministic finite automata (Theorem 2.3) showed that the repetition of patterns within strings accepted by a DFA was a consequence of the nature of the finite description. The finiteness of grammatical descriptions likewise implies a pumping theorem for languages represented by context-free grammars. The proof is greatly simplified by the properties implied by the existence of canonical forms for context-free grammars.

∇ **Theorem 9.7.** Let L be a context-free language over Σ^*. Then

$(\exists n \in \mathbb{N})(\forall z \in L \ni |z| \geq n)(\exists u, v, w, x, y \in \Sigma^*) \ni z = uvwxy, \ |vwx| \leq n, \ |vx| \geq 1,$ and $(\forall i \in \mathbb{N})(uv^iwx^iy \in L)$

Proof. Given a context-free language L, there must exist a PCNF grammar $G = <\Omega, \Sigma, S, P>$ generating $L - \{\lambda\}$. Let $k = \|\Omega\|$. The parse tree generated by this PCNF grammar for any word $z \in L$ is a binary tree with each (terminal) symbol in z

corresponding to a distinct leaf in the tree. Let $n = 2^{k+1}$. Choose a string z generated by G of length at least n (if there are no strings in L that are this long, then the theorem is vacuously true, and we are done). The binary parse tree for any such string z must have depth at least $k + 1$, which implies the existence of a path involving at least $k + 2$ nodes, beginning at the root and terminating with a leaf. The labels on the $k + 1$ interior nodes along the path must all be nonterminals, and since $\|\Omega\| = k$, they cannot all be distinct. Indeed, the repetition must occur within the "bottom" $k + 1$ interior nodes along the path. Call the repeated label R (see Figure 9.12), and note that there must exist a derivation for the parse tree that looks like

$$S \overset{*}{\Rightarrow} u\mathrm{R}y \overset{*}{\Rightarrow} uv\mathrm{R}xy \overset{*}{\Rightarrow} uvwxy$$

where u, v, w, x, and y are all terminal strings and $z = uvwxy$. That is, there are productions in P that allow $\mathrm{R} \overset{*}{\Rightarrow} v\mathrm{R}x$ and $\mathrm{R} \overset{*}{\Rightarrow} w$. Since $S \overset{*}{\Rightarrow} u\mathrm{R}y$ and $\mathrm{R} \overset{*}{\Rightarrow} w$, $S \overset{*}{\Rightarrow} uwy$ is a valid derivation, and uwy is therefore a word in L. Similarly, $S \overset{*}{\Rightarrow} u\mathrm{R}y \overset{*}{\Rightarrow} uv\mathrm{R}xy \overset{*}{\Rightarrow} uvv\mathrm{R}xxy \overset{*}{\Rightarrow} uvvwxxy$, and so $uv^2wx^2y \in \mathrm{L}$. Induction shows that each of the strings uv^iwx^iy belongs to L for $i = 0, 1, 2, \ldots$. If both v and x were empty, these strings would not be distinct words in L. This case cannot arise, as shown next, and thus the existence of z implies that there is an infinite sequence of strings that must belong to L.

The two occurrences of R were in distinct places in the parse tree, and hence at

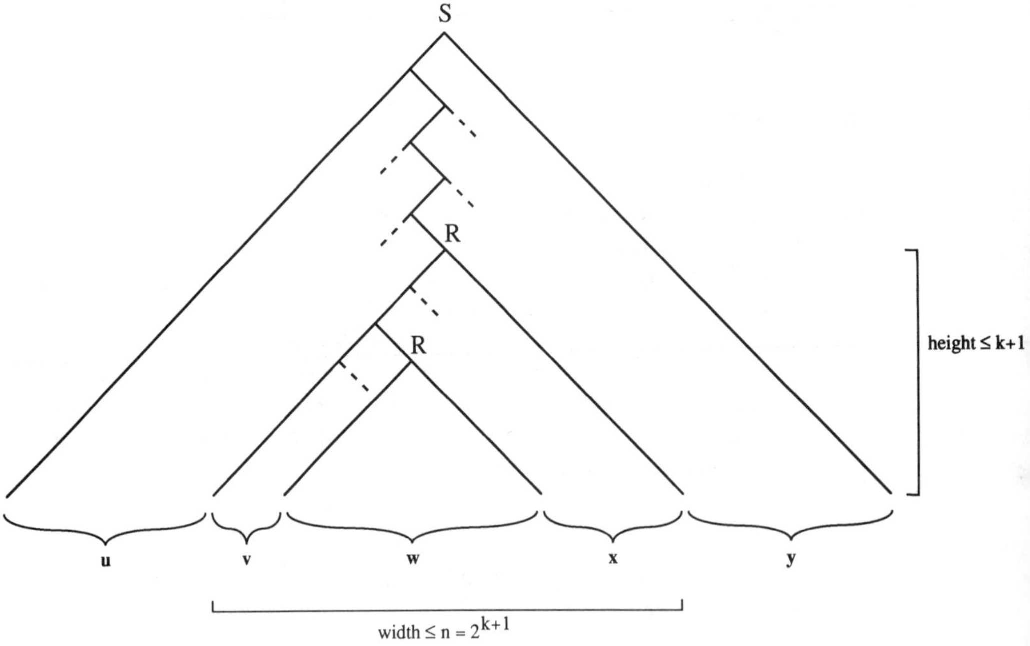

Figure 9.12 The parse tree discussed in the proof of Theorem 9.7

least one production was applied in deriving $uv\mathrm{R}xy$ from $u\mathrm{R}y$. Since the PCNF grammar G contains neither contracting productions nor unit productions, the sentential form $uv\mathrm{R}xy$ must be of greater length than $u\mathrm{R}y$, and hence $|v| + |x| > 0$. Furthermore, the subtree rooted at the higher occurrence of R was of height $k + 1$ or less, and hence accounts for no more than $2^{k+1}(= n)$ terminals. Thus, $|vwx| \leq n$. All the criteria described in the pumping theorem are therefore met.

Since a context-free language must be generated by a CNF grammar with a finite number of nonterminals, there must exist a constant n (such as $n = 2^{\|\Omega\|+1}$) for which the existence of a string of length at least n implies the existence of an infinite sequence of distinct strings that must all belong to L, as stated in the theorem.

Δ

As with the pumping lemma, the pumping theorem is usually applied to justify that certain languages are complex (by proving that the language does not satisfy the pumping theorem and is thus not context free). Such proofs naturally employ the contrapositive of Theorem 9.7, which is stated next.

∇ **Theorem 9.8.** Let L be a language over Σ^*.

if $(\forall n \in \mathbb{N})(\exists z \in \mathrm{L} \ni |z| \geq n)(\forall u, v, w, x, y \in \Sigma^* \ni z = uvwxy,\ |vwx| \leq n,\ |vx| \geq 1)$ $(\exists i \in \mathbb{N} \ni uv^iwx^iy \notin \mathrm{L})$

then L is *not* context free.

Proof. See the exercises.

Δ

Examples 8.5 and 9.17 show that there are context-sensitive languages which are not context free.

EXAMPLE 9.17

The language $\mathrm{L} = \{\mathbf{a}^k\mathbf{b}^k\mathbf{c}^k \mid k \in \mathbb{N}\}$ is not a context-free language. Let n be given, and choose $z = \mathbf{a}^n\mathbf{b}^n\mathbf{c}^n$. Then $z \in \mathrm{L}$ and $|z| = 3n \geq n$. If L were context free, there must be choices for u, v, w, x, and y satisfying the pumping theorem. Every possible choice of these strings leads to a contradiction, and hence L cannot be context free. A sampling of the various cases is outlined below.

If the strings v and x contain only one type of letter (for example, **c**), then uv^2wx^2y will contain more **c**s than **a**s or **b**s, and thus $uv^2wx^2y \notin \mathrm{L}$. If v were, say, all **b**s and x were all **c**s, then uv^2wx^2y would contain too few **a**s and would again not be a member of L. If v were to contain two types of letters such as $v = \mathbf{aabb}$, then $uv^2wx^2y = uvvwxxy = u\mathbf{aabbaabb}wxxy$ and would represent a string that had some **b**s preceding some **a**s, and again $uv^2wx^2y \notin \mathrm{L}$. All other cases are similar to these, and they collectively imply that L is not a context-free language.

Example 9.17 illustrates one major inconvenience of the pumping theorem: the inability to specify which portion of the string is to be "pumped." With the pumping lemma in Chapter 2, variants were explored that allowed the first n letters to be pumped or the last n letters to be pumped. Indeed, any n consecutive letters in a word from an FAD language can be pumped. For context-free languages, such precision is more elusive. The uncertainty as to where the vwx portion of the string was in Example 9.17 led to many subcases, since *all* combinations of u, v, w, x, and y had to be shown to lead to contradictions. The following result, a variant of Ogden's lemma, allows some choice in the placement of the portion of the string to be pumped in a "long" word from a context-free language.

∇ **Theorem 9.9.** Let L be a context-free language over Σ^*. Then
$(\exists n \in \mathbb{N})$
$(\forall z \in \mathrm{L} \ni |z| \geq n$ and z has any n or more positions marked as distinguished$)$
$(\exists u, v, w, x, y \in \Sigma^*) \ni z = uvwxy$,
vwx contains no more than n distinguished positions,
vx contains at least one distinguished position,
w contains at least one distinguished position, and
$(\forall i \in \mathbb{N})(uv^iwx^iy \in \mathrm{L})$

Proof. Given a context-free language L, there must exist a PCNF grammar $G = <\Omega, \Sigma, S, P>$ generating $L - \{\lambda\}$. Let $n = 2^{\|\Omega\|+1}$. The proof is similar to that given for the pumping theorem (Theorem 9.7); the method for choosing the path now depends on the placement of the distinguished positions. A suitable path is constructed by beginning at the root of the binary parse tree and, at each level, descending to the right or left to lengthen the path. The decision to go right or left is determined by observing the number of distinguished positions generated in the right subtree and the number of distinguished positions generated in the left subtree. The path should descend into the subtree that has the larger number of distinguished positions; ties can be broken arbitrarily. The resulting path will terminate at a leaf corresponding to a distinguished position, will be of sufficient length to guarantee a repeated label R within the bottom $\|\Omega\| + 1$ interior nodes, and so on. The conclusions now follow in much the same manner as those given in the pumping theorem.
Δ

EXAMPLE 9.18

For the language $L = \{\mathbf{a}^k\mathbf{b}^k\mathbf{c}^k \mid k \in \mathbb{N}\}$ investigated in Example 9.17, Ogden's lemma could be applied with the first n letters of $\mathbf{a}^n\mathbf{b}^n\mathbf{c}^n$ as the distinguished positions. Since w must have at least one distinguished letter (that is, an **a**), and u and v must precede w, the u and v portions of the string would then be required to be all **a**s. This greatly reduces the number of cases that must be considered. Note that more than n letters can be chosen as the distinguished positions, and they need not be consecutive.

9.5 CLOSURE PROPERTIES

Recall that $\mathscr{C}_\Sigma$ represented the class of context-free languages over Σ. The applications of the pumping theorem show that not every language is context free. The ability to show that specific languages are not context free makes it feasible to decide which language operators preserve context-free languages. The context-free languages are closed under most of the operators considered in Chapter 5; the major exceptions are complement and intersection. We begin with a definition of *substitution* for context-free languages.

∇ **Definition 9.11.** Let $\Sigma = \{\mathbf{a}_1, \mathbf{a}_2, \ldots, \mathbf{a}_m\}$ be an alphabet and let Γ be a second alphabet. Given context-free languages $L_1, L_2, \ldots, L_m$ over Γ, define a *substitution* s: $\Sigma \to \rho(\Gamma^*)$ by $s(\mathbf{a}_i) = L_i$ for each $i = 1, 2, \ldots, m$, which can be extended to $\bar{s}$: $\Sigma^* \to \rho(\Gamma^*)$ by

$$\bar{s}(\lambda) = \lambda$$

and

$$(\forall \mathbf{a} \in \Sigma)\forall x \in \Sigma^*)(\bar{s}(\mathbf{a} \cdot x) = s(\mathbf{a}) \cdot \bar{s}(x))$$

$\bar{s}$ can be further extended to operate on a language $L \subseteq \Sigma^*$ by defining $\bar{s}$: $\rho(\Sigma^*) \to \rho(\Gamma^*)$, where

$$\bar{s}(L) = \bigcup_{z \in L} \bar{s}(z)$$

Δ

A substitution is similar to a language homomorphism (Definition 5.8), where letters were replaced by single words, and to the regular set substitution given by Definition 6.5. For context-free languages, *substitution* denotes the consistent replacement of the individual letters within each word of a context-free language with *sets* of words. Each such set of words must also be a context-free language, although not necessarily over the original alphabet.

EXAMPLE 9.19

Let $L = \boldsymbol{L}(G_t)$, where

$$G_t = <\{T\}, \{\mathbf{a}, \mathbf{b}, \mathbf{c}, \mathbf{d}, -\}, T, \{T \to \mathbf{a} | \mathbf{b} | \mathbf{c} | \mathbf{d} | T - T\}>$$

Let L_1 denote the set of all valid FORTRAN identifiers.

Let L_2 denote the set of all strings denoting integer constants.

Let L_3 denote the set of all strings denoting real constants.

Let L_4 denote the set of all strings denoting double-precision constants.

If the substitution s were defined by $s(\mathbf{a}) = L_1$, $s(\mathbf{b}) = L_2$, $s(\mathbf{c}) = L_3$, $s(\mathbf{d}) = L_4$, then

$\bar{s}$(L) would represent the set of all unparenthesized FORTRAN expressions involving only the subtraction operator.

In this example, $\bar{s}$(L) is a language over a significant portion of the ASCII alphabet, whereas the original alphabet consisted of only five symbols. The result is still context free, and this can be proved for all substitutions of context-free languages into context-free languages. In Example 9.19, the languages L_1 through L_4 were not only context free, but were in fact regular. There are clearly context-free grammars defining each of them, and it should be obvious how to modify G_t to produce a grammar that generates $\bar{s}$(L). If $G_1 = <\Omega_1, \Sigma_1, S_1, P_1>$ is a grammar generating L_1, for example, then occurrences of **a** in the productions of G_t should simply be replaced by the start symbol S_1 of G_1 and the productions of P_1 added to the new grammar that will generate $\bar{s}$(L). This is essentially the technique used to justify Theorem 9.10. The closure theorem is stated for substitutions that do not modify the terminal alphabet, but it is also true in general, as a trivial modification of the following proof would show.

∇ **Theorem 9.10.** Let Σ be an alphabet, and let $s: \Sigma \to \Sigma^*$ be a substitution. Then $\mathscr{C}_\Sigma$ is closed under $\bar{s}$.

Proof. Let $\Sigma = \{\mathbf{a}_1, \mathbf{a}_2, \ldots, \mathbf{a}_m\}$. If L is a context-free language, then there is a context-free grammar $G = <\Omega, \Sigma, S, P>$ that generates L_1. If $s: \Sigma \to \Sigma^*$ is a substitution satisfying Definition 9.11, then for each letter $\mathbf{a}_k \in \Sigma$ there is a corresponding grammar $G_k = <\Omega_k, \Sigma, S_k, P_k>$ for which $L(G_k) = s(\mathbf{a}_k)$. Since nonterminals can be freely renamed, we may assume that $\Omega, \Omega_1, \Omega_2, \ldots, \Omega_m$ have no common symbols. $\bar{s}$(L) will be generated by the context-free grammar

$$G' = <\Omega \cup \Omega_1 \cup \Omega_2 \cup \cdots \cup \Omega_m, \Sigma, S, P' \cup P_1 \cup P_2 \cup \cdots \cup P_m>,$$

where P' consists of the rules of P, with each appearance of $\mathbf{a}_k$ replaced by S_k. From the start symbol S, the rules of P' can be used as they were in the original grammar G, producing strings with the start symbol of the kth grammar where the kth terminal symbol would be. Since the nonterminal sets were assumed to be pairwise disjoint, only the rules in P_k can be used to expand S_k, resulting in the desired terminal strings from $s(\mathbf{a}_k)$. It follows that $L(G') = \bar{s}(L)$, and thus $\bar{s}$(L) is context free.

Δ

∇ **Theorem 9.11.** Let Σ be an alphabet, and let $\psi: \Sigma \to \Sigma^*$ be a homomorphism. Then $\mathscr{C}_\Sigma$ is closed under $\bar{\psi}$.

Proof. Languages that consist of single words are obviously context free. Hence, Theorem 9.10 applies when single words are substituted for letters. Since homomorphisms are therefore special types of substitutions, $\mathscr{C}_\Sigma$ is closed under homomorphism.

Δ

Many of the other closure properties of the collection of context-free grammars follow immediately from the result for substitution. Closure under union could be proved by essentially the same method presented in Theorem 8.4. An alternate proof, based on Theorem 9.10, is given next.

∇ **Theorem 9.12.** Let Σ be an alphabet, and let L_1 and L_2 be context-free languages over Σ. Then $L_1 \cup L_2$ is context free. Thus, $\mathscr{C}_\Sigma$ is closed under union.

Proof. Assume L_1 and L_2 are context-free languages over Σ. The grammar $U = <\{S\}, \{\mathbf{a}, \mathbf{b}\}, S, \{S \to \mathbf{a}, S \to \mathbf{b}\}>$ clearly generates the context-free language $\{\mathbf{a}, \mathbf{b}\}$. The substitution defined by $s(\mathbf{a}) = L_1$ and $s(\mathbf{b}) = L_2$ gives rise to the language $\bar{s}(\{\mathbf{a}, \mathbf{b}\})$, which obviously equals $L_1 \cup L_2$. By Theorem 9.10, this language must be context free.
Δ

A similar technique can be used for concatenation and Kleene closure. It is relatively easy to directly construct appropriate new grammars that combine the generative powers of the original grammars. The exercises explore constructions that prove these closure properties without relying on Theorem 9.10.

∇ **Theorem 9.13.** Let Σ be an alphabet, and let L_1 and L_2 be context-free languages over Σ. Then $L_1 \cdot L_2$ is context free. Thus, $\mathscr{C}_\Sigma$ is closed under concatenation.

Proof. Let L_1 and L_2 be context-free languages over Σ. The pure context-free grammar $C = <\{S\}, \{\mathbf{a}, \mathbf{b}\}, S, \{S \to \mathbf{ab}\}>$ generates the language $\{\mathbf{ab}\}$. The substitution defined by $s(\mathbf{a}) = L_1$ and $s(\mathbf{b}) = L_2$ gives rise to the language $\bar{s}(\{\mathbf{ab}\}) = L_1 \cdot L_2$. By Theorem 9.10, $L_1 \cdot L_2$ must therefore be context free.
Δ

Closure under Kleene closure could be justified by Theorem 9.10 in a similar manner, since the context-free grammar

$$K = <\{Z, S\}, \{\mathbf{a}, \mathbf{b}\}, S, \{Z \to \lambda, Z \to S, S \to \mathbf{a}S, S \to \mathbf{a}\}>$$

generates the language $\mathbf{a}^*$. The substitution defined by $s(\mathbf{a}) = L_1$ gives rise to the language $\bar{s}(\mathbf{a}^*)$, which is L_1^*, and so L_1^* is also context free. The proof of Theorem 9.14 instead illustrates how to modify an existing grammar.

∇ **Theorem 9.14.** Let Σ be an alphabet, and let L_1 be a context-free language over Σ. then L_1^* is context free. Thus, $\mathscr{C}_\Sigma$ is closed under Kleene closure.

Proof. If L_1 is a context-free language, then there is a pure context-free grammar $G_1 = <\Omega_1, \Sigma, S_1, P_1>$ that generates $L_1 - \{\lambda\}$. Choose nonterminals Z' and S' such that $Z' \notin \Omega_1$ and $S' \notin \Omega_1$, and define a new grammar

$$G_* = <\Omega_1 \cup \{S', Z'\}, \Sigma, Z', P_1 \cup \{Z' \to \lambda, Z' \to S', S' \to S'S_1, S' \to S_1\}>.$$

A straightforward induction shows that $L(G_*) = L(G_1)^*$.
Δ

Thus, many of the closure properties of the familiar operators investigated in Chapter 5 for regular languages carry over to the class of context-free languages. Closure under intersection does *not* extend, as the next result shows.

∇ **Lemma 9.3.** $\mathscr{C}_{\{\mathbf{a},\mathbf{b},\mathbf{c}\}}$ is *not* closed under intersection.

Proof. The languages $L_1 = \{\mathbf{a}^i\mathbf{b}^j\mathbf{c}^j \mid i,j \in \mathbb{N}\}$ and $L_2 = \{\mathbf{a}^n\mathbf{b}^n\mathbf{c}^m \mid n,m \in \mathbb{N}\}$ are context free (see the exercises), and yet $L_1 \cap L_2 = \{\mathbf{a}^k\mathbf{b}^k\mathbf{c}^k \mid k \in \mathbb{N}\}$ was shown in Example 9.17 to be a language that was not context free. Hence $\mathscr{C}_{\{\mathbf{a},\mathbf{b},\mathbf{c}\}}$ is not closed under intersection.

Δ

The exercises show that $\mathscr{C}_\Sigma$ is not closed under intersection for any alphabet Σ with two or more letters. It was noted in Chapter 5 that De Morgan's laws implied that any collection of languages that is closed under union and complementation must also be closed under intersection. It therefore follows immediately that $\mathscr{C}_{\{\mathbf{a},\mathbf{b},\mathbf{c}\}}$ cannot be closed under complementation either.

∇ **Lemma 9.4.** $\mathscr{C}_{\{\mathbf{a},\mathbf{b},\mathbf{c}\}}$ is *not* closed under complementation.

Proof. Assume that $\mathscr{C}_{\{\mathbf{a},\mathbf{b},\mathbf{c}\}}$ *is* closed under complementation. Then any two context-free languages L_1 and L_2 would have context-free complements $\sim L_1$ and $\sim L_2$. By Theorem 9.12, $\sim L_1 \cup \sim L_2$ is context free, and the assumption would imply that its complement is also context free. But $\sim(\sim L_1 \cup \sim L_2) = L_1 \cap L_2$, which would contradict Lemma 9.3 (for example, if L_1 were $\{\mathbf{a}^i\mathbf{b}^j\mathbf{c}^j \mid i,j \in \mathbb{N}\}$ and L_2 were $\{\mathbf{a}^n\mathbf{b}^n\mathbf{c}^m \mid n,m \in \mathbb{N}\}$). Hence the assumption must be false and $\mathscr{C}_{\{\mathbf{a},\mathbf{b},\mathbf{c}\}}$ cannot be closed under complementation.

Δ

Thus, the context-free languages do not enjoy all of the closure properties that the regular languages do. However, the distinction between a regular language and a context-free language is lost if the underlying alphabet contains only one letter, as shown by the following theorem. The proof demonstrates that there is a certain regularity in the lengths of *any* context-free language. It is the relationships between the different letters in the words of a context-free language that give it the potential for being non-FAD. If L is a context-free language over the singleton alphabet $\{\mathbf{a}\}$, then no such complex relationships can exist; the character of a word is determined solely by its length.

∇ **Theorem 9.15.** $\mathscr{C}_{\{\mathbf{a}\}} = \mathscr{D}_{\{\mathbf{a}\}}$; that is, every context-free language over a single letter alphabet is regular.

Proof. Let L be a context-free language over the singleton alphabet $\{\mathbf{a}\}$, and assume the CNF grammar $G = <\Omega, \Sigma, S, P>$ generates L. Let $n = 2^{\|\Omega\|+1}$. Consider the words in L that are of length n or greater, choose the smallest such word, and denote it by $\mathbf{a}^{j_1}$. Since $j_1 \geq n$, the pumping theorem can be applied to this word,

and hence $\mathbf{a}^{j_1}$ can be written as $uvwxy$, where $u = \mathbf{a}^{p_1}$, $v = \mathbf{a}^{q_1}$, $w = \mathbf{a}^{r_1}$, $x = \mathbf{a}^{s_1}$, and $y = \mathbf{a}^{t_1}$. Let $i_1 = q_1 + s_1$. Note that $|vwx| \leq n$ implies that $i_1 \leq n$. The pumping theorem then implies that all strings in the set $L_1 = \{\mathbf{a}^{j_1+ki_1} | k = 0, 1, 2, \ldots\}$ must belong to L. These account for many of the large words in L. If there are other large words in L, choose the next smallest word $\mathbf{a}^{j_2}$ that is of length greater than n that belongs to L but is not already in the set L_1. By a similar argument, there is an integer $i_2 \leq n$ for which all strings in the set $L_2 = \{\mathbf{a}^{j_2+ki_2} | k = 0, 1, 2, \ldots\}$ must also belong to L. Note that if i_1 happens to equal i_2, then $j_1 - j_2$ is not a multiple of n, or else $\mathbf{a}^{j_2}$ would belong to L_1. That is, j_1 and j_2 must in this case belong to different equivalence classes modulo n. While large words remain unaccounted for, we continue choosing the next smallest word $\mathbf{a}^{j_{m+1}}$ that is of length greater than n and belongs to L but is not already in the set $L_1 \cup L_2 \cup \cdots \cup L_m$. Since each $i_k \leq n$, there are only n choices for the i_ks, and only n different equivalence classes mod n in which the j_ks may fall, totaling n^2 different combinations. Thus, all the long words in L will be accounted for by the time m reaches n^2. The words in L of length less than n constitute a finite set F, which is regular. Each L_k is represented by the regular expession indicated by $(\mathbf{a}^{i_k})^* \cdot \mathbf{a}^{j_k}$, and there are less than n^2 of these expressions, so L is the finite union of regular sets, and is therefore regular.
Δ

If a regular language is intersected with a context-free language, the result may not be regular, but it will be context free. The proof that $\mathscr{C}_\Sigma$ is closed under intersection with a regular set will use the tools developed in Chapter 10. The constructs in Chapter 10 will also allow us to show that $\mathscr{C}_\Sigma$ is closed under inverse homomorphism. Such results are useful in showing closure under other operators and will also be useful in identifying certain languages as non-context-free. These conclusions will be based on a more powerful type of machine, called a pushdown automaton. The context-free languages will correspond to the languages that can be represented by such recognizers.

EXERCISES

9.1. Characterize the nature of parse trees of left-linear grammars.

9.2. Give context-free grammars for the following languages:
- **(a)** $\{\mathbf{a}^n\mathbf{b}^n\mathbf{c}^m\mathbf{d}^m | n, m \in \mathbb{N}\}$
- **(b)** $\{\mathbf{a}^i\mathbf{b}^j\mathbf{c}^j\mathbf{d}^i | i, j \in \mathbb{N}\}$
- **(c)** $\{\mathbf{a}^n\mathbf{b}^n\mathbf{c}^m\mathbf{d}^m | n, m \in \mathbb{N}\} \cup \{\mathbf{a}^i\mathbf{b}^j\mathbf{c}^j\mathbf{d}^i | i, j \in \mathbb{N}\}$

9.3. **(a)** Find, if possible, unambiguous context-free grammars for each of the languages given in Exercise 9.2.
- **(b)** Prove or disprove: If L_1 and L_2 are unambiguous context-free languages, then $L_1 \cup L_2$ is also an unambiguous context-free language.
- **(c)** Is $\mathscr{U}_\Sigma$ closed under union?

9.4. State and prove the inductive result needed in Theorem 9.2.

9.5. Consider the proof of Theorem 9.4. Let $G = \langle \Omega, \Sigma, S, P \rangle$ be a context-free grammar, with the production set divided up into P^u and P^n (the set of unit productions and the set of nonunit productions, respectively). Devise an automaton-based algorithm that correctly calculates $B^u = \{C \mid B \overset{*}{\Rightarrow} C\}$ for each nonterminal B found in P^u.

9.6. **(a)** What is wrong with proving that $\mathscr{C}_\Sigma$ is closed under concatenation by using the following construction? Let $G_1 = \langle \Omega_1, \Sigma, S_1, P_1 \rangle$ and $G_2 = \langle \Omega_2, \Sigma, S_2, P_2 \rangle$ be two context-free grammars, and without loss of generality assume that $\Omega_1 \cap \Omega_2 = \emptyset$. Choose a new nonterminal Z such that $Z \notin \Omega_1 \cup \Omega_2$, and define a new grammar $G^\bullet = \langle \Omega_1 \cup \Omega_2 \cup \{Z\}, \Sigma, Z, P_1 \cup P_2 \cup \{Z \rightarrow S_1 \cdot S_2\} \rangle$. *Note:* It *is* straightforward to show that $L(G^\bullet) = L(G_1) \cdot L(G_2)$.

(b) Modify $G^\bullet$ so that it reflects an appropriate valid context-free grammars. (*Hint:* Pay careful attention to the treatment of lambda productions.)

(c) Prove that $\mathscr{C}_\Sigma$ is closed under concatenation by using the construction defined in part (b).

9.7. Let $\Sigma = \{\mathbf{a}, \mathbf{b}, \mathbf{c}\}$. Show that $\{\mathbf{a}^i\mathbf{b}^j\mathbf{c}^k \mid i, j, k \in \mathbb{N} \text{ and } i + j = k\}$ is context free.

9.8. **(a)** Show that the following right-linear grammar is ambiguous.

$$G = \langle \{S, A, B\}, \{\mathbf{a}\}, S, \{S \rightarrow A, S \rightarrow B, A \rightarrow \mathbf{aa}A, A \rightarrow \lambda, B \rightarrow \mathbf{aaa}B, B \rightarrow \lambda\} \rangle$$

(b) Use the method outlined in Theorem 9.2 to remove the ambiguity in G.

9.9. The regular expression grammar discussed in Example 9.3 produces strings with needless outermost parentheses, such as **((a∪b)•c)**.

(a) Define a grammar that generates all the words in this language and strings that are stripped of (only) the outermost parentheses, as in **(a∪b)•c**.

(b) Define a grammar that generates all the words in this language and also allows extraneous sets of parentheses, such as **((((a)∪b))•c)**.

9.10. For the regular expression grammar discussed in Example 9.3:

(a) Determine the leftmost derivation for **((a*•b)∪(c•d)*)**.

(b) Determine the rightmost derivation for **((a*•b)∪(c•d)*)**.

9.11. Consider the grammars G and G′ in the proof of Theorem 9.5. Induct on the number of steps in a derivation in G to show that $L(G) = L(G')$.

9.12. For a grammar G in Chomsky normal form, prove by induction that for any string $x \in L(G)$ other than $x = \lambda$ the number of productions applied to derive x is $2|x|$.

9.13. **(a)** For a grammar G in Chomsky normal form and a string $x \in L(G)$, state and prove a lower bound on the depth of the parse tree for x.

(b) For a grammar G in Chomsky normal form and a string $x \in L(G)$, state and prove an upper bound on the depth of the parse tree for x.

9.14. Convert the following grammars to Chomsky normal form.

(a) $\langle \{S, B, C\}, \{\mathbf{a}, \mathbf{b}, \mathbf{c}\}, S, \{S \rightarrow \mathbf{a}B, S \rightarrow \mathbf{ab}C, B \rightarrow \mathbf{bc}, C \rightarrow \mathbf{c}\} \rangle$

(b) $\langle \{S, A, B\}, \{\mathbf{a}, \mathbf{b}, \mathbf{c}\}, S, \{S \rightarrow \mathbf{c}BA, S \rightarrow B, A \rightarrow \mathbf{c}B, A \rightarrow A\mathbf{bb}S, B \rightarrow \mathbf{aaa}\} \rangle$

(c) $\langle \{R\}, \{\mathbf{a}, \mathbf{b}, \mathbf{c}, (,), \epsilon, \emptyset, \cup, \bullet, *\}, R, \{R \rightarrow \mathbf{a} \mid \mathbf{b} \mid \mathbf{c} \mid \epsilon \mid \emptyset \mid (R \bullet R) \mid (R \cup R) \mid R^*\} \rangle$

(d) $\langle \{T\}, \{\mathbf{a}, \mathbf{b}, \mathbf{c}, \mathbf{d}, -, +\}, T, \{T \rightarrow \mathbf{a} \mid \mathbf{b} \mid \mathbf{c} \mid \mathbf{d} \mid T - T \mid T + T\} \rangle$

9.15. Convert the following grammars to Greibach normal form.

(a) $\langle \{S_1, S_2\}, \{\mathbf{a}, \mathbf{b}, \mathbf{c}, \mathbf{d}, \mathbf{e}\}, S_1, \{S_1 \rightarrow S_2S_1\mathbf{e}, S_1 \rightarrow S_2\mathbf{b}, S_2 \rightarrow S_1S_2, S_2 \rightarrow \mathbf{c}\} \rangle$

(b) $\langle \{S_1, S_2, S_3\}, \{\mathbf{a}, \mathbf{b}, \mathbf{c}, \mathbf{d}, \mathbf{e}\}, S_1, \{S_1 \rightarrow S_3S_1, S_1 \rightarrow S_2\mathbf{a}, S_2 \rightarrow \mathbf{be}, S_3 \rightarrow S_2\mathbf{c}\} \rangle$

(c) $\langle \{S_1, S_2, S_3\}, \{\mathbf{a}, \mathbf{b}, \mathbf{c}, \mathbf{d}, \mathbf{e}\}, S_1, \{S_1 \rightarrow S_1S_2\mathbf{c}, S_1 \rightarrow \mathbf{d}S_3, S_2 \rightarrow S_1S_1, S_2 \rightarrow \mathbf{a}, S_3 \rightarrow S_3\mathbf{e}\} \rangle$

9.16. Let G be a context-free grammar, and obtain G′ from G by adding rules of the form

$A \to \lambda$. Prove that there is a context-free grammar G″ that is equivalent to G′. That is, show that apart from the special rule $Z \to \lambda$ all other lambda productions are unnecessary.

9.17. Prove the following generalization of Lemma 9.1. Let $G = \langle \Omega, \Sigma, S, P \rangle$ be a context-free grammar, and assume there are strings α and γ and nonterminals X and B for which $X \to \gamma B \alpha \in P$. Further assume that the set of all B rules is given by $\{B \to \beta_1, B \to \beta_2, \ldots, B \to \beta_m\}$, and let $G' = \langle \Omega, \Sigma, S, P' \rangle$, where

$$P' = P \cup \{X_B \to \gamma\beta_1\alpha, X_B \to \gamma\beta_2\alpha, \ldots, X_B \to \gamma\beta_m\alpha\} - \{X \to \gamma B \alpha\}.$$

Then $\boldsymbol{L}(G) = \boldsymbol{L}(G')$.

9.18. Let $P = \{y \in \{\mathbf{d}\}^* \mid \exists \text{ prime } p \ni y = \mathbf{d}^p\} = \{\mathbf{dd}, \mathbf{ddd}, \mathbf{ddddd}, \mathbf{d}^7, \mathbf{d}^{11}, \mathbf{d}^{13}, \ldots\}$.
- **(a)** Prove that P is not context free by directly applying the pumping theorem.
- **(b)** Prove that P is not context free by using the fact that P is known to be a nonregular language.

9.19. Let $\Gamma = \{x \in \{\mathbf{0}, \mathbf{1}, \mathbf{2}\}^* \mid \exists w \in \{\mathbf{0}, \mathbf{1}\}^* \ni x = w \cdot \mathbf{2} \cdot w\} = \{\mathbf{2}, \mathbf{121}, \mathbf{020}, \mathbf{11211}, \mathbf{10210}, \ldots\}$. Prove that Γ is not context free.

9.20. Let $\Psi = \{x \in \{\mathbf{0}, \mathbf{1}\}^* \mid \exists w \in \{\mathbf{0}, \mathbf{1}\}^* \ni x = w \cdot w\} = \{\lambda, \mathbf{00}, \mathbf{11}, \mathbf{0000}, \mathbf{1010}, \mathbf{1111}, \ldots\}$. Prove that Ψ is not context free.

9.21. Let $\Xi = \{x \in \{\mathbf{b}\}^* \mid \exists j \in \mathbb{N} \ni |x| = 2^j\} = \{\mathbf{b}, \mathbf{bb}, \mathbf{bbbb}, \mathbf{b}^8, \mathbf{b}^{16}, \mathbf{b}^{32}, \ldots\}$. Prove that Ξ is not context free.

9.22. Let $\Phi = \{x \in \{\mathbf{a}\}^* \mid \exists j \in \mathbb{N} \ni |x| = j^2\} = \{\lambda, \mathbf{a}, \mathbf{aaaa}, \mathbf{a}^9, \mathbf{a}^{16}, \mathbf{a}^{25}, \ldots\}$, and let

$$\Phi' = \{x \in \{\mathbf{b}, \mathbf{c}, \mathbf{d}\}^* \mid |x|_{\mathbf{b}} \geq 1 \wedge |x|_{\mathbf{c}} = (|x|_{\mathbf{d}})^2\}.$$

- **(a)** Prove that Φ is not context free.
- **(b)** Use the conclusion of part (a) and the properties of homomorphism to prove that Φ' is not context free.
- **(c)** Use Ogden's lemma to directly prove that Φ' is not context free.
- **(d)** Is it possible to use the pumping theorem to directly prove that Φ' is not context free?

9.23. Consider $L = \{y \in \{\mathbf{0}, \mathbf{1}\}^* \mid |y|_{\mathbf{0}} = |y|_{\mathbf{1}}\}$. Prove or disprove that L is context free.

9.24. Refer to the proof of Theorem 9.9.
- **(a)** Give a formal recursive definition of the path by (1) stating boundary conditions, and (2) giving a rule for choosing the next node on the path.
- **(b)** Show that the conclusions of Theorem 9.9 follow from the properties of this path.

9.25. Show that $\mathscr{C}_\Sigma$ is closed under $\cup$ by directly constructing a new context-free grammar with the appropriate properties.

9.26. Let $\mathscr{X}_\Sigma$ be the set of all languages that are *not* context free. Determine whether or not:
- **(a)** $\mathscr{X}_\Sigma$ is closed under union.
- **(b)** $\mathscr{X}_\Sigma$ is closed under complement.
- **(c)** $\mathscr{X}_\Sigma$ is closed under intersection.
- **(d)** $\mathscr{X}_\Sigma$ is closed under Kleene closure.
- **(e)** $\mathscr{X}_\Sigma$ is closed under concatenation.

9.27. Let Σ be an alphabet, and $x = \mathbf{a}_1\mathbf{a}_2 \cdots \mathbf{a}_{n-1}\mathbf{a}_n \in \Sigma^*$; define $x^{\mathrm{r}} = \mathbf{a}_n\mathbf{a}_{n-1} \cdots \mathbf{a}_2\mathbf{a}_1$. For a language L over Σ, define $L^{\mathrm{r}} = \{x^{\mathrm{r}} \mid x \in L\}$. Note that the (unary) reversal operator r is thus defined by $L^{\mathrm{r}} = \{\mathbf{a}_n\mathbf{a}_{n-1} \cdots \mathbf{a}_3\mathbf{a}_2\mathbf{a}_1 \mid \mathbf{a}_1\mathbf{a}_2\mathbf{a}_3 \cdots \mathbf{a}_{n-1}\mathbf{a}_n \in L\}$, and L^{r} therefore represents all the words in L written backward. Show that $\mathscr{C}_\Sigma$ is closed under the operator r.

9.28. Let $\Sigma = \{\mathbf{a}, \mathbf{b}, \mathbf{c}, \mathbf{d}\}$. Define the (unary) operator T by

$$T(L) = \{\mathbf{a}_n\mathbf{a}_{n-1}\cdots\mathbf{a}_3\mathbf{a}_2\mathbf{a}_1\mathbf{a}_1\mathbf{a}_2\mathbf{a}_3\cdots\mathbf{a}_{n-1}\mathbf{a}_n \mid \mathbf{a}_1\mathbf{a}_2\mathbf{a}_3\cdots\mathbf{a}_{n-1}\mathbf{a}_n \in L\}$$
$$= \{w^r \cdot w \mid w \in L\}$$

(see the definition of w^r in Exercise 9.27). Prove or disprove that $\mathscr{C}_\Sigma$ is closed under the operator T.

9.29. Prove or disprove that $\mathscr{C}_{\{\mathbf{a},\mathbf{b}\}}$ is closed under *relative complement*; that is, if L_1 and L_2 are context free, then $L_1 - L_2$ is also context free.

9.30. **(a)** Prove that $\mathscr{C}_{\{\mathbf{a},\mathbf{b}\}}$ is not closed under intersection, nor is it closed under complement.

(b) By defining an appropriate homomorphism, argue that whenever Σ has more than one symbol $\mathscr{C}_\Sigma$ is not closed under intersection, nor is it closed under complement.

9.31. Consider the iterative method discussed in the proof of Theorem 9.3. Outline an alternative method based on an automaton with states labeled by the sets in $\rho(\Omega)$.

9.32. Consider grammars in Greibach normal form that also satisfy one of the restrictions of Chomsky normal form; that is, no production has more than two symbols on the right side.

(a) Show that this is not a "normal form" for context-free languages by demonstrating that there is a context-free language that cannot be generated by any grammar in this form.

(b) Characterize the languages generated by grammars that *can* be represented by this restrictive form.

9.33. Let L be *any* collection of words over an alphabet Σ. Prove that L^* must be regular.

9.34. If $\|\Sigma\| = 1$, prove or disprove that $\mathscr{C}_\Sigma$ is closed under complementation.

9.35. Prove that $\{\mathbf{a}^n\mathbf{b}^n\mathbf{c}^m \mid n, m \in \mathbb{N}\}$ is context free.

9.36. Use Ogden's lemma to prove that $\{\mathbf{a}^k\mathbf{b}^n\mathbf{c}^m \mid (k \neq n) \wedge (n \neq m)\}$ is not context free.

CHAPTER

10

PUSHDOWN AUTOMATA

In the earlier part of this text, the representation of languages via regular grammars was a generative construct equivalent to the cognitive power of deterministic finite automata and nondeterministic finite automata. Chapter 9 showed that context-free grammars had more generative potential than did regular grammars, and thus defined a significantly larger class of languages. This chapter and the next explore generalizations of the basic automata construct introduced in Chapter 1. In Chapter 4, we discovered that adding nondeterminism did not enhance the language capabilities of an automaton. It seems that more powerful automata will need the ability to store more than a finite amount of state information, and machines with the ability to write and read from an indefinitely long tape will now be considered. Automata that allow unrestricted access to all portions of the tape are the subject of Chapter 11. Such machines are regarded to be as powerful as a general-purpose computer. This chapter will deal with automata with restricted access to the auxiliary tape. One such device is known as a *pushdown automaton* and is strongly related to the context-free languages.

10.1 DEFINITIONS AND EXAMPLES

A language such as $\{\mathbf{a}^n\mathbf{b}^n \mid n \geq 1\}$ can be shown to be non-FAD by the pumping lemma, which uses the observation that a finite-state control cannot distinguish between an unlimited number of essentially different situations. Deterministic finite automata could at best "count" modulo some finite number; unlimited matching was one of the many things beyond the capabilities of a finite-state control. One possible enhancement would be to augment the automaton with a single integer counter, which could be envisioned as a sack in which stones could be placed (or removed) in response to input. The automaton would begin with one stone in the sack and process input much as a nondeterministic finite automaton would. With each transition, the machine would not only choose a new state, but also choose to add another stone to the sack, remove an existing stone from the sack, or leave the contents unchanged. The δ function is independent of the status of the sack; the sack is used only to determine whether the automaton should continue to process input symbols. Perhaps some sort of weight sensor would be used to detect when there were stones in the sack, and the device would continue to operate as long as stones were present; the device would halt when the sack is empty. If all the symbols on the input tape happen to have been consumed at the time the sack empties, the input string is *accepted* by the automaton.

Such devices are called *counting automata* and are general enough to recognize many non-FAD languages. A device to recognize $\{\mathbf{a}^n\mathbf{b}^n \mid n \geq 1\}$ would need three states. The start state will transfer control to a second state when an **a** is read, leaving the sack contents unchanged. The start state will have no valid moves for **b**, causing words that begin with **b** to be rejected since the input tape will not be completely consumed. The automaton will remain in the second state in response to each **a**, adding a stone to the sack each time an **a** is processed. The second state will transfer control to the third state upon receipt of the symbol **b** and withdraw a stone from the sack. The third state has no moves for **a** and remains in that state while removing a stone for each **b** that is processed. For this device, only words of the form $\mathbf{a}^n\mathbf{b}^n$ will consume all the input just when the sack becomes empty.

Another type of counting automaton handles acceptance in the same manner as nondeterministic finite automata. That is, if there is a sequence of transitions that consumes all the input and leaves the device in a final state, the input word is accepted (irrespective of the sack contents). As with NDFAs, the device may halt prematurely if there are no applicable transitions (or if the sack empties).

These counting automata are not quite general enough to recognize all context-free languages. More than one type of "stone" is necessary in order for such an automaton to emulate the power of context-free grammars, at which point the order of the items becomes important. Thus, the sack is replaced by a *stack*, a last-in, first-out (LIFO) list. The most recently added item is positioned at the end called the *top* of the stack. A newly added item is placed above the current top and becomes the new top item as it is *pushed* onto the stack. The action of the finite-state control can be influenced by the type of item that is on the top of the stack. Only the top (that is, the most recently placed) item can affect the state transition function; the device has no ability to reexamine items that have previously been deleted (that is, have been *popped*). The next item below the top of the stack cannot be examined until the top item is popped (and that popped item thereby becomes unavailable for later reinspection). As with counting automata, an empty stack will halt the operation of this type of automaton, called a *pushdown automaton*.

∇ **Definition 10.1.** A *(nondeterministic) pushdown automaton* (NPDA or just PDA) is a septuple $\mathsf{P} = \langle \Sigma, \Gamma, S, s_0, \delta, B, F \rangle$, where

Σ is the *input alphabet*.
Γ is the *stack alphabet*.
S is a finite nonempty set of *states*.
s_0 is the *start state* ($s_0 \in S$).
δ is the *state transition function*,
  $\delta: S \times (\Sigma \cup \lambda) \times \Gamma \to$ the set of finite subsets of $S \times \Gamma^*$.
B is the *bottom of the stack* symbol ($B \in \Gamma$).
F is the set of *final* states ($F \subseteq S$).

Δ

By the definition of alphabet (Definition 1.1), both Σ and Γ must be nonempty. Figure 10.1 presents a conceptualization of a pushdown automaton. As with an NDFA, there is a finite-state control and a read head for the input tape, which only moves forward. The auxiliary tape also has a read/write head, which not only moves forward, but can move backward when an item is popped. The state transition function is meant to signify that, given a current state, an input symbol being currently scanned, and the current top stack symbol, the automaton may choose

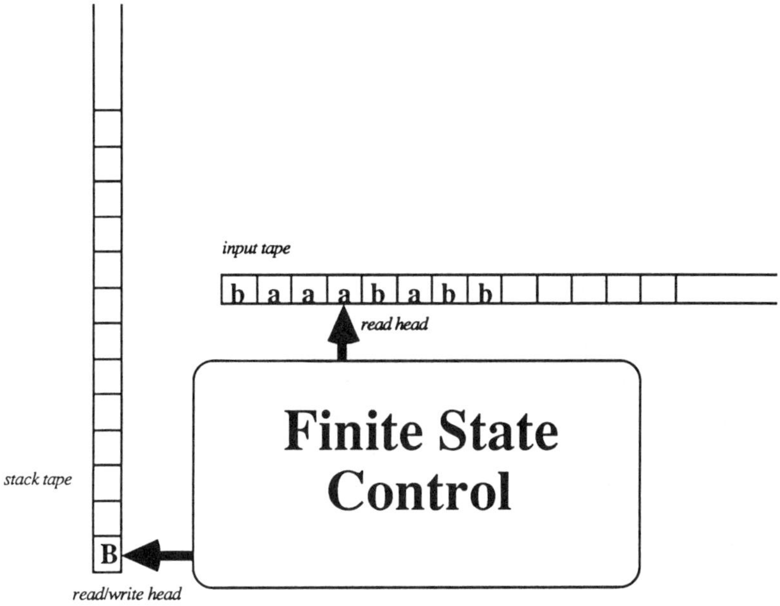

Figure 10.1 A model of a pushdown automaton

both a new current state and a new string of symbols from Γ^* to replace the top stack symbol. This definition allows the machine to behave nondeterministically, since a current state, input letter, and stack symbol are allowed to have any (finite) number of alternatives for state transitions and strings from Γ^* to record on the stack.

The auxiliary tape is similar to that of a finite-state transducer; the second component of the range of the state transition function in a pushdown automaton specifies the string to be written on the stack tape. Thus, the functions δ and ω of a FST are essentially combined in the δ function for pushdown automata. The auxiliary tape differs from that of a FST in that the current symbol from Γ on the tape is sensed by the stack read/write head and can affect the subsequent operation of the automaton. If no symbols are written to tape during a transition, the tape head drops back one position and will then be scanning the previous stack symbol. In essence, a state transition is initiated by the currently scanned symbol on both the input tape and the stack tape and begins with the stack symbol being popped from the stack; the state transition is accompanied by a push operation, which writes a new string of stack symbols on the stack tape. If several symbols are written, the auxiliary read/write head will move ahead an appropriate amount, and the head will be positioned over the last of the symbols written. Thus, if exactly one symbol is written, the stack tape head does not move, and the effect is that the old top-of-stack symbol is overwritten by the new symbol. When the empty string is to be written, the effect is a pop followed by a push of no letters, and the stack tape head retreats one position. If the only remaining stack symbol is removed from the stack in this fashion, the stack tape head moves off the end of the tape. It would then no longer be scanning a valid stack symbol, so no further transitions are possible, and the device *halts*.

It is possible to manipulate the stack and change states without consuming an input letter, which is the intent of the λ-moves in the state transition function. Since at most one symbol can be removed from the stack as a result of a transition, λ-moves allow the stack to be shortened by several symbols before the next input symbol is processed.

Acceptance can be defined by requiring the stack to be empty after the entire input tape is consumed (as was the case with counting automata) or by requiring that the automaton be in a final state after all the input is consumed. The nondeterminism may allow the device to react to a given input string in several distinct ways. As with NDFAs, the input word is considered accepted if at least one of the possible reactions satisfies the criteria for acceptance. For a given PDA, the set of words accepted by the empty stack criterion will likely differ from the set of words accepted by the final state condition.

EXAMPLE 10.1

Consider the PDA defined by $P_1 = <\{\mathbf{a}, \mathbf{b}\}, \{A, B\}, \{q, r\}, q, \delta, B, \emptyset>$, where δ is defined by

$$\delta(q, \mathbf{a}, B) = \{\langle q, A\rangle\}$$
$$\delta(q, \mathbf{a}, A) = \{\langle q, AA\rangle\}$$
$$\delta(q, \mathbf{b}, B) = \{\ \}$$
$$\delta(q, \mathbf{b}, A) = \{\langle r, \lambda\rangle\}$$
$$\delta(r, \mathbf{a}, B) = \{\ \}$$
$$\delta(r, \mathbf{a}, A) = \{\ \}$$
$$\delta(r, \mathbf{b}, B) = \{\ \}$$
$$\delta(r, \mathbf{b}, A) = \{\langle r, \lambda\rangle\}$$

Note that since the set of final states is empty no strings are accepted by final state. We wish to consider the set of strings accepted by empty stack. In general, when the set of final states is nonempty, the PDA will designate a machine designed to accept by final state; $F = \emptyset$ will generally be taken as an indication that acceptance is to be by empty stack.

The action of the state transition function can be displayed much like that of finite-state transducers. Transition arrows are no longer labeled with just a symbol from the input alphabet, since both a stack symbol and an input symbol now govern the action of the automaton. Thus, arrows are labeled by ordered pairs from $\Sigma \times \Gamma$. As with FSTs, this is followed by the output caused by the transition. The diagram corresponding to P_1 is shown in Figure 10.2.

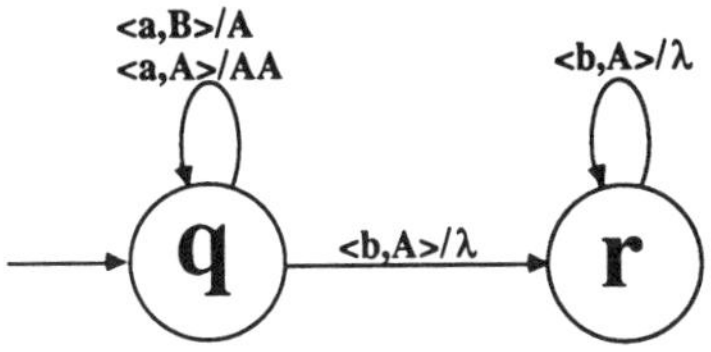

Figure 10.2 The PDA discussed in Example 10.1

The reaction of P_1 to the string **aabb** is the sequence of moves displayed in Figure 10.3. Initially, the heads of the two tapes are positioned as shown in Figure 10.3a, with the (current) initial state highlighted. Since the state is q, the input symbol is **a**, and the stack symbol is B, the first transition rule $\delta(q, \mathbf{a}, B) = \{\langle q, A\rangle\}$ applies; P_1 remains in state q, and the popped stack symbol B is replaced by a single A. Figure 10.3b shows the new state of the automaton. The stack read/write head is in the same position, since the length of the stack did not change. The input read head moves on to the next letter, since the first input symbol was consumed. The second rule now applies, and the single A is replaced by the pair AA as P_1 returns to q again, as shown in Figure 10.3c. Note that the stack tape head advanced as the topmost symbol was written. The rule $\delta(q, \mathbf{b}, A) = \{\langle r, \lambda\rangle\}$ now applies, and the state of the machine switches to r as the (topmost) A is popped and replaced with an

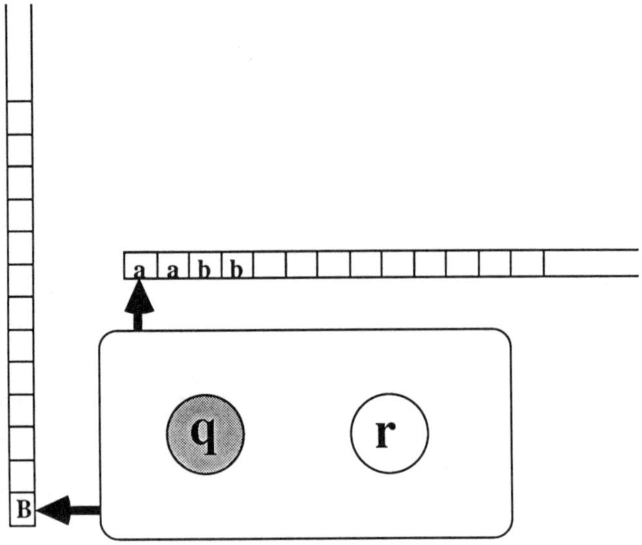

(a)

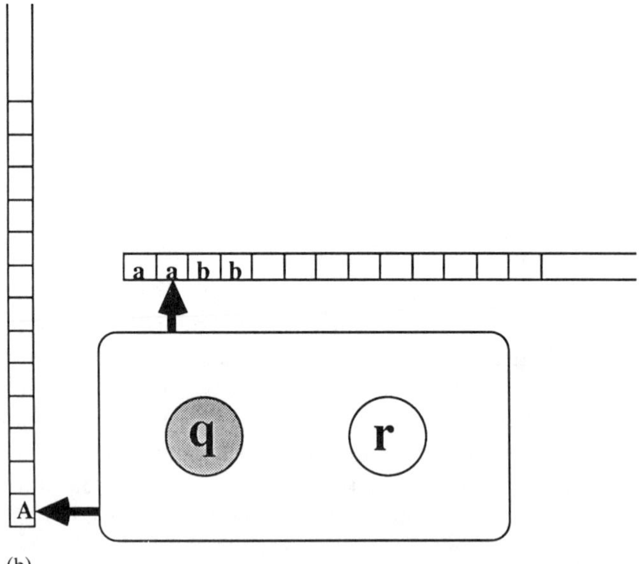

(b)

Figure 10.3 (a–e) Walkthrough of the pushdown automaton discussed in Example 10.1

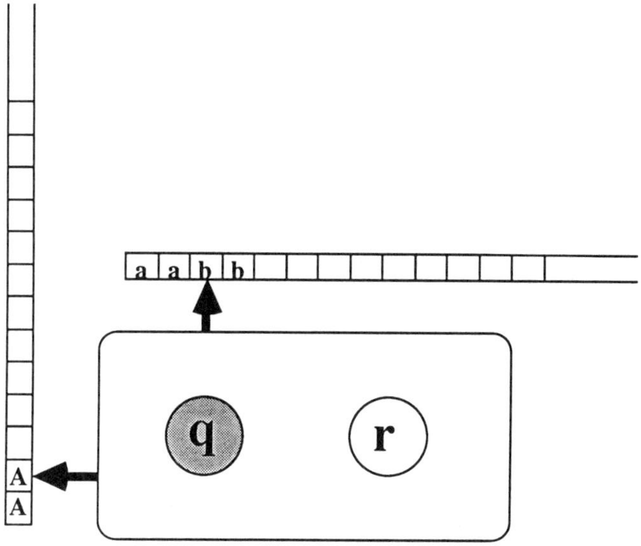

(c)

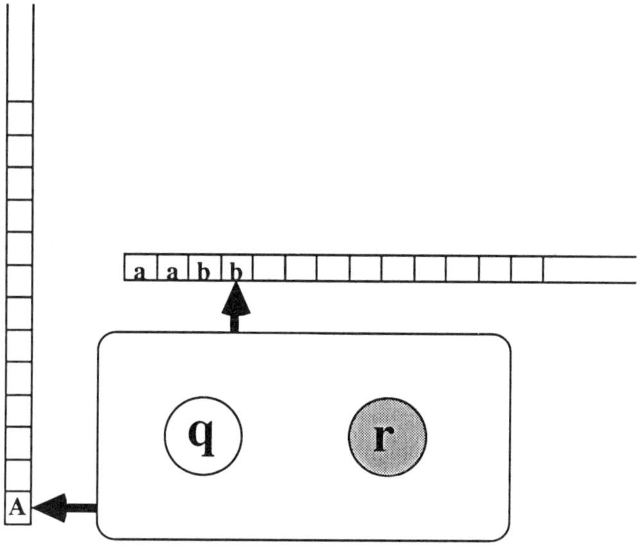

(d)

empty string, leaving the stack shorter than before. This is shown in Figure 10.3d. The last of the eight transition rules now applies, leaving the automaton in the configuration shown by Figure 10.3e. Since the stack is now empty, no further moves are possible. However, since the read head has reached the end of the input string, the word **aabb** is accepted by P_1. The word **aab** would be rejected by P_1, since

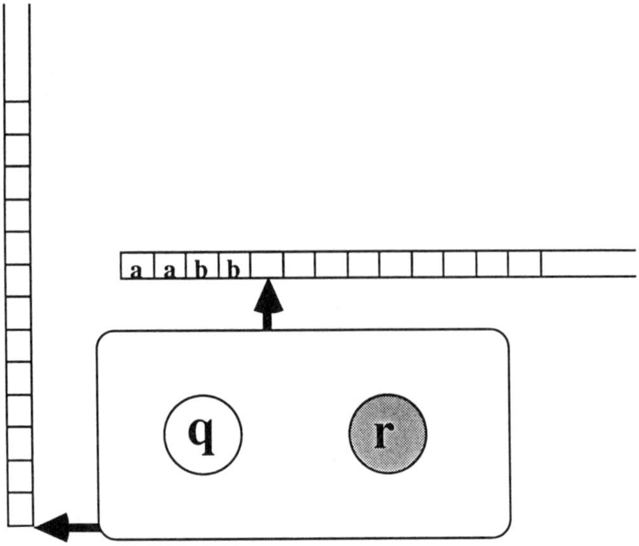

(e)

the automaton would run out of input in a configuration similar to that of Figure 10.3d, in which the stack is not yet empty. The word **aabbb** would not be accepted because the stack would empty prematurely, leaving P_1 stuck in a configuration similar to that of Figure 10.3e, but with the input string incompletely consumed. The word **aaba** would likewise be rejected because there would be no move from the state r with which to process the final input symbol **a**.

As with deterministic finite automata, once an input symbol is consumed, it has no further effect on the operation of the pushdown automaton. The current state of the device, the remaining input symbols, and the current stack contents form a triple that describes the current configuration of the PDA. The triple $\langle q, \mathbf{bb}, AA\rangle$ thus describes the configuration of the PDA in Figure 10.3c. When processing **aabb**, P_1 moved through the following sequence of configurations:

$$\langle q, \mathbf{aabb}, B\rangle$$

$$\langle q, \mathbf{abb}, A\rangle$$

$$\langle q, \mathbf{bb}, AA\rangle$$

$$\langle r, \mathbf{b}, A\rangle$$

$$\langle r, \lambda, \lambda\rangle$$

Successive configurations followed from their predecessors by applying a single rule from the state transition function. These transitions will be described by the operator $\vdash$.

∇ **Definition 10.2.** The current *configuration* of pushdown automaton $P = <\Sigma, \Gamma, S, s_0, \delta, B, F>$ is described by a triple $\langle s, x, \alpha \rangle$, where

s is the current state.

x is the unconsumed portion of the input string.

α is the current stack contents (with the topmost symbol written as the leftmost).

An ordered pair $\langle t, \gamma \rangle$ within the finite set of objects specified by $\delta(s, \mathbf{a}, A)$ can cause a *move* in the pushdown automaton P from the configuration $\langle s, \mathbf{a}y, A\beta \rangle$ to the configuration $\langle t, y, \gamma\beta \rangle$. This transition is denoted as $\langle s, \mathbf{a}y, A\beta \rangle \vdash \langle t, y, \gamma\beta \rangle$.

A sequence of successive moves in which

$$\langle s_1, x_1, \alpha_1 \rangle \vdash \langle s_2, x_2, \alpha_2 \rangle, \langle s_2, x_2, \alpha_2 \rangle \vdash \langle s_3, x_3, \alpha_3 \rangle, \ldots, \langle s_{m-1}, x_{m-1}, \alpha_{m-1} \rangle \vdash \langle s_m, x_m, \alpha_m \rangle$$

is denoted by $\langle s_1, x_1, \alpha_1 \rangle \overset{*}{\vdash} \langle s_m, x_m, \alpha_m \rangle$.

Δ

The operator $\overset{*}{\vdash}$ reflects the reflexive and transitive closure of $\vdash$, and thus we also have $\langle s_1, x_1, \alpha_1 \rangle \overset{*}{\vdash} \langle s_1, x_1, \alpha_1 \rangle$ and clearly $\langle s_1, x_1, \alpha_1 \rangle \vdash \langle s_2, x_2, \alpha_2 \rangle$ implies $\langle s_1, x_1, \alpha_1 \rangle \overset{*}{\vdash} \langle s_2, x_2, \alpha_2 \rangle$.

EXAMPLE 10.2

For the pushdown automaton P_1 in Example 10.1, $\langle q, \mathbf{aabb}, B \rangle \overset{*}{\vdash} \langle r, \lambda, \lambda \rangle$ because $\langle q, \mathbf{aabb}, B \rangle \vdash \langle q, \mathbf{abb}, A \rangle \vdash \langle q, \mathbf{bb}, AA \rangle \vdash \langle r, \mathbf{b}, A \rangle \vdash \langle r, \lambda, \lambda \rangle$.

∇ **Definition 10.3.** For a pushdown automaton $P = <\Sigma, \Gamma, S, s_0, \delta, B, F>$, the *language accepted via final state* by P, $L(P)$, is

$$\{x \in \Sigma^* \mid \exists r \in F, \exists \alpha \in \Gamma^* \ni \langle s_0, x, B \rangle \overset{*}{\vdash} \langle r, \lambda, \alpha \rangle\}$$

The *language accepted via empty stack* by P, $\Lambda(P)$, is

$$\{x \in \Sigma^* \mid \exists r \in S \ni \langle s_0, x, B \rangle \overset{*}{\vdash} \langle r, \lambda, \lambda \rangle\}$$

Δ

EXAMPLE 10.3

Consider the pushdown automaton P_1 in Example 10.1. Since only strings of the form $\mathbf{a}^i\mathbf{b}^i$ (for $i \geq 1$) allow $\langle q, \mathbf{a}^i\mathbf{b}^i, B \rangle \overset{*}{\vdash} \langle r, \lambda, \lambda \rangle$, it follows that $\Lambda(P_1) = \{\mathbf{a}^n\mathbf{b}^n \mid n \geq 1\}$. However, $F = \emptyset$ and thus $L(P_1)$ is clearly $\emptyset$.

The pushdown automaton P_1 in Example 10.1 was *deterministic* in the sense that there will never be more than one choice that can be made from any configuration. The following example illustrates a pushdown automaton that is nondeterministic.

EXAMPLE 10.4

Consider the pushdown automaton defined by $\mathsf{P}_2 = <\{\mathbf{a}, \mathbf{b}\}, \{S, C\}, \{t\}, t, \delta, S, \emptyset>$, where δ is defined by

$$\delta(t, \mathbf{a}, S) = \{\langle t, SC\rangle, \langle t, C\rangle\}$$

$$\delta(t, \mathbf{a}, C) = \{\ \}$$

$$\delta(t, \mathbf{b}, S) = \{\ \}$$

$$\delta(t, \mathbf{b}, C) = \{\langle t, \lambda\rangle\}$$

$$\delta(t, \lambda, S) = \{\ \}$$

$$\delta(t, \lambda, C) = \{\ \}$$

In this automaton, there are two distinct courses of action when the input symbol is **a** and the top stack symbol is S, which leads to several possible options when trying to process the word **aabb**. One option is to apply the first move whenever possible, which leads to the sequence of configurations

$$\langle t, \mathbf{aabb}, S\rangle \vdash \langle t, \mathbf{abb}, SC\rangle \vdash \langle t, \mathbf{bb}, SCC\rangle.$$

Since there are no λ-moves and $\delta(t, \mathbf{b}, S) = \{\ \}$, there are no further moves that can be made, and the input word cannot be completely consumed in this manner. Another option is to choose the second move option exclusively, leading to the abortive sequence $\langle t, \mathbf{aabb}, S\rangle \vdash \langle t, \mathbf{abb}, C\rangle$; $\delta(t, \mathbf{a}, C) = \{\ \}$, and processing again cannot be completed. A mixture of the first and second moves results in the sequence $\langle t, \mathbf{aabb}, S\rangle \vdash \langle t, \mathbf{abb}, SC\rangle \vdash \langle t, \mathbf{bb}, CC\rangle \vdash \langle t, \mathbf{b}, C\rangle \vdash \langle t, \lambda, \lambda\rangle$, and **aabb** is thus accepted by P_2. Further experimentation shows that $\Lambda(\mathsf{P}_2) = \{\mathbf{a}^n\mathbf{b}^n \mid n \geq 1\}$. To successfully empty its stack, this automaton must correctly "guess" when the last **a** is being read and choose the second transition pair, placing only C on the stack.

∇ **Definition 10.4.** Two pushdown automata $\mathsf{M}_1 = <\Sigma, \Gamma_1, S_1, s_{0_1}, \delta_1, B_1, F_1>$ and $\mathsf{M}_2 = <\Sigma, \Gamma_2, S_2, s_{0_2}, \delta_2, B_2, F_2>$ are called *equivalent iff* they accept the same language.
Δ

The pushdown automaton P_1 from Example 10.1 is therefore equivalent to P_2 in Example 10.4. The concept of equivalence will apply even if one device accepts via final state and the other accepts via empty stack. In keeping with the previous broad use of the concept of equivalence, if any two finite descriptors define the same language, those descriptors will be called equivalent. Thus, if a PDA M happens to accept the language described by a regular expression R, we will say that R is equivalent to M.

EXAMPLE 10.5

The following pushdown automaton illustrates the use of λ-moves and acceptance by final state for the language $\{\mathbf{a}^n\mathbf{b}^m \mid n \geq 1 \wedge (n = m \vee n = 2m)\}$. Let $\mathsf{P}_3 = <\{\mathbf{a}, \mathbf{b}\}, \{A\}, \{s_0\}, \{s_0, s_1, s_2, s_3, s_4\}, \delta, A, \{s_2, s_4\}>$, where δ is defined by

$$\delta(s_0, \mathbf{a}, A) = \{\langle s_0, AA\rangle\}$$
$$\delta(s_0, \mathbf{b}, A) = \{\ \}$$
$$\delta(s_0, \lambda, A) = \{\langle s_1, \lambda\rangle, \langle s_3, \lambda\rangle\}$$
$$\delta(s_1, \mathbf{a}, A) = \{\ \}$$
$$\delta(s_1, \mathbf{b}, A) = \{\langle s_1, \lambda\rangle\}$$
$$\delta(s_1, \lambda, A) = \{\langle s_2, \lambda\rangle\}$$
$$\delta(s_2, \mathbf{a}, A) = \{\ \}$$
$$\delta(s_2, \mathbf{b}, A) = \{\ \}$$
$$\delta(s_2, \lambda, A) = \{\ \}$$
$$\delta(s_3, \mathbf{a}, A) = \{\ \}$$
$$\delta(s_3, \mathbf{b}, A) = \{\ \}$$
$$\delta(s_3, \lambda, A) = \{\langle s_4, \lambda\rangle\}$$
$$\delta(s_4, \mathbf{a}, A) = \{\ \}$$
$$\delta(s_4, \mathbf{b}, A) = \{\langle s_3, \lambda\rangle\}$$
$$\delta(s_4, \lambda, A) = \{\ \}$$

The finite-state control for this automaton is diagrammed in Figure 10.4. Note that the λ-move from state s_3 is *not* responsible for any nondeterminism in this machine. From s_3, only one move is permissible: the λ-move to s_4. On the other hand, the λ-move from state s_1 does allow a choice of moving to s_2 (without moving the read head) or staying at s_1 while consuming another input symbol. The choice of moves from state s_0 also contributes to the nondeterminism; the device must "guess" whether the number of **b**s will equal the number of **a**s or whether there will be half as many, and at the appropriate time transfer control to s_1 or s_3, respectively. Notice that the moves defined by states s_3 and s_4 allow *two* stack symbols to be removed for each **b** consumed. Furthermore, a string like **aab** can transfer control to s_3 as the

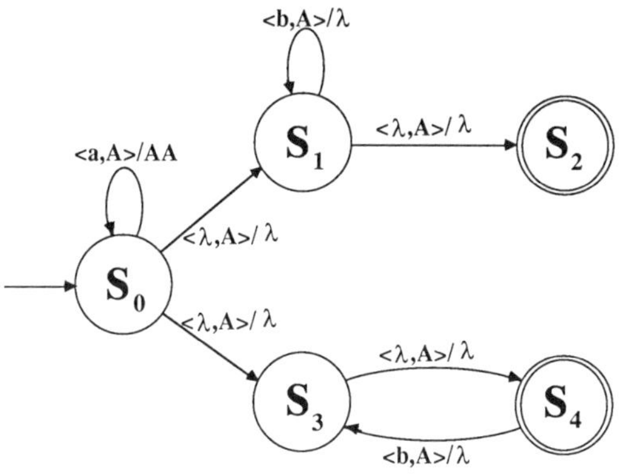

Figure 10.4 The PDA discussed in Example 10.5

final **b** is processed, but the λ-move can then be applied to reach s_4 even though there are no more symbols on the input tape.

Since A was the only stack symbol in P_3, the language could have as easily been described by the sack-and-stone counting device described at the beginning of the section. It should be clear that counting automata are essentially pushdown automata with a singleton stack alphabet. Pushdown automata with only one stack symbol cannot generate all the languages that a PDA with two symbols can [DENN]. However, it can be shown that using more than two stack symbols does not contribute to the generative power of a PDA; for example, a PDA with $\Gamma = \{A, B, C, D\}$ can be converted into an equivalent machine with $\Gamma' = \{0, 1\}$ and the occurrences of the old stack symbols replaced by the encodings $A = 01$, $B = 001$, $C = 0001$, and $D = 00001$.

Every NDFA can be simulated by a PDA that simply ignores its stack. In fact, every NDFA has an equivalent counting automaton, as shown in the following theorem.

∇ **Theorem 10.1.** Given any alphabet Σ, and an NDFA A:

1. There is an equivalent pushdown automaton (counting automaton) A′ for which $\boldsymbol{L}(\mathsf{A}) = \boldsymbol{L}(\mathsf{A}')$.
2. There is an equivalent pushdown automaton (counting automaton) A″ for which $\boldsymbol{L}(\mathsf{A}) = \Lambda(\mathsf{A}'')$.

Proof. The results for pushdown automata will actually follow from the results of the next section, since pushdown automata can define all the context-free languages, and the regular language defined by the NDFA A must be context free. The following constructions will use only the one stack symbol ¢, and hence A′ and A″ are actually *counting* automata for which $\boldsymbol{L}(\mathsf{A}) = \boldsymbol{L}(\mathsf{A}')$ and $\boldsymbol{L}(\mathsf{A}) = \Lambda(\mathsf{A}'')$.

While the construction of a PDA from an NDFA is straightforward, the inductive proofs are simplified if we appeal to Theorem 4.1, and assume that the given automaton is actually a DFA $\mathsf{A} = <\Sigma, S, s_0, \delta, F>$. Define the PDA $\mathsf{A}' = <\Sigma, \{¢\}, S, s_0, \delta', ¢, F>$, where δ' is defined by

$$(\forall s \in S)(\forall \mathbf{a} \in \Sigma)(\delta'(s, \mathbf{a}, ¢) = \{\langle \delta(s, \mathbf{a}), ¢\rangle\})$$

and $(\forall s \in S)(\delta'(s, \lambda, ¢) = \{\ \})$. That is, the PDA makes the same transitions that the DFA does and replaces the ¢ with the same symbol on the stack at each move. The proof that A and A′ are equivalent is by induction on the length of the input string, where $P(n)$ is the statement that

$$(\forall x \in \Sigma^n)(\bar{\delta}(s_0, x) = t \Leftrightarrow \langle s_0, x, ¢\rangle \overset{*}{\vdash} \langle t, \lambda, ¢\rangle)$$

The PDA with a single stack symbol that accepts L via empty stack is quite similar; final states are simply given the added option of removing the only symbol on the stack. That is, $\mathsf{A}'' = <\Sigma, \{¢\}, S, s_0, \delta'', ¢, \emptyset>$, where δ'' is defined by

$$(\forall s \in S)(\forall \mathbf{a} \in \Sigma)(\delta''(s, \mathbf{a}, ¢) = \{\langle \delta(s, \mathbf{a}), ¢\rangle\})$$

and

$$(\forall s \in F)(\delta''(s, \lambda, ¢) = \{\langle s, \lambda\rangle\})$$

while

$$(\forall s \in S - F)(\delta''(s, \lambda, ¢) = \{\ \})$$

The same type of inductive statement proved for A′ holds for A″, and it therefore will follow that exactly those words that terminate in what used to be final states empty the stack, and thus $\boldsymbol{L}(A) = \Lambda(A'')$.
Δ

10.2 EQUIVALENCE OF PDAs AND CFGs

In this section, it will be shown that if L is accepted by a PDA, then L can be generated by a CFG, and, conversely, every context-free language can be recognized by a PDA. We will also show that the class of pushdown automata that accept by empty stack defines exactly the same languages as the class of pushdown automata that accept by final state. In each case, the languages defined are exactly the context-free languages.

∇ **Definition 10.5.** For a given alphabet Σ, let

$$\mathscr{P}_\Sigma = \{L \subseteq \Sigma^* \mid \exists \text{PDA } P \ni L = \Lambda(P)\}$$

$$\mathscr{F}_\Sigma = \{L \subseteq \Sigma^* \mid \exists \text{PDA } P \ni L = \boldsymbol{L}(P)\}$$

Δ

Recall that $\mathscr{C}_\Sigma$ was defined to be the collection of context-free languages. We begin by showing that $\mathscr{C}_\Sigma \subseteq \mathscr{P}_\Sigma$. To do this, we must show that, given a language L generated by a context-free grammar G, there is a PDA P_G that recognizes exactly those words that belong to L. The pushdown automaton given in the next definition simulates leftmost derivations in G. That is, as the symbols on the input tape are scanned, the automaton guesses at the production that produced that letter and remembers the remainder of the sentential form by pushing it on the stack. P_G is constructed in such a way that, when the stack contents are checked against the symbols on the input tape, wrong guesses are discovered and the device halts. Wrong guesses, corresponding to inappropriate or impossible derivations, are thereby prevented from emptying the stack, and yet each word that can be generated by G will be guaranteed to have a sequence of moves that results in acceptance by empty stack.

∇ **Definition 10.6.** Given a context-free grammar $G = <\Omega, \Sigma, S, P>$ in pure Greibach normal form, the single-state *pushdown automaton corresponding to G* is the septuple

$$P_G = <\Sigma, \Omega \cup \Sigma, \{s\}, s, \delta_G, S, \emptyset>,$$

where δ_G is defined by

$$\delta_G(s, \mathbf{a}, \Psi) = \begin{cases} \{\langle s, \alpha\rangle \mid \Psi \to \mathbf{a}\alpha \in P\}, & \text{if } \Psi \in \Omega \\ \{\langle s, \lambda\rangle\}, & \text{if } \Psi \in \Sigma \wedge \Psi = \mathbf{a} \end{cases} \qquad \forall \mathbf{a} \in \Sigma, \forall \Psi \in (\Omega \cup \Sigma)$$

Δ

EXAMPLE 10.6

Consider the pure Greibach normal form grammar

$$G = <\{S\}, \{\mathbf{a}, \mathbf{b}\}, S, \{S \to \mathbf{aSb}, S \to \mathbf{ab}\}>$$

which is perhaps the simplest grammar generating $\{\mathbf{a}^n\mathbf{b}^n \mid n \geq 1\}$. The automaton P_G is then

$$P_G = <\{\mathbf{a}, \mathbf{b}\}, \{S, \mathbf{a}, \mathbf{b}\}, \{s\}, s, \delta_G, S, \emptyset>$$

where δ_G is defined by

$$\delta_G(s, \mathbf{a}, S) = \{\langle s, S\mathbf{b}\rangle, \langle s, \mathbf{b}\rangle\}$$
$$\delta_G(s, \mathbf{a}, \mathbf{a}) = \{\langle s, \lambda\rangle\}$$
$$\delta_G(s, \mathbf{a}, \mathbf{b}) = \{\ \}$$
$$\delta_G(s, \mathbf{b}, S) = \{\ \}$$
$$\delta_G(s, \mathbf{b}, \mathbf{a}) = \{\ \}$$
$$\delta_G(s, \mathbf{b}, \mathbf{b}) = \{\langle s, \lambda\rangle\}$$

This automaton contains no λ-moves and is essentially the same as P_2 in Example 10.4, with the state t now relabeled as s, the stack symbol **b** now playing the role of C, and the unused stack symbol **a** added to Γ. The derivation $S \Rightarrow \mathbf{aSb} \Rightarrow \mathbf{aabb}$ corresponds to the successful move sequence

$$\langle s, \mathbf{aabb}, S\rangle \vdash \langle s, \mathbf{abb}, S\mathbf{b}\rangle \vdash \langle s, \mathbf{bb}, \mathbf{bb}\rangle \vdash \langle s, \mathbf{b}, \mathbf{b}\rangle \vdash \langle s, \lambda, \lambda\rangle.$$

The exact correspondence between derivation steps and move sequences is illustrated in the next example.

EXAMPLE 10.7

For a slightly more complex example, consider the pure Greibach normal form grammar

$$G = <\{R\}, \{\mathbf{a}, \mathbf{b}, \mathbf{c}, (,), \epsilon, \emptyset, \cup, \cdot, {}^*\}, \{R, \{R \to \mathbf{a} \mid \mathbf{b} \mid \mathbf{c} \mid \epsilon \mid \emptyset \mid (R\cdot R) \mid (R \cup R) \mid (R)^*\}>.$$

The automaton P_G is then

$$<\{\mathbf{a}, \mathbf{b}, \mathbf{c}, (,), \epsilon, \emptyset, \cup, \cdot, {}^*\}, \{R, \mathbf{a}, \mathbf{b}, \mathbf{c}, (,), \epsilon, \emptyset, \cup, \cdot, {}^*\}, \{s\}, s, \delta_G, R, \emptyset>,$$

where δ_G is comprised of the following nonempty transitions:

$$\delta_G(s, \mathbf{(}, R) = \{\langle s, R\bullet R\mathbf{)}\rangle, \langle s, R\cup R\mathbf{)}\rangle, \langle s, R\mathbf{)*}\rangle\}$$
$$\delta_G(s, \mathbf{a}, R) = \{\langle s, \lambda\rangle\}$$
$$\delta_G(s, \mathbf{b}, R) = \{\langle s, \lambda\rangle\}$$
$$\delta_G(s, \mathbf{c}, R) = \{\langle s, \lambda\rangle\}$$
$$\delta_G(s, \boldsymbol{\epsilon}, R) = \{\langle s, \lambda\rangle\}$$
$$\delta_G(s, \boldsymbol{\emptyset}, R) = \{\langle s, \lambda\rangle\}$$
$$\delta_G(s, \mathbf{a}, \mathbf{a}) = \{\langle s, \lambda\rangle\}$$
$$\delta_G(s, \mathbf{b}, \mathbf{b}) = \{\langle s, \lambda\rangle\}$$
$$\delta_G(s, \mathbf{c}, \mathbf{c}) = \{\langle s, \lambda\rangle\}$$
$$\delta_G(s, \boldsymbol{\emptyset}, \boldsymbol{\emptyset}) = \{\langle s, \lambda\rangle\}$$
$$\delta_G(s, \boldsymbol{\epsilon}, \boldsymbol{\epsilon}) = \{\langle s, \lambda\rangle\}$$
$$\delta_G(s, \cup, \cup) = \{\langle s, \lambda\rangle\}$$
$$\delta_G(s, \bullet, \bullet) = \{\langle s, \lambda\rangle\}$$
$$\delta_G(s, \mathbf{*}, \mathbf{*}) = \{\langle s, \lambda\rangle\}$$
$$\delta_G(s, \mathbf{)}, \mathbf{)}) = \{\langle s, \lambda\rangle\}$$
$$\delta_G(s, \mathbf{(}, \mathbf{(}) = \{\langle s, \lambda\rangle\}$$

In this grammar, it happens that the symbol **(** is never pushed onto the stack, and so the last transition is not utilized. Transitions not listed are empty; that is, they are of the form $\delta_G(s, \mathbf{d}, A) = \{\ \}$.

Consider the string **(a∪(b•c))**, which has the following (unique) derivation:

$$\begin{aligned} R &\Rightarrow \mathbf{(}R\cup R\mathbf{)} \\ &\Rightarrow \mathbf{(a\cup}R\mathbf{)} \\ &\Rightarrow \mathbf{(a\cup(}R\bullet R\mathbf{))} \\ &\Rightarrow \mathbf{(a\cup(b\bullet}R\mathbf{))} \\ &\Rightarrow \mathbf{(a\cup(b\bullet c))} \end{aligned}$$

P_G simulates this derivation with the following steps:

$$\begin{aligned} \langle s, \mathbf{(a\cup(b\bullet c))}, R\rangle &\vdash \langle s, \mathbf{a\cup(b\bullet c))}, R\cup R\mathbf{)}\rangle \\ &\vdash \langle s, \mathbf{\cup(b\bullet c))}, \cup R\mathbf{)}\rangle \\ &\vdash \langle s, \mathbf{(b\bullet c))}, R\mathbf{)}\rangle \\ &\vdash \langle s, \mathbf{b\bullet c))}, R\bullet R\mathbf{))}\rangle \end{aligned}$$

$\vdash \langle s, \bullet \mathbf{c})), \bullet R)) \rangle$

$\vdash \langle s, \mathbf{c})), R)) \rangle$

$\vdash \langle s,)),)) \rangle$

$\vdash \langle s,),) \rangle$

$\vdash \langle s, \lambda, \lambda \rangle$

Figure 10.5 illustrates the state of the machine at several points during the move sequence. At each point when an R is the top stack symbol and the input tape head is scanning a **(**, there are three choices of productions that might have generated the opening parenthesis, and consequently the automaton has three choices with which to replace the R on the stack. If the wrong choice is taken, P_G will halt at some future point. For example, if the initial move guessed that the first parenthesis was due to a concatenation operation, the move sequence would be

$$\langle s, \mathbf{(a\cup(b\bullet c))}, R\rangle \vdash \langle s, \mathbf{a\cup(b\bullet c))}, R\bullet R)\rangle \vdash \langle s, \mathbf{\cup(b\bullet c))}, \bullet R)\rangle$$

Since there are no λ-moves and the entry for $\delta_G(s, \cup, \bullet)$ is empty, this attempt can go no further. A construction such as the one given in Definition 10.6 can be shown to produce the desired automaton for any context-free grammar in Greibach normal form.

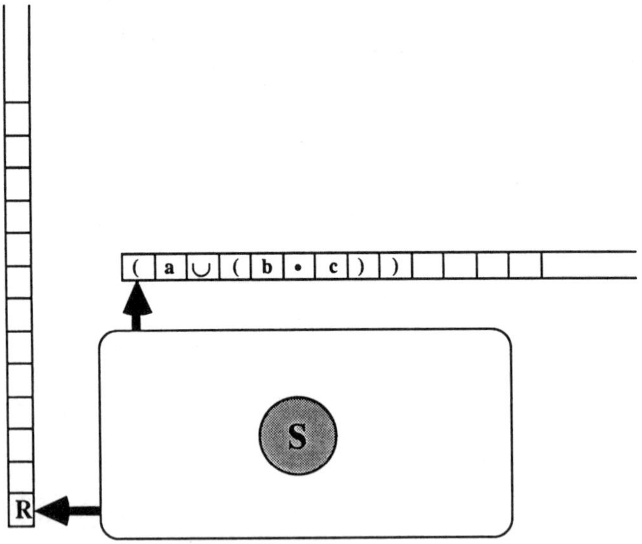

(a)

Figure 10.5 (a–f) Walkthrough of the pushdown automaton discussed in Example 10.7

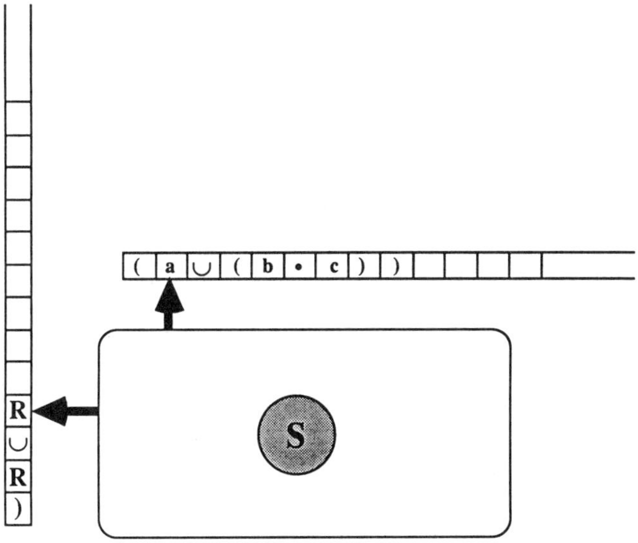

(b)

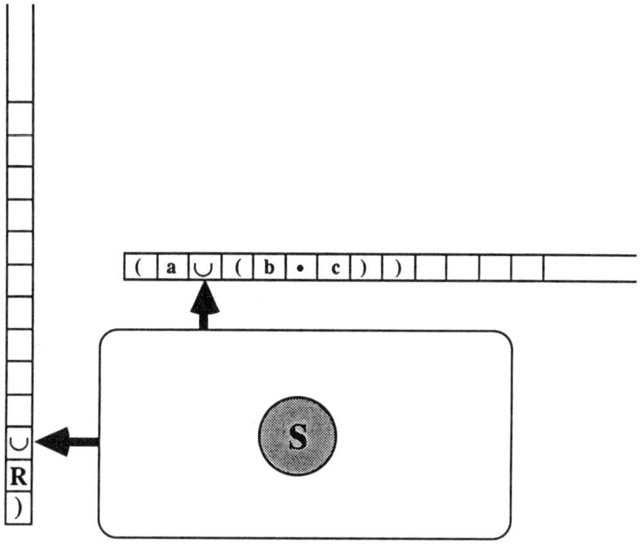

(c)

∇ **Theorem 10.2.** Given any alphabet Σ, $\mathscr{C}_\Sigma \subseteq \mathscr{P}_\Sigma$. In particular, for any context-free grammar G, there is a pushdown automaton that accepts (via empty stack) the language generated by G.

Proof. Let G′ be any context-free grammar. Theorem 9.6 guarantees that there is a pure Greibach normal form grammar $G = \langle \Omega, \Sigma, S, P \rangle$ for which

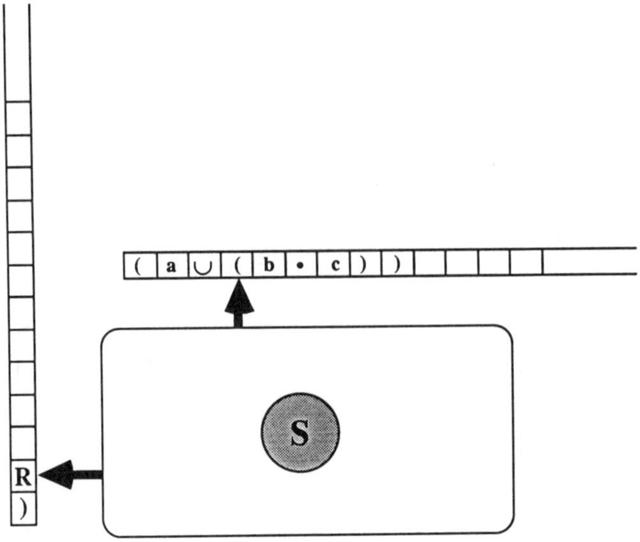

(d)

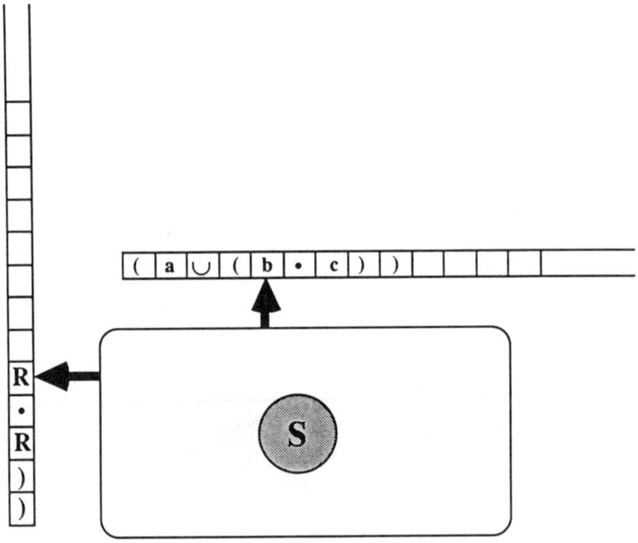

(e)

$L(G) = L(G') - \{\lambda\}$. If $\lambda \notin L(G')$, the PDA P_G from Definition 10.6 can be used directly. If $\lambda \in L(G')$, then there is a Greibach normal form grammar

$$G'' = <\Omega \cup \{Z\}, \Sigma, Z, P \cup \{Z \to S, Z \to \lambda\}>,$$

which generates $L(G')$, and the state transition function for $L(G')$ should then include the move $\delta_G(s, \lambda, Z) = \{\langle s, S\rangle, \langle s, \lambda\rangle\}$ to reflect the two Z-rules. The bottom of the stack symbol would then be Z, the new start symbol.

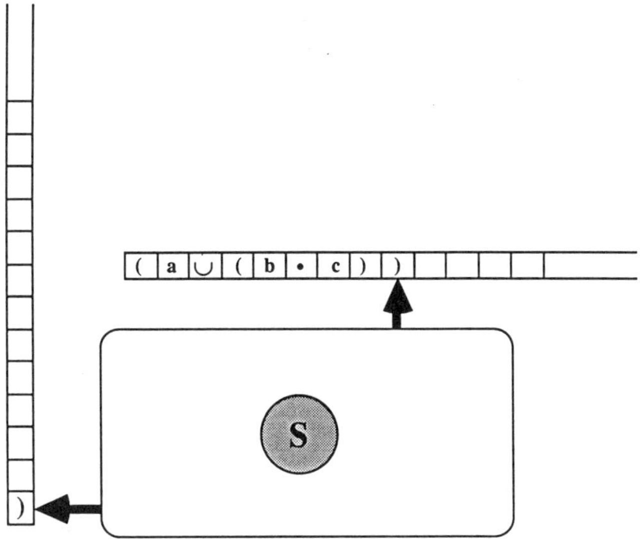

(f)

In either case, induction on the number of moves in a sequence will show that $(\forall x \in \Sigma^*)(\forall \beta \in (\Sigma \cup \Omega)^*)(\langle s, x, S\rangle \overset{*}{\vdash} \langle s, \lambda, \beta\rangle$ *iff* $S \overset{*}{\Rightarrow} x\beta$ as a leftmost derivation). Note that $x\beta$ is likely to be a sentential form that still contains nonterminals. The words x that result in an empty stack ($\beta = \lambda$) will then be exactly those words that produce an entire string of terminal symbols from the start symbol S (or Z in the case where the grammar contains the two special Z-rules). In other words, $L(G') = \Lambda(P_G)$.
Δ

Given a context-free grammar, the definition of an equivalent PDA is easy once an appropriate GNF grammar is in hand. In Example 10.6, the grammar was already in Greibach normal form. To find a PDA for the grammar in Chapters 8 and 9 that generates regular expressions, the grammar

$$<\{R\}, \{\mathbf{a}, \mathbf{b}, \mathbf{c}, \mathbf{(}, \mathbf{)}, \boldsymbol{\epsilon}, \boldsymbol{\emptyset}, \cup, \cdot, {}^*\}, R, \{R \to \mathbf{a} | \mathbf{b} | \mathbf{c} | \boldsymbol{\epsilon} | \boldsymbol{\emptyset} | \mathbf{(}R\cdot R\mathbf{)} | \mathbf{(}R\cup R\mathbf{)} | R^*\}>$$

would have to be converted to Greibach normal form. The offending left-recursive production $R \to R^*$ would have to be replaced, resulting in an extra nonterminal and about three times as many productions. The definition of the PDA for this grammar would be correspondingly more complex (see the exercises).

Since every context-free language can be represented by a pushdown automaton with only one state, one might suspect that more complex PDAs with extra states may be able to define languages that are more complex than those in $\mathscr{C}_\Sigma$. It turns out that extra states yield no more cognitive power; the information stored within the finite-state control can effectively be stored on the stack tape. This will follow from the fact that the converse of Theorem 10.2, that context-free grammars have equivalent pushdown automata, is also true.

Defining a pushdown automaton based on a context-free grammar is not as elegant as the construction presented in Definition 10.6, but the idea is to have the leftmost derivations in the grammar correspond to successful move sequences in the PDA.

∇ **Definition 10.7.** Let $\mathsf{P} = <\Sigma, \Gamma, S, s_0, \delta, B, \emptyset>$ be a pushdown automaton. Define the grammar $\mathsf{G_P} = <\Omega, \Sigma, Z, P_\mathsf{P}>$, where

$$\Omega = \{Z\} \cup \{A^{st} \mid A \in \Gamma,\ s, t \in S\}$$

and

$$P_\mathsf{P} = \{Z \to B^{s_0 t} \mid t \in S\} \cup \{A^{sq} \to \mathbf{a} A_1^{rt_1} A_2^{t_1 t_2} A_3^{t_2 t_3} \cdots A_{m-1}^{t_{m-1} t_m} A_m^{t_m q} \mid A \in \Gamma, \mathbf{a} \in \Sigma \cup \{\lambda\},$$
$$\langle r, A_1 A_2 \cdots A_m \rangle \in \delta(s, \mathbf{a}, A),\ s, q, r, t_1, t_2, \ldots, t_m \in S\}$$
$$\cup \{A^{sr} \to \mathbf{a} \mid s, r \in S, A \in \Gamma,\ \mathbf{a} \in \Sigma \cup \{\lambda\}, \langle r, \lambda \rangle \in \delta(s, \mathbf{a}, A)\}$$

Δ

Note that when $m = 1$, the transition $\langle r, A_1 \rangle \in \delta(s, \mathbf{a}, A)$ gives rise to a rule of the form $A^{sq} \to \mathbf{a} A_1^{rq}$ for each state $q \in S$.

EXAMPLE 10.8

Consider again the pushdown automaton from Example 10.4, defined by $\mathsf{P}_2 = <\{\mathbf{a}, \mathbf{b}\}, \{S, C\}, \{t\}, t, \delta, S, \emptyset>$, where δ is given by

$$\delta(t, \mathbf{a}, S) = \{\langle t, SC \rangle, \langle t, C \rangle\}$$
$$\delta(t, \mathbf{a}, C) = \{\ \}$$
$$\delta(t, \mathbf{b}, S) = \{\ \}$$
$$\delta(t, \mathbf{b}, C) = \{\langle t, \lambda \rangle\}$$

Since there is but one state and two stack symbols, the nonterminals for the corresponding grammar $\mathsf{G}_{\mathsf{P}_2}$ are $\Omega = \{Z, S^{tt}, C^{tt}\}$. P_{P_2} can be calculated as follows: $Z \to S^{tt}$ is the only rule arising from the first criteria for productions. Since $\delta(t, \mathbf{a}, S)$ contains $\langle t, SC \rangle$, a move that produces two stack symbols, $m = 2$ and the resulting production is $S^{tt} \to \mathbf{a} S^{tt} C^{tt}$. The only other rule due to the second criteria arises because $\delta(t, \mathbf{a}, S)$ contains $\langle t, C \rangle$, which with $m = 1$ yields $S^{tt} \to \mathbf{a} C^{tt}$. Finally, $\langle t, \lambda \rangle \in \delta(t, \mathbf{b}, C)$ causes $C^{tt} \to \mathbf{b}$ to be added to the production set. The resulting grammar is therefore

$$\mathsf{G}_{\mathsf{P}_2} = <\{Z, S^{tt}, C^{tt}\}, \{\mathbf{a}, \mathbf{b}\}, Z, \{Z \to S^{tt}, S^{tt} \to \mathbf{a} S^{tt} C^{tt}, S^{tt} \to \mathbf{a} C^{tt}, C^{tt} \to \mathbf{b}\}>$$

and $\mathsf{G}_{\mathsf{P}_2}$ does indeed generate $\{\mathbf{a}^n \mathbf{b}^n \mid n \geq 1\}$ and is therefore equivalent to P_2.

EXAMPLE 10.9

Now consider the pushdown automaton from Example 10.1, defined by

$$\mathsf{P}_1 = <\{\mathbf{a}, \mathbf{b}\}, \{A, B\}, \{q, r\}, q, \delta, B, \emptyset>,$$

where the nonempty transitions were

$$\delta(q, \mathbf{a}, B) = \{\langle q, A\rangle\}$$

$$\delta(q, \mathbf{a}, A) = \{\langle q, AA\rangle\}$$

$$\delta(q, \mathbf{b}, A) = \{\langle r, \lambda\rangle\}$$

$$\delta(r, \mathbf{b}, A) = \{\langle r, \lambda\rangle\}$$

Since there are two stack symbols and two choices for each of the state superscripts, the nonterminal set for the grammar G_{P_1} is $\Gamma = \{Z, B^{qq}, B^{qr}, B^{rq}, B^{rr}, A^{qq}, A^{qr}, A^{rq}, A^{rr}\}$, although some of these will turn out to be useless.

P_{P_1} contains the Z-rules $Z \to B^{qq}$ and $Z \to B^{qr}$ from the first criteria for productions. The transition $\delta(q, \mathbf{a}, B) = \{\langle q, A\rangle\}$ accounts for the productions $B^{qr} \to \mathbf{a}A^{qr}$ and $B^{qq} \to \mathbf{a}A^{qq}$. $\delta(q, \mathbf{a}, A) = \{\langle q, AA\rangle\}$ gives rise to the A^{qq}-rules $A^{qq} \to \mathbf{a}A^{qq}A^{qq}$ and $A^{qq} \to \mathbf{a}A^{qr}A^{rq}$, and the A^{qr}-rules $A^{qr} \to \mathbf{a}A^{qq}A^{qr}$ and $A^{qr} \to \mathbf{a}A^{qr}A^{rr}$. $\delta(q, \mathbf{b}, A) = \{\langle r, \lambda\rangle\}$ accounts for another A^{qr}-rule, $A^{qr} \to \mathbf{b}$. Finally, the transition $\delta(r, \mathbf{b}, A) = \{\langle r, \lambda\rangle\}$ generates the only A^{rr}-rule, $A^{rr} \to \mathbf{b}$.

Note that some of the potential nonterminals (B^{qr}, B^{rq}, B^{rr}) are never generated, and others (A^{qq}, B^{qq}) cannot produce terminal strings. The resulting grammar, with useless items deleted, is given by

$$G_{P_1} = <\{Z, B^{qr}, A^{qr}, A^{rr}\}, \{\mathbf{a}, \mathbf{b}\}, Z, \{Z \to B^{qr}, B^{qr} \to \mathbf{a}A^{qr}, A^{qr} \to \mathbf{a}A^{qr}A^{rr}, A^{qr} \to \mathbf{b}, A^{rr} \to \mathbf{b}\}>$$

and G_{P_1} generates the language P_1 recognizes: $\{\mathbf{a}^n\mathbf{b}^n \mid n \geq 1\}$.

Notice that the move sequence

$$\begin{aligned}\langle q, \mathbf{aaabbb}, B\rangle &\vdash \langle q, \mathbf{aabbb}, A\rangle \\ &\vdash \langle q, \mathbf{abbb}, AA\rangle \\ &\vdash \langle q, \mathbf{bbb}, AAA\rangle \\ &\vdash \langle r, \mathbf{bb}, AA\rangle \\ &\vdash \langle r, \mathbf{b}, A\rangle \\ &\vdash \langle r, \lambda, \lambda\rangle\end{aligned}$$

corresponds to the leftmost derivation

$$\begin{aligned}Z \Rightarrow B^{qr} &\Rightarrow \mathbf{a}A^{qr} \\ &\Rightarrow \mathbf{aa}A^{qr}A^{rr} \\ &\Rightarrow \mathbf{aaa}A^{qr}A^{rr}A^{rr} \\ &\Rightarrow \mathbf{aaab}A^{rr}A^{rr} \\ &\Rightarrow \mathbf{aaabb}A^{rr} \\ &\Rightarrow \mathbf{aaabbb}\end{aligned}$$

Note the relationship between the sequence of stack configurations and the nonterminals in the corresponding sentential form. For example, when **aaa** has been processed by P_1, AAA is on the stack, and when the leftmost derivation has produced **aaa**, the remaining nonterminals are also three A-based symbols ($A^{qr}A^{rr}A^{rr}$). A^{qr} denotes a nonterminal (which corresponds to the stack symbol A) that will eventually produce a terminal string as the stack shrinks below the current size during a sequence of transitions that lead from state q to state r. This finally happens in the last of the following steps, where $\mathbf{aaa}A^{qr}A^{rr}A^{rr} \stackrel{*}{\Rightarrow} \mathbf{aaabbb}$. A^{rr}, by contrast, denotes a nonterminal (again corresponding to the stack symbol A) that will produce a terminal string as the stack shrinks in size during transitions from state r back to state r. In this example, this occurs in the next to the last two steps. The initial stack symbol position held by B is finally vacated during a sequence of transitions from q to r, and hence B^{qr} appears in the leftmost derivation. On the other hand, it was not possible to vacate B's position during a sequence of moves from q to q, so B^{qq} consequently does not participate in significant derivations.

The strong correspondence between profitable move sequences in P and valid leftmost derivations in G_P forms the cornerstone of the following proof.

∇ **Theorem 10.3.** Given any alphabet Σ, $\mathcal{P}_\Sigma \subseteq \mathcal{C}_\Sigma$. In particular, for any pushdown automaton P, there is a context-free grammar G_P for which $L(G_P) = \Lambda(P)$.

Proof. Let $P = <\Sigma, \Gamma, S, s_0, \delta, B, \emptyset>$ be a pushdown automaton, and let G_P be the grammar given in Definition 10.7. The key to the proof is to show that all words accepted by empty stack in the PDA P can be generated by G_P and that only such words can be generated by G_P. That is, we wish to show that the automaton halts in some state t with an empty stack after processing the terminal string x exactly when there is a leftmost derivation of the form

$$Z \Rightarrow A^{s_0t} \stackrel{*}{\Rightarrow} x$$

That is,

$$(\forall x \in \Sigma^*)(Z \Rightarrow B^{s_0t} \stackrel{*}{\Rightarrow} x \Leftrightarrow \langle s_0, x, B\rangle \stackrel{*}{\vdash} \langle t, \lambda, \lambda\rangle)$$

The desired conclusion, that $L(G_P) = \Lambda(P)$, will follow immediately from this equivalence. The equivalence does not easily lend itself to proof by induction on the length of x; indeed, to progress from the mth to the $m+1$st step, a more general statement involving more of the nonterminals of G_P is needed. The following statement can be proved by induction on the number of moves and leads to the desired conclusion when $s = s_0$ and $A = B$:

$$(\forall x \in \Sigma^*)(\forall A \in \Gamma)(\forall s \in S)(\forall t \in S)(A^{st} \stackrel{*}{\Rightarrow} x \Leftrightarrow \langle s, x, A\rangle \stackrel{*}{\vdash} \langle t, \lambda, \lambda\rangle)$$

The resulting grammar will then generate $\Lambda(P)$, but G_P may not be a strict context-free grammar; λ-moves may result in some productions of the form $A^{sr} \to \lambda$, which will then have to be "removed," as specified by Exercise 9.16.

Δ

Thus, $\mathcal{P}_\Sigma = \mathcal{C}_\Sigma$. Furthermore, only one state in a PDA is truly necessary, as noted in the following corollary. In essence, this means that for PDAs that accept by empty stack any state information can be effectively encoded with the information on the stack.

∇ **Corollary 10.1.** For every PDA P that accepts via empty stack, there is an equivalent one-state PDA P′ that also accepts via empty stack.

Proof. Let P be a PDA that accepts via empty stack. Let $P' = P_{G_P}$. That is, from the original PDA P, find the corresponding context-free grammar G_P. By Theorem 10.3, this is equivalent to P. However, by Theorem 10.2, the grammar G_P has an equivalent one-state PDA, which must also be equivalent to P.
Δ

Unlike the pushdown automata discussed in this section, PDAs that accept via final state cannot always make do with a single state. As the exercises will make clear, at least one final and one nonfinal state are necessary. Unlike DFAs, PDAs with only one state *can* accept some nontrivial languages, since selected words can be rejected because there is no appropriate move sequence. However, a single final state and a single nonfinal state *are* sufficient, as shown in the following section.

10.3 EQUIVALENCE OF ACCEPTANCE BY FINAL STATE AND EMPTY STACK

In this section, we explore the ramifications of accepting words according to the criteria that a final state can be reached after processing all the letters on the input tape, rather than the criteria that the stack is emptied. Theorem 10.4 will show that any language that can be accepted via empty stack can also be accepted via final state. In terms of Definition 10.5, this means that $\mathcal{P}_\Sigma \subseteq \mathcal{F}_\Sigma$. Since $\mathcal{P}_\Sigma = \mathcal{C}_\Sigma$, this means that every context-free language can be accepted by a PDA via final state. Theorem 10.5 ensures that no "new" languages can be produced by pushdown automata that accept via final state; $\mathcal{F}_\Sigma \subseteq \mathcal{P}_\Sigma$, and so $\mathcal{F}_\Sigma = \mathcal{P}_\Sigma = \mathcal{C}_\Sigma$.

As in the last section, the key to the correspondence is the definition of an appropriate translation from one finite representation to another. We first consider a scheme for modifying a PDA so that the new device can transfer to a final state whenever the old device was capable of emptying its stack. To do this, we need to place a "buffer" symbol at the bottom of the stack, which will appear when the original automaton would have emptied its stack. The new machine operates in almost the same fashion as the original automaton; the differences amount to an additional transition at the start of operation to install the new buffer symbol and an extra move at the end of operation to transfer to the (new) final state.

∇ **Theorem 10.4.** Every pushdown automaton P that accepts via empty stack has an equivalent two-state pushdown automaton P_f that accepts via final state.

Proof. Corollary 10.1 guaranteed that every pushdown automaton that accepts via empty stack has an equivalent one-state pushdown automaton that also accepts via empty stack. Without loss of generality, we may therefore assume that $P = <\Sigma, \Gamma, \{s\}, s, \delta, B, \emptyset>$. Define P_f by choosing a new state f and two new stack symbols Y and Z such that $Y, Z \notin \Gamma$, and let $P_f = <\Sigma, \Gamma \cup \{Y, Z\}, \{s, f\}, s, \delta_f, Z, \{f\}>$, where δ_f is defined by:

1. $\delta_f(s, \lambda, Z) = \{\langle s, BY\rangle\}$
2. $(\forall \mathbf{a} \in \Sigma)(\forall A \in \Gamma)(\delta_f(s, \mathbf{a}, A) = \delta(s, \mathbf{a}, A))$
3. $(\forall A \in \Gamma)(\delta_f(s, \lambda, A) = \delta(s, \lambda, A))$
4. $\delta_f(s, \lambda, Y) = \{\langle f, Y\rangle\}$
5. $(\forall \mathbf{a} \in \Sigma)(\delta_f(s, \mathbf{a}, Z) = \{\ \} \wedge \delta_f(s, \mathbf{a}, Y) = \{\ \})$
6. $(\forall \mathbf{a} \in \Sigma \cup \{\lambda\})(\forall A \in \Gamma \cup \{Y, Z\})(\delta_f(f, \mathbf{a}, A) = \{\ \})$

Notice that rules 2 and 3 imply that, while the original stack symbols appear on the stack, the machine moves exactly as the original PDA. Rules 5 and 6 indicate that no letters can be consumed while there is a Y or Z on the stack, and no moves are possible once the final state f is reached. Since the bottom of the stack symbol is now the new letter Z, rule 1 is the only rule that initially applies. Its application results in a configuration very much like that of the old PDA, with the symbol Y underneath the old bottom of the stack symbol B. P_f now simulates P until the Y is uncovered (that is, until a point is reached in which the old PDA would have emptied its stack). In such cases (and only in such cases), rule 4 applies, and control can be transferred to the final state f, and P_f must then halt.

By inducting on the number of moves in a sequence, it can be shown for any $\alpha, \beta \in \Gamma^*$ that

$$(\forall x, y \in \Sigma^*)(\langle s, xy, \alpha\rangle \overset{*}{\vdash} \langle s, y, \beta\rangle \text{ in } P \Leftrightarrow \langle s, xy, \alpha Y\rangle \overset{*}{\vdash} \langle s, y, \beta Y\rangle \text{ in } P_f)$$

From this, with $y = \beta = \lambda$ and $\alpha = B$, it follows that

$$(\forall x \in \Sigma^*)(\langle s, x, B\rangle \overset{*}{\vdash} \langle s, \lambda, \lambda\rangle \text{ in } P \Leftrightarrow \langle s, x, BY\rangle \overset{*}{\vdash} \langle s, \lambda, Y\rangle \text{ in } P_f)$$

Consequently, since $\delta_f(s, \lambda, Z) = \{\langle s, BY\rangle\}$ and $\delta_f(s, \lambda, Y) = \{\langle f, Y\rangle\}$,

$$(\forall x \in \Sigma^*)(\langle s, x, B\rangle \overset{*}{\vdash} \langle s, \lambda, \lambda\rangle \text{ in } P \Leftrightarrow \langle s, x, Z\rangle \overset{*}{\vdash} \langle f, \lambda, Y\rangle \text{ in } P_f)$$

which implies that $(\forall x \in \Sigma^*)(x \in \Lambda(P) \Leftrightarrow x \in \boldsymbol{L}(P_f))$, as was to be proved.
Δ

Thus, every language which is $\Lambda(P)$ for some PDA can be recognized by a PDA that accepts via final state, and this PDA need only employ one final and one nonfinal state. Thus, $\mathcal{P}_\Sigma \subseteq \mathcal{F}_\Sigma$. One might conjecture that $\mathcal{F}_\Sigma$ might actually be larger than $\mathcal{P}_\Sigma$, since some added capability might arise if more than two states are used in a pushdown automaton that accepts via final state. This is not the case, as demonstrated by the following theorem. Once again, the information stored in the finite control can effectively be transferred to the stack; only one final and one nonfinal state are needed to accept any context-free language via final state, and context-free languages are the only type accepted via final state.

∇ **Theorem 10.5.** Every pushdown automaton P that accepts via final state has an equivalent pushdown automaton P_λ that accepts via empty stack.

Proof. Assume that $P = <\Sigma, \Gamma, S, s_0, \delta, B, F>$. Define P_λ by choosing a new stack symbols Y and Z such that $Y, Z \notin \Gamma$ and a new state e such that $e \notin S$, and let $P_\lambda = <\Sigma, \Gamma \cup \{Y, Z\}, S \cup \{e\}, s_0, \delta_\lambda, Z, \emptyset>$, where δ_λ is defined by:

1. $\delta_\lambda(s_0, \lambda, Z) = \{\langle s_0, BY\rangle\}$
2. $(\forall \mathbf{a} \in \Sigma)(\forall A \in \Gamma)(\forall s \in S)(\delta_\lambda(s, \mathbf{a}, A) = \delta(s, \mathbf{a}, A))$
3. $(\forall A \in \Gamma)(\forall s \in S - F)(\delta_\lambda(s, \lambda, A) = \delta(s, \lambda, A))$
4. $(\forall A \in \Gamma)(\forall f \in F)(\delta_\lambda(f, \lambda, A) = \delta(f, \lambda, A) \cup \{\langle e, \lambda\rangle\})$
5. $(\forall A \in \Gamma)(\delta_\lambda(e, \lambda, A) = \{\langle e, \lambda\rangle\})$
6. $\delta_\lambda(e, \lambda, Y) = \{\langle e, \lambda\rangle\}$

The first rule guards against P_λ inappropriately accepting if P simply empties its stack (by padding the stack with the new stack symbol Y). The intent of rules 2 through 4 is to arrange for P_λ to simulate the moves of P and allow P_λ to enter the state e when final states can be reached. The state e does not allow any further symbols to be processed, but does allow the stack contents (including the new buffer symbol) to be emptied via rules 5 and 6. Thus, P_λ has a sequence of moves for input x that empties the stack exactly when P has a sequence of moves that leads to a final state.

By inducting on the number of moves in a sequence, it can be shown for any $\alpha, \beta \in \Gamma^*$ that

$$(\forall x, y \in \Sigma^*)(\forall s, t \in S)(\langle s, xy, \alpha\rangle \vdash^* \langle t, y, \beta\rangle \text{ in P} \Leftrightarrow \langle s, xy, \alpha Y\rangle \vdash^* \langle t, y, \beta Y\rangle \text{ in } P_\lambda)$$

From this, with $y = \lambda$, $\alpha = B$, and $t \in F$, it follows that

$$(\forall x, y \in \Sigma^*)(\forall t \in F)(\langle s_0, x, B\rangle \vdash^* \langle t, \lambda, \beta\rangle \text{ in P} \Leftrightarrow \langle s_0, x, BY\rangle \vdash^* \langle t, \lambda, \beta Y\rangle \text{ in } P_\lambda)$$

Consequently, since $\delta_\lambda(s_0, \lambda, Z) = \{\langle s_0, BY\rangle\}$ and $\delta_\lambda(t, \lambda, A)$ contains $\langle e, \lambda\rangle$, repeated application of rules 5 and 6 implies

$$(\forall x, y \in \Sigma^*)(\forall t \in F)(\langle s_0, x, B\rangle \vdash^* \langle t, \lambda, \beta\rangle \text{ in P} \Leftrightarrow \langle s_0, x, Z\rangle \vdash^* \langle t, \lambda, \lambda\rangle \text{ in } P_\lambda)$$

This shows that $(\forall x \in \Sigma^*)(x \in \Lambda(P_\lambda) \Leftrightarrow x \in \boldsymbol{L}(P))$.
Δ

Thus, $\mathcal{F}_\Sigma \subseteq \mathcal{P}_\Sigma$, and so $\mathcal{F}_\Sigma = \mathcal{P}_\Sigma = \mathcal{C}_\Sigma$. Acceptance by final state yields exactly the same class of languages as acceptance by empty stack. This class of languages, described by these cognitive constructs, has been encountered before and can be defined by the generative constructs which comprise the context-free grammars. Note that since the type 3 languages are contained in the type 2 languages, the portion of Theorem 10.1 dealing with pushdown automata follows immediately from the results in this and the previous section.

10.4 CLOSURE PROPERTIES AND DETERMINISTIC PUSHDOWN AUTOMATA

Since the collection of languages recognized by pushdown automata is exactly the collection of context-free languages, the results in Chapter 9 show that $\mathcal{P}_\Sigma$ is closed under substitution, homomorphism, union, concatenation, and Kleene closure. Results for context-free languages likewise imply that $\mathcal{P}_\Sigma$ is not closed under complement or intersection.

It is hard to imagine how to find a method that would combine two context-free grammars to produce a new context-free grammar that might accept the intersection of the original languages. The constructs for regular expressions and regular grammars likewise did not lend themselves to such methods, and yet it *was* possible to find appropriate constructs that *did* represent intersections. As presented in Chapter 5, this was possible by turning to the cognitive representation for this class of languages, the deterministic finite automata. It is instructive to recall the technique that allowed two DFAs A_1 and A_2 to be combined to form a new DFA $A^\cap$ that accepts the intersection of the languages accepted by the original devices and to see why this same method cannot be adapted to pushdown automata.

The automaton $A^\cap$ used a cross product of the states of A_1 and A_2 to simultaneously keep track of the progress of both DFAs through an appropriate revamping of the state transition function. $A^\cap$ only accepted strings that would have reached final states in both A_1 and A_2. Two pushdown automata P_1 and P_2 might be combined into a new PDA $P^\cap$ using the cross-product approach, but the transition function for this composite PDA cannot be reliably defined. A problem arises since the δ function depends on the top stack symbol, and it is impossible to keep track of both the original stacks through any type of stack encoding, since the stack size of P_1 might be increasing while the stack size of P_2 is decreasing. A device like the one depicted in Figure 10.6 could be capable of recognizing the intersection of two context-free languages, but such a machine is inherently more powerful than PDAs. The language $\{\mathbf{a}^n\mathbf{b}^n\mathbf{c}^n \mid n \geq 0\}$ is not context free, yet a two-tape automata could recognize this set of words by storing the initial **a**s on the first stack tape, match them against the incoming **b**s while storing those **b**s on the second tape, and then matching the **c**s against the **b**s on the second tape (see the exercises).

If one were to attempt to intersect a context-free language with a regular language, one would expect the result to be context free, since the corresponding cross-product construct would need only one tape. This is indeed the case, as shown by the following theorem.

∇ **Theorem 10.6.** $\mathcal{C}_\Sigma$ is closed under intersection with a regular set. That is, if L_1 is context free and R_2 is regular, $L_1 \cap R_2$ is always context free.

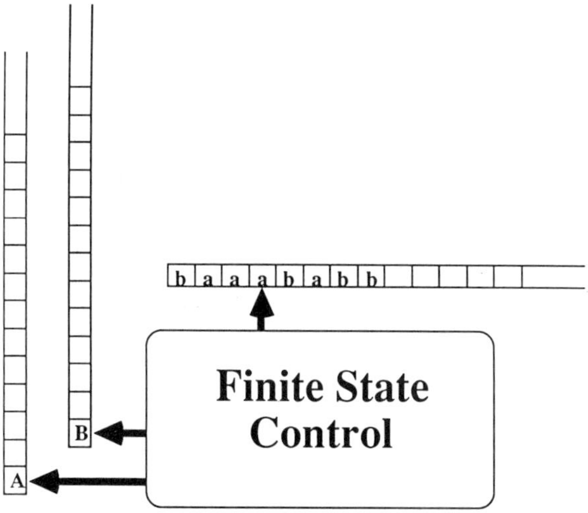

Figure 10.6 A model of a "pushdown automaton" with two tapes

Proof. Let L_1 be a context-free language and let R_2 be a regular set. Since $\mathscr{C}_\Sigma = \mathscr{P}_\Sigma$, there must be a PDA $P_1 = <\Sigma, \Gamma_1, S_1, s_{0_1}, \delta_1, B_1, F_1>$ for which $L_1 = L(P_1)$. Let $A_2 = <\Sigma, S_2, s_{0_2}, \delta_2, F_2>$ be a DFA for which $R_2 = L(A_2)$. Define

$$P^\cap = <\Sigma, \Gamma_1, S_1 \times S_2, \langle s_{0_1}, s_{0_2}\rangle, \delta^\cap, B_1, F_1 \times F_2>,$$

where $\delta^\cap$ is defined by:

1. $(\forall s_1 \in S_1)(\forall s_2 \in S_2)(\forall \mathbf{a} \in \Sigma)(\forall A \in \Gamma_1)$
$(\delta^\cap(\langle s_1, s_2\rangle, \mathbf{a}, A) = \{\langle\langle t_1, t_2\rangle, \beta\rangle \mid \langle t_1, \beta\rangle \in \delta_1(s_1, \mathbf{a}, A) \wedge t_2 = \delta_2(s_2, \mathbf{a})\})$.
2. $(\forall s_1 \in S_1)(\forall s_2 \in S_2)(\forall A \in \Gamma_1)$
$(\delta^\cap(\langle s_1, s_2\rangle, \lambda, A) = \{\langle\langle t_1, t_2\rangle, \beta\rangle \mid \langle t_1, \beta\rangle \in \delta_1(s_1, \lambda, A) \wedge t_2 = s_2\})$.

As with the constructions in the previous sections, induction on the number of moves exhibits the desired correspondence between the behaviors of the machines. In particular, it can be shown for any $\alpha, \beta \in \Gamma^*$ that

$$(\forall x \in \Sigma^*)(\forall s_1, t_1 \in S_1)(\forall s_2, t_2 \in S_2)((\langle\langle s_1, s_2\rangle, xy, \alpha> \overset{*}{\vdash} \langle\langle t_1, t_2\rangle, y, \beta\rangle \text{ in } P_1 \Leftrightarrow$$
$$((\langle s_1, xy, \alpha\rangle \overset{*}{\vdash} \langle t_1, y, \beta\rangle \text{ in } P^\cap) \wedge (t_2 = \overline{\delta}_2(s_2, x))))$$

From this, with $\alpha = B_1$ and the observation that $\langle t_1, t_2\rangle \in F_1 \times F_2$ *iff* $t_1 \in F_1 \wedge t_2 \in F_2$, it follows that $(\forall x \in \Sigma^*)(x \in L(P^\cap) \Leftrightarrow (x \in L(P_1) \wedge x \in L(A_2)))$. Therefore,

$$L(P^\cap) = L(P_1) \cap L(A_2) = L_1 \cap R_2.$$

Since $P^\cap$ is a PDA accepting $L_1 \cap R_2$, $L_1 \cap R_2$ must be context free.
Δ

Closure properties such as this are quite useful in showing that certain languages are not context free. Consider the set $L = \{x \in \{\mathbf{a}, \mathbf{b}, \mathbf{c}\}^* \mid |x|_\mathbf{a} = |x|_\mathbf{b} = |x|_\mathbf{c}\}$. Since the letters in a word can occur in any order, a pumping theorem proof is less straightforward than for the set $\{\mathbf{a}^n\mathbf{b}^n\mathbf{c}^n \mid n \geq 0\}$. However, if L were context free, then $L \cap \mathbf{a}^*\mathbf{b}^*\mathbf{c}^*$ would also be context free. But $L \cap \mathbf{a}^*\mathbf{b}^*\mathbf{c}^* = \{\mathbf{a}^n\mathbf{b}^n\mathbf{c}^n \mid n \geq 0\}$, and thus L cannot be context free. The exercises suggest other occasions for which closure properties are useful in showing certain languages are not context free.

For the machines discussed in the first portion of this text, it was seen that nondeterminism did not add to the computing power of DFAs. In contrast, this is not the case for pushdown automata. There are languages that can be accepted by nondeterministic pushdown automata that cannot be accepted by any deterministic pushdown automaton. The following is the broadest definition of what can constitute a deterministic pushdown automaton.

∇ **Definition 10.8.** A *deterministic pushdown automaton* (DPDA) is a pushdown automaton $P = <\Sigma, \Gamma, S, s_0, \delta, B, F>$ with the following restrictions on the state transition function δ:

1. $(\forall \mathbf{a} \in \Sigma)(\forall A \in \Gamma)(\forall s \in S)(\delta(s, \mathbf{a}, A)$ is empty or contains just one element).
2. $(\forall A \in \Gamma)(\forall s \in S)(\delta(s, \lambda, A)$ is empty or contains just one element).
3. $(\forall A \in \Gamma)(\forall s \in S)(\delta(s, \lambda, A) \neq \emptyset \Rightarrow (\forall \mathbf{a} \in \Sigma)(\delta(s, \mathbf{a}, A) = \emptyset))$.

Δ

Rule 1 states that, for a given input letter, deterministic pushdown automata cannot have two different choices of destination states or two different choices of strings to place on the stack. Rule 2 ensures that there is no choice of λ-moves either. Furthermore, rule 3 guarantees that there will never be a choice between a λ-move and a transition that consumes a letter; states that have a λ-move can have *only* that one move; no other transitions of any type are allowed out of that state. Thus, for any string, there is never any more than one path through the machine. Unlike deterministic finite automata, deterministic pushdown automata may not always completely process the strings in Σ^*; a given string may reach a state that has no further valid moves, or a string may prematurely empty the stack. In each case, the DPDA would halt without processing any further input.

EXAMPLE 10.10

The automaton P_1 in Example 10.1 was deterministic. The PDAs in Examples 10.4 and 10.5 were not deterministic. The automaton P_G derived in Example 10.7 was not deterministic because there were three possible choices of moves listed for δ_G(s, **(**, R): {⟨s, R•R**)**⟩, ⟨s, R∪R**)**⟩, ⟨s, R**)***⟩}. These choices corresponded to the three different operators that might have generated the open parenthesis.

Pushdown automata provide an appropriate mechanism for parsing sentences in programming languages. The regular expression grammar in Example 10.7 is quite similar to the arithmetic expression grammar that describes expressions in many programming languages. Indeed, the transitions taken within the corresponding PDA give an indication of which productions in the underlying grammar were used; such information is of obvious use in compiler construction. A nondeterministic pushdown automaton is at best a very inefficient tool for parsing; a DPDA is much better suited to the task.

As mentioned in the proof of Theorem 10.2, each leftmost derivation in G has a corresponding sequence of moves in P_G. If G is ambiguous, then there is at least one word with two distinct leftmost derivations, and hence if that word appeared on the input tape of P_G, there would be two distinct move sequences leading to acceptance. In this case, P_G cannot possibly be deterministic. On the other hand, if P_G is nondeterministic, this does not mean that G is ambiguous, as demonstrated by Example 10.7. In parsing a string in that automaton, it may not be immediately obvious which production to use (and hence which transition to take), but for any string, there is at most only one correct choice; each word has a unique parse tree and a unique leftmost derivation. The grammar in Example 10.7 is not ambiguous, even though the corresponding PDA was nondeterministic.

EXAMPLE 10.11

The following Greibach normal form grammar is similar to the one used to construct the PDA in Example 10.7, but with the different operators paired with unique delimiters. Let

$$G = <\{R\},\{\mathbf{a},\mathbf{b},\mathbf{c},\mathbf{(},\mathbf{)},\mathbf{\{},\mathbf{\}},[,],\boldsymbol{\epsilon},\boldsymbol{\emptyset},\cup,\bullet,{}^{*}\},R,\ \{R \to \mathbf{a}|\mathbf{b}|\mathbf{c}|\boldsymbol{\epsilon}|\boldsymbol{\emptyset}|\mathbf{(}R\bullet R\mathbf{)}|[R\cup R]|\mathbf{\{}R\mathbf{\}}{}^{*}\}>.$$

The automaton P_G is then

$$<\{\mathbf{a},\mathbf{b},\mathbf{c},\mathbf{(},\mathbf{)},\mathbf{\{},\mathbf{\}},[,],\boldsymbol{\epsilon},\boldsymbol{\emptyset},\cup,\bullet,{}^{*}\},\{R,\mathbf{a},\mathbf{b},\mathbf{c},\mathbf{(},\mathbf{)},\mathbf{\{},\mathbf{\}},[,],\boldsymbol{\epsilon},\boldsymbol{\emptyset},\cup,\bullet,{}^{*}\},\{s\},s,\delta_G,R,\emptyset>$$

where δ_G is comprised of the following nonempty transitions:

$$\delta_G(s,\mathbf{(},R) = \{\langle s, R\bullet R\mathbf{)}\rangle\}$$

$$\delta_G(s,[,R) = \{\langle s, R\cup R]\rangle\}$$

$$\delta_G(s,\mathbf{\{},R) = \{\langle s, R\mathbf{\}}{}^{*}\rangle\}$$

$$\delta_G(s,\mathbf{a},R) = \{\langle s,\lambda\rangle\}$$

$$\delta_G(s,\mathbf{b},R) = \{\langle s,\lambda\rangle\}$$

$$\delta_G(s,\mathbf{c},R) = \{\langle s,\lambda\rangle\}$$

$$\delta_G(s,\boldsymbol{\epsilon},R) = \{\langle s,\lambda\rangle\}$$

$$\delta_G(s,\boldsymbol{\emptyset},R) = \{\langle s,\lambda\rangle\}$$

$$\delta_G(s,\mathbf{a},\mathbf{a}) = \{\langle s,\lambda\rangle\}$$

$$\delta_G(s,\mathbf{b},\mathbf{b}) = \{\langle s,\lambda\rangle\}$$

$$\delta_G(s,\mathbf{c},\mathbf{c}) = \{\langle s,\lambda\rangle\}$$

$$\delta_G(s,\boldsymbol{\emptyset},\boldsymbol{\emptyset}) = \{\langle s,\lambda\rangle\}$$

$$\delta_G(s, \epsilon, \epsilon) = \{\langle s, \lambda\rangle\}$$
$$\delta_G(s, \cup, \cup) = \{\langle s, \lambda\rangle\}$$
$$\delta_G(s, \bullet, \bullet) = \{\langle s, \lambda\rangle\}$$
$$\delta_G(s, *, *) = \{\langle s, \lambda\rangle\}$$
$$\delta_G(s,),)) = \{\langle s, \lambda\rangle\}$$
$$\delta_G(s,],]) = \{\langle s, \lambda\rangle\}$$
$$\delta_G(s, \}, \}) = \{\langle s, \lambda\rangle\}$$
$$\delta_G(s, (, () = \{\langle s, \lambda\rangle\}$$
$$\delta_G(s, [, [) = \{\langle s, \lambda\rangle\}$$
$$\delta_G(s, \{, \{) = \{\langle s, \lambda\rangle\}$$

All other transitions are empty; that is, they are of the form $\delta_G(s, \mathbf{d}, A) = \{\ \}$. The resulting PDA is clearly deterministic, since there are no λ-moves and the other transitions are all singleton sets or are empty. It is instructive to step through the transitions in P_G for a string such as **[{(a•b)}*∪c]**. Upon encountering a delimiter while scanning a prospective string, the parser would immediately know which operation gave rise to that delimiter, and need not "guess" at which of the three productions might have been applied. Note that G was an LL0 grammar (as defined in Section 9.2), and the properties of G resulted in P_G being a deterministic device. An efficient parser for this language follows immediately from the specification of the grammar, whereas the grammar in Example 10.7 gave rise to a nondeterministic device.

Programmers would not be inclined to tolerate remembering which delimiters should be used in conjunction with the various operators, and hence programming language designers take a slightly different approach to the problem. The nondeterminism in Example 10.7 may only be an effect of the particular grammar chosen and not inherent in the language itself. Note that the language $\{\mathbf{a}^n\mathbf{b}^n \mid n \geq 1\}$ had a grammar that produced a nondeterministic PDA (Example 10.4), but it also had a grammar that corresponded to a DPDA (Example 10.1). In compiler construction, designers lean toward syntax that is compatible with determinism, and they seek grammars for the language that reflect that determinism.

EXAMPLE 10.12

Consider again the language discussed in Example 10.7, which can also be expressed by the following grammar

$$H = <\{S, T\}, \{\mathbf{a}, \mathbf{b}, \mathbf{c}, \mathbf{(}, \mathbf{)}, \epsilon, \emptyset, \cup, \bullet, *\}, S, \{S \to (ST \mid \mathbf{a} \mid \mathbf{b} \mid \mathbf{c} \mid \epsilon \mid \emptyset, T \to \bullet S) \mid \cup S) \mid)*\}>$$

The automaton P_H is then

$$<\{\mathbf{a}, \mathbf{b}, \mathbf{c}, \mathbf{(}, \mathbf{)}, \epsilon, \emptyset, \cup, \bullet, *\}, \{S, T, \mathbf{a}, \mathbf{b}, \mathbf{c}, \mathbf{(}, \mathbf{)}, \epsilon, \emptyset, \cup, \bullet, *\}, \{t\}, t, \delta_H, S, \emptyset>$$

where each production of H gives rise to the following transitions in δ_H:

$$\delta_H(t, \mathbf{(}, S) = \{\langle t, ST\rangle\}$$

$$\delta_H(t, \mathbf{a}, S) = \{\langle t, \lambda\rangle\}$$

$$\delta_H(t, \mathbf{b}, S) = \{\langle t, \lambda\rangle\}$$

$$\delta_H(t, \mathbf{c}, S) = \{\langle t, \lambda\rangle\}$$

$$\delta_H(t, \boldsymbol{\epsilon}, S) = \{\langle t, \lambda\rangle\}$$

$$\delta_H(t, \boldsymbol{\emptyset}, S) = \{\langle t, \lambda\rangle\}$$

$$\delta_H(t, \cdot, T) = \{\langle t, S\mathbf{)}\rangle\}$$

$$\delta_H(t, \cup, T) = \{\langle t, S\mathbf{)}\rangle\}$$

$$\delta_H(t, \mathbf{)}, T) = \{\langle t, \mathbf{*}\rangle\}$$

While the formal definition of δ_H specifies several productions of the form $\delta_H(t, \mathbf{d}, \mathbf{d}) = \{\langle t, \lambda\rangle\}$, by observing what can be put on the stack by the above productions, it is clear that the only remaining useful transitions in δ_H are

$$\delta_H(t, \mathbf{*}, \mathbf{*}) = \{\langle t, \lambda\rangle\}$$

and

$$\delta_H(t, \mathbf{)}, \mathbf{)}) = \{\langle t, \lambda\rangle\}$$

Thus, even though the PDA P_G in Example 10.7 turned out to be nondeterministic, this was not a flaw in the language itself, since P_H is an equivalent DPDA. Notice that the grammar G certainly appears to be more straightforward than H. G had fewer nonterminals and fewer productions, and it is a bit harder to understand the relationships between the nonterminals of H. Nevertheless, the LL0 grammar H led to an efficient parser and G did not.

To take advantage of the resulting reduction in complexity, all major programming languages are designed to be recognized by DPDAs. These constructs naturally lead to a mechanical framework for syntactic analysis. In Example 10.12, the application of the production $T \rightarrow \cup S\mathbf{)}$ [that is, the use of the transition $\delta_H(t, \cup, T) = \{\langle t, S\mathbf{)}\rangle\}$] signifies that the previous expression and the expression to which S will expand are to be combined with the union operator. It should be easy to see that a similar grammar and DPDA for arithmetic expressions (using +, −, *, and / rather than ∪, ·, and *) would provide a guide for converting such expressions into their equivalent machine code.

Deterministic pushdown automata have some surprising properties. Recall that $\mathscr{C}_\Sigma$ was not closed under complementation, and since $\mathscr{P}_\Sigma = \mathscr{C}_\Sigma$, there must be some PDAs that define languages whose complement cannot be recognized by any PDA. However, it can be shown that any language accepted by a DPDA must have a complement that can also be recognized by a DPDA. The construction used to prove this statement, in which final and nonfinal states are interchanged in a DPDA that accepts via final state, is similar to the approach used in Theorem 5.1 for deterministic finite automata. It is useful to recall why it was crucial in the proof of Theorem 5.1 to begin with a DFA when interchanging states, rather than using an NDFA. Strings that have multiple paths in an NDFA that lead to both final and nonfinal states would be accepted in the original automaton and also in the machine with the states interchanged. Furthermore, some strings may have no complete paths through the NDFA and be rejected in both the original and new automata. The problem of multiple paths does not arise with DPDAs, since by definition no choice of moves is allowed. However, strings that do not get completely consumed would be rejected in both the original DPDA and the DPDA with final and nonfinal states interchanged. Thus, the proof of closure under complement for DPDAs is not as straightforward as for DFAs. There are three ways an input string might not be completely consumed: the stack might empty prematurely, there may be no transition available at some point, or there might only be a cycle of λ-moves available that consumes no further input. The exercises indicate that it is possible to avoid these problems by padding the stack with a new bottom-of-the-stack symbol, and adding a "garbage state" to which strings that are hopelessly stuck would transfer.

∇ **Theorem 10.7.** If L is a language recognized by a deterministic pushdown automaton, then ~L can also be recognized by a DPDA.

Proof. See the exercises.

Δ

∇ **Definition 10.9.** Given any alphabet Σ, let $\mathcal{A}_\Sigma$ represent the collection of all languages recognized by deterministic pushdown automata. If $L \in \mathcal{A}_\Sigma$, then L is said to be a *deterministic context-free language* (DCFL).

Δ

Theorem 10.7 shows that unlike $\mathcal{P}_\Sigma$, $\mathcal{A}_\Sigma$ is closed under complementation. This divergent behavior has some immediate consequences, as stated below.

∇ **Theorem 10.8.** Let Σ be an alphabet.

If $|\Sigma| = 1$, then $\mathcal{D}_\Sigma = \mathcal{A}_\Sigma = \mathcal{P}_\Sigma$.

If $|\Sigma| > 1$, then $\mathcal{D}_\Sigma$ is properly contained in $\mathcal{A}_\Sigma$, which is properly contained in $\mathcal{P}_\Sigma$.

Proof. For every alphabet Σ, examining the proof of Theorem 10.1 shows that every finite automaton has an equivalent deterministic pushdown automaton, and thus it is always true that $\mathcal{D}_\Sigma \subseteq \mathcal{A}_\Sigma$. Definition 10.7 implies that $\mathcal{A}_\Sigma \subseteq \mathcal{P}_\Sigma$. If $|\Sigma| = 1$, then Theorem 9.15 showed that $\mathcal{D}_\Sigma = \mathcal{C}_\Sigma$ $(= \mathcal{P}_\Sigma)$, from which it follows that $\mathcal{D}_\Sigma = \mathcal{A}_\Sigma = \mathcal{P}_\Sigma$. If $|\Sigma| > 1$, an example such as $\{\mathbf{a}^n\mathbf{b}^n \mid n \geq 1\}$ shows that $\mathcal{D}_\Sigma$ is properly contained in $\mathcal{A}_\Sigma$ (see the exercises). Since $\mathcal{P}_{\{\mathbf{a},\mathbf{b}\}}$ and $\mathcal{A}_{\{\mathbf{a},\mathbf{b}\}}$ have different closure

properties, they cannot represent the same collection, and $\mathcal{A}_\Sigma \subseteq \mathcal{P}_\Sigma$ implies that the containment must be proper.
Δ

In the proof of Theorem 10.6, it is easy to see that if P_1 is deterministic then $\mathsf{P}^\cap$ will be a DPDA, also. Hence $\mathcal{A}_\Sigma$, like $\mathcal{P}_\Sigma$, is closed under intersection with a regular set. Also, the exercises show that both $\mathcal{A}_\Sigma$ and $\mathcal{P}_\Sigma$ are closed under difference with a regular set. However, the closure properties of $\mathcal{A}_\Sigma$ and $\mathcal{P}_\Sigma$ disagree in just about every other case. The languages

$$L_1 = \{\mathbf{a}^n\mathbf{b}^m \mid (n \geq 1) \wedge (n = m)\} \quad \text{and} \quad L_2 = \{\mathbf{a}^n\mathbf{b}^m \mid (n \geq 1) \wedge ((n = 2m)\}$$

are both DCFLs, and yet $L_1 \cup L_2 = \{\mathbf{a}^n\mathbf{b}^m \mid (n \geq 1) \wedge (n = m \vee n = 2m)\}$ is not a DCFL (see the exercises). Thus, unlike $\mathcal{P}_\Sigma$, $\mathcal{A}_\Sigma$ is not closed under union if Σ is comprised of at least two symbols (recall that since $\mathcal{D}_{\{\mathbf{a}\}} = \mathcal{A}_{\{\mathbf{a}\}} = \mathcal{P}_{\{\mathbf{a}\}}$, $\mathcal{A}_{\{\mathbf{a}\}}$ would be closed under union). If $\mathcal{A}_\Sigma$ was closed under intersection, then $\mathcal{A}_\Sigma$ would by De Morgan's law be closed under union, since it is closed under complement. Hence, $\mathcal{A}_\Sigma$ cannot be closed under intersection.

The language $\{\mathbf{c}^n\mathbf{b}^m \mid (n \geq 1) \wedge (n = m)\} \cup \{\mathbf{a}^n\mathbf{b}^m \mid (n \geq 1) \wedge (n = 2m)\}$ is definitely a DCFL, and yet a simple homomorphism can transform it into

$$\{\mathbf{a}^n\mathbf{b}^m \mid (n \geq 1) \wedge ((n = m) \vee (n = 2m))\}$$

(see the exercises). Thus, $\mathcal{A}_\Sigma$ is not closed under homomorphism. Since homomorphisms are special cases of substitutions, $\mathcal{A}_\Sigma$ is not closed under substitution either. $\mathcal{A}_\Sigma$ is also the only collection of languages discussed in this text that is not closed under reversal; $\{\mathbf{c}\mathbf{a}^n\mathbf{b}^m \mid (n \geq 1) \wedge (n = m)\} \cup \{\mathbf{a}^n\mathbf{b}^m \mid (n \geq 1) \wedge (n = 2m)\}$ is a DCFL, but $\{\mathbf{b}^m\mathbf{a}^n\mathbf{c} \mid (n \geq 1) \wedge (n = m)\} \cup \{\mathbf{b}^m\mathbf{a}^n \mid (n \geq 1) \wedge (n = 2m)\}$ is not. These properties are summed up in the following statements.

∇ **Theorem 10.9.** Given any alphabet Σ, $\mathcal{A}_\Sigma$ is closed under complement. $\mathcal{A}_\Sigma$ is also closed under union, intersection, and difference *with a regular set*. That is, if L_1 is a DCFL and R_2 is a FAD language, then the following are deterministic, context-free languages:

$$\begin{gathered} \sim L_1 \\ L_1 \cap R_2 \\ L_1 \cup R_2 \\ L_1 - R_2 \\ R_2 - L_1 \end{gathered}$$

Proof. The proof follows from the above discussion and theorems and the exercises.
Δ

∇ **Lemma 10.1.** Let Σ be an alphabet comprised of at least two symbols. Then $\mathcal{A}_\Sigma$ is not closed under union, intersection, concatenation, Kleene closure, homomorphism, substitution, or reversal. That is, there are examples of deterministic context-free languages L_1 and L_2, a homomorphism h, and a substitution s for which the following are not DCFLs:

$$L_1 \cup L_2$$
$$L_1 \cap L_2$$
$$L_1 \cdot L_2$$
$$L_1^*$$
$$\overline{h}(L_1)$$
$$\overline{s}(L_1)$$
$$L_1^r$$

Proof. The proof follows from the above discussion and theorems and the exercises.
Δ

EXAMPLE 10.13

These closure properties can often be used to justify that certain languages are not DCFLs. For example, the language

$$L = \{x \in \{\mathbf{a}, \mathbf{b}, \mathbf{c}\}^* \mid |x|_{\mathbf{a}} = |x|_{\mathbf{b}}\} \cup \{x \in \{\mathbf{a}, \mathbf{b}, \mathbf{c}\}^* \mid |x|_{\mathbf{b}} = |x|_{\mathbf{c}}\}$$

can be recognized by a PDA but not by a DPDA. If L were a DCFL, then $\sim L = \{x \in \{\mathbf{a}, \mathbf{b}, \mathbf{c}\}^* \mid |x|_{\mathbf{a}} \neq |x|_{\mathbf{b}}\} \cap \{x \in \{\mathbf{a}, \mathbf{b}, \mathbf{c}\}^* \mid |x|_{\mathbf{b}} \neq |x|_{\mathbf{c}}\}$ would also be a DCFL. However, $\sim L \cap \mathbf{a}^*\mathbf{b}^*\mathbf{c}^* = \{\mathbf{a}^k\mathbf{b}^n\mathbf{c}^m \mid (k \neq n) \wedge (n \neq m)\}$, which should also be a DCFL. Ogden's lemma shows that this is not even a CFL (see the exercises), and hence the original hypothesis that L was a DCFL must be false. The interested reader is referred to similar discussions in [HOPC] and [DENN].

The restriction that the head scanning the stack tape could only access the symbol at the top of the stack imposed limitations on the cognitive power of this class of automata. While the current contents of the top of the stack could be stored in the finite-state control and be remembered after the stack was popped, only a finite number of such pops can be recorded within the states of the PDA. At some point, seeking information further down on the stack will cause an irretrievable loss of information. One might suspect that if popped items were not erased (so that they could be revisited and reviewed at some later point) a wider class of languages might be recognizable. Generalized automata that allow such nondestructive "backtracking" are called Turing machines and form a significantly more powerful class of automata. These devices and their derivatives are the subject of the next chapter.

EXERCISES

10.1. Refer to Theorem 10.1 and use induction to show

$$(\forall x \in \Sigma^*)(\overline{\delta}(s_0, x) = t \Leftrightarrow \langle s_0, x, ¢\rangle \overset{*}{\vdash} \langle t, \lambda, ¢\rangle)$$

10.2. Define a *deterministic* pushdown automaton P_1' with only one state for which $\Lambda(P_1') = \{\mathbf{a}^n\mathbf{b}^n \mid n \geq 1\}$.

10.3. Consider the pushdown automaton defined by $P_2' = <\{\mathbf{a}, \mathbf{b}\}, \{S, C\}, \{t\}, t, \delta, S, \{t\}>$, where δ is defined by

$$\delta(t, \mathbf{a}, S) = \{\langle t, SC\rangle, \langle t, C\rangle\}$$

$$\delta(t, \mathbf{a}, C) = \{\ \}$$

$$\delta(t, \mathbf{b}, S) = \{\ \}$$

$$\delta(t, \mathbf{b}, C) = \{\langle t, \lambda\rangle\}$$

(a) Give an inductive proof that

$$(\forall i \in \mathbb{N})(\langle t, \mathbf{a}^i, S\rangle \overset{*}{\vdash} \langle t, \lambda, \alpha\rangle \Rightarrow (\alpha = SC^i \ \vee\ \alpha = C^i))$$

(b) Give an inductive proof that

$$(\forall i \in \mathbb{N})(\langle t, x, C^i\rangle \overset{*}{\vdash} \langle t, \lambda, \beta\rangle \Rightarrow (x = \mathbf{b}^i))$$

(c) Find $L(P_2')$; use parts (a) and (b) to rigorously justify your statements.

10.4. Let $L = \{\mathbf{a}^i\mathbf{b}^j\mathbf{c}^k \mid i, j, k \in \mathbb{N} \text{ and } i + j = k\}$.

(a) Find a pushdown automaton (which accepts via final state) that recognizes L.
(b) Find a pushdown automaton (which accepts via empty stack) that recognizes L.
(c) Is there a counting automaton that accepts L?
(d) Is there a DPDA that accepts L?
(e) Use Definition 10.7 to find a grammar equivalent to the PDA in part (a).

10.5. Let $L = \{x \in \{\mathbf{a}, \mathbf{b}, \mathbf{c}\}^* \mid |x|_\mathbf{a} + |x|_\mathbf{b} = |x|_\mathbf{c}\}$.

(a) Find a pushdown automaton (which accepts via final state) that recognizes L.
(b) Find a pushdown automaton (which accepts via empty stack) that recognizes L.
(c) Is there a counting automaton that accepts L?
(d) Is there a DPDA that accepts L?
(e) Use Definition 10.7 to find a grammar equivalent to the PDA in part (a).

10.6. Prove or disprove that:

(a) $\mathcal{P}_\Sigma$ is closed under inverse homomorphism.
(b) $\mathcal{A}_\Sigma$ is closed under inverse homomorphism.

10.7. Give an example of a finite language that cannot be recognized by any one-state PDA that accepts via final state.

10.8. Let $L = \{\mathbf{a}^n\mathbf{b}^n\mathbf{c}^m\mathbf{d}^m \mid n, m \in \mathbb{N}\}$.

(a) Find a pushdown automaton (which accepts via final state) that recognizes L.
(b) Find a pushdown automaton (which accepts via empty stack) that recognizes L.
(c) Is there a DPDA that accepts L?
(d) Is there a counting automaton that accepts L?
(e) Use Definition 10.7 to find a grammar equivalent to the PDA in part (b).

10.9. Refer to Theorem 10.2 and use induction on the number of moves in a sequence to show that

$$(\forall x \in \Sigma^*)(\forall \beta \in (\Sigma \cup \Omega)^*)(\langle s, x, S\rangle \overset{*}{\vdash} \langle s, \lambda, \beta\rangle \ \textit{iff}\ \ S \overset{*}{\Rightarrow} x\beta \text{ as a leftmost derivation})$$

10.10. Consider the grammar

$$<\{R\}, \{\mathbf{a}, \mathbf{b}, \mathbf{c}, \mathbf{(}, \mathbf{)}, \boldsymbol{\epsilon}, \boldsymbol{\emptyset}, \cup, \bullet, \mathbf{*}\}, R, \{R \to \mathbf{a} \mid \mathbf{b} \mid \mathbf{c} \mid \boldsymbol{\epsilon} \mid \boldsymbol{\emptyset} \mid \mathbf{(}R\bullet R\mathbf{)} \mid \mathbf{(}R\cup R\mathbf{)} \mid R\mathbf{*}\}>$$

(a) Convert this grammar to Greibach normal form, adding the new nonterminal Y.
(b) Use Definition 10.6 on part (a) to find the corresponding PDA.
(c) Use the construct suggested by Theorem 10.4 in part (b) to find the corresponding PDA that accepts via final state.

10.11. Let $L = \{\mathbf{a}^i\mathbf{b}^j\mathbf{c}^j\mathbf{d}^i \mid i, j \in \mathbb{N}\}$.
(a) Find a pushdown automaton (which accepts via final state) that recognizes L.
(b) Find a pushdown automaton (which accepts via empty stack) that recognizes L.
(c) Is there a DPDA that accepts L?
(d) Is there a counting automaton that accepts L?
(e) Use Definition 10.7 to find a grammar equivalent to the PDA in part (b).

10.12. Consider the PDA P_3 in Example 10.5. Use Definition 10.7 to find G_{P_3}.

10.13. Refer to Theorem 10.3 and use induction to show

$$(\forall x \in \Sigma^*)(\forall A \in \Gamma)(\forall s \in S)(\forall t \in S)(A^{st} \stackrel{*}{\Rightarrow} x \Leftrightarrow \langle s, x, A\rangle \stackrel{*}{\vdash} \langle t, \lambda, \lambda\rangle)$$

10.14. Let $L = \{\mathbf{a}^n\mathbf{b}^n\mathbf{c}^m\mathbf{d}^m \mid n, m \in \mathbb{N}\} \cup \{\mathbf{a}^i\mathbf{b}^j\mathbf{c}^j\mathbf{d}^i \mid i, j \in \mathbb{N}\}$.
(a) Find a pushdown automaton (which accepts via final state) that recognizes L.
(b) Find a pushdown automaton (which accepts via empty stack) that recognizes L.
(c) Is there a DPDA that accepts L?
(d) Is there a counting automaton that accepts L?
(e) Use Definition 10.7 to find a grammar equivalent to the PDA in part (b).

10.15. Consider the PDA P_G in Example 10.6. Use Definition 10.7 to find G_{P_G}.

10.16. Refer to Theorem 10.4 and use induction to show

$$(\forall \alpha, \beta \in \Gamma^*)(\forall x, y \in \Sigma^*)(\langle s, xy, \alpha\rangle \stackrel{*}{\vdash} \langle s, y, \beta\rangle \text{ in } P \Leftrightarrow \langle s, xy, \alpha Y\rangle \stackrel{*}{\vdash} \langle s, y, \beta Y\rangle \text{ in } P_f)$$

10.17. Refer to Theorem 10.5 and use induction to show

$$(\forall \alpha, \beta \in \Gamma^*)(\forall x, y \in \Sigma^*)(\forall s, t \in S)(\langle s, xy, \alpha\rangle \stackrel{*}{\vdash} \langle t, y, \beta\rangle \text{ in } P \Leftrightarrow$$
$$\langle s, xy, \alpha Y\rangle \stackrel{*}{\vdash} \langle t, y, \beta Y\rangle \text{ in } P_\lambda)$$

10.18. Prove that $\{x \in \{\mathbf{a}, \mathbf{b}, \mathbf{c}\}^* \mid |x|_\mathbf{a} = |x|_\mathbf{b} \wedge |x|_\mathbf{b} > |x|_\mathbf{c}\}$ is not context free. (*Hint:* Use closure properties.)

10.19. **(a)** Give an appropriate definition for the state transition function of the two-tape automaton pictured in Figure 10.6, stating the new domain and range.
(b) Define a two-tape automaton that accepts $\{\mathbf{a}^n\mathbf{b}^n\mathbf{c}^n \mid n \geq 1\}$ via final state.

10.20. **(a)** Prove that $\{\mathbf{a}^n\mathbf{b}^n\mathbf{c}^n \mid n \geq 1\}$ is not context free.
(b) Prove that $\{x \in \{\mathbf{a}, \mathbf{b}, \mathbf{c}\}^* \mid |x|_\mathbf{a} = |x|_\mathbf{b}\}$ is not context free. [*Hint:* Use closure properties and apply part (a).]

10.21. **(a)** Find a DPDA that accepts

$$\{\mathbf{c}^n\mathbf{b}^m \mid (n \geq 1) \wedge (n = m)\} \cup \{\mathbf{a}^n\mathbf{b}^m \mid (n \geq 1) \wedge (n = 2m)\}$$

(b) Define a homomorphism that transforms part (a) into a language that is not a DCFL.

10.22. Use Ogden's lemma to show that $\{\mathbf{a}^k\mathbf{b}^n\mathbf{c}^m \mid (k \neq n) \wedge (n \neq m)\}$ is not a context-free language.

10.23. Refer to Theorem 10.6 and use induction to show

$$(\forall \alpha, \beta \in \Gamma^*)(\forall x \in \Sigma^*)(\forall s_1, t_1 \in S_1)(\forall s_2, t_2 \in S_2)$$
$$(\langle\langle s_1, s_2\rangle, xy, \alpha\rangle \stackrel{*}{\vdash} \langle\langle t_1, t_2\rangle, y, \beta\rangle \text{ in } P_1 \Leftrightarrow ((\langle s_1, xy, \alpha\rangle \stackrel{*}{\vdash} \langle t_1, y, \beta\rangle \text{ in } P^\cap) \wedge (t_2 = \overline{\delta}_2(s_2, x))))$$

10.24. Assume that P is a DPDA. Prove that there is an equivalent DPDA P′ (which accepts via final state) for which:

(a) P′ always has a move for all combinations of states, input symbols, and stack symbols.

(b) P′ never empties its stack.

(c) For each input string presented to P′, P′ always scans the entire input string.

10.25. Assume the results of Exercise 10.24, and show that $\mathcal{A}_\Sigma$ is closed under complementation. (*Hint:* Exercise 10.24 almost allows the trick of switching final and nonfinal states to work; the main remaining problem involves handling the case where a series of λ-moves may cycle through both final and nonfinal states.)

10.26. Give an example that shows that $\mathcal{A}_\Sigma$ is not closed under concatenation.

10.27. Give an example that shows that $\mathcal{A}_\Sigma$ is not closed under Kleene closure.

10.28. Show that $\{\mathbf{ca}^n\mathbf{b}^m \mid (n \geq 1) \wedge (n = m)\} \cup \{\mathbf{a}^n\mathbf{b}^m \mid (n \geq 1) \wedge (n = 2m)\}$ is a DCFL.

10.29. **(a)** Modify the proof of Theorem 10.6 to show that if L_1 is context free and R_2 is regular, $L_1 - R_2$ is always context free.

(b) Prove the result in part (a) by instead appealing to closure properties for complement and intersection.

10.30. **(a)** Modify the proof of Theorem 10.6 to show that if L_1 is context free and R_2 is regular, $L_1 \cup R_2$ is always context free.

(b) Prove the result in part (a) by instead appealing to closure properties for complement and intersection.

10.31. Argue that if L_1 is a DCFL and R_2 is regular, $R_2 - L_1$ is always a DCFL.

10.32. **(a)** Prove that $\{w\mathbf{2}w^r \mid w \in \{\mathbf{0},\mathbf{1}\}^*\}$ is a DCFL.

(b) Prove that $\{ww^r \mid w \in \{\mathbf{0},\mathbf{1}\}^*\}$ is *not* a DCFL.

10.33. Give examples to show that even if L_1 and L_2 are DCFLs:

(a) $L_1 \cdot L_2$ need not be a DCFL.

(b) $L_1 - L_2$ need not be a DCFL.

(c) L_1^* need not be a DCFL.

(d) L_1^r need not be a DCFL.

10.34. Consider the quotient operator / given by Definition 5.10. Prove or disprove that:

(a) $\mathcal{P}_\Sigma$ is closed under quotient.

(b) $\mathcal{A}_\Sigma$ is closed under quotient.

10.35. Consider the operator b defined in Theorem 5.11. Prove or disprove that:

(a) $\mathcal{P}_\Sigma$ is closed under the operator b.

(b) $\mathcal{A}_\Sigma$ is closed under the operator b.

10.36. Consider the operator Y defined in Theorem 5.7. Prove or disprove that:

(a) $\mathcal{P}_\Sigma$ is closed under the operator Y.

(b) $\mathcal{A}_\Sigma$ is closed under the operator Y.

10.37. Consider the operator P given in Exercise 5.16. Prove or disprove that:

(a) $\mathcal{P}_\Sigma$ is closed under the operator P.

(b) $\mathcal{A}_\Sigma$ is closed under the operator P.

10.38. Consider the operator F given in Exercise 5.19. Prove or disprove that:

(a) $\mathcal{P}_\Sigma$ is closed under the operator F.

(b) $\mathcal{A}_\Sigma$ is closed under the operator F.

CHAPTER

11

TURING MACHINES

In the preceding chapters, we have seen that DFAs and NDFAs represented the type 3 languages and pushdown automata represented the type 2 languages. In this chapter we will explore the machine analog to the type 1 and type 0 grammars. These devices, called *Turing machines*, are the most powerful automata known and can recognize every language considered so far in this text. We will also encounter languages that are too complex to be recognized by any Turing machine. Indeed, we will see that any other such (finite) scheme for the representation of languages is likewise forced to be unable to represent all possible languages over a given alphabet. Turing machines provide a gateway to *undecidability*, discussed in the next chapter, and to the general theory of *computational complexity*, which is rich enough to warrant much broader treatment than would be possible here.

11.1 DEFINITIONS AND EXAMPLES

Pushdown automata turned out to be the appropriate cognitive devices for the type 2 languages, but further enhancements in the capabilities of the automaton model are necessary to achieve the generality inherent in type 0 and type 1 languages. A (seemingly) minor modification will be all that is required. *Turing machines* are comprised of the familiar components that have already been used in previous classes of automata. As with the earlier constructions, the heart of the device is a finite-state control, which reacts to information scanned by the tape head(s). Like finite-state transducers and pushdown automata, information can be written to tape as transitions between states are made. Unlike FSTs and PDAs, Turing machines have only one tape with which to work, which serves both the input and the output needs of the device. Note that with finite-state transducers the presence of a second tape was purely for convenience; a single tape, with input symbols overwritten by the appropriate output symbol as the read head progressed, would have sufficed. Whereas a pushdown automaton could write an entire string of symbols to the stack, a Turing machine is constrained to print a single letter at a time. These new devices would therefore be of less value than PDAs were they not given some other capability. In all previous classes of automata, the read head was forced to move one space to the right on each transition (or, in the case of λ-moves, remain stationary). On each transition, the Turing machine tape head has the option of staying put, moving right, or moving left. The ability to move back to the left and review previously written information accounts for the added power of Turing machines.

It is possible to view a Turing machine as a powerful transducer of computable functions, with an associated function defined much like those for FSTs. That is, as with finite-state transducers, each word that could be placed on an otherwise blank tape is associated with the word formed by allowing the Turing machine to operate on that word. With FSTs, this function was well defined; the machine would process each letter of the word in a unique way, the read head would eventually find the end of the word (that is, it would scan a blank), and the device would then halt. With Turing machines, there is no built-in guarantee that it will always halt; since the tape head can move both right and left, it is possible to define a Turing machine that would reverberate back and forth between two adjacent spaces indefinitely. A Turing machine is also not constrained to halt when it scans a blank symbol; it may overwrite the blank and/or continue moving right indefinitely.

Rather than viewing a Turing machine as a transducer, we will primarily be concerned with employing it as an acceptor of words placed on the tape. Some variants of Turing machines are defined with a set of final states, and the criteria for acceptance would then be that the device both halt and be in a final state. For our purposes, we will employ the writing capabilities of the Turing machine and simply require that acceptance be indicated by printing a **Y** just prior to halting. If such a **Y** is never printed or the machine does not halt, the word will be considered rejected. It may be that there are words that might be placed on the input tape that would prevent the machine from halting, which is at best a serious inconvenience; if the device has been operating for an extraordinary amount of time, we may not be able to tell if it will never halt (and thus reject the word), or whether we simply need to be patient and wait for it to eventually print the **Y**. This uncertainty can in some cases be avoided by finding a superior design for the Turing machine, which would always halt, printing **N** when a word is rejected and **Y** when a word is accepted. This is not always a matter of being clever in defining the machine; we will see that there are some languages that are inherently so complex that this goal is impossible to achieve.

A conceptual model of a Turing machine is shown in Figure 11.1. Note that the tape head is capable of both reading and overwriting the currently scanned symbol. As before, the tape is composed of a series of cells, with one symbol per cell. The

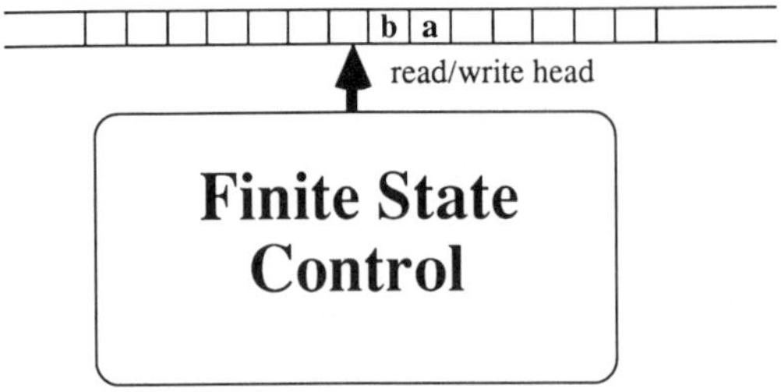

Figure 11.1 A model of a Turing machine

tape head will also be allowed to move one cell to either the left or right during a transition. Note that unlike all previous automata, the tape does not have a "left end"; it extends indefinitely in both directions. This tape will be used for input, output, and as a "scratch pad" for any intermediate calculations. At the start of operation of the device, all but a finite number of contiguous cells are blank. Also, unlike our earlier devices, the following definition implies that Turing machines may continue to operate after scanning a blank.

∇ **Definition 11.1.** A *Turing machine* that recognizes words over an alphabet Σ is a quintuple $\mathsf{M} = <\Sigma, \Gamma, S, s_0, \delta>$, where

Σ is the *input alphabet*.

Γ is the *auxiliary alphabet*, and Σ, Γ, and $\{\mathbf{L}, \mathbf{R}\}$ are pairwise disjoint sets of symbols.

S is a finite nonempty set of *states* (and $S \cap (\Sigma \cup \Gamma) = \emptyset$).

s_0 is the *start state* ($s_0 \in S$).

δ is the *state transition function* $\delta: S \times (\Sigma \cup \Gamma) \to (S \cup \{h\}) \times (\Sigma \cup \Gamma \cup \{\mathbf{L}, \mathbf{R}\})$.

The auxiliary alphabet always includes the *blank symbol* (denoted by #), and neither Σ nor Γ include the special symbols **L** and **R**, which denote moving the tape head left and right, respectively. The state h is a special *halt state*, from which no further transitions are possible; $h \notin S$.

Δ

The alphabet Σ is intended to denote the nonblank symbols that can be expected to be initially present on the input tape. By convention, it is assumed that the tape head is positioned over the leftmost nonblank (in the case of the empty string, though, the head will be scanning a blank). In Definition 11.1, the state transition function is deterministic; for every state in S and every tape symbol scanned, exactly one destination state is specified, and one action is taken by the tape head. The tape head may either:

1. Overprint the cell with a symbol from Σ or Γ (and thus a blank may be printed).

2. Move one cell left (without printing).
3. Move one cell right (also without printing).

In the case where a cell is overprinted, the tape head remains positioned on that cell.

The above definition of a Turing machine is compatible with the construct implemented by Jon Barwise and John Etchemendy in their Turing's World© software package for the Apple® Macintosh. The Turing's World program allows the user to interactively draw a state transition diagram of a Turing machine and watch it operate on any given input string. As indicated by the next example, the same software can be used to produce and test state transition diagrams for deterministic finite automata.

EXAMPLE 11.1

The following simple Turing machine recognizes the set of even-length words over $\{\mathbf{a}, \mathbf{b}\}$. The state transition diagram for this device is shown in Figure 11.2 and conforms to the conventions introduced in Chapter 7. Transitions between states are represented by arrows labeled by the symbol that caused the transition. The symbol after the slash denotes the character to be printed or, in the case of **L** and **R**, the direction to move the tape head. The quintuple is $<\{\mathbf{a}, \mathbf{b}\}, \{\#, \mathbf{Y}, \mathbf{N}\}, \{s_0, s_1\}, s_0, \delta_T>$, where δ_T is given by

$$\delta_T(s_0, \mathbf{a}) = \langle s_1, \mathbf{R}\rangle$$

$$\delta_T(s_0, \mathbf{b}) = \langle s_1, \mathbf{R}\rangle$$

$$\delta_T(s_0, \#) = \langle h, \mathbf{Y}\rangle$$

$$\delta_T(s_1, \mathbf{a}) = \langle s_0, \mathbf{R}\rangle$$

$$\delta_T(s_1, \mathbf{b}) = \langle s_0, \mathbf{R}\rangle$$

$$\delta_T(s_1, \#) = \langle h, \mathbf{N}\rangle$$

This particular Turing machine operates in much the same way as a DFA would, always moving right as it scans each symbol of the word on the input tape.

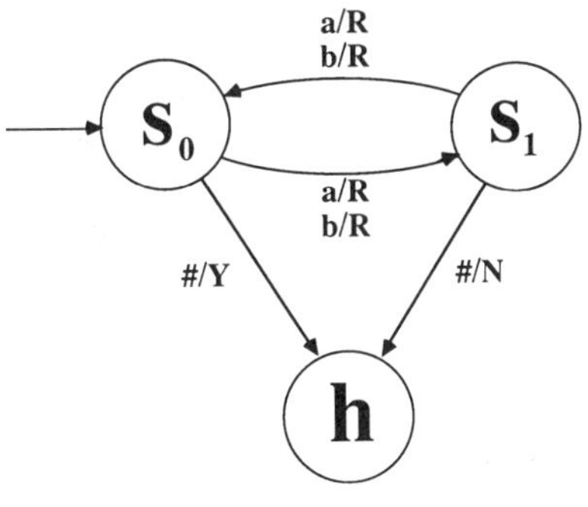

Figure 11.2 The state transition diagram of the Turing machine discussed in Example 11.1

When it reaches the end of the word (that is, when it first scans a blank), it prints **Y** or **N**, depending on which state it is in, and halts. It differs from a DFA in that the accept/reject indication is printed on the tape at the right end of the word. Figure 11.3 shows an alternative way of displaying this machine, in which the halt state is not explicitly shown. Much like the straight start state arrow that denotes where the automaton is entered, the new straight arrows show how the machine is left. This notation is especially appropriate for *submachines*. As with complex programs, a complex Turing machine may be comprised of several submodules. Control may be passed to a submachine, which manipulates the input tape until it halts. Control may then be passed to a second submachine, which then further modifies the tape contents. When this submachine would halt, control may be passed on to a third submachine, or back to the first submachine, and so on. The straight arrows leaving the state transition diagram can be thought of as exit arrows for a submachine, and they function much like a *return* statement in many programming languages. Example 11.4 illustrates a Turing machine that employs submachines.

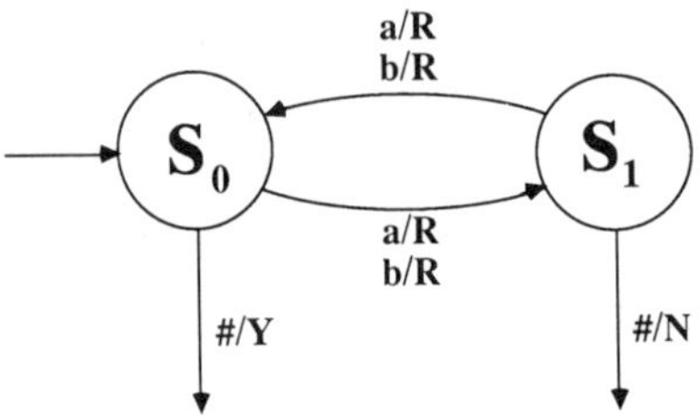

Figure 11.3 An alternate depiction of the Turing machine discussed in Example 11.1

We will see that any DFA can be emulated by a Turing machine in the manner suggested by Example 11.1. The following example shows that Turing machines can recognize languages that are definitely not FAD. In fact, the language accepted in Example 11.2 is not even context free.

EXAMPLE 11.2

The Turing machine M illustrated in Figure 11.4 operates on words over $\{\mathbf{a}, \mathbf{b}, \mathbf{c}\}$. When started at the leftmost end of the word, it is guaranteed to halt at the rightmost end and print **Y** or **N**. It happens to overwrite the symbols comprising the input word as it operates, but this is immaterial. In fact, it is possible to design a slightly more complex machine that restores the word before halting (see Example 11.11). The quintuple is $<\{\mathbf{a}, \mathbf{b}, \mathbf{c}\}, \{\#, \mathbf{X}, \mathbf{Y}, \mathbf{N}\}, \{s_0, s_1, s_2, s_3, s_4, s_5, s_6\}, s_0, \delta>$, where δ is as indicated in the diagram in Figure 11.4. It is intended to recognize the language $\{x \in \{\mathbf{a}, \mathbf{b}, \mathbf{c}\}^* \mid |x|_{\mathbf{a}} = |x|_{\mathbf{b}} = |x|_{\mathbf{c}}\}$. One possible procedure for processing a string to check if it had the same number of **a**s, **b**s, and **c**s is given by the pseudocode below.

while an **a** remains *do*
begin
  replace **a** by **X**
  return to leftmost symbol

find **b**; if none, halt and print **N**
replace **b** by **X**
return to leftmost symbol
find **c**; if none, halt and print **N**
replace **c** by **X**
return to leftmost symbol
end
halt and print **Y** if no more **b**s nor **c**s remain

States s_0 and s_1 in Figure 11.4 check the *while* condition, and states s_2 through s_6 perform the body of the do loop. On each iteration, beginning at the leftmost symbol, state s_0 moves the tape head right, checking for symbols that have not been replaced by **X**. If it reaches the end of the word (that is, if it scans a blank), the **a**s, **b**s, and **c**s all matched, and it halts, printing **Y**. If **b** or **c** is found, state 1 searches for **a**s; if the end of the string is reached without finding a corresponding **a**, the machine halts with **N**, since there were an insufficient number of **a**s. From either s_0 or s_1, control passes to s_2 when an **a** is scanned, and that **a** is replaced by **X**. State s_2, like s_4 and s_6, returns the tape head to the leftmost character. This is done by scanning left until a blank is found and then moving right as control is passed on to the next state. State s_3 searches for **b**, halting with **N** if none is found. The first **b** encountered is otherwise replaced by **X**, and the Turing machine enters s_4, which then passes control on to s_5 after returning to the leftmost symbol. State s_5 operates much like s_3, searching for **c** this time, and s_6 returns the tape head to the extreme left if the previous **a** and **b** have been matched with **c**. The process then repeats from s_0.

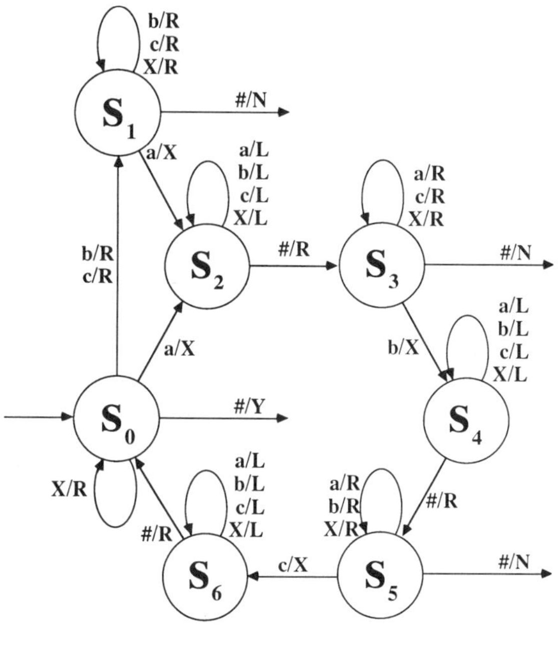

Figure 11.4 The Turing machine M discussed in Example 11.2

To see exactly how the machine operates, it is useful to step through the computation for an input string such as **babcca**. To do this, conventions to designate the status of the device are quite helpful. Like the stack in a PDA, the tape contents may change as transitions occur, and the notation for the configuration of a Turing machine must reflect those changes. Steps in a computation will be represented according to the following conventions.

∇ **Definition 11.2.** Let $M = <\Sigma, \Gamma, S, s_0, \delta>$ be a Turing machine that is operating on a tape containing $\ldots \#\#\#\alpha\mathbf{b}\beta\#\#\# \ldots$, currently in state t with the tape head scanning the **b**, where $\alpha, \beta \in (\Sigma \cup \Gamma)^*$, α contains no leading blanks and β has no trailing blanks. This configuration will be represented by $\alpha t\mathbf{b}\beta$.

$\gamma \vdash \psi$ will be taken to mean that the configuration denoted by ψ is reached in one transition from γ. The symbol $\overset{*}{\vdash}$ will denote the reflexive and transitive closure of $\vdash$.

Δ

That is, the symbol representing the state will be embedded within the string, just to the left of the symbol being scanned. If $\delta(t, \mathbf{b}) = \langle s, \mathbf{R} \rangle$, then $\alpha t\mathbf{b}\beta \vdash \alpha\mathbf{b}s\beta$. The new placement of the state label within the string indicates that the tape head has indeed moved right one symbol. The condition $S \cap (\Sigma \cup \Gamma) = \emptyset$ ensures that there is no confusion as to which symbol in the configuration representation denotes the state. As with PDAs, $\gamma \overset{*}{\vdash} \psi$ means that γ produces ψ in zero or more transitions. Note that the leading and trailing blanks are not represented, but α and β may contain blanks. Indeed, **b** may be a blank. The representation **ac###**t**#** indicates that the tape head has moved past the word **ac** and is scanning the fourth blank to the right of the word ($\alpha = \mathbf{ac\#\#\#}, \mathbf{b} = \#, \beta = \lambda$). At the other extreme, t**##ac** shows the tape head two cells to the left of the word ($\alpha = \lambda, \mathbf{b} = \#, \beta = \mathbf{\#ac}$). A totally blank tape is represented by t#.

∇ **Definition 11.3.** For a Turing machine $M = <\Sigma, \Gamma, S, s_0, \delta>$, the *language accepted by M*, denoted by $L(M)$, is $L(M) = \{x \in \Sigma^* \mid s_0x \overset{*}{\vdash} xh\mathbf{Y}\}$. A language accepted by a Turing machine is called a *Turing-acceptable* language.

Δ

It is generally convenient to assume that the special symbol **Y** is not part of the input alphabet. Note that words can be rejected if the machine does not print a **Y** *or* if the machine never halts.

Several reasonable definitions of acceptance can be applied to Turing machines. One of the most common specifies that the language accepted by M is the set of all words for which M simply halts, irrespective of what the final tape contents are. It might be expected that this more robust definition of acceptance might lead to more (or at least different) languages being recognized. However, this definition turns out to yield a device with the same cognitive power as specified by Definition 11.3, as indicated below. More precisely, let us define

$$L_1(\mathsf{A}) = \{x \in \Sigma^* \mid \exists \alpha, \beta \in (\Sigma \cup \Gamma)^* \ni s_0x \overset{*}{\vdash} \alpha h\beta\}$$

$L_1(\mathsf{A})$ is thus the set of all words that cause A to halt. Let L be a language for which $\mathrm{L} = L_1(\mathsf{B})$ for some Turing machine B. It can be shown that there exists another Turing machine C that accepts L according to Definition 11.3; that is, $L_1(\mathsf{B}) = L(\mathsf{C})$ for some C. The converse is also true: any language of the form $L(\mathsf{M})$ is $L_1(\mathsf{A})$ for some Turing machine A. Other possible definitions of acceptance include

$$L_2(\mathsf{M}) = \{x \in \Sigma^* \mid \exists \alpha, \beta \in (\Sigma \cup \Gamma)^* \ni s_0x \overset{*}{\vdash} \alpha h\mathbf{Y}\beta\}$$

and

$$L_3(\mathsf{M}) = \{x \in \Sigma^* \mid \exists \alpha \in (\Sigma \cup \Gamma)^* \ni s_0x \overset{*}{\vdash} \alpha h\mathbf{Y}\}$$

These distinguish all words that halt with **Y** somewhere on the tape and all words that halt with **Y** at the end of the tape, respectively.

It should be clear that a Turing machine A_1 accepting $\mathrm{L} = L_1(\mathsf{A}_1)$ has an equivalent Turing machine A_2 for which $\mathrm{L} = L_2(\mathsf{A}_2)$. A_2 can be obtained from A_1 by simply adding a new state and changing the transitions to the halt state so that they now all go to the new state. The new state prints **Y** wherever the tape head is and then, upon scanning that **Y**, halts. Similarly, a Turing machine A_3 can be obtained from A_2 by instead requiring the new state to scan right until it finds a blank. It would then print **Y** and halt, and $L_2(\mathsf{A}_2) = L_3(\mathsf{A}_3)$. The technique for modifying such an A_3 to obtain A_4 for which $L_3(\mathsf{A}_3) = L(\mathsf{A}_4)$ is discussed in the next section and illustrated in Example 11.11.

EXAMPLE 11.3

Consider again the machine M in Example 11.2 and the input string **babcca**. By the strict definition of acceptance given in Definition 11.3, $L(\mathsf{M}) = \{\lambda\}$, since λ is the only word that does not get destroyed by M. Using the looser criteria for acceptance yields a more interesting language. The following steps show that $s_0\mathbf{babcca} \overset{*}{\vdash} \mathbf{XXXXXX}h\mathbf{Y}$.

$$\begin{array}{llll}
s_0\mathbf{babcca} \vdash \mathbf{b}s_1\mathbf{abcca} & \vdash \mathbf{b}s_2\mathbf{Xbcca} & \vdash s_2\mathbf{bXbcca} & \vdash \\
s_2\#\mathbf{bXbcca} \vdash s_3\mathbf{bXbcca} & \vdash s_4\mathbf{XXbcca} & \vdash s_4\#\mathbf{XXbcca} & \vdash \\
s_5\mathbf{XXbcca} \vdash \mathbf{X}s_5\mathbf{Xbcca} & \vdash \mathbf{XX}s_5\mathbf{bcca} & \vdash \mathbf{XXb}s_5\mathbf{cca} & \vdash \\
\mathbf{XXb}s_6\mathbf{Xca} \vdash \mathbf{XX}s_6\mathbf{bXca} & \vdash \mathbf{X}s_6\mathbf{XbXca} & \vdash s_6\mathbf{XXbXca} & \vdash \\
s_6\#\mathbf{XXbXca} \vdash s_0\mathbf{XXbXca} & \vdash \mathbf{X}s_0\mathbf{XbXca} & \vdash \mathbf{XX}s_0\mathbf{bXca} & \vdash \\
\mathbf{XXb}s_1\mathbf{Xca} & \overset{*}{\vdash} s_2\#\mathbf{XXbXcX} & & \overset{*}{\vdash} \\
\mathbf{XX}s_3\mathbf{bXcX} & \overset{*}{\vdash} s_4\#\mathbf{XXXXcX} & & \overset{*}{\vdash} \\
\mathbf{XXXX}s_5\mathbf{cX} & \overset{*}{\vdash} s_6\#\mathbf{XXXXXX} & & \overset{*}{\vdash} \\
\mathbf{XXXXXX}s_0 & \vdash \mathbf{XXXXXX}h\mathbf{Y} & &
\end{array}$$

The string **babcca** is therefore accepted. **ac** is rejected since s_0**ac** $\overset{*}{\vdash}$ **XchN**. Further analysis shows that $L_3(\mathsf{M})$ is exactly $\{x \in \{\mathbf{a}, \mathbf{b}, \mathbf{c}\}^* \mid |x|_\mathbf{a} = |x|_\mathbf{b} = |x|_\mathbf{c}\}$. Since the only place **Y** is printed is at the end of the word on the tape, $L_3(\mathsf{M}) = L_2(\mathsf{M})$. Every word eventually causes M to halt with either **Y** or **N** on the tape, and so $L_1(\mathsf{M}) = \Sigma^*$.

EXAMPLE 11.4

The composite Turing machine shown in Figure 11.5 employs several submachines and is based on the parenthesis checker included as a sample in the Turing's World software. The machine will search for correctly matched parentheses, restoring the original string and printing **Y** if the string is syntactically correct, and leaving a **$** to mark the offending position if the string has mismatched parentheses. Asterisks are recorded to the left of the string as left parentheses are found, and these are erased as they are matched with right parentheses.

Figure 11.5a shows the main architecture of the Turing machine. The square nodes represent the submachines illustrated in Figures 11.5b and 11.5c. When s_0 encounters a left parenthesis, it marks the occurrence with **$**, and transfers control to the submachine S_1. S_1 moves the read head to the left end of the string, and deposits one * there. The cells to the left of the original string serve as a scratch area; the asterisks record the number of unmatched left parentheses encountered thus far. Submachine S_1 then scans right until the **$** is found; it then restores the original left parenthesis. At this point, no further internal moves can be made in S_1, and the arrow leaving s_{12} indicates that control should be returned to the parent automaton.

The transition leaving the square S_1 node in Figure 11.5a now applies, and the tape head moves to the right of the left parenthesis that was just processed by S_1, and control is returned to s_0. s_0 continues to move right past the symbols **a** and **b**, uses S_1 to process subsequent left parenthesis, and transfers control to the submachine S_2 whenever a right parenthesis is encountered.

Submachine S_2 attempts to match a right parenthesis with a previous left parenthesis. As control was passed to S_2, the right parenthesis was replaced by **$** so that this spot on the tape can be identified later. The transitions in state s_{20} move the tape head left until a blank cell is scanned. If the cell to the right of this blank does not contain an asterisk, s_{21} has no moves and control is passed back to the parent Turing machine, which will enter s_4 and move right past all the symbols in the word, printing **N** as it halts. The absence of the asterisk implies that no previous matching left parenthesis had been found, so halting with **N** is the appropriate action.

If an asterisk had been found, s_{21} would have replaced it with a blank, and then would have no further moves, and the return arrow would be followed. The blank that is now under the tape head will cause the parent automaton to pass control to s_3, which will move right to **$**, and the **$** is then restored to **)**. Control returns to s_0 as the tape head moves past this parenthesis.

The start state continues checking the remainder of the word in this fashion. When the end of the word is reached, s_6 is used to examine the left end of the string;

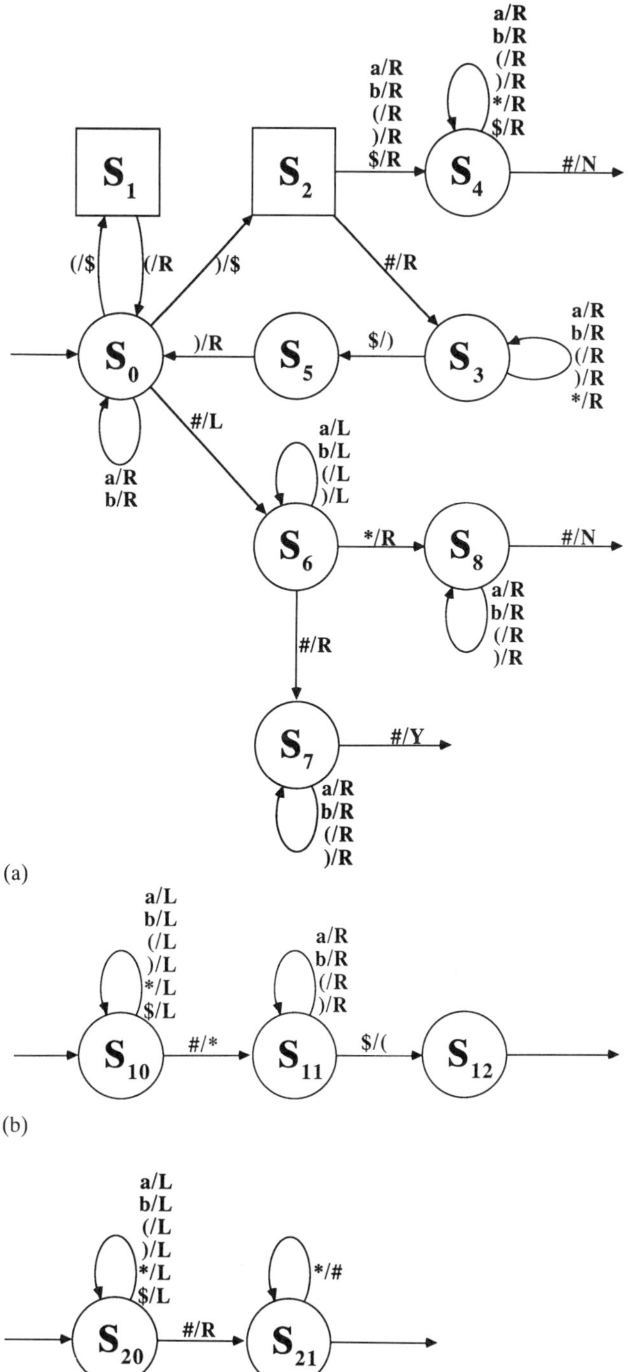

Figure 11.5 (a) The Turing machine discussed in Example 11.4 (b) Submachine S_1 (c) Submachine S_2

remaining asterisks indicate unmatched left parentheses, and will yield **N** as the machine halts from s_8. If s_6 does not encounter *, the Turing machine halts with **Y** and accepts the string from s_7.

As more complex examples are considered, one may begin to suspect that any programming assignment could be carried out on a Turing machine. While it would be truly unwise to try to make a living selling computers with this architecture, these devices are generally regarded to be as powerful as any general-purpose computer. That is, if an algorithm for solving a class of problems can be carried out on a computer, then there should be a Turing machine that can produce identical output for each instance of a problem in that class.

The language $\{x \in \{\mathbf{a}, \mathbf{b}, \mathbf{c}\}^* \mid |x|_\mathbf{a} = |x|_\mathbf{b} = |x|_\mathbf{c}\}$ is not context free, so it cannot be recognized by a PDA. Turing machines can therefore accept some languages that PDAs cannot, and we will see that they can recognize every context-free language. We began with DFAs, which were then extended to the more powerful PDAs, which have now been eclipsed by the Turing machine construct. Each of these classes of automata has been substantially more general than the previous class. If this text were longer, one might wonder when the next class of superior machines would be introduced. Barring the application of magic or divine intuition, there does not seem to be a "next class." That is, any machine that is constrained to operate algorithmically by a well-defined set of rules appears to have no more computing power than do Turing machines.

This constraint, "to behave in an algorithmic fashion," is an intuitive notion without an obvious exact formal expression. Indeed, "behaving like a Turing machine" is generally regarded as the best way to express this notion! A discussion of how Turing machines came to be viewed in this manner is perhaps in order. An excellent in-depth treatment of their history can be found in [BARW].

At the beginning of the twentieth century, mathematicians were searching for a universal algorithm that could be applied to mechanically prove any well-stated mathematical formula. This naturally focused attention on the manipulation of symbols. In 1931, Gödel showed that algorithms of this sort cannot exist. Since this implied that there were classes of problems that could not have an algorithmic solution, this then led to attempts to characterize those problems that could be effectively "computed." In 1936, Turing introduced his formal device for symbol manipulation and suggested that the definition of an algorithm be based on the Turing machine. He also outlined the *halting problem* (discussed later), which demonstrated a problem to which no Turing machine could possibly provide the correct answer in all instances. The search for a better, perhaps more powerful characterization of what constitutes an algorithm continued.

While it cannot be proved that it is impossible to find a better formalization that is truly more powerful, on the basis of the accumulating evidence, no one believes that a better formulation exists. For one thing, other attempts at formalization, including grammars, λ-calculus, μ-recursive functions, and Post systems, have all turned out to yield exactly the same computing power as Turing machines. Second, all attempts at "improving" the capabilities of Turing machines have not expanded the class of languages that can be recognized. Some of these possible improvements will be examined in the next section. We close this section by formalizing what Example 11.1 probably made clear: every DFA can be simulated by a Turing machine.

∇ **Theorem 11.1.** Every FAD language is Turing acceptable.

Proof. We show that given any DFA $A = <\Sigma, S, s_0, \delta, F>$, there is a Turing machine M_A that is equivalent to A. Define $M_A = <\Sigma, \{\#, \mathbf{Y}, \mathbf{N}\}, S, s_0, \delta_A>$, where δ_A is defined by

$$(\forall s \in S)(\forall \mathbf{a} \in \Sigma)(\delta_A(s, \mathbf{a}) = \langle \delta(s, \mathbf{a}), \mathbf{R} \rangle)$$

$$(\forall s \in F)(\delta_A(s, \#) = \langle h, \mathbf{Y} \rangle)$$

$$(\forall s \in S - F)(\delta_A(s, \#) = \langle h, \mathbf{N} \rangle)$$

A simple inductive argument on $|x|$ shows that

$$(\forall x \in \Sigma^*)(\forall \alpha, \beta \in (\Sigma \cup \Gamma)^*)(\alpha t x \beta \overset{*}{\vdash} \alpha x q \beta \text{ iff } \overline{\delta}_A(t, x) = q)$$

From this it follows that

$$(\forall x \in \Sigma^*)(s_0 x \overset{*}{\vdash} x q \# \text{ iff } \overline{\delta}_A(s_0, x) = q)$$

Therefore,

$$(\forall x \in \Sigma^*)(s_0 x \overset{*}{\vdash} x h \mathbf{Y} \text{ iff } \overline{\delta}_A(s_0, x) \in F)$$

which means that $L(M_A) = L(A)$.
Δ

This result actually follows trivially from the much stronger results presented later. Not only is every type 3 language Turing acceptable, but every type 0 language is Turing acceptable (as will be shown by Theorem 11.2). The above proof presents the far more straightforward conversion available to type 3 languages and illustrates the flavor of the inductive arguments needed in other proofs concerning Turing machines. By using this conversion, the Turing's World software can be employed to interactively build and test deterministic finite automata on a Macintosh.

EXAMPLE 11.5

Consider the DFA T shown in Figure 11.6, which recognizes all words of even length over $\{\mathbf{a}, \mathbf{b}\}$. The corresponding Turing machine is illustrated in Example 11.1 (see Figure 11.2).

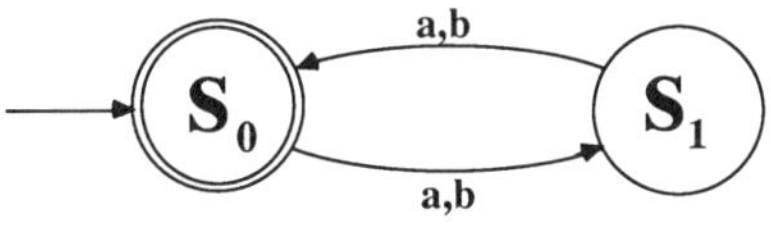

Figure 11.6 The DFA T discussed in Example 11.5

11.2 VARIANTS OF TURING MACHINES

There are several ways in which the basic definition of the Turing machine can be modified. For example, Definition 11.1 disallows the tape head from both moving and printing during a single transition. It should be clear that if such an effect were desired at some point it could be effectively accomplished under the more restrictive Definition 11.1 by adding a state to the finite-state control. The desired symbol could be printed as control is transferred to the new state. The transition out of the new state would then move the tape head in the appropriate fashion, thus accomplishing in two steps what a "fancier" automaton might do in one step. While this modification might be convenient, the ability of Definition 11.1 style machines to simulate this behavior makes it clear that such modified automata are no more powerful than those given by Definition 11.1. That is, every such modified automaton has an equivalent Turing machine.

It is also possible to examine machines that are more restrictive than Definition 11.1. If the machine were constrained to write on only a fixed, finite amount of the tape, this would seriously limit the types of languages that could be recognized. In fact, only the type 3 languages can be accepted by such machines. *Linear bounded automata*, which are Turing machines constrained to write only on the portion of the tape containing the original input word, are also less powerful than unrestricted Turing machines and are discussed in a later section. Having an unbounded area in which to write is therefore an important factor in the cognitive power of Turing machines, but it can be shown that the tape need not be unbounded in both directions. That is, Turing machines that cannot move left of the cell the tape head originally scanned can perform any calculation that can be carried out by the less-restrictive machines given by Definition 11.1 (see the exercises).

In deciding whether a Turing machine can simulate the modified machines suggested below, it is important to remember that the auxiliary alphabet Γ can be expanded as necessary, as long as it remains finite. In particular, it is possible to expand the information content of each cell by adding a second "track" to the tape. For example, we may wish to add check marks to certain designated cells, as shown in Figure 11.7. The lower track would contain the original symbols, and the upper track may or may not have a check mark. This can be accomplished by doubling the

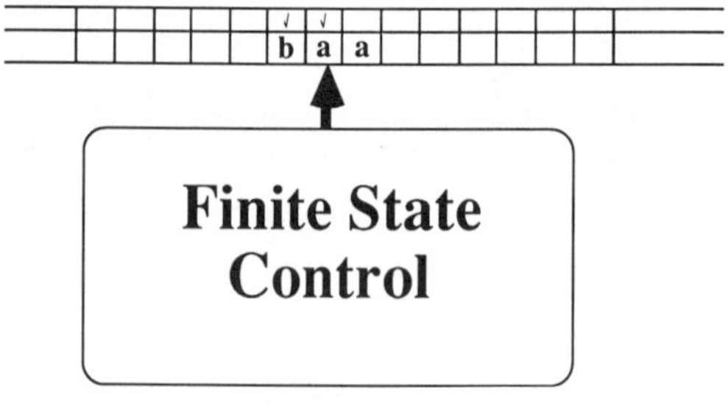

Figure 11.7 A Turing machine with a two-track tape

combined size of the alphabets Σ and Γ to include all symbols without check marks and the same symbols with check marks. The new symbols can be thought of as ordered pairs, and erasing a check mark then amounts to rewriting a pair such as $\langle \mathbf{a}, \surd \rangle$ with $\langle \mathbf{a}, \# \rangle$. A scheme such as this could be used to modify the automaton in Example 11.2. Rather than replacing designated symbols with **X**, a check could instead be placed over the original symbol. Just prior to acceptance, each check mark could be erased, leaving the original string to the left of the **Y** (see Example 11.11).

The foregoing discussion justifies that a Turing machine with a tape head capable of reading two tracks can be simulated by a Definition 11.1 style Turing machine; indeed, it *is* a Turing machine with a slightly more complex alphabet. When convenient, then, we may assume that we have a Turing machine with two tracks. A similar argument shows that, for any finite number k, a k-track machine has an equivalent one-track Turing machine with an expanded alphabet. The symbols on the other tracks can be more varied than just $\surd$ and #; any finite number of symbols may appear on any of the tracks. Indeed, a Turing machine may initially make a copy of the input string on another track to use in a later calculation and/or to restore the tape to its original form. The ability to preserve the input word in this manner illustrates why each language $L = L_3(A)$ for some Turing machine A must be Turing acceptable; that is, $L = L_3(A)$ implies that there is a multitrack Turing machine M for which $L = L(M)$.

EXAMPLE 11.6

Conceptualizing the tape as being divided into tracks simplifies many of the arguments concerning modification of the basic Turing machine design. For example, a modified Turing machine might have two heads that move independently up and down a single tape, both scanning symbols to determine what transition should be made and both capable of moving in either direction (or remaining stationary and overwriting the current cell) as each transition is carried out. Such machines would be handy for recognizing certain languages. The set $\{\mathbf{a}^n\mathbf{b}^n \mid n \geq 1\}$ can be easily recognized by such a machine. If both heads started at the left of the word, one head might first scan right to the first **b** encountered. The two heads could then begin moving in unison to the right, comparing symbols as they progressed, until the leading head encounters a blank and/or the trailing head scans its first **b**. If these two events occurred on the same move, the word would be accepted. A single head Turing machine would have to travel back and forth across the word several times to ascertain if it contained the same number of **a**s as **b**s. The ease with which the two-headed mutation accomplished the same task might make one wonder whether such a modified machine can recognize any languages which the standard Turing machine cannot.

To justify that a two-headed Turing machine is no more powerful than the type described by Definition 11.1, we must show that any two-headed machine can be

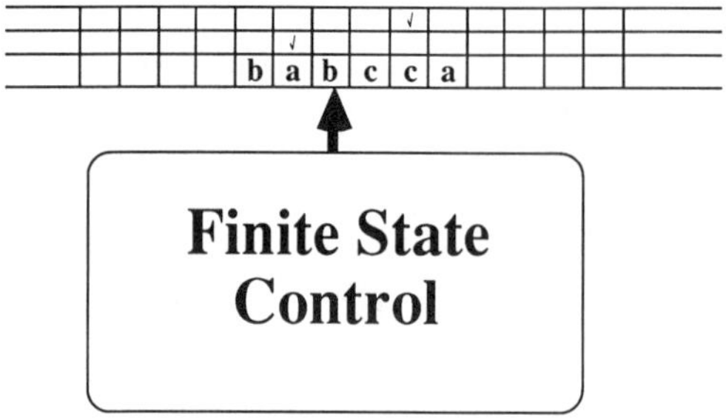

Figure 11.8 Emulating a two-headed Turing machine with a three-track tape

simulated by a corresponding standard Turing machine. As suggested by Figure 11.8, a three-track Turing machine will suffice. The original information would remain on the first track, and check marks will be placed on tracks 2 and 3 to signify the simulated locations of the two heads. Several moves of the single head will be necessary to simulate just one move of the two-headed variant, and the finite-state control must be replicated and augmented to keep track of the stages of the computation. Each simulated move will begin with the single tape head positioned over the leftmost check mark. The tape contents are scanned, and the symbol found is remembered by the finite state control. The tape head then moves right until the second check mark is found. At this point, the device will have available the input symbols that would have been scanned by both heads in the two-headed variant, and hence it can determine what action each of the heads would have taken. The rightmost checkmark would then be moved left or right or the current symbol on track 1 overwritten, whichever is appropriate. The single tape head would then scan left until the other check mark is found, which would then be similarly updated. This would complete the simulation of one move, and the process would then repeat.

Various special cases must be dealt with carefully, such as when both heads would be scanning the same symbol and when the heads "cross" to leave a different head as the leftmost. These cases are tedious but straightforward to sort out, and thus any language that can be recognized by a two-headed machine can be recognized by a standard Turing machine. Similarly, a k-headed Turing machine can be simulated by a machine conforming to Definition 11.1. The number of tracks required would then be $k + 1$, and the set of states must expand so that the device can count the number of check marks scanned on the left and right sweeps of the tape.

Multihead Turing machines are therefore fundamentally no more powerful than the single-head variety. This means that whenever we need to justify that some task can be accomplished by a Turing machine we may employ a variant with several heads whenever this is convenient. We have seen that this variant simplified the justification that $\{\mathbf{a}^n\mathbf{b}^n \mid n \geq 1\}$ was Turing acceptable. It can also be useful in showing that other variants are no more powerful than the type of machines given by Definition 11.1, as illustrated in the next example.

EXAMPLE 11.7

Consider now a device employing several independent tapes with one head for each tape, as depicted in Figure 11.9. If we think of the tapes as stationary and the heads mobile, it is easy to see that we could simply glue the tapes together into one thick tape with several tracks, as indicated in Figure 11.10. The multiple heads would now scan an entire column of cells, but a head would ignore the information on all but the track for which it was responsible. In this fashion, a multitape Turing machine can be simulated by a multihead Turing machine, which can in turn be simulated by a standard Turing machine. Thus, multitape machines are no more powerful than the machines considered earlier.

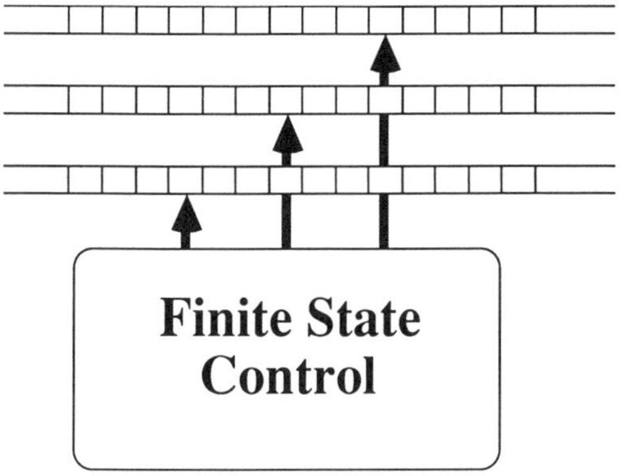

Figure 11.9 A three-tape Turing machine

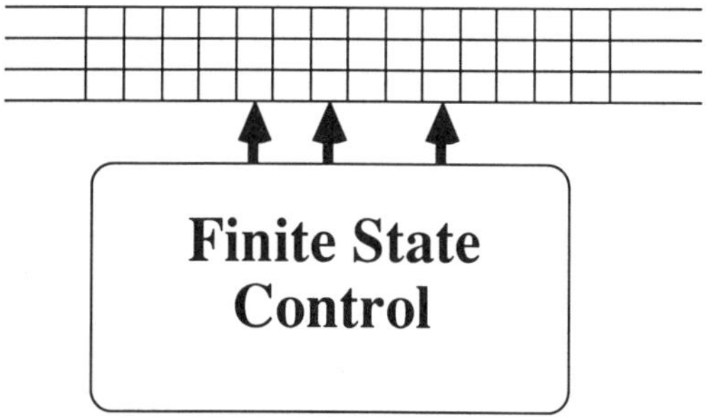

Figure 11.10 Emulating a three-tape Turing machine with a single three-track tape

One of the wilder enhancements involves the use of a two-dimensional tape, which would actually be a surface on which the tape head can move not only left and right, but also up and down to adjacent squares. With some frantic movement of the tape head on a one-dimensional tape, two-dimensional Turing machines can be successfully simulated. Indeed, k-dimensional machines (for finite k} are no more powerful than a standard Turing machine. The interested reader is referred to [HOPC].

EXAMPLE 11.8

A potentially more interesting question involves the effects that nondeterminism might have on the computational power of a Turing machine. With finite automata, it was seen that NDFAs recognized exactly the same class of languages as DFAs. However, deterministic pushdown automata accepted a distinctly smaller class of languages than their nondeterministic cousins. It is consequently hard to develop even an intuition for what "should" happen when nondeterminism is introduced to the Turing machine construct.

Before we can address this question, we must first define what we mean by a nondeterministic Turing machine. As with finite automata and pushdown automata, we may wish to allow a choice of moves from a given configuration, leading to several disparate sequences of moves for a given input string. Like NDFAs and NPDAs, we will consider a word accepted if there is at least one sequence of moves that would have resulted in a **Y** being printed. Simulating such machines with deterministic Turing machines is more involved than it may at first seem. If each possible computation was guaranteed to halt, it would be reasonable to try each sequence of moves, one after the other, halting only when a **Y** was found. If one sequence led to an **N** being printed, we would then move on to the next candidate. Since there may be a countable number of sequences to try, this process may never end. This is not really a problem, since if a sequence resulting in a **Y** exists, it will eventually be found and tried, and the machine will halt and accept the word. If no such sequence resulting in a **Y** exists, and there are an infinite number of negative attempts to be checked, the machine will never halt. By our original definition of acceptance, this will result in the word being rejected, which is the desired result.

The trouble arises in trying to simulate machines that are not guaranteed to halt under all possible circumstances. This is not an inconsequential concern; in Chapter 12, we will identify some languages that are so complex that their corresponding Turing machines cannot halt for all input strings. A problem then arises in trying to switch from one sequence to the next. If, say, the first sequence we tried did not halt and instead simply continued operation without ever producing **Y** or **N**, we would never get the chance to try other possible move sequences. Since the machine will not halt, the word will therefore be rejected, even if some later sequence would have produced **Y**. Simulating the nondeterministic machine in this manner will not be guaranteed to recognize the same language, and an alternative method must be used.

This problem is avoided by simulating the various computations in the following (very inefficient) manner. We begin by simulating the first move of the first sequence. We then start over with the first move of the second sequence, and then begin again and simulate two moves in the first sequence. On the next pass, we simulate the first move of the third sequence, then two moves of the second sequence, and then three moves of the first sequence. On each pass, we start computing a new sequence and move a little further along on the sequences that have already been started. If any of these sequences results in **Y**, we will eventually simulate enough of that sequence to discover that fact and accept the word. In this way, we avoid getting trapped in a dead end with no opportunity to pursue the alternatives.

Implementing the above scheme will produce a deterministic Turing machine that is equivalent to the original nondeterministic machine. It remains to be shown that the Turing machine can indeed *start over* as necessary, and that the possible move sequences can be enumerated in a reasonable fashion so that they can be pursued according to the pattern outlined above. A three-tape (deterministic) Turing machine will suffice. The first tape will keep an inviolate copy of the input string, which will be copied onto the second tape each time a computation begins anew. A specific sequence of steps will be carried out on this second scratch tape, after which the presence of **Y** will be determined. The third tape is responsible for keeping track of the iterations and generating the appropriate sequences to be employed. Enumerating the sequences is much like the problem of generating words over some alphabet in lexicographic order (see the exercises). Methods for generating the "directing sequences" can be found in both [LEWI] and [HOPC]. These references also propose a more efficient approach to the whole simulation, which is based on keeping track of the sets of possible configurations, much as was done in Theorem 4.5 for nondeterministic finite automata.

Thus, neither nondeterminism nor any of the enhancements considered above improved the computational power of these devices. As mentioned previously, no one has yet been able to find any mechanical enhancement that does yield a device that can recognize a language that is not Turing acceptable. Attempts at producing completely different formal systems have fared no better, and there is little cause to believe that such systems exist. We now turn to characterizing what appears to be the largest class of algorithmically definable languages. In the next section, we will see that the Turing-acceptable languages are exactly the type 0 languages introduced in Chapter 8.

∇ **Definition 11.4.** For a given alphabet Σ, let $\mathcal{T}_\Sigma$ be the collection of all Turing-acceptable languages, and let $\mathfrak{Z}_\Sigma$ be the collection of all type 0 languages.
Δ

The freedom to use several tapes and nondeterminism makes it easier to explore the capabilities of Turing machines and relate $\mathcal{T}_\Sigma$ to the previous classes of languages encountered. It is now trivial to justify that every PDA can be simulated by a nondeterministic Turing machine with two tapes. The first tape will hold the input, which will be scanned by the first tape head, which will only have to move right or, at worst, remain stationary and reprint the same character it was scanning. The second tape will function as the stack, with strings pushed or symbols popped in correspondence with what takes place in the PDA. Since a Turing machine can only print one symbol at a time, some new states may be needed in the finite-state control to simulate pushing an entire string, but the translation process is quite direct.

∇ **Lemma 11.1.** Let Σ be an alphabet. Then $\mathscr{P}_\Sigma \subset \mathscr{T}_\Sigma$. That is, every context-free language is Turing acceptable, and the containment is proper.

Proof. Containment follows from the formalization of the above discussion (see the exercises). Example 11.3 presented a language over $\{\mathbf{a}, \mathbf{b}, \mathbf{c}\}$ that is Turing acceptable but not context free. While the distinction between $\mathscr{D}_\Sigma$ and $\mathscr{P}_\Sigma$ disappeared for singleton alphabets, proper containment remains between $\mathscr{P}_{\{\mathbf{a}\}}$ and $\mathscr{T}_{\{\mathbf{a}\}}$, as shown by languages such as $\{\mathbf{a}^n \mid n \text{ is a perfect square}\}$.
Δ

In the next section, an even stronger result is discussed, which shows that the class of Turing-acceptable languages includes much more than just the context-free languages. Lemma 11.1 is actually an immediate corollary of Theorem 11.2. The next section also explores the formal relationship between Turing machines and context-sensitive languages.

11.3 TURING MACHINES, LBAs, AND GRAMMARS

The previous sections have shown that the class of Turing-acceptable languages properly contains the type 2 languages. We now explore how the type 0 and type 1 languages relate to Turing machines. Since the preceding discussions mentioned that no formal systems have been found that surpass Turing machines, one would expect that every language generated by a grammar can be recognized by a Turing machine. This is indeed the case, as indicated by the following theorem.

∇ **Theorem 11.2.** Let Σ be an alphabet. Then $\mathscr{L}_\Sigma \subseteq \mathscr{T}_\Sigma$. That is, every type 0 language is Turing acceptable.

Proof. We justify that, given any type 0 grammar $G = <\Sigma, \Gamma, S, P>$, there must be a Turing machine T_G that is equivalent to G. As with the suggested conversion of a PDA to a Turing machine, T_G will employ two tapes and nondeterminism. The first tape again holds the input, which will be compared to the sentential form generated on the second tape. The second tape begins with only the start symbol on an otherwise blank tape. The finite-state control is responsible for nondeterministically guessing the proper sequence of productions to apply, and with each guess, the second tape is modified to reflect the new sentential form. If at some point the sentential form agrees with the contents of the first tape, the machine prints **Y** and halts. A guess will consist of choosing both an arbitrary position within the current sentential form and a particular production to attempt to substitute for the substring beginning at that position. Only words that can be generated by the grammar will have a sequence of moves that produces **Y**, and no word that cannot be generated will be accepted. Thus, the new Turing machine is equivalent to G.
Δ

EXAMPLE 11.9

Consider the context-sensitive grammar $\mathrm{G} = \langle\{\mathbf{a}, \mathbf{b}, \mathbf{c}\}, \{\mathrm{S}, \mathrm{A}, \mathrm{B}, \mathrm{C}\}, \mathrm{S}, P\rangle$, where P contains the productions

1. $\mathrm{Z} \to \lambda$
2. $\mathrm{Z} \to \mathrm{S}$
3. $\mathrm{S} \to \mathrm{SABC}$
4. $\mathrm{S} \to \mathrm{ABC}$
5. $\mathrm{AB} \to \mathrm{BA}$
6. $\mathrm{BA} \to \mathrm{AB}$
7. $\mathrm{CB} \to \mathrm{BC}$
8. $\mathrm{BC} \to \mathrm{CB}$
9. $\mathrm{CA} \to \mathrm{AC}$
10. $\mathrm{AC} \to \mathrm{CA}$
11. $\mathrm{A} \to \mathbf{a}$
12. $\mathrm{B} \to \mathbf{b}$
13. $\mathrm{C} \to \mathbf{c}$

It is quite easy to show that $\boldsymbol{L}(\mathrm{G}) = \{x \in \{\mathbf{a}, \mathbf{b}, \mathbf{c}\}^* \mid |x|_{\mathbf{a}} = |x|_{\mathbf{b}} = |x|_{\mathbf{c}}\}$ by observing that no production changes the relative numbers of (lowercase and capital) As, Bs, and Cs, and the six context-sensitive rules allow them to be arbitrarily reordered. One of the attempted "guesses" made by thc Turing machine $\mathrm{T_G}$ concerning how the productions might be applied is:

Use (2) beginning at position 1.
Use (4) beginning at position 1.
Use (6) beginning at position 2 . . . .

This would lead to a failed attempt, since it corresponds to $\mathrm{Z} \Rightarrow \mathrm{S} \Rightarrow \mathrm{ABC}$, and the substring BC beginning at position 2 does not match BA, the left side of rule 6. On the other hand, there is a pattern of guesses that would cause the following sequence of symbols to appear on the second tape:

$$\mathrm{Z} \Rightarrow \mathrm{S} \Rightarrow \mathrm{ABC} \Rightarrow \mathrm{BAC} \Rightarrow \mathrm{BCA} \Rightarrow \mathrm{B}\mathbf{c}\mathrm{A} \Rightarrow \mathrm{B}\mathbf{ca} \Rightarrow \mathbf{bca}$$

This would lead to a favorable comparison if **bca** was the word on the input tape. Note that the Turing machine may have to handle shifting over existing symbols on the scratch tape to accommodate increases in the size of the sentential form. Since type 0 grammars allow length-reducing productions, the machine may also be required to shrink the sentential form when a string of symbols is replaced by a smaller string.

A rather nice feature of type 1 languages is that the length of the sentential form could never decrease (except perhaps for the application of the initial production $Z \to \lambda$), and hence sentential forms that become longer than the desired word are known to be hopeless. All context-sensitive (that is, type 1) languages can therefore be recognized by a Turing machine that use an amount of tape proportional to the length of the input string, as outlined below.

∇ **Definition 11.5.** A *linear bounded automaton* (LBA) is a nondeterministic Turing machine that recognizes words over an alphabet Σ given by the quintuple $M = <\Sigma, \Gamma, S, s_0, \delta>$, where

Σ is the *input alphabet*
Γ is the *auxiliary alphabet* containing the special markers $<$ and $>$ and Σ, Γ, and $\{\mathbf{L}, \mathbf{R}\}$ are pairwise disjoint sets (and thus $<, > \notin \Sigma$).
S is a finite nonempty set of *states* (and $S \cap (\Sigma \cup \Gamma) = \emptyset$).
s_0 is the *start state* ($s_0 \in S$).
δ is the *state transition function* $\delta: S \times (\Sigma \cup \Gamma) \to (S \cup \{h\}) \times (\Sigma \cup \Gamma \cup \{\mathbf{L}, \mathbf{R}\})$, where
$(\forall s \in S)(\delta(s, <) = \langle q, \mathbf{R} \rangle$ for some $q \in S \cup \{h\})$, and
$(\forall s \in S)(\delta(s, >) = \langle q, \mathbf{L} \rangle$ for some $q \in S \cup \{h\}$, or
$\delta(s, >) = \langle h, \mathbf{Y} \rangle$ or $\delta(s, >) = \langle h, \mathbf{N} \rangle)$

Δ

That is, the automaton cannot move left of the symbol $<$ nor overwrite it. The LBA likewise cannot move right of the symbol $>$, and it can only overwrite it with **Y** or **N** just prior to halting. The symbols #, **L**, **R**, **Y**, and **N** retain their former meaning, although # can be dropped from Γ since it will never be scanned. As implied by the following definition, the special markers $<$ and $>$ are intended to delimit the input string, and Definition 11.5 ensures that the automaton cannot move past these limits. As has been seen, the use of several tracks can easily multiply the amount of information that can be stored in a fixed amount of space, and thus the restriction is essentially that the amount of available tape is a linear function of the length of the input string. In practice, any Turing machine variant for which each tape head is constrained to operate within an area that is a multiple of the length of the input string is called a linear bounded automaton.

∇ **Definition 11.6.** For a linear bounded automaton $M = <\Sigma, \Gamma, S, s_0, \delta>$, the *language accepted by M*, denoted by $L(M)$, is $L(M) = \{x \in \Sigma^* \mid <s_0x> \overset{*}{\vdash} <xh\mathbf{Y}\}$. A language accepted by a linear bounded automaton is called a *linear bounded language* (LBL).

Δ

Note that while the endmarkers must enclose the string x, it is the word x (rather than $<x>$) that is considered to belong to $L(M)$. As before, other criteria for acceptance are equivalent to Definition 11.6. The set of all words for which a LBA merely halts can be shown to be a LBL according to the above definition. The following example illustrates a linear bounded automaton that is intended to recognize all words that cause the machine to print **Y** at the end of the (obliterated) word. Example 11.13 illustrates a general technique for restoring the input word, producing an LBA that accepts according to Definition 11.6.

EXAMPLE 11.10

Consider the machine L shown in Figure 11.11 and the input string **babcca**. The following steps show that $<s_0\mathbf{babcca}> \overset{*}{\vdash} <\mathbf{XXXXXX}h\mathbf{Y}$.

$$
\begin{array}{lllll}
<s_0\mathbf{babcca}> \vdash <\mathbf{b}s_1\mathbf{abcca}> & \vdash <\mathbf{b}s_2\mathbf{Xbcca}> & \vdash <s_2\mathbf{bXbcca}> & \vdash \\
s_2<\mathbf{bXbcca}> \vdash <s_3\mathbf{bXbcca}> & \vdash <s_4\mathbf{XXbcca}> & \vdash s_4<\mathbf{XXbcca}> & \vdash \\
<s_5\mathbf{XXbcca}> \vdash <\mathbf{X}s_5\mathbf{Xbcca}> & \vdash <\mathbf{XX}s_5\mathbf{bcca}> & \vdash <\mathbf{XXb}s_5\mathbf{cca}> & \vdash \\
<\mathbf{XXb}s_6\mathbf{Xca}> \vdash <\mathbf{XX}s_6\mathbf{bXca}> & \vdash <\mathbf{X}s_6\mathbf{XbXca}> & \vdash <s_6\mathbf{XXbXca}> & \vdash \\
s_6<\mathbf{XXbXca}> \vdash <s_0\mathbf{XXbXca}> & \vdash <\mathbf{X}s_0\mathbf{XbXca}> & \vdash <\mathbf{XX}s_0\mathbf{bXca}> & \vdash \\
<\mathbf{XXb}s_1\mathbf{Xca}> & \overset{*}{\vdash} s_2<\mathbf{XXbXcX}> & & \overset{*}{\vdash} \\
<\mathbf{XX}s_3\mathbf{bXcX}> & \overset{*}{\vdash} s_4<\mathbf{XXXXcX}> & & \overset{*}{\vdash} \\
<\mathbf{XXXX}s_5\mathbf{cX}> & \overset{*}{\vdash} s_6<\mathbf{XXXXXX}> & & \overset{*}{\vdash} \\
<\mathbf{XXXXXX}s_0> & \vdash <\mathbf{XXXXXX}h\mathbf{Y} & &
\end{array}
$$

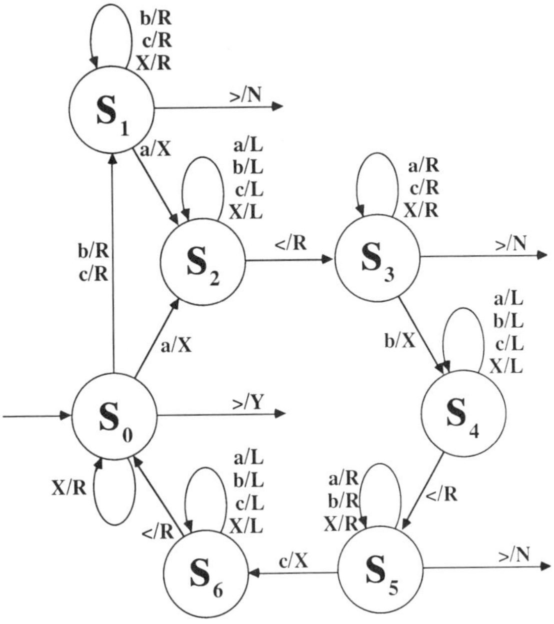

Figure 11.11 The Turing machine discussed in Example 11.10

∇ **Definition 11.7.** For a given alphabet Σ, let $\mathscr{L}_\Sigma$ be the collection of all linear bounded languages, and let $\mathfrak{O}_\Sigma$ be the collection of all context-sensitive (type 1) languages.
Δ

The proof of Theorem 11.2 can be modified to show that all context-sensitive languages can be recognized by linear bounded automata. Since context-sensitive languages do not contain contracting productions, no sentential forms that are longer than the desired word need be considered. Consequently, the two-tape Turing machine in Theorem 11.2 can operate as a linear bounded automaton. The first tape with the input word never changes and thus satisfies the boundary restriction, while the finite-state control can simply abort any computation on the second tape that violates the length restriction. Just as Theorem 11.2 showed that $\mathfrak{Z}_\Sigma \subseteq \mathcal{T}_\Sigma$, we now have a relationship between another pair of cognitive and generative classes.

∇ **Theorem 11.3.** Let Σ be an alphabet. Then $\mathfrak{O}_\Sigma \subseteq \mathscr{L}_\Sigma$. That is, every type 1 language is a LBL.

Proof. The proof follows from the formalization of the above discussion (see the exercises).
Δ

We have argued that every type 0 grammar must have an equivalent Turing machine, and it can conversely be shown that every Turing-acceptable language can be generated by a type 0 grammar. To do this, it is most convenient to use the very restrictive criteria for a Turing-acceptable language given in Definition 11.3, in which the original input string is not destroyed. For Turing machines which behave in this fashion, the descriptions of the device configurations bear a remarkable resemblance to the derivations in a grammar.

EXAMPLE 11.11

Consider again the language $\{x \in \{\mathbf{a}, \mathbf{b}, \mathbf{c}\}^* \mid |x|_\mathbf{a} = |x|_\mathbf{b} = |x|_\mathbf{c}\}$. As discussed in Example 11.3, the Turing machine in Figure 11.4 destroys the word originally on the input tape. Figure 11.12 depicts a slightly more complex Turing machine that restores the original word just prior to acceptance. It will (fortunately) not generally be necessary for our purposes to restore rejected words, since there are intricate languages for which this is not always possible. The modified quintuple is $\mathsf{T} = <\{\mathbf{a}, \mathbf{b}, \mathbf{c}\}, \{\#, \mathbf{A}, \mathbf{B}, \mathbf{C}, \mathbf{Y}, \mathbf{N}\}, \{s_0, s_1, s_2, s_3, s_4, s_5, s_6, s_7, s_8\}, s_0, \delta>$, where δ is as indicated in the diagram in Figure 11.13. "Saving" the original input string is accomplished by replacing occurrences of the different letters by distinct symbols and restoring them later. The implementation reflects one of the first uses suggested for multiple-track machines: using the second track to check off input symbols. For legibility, an **a** with a check mark above it is denoted by **A**, while an **a** with no check

Figure 11.12 The Turing machine discussed in Example 11.11

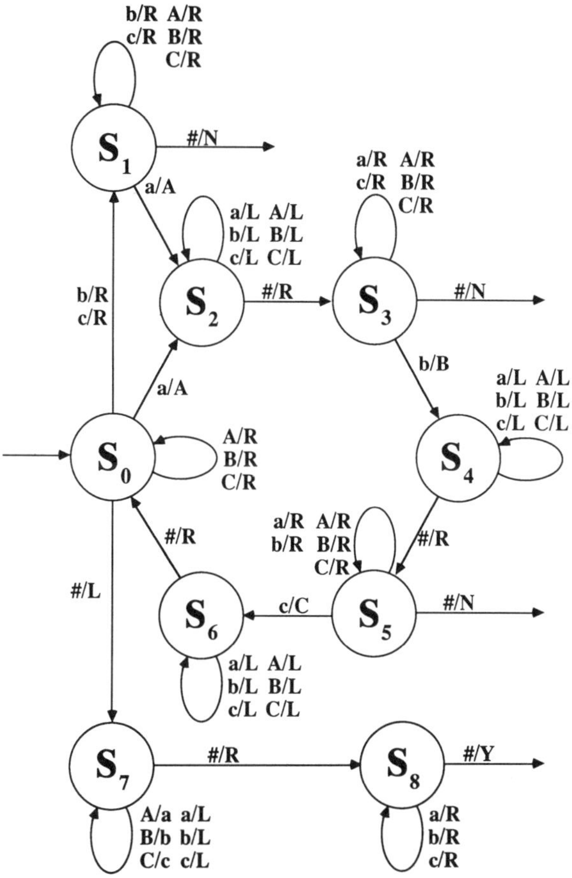

Figure 11.13 The state transition diagram discussed in Example 11.11

mark remains an **a**. Similarly, checked **b**s are represented by **B** and checked **c**s by **C**. Thus, if the string **BAbCca** were on a two-track tape employing check marks, it would look like

√√ √
babcca

The additional states s_7 and s_8 essentially erase the check marks just before halting by replacing **A** with **a**, **B** with **b**, and **C** with **c**.

Consider again the input string **babcca** processed by the Turing machine in Example 11.3. It is also accepted by this Turing machine because the following steps show that $s_0\mathbf{babcca} \overset{*}{\vdash} \mathbf{babcca}h\mathbf{Y}$. Note how closely the steps correspond with those in Example 11.3. The sequence below also illustrates how s_7 converts the string back to lowercase, after which s_8 returns the tape head to the right for acceptance.

$$\begin{array}{lllll}
s_0\mathbf{babcca} \vdash \mathbf{b}s_1\mathbf{abcca} & \vdash \mathbf{b}s_2\mathbf{Abcca} & \vdash s_2\mathbf{bAbcca} & & \vdash \\
s_2\#\mathbf{bAbcca} \vdash s_3\mathbf{bAbcca} & \vdash s_4\mathbf{BAbcca} & \vdash s_4\#\mathbf{BAbcca} & & \vdash \\
s_5\mathbf{BAbcca} \vdash \mathbf{B}s_5\mathbf{Abcca} & \vdash \mathbf{BA}s_5\mathbf{bcca} & \vdash \mathbf{BAb}s_5\mathbf{cca} & & \vdash \\
\mathbf{BAb}s_6\mathbf{Cca} \vdash \mathbf{BA}s_6\mathbf{bCca} & \vdash \mathbf{B}s_6\mathbf{AbCca} & \vdash s_6\mathbf{BAbCca} & & \vdash \\
s_6\#\mathbf{BAbCca} \vdash s_0\mathbf{BAbCca} & \vdash \mathbf{B}s_0\mathbf{AbCca} & \vdash \mathbf{BA}s_0\mathbf{bCca} & & \vdash \\
\mathbf{BAb}s_1\mathbf{Cca} & \overset{*}{\vdash} s_2\#\mathbf{BAbCcA} & & & \overset{*}{\vdash} \\
\mathbf{BA}s_3\mathbf{bCca} & \overset{*}{\vdash} s_4\#\mathbf{BABCcA} & & & \overset{*}{\vdash} \\
\mathbf{BABC}s_5\mathbf{cA} & \overset{*}{\vdash} s_6\#\mathbf{BABCCA} & & & \overset{*}{\vdash} \\
\mathbf{BABCCA}s_0 \vdash \mathbf{BABCC}s_7\mathbf{A} & \vdash \mathbf{BABCC}s_7\mathbf{a} & \vdash \mathbf{BABC}s_7\mathbf{Ca} & & \vdash \\
\mathbf{BABC}s_7\mathbf{ca} & \overset{*}{\vdash} s_7\mathbf{babcca} & \vdash s_7\#\mathbf{babcca} & & \vdash \\
s_8\mathbf{babcca} \vdash \mathbf{b}s_8\mathbf{abcca} & \overset{*}{\vdash} \mathbf{babcca}s_8 & & & \vdash \\
\mathbf{babcca}h\mathbf{Y} & & & &
\end{array}$$

If occurrences of the machine transition symbol $\vdash$ are replaced by the derivation symbol $\Rightarrow$, the above sequence would look remarkably like a derivation in a type 0 grammar. Indeed, we would like to construct a grammar in which sentential forms like $\mathbf{b}s_1\mathbf{abcca}$ could be derived from $s_0\mathbf{babcca}$ in one step. Since the machine changed configurations because of the transition rule $\delta(s_0, \mathbf{b}) = \langle s_1, \mathbf{R}\rangle$, this transition should have a corresponding production of the form $s_0\mathbf{b} \rightarrow \mathbf{b}s_1$. Each transition in the Turing machine will be responsible for similar productions.

Unfortunately, the correspondence between transition rules and productions is complicated by the fact that the tape head may occasionally scan blank cells, which must then be added to the sentential form. The special characters [and] will bracket the sentential form throughout this stage of the derivation and will indicate the current left and right limits of the tape head travel, respectively. Attempting to move left past the conceptual position of [(or right past the position of]) will result in the addition of a blank symbol to the sentential form.

To generate the words accepted by a Turing machine, our grammar will randomly generate a word over Σ, delimit it by brackets, and insert the symbol for the start state at the left edge. The rules derived from the transitions should then be able to transform a string such as $[s_0\mathbf{babcca}\#]$ into $[\#\mathbf{babccahY}\#]$. Since only the letters in Σ will be considered terminal symbols, the symbols [,], #, and **Y** are nonterminals, and the derivation will not yet be complete. To derive terminal strings for just the accepted words, the presence of **Y** will allow further productions to delete the remaining nonterminals.

∇ **Definition 11.8.** Given a Turing machine $M = <\Sigma, \Gamma, S, s_0, \delta>$, the grammar corresponding to M, G_M, is given by $G_M = <\Sigma, \Gamma \cup S \cup \{Z, W, U, V, [,]\}, Z, P_M>$, where P_M contains the following classes of productions:

1. $Z \to [W\#] \in P_M$
   $(\forall \mathbf{a} \in \Sigma)([W \to [W\mathbf{a} \in P_M)$
   $W \to s_0 \in P_M$
2. Each printing transition gives rise to a production rule as follows

   $$(\forall s \in S)(\forall t \in S \cup \{h\})(\forall \mathbf{a}, \mathbf{b} \in \Sigma \cup \Gamma)(\text{if } \delta(s, \mathbf{a}) = \langle t, \mathbf{b} \rangle, \text{ then } s\mathbf{a} \to t\mathbf{b} \in P_M)$$

   Each move right gives rise to a production rule as follows

   $$(\forall s, t \in S)(\forall \mathbf{a} \in \Sigma \cup \Gamma)(\text{if } \delta(s, \mathbf{a}) = \langle t, \mathbf{R} \rangle, \text{ then } s\mathbf{a} \to \mathbf{a}t \in P_M)$$

   If $\mathbf{a} = \#$, an additional production is needed:

   $$(\forall s, t \in S)(\text{if } \delta(s, \#) = \langle t, \mathbf{R} \rangle, \text{ then } s] \to \#t] \in P_M)$$

   Each move left gives rise to a production rule as follows

   $$(\forall s, t \in S)(\forall \mathbf{a} \in \Sigma \cup \Gamma)$$
   $$(\text{if } \delta(s, \mathbf{a}) = \langle t, \mathbf{L} \rangle, \text{ then } [s\mathbf{a} \to [t\#\mathbf{a} \in P_M \wedge (\forall \mathbf{d} \in \Sigma \cup \Gamma)(\mathbf{d}s\mathbf{a} \to t\mathbf{d}\mathbf{a} \in P_M))$$
3. $h\mathbf{Y} \to U \in P_M$
   $U\# \to U \in P_M$
   $U] \to V \in P_M$
   $(\forall \mathbf{a} \in \Sigma)(\mathbf{a}V \to V\mathbf{a} \in P_M)$
   $\#V \to V \in P_M$
   $[V \to \lambda \in P_M$

Δ

The rules in class 1 are intended to generate all words of the form $[s_0x\#]$, where x is an arbitrary member of Σ^*. The remaining rules are defined in such a way that only those strings x that are recognized by M can successfully produce a terminal string. Note that once W is replaced by s_0 neither Z nor W can appear in a later sentential form. After s_0 is generated, the rules in class 2 may apply. It can be inductively argued that the derivations arising from the application of these rules directly reflect the changes in the configuration of the Turing machine (see Theorem 11.4).

None of the class 3 productions can be used until the point at which the halt state would be reached in the corresponding computation. Since $h \notin S$, none of the class 2 productions can then be used. Only if **Y** was written to tape as the Turing machine halted will the production $h\mathbf{Y} \to U$ be applicable. U will then delete the trailing blanks and] from the sentential form, and then V will percolate to the left, removing the leading blanks and the final nonterminal [, leaving only the terminal string x in the (completed) sentential form. The following example illustrates a derivation stemming from a typical Turing machine.

EXAMPLE 11.12

Consider the Turing machine T in Figure 11.13 and the corresponding grammar G_T. Among the many possible derivations involving the class 1 productions is

$$Z \Rightarrow [W\mathbf{\#}] \Rightarrow [W\mathbf{a\#}] \Rightarrow [W\mathbf{ca\#}] \Rightarrow [W\mathbf{cca\#}] \Rightarrow [W\mathbf{bcca\#}] \Rightarrow [W\mathbf{abcca\#}]$$

$$\Rightarrow [W\mathbf{babcca\#}] \Rightarrow [s_0\mathbf{babcca\#}]$$

Only class 2 productions apply at this point, and there is exactly one derivation applicable at each step in the following sequence.

$$[s_0\mathbf{babcca\#}] \Rightarrow [\mathbf{b}s_1\mathbf{abcca\#}] \Rightarrow [\mathbf{b}s_2\mathbf{Abcca\#}] \Rightarrow [s_2\mathbf{bAbcca\#}] \Rightarrow$$

$$[s_2\mathbf{\#bAbcca\#}] \Rightarrow [\mathbf{\#}s_3\mathbf{bAbcca\#}] \Rightarrow [\mathbf{\#}s_4\mathbf{BAbcca\#}] \Rightarrow [s_4\mathbf{\#BAbcca\#}] \Rightarrow$$

$$[\mathbf{\#}s_5\mathbf{BAbcca\#}] \Rightarrow [\mathbf{\#B}s_5\mathbf{Abcca\#}] \Rightarrow [\mathbf{\#BA}s_5\mathbf{bcca\#}] \Rightarrow [\mathbf{\#BAb}s_5\mathbf{cca\#}] \Rightarrow$$

$$[\mathbf{\#BAb}s_6\mathbf{Cca\#}] \Rightarrow [\mathbf{\#BA}s_6\mathbf{bCca\#}] \Rightarrow [\mathbf{\#B}s_6\mathbf{AbCca\#}] \Rightarrow [\mathbf{\#}s_6\mathbf{BAbCca\#}] \Rightarrow$$

$$[s_6\mathbf{\#BAbCca\#}] \Rightarrow [\mathbf{\#}s_0\mathbf{BAbCca\#}] \Rightarrow [\mathbf{\#B}s_0\mathbf{AbCca\#}] \Rightarrow [\mathbf{\#BA}s_0\mathbf{bCca\#}] \Rightarrow$$

$$[\mathbf{\#BAb}s_1\mathbf{Cca\#}] \stackrel{*}{\Rightarrow} [s_2\mathbf{\#BAbCcA\#}] \stackrel{*}{\Rightarrow}$$

$$[\mathbf{\#BA}s_3\mathbf{bCcA\#}] \stackrel{*}{\Rightarrow} [s_4\mathbf{\#BABCcA\#}] \stackrel{*}{\Rightarrow}$$

$$[\mathbf{\#BABC}s_5\mathbf{cA\#}] \stackrel{*}{\Rightarrow} [s_6\mathbf{\#BABCCA\#}] \stackrel{*}{\Rightarrow}$$

$$[\mathbf{\#BABCCA}s_0\mathbf{\#}] \Rightarrow [\mathbf{\#BABCC}s_7\mathbf{A\#}] \Rightarrow [\mathbf{\#BABCC}s_7\mathbf{a\#}] \Rightarrow [\mathbf{\#BABC}s_7\mathbf{Ca\#}] \Rightarrow$$

$$[\mathbf{\#BABC}s_7\mathbf{ca\#}] \stackrel{*}{\Rightarrow} [\mathbf{\#}s_7\mathbf{babcca\#}] \Rightarrow [s_7\mathbf{\#babcca\#}] \Rightarrow$$

$$[\mathbf{\#}s_8\mathbf{babcca\#}] \Rightarrow [\mathbf{\#b}s_8\mathbf{abcca\#}] \stackrel{*}{\Rightarrow} [\mathbf{\#babcca}s_8\mathbf{\#}] \Rightarrow$$

$$[\mathbf{\#babcca}h\mathbf{Y}]$$

In Turing machines where the tape head travels further afield, there may be many more blanks enclosed within the brackets. At this point, the class 3 productions take over to tidy up the string:

$$[\mathbf{\#babcca}h\mathbf{Y}] \Rightarrow [\mathbf{\#babcca}U] \Rightarrow [\mathbf{\#babcca}V \Rightarrow [\mathbf{\#babcc}V\mathbf{a}$$

$$\Rightarrow [\mathbf{\#babc}V\mathbf{ca} \Rightarrow [\mathbf{\#bab}V\mathbf{cca} \Rightarrow [\mathbf{\#ba}V\mathbf{bcca} \Rightarrow [\mathbf{\#b}V\mathbf{abcca}$$

$$\Rightarrow [\mathbf{\#}V\mathbf{babcca} \Rightarrow [V\mathbf{babcca} \Rightarrow \mathbf{babcca}$$

As expected, $\mathbf{babcca} \in L(G_T)$.

It is interesting to observe that only stage in which a choice of productions is available is during the replacement of the nonterminal W. Once a candidate string is so chosen, the determinism of the Turing machine forces the remainder of the derivation to be unique. This is true even for strings that were not accepted by the Turing machine: if class 2 productions are applied to [s_0**baa**#], there is exactly one derivation sequence for this sequential form, and it leads to [**BAa**s_5#] and then [**BAahN**]. No productions apply to this sentential form, and thus no terminal string will be generated. The relationship between strings accepted by the Turing machine and the strings generated by the corresponding grammar is at the heart of the following theorem.

∇ **Theorem 11.4.** Let Σ be an alphabet. Then $\mathcal{T}_\Sigma \subseteq \mathfrak{Z}_\Sigma$. That is, every Turing-acceptable languge can be generated by a type 0 grammar.

Proof. Let M be a Turing machine $\mathsf{M} = \langle\Sigma, \Gamma, S, s_0, \delta\rangle$, and let

$$L(\mathsf{M}) = \{x \in \Sigma^* \mid s_0x \overset{*}{\vdash} xh\mathbf{Y}\},$$

as specified in the most restrictive sense of a Turing-acceptable language (Definition 11.3). Consider the grammar G_M corresponding to M, as given in Definition 11.8. The previous discussion of G_M provided a general sense of the way in which the productions could be used and justified that they could not be combined in unexpected ways. A rigorous proof requires an explicit formal statement of the general properties that have been discussed. A trivial induction on the length of x shows that by using just the productions in class 1

$$(\forall x \in \Sigma^*)(Z \overset{*}{\Rightarrow} [s_0x\#])$$

Another induction argument establishes the correspondence between sequences of applications of the class 2 productions and sequences of moves in the Turing machine. Specifically, by inducting on the number of transitions, it can be shown that

$$(\forall s, t \in S \cup \{h\})(\forall \alpha, \beta, \gamma, \omega \in (\Sigma \cup \Gamma)^*)$$
$$(\alpha s\beta \overset{*}{\vdash} \gamma t\omega \textit{ iff } (\exists i, j, m, n \in \mathbb{N})([\#^i\alpha s\beta\#^j] \overset{*}{\Rightarrow} [\#^m\gamma t\omega\#^n]))$$

The actual number of padded blanks is related to the extent of the tape head movement, but this is not important for our purposes. The essential observation is that a move sequence in M is related to a derivation sequence in G_M, with perhaps some change in the number of blanks at either end. The above statement was stated in full generality to facilitate the induction proof (see the exercises). We need apply it in a very limited sense, as stated below.

$$(\forall \alpha, \beta, \gamma, \omega \in (\Sigma \cup \Gamma)^*)(s_0x \overset{*}{\vdash} xh\mathbf{Y} \textit{ iff } (\exists m, n \in \mathbb{N})([s_0x\#] \overset{*}{\Rightarrow} [\#^m xh\mathbf{Y}\#^n]))$$

Observe that the productions in class 3 cannot be used unless **hY** appears on the tape after a finite number of steps. As discussed earlier, the presence of **hY** triggers the class 3 productions, which remove all the remaining nonterminals. Thus,

$$(\forall x \in \Sigma^*)(s_0x \overset{*}{\vdash} x\text{h}\mathbf{Y} \textit{ iff } Z \overset{*}{\Rightarrow} [s_0x\#] \overset{*}{\Rightarrow} [\#^m x\text{h}\mathbf{Y}\#^n] \overset{*}{\Rightarrow} x)$$

which implies that $\boldsymbol{L}(\mathsf{M}) = \boldsymbol{L}(\mathsf{G_M})$.
Δ

Since every Turing machine has an equivalent type 0 grammar and every type 0 grammar generates a Turing-acceptable language, we have two ways of representing the same class of languages.

∇ **Corollary 11.1.** The class of languages generated by type 0 grammars is exactly the Turing-acceptable languages. That is, $\mathcal{Z}_\Sigma = \mathcal{T}_\Sigma$.

Proof. The proof follows immediately from Theorems 11.2 and 11.4.
Δ

As will be seen in Chapter 12, the linear bounded languages are a distinctly smaller class than the Turing-acceptable languages. Theorem 11.3 showed that $\mathcal{O}_\Sigma \subseteq \mathcal{L}_\Sigma$, and a technique similar to that used in Theorem 11.4 will show that $\mathcal{L}_\Sigma \subseteq \mathcal{O}_\Sigma$. That is, we can show that every linear bounded automaton has an equivalent context-sensitive grammar. Note that the class 1 and 2 productions in Definition 11.8 contained no contracting productions; it was only when the class 3 productions were applied that the sentential form might shrink. When dealing with linear bounded automata, the tape head is restricted to the portion of the tape containing the input string, so there will be no extraneous blanks to delete. The input word on the tape of a linear bounded automaton is bracketed by distinct symbols $<$ and $>$, which might be used in the corresponding grammar in a fashion similar to [and]. These would be *immovable* in the sense that no new blanks would be inserted between them and the rest of the bracketed word. Unfortunately, in Definition 11.8 the delimiters [and] must eventually disappear, shortening the sentential form. No such shrinking can occur if we hope to produce a context-sensitive grammar.

To overcome this difficulty, it is useful to imagine a three-track tape with the input word on the middle track and the delimiter – on the upper track of the tape above the first symbol of the word. Another – will occur on the lower track below the last character of the input string. These markers will serve as guides to prevent the tape head from moving past the limits of the input word. For example, if the linear bounded automaton contained the word **<babcca>** on its input tape, the tape for the corresponding three-track automaton would be as pictured in Figure 11.14a. If the word were accepted, the tape would eventually reach the configuration shown in Figure 11.14b as it halted, printing **Y** on the lower track. It is a relatively simple task to convert a linear bounded automaton into a three-track automaton, where the tape head never moves left of the tape cell with the – in the upper track, and never moves right of the cell with the – in the lower track (see the exercises). We will refer to such an automaton as a *strict linear bounded automaton*. The definitions

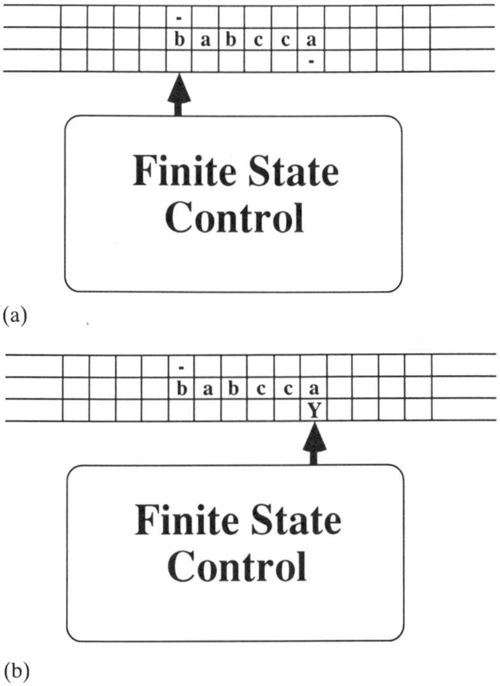

Figure 11.14 (a) A three-track Turing machine employing delimiters (b) An accepting configuration

used will depend on the upper and lower track markers occurring in different cells, which makes the representation of words of length less than two awkward. Since this construct is motivated by a need to find a context-sensitive grammar, we will simply modify the resulting grammar to explicitly generate any such short words and not rely on the above formalism.

EXAMPLE 11.13

Consider the linear-bounded automaton discussed in Example 11.10, which accepted $\{x \in \{\mathbf{a},\mathbf{b},\mathbf{c}\}^* \mid |x|_\mathbf{a} = |x|_\mathbf{b} = |x|_\mathbf{c}\}$. As suggested by the exercises, this can be modified to form the three-track strict linear bounded automaton shown in Figure 11.15, which accepts $\{x \in \{\mathbf{a},\mathbf{b},\mathbf{c}\}^* \mid |x| \geq 2 \wedge |x|_\mathbf{a} = |x|_\mathbf{b} = |x|_\mathbf{c}\}$. To avoid explicitly mentioning the three tracks, a cell containing **b** on the middle track and $-$ on the upper track is denoted by the single symbol **b**, a cell containing **A** on the middle track and $-$ on the lower track is shown as $\underline{\mathbf{A}}$, and so on. Thus, the six original symbols in $\{\mathbf{a},\mathbf{b},\mathbf{c},\mathbf{A},\mathbf{B},\mathbf{C}\}$ give rise to six other symbols employing the overbar $\bar{\ }$, six more using the underscore _, and some symbols indicating acceptance (or possibly rejection), such as $\mathbf{a}_\mathbf{Y}$ (or $\mathbf{C}_\mathbf{N}$). For clarity, only those combinations that can actually occur in a transition sequence are shown in Figure 11.15. The sequence of moves that would transform the tape from the configuration shown in Figure 11.14a to that of Figure 11.14b is shown below.

$$s_0\overline{\mathbf{b}}\mathbf{abcc}\underline{\mathbf{a}} \vdash \overline{\mathbf{b}}s_1\mathbf{abcc}\underline{\mathbf{a}} \vdash \overline{\mathbf{b}}s_2\mathbf{Abcc}\underline{\mathbf{a}} \vdash s_2\overline{\mathbf{b}}\mathbf{Abcc}\underline{\mathbf{a}} \vdash$$

$$s_3\mathbf{bAbcc}\underline{\mathbf{a}} \vdash s_4\mathbf{BAbcc}\underline{\mathbf{a}} \vdash$$

$$s_5\overline{\mathbf{B}}\mathbf{Abcc}\underline{\mathbf{a}} \vdash \overline{\mathbf{B}}s_5\mathbf{Abcc}\underline{\mathbf{a}} \vdash \overline{\mathbf{B}}\mathbf{A}s_5\mathbf{bcc}\underline{\mathbf{a}} \vdash \overline{\mathbf{B}}\mathbf{Ab}s_5\mathbf{cc}\underline{\mathbf{a}} \vdash$$

$$\mathbf{BAb}s_6\mathbf{Cc}\underline{\mathbf{a}} \vdash \overline{\mathbf{B}}\mathbf{A}s_6\mathbf{bCc}\underline{\mathbf{a}} \vdash \overline{\mathbf{B}}s_6\mathbf{AbCc}\underline{\mathbf{a}} \vdash s_6\overline{\mathbf{B}}\mathbf{AbCc}\underline{\mathbf{a}} \vdash$$

$$s_0\overline{\mathbf{B}}\mathbf{AbCc}\underline{\mathbf{a}} \vdash \overline{\mathbf{B}}s_0\mathbf{AbCc}\underline{\mathbf{a}} \vdash \overline{\mathbf{B}}\mathbf{A}s_0\mathbf{bCc}\underline{\mathbf{a}} \vdash$$

$$\overline{\mathbf{B}}\mathbf{Ab}s_1\mathbf{Cc}\underline{\mathbf{a}} \overset{*}{\vdash} s_2\overline{\mathbf{B}}\mathbf{AbCc}\underline{\mathbf{A}} \overset{*}{\vdash}$$

$$\overline{\mathbf{B}}\mathbf{A}s_3\mathbf{bCc}\underline{\mathbf{A}} \overset{*}{\vdash} s_4\overline{\mathbf{B}}\mathbf{ABCc}\underline{\mathbf{A}} \overset{*}{\vdash}$$

$$\overline{\mathbf{B}}\mathbf{ABC}s_5\mathbf{c}\underline{\mathbf{A}} \overset{*}{\vdash} s_6\overline{\mathbf{B}}\mathbf{ABCC}\underline{\mathbf{A}} \overset{*}{\vdash}$$

$$\overline{\mathbf{B}}\mathbf{ABCC}s_0\underline{\mathbf{A}} \vdash \overline{\mathbf{B}}\mathbf{ABCC}s_7\underline{\mathbf{a}} \vdash \overline{\mathbf{B}}\mathbf{ABC}s_7\mathbf{C}\underline{\mathbf{a}} \vdash$$

$$\overline{\mathbf{B}}\mathbf{ABC}s_7\mathbf{c}\underline{\mathbf{a}} \overset{*}{\vdash} s_7\overline{\mathbf{B}}\mathbf{abcc}\underline{\mathbf{a}} \vdash$$

$$s_8\overline{\mathbf{b}}\mathbf{abcc}\underline{\mathbf{a}} \vdash \overline{\mathbf{b}}s_8\mathbf{abcc}\underline{\mathbf{a}} \overset{*}{\vdash} \overline{\mathbf{b}}\mathbf{abcc}s_8\underline{\mathbf{a}} \vdash$$

$$\overline{\mathbf{b}}\mathbf{abccha}_{\mathbf{Y}}$$

Consider implementing a grammar similar to that given in Definition 11.8, but applied to a strict linear bounded automaton incorporating the two delimiting markers on separate tracks. The new symbols will eliminate the need for [and] and avoid the contracting productions that were required to delete [and] from the sentential form. The class 3 productions would simply replace a symbol such as $\mathbf{a}_{\mathbf{Y}}$ with **a** and $\overline{\mathbf{b}}$ with **b**.

Unfortunately, it will not be possible to explicitly use distinct symbols to keep track of the state and the placement of the state head, as was done with $s_0, s_1, \ldots, s_n$ and h in the previous production sets. This extraneous symbol will also have to disappear to form a terminal string, and this must be done in a way that does not use contracting productions. As with the underscore and overbar, the state name will be encoded as a subscript attached to one symbol in the sentential form. Thus, each original symbol **d**, which has already given rise to additional nonterminals $\overline{\mathbf{d}}$ and $\underline{\mathbf{d}}$, will also require nonterminals such as $\mathbf{d}_0, \mathbf{d}_1, \ldots, \mathbf{d}_n$ to be added to Γ. The inclusion of $\mathbf{d}_i$ within a sentential form will reflect that the tape head is currently scanning this **d** while the finite-state control is in state s_i. Further symbols will also be needed; $\overline{\mathbf{d}}_i$ indicates that the tape head is scanning the leftmost symbol, which happens to be **d**, while the finite-state control is in state s_i, and $\underline{\mathbf{d}}_i$ indicates a similar situation involving the rightmost symbol.

This plethora of nonterminals can be used to define a context-sensitive grammar that generates the language recognized by a strict linear bounded automaton. For the automaton given in Example 11.13, generating the terminal string **babcca** will begin with the random generations of the six-symbol sentential form $\overline{\mathbf{b}}_0\mathbf{abcc}\underline{\mathbf{a}}$ with the class 1 productions, which will be transformed into $\overline{\mathbf{b}}\mathbf{abcca}_{\mathbf{Y}}$ by the class 2 productions, and finally into **babcca** via the class 3 productions. In the

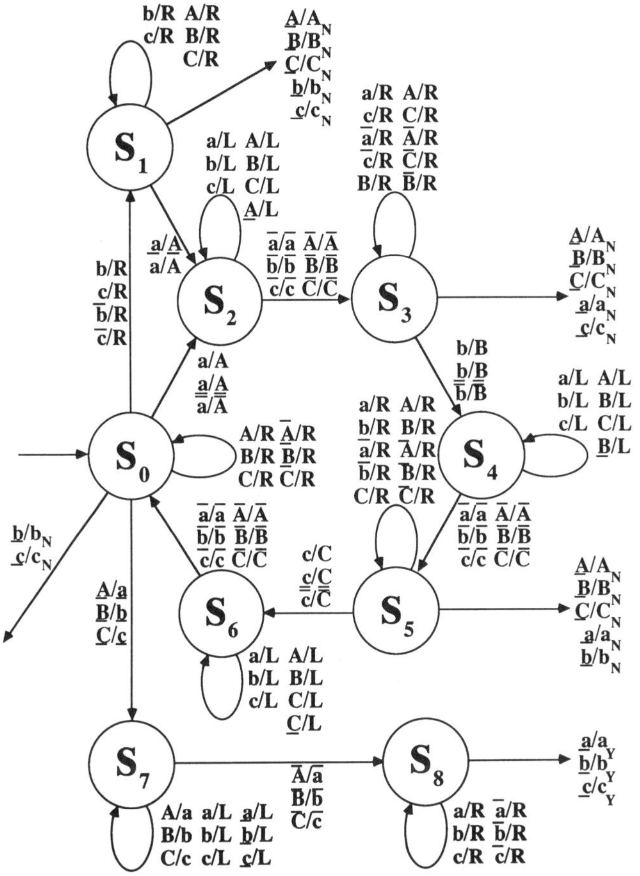

Figure 11.15 The Turing machine discussed in Example 11.13

following definition, note that by the conditions placed on a strict linear bounded automaton Γ already contains symbols of the form $\overline{\mathbf{A}}$ and $\underline{\mathbf{A}}$, and hence so will Γ_{B}. For simplicity, the state set is required to be of the form $\{s_0, s_1, \ldots, s_n\}$, but clearly the state names of any automaton could be renumbered sequentially to fit the given definition.

∇ **Definition 11.9.** Given a strict linear bounded automaton

$$\mathsf{B} = \langle \Sigma, \Gamma, \{s_0, s_1, \ldots, s_n\}, s_0, \delta \rangle,$$

the context-sensitive grammar corresponding to B, G_{B}, is given by

$$\mathsf{G}_{\mathsf{B}} = \langle \Sigma, \Gamma_{\mathsf{B}}, Z, P_{\mathsf{B}} \rangle,$$

where Γ_{B} is given by

$$\Gamma_{\mathsf{B}} = \Gamma \cup \{\mathbf{d}_i \mid \mathbf{d} \in \Sigma \cup \Gamma, i = 1, 2, \ldots, n, \text{ or } i = \mathrm{Y}\} \cup \{Z, S, W\}$$

P_B contains the following classes of productions:

1. If $\lambda \in \boldsymbol{L}(B)$, then $Z \to \lambda \in P_B$
$Z \to S \in P_B$
$(\forall \mathbf{d} \in \Sigma)(\text{if } \mathbf{d} \in \boldsymbol{L}(B), \text{ then } S \to \mathbf{d} \in P_B)$
$(\forall \mathbf{d} \in \Sigma)(S \to W\underline{\mathbf{d}} \in P_B)$
$(\forall \mathbf{d} \in \Sigma)(W \to W\mathbf{d} \in P_B)$
$(\forall \mathbf{d} \in \Sigma)(W \to \overline{\mathbf{d}}_0 \in P_B)$

2. Each printing transition gives rise to a production rule as follows:

$$(\forall s_i, s_j \in S)(\forall \mathbf{a}, \mathbf{b} \in \Sigma \cup \Gamma)(\text{if } \delta(s_i, \mathbf{a}) = \langle s_j, \mathbf{b}\rangle, \text{ then } \mathbf{a}_i \to \mathbf{b}_j \in P_B)$$

Each move right gives rise to a production rule as follows:

$$(\forall s_i, s_j \in S)(\forall \mathbf{a} \in \Sigma \cup \Gamma)(\text{if } \delta(s_i, \mathbf{a}) = \langle s_j, \mathbf{R}\rangle, \text{ then } (\forall \mathbf{d} \in \Sigma \cup \Gamma)(\mathbf{a}_i\mathbf{d} \to \mathbf{a}\mathbf{d}_j \in P_B)$$

Each move left gives rise to a production rule as follows:

$$(\forall s_i, s_j \in S)(\forall \mathbf{a} \in \Sigma \cup \Gamma)(\text{if } \delta(s_i, \mathbf{a}) = \langle s_j, \mathbf{L}\rangle, \text{ then } (\forall \mathbf{d} \in \Sigma \cup \Gamma)(\mathbf{d}\mathbf{a}_i \to \mathbf{d}_j\mathbf{a} \in P_B)$$

Each halt with acceptance gives rise to a production rule as follows:

$$(\forall s_i \in S)(\forall \mathbf{b} \in \Sigma \cup \Gamma)(\forall \mathbf{a} \in \Sigma)(\text{if } \delta(s_i, \mathbf{b}) = \langle h, \mathbf{a}_Y\rangle, \text{ then } \mathbf{b}_i \to \mathbf{a}_Y \in P_B)$$

3. $(\forall \mathbf{a}, \mathbf{b} \in \Sigma)(\mathbf{b}\mathbf{a}_Y \to \mathbf{b}_Y\mathbf{a} \in P_B)$

$(\forall \mathbf{a}, \mathbf{b} \in \Sigma)(\overline{\mathbf{b}}\mathbf{a}_Y \to \mathbf{b}\mathbf{a} \in P_B)$

Δ

EXAMPLE 11.14

Consider again the strict linear bounded automaton B given in Figure 11.15 and the corresponding context-sensitive grammar G_B. The following derivation sequences show that **babcca** $\in \boldsymbol{L}(G_B)$:

$$Z \Rightarrow S \Rightarrow W\underline{\mathbf{a}} \Rightarrow W\mathbf{c}\underline{\mathbf{a}} \Rightarrow W\mathbf{cc}\underline{\mathbf{a}} \Rightarrow W\mathbf{bcc}\underline{\mathbf{a}} \Rightarrow W\mathbf{abcc}\underline{\mathbf{a}} \Rightarrow \overline{\mathbf{b}}_0\mathbf{abcc}\underline{\mathbf{a}}$$

At this point, only the class 2 productions can be employed, yielding:

$$\overline{\mathbf{b}}_0\mathbf{abcc}\underline{\mathbf{a}} \Rightarrow \overline{\mathbf{b}}\mathbf{a}_1\mathbf{bcc}\underline{\mathbf{a}} \Rightarrow \overline{\mathbf{b}}\mathbf{A}_2\mathbf{bcc}\underline{\mathbf{a}} \Rightarrow \overline{\mathbf{b}}_2\mathbf{Abcc}\underline{\mathbf{a}} \Rightarrow$$
$$\overline{\mathbf{b}}_3\mathbf{Abcc}\underline{\mathbf{a}} \Rightarrow \overline{\mathbf{B}}_4\mathbf{Abcc}\underline{\mathbf{a}} \Rightarrow$$
$$\overline{\mathbf{B}}_5\mathbf{Abcc}\underline{\mathbf{a}} \Rightarrow \overline{\mathbf{B}}\mathbf{A}_5\mathbf{bcc}\underline{\mathbf{a}} \Rightarrow \overline{\mathbf{B}}\mathbf{Ab}_5\mathbf{cc}\underline{\mathbf{a}} \Rightarrow \overline{\mathbf{B}}\mathbf{Abc}_5\mathbf{c}\underline{\mathbf{a}} \Rightarrow$$
$$\overline{\mathbf{B}}\mathbf{AbC}_6\mathbf{c}\underline{\mathbf{a}} \Rightarrow \overline{\mathbf{B}}\mathbf{Ab}_6\mathbf{Cc}\underline{\mathbf{a}} \Rightarrow \overline{\mathbf{B}}\mathbf{A}_6\mathbf{bCc}\underline{\mathbf{a}} \Rightarrow \overline{\mathbf{B}}_6\mathbf{AbCc}\underline{\mathbf{a}} \Rightarrow$$
$$\overline{\mathbf{B}}_0\mathbf{AbCc}\underline{\mathbf{a}} \Rightarrow \overline{\mathbf{B}}\mathbf{A}_0\mathbf{bCc}\underline{\mathbf{a}} \Rightarrow \overline{\mathbf{B}}\mathbf{Ab}_0\mathbf{Cc}\underline{\mathbf{a}} \Rightarrow$$
$$\overline{\mathbf{B}}\mathbf{AbC}_1\mathbf{c}\underline{\mathbf{a}} \overset{*}{\Rightarrow} \overline{\mathbf{B}}_2\mathbf{AbCc}\underline{\mathbf{A}} \overset{*}{\Rightarrow}$$
$$\overline{\mathbf{B}}\mathbf{Ab}_3\mathbf{Cc}\underline{\mathbf{A}} \overset{*}{\Rightarrow} \overline{\mathbf{B}}_4\mathbf{ABCc}\underline{\mathbf{A}} \overset{*}{\Rightarrow}$$
$$\overline{\mathbf{B}}\mathbf{ABCc}_5\underline{\mathbf{A}} \overset{*}{\Rightarrow} \overline{\mathbf{B}}_6\mathbf{ABCC}\underline{\mathbf{A}} \overset{*}{\Rightarrow}$$

$$\bar{\mathbf{B}}\mathbf{ABCC}\underline{\mathbf{A}}_0 \Rightarrow \bar{\mathbf{B}}\mathbf{ABCC}\underline{\mathbf{a}}_7 \Rightarrow \bar{\mathbf{B}}\mathbf{ABCC}_7\underline{\mathbf{a}} \Rightarrow$$

$$\bar{\mathbf{B}}\mathbf{ABCc}_7\underline{\mathbf{a}} \stackrel{*}{\Rightarrow} \bar{\mathbf{B}}_7\mathbf{abcc}\underline{\mathbf{a}} \Rightarrow$$

$$\bar{\mathbf{b}}_8\mathbf{abcc}\underline{\mathbf{a}} \Rightarrow \bar{\mathbf{b}}\mathbf{a}_8\mathbf{bcc}\underline{\mathbf{a}} \stackrel{*}{\Rightarrow} \bar{\mathbf{b}}\mathbf{abcc}\underline{\mathbf{a}}_8$$

Finally, since $\delta(s_8, \underline{\mathbf{a}}) = \langle h, \mathbf{a}_Y \rangle$, the class 3 productions now apply:

$$\bar{\mathbf{b}}\mathbf{abcc}\underline{\mathbf{a}}_8 \Rightarrow \bar{\mathbf{b}}\mathbf{abcca}_Y \Rightarrow \bar{\mathbf{b}}\mathbf{abcc}_Y\mathbf{a} \Rightarrow \bar{\mathbf{b}}\mathbf{abc}_Y\mathbf{ca} \Rightarrow \bar{\mathbf{b}}\mathbf{ab}_Y\mathbf{cca} \Rightarrow \bar{\mathbf{b}}\mathbf{a}_Y\mathbf{bcca} \Rightarrow \mathbf{babcca}$$

Once again, the grammars springing from Definition 11.9 can generate sentential forms corresponding to any string in Σ^*, as long as the length of the string is at least two. As with the grammars arising from Definition 11.8, only strings that would have been accepted by the original machine will lead to a terminal string. If the productions of this example were applied to the sentential form $\bar{\mathbf{b}}_0\mathbf{a}\underline{\mathbf{a}}$, at each step there will be exactly one choice of applicable production, until eventually the form $\bar{\mathbf{B}}\mathbf{A}\underline{\mathbf{a}}_5$ is obtained. At this step, no production will apply, and therefore a terminal string cannot be generated from $\bar{\mathbf{b}}_0\mathbf{a}\underline{\mathbf{a}}$. This correspondence between words accepted by the machine B and words generated by the context-sensitive grammar G_B given in Definition 11.9 is the foundation of the following theorem.

∇ **Theorem 11.5.** Let Σ be an alphabet. Then $\mathscr{L}_\Sigma \subseteq \mathcal{O}_\Sigma$. That is, every linear bounded language can be generated by a type 1 grammar.

Proof. Any linear bounded language can be recognized by a strict linear bounded automaton (see the exercises). Hence, if L is a linear bounded language, there exists a strict linear bounded automaton $B = <\Sigma, \Gamma, \{s_0, s_1, \ldots, s_n\}, s_0, \delta>$ which accepts exactly the words in L by printing **Y** on the lowest of the three tracks after restoring the original word to the middle track. We will employ the grammar G_B corresponding to B, as given in Definition 11.9. Example 11.14 illustrated that these productions can be used in a manner similar to those of Definition 11.8, and it is easy to justify that they cannot be combined in unexpected ways. Induction on the length of x will show that by using just the productions in class 1,

$$(\forall x \in \Sigma^*)(\forall \mathbf{a}, \mathbf{b} \in \Sigma)(Z \stackrel{*}{\Rightarrow} \bar{\mathbf{a}}_0 x \underline{\mathbf{b}})$$

The correspondence between sequences of applications of the class 2 productions and sequences of moves in B follows as in Theorem 11.4. Due to the myriad positions that the integer subscript can occupy, and the special cases caused by the presence of the overbars and underscores, the general induction statement is quite tedious to state and is left as an exercise. The statement will again be applied to the special case in which we are interested, as stated below.

$$(\forall x \in \Sigma^*)(\forall \mathbf{a}, \mathbf{b} \in \Sigma)(s_0 \mathbf{a} x \mathbf{b} \stackrel{*}{\vdash} \mathbf{a} x h \mathbf{b}_Y \textit{ iff } \bar{\mathbf{a}}_0 x \underline{\mathbf{b}} \stackrel{*}{\Rightarrow} \bar{\mathbf{a}} x \mathbf{b}_Y)$$

A final induction argument will show that $\bar{\mathbf{a}} x \mathbf{b}_Y \stackrel{*}{\Rightarrow} \mathbf{a} x \mathbf{b}$. Thus,

$$(\forall x \in \Sigma^*)(\forall \mathbf{a}, \mathbf{b} \in \Sigma)(s_0 \mathbf{a} x \mathbf{b} \stackrel{*}{\vdash} \mathbf{a} x h \mathbf{b}_Y \textit{ iff } Z \stackrel{*}{\Rightarrow} \bar{\mathbf{a}}_0 x \underline{\mathbf{b}} \stackrel{*}{\Rightarrow} \bar{\mathbf{a}} x \mathbf{b}_Y \stackrel{*}{\Rightarrow} \mathbf{a} x \mathbf{b})$$

This establishes the correspondence between words *of length at least two* accepted by B and those generated by G_B. Definition 11.9 included specific productions of the form $Z \rightarrow \lambda$ and $S \rightarrow \mathbf{d}$ to ensure that words of length 0 and 1 also corresponded. This implies that $L(B) = L(G_B)$, as was to be shown.

Δ

The proof of Theorem 11.5 argues that there exists a context-sensitive grammar G_B for each strict linear bounded automaton B, and it certainly appears that given an automaton B we can immediately write down all the productions in P_B, as specified by Definition 11.9. However, some of the class 1 productions may cause some trouble. For example, determining whether the production $Z \rightarrow \lambda$ is included in P_B depends on whether the automaton halts with **Y** when presented with a blank tape. In the next chapter, we will see that even this simple question cannot be effectively answered for arbitrary Turing machines! That is, it is impossible to find an algorithm that, when presented with the state diagram of a Turing machine, can reliably determine whether or not the machine accepts the empty string. It will be shown that any such proposed algorithm is guaranteed to give the wrong answer for some Turing machines. Similarly, it now seems that there might be some uncertainty about which members of Σ give rise to productions of the form $S \rightarrow \mathbf{d}$.

The productions specified by Definition 11.9 were otherwise quite explicit; only the productions relating to the immediate generation of a single character or the empty string were in any way questionable. There are only $|\Sigma| + 1$ such productions, and some combination of them has to be the correct set of productions to include in P_B. Thus, as stated in the theorem, we *are* assured that a context-sensitive grammar does exist, even if we are unclear as to exactly what productions it should contain.

As will be seen in Chapter 12, it *is* possible to determine which words are accepted (and which are rejected) by linear bounded automata. Unlike unrestricted Turing machines, there is only a finite span of tape upon which symbols can be placed. Furthermore, there are only a finite number of characters that can appear in those cells, a finite number of positions the tape head can be in, and a finite number of states to consider. The limited number of configurations makes it possible to determine exactly which words of a given size are recognized by the LBA.

We have seen that every linear bounded automaton is equivalent to a strict linear bounded automaton, and these have equivalent type 1 grammars. Conversely, every type 1 grammar generates a linear bounded language, which implies there is another correspondence between a generative construct and a cognitive construct.

∇ **Corollary 11.2.** The class of languages generated by context-sensitive grammars is exactly the linear bounded languages. That is, $\mathscr{L}_\Sigma = \mathscr{O}_\Sigma$.

Proof. The proof follows immediately from Theorems 11.3 and 11.5.

Δ

11.4 CLOSURE PROPERTIES AND THE HIERARCHY THEOREM

Finally, we consider some of the closure properties of the classes of languages explored in this chapter. Since $\mathcal{T}_\Sigma = \mathfrak{L}_\Sigma$, we may use either cognitive or generative constructs for this class, whichever is most convenient. The fact that $\mathcal{L}_\Sigma = \mathcal{O}_\Sigma$ will allow the same choice for the type 1 languages. The next theorem illustrates a case in which the grammatical construct is the easier to use.

∇ **Theorem 11.6.** Let Σ be an alphabet. Then $\mathcal{T}_\Sigma$ is closed under union.

Proof. If L_1 and L_2 are two Turing-acceptable languages, then by Theorem 11.4 there are type 0 grammars $G_1 = <\Omega_1, \Sigma, S_1, P_1>$ and $G_2 = <\Omega_2, \Sigma, S_2, P_2>$ that recognize L_1 and L_2. Without loss of generality, assume that $\Omega_1 \cap \Omega_2 = \emptyset$. Choose a new nonterminal Z such that $Z \notin \Omega_1 \cup \Omega_2$, and consider the new type 0 grammar $G^\cup$ defined by $G^\cup = <\Omega_1 \cup \Omega_2 \cup \{Z\}, \Sigma, Z, P_1 \cup P_2 \cup \{Z \to S_1, Z \to S_2\}>$. Clearly, $\boldsymbol{L}(G^\cup) = \boldsymbol{L}(G_1) \cup \boldsymbol{L}(G_2)$. By Theorem 11.2, there is a Turing machine equivalent to $G^\cup$, and hence $L_1 \cup L_2$ is Turing acceptable.
Δ

Theorem 11.6 could be proved directly by constructing a new Turing machine from Turing machines T_1 and T_2 accepting L_1 and L_2. It is a bit harder to give a concrete proof and care must be taken to avoid inappropriate constructions. For example, it would be incorrect to build the new machine in such a way that it first simulates T_1, halting with **Y** if T_1 does, and then simulating T_2 if T_1 would have halted with **N**. It must be remembered that there is no guarantee that a Turing machine will *ever* halt for a given word. The above construction will incorrectly reject words that could be recognized by T_2 but which were rejected by T_1 because T_1 never halted; the new machine would never get a chance to simulate T_2. One valid construction involves a two-tape Turing machine, which immediately copies the input word onto the second tape. By using a cross product of the states of the T_1 and T_2 and appropriate transitions, the action of both machines could be simultaneously simulated, and the new machine would accept as soon as either simulation indicated that the word should be accepted. A slight modification of this construct would show that $\mathcal{T}_\Sigma$ is also closed under intersection, but the next theorem outlines a superior method.

∇ **Theorem 11.7.** Let Σ be an alphabet. Then $\mathcal{T}_\Sigma$ is closed under intersection.

Proof. L_1 and L_2 are two Turing-acceptable languages recognized by the Turing machines T_1 and T_2, respectively. We build a new Turing machine $T^\cap$ with T_1 and T_2 as submachines. $T^\cap$ transfers control to the submachine T_1. If T_1 never halts, the input will be rejected, which is the desired result. If T_1 halts, $T^\cap$ erases the **Y** and moves the tape head back to the leftmost character and transfers control to the submachine T_2. $T^\cap$ will halt if T_2 does, and if T_2 also accepts, **Y** will be left in the

proper place on the tape. $T^{\cap}$ therefore accepts if and only if both T_1 and T_2 accept, and hence $L_1 \cap L_2$ is Turing acceptable.
Δ

Note that it was important that, except for the presence of **Y** after the input word, T_1 left the tape in the same condition it found it, with the input string intact for T_2. As with type 3 and type 2 grammars, there is no pleasant way to combine type 0 grammars to produce a grammar that generates the intersection of type 0 languages, although Theorem 11.7 guarantees that such a grammar must surely exist.

∇ **Theorem 11.8.** Let Σ be an alphabet. Then $\mathcal{T}_\Sigma$ is closed under reversal, homomorphism, inverse homomorphism, substitution, concatenation, and Kleene closure.

Proof. The proof for reversal is almost trivial; it is almost as simple as replacing every transition that moves the tape head to the right with a transition to the left, and likewise making left moves into right moves. This will yield a mirror image machine, which when started at the *right*most character will print **Y** just past the *left*most character. We therefore have to modify this machine by adding a preliminary states that will move the tape head from its traditional leftmost starting position to the opposite end of the word. Similarly, just before the **Y** would be printed, we must again move the tape head to the right.

The description of the modifications necessary to convert a type 0 grammar into one that generates the reverse of the original is even more succinct: Each rule in the original grammar is modified by writing the characters to the left of the production symbol $\rightarrow$ backward, and similarly reversing the string on the right of $\rightarrow$. That is, a production like **Dc**$\rightarrow$**ABe** would become **cD**$\rightarrow$**eBA**. A relatively trivial induction on the number of steps in a derivation proves that the new grammar accepts the reverse of the original language. The proofs of closure under the remaining operators are left for the exercises.
Δ

As shown in Chapter 12, there are some operators under which $\mathcal{T}_\Sigma$ is not closed. Complementation is perhaps the most glaring exception. The closure properties of $\mathcal{L}_\Sigma$ are very similar to those of $\mathcal{T}_\Sigma$. In most cases, slight modifications of the above proofs carry over to the type 1 languages.

∇ **Theorem 11.9.** Let Σ be an alphabet. Then $\mathfrak{O}_\Sigma$ is closed under reversal, homomorphism, inverse homomorphism, substitution, concatenation, union, and intersection.

Proof. Both proofs given for reversal carry over without modification. In the cognitive approach, the states added to the mirror image Turing machine keep the tape head within the confines of the input word, and hence if the original machine was a LBA, the new version will also be a LBA. In the generative approach, reversing the characters in type 1 productions still results in a type 1 grammar. That is, if the original grammar had no contracting productions, neither will the new grammar.

Proving that the union of two type 1 languages is type 1 is similar to the proof given in Theorem 11.6, although care must be taken to avoid extraneous productions of the form $Z_1 \to \lambda$. Building an intersection machine from two linear bounded automata can be done exactly as described in Theorem 11.7. The remaining closure properties are left for the exercises.
Δ

It is clear from our definitions that $\mathcal{O}_\Sigma \subseteq \mathfrak{X}_\Sigma$, but we have yet to prove that $\mathcal{O}_\Sigma \subset \mathfrak{X}_\Sigma$. That the inclusion is proper and $\mathfrak{X}_\Sigma$ is truly a larger class than $\mathcal{O}_\Sigma$ will be shown to be a consequence of the material considered in Chapter 12. Apart from this one missing piece, we have over the course of several chapters encountered the major components of the following *hierarchy theorem*.

∇ **Theorem 11.10.** Let Σ be an alphabet for which $\|\Sigma\| \geq 2$. Then

$$\mathcal{D}_\Sigma = \mathcal{W}_\Sigma = \mathcal{R}_\Sigma = \mathcal{G}_\Sigma \subset \mathcal{U}_\Sigma \subset \mathcal{C}_\Sigma = \mathcal{P}_\Sigma \subset \mathcal{L}_\Sigma = \mathcal{O}_\Sigma \subset \mathfrak{X}_\Sigma = \mathcal{T}_\Sigma$$

Proof. The cognitive power of deterministic and nondeterministic finite automata was shown to be equivalent in Chapter 4, and their relation to regular expressions was investigated in Chapter 6. These were all shown to describe the type 3 languages in Chapter 8. In Chapter 9, Theorem 9.1 and Corollary 9.1 showed that the context-free languages (over alphabets with at least two symbols) properly contained the unambiguous context-free languages, which in turn properly contained the regular languages. In Chapter 10, the (nondeterministic) pushdown automata were shown to recognize exactly the type 2 languages. The context-sensitive language $\{x \in \{\mathbf{a}, \mathbf{b}, \mathbf{c}\}^* \mid |x|_\mathbf{a} = |x|_\mathbf{b} = |x|_\mathbf{c}\}$ is not context free, so the type 1 languages properly contain the type 2 languages. In this chapter, the linear bounded automata were shown to be recognize exactly the type 1 languages and Turing machines were shown to accept the type 0 languages. Corollary 12.4 will show that the type 1 languages are properly included in the type 0 languages.
Δ

EXERCISES

11.1. By making the appropriate analogies for states and input, answer the musical question "How is a Turing machine like an elevator?" What essential (missing) component prevents an elevator from modeling a general computing device?

11.2. Let $\Sigma = \{\mathbf{a}, \mathbf{b}, \mathbf{c}\}$ and let $L = \{w \mid w = w^r\}$.

(a) Explicitly define a deterministic, one-tape, one-head Turing machine that will recognize L.

(b) Justify that there exists a linear bounded automaton that accepts L.

(c) Describe how nondeterminism or additional tapes and heads might be employed to recognize L.

11.3. Let $\Sigma = \{\mathbf{a}\}$. Explicitly define a deterministic, one-tape, one-head Turing machine that will recognize $\{\mathbf{a}^n \mid n \text{ is a perfect square}\}$.

11.4. Let $\Sigma = \{\mathbf{a}, \mathbf{b}, \mathbf{c}\}$.

(a) Explicitly define a deterministic, one-tape, one-head Turing machine that will recognize $\{\mathbf{a}^k\mathbf{b}^n\mathbf{c}^m \mid (k \neq n) \wedge (n \neq m)\}$.

(b) Explicitly define a deterministic, one-tape, one-head Turing machine that will recognize $\{x \in \{\mathbf{a}, \mathbf{b}, \mathbf{c}\}^* \mid \ |x|_{\mathbf{a}} \neq |x|_{\mathbf{b}} \wedge |x|_{\mathbf{b}} \neq |x|_{\mathbf{c}}\}$.

11.5. **(a)** Recall that there are several common definitions of acceptance that can be applied to Turing machines. Design a machine M for which

$$L(\mathsf{M}) = L_1(\mathsf{M}) = L_2(\mathsf{M}) = L_3(\mathsf{M}) = \{x \in \{\mathbf{a}, \mathbf{b}, \mathbf{c}\}^* \mid \ |x|_{\mathbf{a}} = |x|_{\mathbf{b}} = |x|_{\mathbf{c}}\}.$$

(b) For any Turing-acceptable language L, is it always possible to find a corresponding machine for which $L(\mathsf{M}) = L_1(\mathsf{M}) = L_2(\mathsf{M}) = L_3(\mathsf{M}) = \mathrm{L}$? Justify your answer.

11.6. Let $\mathrm{L} = \{ww \mid w \in \{\mathbf{a}, \mathbf{b}, \mathbf{c}\}^*\}$.

(a) Explicitly define a deterministic, one-tape, one-head Turing machine that will recognize L.

(b) Justify that there exists a linear bounded automaton that accepts L.

(c) Describe how nondeterminism or additional tapes and heads might be employed to recognize L.

11.7. Given an alphabet $\Sigma = \{\mathbf{a}_1, \mathbf{a}_2, \mathbf{a}_3, \ldots, \mathbf{a}_n\}$, associate each word with the base n number derived from the subscripts. Thus, $\mathbf{a}_3\mathbf{a}_2\mathbf{a}_4$ is associated with 324, $\mathbf{a}_1$ with 1, and λ with 0. These associated numbers then imply a *lexicographic* ordering of Σ^*, with

$$\lambda < \mathbf{a}_1 < \mathbf{a}_2 < \mathbf{a}_3 < \cdots < \mathbf{a}_1\mathbf{a}_1 < \mathbf{a}_1\mathbf{a}_2 < \mathbf{a}_1\mathbf{a}_3 < \cdots < \mathbf{a}_2\mathbf{a}_1 < \mathbf{a}_2\mathbf{a}_2 < \cdots < \mathbf{a}_1\mathbf{a}_1\mathbf{a}_1 < \cdots$$

(a) Given an alphabet Σ, build a Turing machine that, given an input word x, will replace that word with the string that follows x in lexicographic order.

(b) Using the machine in part (a) as a submachine, build a Turing machine that will start with a blank tape and sequentially generate the words in Σ^* in lexicographic order, erasing the previous word as the following word is generated.

(c) Using the machine in part (a) as a submachine, build a Turing machine that will start with a blank tape and sequentially enumerate the words in Σ^* in lexicographic order, placing each successive word to the right of the previous word on the tape, separated by a blank.

(d) Explain how these techniques can be used in building a deterministic version of a nondeterministic Turing machine.

11.8. Define a *semi-infinite tape* as one that has a distinct left boundary but extends indefinitely to the right, such as those employed by DFAs.

(a) Given a Turing machine satisfying Definition 11.1, define an equivalent two-track Turing machine with a semi-infinite tape.

(b) Prove that your construction is equivalent to the original.

11.9. Let $\Sigma = \{\mathbf{a}\}$. Explicitly define a deterministic, one-tape, one-head Turing machine that will recognize $\{\mathbf{a}^n \mid n \text{ is a power of } 2\} = \{\mathbf{a}, \mathbf{aa}, \mathbf{aaaa}, \ldots\}$.

11.10. Define a three-head Turing machine that accepts $\{x \in \{\mathbf{a}, \mathbf{b}, \mathbf{c}\}^* \mid \ |x|_{\mathbf{a}} = |x|_{\mathbf{b}} = |x|_{\mathbf{c}}\}$.

Assume that all three heads start on the leftmost character. Is there any need for any of the heads to ever move left?

11.11. Let Σ be an alphabet. Prove that every context-free language is Turing-acceptable by providing the details for the construction discussed in Lemma 11.1.

11.12. Let Σ be an alphabet. Prove that every type 1 language is a LBL by providing the details for the construction discussed in Theorem 11.3.

11.13. Let $\mathsf{M} = <\Sigma, \Gamma, S, s_0, \delta>$ be a linear bounded automaton. Show how to convert M into a three-track automaton that never scans any cells but those containing the original word by:

(a) Explicitly defining the new alphabets.

(b) Explicitly defining the new transitions from the old. (*Hint:* From any state, an old transition "leaving" the word to scan one of the delimiters must return to the word in a unique manner.)

(c) Prove that for words of length at least 2 your new strict linear bounded automaton accepts exactly when M does.

11.14. By adding appropriate new symbols (of the form $\overline{\mathrm{b}}$) and suitable transitions:

(a) Modify the strict linear bounded automaton defined in Exercise 11.13 so that it correctly handles strings of length 1.

(b) Assume that a strict LBA that initially scans a blank is actually scanning an empty tape. If we expect to handle the empty string, we cannot insist that a strict linear bounded automaton never scan a cell that is not part of the input string, since the tape head must initially look at something. If we instead require that the tape head of a strict LBA may never *actively move to* a cell that is not part of the input string, then the dilemma is solved. Show that such a strict LBA can be found for any type 1 language.

11.15. Refer to Theorem 11.4 and show, by inducting on the number of transitions, that

$$(\forall s, t \in S \cup \{h\})(\forall \alpha, \beta, \gamma, \omega \in (\Sigma \cup \Gamma)^*)$$

$$(\alpha s \beta \overset{*}{\vdash} \gamma t \omega \ \ \textit{iff} \ \ (\exists i, j, m, n \in \mathbb{N})([\#^i \alpha s \beta \#^j] \overset{*}{\Rightarrow} [\#^m \gamma t \omega \#^n]))$$

11.16. State and prove the general induction statement needed to rigorously prove Theorem 11.5.

11.17. If $\mathsf{G} = <\Sigma, \Gamma, \mathrm{Z}, P>$ is a grammar for a type 0 language:

(a) Explain why the following construction may not accept $L(\mathsf{G})^*$: Choose a new start symbol W, and form $\mathsf{G}_* = <\Sigma, \Gamma \cup \{\mathrm{W}\}, \mathrm{W}, P \cup \{\mathrm{W} \to \lambda, \mathrm{W} \to \mathrm{WW}, \mathrm{W} \to \mathrm{Z}\}>$.

(b) Give an example of a grammar that illustrates this flaw.

(c) Given a type 0 grammar $\mathsf{G} = <\Sigma, \Gamma, \mathrm{Z}, P>$, define an appropriate grammar G_* that should accept the Kleene closure of $L(\mathsf{G})$.

(d) Prove that the construction defined in part (c) has the property that

$$L(\mathsf{G}_*) = L(\mathsf{G})^*.$$

11.18. Let Σ be an alphabet. Prove that $\mathcal{T}_\Sigma$ is closed under:

(a) Homomorphism

(b) Inverse homomorphism

(c) Concatenation

(d) Substitution

11.19. **(a)** Show that any Turing machine A_1 accepting $\mathrm{L} = L_1(\mathsf{A}_1)$ has an equivalent Turing machine A_2 for which $\mathrm{L} = L_2(\mathsf{A}_2)$ by explicitly modifying the quintuple for A_1 and proving that your construction behaves as desired.

(b) Show that any Turing machine A_2 accepting $\mathrm{L} = L_2(\mathsf{A}_2)$ has an equivalent Turing machine A_3 for which $\mathrm{L} = L_3(\mathsf{A}_3)$ by explicitly modifying the quintuple for A_2 and proving that your construction behaves as desired.

11.20. Let Σ be an alphabet. Prove that $\mathcal{O}_\Sigma$ is closed under:

(a) Homomorphism
(b) Inverse homomorphism
(c) Concatenation
(d) Substitution

CHAPTER

12

DECIDABILITY

In this chapter, the nature and limitations of algorithms are explored. We will first look at the general properties that can be ascertained about finite automata and FAD languages. For example, we might like to be able to enter the state transition table of a DFA into a suitably sized array and then run a program that determines whether the DFA was connected. An algorithm for checking this property was outlined in Chapter 3. Similarly, we have seen that it is possible to write a program to check whether an arbitrary DFA is minimal. We know this property can be reliably checked because we proved that the algorithms in Chapter 3 could be applied to ascertain the correct answer for virtually every conceivable DFA. There are an infinite number of DFAs about which the question can be posed, and yet our algorithm decides the question correctly in all cases. In the following section we consider questions that can be asked about more complex languages and machines.

In the latter part of this chapter, we will see that unlike the questions in Sections 12.1 and 12.2, there are some questions that are in a fundamental sense unanswerable in the general case. That is, there cannot exist an algorithm that correctly answers such a question in all cases. These questions will be called *undecidable*. An undecidable question about Pascal programs is considered in detail in Section 12.3 and is independent of advanced machine theory. The concept of undecidability is addressed formally in Section 12.4, and other undecidable problems are also presented.

12.1 DECIDABLE QUESTIONS ABOUT REGULAR LANGUAGES

Recall that a procedure is a finite set of instructions that unambiguously specifies deterministic, discrete steps for performing some task. In this chapter, the task will generally involve providing the correct answer to some yes–no question. Most questions that involve a numerical answer can be rephrased as a yes–no question of similar complexity. For example, the question "What is the minimum number of states necessary for a DFA to accept the language represented by the regular expression R?" has the yes–no analog "Does there exist a DFA with fewer than, say, five states that accepts the language represented by the regular expression R?" Clearly, if we can answer the first question, the second question is easy to answer. Conversely, if questions like the second one can be answered for any number we wish (rather than just five), then the answer to the first question can be deduced.

Recall also that an algorithm is a procedure that is guaranteed to halt in all instances. Note that "guaranteed to halt" does not mean that there is a fixed time limit on how long it may take to finish the procedure for all inputs; some instances may take far longer than others. For example, the question "Does there exist a DFA with fewer than ten states that accepts the language represented by $\mathbf{ab}(\mathbf{b} \cup \mathbf{c})^*$?" will probably take less time to answer than "Does there exist a DFA with fewer than ten states that accepts the language represented by $\mathbf{a}^*\mathbf{b}((\mathbf{b}^*\mathbf{d} \cup \mathbf{c}^*\mathbf{b})\mathbf{d} \cup \mathbf{e})^*$?"

It is important to keep in mind that algorithms are intended to provide a general solution to a vast array of similar problems and are (usually) not limited to a single specific instance. As an example, consider the task of sorting a file containing the three names:

Williams
Jones
Smith

A variety of sorting algorithms, when applied to this file, will produce the correct output. It is also possible to write a program that ignores its input and always prints the lines

Jones
Smith
Williams

This program does yield the correct answer for the particular problem we wished to solve, and indeed it solves the sorting problem for all files that contain exactly these three particular names in some arbitrary order (there are six such files). Thus, this trivial program is an algorithm that solves the sorting problem for these six specific instances. A slightly more complex program might be capable of printing two or three distinct answers, depending on the input, and thus solve the sorting problem for an even larger (but still finite) class of instances.

It should be clear that producing an algorithm that solves a finite set of instances is no great accomplishment, since these algorithms are guaranteed to exist. Such an algorithm could be programmed as one big `case` statement, which identifies the particular input instance and produces the corresponding output for that instance. Algorithms that apply to an infinite set of instances are of much more theoretical and practical interest.

∇ **Definition 12.1.** Given a set of *instances* and a yes–no *question* that can be applied to those instances, we will say that the question is *decidable* if there is an algorithm for determining in each instance the (correct) answer to the question. Δ

A more precise definition of decidability is presented in Section 12.4, based on the perceived relationship between Turing machines and algorithms. As mentioned earlier, if the set of instances is finite, an algorithm is guaranteed to exist, no matter how complex the question appears to be.

EXAMPLE 12.1

A typical set of instances might be the set of all deterministic finite automata over a given alphabet Σ; a typical question might be whether a given automaton accepts at least one string in Σ^*.

It is possible to devise an algorithm to correctly answer the question posed in Example 12.1 for every finite automaton $A = <\Sigma, S, s_0, \delta, F>$. The first idea that might come to mind is to simply look at strings from Σ^* in an orderly manner and use $\bar{\delta}$ to determine whether that string is accepted by A; if we find a string that does reach a final state, it is clear that the answer to the question should be "YES–$L(A) \neq \emptyset$," while if we never find a string that is accepted, the answer should be "NO–$L(A) = \emptyset$." This procedure is guaranteed to halt and give the correct answer if the language is indeed nonempty. However, the procedure will never halt and answer NO (in a finite amount of time) because there are an infinite number of strings in Σ^* that must be checked. A modification of this basic idea is necessary to produce a procedure that will halt under all circumstances (that is, to produce an *algorithm*).

∇ **Theorem 12.1.** Given any alphabet Σ and a DFA $A = <\Sigma, S, s_0, \delta, F>$, it is decidable whether $L(A) = \emptyset$.

Proof. Let $n = \|S\|$. Since both Σ and S are finite sets,

$$B = \{\lambda\} \cup \Sigma \cup \Sigma^2 \cup \cdots \cup \Sigma^{n-1}$$

is a finite set, and we can examine each string of this set and still have a procedure that halts. There is clearly an algorithm for determining the set C of all states that are reached by these few strings. Specifically,

$$C = \{\bar{\delta}(s_0, x) \mid x \in \Sigma^* \wedge |x| < n\} = \{\bar{\delta}(s_0, x) \mid x \in B\}.$$

Note that Theorem 2.7 implies that if a string (of *any* length) is accepted by A then there is another string of length less than n that is also accepted by A. Consequently, it is sufficient to examine only the "short" strings contained in B rather than examine all of Σ^*. If any of the strings in B lead to a final state (that is, if $C \cap F \neq \emptyset$), then the answer to the question is clearly "NO–L(A) is *not* empty," while if $C \cap F = \emptyset$, then Theorem 2.7 guarantees that "YES–L(A) *is* empty" is the correct answer. We have therefore constructed an algorithm (which computes C and then examines $C \cap F$, both of which can be done in a finite amount of time) for determining whether the language accepted by a given machine is empty.
Δ

The definition of C does not suggest the most efficient algorithm for calculating the set C; better strategies are available. The technique is similar to that employed to find the state equivalence relation E_A. C is actually the set of connected states S^c, which can be calculated recursively as indicated in Definition 3.10. Note that Theorem 12.1 answers the question posed in Example 12.1. The set of instances to which this question applies can easily be expanded. It can be shown that it is decidable whether $L(A) = \emptyset$ for any NDFA A by first employing Definition 4.5 to find the equivalent DFA A^d and then applying the method outlined in Theorem 12.1 to that machine. It is possible to find a much more efficient algorithm for answering this question that does not rely on the conversion to a DFA (see the exercises).

Just as the algorithm for converting an NDFA into a DFA allows the emptiness question to be answered for NDFAs, the techniques in Chapter 6 justify that the similar question for regular expressions is decidable. That is, since every regular expression has an equivalent DFA, the question of whether a regular expression describes any strings is clearly decidable. Similar extensions can be applied to most of the results in this section. Just as we can decide whether a DFA A accepts any strings, we can also decide if A accepts an infinity of strings, as shown by Theorem 12.2. This can be proved by a related appeal to Theorem 12.1, but an efficient algorithm for answering this question depends on the following lemma.

∇ **Lemma 12.1.** Let Σ be an alphabet, $A = <\Sigma, S, s_0, \delta, F>$ be a finite automaton, $n = \|S\|$, and $M = \{x \mid x \in L(A) \wedge |x| \geq n\}$. Then, if $M \neq \emptyset$, M must contain a string of minimal length (call it x_m), and furthermore $|x_m| < 2n$.

Proof. The proof is obtained by repeated application of the pumping lemma with $i = 0$ (see the exercises and Theorem 2.7).
Δ

A question similar to the one posed in Theorem 12.1 is "Does a given DFA accept a finite or an infinite number of strings?" This is also a decidable question, as demonstrated by the following theorem. The proof is based on the observation that a DFA A that accepts no strings of length greater than some fixed constant must by definition recognize a finite set, while the pumping lemma implies that if L(A) contains a sufficiently long string, then $L(\mathsf{A})$ must contain an infinite number of related strings.

∇ **Theorem 12.2.** Given any alphabet Σ and a DFA $\mathsf{A} = <\Sigma, S, s_0, \delta, F>$, it is decidable whether $L(\mathsf{A})$ is an infinite set.

Proof. Let $n = \|S\|$. Clearly, if A accepts no strings of length n or greater, then $L(\mathsf{A})$ is finite. From the pumping lemma, we know that if A accepts even one string of length equal to or greater than n, then A must accept an infinite number of strings. We still cannot check all the strings of length greater than n and have a procedure that halts, so Lemma 12.1 will be invoked to argue that if a long string is accepted by A, then a string whose length is in the range $n \leq |x| < 2n$ must be accepted, and it is therefore sufficient to check the strings in this limited range. Thus, our algorithm will consist of computing the intersection of $\{\overline{\delta}(s_0, y) \mid y \in \Sigma^* \wedge n \leq |y| < 2n\}$ and F. $L(\mathsf{A})$ is infinite ***iff*** this intersection is nonempty.
Δ

If we were to write a program that consulted the matrix containing the state transition table for A to actually determine $\{\overline{\delta}(s_0, y) \mid y \in \Sigma^* \wedge n \leq |y| < 2n\}$, it would be very inefficient to implement this computation as implied by the definition. Repeatedly looking up entries in the state transition table to determine $\overline{\delta}$ for each word in this large class of specified strings would involve an enormous duplication of effort. It is far better to recursively calculate $R_i = \{\overline{\delta}(s_0, x) \mid x \in \Sigma^i\}$, which represents the set of all states that can be reached by strings of length exactly i. This can be easily computed by defining $R_0 = \{s_0\}$ and using the recursive formula

$$R_{i+1} = \{\delta(s, \mathbf{a}) \mid \mathbf{a} \in \Sigma, s \in R_i\}$$

Successive sets can thereby be calculated from R_0. When R_n is reached, it is checked against F, and the algorithm halts and returns Yes if they have a common state. Otherwise, R_{n+1} through R_{2n-1} are checked, and No is returned if no final state appears in this group. This method is easily adaptable to nondeterministic finite automata by setting R_0 to be the set of all start states and adjusting the definition of R_{i+1} to conform to NDFA notation.

The involved arguments presented in Lemma 12.1 and the proof of Theorem 12.2 are necessary to justify that the above efficient recursive algorithm correctly answers the question of whether a finite automaton accepts an infinite number of strings. However, if we were simply interested in justifying that it is decidable whether $L(\mathsf{A})$ is infinite, it would have been much more convenient to simply adapt the result of Theorem 12.1. In particular, we could have easily built a DFA that accepts all strings of length at least n, form the "intersection" machine, and apply Theorem 12.1 to the new machine.

Specifically, if A is an n-state deterministic finite automaton, consider the DFA $\mathsf{A}_n = <\Sigma, \{r_0, r_1, r_2, \ldots, r_n\}, r_0, \delta_n, \{r_n\}>$, where δ_n is defined by

$$(\forall i = 0, 1, \ldots, n)(\forall \mathbf{a} \in \Sigma)(\delta_n(\mathrm{r}_i, \mathbf{a}) = \mathrm{r}_{max\{i+1,n\}})$$

It is easy to show that $L(\mathsf{A}_n) = \{x \in \Sigma^* \mid |x| \geq n\}$, and building $\mathsf{A}^\cap$ as specified in Lemma 5.1 produces a DFA for which $L(\mathsf{A}^\cap) = \{x \in L(\mathsf{A}) \mid |x| \geq n\}$. The question of whether $L(\mathsf{A})$ is infinite now becomes the question of whether $L(\mathsf{A}^\cap)$ is nonempty, which was shown to be decidable by Theorem 12.1.

An indication of the nature of the automaton A_n is given in Figure 12.1. The above argument provides a much shorter and clearer proof of Theorem 12.2, but it should not be construed to be the basis of an efficient algorithm. Forming the intersection of A and A_n involves well over n^2 states, and thus applying the technique described in Theorem 12.1 to $\mathsf{A}^\cap$ may involve more than n^2 iterations. For our purposes, we will henceforth be content to discover whether various tasks are merely possible and not be concerned with efficiency.

Figure 12.1 The automaton A_n

The following theorem answers a major question about DFAs: "Are two given deterministic finite automata equivalent?" At first glance, this appears to be a hard question; an initial strategy might be to check longer and longer strings, and answer "No, they are not equivalent" if a string is found that is accepted by one machine but is not accepted by the other. As in the proof of Theorems 12.1 and 12.2, we would again be faced with the task of determining when we could confidently stop checking strings and answer "Yes, they are equivalent."

Such a strategy can be made to work, but an easier method is again available. We are essentially checking whether the start state of the first machine treats strings differently than does the start state of the second machine. This problem was addressed in Chapter 3, and an algorithm that accomplished this sort of checking has already been presented. This observation provides the basis for the proof of the following theorem.

∇ **Theorem 12.3.** Given any alphabet Σ and two DFAs $\mathsf{A}_1 = <\Sigma, S_1, s_{0_1}, \delta_1, F_1>$ and $\mathsf{A}_2 = <\Sigma, S_2, s_{0_2}, \delta_2, F_2>$, it is decidable whether $L(\mathsf{A}_1) = L(\mathsf{A}_2)$.

Proof. Without loss of generality, assume that $S_1 \cap S_2 = \emptyset$, and construct a new DFA defined by $\mathsf{A} = <\Sigma, S_1 \cup S_2, s_{0_1}, \delta, F_1 \cup F_2>$, where

$$(\forall s \in S_1 \cup S_2)(\forall \mathbf{a} \in \Sigma)\ \delta(s, \mathbf{a}) = \begin{cases} \delta_1(s, \mathbf{a}), & \textit{iff } s \in S_1 \\ \delta_2(s, \mathbf{a}), & \textit{iff } s \in S_2 \end{cases}$$

Corollary 3.5 outlines the algorithm for constructing E_{A} for this machine, and it should be clear from the definition of A that $s_{0_1} E_{\mathsf{A}} s_{0_2} \Leftrightarrow L(\mathsf{A}_1) = L(\mathsf{A}_2)$.

EXAMPLE 12.2

Consider the two machines A_1 and A_2 displayed in Figure 12.2. The machine A constructed according to Theorem 12.3 would look like the diagram inside the dotted box shown in Figure 12.3. This new machine is very definitely disconnected, and in this example s_{0_1} is not related to s_{0_2} by E_A since these two states treat **ab** differently (**ab** is accepted by A_1 and rejected by A_2). The reader is encouraged to generate another example using two equivalent machines, and verify that the two original start states would indeed be related by E_A.

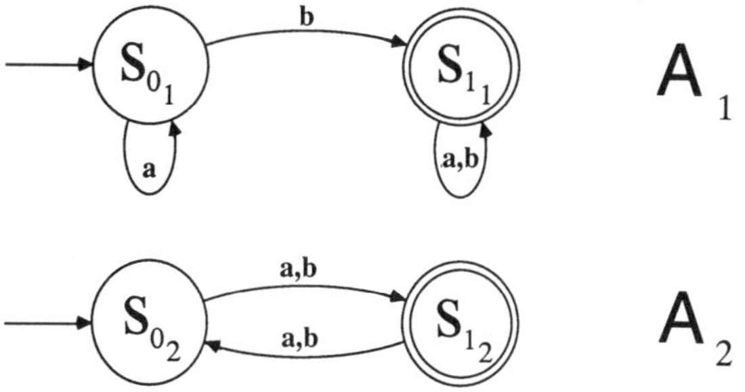

Figure 12.2 The automata discussed in Example 12.2

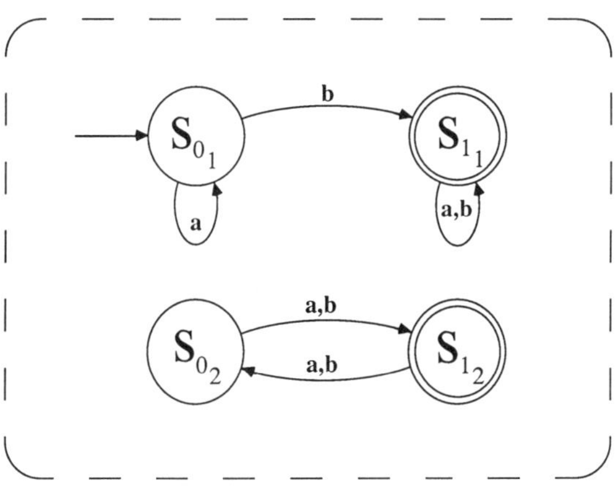

Figure 12.3 The composite machine discussed in Example 12.2

The following theorem explores the relationship between the complexity of a given regular expression and the size of the corresponding minimal DFA.

∇ **Theorem 12.4.** Given any alphabet Σ and a regular expression R over Σ, it is decidable whether there exists a DFA with fewer than five final states that accepts the language described by R.

Proof. Given R, Lemma 6.2 indicates the algorithm (generated by the constructions presented in Theorems 5.2, 5.4, and 5.5) for building some NDFA that accepts the regular set corresponding to R. Definition 4.5 outlines the algorithm for

converting this NDFA into a DFA. Theorem 3.7 and Corollary 3.5 indicate the algorithms for minimizing this DFA. Counting the number of final states in this minimal machine will allow the question to be answered correctly.
Δ

The careful reader may have noticed that the minimal machine described in Chapters 2 and 3 was only advertised to have the minimum *total* number of states and has not yet been guaranteed to have the smallest number of *final* states (perhaps there is an equivalent machine with many more nonfinal states but fewer final states). An investigation of the relationship between the final states of the minimal machine and the equivalence classes comprising the right congruence generated by this language will show that no equivalent machine can have fewer final states than the minimal machine has (see the exercises).

The proofs of Theorems 12.3 and 12.4 are good examples of using existing algorithms to build new algorithms. This technique should be applied whenever possible in the following exercises. It is certainly useful in resolving the following question about grammars.

Given two right linear grammars $G_1 = <\Omega_1, \Sigma, S_1, P_1>$ and $G_2 = <\Omega_2, \Sigma, S_2, P_2>$, it is clearly *decidable* whether G_2 is equivalent to G_1. An algorithm can be formed that simply:

1. Uses the construction presented in Lemma 8.2 to find A_{G_1} and A_{G_2}.
2. Converts these NDFAs to two DFAs called A_1 and A_2.
3. Appeals to the algorithm presented in Theorem 12.3 to correctly answer the question.

A trivial extension of this idea proves the following theorem.

∇ **Theorem 12.5.** It is decidable whether two given regular grammars $G_1 = <\Omega_1, \Sigma, S_1, P_1>$ and $G_2 = <\Omega_2, \Sigma, S_2, P_2>$ are equivalent.

Proof. See the exercises.
Δ

Most of the decidability questions we have asked about languages recognized by finite automata or described by regular expressions can also be answered for languages generated by grammars through a similar transformation of existing algorithms. Such algorithms are generally not the most efficient ones available, and it can often be instructive to develop a new method from scratch. This is especially true of the following question, which has no analog in the realms of finite automata or regular expressions.

∇ **Theorem 12.6.** It is decidable whether a given right-linear grammar $G = <\Omega, \Sigma, S, P>$ contains any useless nonterminals.

Proof. Recall that a nonterminal is *useless* if it can never appear in the derivation of *any* valid terminal string. Essentially, only two things can prevent a nonterminal X from being effectively used somewhere in a valid derivation: either X can never appear as part of a partial derivation that begins with only the start symbol (no matter how many productions we apply), or, once X is generated, it can never lead to a valid *terminal* string.

Finding the members of Ω that *can* be produced from S is a simple recursive procedure: Begin with $Z_0 = \{S\}$ and form Z_1 by adding to Z_0 all the nonterminals that appear on the right side of productions that are used to replace S. Then form Z_2 by adding to Z_1 all the nonterminals that appear on the right side of productions that are used to replace members of Z_1, and so on. More formally:

$$Z_0 = \{S\}$$

and for $i \geq 1$,

$$Z_{i+1} = Z_i \cup \{Y \in \Omega \mid (\exists x \in \Sigma^*)(\exists T \in Z_i) \ni T \to xY \text{ is a production in } P\}$$

Clearly, $Z_0 \subseteq Z_1 \subseteq \cdots \subseteq Z_n \subseteq \cdots \subseteq \Omega$, and as was shown for similar collections of nested entities (such as $E_{0A}, E_{1A}, \ldots$ in Chapter 3), after a finite number of steps we will reach the point where $Z_m = Z_{m+1}$ and Z_m will then represent the set of *all* nonterminals that can be reached from the start symbol S.

In a similar fashion, we can generate another nested sequence of sets $W_0, W_1, \ldots,$ where W_i represents the set of all nonterminals that can produce a *terminal* string in i or fewer steps. We are again guaranteed to reach a point where $W_n = W_{n+1}$, and W_n will indeed be the set of all nonterminals that can *ever* produce a valid terminal string.

$Z_m \cap W_n$ is thus the set of all use*ful* members of Ω, and $\Omega - (Z_m \cap W_n)$ is therefore the set of all useless nonterminals.

Δ

EXAMPLE 12.3

$G_4 = <\{S, A, B, C, V, W, X\}, \{\mathbf{a}, \mathbf{b}, \mathbf{c}\}, S, \{S \to \mathbf{ab}A \mid \mathbf{bb}B \mid \mathbf{cc}V, A \to \mathbf{b}C \mid \mathbf{c}X, B \to \mathbf{ab}, C \to \lambda \mid \mathbf{c}S, V \to \mathbf{a}V \mid \mathbf{c}X, W \to \mathbf{aa} \mid \mathbf{a}W, X \to \mathbf{b}V \mid \mathbf{aa}X\}>$ contains three useless nonterminals, V, W, and X. Recursively calculating the sets described in the above proof yields:

$$Z_0 = \{S\} \qquad W_0 = \{\ \}$$

$$Z_1 = \{S, A, B, V\} \qquad W_1 = \{C, B, W\}$$

$$Z_2 = \{S, A, B, V, C, X\} \qquad W_2 = \{C, B, W, A, S\}$$

$$Z_3 = \{S, A, B, V, C, X\} \qquad W_3 = \{C, B, W, A, S\}$$

Thus W cannot be generated from the start symbol, and V and X cannot produce terminal strings. The use*ful* symbols are $Z_2 \cap W_2 = \{S, A, B, C\}$.

The techniques employed here should look somewhat familiar. They involve iteration methods similar to those developed in Chapter 3. In fact, it is possible to apply the connectivity algorithms for nondeterministic finite automata to this problem by transforming the right-linear grammar G into the NDFA A_G, as defined in the proof of Lemma 8.1. The automaton corresponding to the grammar in Example 12.3 is shown in Figure 12.4. Note that the state labeled <W> is inaccessible, which means that it cannot be reached from <S>. This indicates that there is no sequence of productions starting with the start symbol S that will produce a string containing W.

Checking whether a nonterminal such as V can produce a terminal string is tantamount to checking whether the language accepted by A_G^V is nonempty, where A_G^V is A_G with the start state moved to the state labeled <V>. Since both $L(A_G^V)$ and $L(A_G^X)$ are empty, V and X are useless.

12.2 OTHER DECIDABLE QUESTIONS

It is fairly easy to find succinct algorithms that answer most of the reasonable questions one might ask about representations of regular languages. For each of the more complex classes of languages, there are many reasonable questions that are not decidable. Several of these will be presented in the following sections. In this section, we consider some of the answerable questions that can be asked about the more robust machines and grammars.

∇ **Theorem 12.7.** Given any context-free grammar G, it is decidable whether $L(G) = \emptyset$.

Proof. In Theorem 9.3, a scheme was presented that specified how to build several automata that would be used to identify the useless nonterminals in $G = <\Sigma, \Gamma, S, P>$. Since $L(G) = \emptyset$ ***iff*** the start symbol S is useless, there is an algorithm for testing whether $L(G) = \emptyset$.
Δ

It is also possible to tell whether a context-free grammar generates a finite or an infinite number of distinct words. The proof is based on the same principle that was employed in the pumping theorem proof: the presence of long strings implies that some useful nonterminal A must derive a nontrivial sentential form containing A. The start state S must produce a useful sentential form containing A, and A can then be used to generate an infinite series of distinct strings.

∇ **Theorem 12.8.** Given any context-free grammar G, it is decidable whether $L(G)$ is infinite.

Proof. Let $G = <\Sigma, \Gamma, S, P>$ be a context-free grammar. By Theorem 9.5, there exists a Chomsky normal form grammar $G' = <\Sigma, \Gamma', S, P'>$ that is equiv-

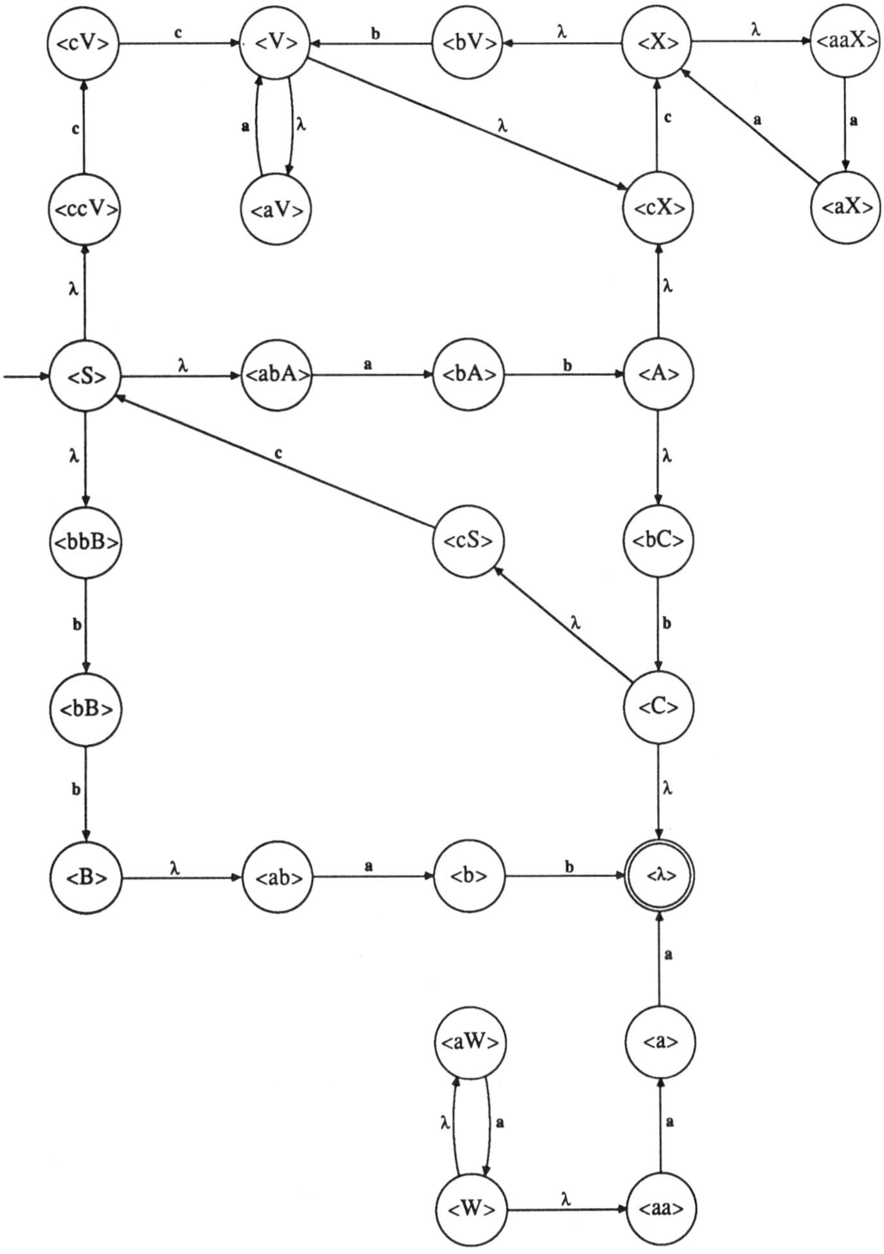

Figure 12.4 The automaton discussed in Example 12.3

alent to G. Let $n = 2^{|\Gamma'|}$. By Theorem 9.7, any string in L(G) of length n or greater can be pumped and will imply that L(G) is infinite. An argument similar to that of Lemma 12.1 will show that it is sufficient to check strings in the set $\{y \mid y \in \Sigma^* \wedge n \leq |y| < 2n\}$ for membership in L(G). There are only a finite number of derivation sequences that can produce words in this range. The algorithm for determining whether L(G) is infinite will check whether

$$\{y \mid y \in L(\mathrm{G}) \wedge n \leq |y| < 2n\}$$

is empty; if so, L(G) is finite, and L(G) is infinite otherwise.
Δ

The exercises explore more efficient methods for searching for a string that can be pumped. The intimate correspondence between context-free grammars and pushdown automata guarantees that similar questions about PDAs are decidable.

∇ **Corollary 12.1.** Given any pushdown automaton P, it is decidable whether:

a. L(P) is empty.
b. L(P) is finite.
c. L(P) is infinite.

Proof. By Theorem 10.3, every PDA P has a corresponding context-free grammar G_P. The algorithms described in Theorems 12.7 and 12.8 can be applied to G_P to determine the nature of $L(G_P)$, and since $L(P) = L(G_P)$, the same questions about P are likewise decidable.
Δ

Given a particular word x and a context-free grammar G, it is decidable whether x can be generated by G. In fact, this question can be decided for context-sensitive grammars, too. The proof heavily relies on the fact that no sentential form longer than x can possibly generate x in the absence of contracting productions in the grammar.

∇ **Theorem 12.9.** Given any context-sensitive grammar G and any word x, it is decidable whether $x \in L$(G).

Proof. Let $G = \langle\Sigma, \Gamma, S, P\rangle$ be a context-sensitive grammar and let $x \in \Sigma^*$. It is possible to construct a (finite) graph and apply existing algorithms from graph theory to answer the question of whether G generates x. The nodes of the graph will correspond to the strings from $(\Sigma \cup \Gamma)^*$ of length n or less. The (directed) edges from a node representing a given sentential form w lead to the strings (of length n or less) that can be generated from w by applying a single production from P. Both the sentential form x and S will appear in this graph, and the question of whether $x \in L$(G) is equivalent to the question of whether there is a path from S to x. There

are many standard algorithms for determining paths and components in a graph, and thus the question of whether $x \in \boldsymbol{L}(\mathrm{G})$ is decidable.
Δ

The generation of all the edges in the graph generally involves more effort than is needed to answer the question. A more efficient method is similar to the recursive calculations used to find the set of connected states in a DFA. Beginning with {S}, the production set P can be consulted to determine the labels of nodes that can be derived from S in one step. These new labels can be added to the set of accessible sentential forms, and the added nodes can be checked until no new labels are found. The set of sentential forms will then consist of

$$\{w \in (\Sigma \cup \Gamma)^* \mid S \stackrel{*}{\Rightarrow} w \wedge |w| \leq n\}$$

and contain all words in $\boldsymbol{L}(\mathrm{G})$ of length $\leq n$. If we are only interested in the specific word x, then the algorithm can return Yes as soon as x appears in the set of accessible sentential forms and would return No if x did not appear by the time the set stopped growing.

The above algorithm will suffice for any grammar that does not contain contracting productions, but can clearly give the wrong answers when applied to type 0 grammars. Since the length of sentential forms can both grow and shrink in unrestricted grammars, the word x may actually be generated by a sequence of productions that at some point generates a sentential form longer than x. Such a sequence would not be considered by the method outlined in Theorem 12.9, and the algorithm might answer No when the correct answer is Yes. We could define a procedure that looked at larger and larger graphs (consisting of more and longer sentential forms), which would halt and answer Yes if a derivation sequence for x was discovered. If x actually can be generated by G, this method will eventually uncover the appropriate sequence. We therefore have a procedure that will reliably tell us if a word can be generated by an unrestricted grammar. Unless we include a specification of when to stop and answer No, this procedure is not an algorithm. In later sections, we will see that it is *impossible* to determine, for an arbitrary type 0 grammar G, if an arbitrary word x is not generated by G. The question of whether $x \in \boldsymbol{L}(\mathrm{G})$ is not decidable for arbitrary grammars.

It turns out that there are many reasonable questions such as this one that cannot be determined algorithmically. We begin our overview of undecidable problems with an analysis of a very reasonable question concerning Pascal programs. Subsequent sections consider undecidable questions concerning the grammars and machines covered in this text.

12.3 AN UNDECIDABLE PROBLEM

Having now developed a false sense of security about our ability to produce algorithms for determining many properties about machines and languages, we now step back and see whether there is anything we cannot do algorithmically. A simple counting argument will show that there are too many things to calculate and not enough algorithms with which to calculate them all. It may be helpful to review the section on cardinality in Chapter 0 and recall that there are different orders of infinity. A diagonalization argument showed that the natural numbers could not be put in one-to-one correspondence with the real numbers; there are simply too many real numbers to allow such a matching to occur. A similar mismatch occurs when comparing the (countable) number of algorithms to the (uncountable) number of possible yes–no functions.

By definition, an algorithm is a *finite* list of instructions, written over some finite character set. As such, there are only a countable number of different algorithms that can be written. It may be helpful to consider the set of all Pascal programs and view each file that contains the ASCII code for a program, which is essentially a sequence of zeros and ones, as one very long binary integer. Clearly, an infinite number of Pascal programs can be written, but no more programs than there are binary integers, so the number of such files is indeed countable.

Now consider the possible lists of answers that could be given to questions involving a countable number of instances. We will argue that there are an uncountable number of yes–no patterns that might describe the answers to such questions. Notice that the descriptions for automata, grammars, and the like are also finite, and thus there are a countable number of DFAs, a countable number of grammars, and so on, that can be described. The questions we asked in the previous sections were therefore applied to a countable number of instances, and these instances could be ordered in some well-defined way, much as the natural numbers are ordered. If we think of a yes response corresponding to the digit 1 and a no response corresponding to 0, then the corresponding series of answers to a particular question can be thought of as an unending sequence of 0s and 1s. By placing a decimal point at the beginning of the sequence, each such pattern can be thought of as a binary fraction, representing a real number between $.00000\ldots = 0$ and $.111111\ldots = 1$. Conversely, each such real number in this range represents a sequence of yes–no answers to some question. Since there are an uncountable number of real numbers between 0 and 1, there are an uncountable number of answers that might be of interest to us. Some of these answers cannot be obtained by algorithms, since there are not enough algorithms to go around. Thus, there must be many questions that are not decidable.

It is not immediately apparent that the existence of undecidable questions is much of a drawback; perhaps all the "interesting" questions are decidable. After all, there are an uncountable number of real numbers, yet all computers and many humans seem to make do with just the countable number of rational numbers. Unfortunately, there are many simple and meaningful questions that are undecidable. We discuss one such question now; others are considered in the next section.

Just about every programmer has had the experience of running a program that never produces any output and never shows any sign of halting. For programs that are fairly short, this is usually not a problem. For major projects that are expected to take a very long time, there comes an agonizing moment when we have to give up hope that it is on the verge of producing a useful answer and stop the program on the assumption that it has entered an infinite loop. While it would be very nice to have a utility that would look over a program and predict how long it would run, most of us would settle for a device that would simply predict whether or not it will ever halt.

It's a good bet that you have never used such a device, which may at first seem strange since a solution to the halting problem would certainly provide information that would often be useful. If you have never thought about this before, you might surmise that the scarcity of such programs is a consequence of any one of several limiting factors. Perhaps they are inordinately expensive to run, or no one has taken the time to implement an existing scheme, or perhaps no one has yet figured out how to develop the appropriate algorithms. In actuality, no one is even looking for a "halting" algorithm, since no such algorithm can possibly exist.

Let us consider the implications that would arise if such an algorithm could be programmed in, say, Pascal. We can consider such an algorithm to be implemented as a Boolean function called HALT, which looks at whatever program happens to be in the file named data.p and returns the value TRUE if that program will halt, and returns FALSE if the program in data.p would never halt. Perhaps this function is general enough to look at source code for many different languages, but we will see that it is impossible for it to simply respond correctly even when looking solely at Pascal programs.

The programmer of the function HALT would likely have envisioned it to be used in a program such as CHECK, shown in Figure 12.5. We will use it in a slightly different way and show that a contradiction arises if HALT really did solve the halting problem. Our specific assumptions are that:

1. HALT is written in Pascal.
2. HALT always gives a correct answer to the halting problem, which means:
   a. It always returns an answer after a finite amount of time.
   b. The answer returned is FALSE if the Pascal program in data.p would never halt.
   c. The answer returned is TRUE if the Pascal program in data.p would halt (or if the program in data.p will not compile).

Consider the program TEST in Figure 12.6, which is structured so that it will run forever if the function HALT indicates that the program in the file data.p would halt, and simply quits if HALT indicates that the program in data.p would not halt. Some interesting things happen if we run this program after putting a copy of the source code for TEST in data.p.

If HALT does not produce an answer, then HALT certainly does not behave as advertised, and we have an immediate contradiction. HALT is supposed to be an algorithm, so it must eventually return with an answer. Since HALT is a Boolean function, we have only two cases to consider.

```
program CHECK;
{ envisioned usage of HALT }
   function HALT:boolean;
   begin
      { marvelous code goes here }
   end { HALT }

begin { CHECK }
if HALT then
   writeln('The program in file data.p will halt')
else
   writeln('The program in file data.p will not halt')
end { CHECK }.
```

Figure 12.5 A possible usage of HALT

Case 1: HALT returns a value of TRUE to the calling program TEST. This has two consequences, the first of which is implied by the asserted behavior of HALT.

i. If halt does what it is supposed to do, this means that the program in data.p halts. We ran this program with the source code for TEST in data.p, so TEST must actually halt.

The second consequence comes from examining the code for TEST, and noting what happens when HALT returns TRUE.

ii. The `if` statement in the program TEST then causes the infinite loop to be entered, and TEST runs forever, doing nothing particularly useful.

Our two consequences are that TEST halts and TEST does not halt. This is a clear contradiction, and so case 1 never occurs.

Case 2: HALT returns a value of FALSE to the calling program TEST. This likewise has two consequences. Considering the advertised behavior of HALT, this must mean that the program in data.p, TEST, must not halt. However, the code for TEST shows that if HALT returns FALSE we execute the `else` statement, write one line, and then stop. TEST therefore halts. TEST must again both halt and not halt.

Whichever way we turn, we reach a contradiction. The only possible conclusion is that the function HALT does not behave as advertised. It must either return no answer, or give an incorrect answer.

It should be clear that the problem cannot be fixed by having the programmer who proposed the function HALT fiddle with the code; the above contradiction will be reached regardless of what code appears between the `begin` and `end` statements in the function HALT. We have shown that any such proposed function is *guaranteed* to behave inappropriately when fed a program such as TEST. In actuality,

```
program TEST;
{ to be placed in the file data.p }
var FOREVER: boolean;
   function HALT : boolean;
   begin
      { marvelous code goes here }
   end; { HALT }

begin { TEST }
FOREVER := false;
if HALT then
   repeat
      FOREVER := false;
   until FOREVER
else
   writeln('This program halts')
end { TEST }.
```

Figure 12.6 Another program incorporating HALT

there are an infinite number of programs that cause HALT to misbehave, but it was sufficient to demonstrate just one failure to justify that no such function can solve the general problem.

The above argument demonstrates that the *halting problem* for Pascal programs is *undecidable* or *unsolvable*. That is, there does not exist a Pascal program that can always decide correctly, when fed an arbitrary Pascal program, whether that program halts.

If we were to define an algorithm as "something that can be programmed in Pascal," we would have shown that there is no algorithm for deciding whether an arbitrary Pascal program halts. One might suspect that this is therefore not a very satisfying definition of what an algorithm is, since we have a concise, well-stated problem that cannot be solved using Pascal. It is generally agreed that the problem does not lie with some overlooked feature that was inadvertently not incorporated into Pascal. Clearly, all programming languages suffer from similar inadequacies. For example, an argument similar to the one presented for Pascal would show that no C program can be devised that can tell which C programs can halt. Thus, no other programming language can provide a more robust definition of what an algorithm is.

There are variations on this theme that likewise lead to contradictions. Might there be a Pascal program that can check which C programs can halt? If you believe that every Pascal program can be rewritten as an equivalent C program, the answer is definitely no; a Pascal program that checks C programs could then be rewritten as a C program (which checks C programs), and we again reach a contradiction.

It is generally agreed that the limitations do not arise from some correctable inadequacy in our current methods of implementing algorithms. That is, the limitations of algorithmic solutions seem to be inherent in the nature of algorithms. Programming languages, Turing machines, grammars, and all other proposed systems for implementing algorithms have been shown to be subject to the same limitations in computational power. The use of Turing machines to implement algorithms has several implications that apply to the theory of languages. These are explored in the following sections.

12.4 TURING DECIDABILITY

In the previous section, we saw that no Pascal program could always correctly predict when another Pascal program would halt. A similar statement was true for C programs, and Turing machines, considered as computing devices, are no different; no Turing machine solves the halting problem.

Each of us is probably familiar with the way in which a Pascal program reads a file, and hence it is not hard to imagine a Pascal program that reacts to the code for another Pascal program. As long as the input alphabet contains at least two symbols, encodings can be defined for the structure of a Turing machine, which allows the blueprint for its finite state control to be placed on the input tape of another Turing machine. A binary encoding might be given for the number of states, followed by codes that enumerate the moves from each of the states. Just as we are not presently concerned about the exact ASCII codes that define the individual characters in a file containing a Pascal program, we need not be concerned with the specific representation used to encode a Turing machine on an input tape.

Consider input tapes that contain the encoding of a Turing machine, followed by some delimiter, followed by an input word. Assume there exists a Turing machine H that, given such an encoding of an arbitrary machine and an input word, always correctly predicts whether the Turing machine represented by that encoding halts for that particular word. This assumption leads to a contradiction exactly as shown in the last section for Pascal programs. We would be able to use the machine H as a submachine in another Turing machine that halts exactly when it is not supposed to halt, and thereby show that H cannot possibly behave properly.

∇ **Theorem 12.10.** Given a Turing machine M and a word w, it is undecidable whether M halts when the string w is placed on the input tape.

Proof. The proof is essentially the same argument that was presented in the last section.

Δ

We will see that the unsolvability of the halting problem will imply that it is not decidable whether a given string will cause a Turing machine to halt and print **Y**. If a word is accepted, this fact can eventually be discovered, but we cannot reliably tell which words are rejected by an arbitrary Turing machine. If we could, we would have an algorithm for computing the complement of any Turing-acceptable language. In the next section, we will show that there are Turing-acceptable languages that have complements that are not Turing-acceptable, which means that a general algorithm for computing complements cannot exist.

A problem equivalent to the halting problem involves the question of whether an arbitrary type 0 grammar accepts a given word. This can be seen to be almost the same question as was asked of Turing machines.

∇ **Theorem 12.11.** Given a type 0 grammar G and a word w, it is undecidable whether G generates w.

Proof. If this question were decidable, it would provide an algorithm for solving the halting problem, which is known to be undecidable. That is, if there existed an algorithm for deciding whether $w \in L(G)$, there would also be an algorithm for deciding whether w is accepted by a Turing machine. The Turing machine algorithm would operate as follows:

Given an arbitrary Turing machine M, modify M to produce M′, an equivalent machine that halts only when it accepts. Use Definition 11.8 to find the corresponding type 0 grammar $G_{M'}$, which is also equivalent to M. The algorithm that predicts whether $w \in L(G_{M'})$ can now be used to decide whether M halts on input w.

This scheme would therefore solve the halting problem for an arbitrary Turing machine, and hence the algorithm that predicts whether $w \in L(G)$ cannot exist. Thus, $w \in L(G)$ is undecidable for arbitrary type 0 grammars.
Δ

Given the intimate correspondence between Turing machines and type 0 grammars, it is perhaps not surprising that it is just as hard to solve the membership question for type 0 grammars as it was to solve the halting problem for Turing machines. We now consider a question that may initially appear to be more tractable than the halting problem. However, it will be shown to be unsolvable by the same reasoning used in the last theorem: if this question could be decided, then the halting problem would be decidable.

∇ **Theorem 12.12.** Given an arbitrary Turing machine T, it is undecidable whether T accepts λ.

Proof. Assume that there exists an algorithm for deciding whether T accepts λ. That is, assume that there exists a Turing machine X that, when fed an encoding of any Turing machine T, halts with **Y** when T would accept λ and halts with **N** whenever T rejects λ. X can then be used to determine whether an arbitrary Turing machine M would accept an arbitrary word x. Given a machine M and a string x, it is easy to modify M to produce a new Turing machine T_{M_x}, which accepts λ exactly when M accepts x. T_{M_x} is formed by adding a new start state that checks whether the read head is initially scanning a blank (that is, if λ is on the input tape). If not, control remains in this state, and T_{M_x} never halts. However, if the initially scanned symbol is a blank, new states are used to write x on the input tape and return the read head to the leftmost symbol of x. Control then passes to the original start state of M. In this manner, T_{M_x} accepts λ exactly when M accepts x.

This correspondence makes it possible to use the Turing machine X as a submachine in another Turing machine X_H that solves the halting problem. That is, given an input tape with an encoding of a machine M followed by the symbols for a word x, X_H can be easily programmed to modify the encoding of M to produce the encoding of T_{M_x} and leave this new encoding on the input tape before passing control to the submachine X. X_H then accepts exactly when T_{M_x} accepts λ, which happens exactly when M halts on input x. X_H would therefore represent an algorithm for solving the halting problem, which we know cannot exist. The portion of the machine that modifies the encoding of M is quite elementary, so it must be the submachine X that cannot exist. Thus, there is no algorithm that can accomplish the task for which X was designed, that is, determining whether an arbitrary Turing machine T accepts the empty string.
Δ

The conclusion that X was the portion of X_H that behaves improperly is akin to the observation in the previous section that the main part of the Pascal program TEST was valid, and hence it must be the function HALT that behaves incorrectly.

12.5 TURING-DECIDABLE LANGUAGES

We now consider languages whose criteria for membership is related to the halting problem. Define the language D to be those words that either are not encodings of Turing machines or are encodings of machines that would halt with **Y** when presented with their own encoding on their input tape. The language D is Turing acceptable, since a multitape machine could copy the input word to a second tape, check whether the encoding truly represented a valid Turing machine, and then use the "directions" on the second tape to simulate the action of the encoded machine on the original input. The multitape machine would halt with **Y** if the encoding was invalid or if the simulated machine ever accepts.

On the other hand, the complement of D is not Turing acceptable. Let U be the set of all valid encodings of Turing machines that do *not* halt when fed their own encodings. Then U = ~D, and there does not exist a machine T for which $L(\mathsf{T}) = \mathrm{U}$. If such a machine existed, it would have an encoding, and this leads to the same problem encountered with the HALT function in Pascal. This encoding of T is either a word in U or is not a word in U; both cases lead to contradictions. If the encoding of T belongs to U, then by definition of U it does not halt when fed its own encoding. But the assumption that $L(\mathsf{T}) = \mathrm{U}$ requires that T halt with **Y** for all encodings belonging to U, which means T must halt when fed its own encoding. A similar contradiction is also reached if the encoding of T does not belong to U. Therefore, no such Turing machine T can exist, and U is an example of a language that is not Turing-acceptable.

We have finally found a language that is not type 0. A counting argument would have shown that, since there are only a countable number of type 0 grammars and an uncountable number of subsets of Σ^*, there had to be many languages over Σ that are not in $\mathfrak{L}_\Sigma$ ($= \mathcal{T}_\Sigma$). We now see that some of these unrepresentable languages are meaningful sets for which it would be quite desirable to be able to recognize or generate.

∇ **Theorem 12.13.** If $\|\Sigma\| \geq 2$, then $\mathcal{T}_\Sigma$ is not closed under complementation.

Proof. Encodings of arbitrary Turing machines can be effectively accomplished with only two distinct symbols in the alphabet. The Turing-acceptable language D described above has a complement U that is not Turing-acceptable.
Δ

Our original criteria for belonging to the language L accepted by a Turing machine M implied that M would eventually halt when presented with any word in L, but we had no guarantees about how M will behave when presented with a word that is not in L. M may halt with **N** on the tape, or M may run forever. Indeed, we have just seen a Turing-acceptable language for which this will be the best we can hope for. Turing machines therefore embody *procedures*, which are essentially a deterministic set of step-by-step instructions. We now consider the languages accepted by the subclass of Turing machines that correspond to *algorithms*, procedures that are guaranteed to eventually halt under all circumstances.

∇ **Definition 12.2.** Let Σ be an alphabet. Define $\mathcal{H}_\Sigma$ to be the collection of all languages that can be recognized by Turing machines that halt on all input.
Δ

Languages in $\mathcal{H}_\Sigma$ are called *Turing-decidable* languages. A trivial modification shows that $L \in \mathcal{H}_\Sigma$ if there exists a Turing machine that not only halts upon placing a **Y** after the input word on an otherwise blank tape for accepted words, but similarly preserves the input word and prints **N** for each rejected string. Such devices will be referred to as *halting* Turing machines.

∇ **Theorem 12.14.** $\mathcal{H}_\Sigma$ is closed under complementation.

Proof. Let L be a Turing-decidable language. Then there must exist a Turing machine H for which $\boldsymbol{L}(\mathsf{H}) = L$ and that halts with **Y** or **N** for all strings in Σ^*. The finite-state control of H can be easily modified to produce a Turing machine H′ for which $\boldsymbol{L}(\mathsf{H}') = \sim L$. All that is required is to replace every transition in H that prints **N** with a similar transition that prints **Y** and likewise make sure that **N** will be printed by H′ whenever H prints **Y**.
Δ

This result has some immediate consequences.

∇ **Corollary 12.2.** There is a language that is Turing acceptable but not Turing decidable. That is, $\mathcal{H}_\Sigma \subset \mathcal{T}_\Sigma$.

Proof. Definition 12.2 implies that $\mathcal{H}_\Sigma \subseteq \mathcal{T}_\Sigma$. By Theorems 12.13 and 12.14, these two classes have different closure properties, and thus they cannot be equal. Therefore, $\mathcal{H}_\Sigma \subset \mathcal{T}_\Sigma$.
Δ

Actually, we have already seen a language that is Turing acceptable but not Turing decidable. D was shown to be Turing acceptable, but if D were Turing decidable, then its complement would be Turing decidable by Theorem 12.14. However, $\sim$D = U, and U is definitely not Turing decidable since it is not even Turing acceptable.

$\mathcal{O}_\Sigma$, the context-sensitive languages, is another subclass of $\mathcal{T}_\Sigma$. It is possible to determine how $\mathcal{H}_\Sigma$ relates to $\mathcal{O}_\Sigma$ and thereby insert $\mathcal{H}_\Sigma$ into the language hierarchy.

∇ **Corollary 12.3.** Every context-sensitive language is Turing decidable. That is, $\mathcal{O}_\Sigma \subseteq \mathcal{H}_\Sigma$.

Proof. This is actually a corollary of Theorem 12.9. Given a type 1 language L, there is a context-sensitive grammar G that generates L. The proof of Theorem 12.9 presented an algorithm for determining whether an arbitrary word can be generated by G. This algorithm can be implemented as a Turing machine T_G that can determine whether a given word can be generated by G and always halts with the correct answer. Thus, L is Turing decidable.
Δ

These implications provide the missing element in the proof of Theorem 11.10, as stated in the next corollary.

∇ **Corollary 12.4.** The class of context-sensitive languages is properly contained in the class of Turing acceptable languages. That is, $\mathcal{O}_\Sigma \subset \mathcal{T}_\Sigma$.

Proof. By the previous corollaries, $\mathcal{O}_\Sigma \subseteq \mathcal{H}_\Sigma$ and $\mathcal{H}_\Sigma \subset \mathcal{T}_\Sigma$.
Δ

Actually, the context-sensitive languages are properly contained in $\mathcal{H}_\Sigma$. This will be shown by exhibiting a language that is recognized by a Turing machine that halts on all inputs, but that cannot be generated by any context-sensitive language. The following proof, based on diagonalization, should by now look familiar.

∇ **Theorem 12.15.** Let Σ be an alphabet for which $\|\Sigma\| \geq 2$. There is a language that is Turing decidable but not context sensitive. That is, $\mathcal{O}_\Sigma \subset \mathcal{H}_\Sigma$.

Proof. By Corollary 12.3, $\mathcal{O}_\Sigma \subseteq \mathcal{H}_\Sigma$, and it remains to be shown that there is a member of $\mathcal{H}_\Sigma$ that is not a member of $\mathcal{O}_\Sigma$. By the technique described in Theorem

12.9, every context-sensitive grammar can be represented by a halting Turing machine, and each such Turing machine has an encoding of its finite-state control. Define L to be the set of all encodings of Turing machines that:

1. Represent context-sensitive grammars.
2. Reject their own encoding.

Providing a scheme for encoding the quadruple for a context-sensitive grammar is left for the exercises. Any reasonable encoding scheme will make it a simple task to determine whether a candidate string represents nonsense or a valid context-sensitive grammar.

L can therefore be recognized by a halting Turing machine that:

1. Checks if the string on the input tape represents the encoding of a valid context-sensitive grammar.
2. Calculates the encoding of the corresponding Turing machine.
3. Simulates that Turing machine being fed its own encoding.

This process is guaranteed to halt, since the Turing machine being simulated is known to be a halting Turing machine. Thus, $L \in \mathcal{H}_\Sigma$. However, if $L \in \mathcal{O}_\Sigma$, we find ourselves in a familiar dilemma. If there is a context-sensitive grammar G_L that generates L, then this grammar would have a corresponding Turing machine T_L, which would have an encoding x_L. If x_L did not belong to L, then by definition of L it would be an encoding of a machine (T_L) that did not reject its own encoding (x_L). Thus, T_L recognizes x_L, and therefore the corresponding grammar G_L must generate x_L. But then $x_L \in L(G_L) = L$, contradicting the assumption that x_L did not belong to L. If on the other hand x_L belongs to L, then, by definition of L, T_L must reject its own encoding (x_L), and thus $x_L \notin L(T_L) = L(G_L) = L$, which is another contradiction. Thus, no such context-sensitive grammar G_L can exist, and L is not a context-sensitive language.

Δ

The above diagonalization technique can be generalized; given any enumerable class $\mathcal{C}$ of languages whose members are all represented by halting Turing machines, there must exist a halting Turing machine that recognizes a language not in $\mathcal{C}$ (see the exercises). The following theorem summarizes how the other classes of languages discussed in the text fit in the language hierarchy.

∇ **Theorem 12.16.** Let Σ be an alphabet for which $\|\Sigma\| \geq 2$. Then

$$\mathcal{D}_\Sigma = \mathcal{W}_\Sigma = \mathcal{R}_\Sigma = \mathcal{G}_\Sigma \subset \mathcal{A}_\Sigma \subset \mathcal{C}_\Sigma = \mathcal{P}_\Sigma \subset \mathcal{L}_\Sigma = \mathcal{O}_\Sigma \subset \mathcal{H}_\Sigma \subset \mathcal{Z}_\Sigma = \mathcal{T}_\Sigma \subset \rho(\Sigma^*)$$

Proof. The relationship between the type 0, type 1, type 2, and type 3 languages was outlined in Theorem 11.10. Theorem 10.8 showed that $\mathcal{A}_\Sigma$ properly

lies between the type 3 and type 2 languages. Corollary 12.2 and Theorem 12.15 show that $\mathcal{H}_\Sigma$ properly lies between the type 1 and type 0 languages and also show that the type 1 languages are a proper subset of the type 0 languages. The existence of languages that are not Turing acceptable shows that $\mathcal{T}_\Sigma$ is properly contained in $\rho(\Sigma^*)$. A counting argument shows that proper containment of $\mathcal{T}_\Sigma$ in $\rho(\Sigma^*)$ also holds even if Σ is a singleton set.
Δ

The relationships between six distinct and nontrivial classes of languages are characterized by Theorem 12.16. Each of these classes is defined by a particular type of automaton. The trivial class of all languages, $\rho(\Sigma^*)$, was shown to have no mechanical counterpart. We have seen that type 3 languages appear in many useful applications. Program design, lexical analysis, and various engineering problems are aided by the use of finite automata concepts. Programming languages are always defined in such a way that they belong to the class $\mathcal{A}_\Sigma$, since compilers should operate deterministically. The theory of compiler construction builds on the material presented here; syntactic analysis, the translation from source code to machine code, is guided by the generation of parse trees for the sentences in the program, which in turn give meaning to the code. The type 0 languages represent the fundamental limits of mechanical computation. The concepts presented in this text provide a foundation for the study of computational complexity and other elements of computation theory.

EXERCISES

12.1. Verify the assertions made in the proof of Theorem 12.1 concerning Theorem 2.7.

12.2. Prove Lemma 12.1.

12.3. Given an FAD language L, the minimal DFA accepting L, and another machine B for which $L(\mathrm{B}) = \mathrm{L}$, prove that the number of *non*final states in the minimal machine must be equal to or less than the number of *non*final states in B.

12.4. Given two DFAs $\mathrm{A}_1 = <\Sigma, S_1, s_{0_1}, \delta_1, F_1>$ and $\mathrm{A}_2 = <\Sigma, S_2, s_{0_2}, \delta_2, F_2>$, show that it is decidable whether $L(\mathrm{A}_1) \subseteq L(\mathrm{A}_2)$.

12.5. Given any alphabet Σ and a DFA $\mathrm{A} = <\Sigma, S, s_0, \delta, F>$, show that it is decidable whether $L(\mathrm{A})$ is cofinite. (*Note:* A set L is cofinite ***iff*** its complement is finite, that is, ***iff*** $\Sigma^* - \mathrm{L}$ is finite.)

12.6. Given any alphabet Σ and a DFA $\mathrm{A} = <\Sigma, S, s_0, \delta, F>$, show that it is decidable whether $L(\mathrm{A})$ contains any string of length greater than 1228.

12.7. Given any alphabet Σ and a DFA $\mathrm{A} = <\Sigma, S, s_0, \delta, F>$, show that it is decidable whether A accepts any even-length strings.

12.8. Given any alphabet Σ and regular expressions R_1 and R_2 over Σ, show that it is decidable whether R_1 and R_2 represent languages that are complements of each other.

12.9. Given any alphabet Σ and regular expressions R_1 and R_2 over Σ, show that it is decidable whether R_1 and R_2 describe any common strings.

12.10. Given any alphabet Σ and a regular expression R_1 over Σ, show that it is decidable whether there is a DFA with less than 31 states that accepts the language described by R_1.

12.11. Given any alphabet Σ and a regular expressions R_1 over Σ, show that it is decidable whether there is a DFA with *more* than 31 states that accepts the language described by R_1. (You should be able to argue that there is a *one*-step algorithm that always supplies the correct yes–no answer to this question.)

12.12. Given any alphabet Σ and a regular expression R over Σ, show that it is decidable whether there exists a NDFA (*with* λ-moves) with at most one final state that accepts R.

12.13. Given any alphabet Σ and a DFA $A = \langle\Sigma, S, s_0, \delta, F\rangle$, show that it is decidable whether there exists a NDFA (with*out* λ-moves) with at most one final state that accepts the same language A does.

12.14. Given any alphabet Σ and regular expressions R_1 and R_2 over Σ, show that it is decidable whether $R_1 = R_2$.

12.15. Given any alphabet Σ and regular expressions R_1 and R_2 over Σ (which represent languages L_1 and L_2, respectively), show that it is decidable whether they generate the same right congruences (that is, whether $R_{L_1} = R_{L_2}$).

12.16. Prove Theorem 12.5.

12.17. Outline an *efficient* algorithm for computing $\{\overline{\delta}(s_0, y) \mid y \in \Sigma^* \wedge n \leq |y| < 2n\}$ in the proof of Theorem 12.2, and justify why your procedure always halts.

12.18. Consider intersecting the set $\{\overline{\delta}(s_0, y) \mid y \in \Sigma^* \wedge 5n \leq |y| < 6n\}$ with F to answer the question posed in Theorem 12.2. Would this strategy always produce the correct answer? Justify your claims.

12.19. Show that it is decidable whether two Mealy machines are equivalent.

12.20. Show that it is decidable whether two Moore machines are equivalent.

12.21. Given any alphabet Σ and a regular expression R, show that it is decidable whether R represents any strings of length greater than 28. Give an argument that does not depend on finite automata or grammars.

12.22. Given any alphabet Σ and a right-linear grammar G, show that it is decidable whether $L(G)$ contains any string of length greater than 28. Give an argument that does not depend on finite automata or regular expressions.

12.23. Refer to the proof of Theorem 12.6 and prove that $Z_0 \subseteq Z_1 \subseteq \cdots \subseteq Z_n \subseteq \cdots \subseteq \Omega$.

12.24. Refer to the proof of Theorem 12.6 and prove that if $(\exists m \in \mathbb{N})(Z_m = Z_{m+1})$ then Z_m will then represent the set of *all* nonterminals that can be reached from the start symbol S.

12.25. Refer to the proof of Theorem 12.6 and prove that $(\exists m \in \mathbb{N})(Z_m = Z_{m+1})$.

12.26. **(a)** Refer to the proof of Theorem 12.6 and give a formal definition of W_i.
(b) Prove that $W_0 \subseteq W_1 \subseteq \cdots \subseteq W_n \subseteq \cdots \subseteq \Omega$.

12.27. Refer to the proof of Theorem 12.6 and prove that if $(\exists m \in \mathbb{N})(W_m = W_{m+1})$ then W_m will represent the set of *all* nonterminals that can produce valid terminal strings.

12.28. Refer to the proof of Theorem 12.6 and prove that $(\exists m \in \mathbb{N})(W_m = W_{m+1})$.

12.29. Let A be an arbitrary NDFA (with λ-moves). A string processed by A may successfully find several paths through the machine; it is also possible that a string will be rejected because there are no complete paths available.

(a) Show that it is decidable whether there exists a string with no complete path in A.
(b) Show that it is decidable whether there exists a string that has at least one path through A that leads to a nonfinal state.
(c) Show that it is decidable whether there exists a string accepted by A for which all complete paths lead to final states.
(d) Show that it is decidable whether all strings accepted by A have the property that all their complete paths lead to final states.
(e) Show that it is decidable whether all strings have unique paths through A.

12.30. Given two DFAs $A_1 = \langle \Sigma, S_1, s_{0_1}, \delta_1, F_1 \rangle$ and $A_2 = \langle \Sigma, S_2, s_{0_2}, \delta_2, F_2 \rangle$:
(a) Show that it is decidable whether there exists a homomorphism between A_1 and A_2.
(b) Show that it is decidable whether there exists an isomorphism between A_1 and A_2.
(c) Show that it is decidable whether there exist more than three isomorphisms between A_1 and A_2. (*Note:* There are examples of disconnected DFAs for which more than three isomorphisms *do* exist!)

12.31. Given any alphabet Σ and a regular expression R_1 over Σ, show that it is decidable whether R_1 describes an infinite number of strings. Do this by developing an algorithm that does not depend on the construction of a DFA, that is, does not depend on Theorem 12.2.

12.32. Given a Mealy machine M and a Moore machine A, show that it is decidable whether M is equivalent to A.

12.33. Given any alphabet Σ and regular expressions R_1 and R_2 over Σ, show that it is decidable whether the language represented by R_2 properly contains that of R_1.

12.34. It can be shown that it is decidable whether $L(A) = \emptyset$ for any NDFA A by first finding the equivalent DFA A^d and applying Theorem 12.1 to that machine.
(a) Give an efficient method for answering this question that does not rely on the conversion to a DFA.
(b) Give an efficient method for testing whether $L(A)$ is infinite for any NDFA A. Your method should likewise not rely on the conversion to a DFA.

12.35. Given a DPDA M, show that it is decidable whether $L(M)$ is a regular set.

12.36. (a) Refer to Theorem 12.9 and outline an appropriate algorithm for determining paths in the graphs discussed.
(b) Give the details for a more efficient recursive algorithm.

12.37. Prove that $\mathscr{H}_\Sigma$ is closed under:
(a) Union
(b) Intersection
(c) Concatenation
(d) Reversal

12.38. Let $L = L_2(T)$ for some Turing machine T that halts on all inputs. That is, let L consist of all strings that cause T to halt with **Y** somewhere on the tape. Prove that there exists a halting Turing machine T′ for which $L = L_2(T) = L(T')$. T′ must:
1. Halt on all input.
2. Place a **Y** after the input word on an otherwise blank tape for accepted words.
3. Place an **N** after the input word on an otherwise blank tape for rejected words.

12.39. (a) Assume there is a Turing machine $M_{\mathscr{C}}$ that determines whether an encoding of a Turing machine T belongs to some set X. Let the class of languages recognized by

Turing machines with encodings in X be denoted by $\mathscr{C}$. Prove that if every encoding in X represents a halting Turing machine then there must exist a halting Turing machine that recognizes a language not in $\mathscr{C}$.

(b) Apply part (a) to prove Theorem 12.15.

12.40. **(a)** Outline a scheme for encoding the quadruple of context-sensitive grammars suitable for use by a Turing machine. You may assume that there are exactly two terminal symbols, but note that your scheme must be able to handle an unrestricted number of nonterminals.

(b) Outline the algorithm that a Turing machine might use to decide whether an input string represented the encoding of a valid context-sensitive grammar.

12.41. Show that it is undecidable whether $L(\text{X}) = \emptyset$ for:

(a) Arbitrary Turing machines X
(b) Arbitrary halting Turing machines X
(c) Arbitrary context-sensitive grammars X
(d) Arbitrary linear bounded automata X

12.42. Show that it is undecidable whether $L(\text{X}) = \Sigma^*$ for:

(a) Arbitrary Turing machines X
(b) Arbitrary halting Turing machines X
(c) Arbitrary context-sensitive grammars X
(d) Arbitrary linear bounded automata X
(e) Arbitrary context-free grammars X
(f) Arbitrary pushdown automata X

12.43. Consider the set E of all encodings of Turing machines that halt on input λ. Prove or disprove:

(a) $\text{E} \in \mathscr{T}_\Sigma$
(b) $\text{E} \in \mathscr{H}_\Sigma$
(c) $\text{E} \in \mathscr{O}_\Sigma$

12.44. Consider the set N of all encodings of Turing machines that do not halt on input λ. Prove or disprove:

(a) $\text{N} \in \mathscr{T}_\Sigma$
(b) $\text{N} \in \mathscr{H}_\Sigma$
(c) $\text{N} \in \mathscr{O}_\Sigma$

REFERENCES

[ALEK] I. ALEKSANDER and F. HANNA, *Automata Theory: An Engineering Approach*. Crane Russak, New York, 1975.

[BARW] J. BARWISE and J. ETCHEMENDY, *Turing's World: A Computer-Based Introduction to Computability Theory*. Kinko's Academic Courseware Exchange, Santa Barbara, 1986.

[BOOT] T. BOOTH, *Sequential Machines and Automata Theory*. Wiley, New York, 1967.

[BAVE] Z. BAVEL, *Introduction to the Theory of Automata*. Prentice Hall, Englewood Cliffs, N.J., 1983.

[DACR] F. DA CRUZ, *KERMIT Protocol Manual*. Columbia University Press, New York, 1984.

[DENN] P. DENNING, J. DENNIS, and J. QUALITZ, *Machines, Languages, and Computation*. Prentice Hall, Englewood Cliffs, N.J., 1978.

[FERR] D. FERRARI, *Computer Systems Performance Evaluation*. Prentice Hall, Englewood Cliffs, N.J., 1978.

[GIN1] A. GINZBURG, *Algebraic Theory of Automata*. Academic Press, New York.

[GIN2] S. GINSBURG, *Introduction to Mathematical Machine Theory*. Addison-Wesley, Reading, Mass.

[HART] J. HARTMANIS and R. E. STEARNS, *Algebraic Structure Theory of Sequential Machines*. Prentice Hall, Englewood Cliffs, N.J.

[HOPC] J. E. HOPCROFT and J. D. ULLMAN, *Introduction to Automata Theory, Languages, and Computation*. Addison-Wesley, Reading, Mass., 1979.

[KAIN] R. KAIN, *Automata Theory: Machines and Languages*. McGraw-Hill, New York.

[KOHA] Z. KOHAVI, *Switching and Finite Automata Theory*. McGraw-Hill, New York, 1978.

[LEWI] H. LEWIS and C. PAPADIMITRIOU, *Elements of the Theory of Computation*. Prentice Hall, Englewood Cliffs, N.J., 1984.

[MCNA] R. MCNAUGHTON, *Elementary Computability, Formal Languages, and Automata*. Prentice Hall, Englewood Cliffs, N.J., 1982.

[MINS] M. MINSKY, *Computation, Finite and Infinite Machines*. Prentice Hall, Englewood, N.J., 1967.

[MOOR] E. F. MOORE, editor, *Sequential Machines, Selected Papers*. Addison-Wesley, Reading, Mass., 1964.

[NELS] R. J. NELSON, *Introduction to Automata*. Wiley, New York.

[SALO] A. SALOMAA, *Theory of Automata*. Pergamon Press, New York, 1969.

[SAVI] W. SAVITCH, *Abstract Machines and Grammars*. Little, Brown, Boston, 1982.

[SHIE] M. SHIELDS, *An Introduction to Automata Theory*. Blackwell Scientific Publications, London, 1987.

[TANE] A. S. TANENBAUM, *Computer Networks*. Prentice Hall, Englewood Cliffs, N.J., 1981.

INDEX